D1734228

European Yearbook of International Economic Law

More information about this series at http://www.springer.com/series/8165

Marc Bungenberg • Markus Krajewski •
Christian Tams • Jörg Philipp Terhechte •
Andreas R. Ziegler
Editors

European Yearbook of International Economic Law 2017

Editors
Marc Bungenberg
Faculty of Law
Saarland University
Saarbrücken, Germany

Markus Krajewski
Faculty of Law
University of Erlangen-Nürnberg
Erlangen, Germany

Christian Tams
School of Law
University of Glasgow
Glasgow, United Kingdom

Jörg Philipp Terhechte
Competition and Regulation Institute
Leuphana University of Lüneburg
Lüneburg, Germany

Andreas R. Ziegler
Faculty of Law and Criminal Sciences
University of Lausanne
Lausanne, Switzerland

ISSN 2364-8392 ISSN 2364-8406 (electronic)
European Yearbook of International Economic Law
ISBN 978-3-319-58831-5 ISBN 978-3-319-58832-2 (eBook)
DOI 10.1007/978-3-319-58832-2

Printed on acid-free paper

This Springer imprint is published by Springer Nature
The registered company is Springer International Publishing AG
The registered company address is: Gewerbestrasse 11, 6330 Cham, Switzerland

Editorial EYIEL 8 (2017)

The *EYIEL*, already in its eighth volume, focuses particularly on the EU and its international economic relations and thereby also on the EU's role in international trade negotiations as well as in international organisations.

Until a short while ago, the external economic relations of the EU attracted the attention of very few experts—as is still reflected by most textbooks on EU law. This has obviously changed. TTIP and CETA especially and other EU-FTAs in general, as well as popular issues such as investor-state dispute settlement and imports from China in particular, now attract the attention of tens of thousands of people and are discussed in parliamentary hearings at regional, national and European levels. National courts as well as the Court of Justice of the European Union decide on different elements of international trade and investment issues with regard to their (national) constitutionality as well as on their conformity with EU law.

The different contributions in this volume aim to shed light on the EU and its external economic relations from as many different angles as possible. The 2009 Treaty of Lisbon restructured the constitutional background of the EU common commercial policy to a large degree. The result of these developments is visible in the EU mode of negotiating agreements with third states, its appearance in international organisations and unilateral answers given by the EU institutions when adopting import or export regulations. *Marise Cremona* in her distinguished essay draws on "A Quiet Revolution—The Changing Nature of the EU's Common Commercial Policy" and thereby gives an insight into the current state of play and background of the EU common commercial policy.

The first part of this *EYIEL* volume highlights the primary and secondary EU law developments with a specific focus on federal, democratic and cooperative exercises and implementation of the EU common commercial policy by the EU and its Member States. As a consequence of the often discussed but more than complicated vertical and horizontal distribution of competences between the EU and its Member States as well as among the EU institutions, *Thomas Cottier* proposes a possible solution to the now almost permanent discussion of mixed agreements by "Front-Loading Trade Policy-Making in the European Union: Towards a Trade Act". *Mattias Wendel* discusses "International Trade Agreements and Democratic Participation" and *Joris Larik* a "Sincere Cooperation in the Common Commercial Policy: Lisbon, a 'Joined-up' Union, and 'Brexit'". *Wendel* puts special focus on the widely debated transparency issue as a necessary element of democratic legitimisation. *Larik* considers the vertical relationship between the EU and its Member States and discusses the basic EU principle of *Unionstreue*. *Alessandra Asteriti* sheds light on non-economic objectives named in Article 21 TEU and their relevance for the EU's common commercial policy; she sees in this "A Test of Coherence", before *Christina Binder* and *Jane A. Hofbauer* analyse "The Perception of the EU Legal Order in International Law" and in this regard undertake "An In- and Outside View".

The authors in this part have then followed specific policy-related approaches and focus not only on the central and traditional issues of the common commercial policy but also on the more recent features of EU external relations law. This approach can be seen, on the one hand, through *Wolfgang Müller's* evaluation of "The EU's Trade Defence Instruments: Recent Judicial and Policy Developments", encompassing the traditional issues of the application of import rules, and, on the other hand, through the directly related issues of investment, competition, procurement and raw materials law, which are dealt with in individual contributions. In the field of investment law, as one of the more recent features of the EU external relations law, *Christoph Ohler* firstly discusses the "Democratic Legitimacy and the Rule of Law in Investor-State Dispute Settlement under CETA", and secondly *August Reinisch* puts the spotlight on the most recent idea of a permanent investment court system in his contribution—"The EU and Investor-State Dispute Settlement: WTO Litigators Going 'Investor-State Arbitration' and Back to a Permanent 'Investment Court'". In the field of competition law, another hot topic in EU external economic relations, *Florian Wagner-von Papp* closely analyses "Competition Law in EU Free Trade and Cooperation Agreements" and additionally covers the extraterritorial application of EU competition law and gives a firsthand analysis of "What the UK Can Expect after Brexit" in this field of law and politics. *Stephen Woolcock* then presents an in-depth treatment of "The European Union's Policy on Public Procurement in Preferential Trade Agreements", before *Karsten Nowrot* covers the more recent developments of EU raw materials law as part of the common commercial policy in his piece on "Good Raw Materials Governance: Towards a European Approach Contributing to a Constitutionalised International Economic Law", which in a turn of course takes Article 21 TEU as a normative starting point for its development.

The second part of *EYIEL* traditionally focuses on "regions"—this volume, therefore, places the ongoing bi- and multilateral negotiations of the EU under scrutiny. *Frank Hoffmeister* gives a detailed overview with "Bruxelles" insights when he summarises the "Bilateral Developments in EU Trade Policy Seven Years

After Lisbon: A Look into the Spaghetti-Bowl à la Bruxelloise (2010–2016)". In the articles following it, specific concluded agreements, ongoing negotiations and envisaged new agreements are discussed. *Armand de Mestral* starts out with some pronounced Canadian observations on the recently signed CETA and the current EU difficulties in negotiating such agreements at all in his contribution "Negotiating CETA with the European Union and Some Thoughts on the Impact of Mega-Regional Trade Agreements on Agreements Inter Partes and Agreements with Third Parties". *Yumiko Nakanishi* describes the Japanese perspective on "Characteristics of EU Free Trade Agreements in a Legal Context", before *Manjiao Chi* reflects on ongoing negotiations in "The China-EU BIT as a Stepping Stone Towards a China-EU FTA: A Policy Analysis" and thus also draws attention to future issues when relations with the "East" might become easier to sell to the citizens than those with longstanding allies from the "West". The Commission's 2015 "Trade for All" communication already has some ideas about which bilateral negotiations might be next in line; therefore, *Leon Trakman*, *Robert Walters* and *Bruno Zeller* discuss "The Proposed European and Australian Free Trade Agreement" especially from a small and medium-sized enterprise perspective. As a final contribution in this chapter—with an economics-based approach—*Roy Chun Lee* tackles an issue that might be still a long way down the road: "EU-Taiwan" as "New Partners in International Trade Negotiations".

While the second part of *EYIEL* generally deals with "regions", the focus of the third part is on international organisations. *Anna-Luise Chané* and *Jan Wouters* evaluate the relationship between the EU and the "United Nations Economic Governance Fora"; *Päivi Leino* then deals with more international financial matters when discussing "The Duty of Cooperation, Consistency and Influence in the External Relations of the Euro-Zone: Representation of EU and EU Member States in the International Monetary Fund". Finally, in the last contribution, *Jan Bohanes* and *Kholofelo Kugler* give an "Overview of WTO Jurisprudence in 2015 Involving the EU as a Main Party and Selected Cases with Third-Party Participation by the EU".

The editing of this volume would not have been possible without the help and assistance of *Anja Trautmann* who together with *Lukas Kleinert* and *Fabian Blandfort* had to take care of inter alia the final adaptation of manuscripts to form and style guidelines or had to remind some authors of deadlines. Last but not least, we thank *Brigitte Reschke* of Springer for cooperating with us once again and ensuring that this volume could be published as scheduled.

Saarbrücken, Germany	Marc Bungenberg
Erlangen, Germany	Markus Krajewski
Glasgow, UK	Christian Tams
Lüneburg, Germany	Jörg Philipp Terhechte
Lausanne, Switzerland	Andreas R. Ziegler
March 2017	

Contents

List of Contributors

Alessandra Asteriti is junior professor of international economic law at Leuphana University, Competition and Regulation Institute; she is also a postdoctoral research associate in international law at the University of Glasgow. She has an M.A. (summa cum laude) in ancient history from the University of Rome, an M.A. in the theory and practice of human rights from the University of Essex and an LL.M. and Ph.D. in international law from the University of Glasgow.

Christina Binder is professor of international law and international human rights law at the University of the Federal Armed Forces in Munich and lecturer at the Department of European, International and Comparative Law at the University of Vienna. She was visiting fellow at the Lauterpacht Centre for International Law in Cambridge (2007–2008), at the Max Planck Institute for Comparative Public Law and International Law in Heidelberg (2008–2010) and at McGill University in Montréal (summer 2015). She is a member of the Young Academy of the Austrian Academy of Sciences and of the ILA Committees on the Implementation of the Rights of Indigenous Peoples and on Feminism in International Law. Christina is member of the executive board of the European Society of International Law (ESIL).

Jan Bohanes has served as senior counsel at the Advisory Centre on WTO Law (ACWL) since 2010. He assists developing countries in WTO dispute settlement proceedings and has advised on a broad scope of WTO legal issues. Prior to joining the ACWL, Jan was associate attorney at the Geneva office of Sidley Austin LLP, where he advised governments and large commercial stakeholders on all issues of WTO law, including WTO dispute settlement. Between 2002 and 2006, he worked as legal officer at the Appellate Body Secretariat of the World Trade Organization, assisting Appellate Body members on appeals in the WTO dispute settlement system.

Anna-Luise Chané is a research fellow and Ph.D. candidate in law at the Leuven Centre for Global Governance Studies and at the Institute for International Law, University of Leuven. Her research focuses on the relationship between multilateral organisations, in particular the United Nations and the EU, on the EU and human rights and on human dignity in the case law of international courts and tribunals. She is a researcher on the large-scale FP7 project "Fostering Human Rights Among European Policies" (FRAME). Anna-Luise studied law at the University of Cologne and the University of Leuven and passed her first and second juridical state examination with distinction. She holds a master of laws degree from Harvard Law School, where she was an ERP scholar of the German Ministry of Economy and Technology and the German National Academic Foundation.

Manjiao Chi is professor of international law, Law School, Xiamen University, China. His major teaching and research interests cover international trade and investment law and dispute settlement, commercial arbitration, natural resource law and sustainable development law. Manjiao publishes extensively in these fields in both Chinese and English. His recent articles appear in various leading law journals, such as the *Journal of International Economic Law*, the *Journal of World Trade*, *ZEuS* and the *Asian International Arbitration Journal*. Among his many academic affiliations, Manjiao is deputy secretary-general of the Administrative Council of Xiamen Academy of International Law and member of the ILA Committee on Rule of Law and International Investment Law. He also serves as arbitrator, consultant and expert witness in numerous foreign-related and domestic arbitration cases. He was Li Ka Shing professor of practice, Faculty of Law, McGill University, Canada, and senior fellow, Centre for Global Cooperation Research, Germany, as well as visiting fellow of Max Planck Institute of International Law in Heidelberg, Columbia Law School and UNIDROIT.

Thomas Cottier is professor emeritus of European and international economic law at the University of Bern, a senior research fellow at the World Trade Institute and adjunct professor at the University of Ottawa, Faculty of Law, and a board member of EYIEL. He was the founder and managing director of the World Trade Institute from 1994 to 2015 and SNF National Centre of Competence NCCR on International Trade Regulation and, previously, the deputy director general of the Swiss Intellectual Property Office. He served on the Swiss negotiating team of the Uruguay Round and on EFTA-EU EEA negotiations. Thomas has been a member and chair of several GATT and WTO panels and has published widely in international economic law.

Marise Cremona has been a professor in the Law Department of the European University Institute since 2006. She is a codirector of the Academy of European Law and a general editor (with Profs. Nehal Bhuta and Claire Kilpatrick) of *The Collected Courses of the Academy of European Law*, Oxford University Press. Between November 2009 and June 2012, she was head of the Department of Law at the EUI, and between June 2012 and August 2013, she was president ad interim of the EUI. Before joining the EUI, she held the chair of European Commercial Law at the Centre for Commercial Law Studies, Queen Mary University of London. She is a member of the International Advisory Board of the Centre for European Research, University of Göteborg; member of the Scientific Advisory Board of the Lichtenberg-Kolleg Institute for Advanced Study in Humanities and Social Sciences, University of Göttingen; member of the editorial board of the *Common Market Law Review*; member of the advisory board of the *European Foreign Affairs Review*; member of the editorial board of the *Studies in EU External Relations*, Martinus Nijhoff Publishers; and former member of the editorial board of the *European Law Review*. Marise's research interests are in the external relations law of the EU; she is particularly interested in the constitutional basis for EU external relations law and the legal and institutional dimensions of the EU's foreign policy, the interaction between national, regional and international legal and policy regimes, EU common commercial policy and the EU as an exporter of values and norms. She has published extensively on the external relations law of the EU, including *Developments in EU External Relations Law* (Oxford University Press, 2008); *EU Foreign Relations Law: Constitutional Fundamentals*, edited with Bruno de Witte (Hart Publishing, 2008); *The European Court of Justice and External Relations Law: Constitutional Challenges*, edited with Anne Thies (Hart Publishing, 2014); and *Private Law in the External Relations of the EU*, edited with Hans-W. Micklitz (Oxford University Press, 2016).

Jane Alice Hofbauer is currently a postdoctoral researcher and lecturer at the Department of European, International and Comparative Law at the University of Vienna. She is the managing editor of the *Austrian Review of International and European Law* (*ARIEL*). She was legal researcher at the Boltzmann Institute of Human Rights in Vienna, Austria (2014–2016), focusing particularly on the effects of the implementation of climate policies in third states. Previously, she studied in Vienna and Amsterdam and obtained her LL.M. from the University of Iceland, before writing her doctorate in legal anthropology and international law at the University of Vienna (with distinction). During this time, she also worked for the University of Vienna as a predoctoral researcher (2010–2014).

Frank Hoffmeister studied law in Frankfurt, Geneva and Heidelberg (1989–1994) and received a Ph.D. at the Max Planck Institute for Foreign Public Law and International Law (1998). Between 1998 and 2001, he researched and taught as university assistant at the Walter Hallstein Institute for European Constitutional Law at Humboldt University of Berlin. He then entered the European Commission, first on the Cyprus desk at DG Enlargement and afterwards as a member of the Legal Service, where he specialised in international law and WTO issues. From 2010 to 2014, he served as the deputy head of cabinet of EU Trade Commissioner De Gucht, and as of 2015, he is head of unit dealing with anti-dumping at DG Trade. In addition, Frank teaches international economic law at the Free University of Brussels and has published numerous articles on topics of European and international law. Most recently he co-authored *The Law of EU External Relations: Cases, Materials, and Commentary on the EU as an International Legal Actor* (Oxford University Press, 2nd edition, 2016) together with Pieter Jan Kuijper, Jan Wouters, Geert de Baere and Thomas Ramopoulos.

Kholofelo Kugler has served as counsel at the Advisory Centre on WTO Law (ACWL) since 2015. She assists developing countries in WTO dispute settlement proceedings and advises on diverse WTO legal issues. Prior to joining the ACWL, Kholofelo served as a research assistant for Prof. Markus Krajewski at the University of Erlangen-Nuremberg, Germany, and as a junior associate at WTI Advisors in Geneva. In the latter role, she provided trade policy advice on trade in services and technical assistance to developing countries on WTO matters. From 2011 to 2013, Kholofelo worked in private legal practice at Bowman Gilfillan Inc. in Johannesburg, South Africa.

Joris Larik is assistant professor of comparative, EU and international law at Leiden University, senior researcher at The Hague Institute for Global Justice and associate fellow at the Leuven Centre for Global Governance Studies. His work has been acknowledged with NATO's Manfred Wörner Essay Award (2008) and the Mauro Cappelletti Prize for the Best Doctoral Thesis in Comparative Law (2014) from the EUI. He is the author of *Foreign Policy Objectives in European Constitutional Law* (Oxford University Press, 2016) and co-author of *ASEAN's External Agreements: Law, Practice and the Quest for Collective Action* (Cambridge University Press, 2015). Larik has worked on several policy-oriented research projects, including for the Ministry of Foreign Affairs of the Netherlands, the European Commission and the Commission on Global Security, Justice & Governance, which was co-chaired by former US Secretary of State Madeleine Albright and former Nigerian Foreign Minister Ibrahim Gambari. In 2013/2014, he convened a Massive Open Online Course (MOOC) on the EU in global governance. Larik studied law and international relations in Dresden (B.A.), Leiden (LL.M.), the College of Europe (M.A.) and the European University Institute (Ph.D.).

Roy Chun Lee specialised in non-tariff measures (NTMs), trade in services, regional integration, the WTO and the cross-strait (Taiwan-China) economic issues. He is policy advisor for the general liberalisation policy as well as for Taiwan's trade negotiations with China, New Zealand and Singapore and serves as capital-based expert for Taiwan's delegation for WTO services trade and TBT meetings. He writes frequently on liberalisation policy for major newspapers in Taiwan. In his other capacity, he has served as the first secretary-general for the Taiwan Communications Society between 2008 and 2014. Before joining CIER in 2006, Roy Chun Lee worked as a regulatory expert project consultant for the Pacific Economic Cooperation Council (PECC) and the ASEAN-Australia Development Cooperation Program (AADCP). He holds LL.B. and LL.M. degrees and received his Ph.D. in public policy from the Australian National University.

Päivi Leino holds an LL.D. from the University of Helsinki, an LL.M. (with distinction) from the London School of Economics and an M.Pol.Sc. from Åbo Akademi University. She is professor of international and European law at UEF Law School, research fellow at the Academy of Finland and a visiting fellow at the EUI Law Department. She also holds the title of adjunct professor of EU law at the University of Helsinki. She has previously (2005–2015) worked as legal counsellor for the Finnish government participating in various EU and international negotiations.

Armand de Mestral is emeritus professor at McGill University, holds the Jean Monnet chair in law, was codirector of the Institute of European Studies at McGill Université de Montréal (2002–2008), was interim director at the Institute of Air and Space Law at McGill University (1998–2002) and senior fellow at CIGI (2014). His recent publications include *International Law* (7th edn. 2006, co-author), *Law and Practice of International Trade* (2nd edn. 1999) and *The North American Free Trade Agreement: A Comparative Study*, Hague Academy of International Law, Receuil des cours (2000). He served as a panellist and arbitrator in disputes under WTO, CUFTA and NAFTA, was a member of the Canadian delegation to the UN Law of the Sea Conference (1973–1980), was a consultant to NACEC and Law Commission of Canada and was president of the Canadian Red Cross Society (1999–2001).

Wolfgang Müller has been head of the Policy Unit of the European Commission's Trade Defence Directorate since 2015, which is part of DG Trade. He previously had various positions within DG Trade and within the Daimler Benz Group from 1989 to 1993. From 1987 to 1989, Wolfgang was a research assistant at the Universität Konstanz (Germany). He teaches at the Université Nice Sophia Antipolis (France) and has published extensively on trade remedies (the publication of a comprehensive article by article commentary on the WTO ASCM is scheduled for summer 2017).

Yumiko Nakanishi is professor of EU law at the Graduate School of Law, Hitotsubashi University, Tokyo. She studied European law at Hitotsubashi University and Münster University (Germany). She earned a master of laws degree from Hitotsubashi University (1993) and an LL.M. (1995) and a doctor of law degree (1998) from the University of Münster. She is a member of the board of directors of the European Union Studies Association—Japan and a member of the Japanese Society of International Law and the Japan Association of Environmental Law and Policy. She is the founder and representative of the Hitotsubashi Association of European Union Law. She is also the editor responsible for the *Review of European Law* (Shinzansha). Her fields of research are EU external relations law, EU constitutional law and EU environmental law.

Karsten Nowrot is professor of public law, European law and international economic law and director at the Research Institute for Economic Law and Labour Law as well as the current head of the Department of Law at the School of Socio-Economics of the Faculty of Business, Economics and Social Sciences at Hamburg University, Germany. He is also an affiliated professor at the Faculty of Law at Hamburg University and serves as deputy director of the master programme "European and European Legal Studies" at the Institute for European Integration of the Europa-Kolleg in Hamburg.

Christoph Ohler holds a chair in public law, European law, public international law and international economic law at the Friedrich-Schiller University of Jena since 2006. He studied law at the University of Bayreuth and at the College of Europe. In 1997, he received his Ph.D. (Dr. iur.) from the University of Bayreuth and in 2005 his venia legendi from Ludwig Maximilians University of Munich. From 2008 to 2014, he was the spokesperson of the interdisciplinary graduate programme "Global Financial Markets" at the universities of Jena and Halle. In 2015, he was elected as member of the Constitutional Court of the Free State of Thuringia. Christoph publishes extensively on German and EU constitutional law with a special focus on the European Monetary Union and the regulation of financial markets in international and European law.

August Reinisch has been a professor of international and European law at the University of Vienna since 1998. He currently serves as head of the Section of International Law and International Relations and as director of the LL.M. programme in international legal studies. He is a member of the International Law Commission, an associate member of the Institut de droit international, president of the Austrian Branch of the ILA and executive board member of the German Society of International Law. August has served as arbitrator in investment cases mostly under ICSID and UNCITRAL Rules and frequently provided expert opinions in the field. He is a member of the ICSID Panels of Conciliators and of Arbitrators and of the Permanent Court of Arbitration.

Peter Rott is professor in civil law, European private law and consumer law at the University of Kassel, Germany. He graduated as a fully qualified German lawyer in 1996 and obtained his doctorate in 2001. Peter has worked in academia ever since, among other positions as a lecturer at the University of Sheffield from 2000 to 2003, as associate professor at the University of Bremen from 2003 to 2010 and as associate professor at the University of Copenhagen from 2010 to 2014, after which he joined the University of Kassel. He has published widely in the area of European private law, mostly with a focus on consumer law in its broadest sense.

Charlotte Sieber-Gasser is a senior research fellow and lecturer at the Centre for Law and Sustainability, University of Lucerne, and previously worked as postdoc fellow at the World Trade Institute in Bern. She studied law in Fribourg and Bern,

Switzerland, and development studies in Manchester, UK. In her Ph.D. ("Developing Countries and Preferential Services Trade", available at Cambridge University Press), Charlotte analysed the level of compliance in Preferential Trade Agreements (PTAs) in services with WTO law in general and the legal scope for flexibility in PTAs between developing countries in particular.

Leon Trakman is professor of law and former dean of the Faculty of Law at the University of New South Wales. He is the recipient of a doctorate from Harvard and is the author of eight books and over 100 articles in international journals. His academic appointments include, among others, distinguished visiting professor at the University of California (Davis); visiting professor at Wisconsin Law School, Tulane Law School and the University of Cape Town; professor of law at Dalhousie University; and Bolton visiting professor at McGill University. He has served extensively as an international commercial arbitrator and as a panellist appointed by the US, Canadian and Mexican governments to decide anti-dumping, countervailing duty and injury disputes under the NAFTA.

Anja Trautmann has recently finished her Ph.D. at the Europa-Institut of Saarland University in which she analysed the question of competence in the European foreign investment policy. She is the managing editor of the *Zeitschrift für Europarechtliche Studien* (*ZEuS*). Anja studied law in Dresden and obtained her LL.M. from the Europa-Institut where she has also worked as a research assistant since 2006.

Florian Wagner-von Papp is associate professor (reader) at University College London, Faculty of Laws, where he is also director of the UCL Centre for Law and Economics. He holds a master's degree from Columbia Law School (New York) and a doctorate degree from the University of Tubingen (Germany). His research focuses on competition law, comparative law and law and economics.

Robert Walters has recently completed his thesis comparing citizenship, immigration, human rights and private international laws of Australia, Slovenia and the EU. He has more than two decades' experience in policy and law within the government, developing and implementing major law reforms for the primary industry sectors. Robert is working in emerging areas of transnational law (private, trade, investment and economics) and cyber, corporate and business law.

Wolfgang Weiß holds a chair in Public Law, European Law and Public International Law at the German University of Administrative Sciences in Speyer/FRG. He studied law and economics at the University of Bayreuth from 1988 to 1993. After completing his Dr. juris (1995), he became a fully qualified lawyer after passing the second state exam in 1997 and a legal scholar. After completing his second book in law (*Habilitation*) in 2000 and working as acting professor at different German universities, he became a reader and, as from October 2006, a professor in international law at Oxford Brookes University. From 2006 to 2008, he was also professor in public law, European law and public international law at the

University of Erlangen-Nuremberg. In 2015, he also became a senior fellow to the German Research Institute for Public Administration in Speyer. He is still affiliated with Oxford Brookes University as an honorary research fellow. Wolfgang Weiss' main research areas are European constitutional and administrative law, German public law, public international law and WTO law. He contributes to three of the leading German language article by article commentaries on EU law; is author of three books on European law, two on German public law and one on WTO law; and publishes regularly in English or German language journals.

Mattias Wendel is fellow and lecturer at Humboldt University of Berlin and holds an interim professorship at the University of Freiburg in the winter term 2016/2017. He received his doctorate in 2010 from Humboldt University of Berlin with a comparative work on integration clauses at the national and EU level for which he was awarded the Doctoral Thesis Price of the Faculty of Law. He is author of several articles and contributions in the field of EU law, public law and comparative law and a member of the editorial board of the *European Constitutional Law Review* and the *Cahiers de droit européen*. Matthias studied and carried out research i.a. at Berlin, Paris and Oxford.

Stephen Woolcock is an associate professor in international relations at the London School of Economics, where he teaches international political economy, the political economy of international trade and economic diplomacy as well as heads the LSE's International Trade Policy Unit. Stephen has worked on international trade policy, both at the multilateral and preferential level, and written on EU trade and investment policy. For the past 18 years, he has helped coordinate an LSE programme on economic diplomacy that has focused on the process of economic negotiations. His recent books include *The New Economic Diplomacy: Decision-Making and Negotiation in International Economic Relations* (Stephen Woolcock and Nicholas Bayne (eds); Aldershot: Ashgate, 4th edn. 2016) and *European Union Economic Diplomacy* (Stephen Woolcock; Ashgate, 2012).

Jan Wouters is full professor of international law and international organisations, Jean Monnet chair ad personam EU and Global Governance and founding director of the Institute for International Law and of the Leuven Centre for Global Governance Studies at the University of Leuven. He is adjunct professor at Columbia University and visiting professor at Sciences Po (Paris), Luiss University (Rome) and the College of Europe (Bruges). He is a member of the Royal Academy of Belgium for Sciences and Arts, president of the United Nations Association Flanders Belgium and of counsel at Linklaters, Brussels. He has published widely on international and EU law, international organisations, global governance and financial law. He is coordinator of a number of major research projects, including FRAME (a large-scale FP7 programme on human rights in EU Policies), advises various international organisations and governments, trains officials and often comments on international events in the media.

Bruno Zeller is a professor in transnational commercial law at The University of Western Australia, Perth. His teaching interests include international trade law, conflict of laws, international arbitration and maritime law. His research contributes to the understanding of uniform international laws, which have been developed under the auspices of the United Nations, especially the United Nations Convention on Contracts for the International Sale of Goods. In addition, he has also published on alternative dispute resolution mechanisms and free trade agreements. He is an adjunct professor at Murdoch University, Perth, and an adjunct professor at the Sir Zelman Cowan Centre, Victoria University, Melbourne. Bruno is also a visiting professor at La Trobe University, Melbourne, and Humboldt University of Berlin. He is also a fellow of The Australian Institute for Commercial Arbitrations and listed as an arbitrator with the Maritime Law Association of Australia and New Zealand (MLAANZ).

Part I
Special Focus External Economic Relations of the European Union

Distinguished Essay: A Quiet Revolution—The Changing Nature of the EU's Common Commercial Policy

Marise Cremona

Abstract This paper assesses the development of the EU's Common Commercial Policy (CCP) since the coming into force of the Lisbon Treaty. It argues that we have witnessed a "quiet revolution" in EU trade policy. Three major changes are identified. First, the extension of the CCP to include trade in services, the commercial aspects of intellectual property and foreign direct investment. Second is the embedding of EU trade policy into the Union's overall principles and objectives, providing a framework for the broad discretion left by the Treaty to trade policy-makers. Third is the change to the decision-making structures of trade policy. The Commission still plays a key strategic role, but the Commission's key interlocutors now include the European Parliament as well as the Council. The European Parliament has the power to consent to—or to withhold consent from—trade agreements and has proved willing to use its power.

Working together with a renewed political and public interest in trade policy, in the wake of several contentious agreements, this new dynamic has led to calls for, and significant progress towards, greater transparency in the negotiation of trade agreements.

Contents

This is an updated, substantially revised and shortened version of the author's "A Quiet Revolution: The Common Commercial Policy Six Years after the Treaty of Lisbon" SIEPS 2017:2.

M. Cremona (✉)
European University Institute, Villa Salviati, Via Bolognese 156, 50139 Florence, Italy
e-mail: Marise.Cremona@eui.eu

M. Bungenberg et al. (eds.), *European Yearbook of International Economic Law 2017*, European Yearbook of International Economic Law 8,
DOI 10.1007/978-3-319-58832-2_1

1 Introduction

The common commercial policy (CCP) has often been hailed as the most supranational, and the most successful, of the EU's external policies, through which it demonstrates real weight and influence in the world. This success has been attributed in part to the CCP's decision-making processes which were held up as a model of the "Community method", as well as to the fact that the CCP has been accepted as an exclusive competence since the early 1970s[1]; its description as a "common" policy is witness to a substantial degree of integration.[2] The Commission represents the Union in international trade negotiations, trade agreements are concluded by the Union alone without the need for lengthy Member State ratification, and internal decision-making under qualified majority voting is free of the threat of the national veto and ostensibly directed at Union—rather than narrow state or sectoral—interests.

In reality the picture before the coming into force of the Lisbon Treaty had long been more mixed. In terms of scope, the CCP no longer reflected the content of modern trade agreements, which therefore had to be concluded under multiple legal bases.[3] The decision-making processes and the interaction between the provisions applying to different sectors had become extremely complex as a result of amendments introduced by the Treaty of Nice; and that Treaty had also made inroads into the exclusivity of the CCP by introducing shared competence for some aspects of trade in services. The formal exclusion of the European Parliament from involvement in trade legislation and the conclusion of trade agreements was anachronistic

[1]Meunier and Nicolaidis (1999).

[2]Although the relevant chapter of the original Treaty of Rome was headed simply "Commercial Policy", Article 113 EEC referred from the start to the establishment of a "common commercial policy". Among the EU's external policies, only the common commercial policy, the common foreign and security policy and (since the Lisbon Treaty) the common security and defence policy are referred to as *common* policies: Koutrakos (2015).

[3]A high watermark of this fragmentation might be the Decision concluding the WTO agreements in 1994 which was based on 11 substantive legal bases, including the CCP (Articles 43, 54, 57, 66, 75, 84(2), 99, 100, 100a, 113, and 235 EC): Council Decision 94/800/EC of 22 December 1994 concerning the conclusion on behalf of the European Community, as regards matters within its competence, of the agreements reached in the Uruguay Round multilateral negotiations (1986–1994), OJ 1994 L 336/1.

given the expansion of co-decision elsewhere in EC decision-making and increasingly hard to justify as the CCP now covered at least some aspects of services trade (including sensitive sectors such as health and culture) and trade agreements routinely included substantial regulatory commitments.

The Lisbon Treaty represented a serious attempt to address these shortcomings, and it is in the provisions on the CCP that the Union's external policy underwent some of its most significant changes. Seven years after the coming into force of the Lisbon Treaty, we can assess those changes and whether they do in fact represent, or have facilitated, a revolution in EU trade policy-making. In these years some, but certainly not all, of the uncertainties over the revised Treaty provisions on the CCP have been resolved and new questions have emerged.

The Lisbon Treaty presents us, in fact, with an impetus in two different directions: on the one hand towards a greater coherence between internal and external policies and on the other towards a more fully integrated range of external policies operating under an express external mandate and with a set of overall governing principles and objectives. The CCP represents both these tendencies. The link between the CCP and internal policies (in particular the internal market) appears closer as a result of the Treaty of Lisbon, which expanded the scope of the CCP, introduced the ordinary legislative procedure into its decision-making, and attempted to ensure coherence between internal and external objectives. However the CCP is not simply a conduit for transmitting internal policy priorities into external policy-making; we cannot see the CCP as simply an extension of the internal market into the external sphere. The CCP has since the beginning had a close connection to the GATT, and now WTO. Much of the discussion on reforming the CCP over generations of Treaty revision has centred on the need to facilitate the EU's engagement with the GATT/WTO. So we can also see the CCP as concerned with guiding the EU's contribution to international trade and economic policy-making within the framework of the WTO, including a growing number of WTO-compatible bilateral free trade agreements.

The Lisbon Treaty, furthermore, for the first time mandates the Union to develop an external policy with its own set of wide-ranging objectives intended to uphold and promote its values and interests, and the CCP is embedded into this framework for external action. It is one of only two express external competences granted to the EEC from the very earliest days, was declared exclusive in 1975 (its exclusivity now enshrined in Article 3(1) TFEU) and was therefore a foundational plank of the EU's external identity. The controversy surrounding recent trade negotiations such as the Comprehensive Trade and Economic Agreement with Canada (CETA) and the Transatlantic Trade and Investment Partnership with the USA (TTIP) both exemplifies the continuing importance of trade policy and illustrates the close connection and potential tension between EU external economic policy, its broader foreign policy objectives and its own internal policy preferences. These controversies are also a manifestation of another shift in trade policy-making over the last few years. Once seen as the epitome of technocratic policy-making, dominated by trade diplomats and debated behind closed doors out of the public eye, external trade policy has been brought back into the arena of public debate. The integration of the CCP into ordinary legislative and comitology procedures, with the resulting involvement of the European Parliament, is both a catalyst and a symptom of this shift, while trade policy has acquired renewed political salience in national (and even sub-national) parliaments. Trade negotiations are politicised as never before.

In autumn 2015 DG Trade adopted a new trade strategy, "Trade for All: Towards a more responsible trade and investment strategy".[4] While the policy, given new impetus in 2006, of negotiating ambitious preferential trade agreements (PTAs) with strategic and economically important trade partners has not changed, the title of this document tells a story. In the decade 2000–2010 the political debate largely concerned the type of trade agreement the EU was prepared to negotiate with developing countries in the framework of the Cotonou Convention. In the last decade and especially in the last 5 or 6 years, as the EU began to negotiate PTAs with highly developed economies such as South Korea, Singapore, Japan, Canada and the USA, the debate has turned to the impact of trade agreements on the EU itself, in both economic and regulatory terms. These concerns are reflected in the Trade Strategy. DG Trade recognises the need to explain its strategy to a wider audience, to make the case for its approach to trade liberalisation, and to be more transparent about what is being proposed and negotiated. We will discuss these different aspects of the Strategy in what follows; for now, we may note three features.

First, the document puts a strong emphasis on the economic benefits of trade and the contribution made by trade to jobs and growth in the EU. The Commission claims that over 30 million jobs (one in seven) in the EU are supported by exports. It is "trade for all" in this sense. Second, the Commission stresses the need to ensure that trade is "for all" in the sense of supporting developing economies and sustainable development. This is not only a matter of EU trade policy towards developing countries directly (through the Generalised System of Preferences (GSP) or the Economic Partnership Agreements (EPAs)), but also (and this is new) an awareness of the impact on developing countries of EU PTAs with advanced economies. Third, there is an emphasis on values, on a "responsible" trade and investment policy. This includes protecting the EU's own regulatory, social and environmental standards as well as the external dimension based on Articles 3(5) and 21 TEU: respect for human rights and the social (including labour rights) and environmental aspects of trade.[5]

In this context, we may note that the Council's mandate for the negotiation of TTIP requires that "[t]he Agreement should confirm that the transatlantic trade and investment partnership is based on common values, including the protection and

---

[4]European Commission, Trade for All—Towards a more responsible trade and investment policy, 14 October 2015 ("Trade for All").

[5]European Commission, Trade for All, p. 20.

promotion of human rights and international security".[6] More recently, Commissioner Malmström commented on the signing of CETA, "Trade will happen with or without trade agreements. But by signing a progressive, gold-standard trade deal that upholds our ideals and sets a new model for international commerce, we are demonstrating how to shape globalisation."[7] Trade policy is seen as one instrument to be deployed by the EU in promoting its "milieu goals": the shaping of its international environment.[8] The objectives of the EU's trade policy, and the translation of these objectives into its trade strategy, will be the subject of the next section. We will then turn to a consideration of the scope of the CCP and finally to some of the institutional issues raised by the making of trade policy.

2 The Objectives of the Common Commercial Policy

The Lisbon Treaty for the first time gives the EU an explicit mandate for external action, and a set of objectives to which that action should be directed and principles by which it should be guided. These provisions, which expressly apply to the CCP, are potentially of great significance, embedding it into the Union's broader foreign policy objectives and making it clear that the "uniform principles" on which it is based are not simply a necessary instrument for achieving a common policy (although they do serve that function). In fact, to some extent these changes reflect a long-standing understanding of the CCP as an autonomous external policy and the uses to which CCP powers may be put.

In this section we will examine CCP objectives from three different perspectives: the objectives of the CCP itself; the extent to which the Treaties mandate furtherance of, and compatibility with, internal objectives; and the relevance of the Union's general foreign policy objectives. Underpinning these questions is the greater emphasis on policy coherence in the post-Lisbon Treaties, and in particular on coherence between internal and external policies. Thus while the Treaties mandate the Union to develop an explicitly external commercial policy, they also require the Union to "ensure consistency between the different areas of its external action and between these and its other policies".[9]

[6]Council Directives for the negotiation on the Transatlantic Trade and Investment Partnership between the European Union and the United States of America, 17 June 2013, Council doc. 11103/13, declassified 9 October 2014.

[7]Cecilia Malmström, Signing our trade agreement with Canada, blog post 30 October 2016, http://ec.europa.eu/commission/2014-2019/malmstrom/blog/signing-our-trade-agreement-canada_en (last accessed 1 March 2017).

[8]On milieu goals, see Tocci (2007), p. 5.

[9]Article 21(3) TFEU.

2.1 Specific Objectives for the Common Commercial Policy

In historical terms two objectives of the CCP may be said to have been explicitly mandated by the Treaty of Rome, and they are still present in the TFEU. The first is perhaps not so much an objective in itself as a reflection of the underlying rationale of the CCP: the CCP is to be based on "uniform principles". The purpose of the CCP was to ensure the functioning of the customs union, common market and later the internal market by ensuring the uniformity of external trade rules for all Member States. This was the basis from which the Court in opinion 1/75 derived the exclusive nature of CCP powers, in which the common market was linked to the common interest.[10]

Little was said in the Treaty of Rome about the content of the uniform principles on which the policy was to be based, except that the Union was to "aim to contribute" to the liberalisation of world trade. This second objective linked the nascent common market and its "common interests" to the aims of the GATT.[11] It has clearly influenced Community (and now Union) trade policy.[12] Agreements on trade liberalisation, whether multilateral (within the WTO), plurilateral (e.g. the Agreement on Government Procurement, or the Agreement on Trade in Services, TiSA) or bilateral, are the cornerstone of the EU's CCP. However it has always been recognised that trade liberalisation is not an absolute obligation for the EU and is subject to the policy discretion of the legislature; as the Court strikingly expressed it in 1998, "[the] objective of contributing to the progressive abolition of restrictions on international trade cannot compel the institutions to liberalise imports from non-member countries where to do so would be contrary to the interests of the Community".[13] This approach, balancing liberalisation against other EU interests, has enabled trade policy instruments to be used for non-trade purposes which are not necessarily facilitative of trade, ranging from environmental protection[14] to public health,[15] and even economic sanctions.[16]

---

[10]CJEU, opinion 1/75, *Local Costs*, ECLI:EU:C:1975:145.

[11]CJEU, joined cases 21 to 24/72, *International Fruit Company NV and others v Produktschap voor Groenten en Fruit*, ECLI:EU:C:1972:115, paras. 10–13.

[12]The preambles of the early regulations establishing common rules for imports claimed that "the liberalization of imports [. . .] is the starting point for common rules in this field". See e.g. Council Regulation 288/82/EEC on common rules for imports, OJ 1982 L 35/1.

[13]CJEU, case C-150/94, *UK v Council*, ECLI:EU:C:1998:547, para. 67.

[14]See e.g. Agreement between the Government of the United States of America and the European Community on the coordination of energy-efficient labelling programs for office equipment, OJ 2001 L 172/1; CJEU, case C-281/01, *Commission v Council*, ECLI:EU:C:2002:761.

[15]See e.g. Council Decision 2004/513/EC concerning the conclusion of the WHO Framework Convention on Tobacco Control, OJ 2004 L 213/8.

[16]Before the introduction of a specific legal basis for economic sanctions, CCP powers were used for this purpose; see e.g. CJEU, case C-124/95, *The Queen, ex parte Centro-Com Srl v HM Treasury and Bank of England*, ECLI:EU:C:1997:8.

The Lisbon Treaty increases the level of commitment to liberalisation in Article 206 TFEU, by providing that "the Union *shall* contribute, in the common interest, to the harmonious development of world trade, the progressive abolition of restrictions on international trade and on foreign direct investment, and the lowering of customs and other barriers" (emphasis added). The wording is stronger,[17] but we cannot therefore conclude that trade liberalisation is necessarily an overriding objective. The requirement is to "contribute" to the development of world trade: the commitment is to participate in the process of reciprocal and balanced progressive removal of restrictions, through multilateral and bilateral agreements as well as autonomous trade measures. And the removal of restrictions is to operate in the "common interest" and as part of the Union's contribution to the "harmonious development" of world trade. This clearly leaves room to place liberalisation in a context of environmental regulation and sustainable development, as well as to take account of the social and economic needs of its trading partners. This in turn suggests that trade policy-makers will need to consider not only the specific priorities of the CCP but also the objectives of the EU's other policies, ranging from energy to public health, from environmental protection to migration, and its broader external policy framework.

2.2 *Internal Policy Objectives*

In a sense the very existence of the CCP reflects the needs of the common or internal market; without uniform rules on imports and exports, internal frontier-free movements of goods and services cannot be fully achieved. But does the CCP go beyond the need for uniformity in furthering internal market objectives? Hitherto, this has largely been a matter of political choice. In the last decade, increasing emphasis has been placed by the Commission on the contribution of trade policy to the EU's growth and competitiveness strategies. The focus has shifted from ensuring internal free movement (essentially, the treatment of imports) to assisting EU businesses by opening up third country markets, seeking to ensure that EU regulation does not create barriers for EU exporters and facilitating both inward and outward investment.[18] This message is also at the forefront of the Commission's 2015 trade strategy paper which argues that "trade and investment are powerful engines for growth and job creation".[19]

[17]Dimopoulos (2010), p. 161 argues that the strengthened obligation carries at least the obligation not to move backwards in terms of liberalisation.

[18]European Commission, Trade, Growth and World Affairs: Trade Policy as a Core Component of the EU's 2020 Strategy, COM (2010) 612; Cremona (2010a).

[19]European Commission, Trade for All, p. 8.

This focus has now acquired a Treaty basis. The Treaties, as already mentioned, now explicitly require consistency between external and internal policies (Article 21(3) TFEU), and Article 207 contains a specific provision to this effect. Under Article 207(3) the Council and Commission are to ensure that the EU's international trade agreements are "compatible with internal Union policies and rules". Despite its peremptory wording this provision can be read as an injunction to maintain consistent objectives without establishing a priority rule—a reading supported by the ambiguity of the concept of "internal" policies as a legal category to be afforded priority. This is the sentiment behind the Commission's 2015 trade strategy: "While trade policy must deliver growth, jobs and innovation, it must also be consistent with the principles of the European model [. . .]. It must promote and defend European values".[20] More specifically, the Commission has pledged that "no EU trade agreement will lead to lower levels of consumer, environmental or social and labour protection than offered today in the European Union, nor will they constrain the ability of the EU and Member States to take measures in the future to achieve legitimate public policy objectives on the basis of the level of protection they deem appropriate."[21]

2.3 General External Objectives

The reference to "European values" in the 2015 trade strategy signals one of the most potentially significant changes introduced by the Lisbon Treaty to the governance of EU external policy. A series of Treaty articles establishes principles, values and general objectives which are to guide, or constrain, EU external action in general and its external economic policy in particular. According to Article 205 TFEU, EU external action—including the CCP—shall be "guided by the principles, pursue the objectives and conducted in accordance with the general provisions laid down" in Articles 21 and 22 TEU. And Article 207(1) TFEU provides that the CCP "shall be conducted in the context of the principles and the objectives of the Union's external action". A number of these principles and objectives are likely to be relevant to an external commercial policy, including free and fair trade, the protection and promotion of human rights, sustainable economic, social and environmental development, the eradication of poverty, the integration of all countries into world economy, the sustainable management of global natural resources, and good global governance.[22] Whereas in the past certain specific objectives (in particular environmental protection and development) were to be taken into account in the construction and implementation of other policies, this is a much more extensive attempt to ensure that overall external policy concerns permeate sectoral policies such as the CCP. How important is this change?

[20]European Commission, Trade for All, p. 7.

[21]European Commission, Trade for All, p. 21.

[22]Articles 3(5) and 21 TEU.

We should first recall that the use of trade policy to achieve broader political and non-trade objectives has been part of its historical development.[23] In one sense, then, these provisions give a Treaty-based sanction to what has always been a characteristic of the CCP.

Second, although the EU has a tradition of linking trade to its broader policy agenda, this carries risks. If the Union is heavy in the non-economic demands it makes of its negotiating partners, it may need to make greater economic concessions in return. For these and other reasons we are probably more likely to see the impact of these general external objectives on the broader strategic framing of EU trade policy than used as a component of specific trade agreements. That said, "trade and sustainable development" chapters are a notable feature of the new generation of free trade agreements.[24]

Third, Article 205 TFEU refers us not only to the "principles and objectives" set out in Article 21 TFEU, but also to Article 22, according to which the European Council will, on the basis of these principles and objectives, "define the strategic interests and objectives" of the Union. Thus CCP policy choices will also be mediated through this strategic and more political agenda-setting. An example of this process can be found in the European Council Declaration on serious flooding in Pakistan attached to its conclusions of 16 September 2010. The European Council mandated ministers to agree a package of measures to support Pakistan, and included a "firm commitment to grant exclusively to Pakistan increased market access to the EU through the immediate and time limited reduction of duties on key imports from Pakistan in conformity with WTO rules, to be implemented as soon as possible".[25] The Commission was invited to present proposals. The resulting regulation refers in its preamble to the (not only humanitarian) policy reasons behind the trade preferences:

> The severity of this natural disaster demands an immediate and substantial response, which would take into account the geostrategic importance of Pakistan's partnership with the Union, mainly through Pakistan's key role in the fight against terrorism, while contributing to the overall development, security and stability of the region.[26]

---

[23]In CJEU, opinion 1/78, ECLI:EU:C:1979:224, para. 41 et seq., for example, the Court accepted that trade instruments could be used to advance development objectives. Trade powers may also be used to further environmental objectives (see e.g. CJEU, case C-281/01, *Commission v Council*, ECLI:EU:C:2002:761) and broader foreign policy objectives via the imposition of economic sanctions (see e.g. CJEU, case C-124/95, *R v HM Treasury and Bank of England ex parte Centro-Com*, ECLI:EU:C:1997:8). Such cases may prompt disputes over the appropriate legal basis for the measure; see further Koutrakos (2008), Cremona (2012).

[24]See for example the free trade agreements with Korea, Colombia and Peru, Singapore and Canada.

[25]European Council Conclusions, 16 September 2010, Council doc. EUCO 21/1/10 REV 1; CO EUR 16 CONCL 3, Annex II.

[26]Regulation 1029/2012/EU introducing emergency autonomous trade preferences for Pakistan, OJ 2012 L 316/43, recital 5. It may be noted that despite the emergency it took 2 years for this Regulation to be adopted, witness to the debate engendered in the European Parliament, as well as the need for a WTO waiver.

The explicit recognition we now find in the Treaties of the link between trade policy and strategic foreign policy considerations presents challenges in a context where trade policy has traditionally been seen as technocratic and de-politicized. As has already been argued, this has always been somewhat of a myth: EU trade policy has from the start carried a strong political dimension. But there is a difference between harnessing trade policy instruments for political objectives (a familiar practice) and ensuring that trade policy and foreign policy goals go hand-in-hand, a more complex and delicate task, especially when we consider that foreign policy in the sense of the Common Foreign and Security Policy remains a competence shared with the Member States. This is particularly the case, perhaps, when trade is embedded in a broader politically important agreement: the EU's Association Agreement with Ukraine including a "Deep and Comprehensive Free Trade Area" would be an obvious case in point.

Finally, the political institutions are recognised as having an extensive discretion when it comes to the CCP, and the way in which these "principles and objectives" are worded (general and non-prioritised) leaves much scope for that discretion in translating them into specific policy choices. From that perspective, it is significant that the Commission's 2015 trade strategy makes explicit reference to these objectives: "One of the aims of the EU is to ensure that economic growth goes hand in hand with social justice, respect for human rights, high labour and environmental standards, and health and safety protection. This applies to external as well as internal policies, and so also includes trade and investment policy."[27]

In June 2012 the Council adopted an EU Strategic Framework and Action Plan on Human Rights and Democracy,[28] in which it undertakes to "promote human rights in all areas of its external action without exception" and *inter alia* to integrate the promotion of human rights into its trade and investment policies. Listed in the Action Plan is a commitment to include human rights in Impact Assessments carried out for trade agreements with "significant economic, social and environmental impacts".[29] This commitment was reiterated in May 2014.[30] While this is a political commitment, this does not mean it is without effect. In March 2015 the European Ombudsman adopted a recommendation following a complaint that the

[27]European Commission, Trade for All, p. 22.

[28]EU Strategic Framework and Action Plan on Human Rights and Democracy, 25 June 2012, Council doc. 11855/12.

[29]EU Strategic Framework and Action Plan on Human Rights and Democracy, 25 June 2012, Council doc. 11855/12, Action Plan point 1.

[30]Council conclusions on a rights-based approach to development cooperation, Foreign Affairs (Development) Council, 19 May 2014, Council doc. 10020/14, para. 8. See further DG Trade Guidelines on the analysis of human rights impacts in impact assessments for trade-related policy initiatives, 2 July 2015, tradoc 153591. On Impact Assessment generally see Commission Staff Working Document, Better Regulation Guidelines, 19 May 2015, SWD (2015)111, pp. 16–32.

Commission had not carried out a human rights Impact Assessment in respect of the trade agreement under negotiation with Vietnam. The Ombudsman affirmed that good administration—which it is her role to supervise—includes observance of and respect for fundamental rights: "In fact, where fundamental rights are not respected, there cannot be good administration". Thus, the EU institutions "must always consider the compliance of their actions with fundamental rights and the possible impact of their actions on fundamental rights [...] [and this applies] also with respect to administrative activities in the context of international treaty negotiations".[31] Citing Article 21 TEU, the Ombudsman takes the view that "it would be in the spirit of the legal provisions mentioned above to carry out an HR [human rights] impact assessment", as well as consistent with the Commission's current practice and with the 2012 Action Plan already mentioned.[32] The Ombudsman found that the refusal to carry out a human rights Impact Assessment was an instance of maladministration. In its response to the draft recommendation, the Commission rejected this view, arguing that the range of instruments that it uses to promote human rights (such as the human rights "essential elements" clause in its Partnership and Cooperation Agreement with Vietnam; the trade and sustainable development chapter in the free trade agreement under negotiation; and its human rights dialogue with Vietnam), fulfil the same purpose as an HR Impact Assessment.[33] In her final decision in the case the Ombudsman found these reasons unpersuasive and confirmed her finding of maladministration:

> The Ombudsman does not believe that it is sufficient to develop a range of general policies and instruments to promote human rights compliance while at the same time concluding a Free Trade Agreement which may, in fact, result in non-compliance with human rights requirements. In the view of the Ombudsman, it is far preferable, when negotiating such an Agreement, that any measures intended to prevent or mitigate human rights abuses should be informed by a prior human rights impact assessment.[34]

This case thus raises important questions as to the most appropriate "mix" of instruments in determining how the EU's non-trade objectives may be adequately addressed, including tools deployed in the adoption of trade instruments, such as *ex ante* impact assessments, and non-trade policy instruments such as human rights dialogues. It also shows that the integration of non-trade objectives and in particular the EU's human rights objectives into its trade policy-making processes may be liable to administrative assessment and challenge.[35]

---

[31] Draft recommendation of the European Ombudsman in the inquiry into complaint 1409/2014/JN against the European Commission, para. 21 et seq. The complainants were the International Federation for Human Rights (FIDH) and the Vietnam Committee on Human Rights (VCHR).

[32] Draft recommendation of the European Ombudsman in the inquiry into complaint 1409/2014/JN against the European Commission, para. 24 et seq.

[33] See the joint FIDH-VCHR observations on the opinion of the Commission on the European Ombudsman's draft recommendation ref. 1409/2014/JN, 30 September 2015.

[34] Decision in case 1409/2014/MHZ on the European Commission's failure to carry out a prior human rights impact assessment of the EU-Vietnam free trade agreement, para. 28.

[35] See further Vianello (2016).

What of judicial assessment? In *Front Polisario*,[36] the applicant challenged the legality of the Council decision concluding an agreement with Morocco on trade in agricultural and fisheries products on grounds, *inter alia*, of breach of the EU's values (including fundamental rights) and breach of the principles governing the EU's external action. It was argued that the agreement would *de facto* be applied by Morocco to the territory of Western Sahara, sovereignty over which is disputed. While emphasising the wide discretion enjoyed by the Council in deciding to conclude such an agreement, the General Court nevertheless held that the exercise of that discretion was subject to review on grounds of a manifest error of appraisal, and in particular an assessment of whether the Council has, before taking its decision, carefully and impartially examined all the relevant facts.[37] Although, in the General Court's view, no rule of EU or international law prohibited the Council from concluding the agreement on the ground that it would be applied by Morocco in the disputed territory of Western Sahara, nevertheless the effect of the agreement on the fundamental rights of the population of Western Sahara was a factor which should have been taken into account. Its failure to do so led the Court to annul the decision insofar as it approved the application of the agreement to the Western Sahara. In his opinion on the Council's appeal against the General Court judgment, Advocate General *Wathelet* agreed that the EU institutions are under an obligation "to examine, before adopting the contested decision, the human rights situation in Western Sahara and the impact which the conclusion of the agreement at issue could have there in this regard."[38] However he disagreed with the General Court's application of the Charter of Fundamental Rights on the grounds that the territory of Western Sahara is not within the jurisdiction of EU law nor under the control of the EU or its Member States.[39]

The judgment of the General Court was reversed on appeal by the CJEU,[40] on the ground that there was no legal basis for interpreting the EU-Morocco agreement as applicable to the territory of the Western Sahara, and therefore the decision concluding it could not be of direct and individual concern to the applicant, who therefore lacked standing to bring the action.[41] The CJEU did not, as a result, rule

---

[36] GC, case T-512/12, *Polisario Front*, ECLI:EU:T:2015:953.

[37] GC, case T-512/12, *Polisario Front*, ECLI:EU:T:2015:953, para. 225.

[38] Opinion of AG Wathelet to CJEU, case C-104/16 P, *Polisario Front*, ECLI:EU:C:2016:677, para. 274.

[39] Opinion of AG Wathelet to CJEU, case C-104/16 P, *Polisario Front*, ECLI:EU:C:2016:677, paras. 270–274. The General Court referred to a number of rights contained in the EU's Charter of Fundamental Rights, including Article 1 (human dignity), Article 5 (prohibition of slavery and forced labour), Articles 31 and 32 (fair working conditions and prohibition of child labour).

[40] CJEU, case C-104/16 P, *Council v Front Polisario*, ECLI:EU:C:2016:973.

[41] Although not directly relevant to our discussion here, the Court's ruling is of legal and practical significance in holding that the EU's Association Agreement with Morocco does not apply to the Western Sahara, and therefore that the practice of accepting products from the region as of Moroccan origin will have to be altered.

on the General Court's review of the Council's discretion in matters of external economic policy or whether the Council's duty to take account of all relevant facts included the requirement to assess to human rights implications of concluding the agreement. However in the General Court judgment and the Advocate General's opinion, taken together with the Ombudsman's decision in the Vietnam case, we are starting to see some procedural principles emerge, guiding the policy-making process even in fields of external action where traditionally the institutions have the widest discretion. Note, however, that the standard applied is procedural and not substantive: the Council has an obligation to take account of the human rights implications of its trade policy, but the Court has not (yet) imposed a substantive human rights compliance threshold.[42]

This final point is of importance when considering the significance of Treaty-based CCP objectives more generally, such as sustainable development or the need to contribute to the development of world trade. We are some way from envisaging a review by the Court of whether any one of these objectives has been given sufficient priority. But the procedural requirement that is emerging is significant, and in requiring the Commission and Council to provide evidence of the facts on which policy decisions are based it gives support to more accountability in policy-making.

2.4 Turning Objectives into Strategy

Alongside its external mandate and objectives, the drafters of the Lisbon Treaty made a serious attempt to improve the institutional framework for foreign policy strategy, giving a strategic mandate for external policy to the European Council,[43] and introducing the European External Action Service (EEAS) under the High Representative.[44] Trade policy was not brought within the EEAS, and DG Trade continues to have a strong independent presence; it might be thought to be still operating according to its own strategic agenda. Certainly the major focus of DG Trade's strategy paper of 2010 was the contribution of trade policy to growth, job

[42]Nevertheless we see a move in this direction in the Court of Justice's judgment in *Polisario Front*: in its interpretation of the territorial application of the agreement with Morocco, and the effect of practice in implementing the agreement, the Court took account of principles of international law, including the principle of self-determination.

[43]According the Article 15(1) TEU the European Council is to "define the general political directions and priorities" of the EU in general terms; in the external context, Article 22(1) TEU provides that the European Council "shall identify the strategic interests and objectives of the Union in matters of foreign and security policy and other areas of the external action of the Union". The Foreign Affairs Council, according to Article 16(6) TEU, "shall elaborate the Union's external action on the basis of strategic guidelines laid down by the European Council and ensure that the Union's action is consistent".

[44]Article 27(3) TEU; the EEAS was established by Council Decision 2010/427/EU.

creation and competitiveness within the EU; it contained only the briefest of references to the place of trade policy within the EU's overall foreign policy agenda, remarking that trade policy "has its own distinct economic logic and contribution to make to the external action of the Union" and that "the Union's trade and foreign policies can and should be mutually reinforcing".[45]

However there are signs that the Lisbon Treaty's attempt to integrate trade policy into the broader strategic objectives of EU foreign policy are having an effect, albeit gradually. The 2015 trade strategy, while stressing the contribution of trade policy to the EU's economy, also emphasises the synergies between trade policy and other external policies and the need for consistency with other instruments of EU external action.[46] In addition, while DG Trade of course takes primary responsibility, input from other institutional actors is becoming increasingly important. The use of trade preferences as a response to the floods in Pakistan has already been mentioned and it will be recalled that it was the European Council that initially made this commitment. The Global Strategy for EU foreign policy published by HR/VP Mogherini in June 2016 makes frequent references to trade policy.[47] The new generation of trade agreements, the "Deep and Comprehensive Free Trade Agreements", with their emphasis on regulatory cooperation, services, energy and sustainable development, require a greater involvement of sectoral expertise within the Commission. More significant, at least potentially, is the impact of the increased role of the European Parliament. Within Parliament, trade strategy is discussed not only by the international trade committee (INTA) but also by the foreign affairs committee (AFET). At present it is fair to say that the Parliament's input is primarily reactive to specific proposals, although its own initiative reports are becoming more important.[48] As it develops greater capacity, however, it could play a more important part in shaping EU trade strategy. What then have been the major trends in the EU's trade strategy since 2010?

First, as already mentioned, more attention is being paid to embedding trade policy into the EU's broader political strategies. There are two primary contexts here. The first is EU economic policy and competitiveness. Since (at least) 2010 we can point to a concern with the competitiveness of EU industry and the EU economy more generally, especially the ways in which trade can help the EU maintain its global competitive position in the wake of the economic crisis.[49] As

[45]European Commission, Trade, Growth and World Affairs: Trade Policy as a Core Component of the EU's 2020 Strategy, COM (2010) 612, p. 15.

[46]European Commission, Trade for All, p. 22.

[47]Shared Vision, Common Action: A Stronger Europe A Global Strategy for the European Union's Foreign And Security Policy, 28 June 2016.

[48]Recent examples include own-initiative reports on the Trade in Services agreement (TiSA) under negotiation (2015/2233 (INI)), and on future trade and investment strategy (2015/2015 (INI)).

[49]European Commission, Trade, Growth and World Affairs: Trade Policy as a Core Component of the EU's 2020 Strategy, COM (2010) 612; Bendini R, The future of the EU trade policy, European Parliament In-Depth Analysis, DG EXPO/B/PolDep/Note/2015_227 EN, July 2015-PE 549.054, p. 7.

the 2015 Trade Strategy puts it, "[t]he recent crisis brought a realisation that trade could be a stabilising force in tough times."[50] The argument is both that the EU will need to forge trading links with new sources of economic growth, and that the EU's export industry depends on imported raw materials and components. The second policy context for trade is, as we have seen, foreign policy more generally: "An effective trade policy should [. . .] dovetail with the EU's development and broader foreign policies, as well as the external objectives of EU internal policies, so that they mutually reinforce each other."[51]

The second trend is a reinforcement of the importance of securing bilateral and plurilateral trade deals with key trading partners. Until a decade ago, the EU's bilateral agreements were primarily aimed at developing countries and forging close relationships with its neighbours; trade relations with developed trading partners operated through the WTO. This policy started to change in 2006 and the change has accelerated since 2010, the EU negotiating far-reaching trade agreements with strategic trading partners, including Korea, Singapore, Canada, Japan and the trade and investment agreement with the USA (TTIP) currently under negotiation. In addition to these bilateral agreements, the EU has put its support behind a major plurilateral agreement on services, designed to build upon the GATS (the so-called TiSA).

Third, these trade agreements have changed in character. They attempt to go beyond WTO levels of liberalisation, especially in services, and to include new trade-related policies such as regulatory cooperation, investment, competition, intellectual property and procurement. They also typically contain a chapter on trade and sustainable development in which measures may be included to promote trade in environmentally sustainable goods as well as commitments to maintain labour standards. In addition to the increased political debate surrounding this new generation of trade agreements, their broader scope, although partly reflecting the extended scope of the CCP (discussed further below) also raises the possibility of Member State participation, insofar as they may include commitments going beyond the scope of the (exclusive) CCP. Trade agreements thus become very large packages, cumbersome both to negotiate and to steer through the institutional process of signature, provisional application and conclusion.

Fourth, and perhaps also reflecting the degree to which this new generation of trade agreements are taking over the initiative from multilateral liberalisation within the framework of the WTO: since the signature of the FTA with Korea in 2010 the Union has progressively adopted a practice of explicitly denying direct effect to trade agreements. The decision concluding the WTO agreements in 1994 stated in its Preamble that "by its nature, the Agreement establishing the World Trade Organization, including the Annexes thereto, is not susceptible to being directly invoked in Community or Member State courts".[52] However it was not

[50]European Commission, Trade for All, p. 8.

[51]European Commission, Trade for All, p. 7.

[52]Council Decision 94/800/EC, OJ 1994 L 336/1.

until 2010 that such a statement found its way into the operative provisions of the decision.[53] Such a provision in the Council decision of course only affects the Union; however more recent trade agreements have included a similar provision in the text of the agreement itself.[54] For example, the EU's agreement with Columbia and Peru provides in Article 336 that

> Nothing in this Agreement shall be construed as conferring rights or imposing obligations on persons, other than those created between the Parties under public international law.[55]

The Union's new generation of trade agreements, then, will share with the WTO the inability to be directly invoked in Member State or Union courts. Their enforcement will be governed by their provisions on dispute settlement which typically contain detailed provision for arbitration to resolve disputes between the parties. The move is away from enforcement via ordinary courts. From this perspective the possibility of investor-state arbitration, included in the Vietnam, Singapore and Canada agreements, would result in individual enforcement being possible only for those defined as "investors" and only via arbitration. This is a long way from the possibility of individual enforcement in the courts pioneered in such cases as *Kupferberg*.[56]

The exclusion of direct effect, and therefore of enforcement by individuals, has an additional significance if we take into account the fact that recent studies show a distinct reluctance on the part of the EU and its trade partners to use the dispute settlement procedures established in trade agreements. Evenett demonstrates a decreasing use of WTO dispute settlement by the EU since 2008.[57] According to Mavroidis and Sapir, the signing of a preferential trade agreement by the EU (and the US) is strongly correlated with an absence of trade litigation, both under

[53]Council Decision 2011/265/EU of 16 September 2010 on the signing, on behalf of the European Union, and provisional application of the Free Trade Agreement between the European Union and its Member States, of the one part, and the Republic of Korea, of the other part OJ 2011 L 127/1. Article 8 of the decision provides: "The Agreement shall not be construed as conferring rights or imposing obligations which can be directly invoked before Union or Member State courts and tribunals." Decision 2015/2169/EU of 1 October 2015 on the conclusion of the FTA (OJ 2015 L 307/2) contains an identical provision.

[54]See further Semertzi (2014), p. 1125.

[55]Trade Agreement between the European Union and its Member States, of the one part, and Colombia and Peru, of the other part, OJ 2012 L 354/3. See also the agreement with Central America, Article 356; the agreement with Singapore, Article 17.5. In the Association Agreement with Ukraine, a footnote to chapter 14 of Title IV (the DCFTA) provides: "For the avoidance of doubt, this Title shall not be construed as conferring rights or imposing obligations which can be directly invoked before the domestic courts of the Parties." The Council decision 2014/668/EU, OJ 2014 L 278/1, Article 7 on the signature and provisional application of this agreement includes a similar statement as regards the agreement as a whole, not merely its trade provisions.

[56]CJEU, case 104/81, *Hauptzollamt Mainz v Kupferberg*, ECLI:EU:C:1982:362.

[57]Evenett S (2016) Paper tiger? EU trade enforcement as if binding pacts mattered. New Direction – The Foundation for European Reform, http://europeanreform.org/index.php/site/publications-article/paper-tiger-eu-trade-enforcement-as-if-binding-pacts-mattered (last accessed on 1 March 2017).

the trade agreement's dispute settlement procedures and in the WTO.[58] This suggests that enforceability of trade agreements, whether through courts or via arbitration or other quasi-judicial dispute settlement processes, is not a priority in EU trade policy.

3 The Scope of the Common Commercial Policy

In the evolution of the CCP from the Treaty of Rome to the Treaty of Lisbon, two issues have shaped the debate. One is the identification of the CCP as the policy competence enabling the EU to engage with and play a part in the development of the governance of international trade, especially within the GATT and then the WTO. The other is the extent to which CCP should become the external face of the common and then the internal market.[59] The two are not mutually exclusive, and indeed are in practice closely connected as the process of economic integration both within the EU and at a multilateral/bilateral level has broadened and deepened to cover a wider range of economic activity and different types of regulatory trade barrier. To what extent is there a match between the scope of the CCP and the range of activity that may be covered by an external economic policy: trade in goods, provision of services, rights of establishment and investment and capital movements in particular?

3.1 From Goods to Services and Intellectual Property Rights

In its earliest incarnation the CCP was concerned with trade in goods. It was indeed the policy competence granted as a necessary corollary to the establishment of the customs union and internal free movement of goods. A common external tariff requires that the EU not only adopts autonomous legislation on customs and tariffs but also negotiates tariff and trade agreements. Internal free movement encompassing goods in free circulation[60] requires common rules regulating the initial release of goods into free circulation within the Community market.[61] Other

[58]Mavroidis and Sapir (2015), p. 357: "our data supports the view that the EU and the US become 'doves' after the signature of an FTA. [. . .] We are not suggesting that the EU and the US become 'doves' because of the signing of the FTA. We are simply stating that they become 'doves' after this event."

[59]Kuijper et al. (2013), p. 373.

[60]See now Article 28 TFEU.

[61]CJEU, case 41/76, *Suzanne Criel, née Donckerwolcke and Henri Schou v Procureur de la Ré publique*, ECLI:EU:C:1976:182. Despite the establishment of the common external tariff in 1961 it was not until the completion of the internal market in the 1990s with its removal of internal border controls that all national-based quotas on goods imported from outside the Community were abolished.

components of the common (now internal) market such as rights of establishment or the provision of services did not feature as part of the CCP at this stage. The CCP has always had a broad reach in terms of trade in goods. Goods that are subject to specific regimes internally, such as agricultural and fisheries products, nevertheless fall within the CCP as far as external trade is concerned.[62] The CCP was even held to cover products otherwise falling within the Euratom and European Coal and Steel Community (ECSC) Treaties.[63]

The possible extension of the CCP to cover trade in services came to the fore in the early 1990s in the context of the increased importance of services within the internal market legislative programme and the Uruguay Round negotiations leading to the formation of the WTO, which included agreements on both trade in services (GATS) and intellectual property rights (TRIPS).[64] In opinion 1/94 on the conclusion of the WTO Agreements the Court adopted the WTO/GATS distinction between different "modes of supply" of services and while refusing to exclude trade in services as a matter of principle from the CCP, found that only one of these modes of supply—direct cross-border supply not involving the movement of persons—fell within the CCP as it then stood.[65] The WTO negotiations also raised the issue of trade-related intellectual property rights covered by the TRIPS agreement. Again, the Court in opinion 1/94 found that although some aspects of intellectual property enforcement which related to cross-border trade—in particular those concerned with preventing the release into free circulation of counterfeit goods—could be said to fall within the CCP as it then stood, the TRIPS agreement as whole did not.

Over the course of the next 15 years, the question of the scope of the CCP was revisited several times, in three Treaty revisions.[66] The Nice Treaty did address both trade in services and what was referred to as the "commercial aspects" of intellectual property rights (IPR), in a treaty revision which resulted in a formidably complex set of provisions, special rules on decision-making and limits on the transfer of exclusive competence to the Community.[67] The substantially revised

[62]Although the CCP provides the basis for entering into international commitments, their implementation may be adopted under the EU's agricultural policy competence.

[63]CJEU, opinion 1/94, *WTO*, ECLI:EU:C:1994:384, paras. 24–27. Agreements that specifically concerned coal or steel products were, until the end of that Treaty's life, concluded under the ECSC Treaty.

[64]For an account, see Maresceau (1993), Eeckhout (1994).

[65]CJEU, opinion 1/94, *WTO*, ECLI:EU:C:1994:384, paras. 38–47. The other modes of supply are: consumption abroad, where the consumer moves to the country in which the services are supplied; commercial presence, i.e. the presence of a subsidiary or branch; and the supply of services through the presence of natural persons. The reasons for defining the CCP to include this mode of cross-border supply of services were not very clear, the Court saying simply that it was "not unlike" trade in goods and that there was "no particular reason" why such a supply should not fall within the CCP.

[66]Krajewski (2008).

[67]See further Krenzler and Pitschas (2001), Herrmann (2002), Cremona (2002).

text introduced by the Lisbon Treaty, although inevitably raising some questions of interpretation, is certainly clearer.[68] Under Article 207(1) TFEU:

> The common commercial policy shall be based on uniform principles, particularly with regard to changes in tariff rates, the conclusion of tariff and trade agreements relating to trade in goods and services, and the commercial aspects of intellectual property, foreign direct investment, the achievement of uniformity in measures of liberalisation, export policy and measures to protect trade such as those to be taken in the event of dumping or subsidies.

As well as trade in services and the commercial aspects of intellectual property, it will be noticed that the revised CCP also includes "foreign direct investment" (FDI), an important extension discussed below. The CCP is expressly declared in Article 3(1) TFEU to be an exclusive competence of the EU. This is a codification of the Court's case law on the CCP going back to the 1970s,[69] and apart from being expressly stated in the Treaties, it now applies to the CCP as a whole, without any special sectoral exceptions.[70] As a result, establishing the scope of the newly-extended CCP is particularly significant. The Court has had an opportunity to define its approach to the interpretation of trade in services and the commercial aspects of intellectual property, but not yet at the time of writing the scope of foreign direct investment, the most difficult to delimit in terms of both the international regimes involved and its relation with other competences.

As far as IPR is concerned the question has been the extent to which the WTO TRIPS agreement falls within the scope of the CCP, or instead of other implied external powers based on the existence of internal legislation. In *Daiichi Sankyo* the issue came before the Court in terms of its jurisdiction to interpret the TRIPS in the context of patents for pharmaceuticals, and the Court took the opportunity to consider the impact of the Lisbon Treaty on the CCP.[71] The Member States submitting observations in the case took the view, following earlier case law,[72] that intellectual property should be seen as a shared competence within the framework of the internal market and that the Court's jurisdiction to interpret the TRIPS depends on the degree to which the Union has exercised its competence in the field covered by the agreement. The Commission in contrast argued that the whole of the TRIPS now falls within the EU's exclusive competence under the CCP as being concerned with "the commercial aspects of intellectual property" and must therefore be subject as a whole to the interpretational jurisdiction of the Court.

---

[68]For general comment, see Krajewski (2005), Dimopoulos (2008), Bungenberg (2010), Krajewski (2011).

[69]CJEU, opinion 1/75, *Local Costs*, ECLI:EU:C:1975:145.

[70]Some specific sectoral rules still persist, however, in the manner of decision-making, with unanimity required in the Council for agreements "in the field of" certain services sectors: Article 207(4) TFEU, see further below.

[71]CJEU, case C-414/11, *Daiichi Sankyo Co. Ltd.*, ECLI:EU:C:2013:520.

[72]CJEU, joined cases C-300/98 and C-392/98, *Dior and others*, ECLI:EU:C:2000:688; CJEU, case C-431/05, *Merck Genéricos – Produtos Farmacêuticos*, ECLI:EU:C:2007:496.

Instead of seeking to identify aspects of IPR which may be classified as "commercial", the Court started with the nature of the EU's trade policy. The CCP, the Court said, is first of all concerned with trade with non-member countries. Then the Court turned to its tried-and-tested formula[73] for the scope of the CCP:

> [A] European Union act falls within the common commercial policy if it relates specifically to international trade in that it is essentially intended to promote, facilitate or govern trade and has direct and immediate effects on trade.[74]

Applying this to IPR, only those rules "with a specific link to international trade" would fall within the scope of the CCP.[75] The next step was to focus on the TRIPS, the Court taking the view that the whole of TRIPS has a "specific link to international trade". It is an integral part of the WTO system and is linked to the other WTO agreements *inter alia* through the possibility of cross-retaliation. The Court rejected the argument that those parts of TRIPS which deal with the *substance* of IPR fall rather within the scope of the internal market. The objective of those rules in TRIPS, it said, is the liberalisation of international trade and not the harmonisation of Member State laws. However this ruling that TRIPS as a whole falls within the CCP does not mean means that every international agreement in the field of IPR will likewise fall under the CCP. In opinion 3/15, for example, the issue before the Court was whether the EU had exclusive competence to conclude the Marrakesh Treaty to facilitate access to published works for persons who are blind or visually impaired.[76] Its first conclusion was that exclusive competence could not be based on CCP powers: the main purpose of the agreement is not commercial, nor "to promote, facilitate or govern international trade in accessible format copies" but to improve access to published works for blind and visually impaired people.[77] Although some of its provisions are concerned with cross-border exchange of goods, this "cannot be equated with international trade for commercial purposes."[78]

The Court in *Daiichi Sankyo* adopts an approach to defining the scope of the CCP which allows this external policy to cover a broad spectrum of rules operating at the international level without however displacing the operation of the internal competence where rules are adopted within the EU.[79] We find a similar approach to

[73]A formulation hitherto used primarily in the context of discussion of the purposes for which trade instruments may be used; see e.g. CJEU, case C-411/06, *Commission v Parliament and Council*, ECLI:EU:C:2009:518.

[74]CJEU, case C-414/11, *Daiichi Sankyo Co. Ltd.*, ECLI:EU:C:2013:520, para. 51.

[75]CJEU, case C-414/11, *Daiichi Sankyo Co. Ltd.*, ECLI:EU:C:2013:520, para. 52.

[76]CJEU, opinion 3/15, *Marrakesh Treaty*, ECLI:EU:C:2017:114.

[77]CJEU, opinion 3/15, *Marrakesh Treaty*, ECLI:EU:C:2017:114, para. 82.

[78]CJEU, opinion 3/15, *Marrakesh Treaty*, ECLI:EU:C:2017:114, para. 91. The Court then went on to consider competence to conclude the Treaty under implied powers based on the existence of secondary legislation dealing with copyright, finding that on this basis EU competence was indeed exclusive.

[79]It thus reflects Article 207(6) TFEU, which although not referred to by the Court can be sensed in the background to this judgment (see further below). It is an approach which follows the same logic as that applied by the Court in relation to the SPS and TBT agreements in CJEU, opinion 1/94, *WTO*, ECLI:EU:C:1994:384, paras. 30–33.

the relation between the CCP and internal competences as regards services in the *conditional access services* case.[80] The Court was asked to determine the appropriate legal basis for the signature of a Convention on the legal protection of those offering conditional (i.e. authorised) access to television, radio and information society services. The Council had concluded the Convention on the basis of implied external competence relating to the internal market (Article 114 TFEU), whereas the Commission argued that the Convention fell within the scope of the CCP and thus exclusive competence.[81] Internal legislation, coinciding in part with the scope of the Convention, had been adopted under Article 114 and it was clear that the Convention would have the effect of extending this internal market harmonisation to third country parties, as well as providing for additional measures on enforcement and remedies for unlawful activity, which went beyond the current internal EU legislation.

The Court follows the line of reasoning it used in *Daiichi Sankyo*, defining the scope of the CCP and then analysing the Convention to see whether it is concerned with international trade. It found that the Convention was concerned, not with trade in services between Member States, but with trade in services between Member States and third countries. Although aspects of the Convention go beyond the existing EU legislation, and thus can be seen as aimed at improving the functioning of the internal market, the Court held that these were "incidental" effects and not its main purpose.[82] Article 207 does not distinguish between modes of supply,[83] and in *conditional access services* no distinction is made between the different modes of supply of services, either in the Convention at issue or in the judgment of the Court. The concept of "trade in services" in Article 207 (unlike "services" in Article 56 TFEU) is not a residual category; it covers activity, such as the provision of services through commercial presence abroad, which within the internal market would be treated as establishment.

3.2 And Foreign Direct Investment

The precise scope of "foreign direct investment" (FDI) in Article 207(1) TFEU has given rise to much debate and at the time of writing the Court has not yet addressed

[80]CJEU, case C-137/12, *Commission v Council*, ECLI:EU:C:2013:675.

[81]The Commission challenged the validity of Council Decision 2011/853/EU on the signature of the Convention, which was based on Article 114 TFEU.

[82]The legal basis of an international agreement will represent its main or predominant purpose; incidental elements need not be reflected in a separate legal basis; see e.g. CJEU, case C-377/12, *Commission v Council*, ECLI:EU:C:2014:1903.

[83]Bungenberg (2010), p. 132; Devuyst (2011), p. 654.

the question.[84] We cannot engage in a full discussion here,[85] but it seems clear that portfolio investment falls outside the scope of the CCP since it cannot be regarded as "direct",[86] while measures that relate to pre-establishment market access are covered. Less clear is whether Article 207(1) also includes post-establishment investor protection, including non-discrimination, fair and equitable treatment and protection against expropriation. It will be remembered that the Court has already held that the concept of trade in services goes beyond market access to cover also an agreement establishing a regulatory framework for specific services, and that a measure will fall within the CCP is it is "intended to promote, facilitate or govern trade and has direct and immediate effects on trade",[87] a formulation broad enough to cover post-establishment regulation.[88]

The extension of the CCP to cover FDI raises the question of the relationship between the free movement of capital under Articles 63–66 TFEU, which apply to direct investment, and the CCP. Unlike those on establishment and services the Treaty provisions on movement of capital expressly refer to capital movements between the EU and third countries. These provisions certainly have implications for the Member States' bilateral investment treaties,[89] but what part do they play in the EU's own external policy on investment? To what extent could Articles 63–66 TFEU cover aspects of investment agreements (including provisions on portfolio investment) that would not fall within the CCP? Here again views differ, with the Commission arguing that the Treaty provisions on capital and payments provide not just implied but exclusive treaty-making powers: "to the extent that international agreements on investment affect the scope of the common rules set by the Treaty's Chapter on capitals and payments, the exclusive Union competence to conclude

---

[84] A request for an opinion concerning the EU's competence to conclude the proposed Free Trade Agreement with Singapore, which should throw light on this question, has been submitted by the Commission under Article 218(11) TFEU: CJEU, opinion 2/15, *Singapore Agreement*, pending. The opinion of AG Sharpston was delivered on 21 December 2016, ECLI:EU:C:2016:992.

[85] See, inter alia, Karl (2004), Ceyssens (2005), Dimopoulos (2008), Bungenberg (2010), Ortino and Eeckhout (2011), Bischoff (2011).

[86] The concept of direct investment, as contrasted with portfolio investment, has been interpreted by the Court in the context of the Treaty rules on free movement of capital; see e.g. CJEU, case C-446/04, *Test Claimants in the FII Group Litigation v Commissioners of Inland Revenue*, ECLI:EU:C:2006:774, paras. 180–182.

[87] CJEU, case C-137/12, *Commission v Council*, ECLI:EU:C:2013:675, para. 57.

[88] A position also adopted by AG Sharpston to CJEU, opinion 2/15, *Singapore Agreement*, ECLI:EU:C:2016:992, paras. 330–336.

[89] CJEU, case C-205/06, *Commission v Austria*, ECLI:EU:C:2009:118; CJEU, case C-249/06, *Commission v Sweden*, ECLI:EU:C:2009:119; CJEU, case C-118/07, *Commission v Finland*, ECLI:EU:C:2009:715.

agreements in this area would be implied."[90] Thus for the Commission, matters typically included in international investment agreements will fall within exclusive competence, if not as part of the CCP then by virtue of implied powers as a result of Article 3(2) TFEU. Other authors take the view that given the absence of secondary legislation adopted under Article 64(2) TFEU an exclusive competence cannot be derived from Article 63,[91] and this view was also adopted by Advocate General Sharpston in the context of the request for an opinion on the competence to conclude the Free Trade Agreement with Singapore.[92]

3.3 Limits to the Common Commercial Policy

There are other ways in which the CCP may not be able to provide the sole legal basis for modern trade agreements. Agreements in the field of transport are expressly excluded from the CCP by Article 207(5) TFEU and are thus also covered by implied powers. The equivalent exclusion in Article 133(6) EC was interpreted in opinion 1/08 to cover any agreement which deals with transport, including general services agreements which cover transport services, even if transport is not the predominant purpose of the agreement.[93] The Lisbon Treaty has not altered this position.[94] The external dimensions of competition policy and social policy are based upon implied powers,[95] and the question whether a separate legal basis would be needed will depend on whether the relevant provisions in the agreement impose "obligations so extensive that they constitute distinct objectives that are neither secondary nor indirect" in relation to the agreement's predominant (trade) objectives.[96]

Our conclusion must be therefore, that the Lisbon Treaty has introduced a very considerable expansion of the CCP, and its extension to include trade in services

[90]European Commission, Towards a comprehensive European international investment policy, COM (2010) 343, p. 8. The Commission has relied on this argument in its submissions in opinion 2/15, seeking to establish that if competence is not exclusive on the basis of Article 207 TFEU, then it should nevertheless be exclusive on the basis of Articles 63 and 3(2) TFEU. Exclusivity of the type described in the last phrase of Article 3(2) TFEU (effect on common rules) has not so far been founded directly on a Treaty provision rather than secondary legislation.

[91]See e.g. Ortino and Eeckhout (2011), pp. 315–318.

[92]Opinion of AG Sharpston to CJEU, opinion 2/15, *Singapore Agreement*, ECLI:EU:C:2016:992, paras. 350–359.

[93]CJEU, opinion 1/08, *GATS*, ECLI:EU:C:2009:739, paras. 152–173. This is a departure from the Court's standard "predominant purpose" approach to the legal basis of international agreements; see further Cremona (2010b).

[94]Opinion of AG Sharpston to CJEU, opinion 2/15, Singapore Agreement, ECLI:EU:C:2016:992, para. 114 et seq.

[95]Thus, international agreements in the field of competition are based upon Article 103 TFEU; for a recent example see Council Decision 2014/866/EU on the conclusion of an Agreement between the European Union and the Swiss Confederation concerning cooperation on the application of their competition laws OJ 2014 L 347/1.

[96]CJEU, case C-377/12, *Commission v Council*, ECLI:EU:C:2014:1903, para. 48.

and FDI are both highly significant. However, the CCP does not necessarily offer a complete "one-stop-shop" for wide-ranging contemporary trade and investment agreements. Whatever the final answers to the scope of FDI in Article 207 TFEU, it is clear that the introduction of investment into the EU's trade agreements will have an undeniable (but so far not fully foreseeable) impact on EU policy: it is the investment chapters of new agreements that have proved to be the most controversial for the EU public and European Parliament,[97] and this involvement in international investment has led the Union to seek to lead international initiatives for reform of investment protection and investor-state dispute settlement.[98]

4 Decision-Making

The decision-making procedures under the pre-Lisbon CCP were something of a paradox. While held out as an exemplar of the "Community method", in fact the CCP was subject to special decision-making rules and did not include the normal features of the "Community method", in particular co-decision and comitology. The Lisbon Treaty has integrated the CCP into the ordinary legislative and comitology procedures, a change which represents an important shift in the institutional balance in trade policy making. Although the procedures for the adoption of internal legislation in the field of CCP have posed some challenges, for reasons of space we will here focus on two developments that impact the conclusion of international agreements: the increased role of the European Parliament, and the changes to the voting rules for decision-making in the Council.

4.1 *The European Parliament: Consent, Transparency and Public Debate*

The position of the European Parliament in relation to trade agreements has radically changed. Article 218(6)(a)(v) TFEU provides that the conclusion of an international agreement requires the consent of the European Parliament where it covers a field to which the ordinary legislative procedure applies, and this now includes the CCP. In this, and other cases where the Parliament must now give its consent, the Parliament has shown itself willing to exercise that veto. Its rejection of the Anti-Counterfeiting Trade Agreement (ACTA) illustrates graphically just how much things have changed: the Parliament is now able to veto agreements based on

---

[97]See e.g. European Parliament, resolution of 5 July 2016 on a new forward-looking and innovative future strategy for trade and investment, P8_TA(2016)0299, A8-0220/2016 (2015/2105(INI)).

[98]See e.g. European Commission, Investment in TTIP and beyond – the path for reform, 12 May 2015.

trade policy powers where 7 years ago, before the Lisbon Treaty, it did not even possess the formal right to be consulted.[99] However the negotiation of the ACTA also illustrates that the right to consent to an agreement's conclusion raises questions as to the role of the Parliament in the earlier stages of negotiation. Article 218 (10) TFEU requires that the Parliament is to be kept informed at all stages of the procedure, and Article 207(3) TFEU requires the Commission to report regularly on the progress of negotiations both to the Parliament and to a committee of Member State representatives appointed by the Council. Questions arise as to what being "immediately and fully informed"—as required by Article 218(10)—entails. A 2010 inter-institutional agreement between the Parliament and the Commission contains rules for the implementation of these provisions, including a commitment from the Commission to facilitate the inclusion of Parliamentary observers within the Union delegation in treaty negotiations.[100] On the provision of information, the Commission undertakes to inform the Parliament in the same way as the Council or its special committee.[101]

Among the issues raised by the ACTA, and symptomatic of the direction in which modern trade policy is moving, are those surrounding the pursuit of regulatory objectives via international treaties. Since the procedure for negotiating treaties is not the same as for the adoption of domestic legislation, the use of treaties to shape new regulatory norms raises the question of the need for public debate over international agreements which will have a quasi-legislative impact and may carry fundamental rights implications, as well as the difficulty in balancing this need with the traditional processes of international negotiations, seen as executive rather than legislative activity. Here we turn to the basic procedural complaint of the European Parliament in the case of ACTA: the lack of transparency in the negotiation process and limited possibilities for Parliamentary input. During the ACTA negotiations the Parliament expressed concern over the lack of information on the negotiating text, pointing out that in due course it would need to consent to the agreement.[102] The Commission argued that the negotiation of international trade agreements is generally confidential since the parties do not wish their negotiating positions to be made public in advance of the final result, but that within those constraints it had in fact kept the Parliament informed of the progress of negotiations.[103] The

[99]See further Cremona (2014).

[100]Framework Agreement on relations between the European Parliament and the Commission, 20 October 2010, P7_TA(2010)0366, paras. 23–27 and Annex 3 deal with international negotiations; Annex 2 deals with Parliamentary access to classified information.

[101]Framework Agreement on relations between the European Parliament and the Commission, 20 October 2010, P7_TA(2010)0366, Annex 3, para. 5.

[102]European Parliament, resolution of 10 March 2010 on the transparency and state of play of the ACTA negotiations, P7_TA(2010)0058. See also European Parliament, declaration of 9 September 2010 on the lack of a transparent process for the Anti-Counterfeiting Trade Agreement (ACTA) and potentially objectionable content, P7_TA(2010)0317.

[103]Reply by Commissioner De Gucht on behalf of the Commission to Written question E-0147/10 by Alexander Alvaro (ALDE); see also Transparency of ACTA Negotiations, MEMO 12/99, 13 February 2012.

Parliament's Resolution of November 2010 did recognise the efforts that have been made by the Commission and the greater transparency of the later stages of negotiation.[104]

These political exchanges were accompanied by legal moves. During the earlier SWIFT negotiation, and then in the ACTA case, MEPs used Regulation 1049/2001 on public access to documents to challenge Council and Commission refusals to grant access to information during negotiations.[105] In a first case involving the SWIFT agreement,[106] the General Court held that since international negotiations fall in principle within the domain of the executive and the Council is not acting in its legislative capacity, public participation in the procedure "is necessarily restricted, in view of the legitimate interest in not revealing strategic elements of the negotiations". Nevertheless, the principle of the transparency of the decision-making process of the European Union "cannot be ruled out in international affairs", especially where the international agreement may have an impact on the EU's legislative activity. The ACTA cases concerned documents containing the negotiating mandate and EU negotiating positions. In July 2010, MEP *In't Veld* brought an annulment action against the Commission's refusal to grant her full access under Regulation 1049/2001 to the ACTA negotiating documents.[107] Her action was partially successful but the Court generally supported the Commission position that public disclosure of negotiating positions and discussions during a negotiation could compromise the EU's position and be contrary to its interests. The Court argued that the negotiations "do not in any way prejudice the public debate that may develop once the international agreement is signed, in the context of the ratification procedure."[108]

The Court here takes a traditional view of international treaty negotiation and public debate: that the time for debate is not during negotiations but once they are completed and the treaty needs parliamentary ratification. But is this the most appropriate approach in the case of quasi-legislative treaties? It is not only that in the case of such treaties technical discussion may mask fundamental policy choices. It is also that if the Parliament is expected to assent (or not) without having been involved in the ongoing discussion it will not feel any "ownership" of the resulting text. It is worth recalling, too, that the European Parliament is not subject to the same parliamentary-majority-based disciplines as national Parliaments and its

[104]European Parliament, resolution of 24 November 2010 on the Anti-Counterfeiting Trade Agreement (ACTA), P7_TA(2010)0432.

[105]Article 15(3) TFEU; Regulation 1049/2001 regarding public access to European Parliament, Council and Commission documents, OJ 2001 L 145/43.

[106]GC, case T-529/09, *In't Veld v Council*, ECLI:EU:T:2012:215; CJEU, case C-350/12 P, *Council v In't Veld*, ECLI:EU:C:2014:2039. The General Court, upheld by the Court of Justice partially annulled the Council's refusal to allow access to the opinion of the Council's Legal Service concerning the Commission's recommendation to the Council to authorise the opening of the SWIFT negotiations. The declassified document was made available on 16 February 2015 as Council doc. 11897/09 DCL 1.

[107]GC, case T-301/10, *In't Veld v Commission*, ECLI:EU:T:2013:135.

[108]GC, case T-301/10, *In't Veld v Commission*, ECLI:EU:T:2013:135, para. 181.

support cannot be taken for granted.[109] In an era of widespread communication and social media, it is in practice impossible to keep such negotiations under wraps until they are complete. As the Commission has discovered, campaigns mobilise and take on a life of their own; all kinds of leaks occur; myths may proliferate; it is difficult at the end of such a process to put the agreement to a take-it-or-leave-it vote and expect to have a balanced and well-informed debate. By that stage it is too late. This is a question for national parliaments as well as the European Parliament as the recent difficulties over Belgian acceptance of the signature of the CETA illustrate.

All these factors are no doubt behind the Commission's change of practice. Faced with the widespread and sceptical public debate on the trade and investment agreement under negotiation with the USA (TTIP), not only was the negotiating mandate released,[110] but the Commission also made public many of its position papers and textual proposals.[111] Some of this material had already been the subject of an access to documents request under Regulation 1049/2001 and a consequent complaint to the Ombudsman.[112] The 2015 trade strategy paper contains a chapter on transparency which summarises the Commission's new approach. It undertakes to invite the Council to disclose FTA negotiating directives as soon as they are adopted; to "make its closer engagement with the European Parliament in the context of TTIP the rule for all negotiations"; and to "extend TTIP practices of publishing EU texts online for all trade and investment negotiations and make it clear to all new partners that negotiations will have to follow a transparent approach".[113] In the medium term, these changes will impact the quality and level of the public debate on trade policy. Although transparency could certainly be improved and practice is still evolving, it is important that the hitherto barely-challenged argument that all trade negotiations must be conducted in near-secrecy has been abandoned. The increased role given to the Parliament by the Lisbon Treaty was of course not the only driver of change but it has had a catalytic effect.

4.2 *The Member States: Exclusivity and Unanimity*

Two hall-marks of the CCP since the 1970s have been its nature as an exclusive competence and qualified majority voting. The Nice Treaty amendments, while

---

[109]Monar (2010), p. 148.

[110]Council Directives for the negotiation on the Transatlantic Trade and Investment Partnership between the European Union and the United States of America, 17 June 2013, Council doc. 11103/13, declassified 9 October 2014.

[111]These have been made available on the DG Trade web pages, http://trade.ec.europa.eu/doclib/press/index.cfm?id=1230 (last accessed 1 March 2017).

[112]European Ombudsman, case 119/2015/PHP, opened 18 February 2015, decision 4 November 2015. The Ombudsman has also undertaken an own-initiative inquiry into the transparency of the TTIP negotiations, see European Ombudsman, case OI/10/2014/RA, opened 29 July 2014, decision 6 January 2015.

[113]European Commission, Trade for All, p. 18 et seq.

bringing agreements on trade in services and IPR within the CCP, made significant inroads into the principle of exclusivity through a complex set of linked provisions designed to maintain the presence of the Member States in negotiations involving these new fields.[114] The Lisbon Treaty, in contrast, while extending the scope of the CCP even further, returns to the principle of exclusivity. The CCP is one of the few policy fields declared to be exclusive by Article 3(1) TFEU and there are no sectoral exceptions within the policy field. On the other hand, the Lisbon Treaty protects the interests of the Member States in a different way; instead of participation via shared competence there is provision for unanimous voting in three circumstances—each relating to the conclusion of international agreements (not the adoption of autonomous measures) in "new" CCP fields of services, IPR and FDI.

The first of these requires agreements "in the fields of" trade in services, commercial aspects of IPR and FDI to be subject to unanimous voting in the Council where they contain provisions for which unanimity is required for the adoption of internal rules.[115] Examples would include language arrangements for IPR under Article 118 TFEU; measures which involve "a step backwards" as regards liberalisation of movement of capital involving direct investment under Article 64(3) TFEU; and conditions of employment for third country nationals in Union territory under Article 153(1)(g) and (2) TFEU, if applicable in the context of the supply of services under Modes 3 or 4 (commercial presence and presence of natural persons respectively). Although the precise meaning of "in the field of" is not clear, in this case the necessary clarity is provided by the additional requirement that the agreement must contain "provisions" for which unanimity would be required internally. The same is not true of the other two cases where unanimity is required:

> (a) in the field of trade in cultural and audiovisual services, where these agreements risk prejudicing the Union's cultural and linguistic diversity;
>
> (b) in the field of trade in social, education and health services, where these agreements risk seriously disturbing the national organisation of such services and prejudicing the responsibility of Member States to deliver them.[116]

What does it mean to say that an agreement is "in the field of" cultural services, or health services? Interpreting a similar phrase in the context of the pre-Lisbon Article 133 EC in opinion 1/08, the Court refused to limit its application to cases where the agreement was exclusively or predominantly concerned with specific services sectors and held that it also covers agreements which deal with trade in services generally, but which include these sensitive sectors.[117] It seems likely that a similar interpretation would prevail here. However, the unanimity rule requires a second condition to be met: that the agreement "risks prejudicing" the Union's cultural and linguistic diversity, or "risks seriously disturbing" the national organisations of social, education or health services. These conditions imply complex

[114] On their interpretation, see CJEU, opinion 1/08, *GATS*, ECLI:EU:C:2009:739.

[115] Article 207(4) para. 2 TFEU.

[116] Article 207(4) para. 3 TFEU.

[117] CJEU, opinion 1/08, *GATS*, ECLI:EU:C:2009:739.

judgments and immediately raise the question: who decides when they are fulfilled? There is, in Article 207(4), no emergency brake of the kind provided by Article 48 TFEU in relation to social security, which makes it clear that one Member State may declare its interests affected. Should the decision therefore be a collective decision of the Council? The unanimity rule itself suggests that there may be a need to protect the sensitivities of one or more Member States against a qualified majority; it is then somewhat counter-intuitive to require unanimity for a decision to apply the unanimity exception. It is notable that while paragraph (a) refers to the *Union's* cultural and linguistic diversity, paragraph (b) refers clearly to the *national* organisations of specific public services. This might suggest that a decision to act by unanimous vote under paragraph (a) should be a collective one within the Council as the interest to be protected is identified as belonging to the Union; whereas it should be possible for any one Member State to call on paragraph (b) on the grounds of the impact of the agreement on its national organisation of social, education or health services.

These voting rules, designed to protect the interests of Member States, operate against a background of exclusive Union competence. The extension of exclusive competence over trade in services, IPR and FDI no doubt represents a major competence shift; however, it has been limited in its effect both by the Treaty and by institutional practice. First, Article 207(6) TFEU provides that the granting of an exclusive *external* competence does not imply that internal legislative powers are also exclusive. Thus, an international agreement concluded by the Union, Article 207(4) implies, *may* affect the provision of national social services (in which case its negotiation and conclusion must be decided unanimously); however this does not mean that the Union has an exclusive competence to adopt internal legislation regulating social services. Implementation of such an agreement would be a matter of shared competence under internal decision-making rules.

Second, the move to exclusive external competence over FDI created potentially serious problems for the many hundreds of bilateral investment treaties (BITs) concluded by the Member States. As a transitional measure the Member States have been authorised, under certain conditions, to maintain and conclude BITs with third countries.[118]

And third, given the broad scope of modern PTAs, it is not a foregone conclusion that the CCP's exclusive competence will cover the whole agreement. In the case of CETA the Commission came under political pressure to agree that it should be signed as a mixed agreement. The question of whether the Singapore FTA falls under exclusive competence has been referred to the Court in opinion 2/15.[119] It seems likely that the Member States will continue to be involved in the conclusion of wide-ranging PTAs, a circumstance which poses increasing challenges for EU negotiators.

[118]Regulation 1219/2012/EU establishing transitional arrangements for bilateral investment agreements between Member States and third countries, OJ 2012 L 351/40.

[119]AG Sharpston's opinion in the case concludes that although substantial parts of the FTA are within exclusive competence, either via Article 207(1) TFEU or via Article 3(2) TFEU, some aspects fall within shared competence. See opinion of AG Sharpston to CJEU, opinion 2/15, *Singapore Agreement*, ECLI:EU:C:2016:992.

The "Lisbon settlement", whereby extended exclusivity in the CCP was balanced by requiring the assent of the European Parliament and unanimous voting in Council in some cases, has in practice led to a situation in which both the European Parliament and national parliaments may act as veto players. In the past the trade provisions of mixed agreements were sometimes brought into force early, as exclusively EU agreements which were then automatically terminated on the coming into force of the full agreement. More recent practice has preferred to agree the provisional application of (parts of) an agreement on signature and pending full ratification. A couple of points are of note here. First, although the Treaty rules on provisional application do not require this, the Commission and Council have in some cases agreed that no decision on provisional application will be taken without European Parliamentary approval.[120] Second, difficulties may be encountered in ratifying an agreement which has been signed and is being provisionally applied, raising questions as to the propriety of an indefinite extension of provisional application.[121]

5 Conclusion

How may we evaluate the changes to the Common Commercial Policy brought about by the Lisbon Treaty? To what extent do they represent a revolution? The changes have essentially been three-fold. First, the wider scope of the CCP, its extension to include trade in services, the commercial aspects of intellectual property and foreign direct investment. These are significant, in part because of the link to the scope of the WTO agreements, in part because of the significance of direct investment for modern commercial policy and the consequent ability of the EU to develop a trade and investment policy. The scope of FDI, insofar as it falls within the scope of the CCP, is still contested and we await a definitive judgment on this issue. The Court of Justice has given readings of trade in services and IPR which focus on the effects on trade with third countries rather than on any conceptualisation of the field.

The second major change has been the embedding of EU trade policy into the Union's overall principles and objectives, especially as they refer to external action. The Treaty provisions on trade policy have always left very wide scope for the

[120]CETA is a recent example. See European Commission, Press release, 30 October 2016, http://trade.ec.europa.eu/doclib/press/index.cfm?id=1569 (last accessed 1 March 2017). In the case of the FTA with Korea, the Council agreed that the agreement should not be given provisional application before the adoption of internal legislation of safeguard measures: Council Decision 2011/265/EU, OJ 2011 L 127/1. Article 3(2) provides: "The Council shall coordinate the effective date of provisional application with the date of the entry into force of the proposed Regulation of the European Parliament and of the Council implementing the bilateral safeguard clause of the EU-Korea Free Trade Agreement."

[121]The Association Agreement with Ukraine is a case in point; a mixed agreement, it is currently being provisionally applied. Following a negative referendum, ratification by the Netherlands has been delayed, raising questions as to the future of the agreement.

discretion of the policy-makers; now this discretion should be exercised within the framework of the Treaties' general external objectives, which include sustainable development, "free and fair trade" and the promotion of human rights. The implications are still not worked out, but there are signs, both from the Commission and from the Court, that this normative framework is being taken seriously.

The third change is to the decision-making structures of trade policy. The Commission still plays a key strategic role, but the adoption of the ordinary legislative procedure means that the Commission's key interlocutors now include the European Parliament as well as the Council. The European Parliament has the power to consent to—or to withhold consent from—trade agreements and has proved willing to use its power. Working together with a renewed political and public interest in trade policy, in the wake of several contentious agreements, this new dynamic has led to calls for, and significant progress towards, greater transparency in the negotiation of trade agreements. On the other hand, the Union's recent practice has been to attempt to exclude the courts from the direct enforcement of these agreements, a marked change of practice for bilateral agreements and perhaps an indication of the degree to which the new generation of bilateral trade agreements are seen as at least as—or more—significant than the WTO.

We cannot yet look back from 2016 to 2009 and see a true revolution in trade policy. But the Lisbon Treaty put in place mechanisms which could progressively lead to a "quiet revolution"—a trade policy that looks very different from the paradigm of the last 40 years. Whether this happens, and indeed what such a trade policy might look like, will depend on the choices made by the Commission over the next few years, but also on the ways in which the Parliament rises to the challenge to exercise a strategic influence, and the degree and nature of public engagement in the policy choices to be made.

References

Bischoff JA (2011) Just a little BIT of "mixity"? The EU's role in the field of international investment protection law. Common Mark Law Rev 48(5):1527–1569

Bungenberg M (2010) Going global? The EU's common commercial policy after Lisbon. In: Hermann C, Terhechte J (eds) European yearbook of international economic law, vol 1. Springer, Heidelberg, pp 123–151

Ceyssens J (2005) Towards a common foreign investment policy? Foreign investment in the European constitution. Leg Issues Econ Integr 32(3):259–291

Cremona M (2002) A policy of bits and pieces. The common commercial policy after Nice. Cambridge yearbook of European legal studies, vol 4. Cambridge University Press, Cambridge, pp 61–91

Cremona M (2010a) Balancing Union and Member State interests: opinion 1/2008, choice of legal base and the common commercial policy under the Treaty of Lisbon. Eur Law Rev 35 (5):678–694

Cremona M (2010b) The single market as a global export brand. Eur Bus Law Rev 21(5):663–680

Cremona M (2012) Coherence and EU external environmental policy. In: Morgera E (ed) The external environmental policy of the European Union. Cambridge University Press, Cambridge, pp 33–54

Cremona M (2014) The EU's international regulatory policy, democratic accountability and the ACTA: a cautionary tale. In: Cremona M, Takács T (eds) Trade liberalisation and standardisation – new directions in the 'low politics' of EU foreign policy. EUI/AEL Working Paper 2014/01, European University Institute, Florence

Devuyst Y (2011) The European Union's competence in international trade after the treaty of Lisbon. Georgia J Int Comp Law 39(3):639–661

Dimopoulos A (2008) The common commercial policy after Lisbon: establishing parallelism between internal and external economic policy. Croatian yearbook of European law and policy, vol 4. University of Zagreb, Faculty of Law, Zagreb, pp 101–129

Dimopoulos A (2010) The effects of the Lisbon treaty on the principles and objectives of the common commercial policy. Eur Foreign Aff Rev 15(2):153–170

Eeckhout P (1994) The European internal market and international trade – a legal analysis. Oxford University Press, Oxford

Herrmann C (2002) Common commercial policy after nice: Sisyphus would have done a better job. Common Mark Law Rev 39(1):7–29

Karl J (2004) The competence for foreign direct investment – new powers for the EU. J World Invest Trade 5(3):413–448

Koutrakos P (2008) Legal basis and delimitation of competence in EU external relations. In: Cremona M, de Witte B (eds) EU foreign relations law: constitutional fundamentals. Hart, Oxford, pp 171–198

Koutrakos P (2015) External action: common commercial policy, common foreign and security policy, common security and defence policy. In: Chalmers D, Arnull A (eds) The Oxford handbook of European Union law. Oxford University Press, Oxford, pp 271–299

Krajewski M (2005) External trade law and the constitutional treaty: towards a federal and more democratic common commercial policy. Common Mark Law Rev 42(1):91–127

Krajewski M (2008) Of modes and sectors – external relations, internal debates and the special case of (trade in) services. In: Cremona M (ed) Developments in EU external relations law. Oxford University Press, Oxford, pp 172–214

Krajewski M (2011) The reform of the common commercial policy. In: Biondi A, Eeckhout P, Ripley S (eds) EU law after Lisbon. Oxford University Press, Oxford, pp 292–311

Krenzler HG, Pitschas C (2001) Progress or stagnation? The common commercial policy after Nice. Eur Foreign Aff Rev 6:291–313

Kuijper PJ, Wouters J, Hoffmeister F, de Baere G, Ramopoulos T (2013) The law of EU external relations. Oxford University Press, Oxford

Maresceau M (1993) The concept "Common Commercial Policy" and the difficult road to Maastricht. In: Maresceau M (ed) The EC's commercial policy after 1992: the legal dimension. Martinus Nijhoff, Dordrecht, pp 3–19

Mavroidis PC, Sapir A (2015) Dial PTAs for peace: the influence of preferential trade agreements on litigation between trading partners. J World Trade 49(3):351–372

Meunier S, Nicolaidis K (1999) Who speaks for Europe? The delegation of trade authority in the EU. J Common Mark Stud 37(3):477–501

Monar J (2010) The rejection of the EU-US SWIFT interim agreement by the European Parliament: a historic vote and its implications. Eur Foreign Aff Rev 15(2):143–151

Ortino F, Eeckhout P (2011) Towards an EU policy on foreign direct investment. In: Biondi A, Eeckhout P, Ripley S (eds) EU law after Lisbon. Oxford University Press, Oxford, pp 312–329

Semertzi A (2014) The preclusion of direct effect in the recently concluded EU free trade agreements. Common Mark Law Rev 51(4):1125–1158

Tocci N (2007) Profiling normative foreign policy: The European Union and its global partners. CEPS Working Document No. 279, Brussels

Vianello I (2016) Guaranteeing respect for human rights in the EU's external relations: what role for administrative law? In: Poli S (ed) Protecting human rights in the European Union's external relations. CLEER Papers 2016/5, Asser Institute, The Hague, pp 21–36

Front-Loading Trade Policy-Making in the European Union: Towards a Trade Act

Thomas Cottier

Abstract The shift to non-tariff measures and regulatory behind-the-border issues in commercial policy—and thus to matters traditionally pertaining to domestic law of Member States and the European Union—call for enhanced inclusiveness in policy-making. Such inclusiveness, under current rules of exclusive powers and mixed agreements, mainly focuses on the final stages of negotiations. It undermines the authority and treaty-making powers of the Union, frustrating legitimate expectations and trust of trading partners. Instead, major issues and debates on trade policy should be front-loaded and not taking place at the stage of consent and signature, prior to ratification and the adoption of implementing legislation. In assessing current procedures and its shortcomings under the practice of mixed agreements, the paper suggest developing and introducing a European Trade Act, perhaps called International Trade, Investment and Co-operation Regulation (ITICR). In comparison with, and referring to, the United States Trade Act, the paper expounds the potential scope and functions of a European Trade Act under the Lisbon Treaties and its assistance in achieving the goal of front-loading trade policy and investment policy debates within the Union. A Trade Act reduces the risks under the bifurcated system of exclusive and mixed competences of the Union in international economic law. It bears the potential to enhance inclusiveness and thus democratic legitimacy while at the same time supporting effective treaty-making powers of the European Union.

Contents

The author is indebted to Mathias Kende for valuable comments and to the editors and Anja Trautmann for carefully reviewing the paper.

T. Cottier (✉)
World Trade Institute, University of Bern, Bern, Switzerland
e-mail: thomas.cottier@wti.org

M. Bungenberg et al. (eds.), *European Yearbook of International Economic Law 2017*, European Yearbook of International Economic Law 8,
DOI 10.1007/978-3-319-58832-2_2

1 The Problem

The bifurcated nature of external relations of the European Union is an endemic problem. Powers of the Union in foreign affairs and international trade do not match the canon of exclusive competences, even in the traditional field of trade policy which ever since has been one of the few exclusive powers due to the Customs Union. International negotiations inherently tend to go beyond the boundaries defined internally, thus requiring to resorting to the format of mixed agreements.[1] Unlike agreements concluded under exclusive powers, mixed agreements depend upon consent of all Members States, their parliaments prior to the entry into force, in addition to qualified majority approval by the Council and consent by a simple majority of European Parliament. The increasing importance of addressing non-tariff measures (NTMs) and other regulatory behind-the-border issues pertaining to domestic legislation of Member States further reinforces the category of mixed agreements, rather than reducing it. Commercial policy as a field of exclusive competence is outfoxed by the process of globalization and the need to respond to it and to harness it. True, it does not affect the negotiating powers of the Union, and of the Commission in particular. There is no difference in negotiating agreements under exclusive and mixed powers. Under a mandate of the Council and thus Member States, the Commission negotiates upon regular consultations with Member States, taking into account feedback obtained in the process. Internal consultations do not distinguish between exclusive and mixed powers. Member

[1] For a recent discussion of mixed agreements and further references see Cottier (2016).

States are consulted at all stages on all issues alike. For example, in WTO negotiations it does not matter and does not influence the formal standing and role of Member States for practical purposes whether an issue forms part of exclusive or shared powers, albeit the potential of a mixed agreement obliges to take concerns of each of the Member State on its own and does not allow to work with majorities. Whether or not a mixed agreement results often can only be determined results are achieved. The difference between exclusive and mixed agreements thus often arises at a late stage prior to signature and the process of parliamentary approval and ratification. The discussion held on the Comprehensive Economic and Trade Agreement with Canada (CETA) with the Commission reluctantly conceding to a mixed agreement is just a recent example in point.[2]

It may be argued that the requirement of unanimity—otherwise limited to very few areas today of economic regulation, in particular taxation—offers an opportunity to strengthen treaty-making powers of the European Union vis-à-vis the rest of the World. The Commission is in a position to fend-off claims and demands by pointing to difficulties to pass them in all parliaments of Member States back home. The resulting rigidity may be considered an advantage in defending European interests, for example in addressing agricultural policy, environmental or labour migration or labour standards. The reality, however, is that European interests in making progress in international law are often impaired, hampered and paralysed. The need to submit results to Parliaments of all Member States for consent undermines the treaty-making powers of the Union. Partners are not willing to engage in costly negotiations knowing that any result may be taken hostage by the whims and manoeuvers of domestic politics in Member States. Obviously, it is tempting for politicians to generate electoral support by opposing impending negotiations and to create pressures to extract concessions which may not be directly related to the issue. The increasing trend to hold referenda on international agreements further reinforces such temptation. The rejection of the EU-Ukraine Trade Agreements by Dutch voters on 6 April 2016 in a ratio of 61.28% is a recent example in point.[3] Mainly motivated by domestic affairs and the opportunity to express mistrust vis-à-vis the own Government and Cabinet, the negative vote amplified international problems and undermines the credibility of the Union to engage and do business on the basis of mutual trust. The legal complaint lodged in September 2016 before the German Constitutional Court to stop signing the

[2]European Commission, Press Release, European Commission proposes signature and conclusion of EU-Canada trade deal, IP-16-2371, 5 July 2016: "The deal is set to benefit people and businesses – big and small – across Europe as of the first day of its implementation. To allow for a swift signature and provisional application, so that the expected benefits are reaped without unnecessary delay, the Commission has decided to propose CETA as 'mixed' agreement. This is without prejudice to its legal view, as expressed in a case currently being examined by the European Court of Justice concerning the trade deal reached between the EU and Singapore. With this step, the Commission makes its contribution for the deal to be signed during the next EU-Canada Summit, in October."

[3]Marmon (2016).

Comprehensive Economic and Trade Agreement (CETA) with Canada shortly before closing negotiations, requesting in vain urgent and provisional measures, and prohibiting approval of the agreement by the German Government, came at an odd and very late stage in the process.[4] Likewise, the temporary opposition of the Wallonia Parliament in Belgium (representing 3.6 million out of 545 in the Union or 0.66%) to approve CETA with Canada on 24 October 2016 not only upheld the conclusion and signature of the Agreement.[5] It seriously questions the treaty-making powers of the Union and its ability to deliver and implement results in light of the Belgian declaration issued on CETA and option to submit the agreement to the European Court of Justice. A comment was timely entitled the *Age of Vetocracy*.[6]

The same problem is likely to be repeated with increasing resistance to the complex Transatlantic Trade and Investment Partnership (TTIP) with the United States. The cliff-hanger experience with CETA may be a precursor to even more serious challenges to EU treaty-making powers in areas which ever since have been an exclusive competence and stronghold of the EEC and the European Union, in particular technical barriers to trade. Like CETA, TTIP entails new and novel concepts not inherently covered by exclusive powers, in particular regulatory cooperation beyond technical barriers to trade. Thus for legal, but also political reasons, they are qualified to be of a mixed nature. The repeated opposition to TTIP by cabinet members in particular in Germany[7] and Austria[8] during ongoing negotiations in 2016 strongly undermine both the authority and credibility of national governments previously committed to the project, and of the credibility of the European Union as a negotiating partner. Potential early harvests, such as the revision of the 1998 Mutual Recognition Agreement and the recognition of best manufacturing practices in the pharmaceutical sector were put at risk. Again, mainly domestic political motives translate into complicating international relations, weakening the standing of Europe in the World.

---

[4]German Constitutional Court, Applications for a Preliminary Injunction in the “CETA” Proceedings Unsuccessful; Press Release No. 71/2016 of 13 October 2016.

[5]BBC News, Belgium Walloons block key EU Ceta trade deal with Canada, 24 October 2016. The Wallon Parliament, upon further negotiations with capital and the EU agreed to consent on 27 October 2016 and CETA was signed on 30 October 2016; The Guardian, Belgian politicians drop opposition to EU-Canada trade deal, 27 October 2016.

[6]Charlemagne, The age of vetocracy, The Economist, 29 October 2016, p. 26.

[7]TTIP has failed – but no one is admitting it, says German Vice-Chancellor Sigmar Gabriel: Germany’s Vice-Chancellor said in 14 rounds of talks neither side had agreed on a single common chapter out of the 27 being deliberated, Independent, 28 August 2016.

[8]Austrian economy minister adds his “nein” to TTIP debate, EurActive.com, 31 August 2016, https://www.euractiv.com/section/trade-society/news/austrian-economy-minister-adds-his-nein-to-ttip-debate/ (last accessed 1 March 2017).

2 Forum Shifting in Law-Making

It is not a matter of deploring such interventions, or even taking a moralising stand. They essentially relate to the fact of forum shifting in the process of globalization. The phenomenon of *vetocracy* is not an accident of history. It indicates apparent deficiencies in inclusiveness and democratic legitimacy of traditional processes. Matters formerly pertaining to domestic law and parliamentary debate and decision-making, and thus controlled by the electorate, have been shifting to the European and international realms. These shifts mainly took place by recourse to modes of diplomatic negotiations, eventually translating and developing into more inclusive procedures within the European Union. Working on non-tariff barriers—the origin of what we call behind-the-border issues—eventually developed into expert committees open to participation by industry and eventual civil society within the internal market. The extension into other areas of law-making accelerated the rise of the European Parliament to become on par with the Council in terms of internal legislation. The increase in treaty-making powers in external relations also strengthened the position of parliament, albeit not to a comparable extent. It will be seen that the same shift to non-tariff measures, much earlier, triggered the 1974 Trade Act in United States. Importantly, these shifts need to catch up in terms of procedures with the substance and to create appropriate substance-structure pairings are long-term constitutional processes.[9] In Europe, they have not been sufficiently developed and realised in the field of external economic relations and foreign policy in general terms.

The main approach addressing the extension of subject matter in international negotiations ever since the conclusion of the Uruguay Round of the WTO has been to enlarge exclusive trade policy prerogatives of the Union. Following the landmark Advisory Opinion 1/94 relating to the WTO agreements, powers were extended in a complex and somewhat contradictory manner by the Treaty of Amsterdam. New areas of services and intellectual property were included but partly subjected to unanimity. Others remained explicitly excluded. The Treaty of Lisbon made further progress in consolidation of trade policy prerogatives of the Union, adding new powers on investment protection, yet short of portfolio investment. Areas subject to unanimity in domestic affairs, such as taxation, are equally subject to unanimity, as well as other enumerated areas, in particular audio-visual services, social and educational services. The provision of Article 207(6) TFEU carefully avoids that trade policy and international negotiations affect the allocation of internal allocations of powers relating to the internal market.

As indicated, the problem with enumerative powers in the field of external economic policy is that they will always fall short of international developments and efforts to harness globalization. Each of the agreements inherently adds subject matter which constitutionally still pertains to Member States. It is for that reason

[9]For the evolutionary interdependence of substance and decision-making structures see Cottier (1993).

that the Commission conceded that CETA is a mixed agreements—exposing it thus to unanimity of national parliaments (including regional bodies in Belgium). The same is likely to be true for TTIP, the other water-front treaty in the making. Allocating all foreign powers to the Union, of course, would be the best solution in terms of safeguarding effective treaty-making powers. Yet this would imply a shift to a federacy and formal federal structures, away from the *sui generis* legal nature of the EU as a confederation and what in German law is called *Staatenverbund* under past and current treaty law.[10] There is, at this point in time of devolution and fragmentation, no political will to move towards unitary powers in foreign affairs.[11] Importantly, such a move may not sufficiently address the constitutional problem behind shared powers and mixed agreements: the challenge to secure and bring about sufficient inclusion and thus democratic legitimacy of internationally negotiated rules affecting legislative powers which traditionally pertain to national or regional parliaments, legislators or executive branches.

3 The Challenge of Inclusive Participation

The shift from reducing tariffs to non-tariff measures in the late 1980s, and ever since the inclusion of services and intellectual property protection in the WTO, has not been accompanied by more inclusive processes of policy making in international law. Nothing has changed in the *modus operandi* of WTO talks ever since non-tariff barriers were firstly addressed in the Kennedy Round in 1964. They are essentially diplomatic and governmental, at the exclusion of civil society, at least in formal stages. More inclusive procedures all depend upon domestic reform and approaches. It is up to each of the Members of the WTO to define the impact of their parliaments, business and of civil society in the preparatory phase of a negotiation, during and upon completion of the process.

[10]For example German Constitutional Court, Judgment of 30 June 2009, 2 BvE 2/08—*Lisbon Treaty*, headnote 1: "Article 23 of the Basic Law grants powers to take part in and develop a European Union designed as an association of sovereign states (*Staatenverbund*). The concept of *Verbund* covers a close long-term association of states which remain sovereign, a treaty-based association which exercises public authority, but whose fundamental order is subject to the decision-making power of the Member States and in which the peoples, i.e. the citizens, of the Member States remain the subjects of democratic legitimation." The notion of *Staatenverbund* was introduced in case law in assessing the Maastricht Treaty, BVerfGE 89, 155 (Judgment of 12 October 1993).

[11]"Mixity is there to stay", Rosas (2010), p. 367. For further references see Cottier (2016), p. 12, fn. 1.

3.1 International Law and Diplomacy

There are no international standards on inclusiveness as international law is not concerned with the political process at home, except for transparency and the obligation to provide judicial review of trade-related administrative decisions. International law at this stage, and based upon the principle of sovereignty and self-determination, does not know a right to democracy and essentially has remained a black box open to all forms of government. Keeping peace among nations cannot afford to exclude authoritarian governments, even dictatorships, from the international community. The structure of contemporary international law is not inclusive and thus badly prepared to absorb the shift of fora in the wake of globalisation and the need to harness it.

Matters addressing non-tariff barriers and measures traditionally pertaining to domestic law thus today are addressed and settled by way of diplomatic negotiations, often perceived to be exclusive and not sufficiently transparent and accountable. This creates suspicion and resistance. The legitimacy of the WTO and of international agreements negotiated by governments has been increasingly challenged, ever since the 1999 Seattle Ministerial Conference.[12] The shift to preferential trade agreements ever since the end of the Cold War and the accession of China to the WTO in 2001 extended the issue of legitimacy to preferential trade agreements and plurilateral, critical mass agreements formally negotiated and concluded outside the WTO. The decline of the Doha Development agenda eased criticism of the WTO, and turned criticism to agreements like CETA and TTIP. The public perception of these processes and projects, perhaps, is more important than reality which lacks appropriate communication to the public. In reality, diplomatic processes follow strict protocols. They operate on the basis of government instructions and reporting. They are much more rational and interest driven and operating with variable coalitions than generally perceived by the public at large. Indirectly, negotiating tasks and directions in democracies are democratically legitimate as they are founded and supported by prevailing views in Parliament and the executive branch. Yet, these linkages often are not sufficiently visible to outsiders in the tradition of confidential negotiations behind closed doors.

It will take a long time to build more transparent processes on the international level, equivalent to domestic democracy. A proper balance of confidentiality and transparency needs to be found. This is difficult. But it is not impossible within multilevel governance as domestic processes respond to the same needs. Neither are domestic procedures in democracy fully transparent nor confidential, but ideally operate in a way to maintain checks and balances domestically. Primarily, domestic procedures within States and the EU need to be developed and extended to international affairs and thus trade and investment related policies. The matter primarily pertains to each member of the international community to develop appropriate tools of inclusiveness as a matter of home work. Obviously, they will

[12] For a discussion see Cottier (2009a).

move with different speed and needs. Eventually a common ground for international standards of inclusiveness may emerge. We expect the European Union to develop a leading role, given its bifurcated structure and pressing needs to address the issue with a view to safeguard its authority and treaty-making powers.

3.2 European Union Law Treaty-Making

Within the European Union, structures of decision-making in foreign affairs have not fundamentally changed up to now—despite the shift of fora described in the field on non-tariff measures. Democratic control in treaty-making mainly rests upon ex post consent or refusal of negotiated results. The decision to take up negotiations is a matter for the Council, upon proposal by the Commission. Likewise, the Council adopts the negotiating mandate based upon which the Commission engages the negotiating process. The European Parliament is consulted, but not required to consent. During negotiations, Member States and the European Parliament may influence processes politically, but cannot formally influence directions. Adjustments to the negotiating mandates are taken by the Council alone. The European Parliament and National Parliaments of Member States are essentially limited to ex-post controls in the process of consent and ratification and implementation. Given this configuration, it is not astonishing that Member States and their representatives—during ongoing negotiations seek to informally using appropriate means of political communication, and to advance their own interests in doing so. Objections made by civil society, national or regional parliaments, at the time to the WTO Agreements, and more recently to preferential trade agreements with Ukraine, Canada and likely the United States thus are not accidental, but inherent to a system which largely excludes these actors in conceptualising future agreements and in defining their scope and boundaries.

In this vacuum of appropriate structures of inclusive participation prior and during the negotiating phase, it cannot be astonishing that Governments of Member States insist on their treaty-making powers and thus upon the anomaly of mixed agreements within the European Union. Mixity remains the main instrument to influence new and emerging subjects under negotiations. Unless a model of unitary powers can be found and developed in practice which offers enhanced inclusiveness, mixed agreements indeed are likely to stay in trade policy and other areas of foreign affairs of the Union and its Member States.

4 Front-Loading of Trade and Investment Policy-Making

At this point in time, it is not a matter of suggesting on my part to remove mixed agreements, but to complement treaty-making under the Lisbon Treaty with procedures and structures enabling Member States to effectively defend their interests at all critical stages of the negotiating process, in particular at its inception when directions are set. It is a matter of framing the process in a manner that these concerns are effectively heard at the outside and settled prior to engaging talks on the international level, or during such talks. Moreover, it is important to shape these procedures in a way to create the necessary trust and confidence with partners that engaging in talks is worthwhile and obstacles to success remain reasonably limited at the exclusion of arbitrary and capricious captivation of negotiations for whatever political ends. It is submitted that the emphasis of participation should be upon the preparation and inception of negotiations in broadly defining the objectives, scope and strategy of talks. In other words, international trade policy making should be front-loaded, rather than primarily assessed ex-post in internal processes. There should be a broad and robust debate on scope, objectives, goals and conditions of EU commercial policy, upon which international negotiations would build upon. Legal foundations to this effect are currently lacking.

4.1 The Lack of Specific Objectives in Primary Law

Normative goals in primary EU law on commercial policy remain generic and very general. They do not offer more specific guidance as to the conduct of external economic relations and as to how broadly define goals and its interests should best be protected and promoted. Articles 206 and 207 TFEU do not offer much guidance in terms of detailed goals, objectives and conditions of EU commercial policy. Article 206 TFEU commits the Union to contribute to harmonious development of world trade, the progressive abolition of restrictions on international trade and foreign investment and the lowering of customs and other barriers. The provisions refers to Article 21 TEU, stating the general objectives of external action which shall be guided by the principles which had inspired the creation of the Union domestically, in particular democracy the rule of law, human rights and fundamental freedoms. It seeks to build international partnerships and intensive international cooperation with a view to preserve its core values, its interests and security, independence and integrity and, inter alia, to promote the integration of countries into the World economy by lowering trade barriers and to foster sustainable developments. Likewise, Article 208 TFEU on development co-operation refers to Article 21 TEU and generally focuses on poverty alleviation.

Article 207 TFEU is limited to a detailed regulation of powers in external economic relations, the role of EU bodies and EU Member States in trade and investment policy making; it does not state particular goals.[13] One would assume that more precise goals can be found and traced in different regulatory chapters of EU law. Yet, neither the provisions on the internal market and in particular on trade in agricultural, nor on fundamental freedoms (except freedom of capital in

[13]See Cottier and Trimberg (2015).

Articles 63–66 TFEU) offers more precise guidance as to third party relations. In fact, related powers were defined in early developments as implied powers[14] and subsequently assessed and codified in trade policy provisions.

It can be argued that there are good reasons to leave the constitutional level with generic goals and terms, given the difficulty to amend primary law due to the requirement of unanimity in treaty-making. Moreover, it constitutionally grants flexibility and adjustment to new needs and developments without changing the treaty in a cumbersome manner. Most States have been operating on this model emphasising executive powers in foreign affairs. Yet at the same time, the provisions are unable to arbitrate in setting goals and defining interests at stake more precisely. Such decisions could be expected to be found in secondary law and the regulations relating to the conduct of commercial policy. But the level of secondary law has been limited, so far, to implement the results of agreements concluded, in particular within the World Trade Organization. Except for the Trade Barriers Regulation, defining procedural rights of private actors with view to instigate WTO and PTA dispute settlement mechanism on the level of international law,[15] these instruments translate existing treaties and instruments into domestic law, allocating powers and jurisdictions.

4.2 The Role of Negotiating Directives

Defining more precise goals therefore has remained with the elaboration of mandates of negotiations and the negotiating process. Proposed by the Commission, directives are subject to discussion by the European Parliament's Trade Policy Committee and approval and adoption by the Council as prepared by the Trade Policy Committee (*Comité 113*) in accordance with Article 207(3) para. 1 TFEU. Directives of negotiations (negotiating mandates), for a long time, were classified and not made available to the public at large. Goals and objectives for a long time were not meant to be officially known to the negotiating partner and own constituencies, maximising leeway for the Commission. For example, the mandate relating to CETA was adopted on 24 April 2009, revised in 2011, but only released on 15 December 2015.[16] Recently, this has significantly changed and the Trade Policy

[14]CJEU, case 22/70, *Commission v. Council (AETR)*, ECLI:EU:C:1971:32.

[15]Regulation (EU) No 654/2014 of the European Parliament and of the Council of 15 May 2014 concerning the exercise of the Union's rights for the application and enforcement of international trade rules and amending Council Regulation (EC) No 3286/94 laying down Community procedures in the field of the common commercial policy in order to ensure the exercise of the Community's rights under international trade rules, in particular those established under the auspices of the World Trade Organization Regulation (EC) No 3286/94 – procedures to ensure the exercise of the EU's rights under international trade rules, in particular those established under the auspices of the World Trade Organization, OJ 2014 L 189/50.

[16]Council of the European Union, Partial Declassification 9036/09, 14 December 2015.

Committee adopted an ad hoc approach. Under new policies of transparency, developed within TTIP negotiations, the mandate adopted on 17 June 2013 eventually was declassified and made available within 16 months on 9 October 2014.[17] It was a major shift towards greater transparency. It was part of the overall (but not complete) release of preparatory documents stating EU positions and proposals in greater detail. TTIP negotiations thus brought about an unprecedented, unilateral and welcome shift towards greater transparency of negotiating documents.[18] The policy so far has not been reciprocated by the United States and agreed texts thus remain confidential until negotiations are concluded.

Directives of negotiations of the European Council essentially follow the structure of WTO law. Taking the example of directives for negotiations on TTIP,[19] they sets out the contours of a free trade agreement compatible within Article XXIV GATT and Article V GATS and other WTO rules (para. 2), yet without engaging in detailed instructions for most of its parts. A number of issues are addressed more precisely. For example, the directives call for investor state dispute settlement (ISDS, para. 22), European standards on investment protection (para. 23), regulatory coherence and regulatory compatibility without prejudice to existing health standards, for the inclusion of geographical indications (para. 29), government procurement to extend to local authorities (para. 24), the inclusion of core labour standards, the inclusion on disciplines on competition policy (para. 36) and the inclusion of trade in energy (para. 37). The directives explicitly reserve "the most sensitive tariffs" (para. 10) and exclude negotiations on audio-visual services (para. 21).

Interestingly, the TTIP directives do not address specific trade issues looming large in transatlantic relations which one would expect to be addressed. Issues in agricultural policies are not addressed except for sensitive tariffs. Specific subsidies are not addressed. To name a few: the directives remain silent on dual use goods and restrictions for national security and coordination on economic counter measures outside of UN sanctions; investment in key areas of infrastructure for national interest, data protection and trade in genetically modified organisms (GMOs), parallel trade and competition in the field of IPRs, in particular trademarked goods, common rules on transfer of technology, of increasing importance in the age of climate change mitigation and adaption, carbon subsidies, control of electronic data, internet and safe havens for providers, restrictions on exports of oil and gas, and highly controversial liberalization of services in education and health, or the issue of strategic investment in infrastructure and its control.

---

[17] Council of the European Union, Declassification 11103/B DCL 1, 9 October 2014.

[18] European Commission, DG Trade, TTIP, http://ec.europa.eu/trade/policy/in-focus/ttip/about-ttip/ (last accessed 1 March 2017).

[19] Directives for the Negotiation on a Comprehensive Trade and Investment Agreement, called the Transatlantic Trade and Investment Partnership, between the European Union and the United States of America, Council of the European Union, Doc. 11103/13 DCL 1, 17 June 2013.

The TTIP directives thus merely provide a broad framework without defining instructions to negotiators in a precise manner. They contain 18 pages of text only. The laconic approach bears the advantage of flexibility and adjustment to US claims. But it also bears the disadvantage of missing *ex ante* clarification of important issues in preparing the negotiations. Increasing attention and resistance to TTIP negotiations during the process indicate that major issues have not been addressed prior the launch of the talks, but eventually emerged during negotiation and the process of impact assessment the result of which partly complements negotiating directives. There certainly is the need to adjust a negotiating mandate during negotiations, reflecting the needs of the negotiating partner or due to domestic pressures, as it was the case on investment protection. Even large markets and powers cannot fully control outcomes of negotiations. Yet, they can define topics and redlines *ex ante* to a considerable amount in domestic processes including impact assessment prior to engaging the talks as such.

4.3 The Challenge Ahead

The lack of sufficiently precise operational goals in primary and secondary legislation and a tradition of fairly general directives for negotiations results in postponing domestic debate to the stage of negotiations, and thus complicating and delaying the process. To some extent this is unavoidable as new issues and perceptions and needs emerge in due course. However, more internal decision-making and detailed agenda setting could be front-loaded prior to engaging the talks. For example, in hind side, it would have been highly beneficial to have a more extensive internal debate and decision-making on the future of investment protection and its modalities of dispute settlement in relations among industrialised countries prior to taking up negotiations on the subject matter on the basis of a laconic negotiating mandate including investor-state arbitration. Basic operational goals of general importance should be defined ex ante, and directives of negotiations should also include difficult issues where internal consensus takes more time to build.

With a view to front-load the agenda of negotiations and major operational goals in general and with a view to prepare specific talks, it is interesting to draw attention to the US Trade Act as a potential model for European trade policy-making. The size of the European market implies substantial negotiating power allowing for such comparison with a model which emerged for domestic reasons when the United States still largely dominated international trade policy and was able to impose its domestic and legally defined objectives. While domestic concerns vary according to differences in constitutional law, the US and the EU share common goals in combining inclusive and effective treaty-making powers. It is an exercise of combining and interfacing democracy, predictability, reliance and trust. It may be added, though, that the model may also be of interest to other Members of the WTO facing comparable challenges in trade-policy making.

5 The US Trade Act and Trade Promotion Authority (TPA)

As international trade is a constitutional prerogative of Congress (Article I section 8 US Constitution), the President only engages in trade talks and negotiations to the extent the Administration is authorized by Congress. Short of appropriate legislation, the executive branch would essentially depend upon consent by two-thirds by the Senate and regular legislation controlled by the two Houses. In other words, the Presidency, despite extensive foreign policy powers and Commander in-chief, is not in a position to meet legitimate expectations of trading partners on its own. It depends upon close co-operation with Congress. Trade agreements in the US are thus concluded as so called Congressional-executive agreements, involving both Houses of Congress and the President.[20]

This regime developed over time, and eventually solved the tensions between extensive foreign policy powers and the prerogatives of the Congress in international trade. At the outset of post-World War II efforts, the GATT 1947 and the provisional protocol of application passed under executive powers of the President. It was never adopted as formal treaty upon consent by the Senate with a view to avoid high hurdles of an often introverted and even protectionist majority in Congress. The monist tradition of US constitutional law allowed, in principle, for direct effect of executive agreements in international law.[21] Early developments to this effect however were eventually frustrated by Congress requiring implementing legislation and enacting a ban on direct effect upon adoption of the Tokyo Round and Uruguay Round agreements, thus in fact imposing a dualist system in the field of international trade. The Administration, henceforth, depended upon full implementing legislation passed by Congress.

The Trade Act of the United States, as regularly emended since its introduction in 1934 by the Roosevelt Administration under the name of Reciprocal Trade Agreements Act (RTAA),[22] establishing the authority of the President to negotiate reciprocal trade agreements and reversing protectionist tariffs, contains main goals and conditions which treaties negotiated by the Administration need to pursue. The trade prerogatives of Congress—very different from European traditions of trade being a power of the executive branch—thus allow to front-load major and fairly detailed policy goals in the course of ordinary bicameral legislation, subject to the veto powers of the President. It is important to note, in particular from a European perspective that the shift towards non-tariff measures and barriers and thus substantial intrusion into legislative tasks of Congress and of States called for a new

[20]See generally Jackson (1984), Jackson (1997), adapted in Jackson (2000), p. 367; Leebron (1997); Fergusson IF, Trade Promotion Authority (TPA) and the Role of Congress in Trade Policy, Congressional Research Service 15 June 2015, https://fas.org/sgp/crs/misc/RL33743.pdf (last accessed 1 March 2017).

[21]Jackson (1967), adapted in Jackson (2000), pp. 195–259.

[22]An Act to Amend the Tariff Act of 1930, Part III, Pub. L. No. 316, 48 Stat. 943 (1934).

model of co-operation and interaction between Congress and the President upon the failure to enact the agreements on non-tariff barriers by Congress[23] and the expiry of the 1962 Trade Expansion Act upon the conclusion of the Kennedy Round in 1967. The need for enhanced inclusiveness and new procedures showed with the advent of non-tariff barriers and beginning shift from trade liberalization and de-regulation to international trade regulation and re-regulation.[24]

5.1 The 1974 Trade Act and Amendments

As of 1974, the US Trade Act,[25] as extended in 1979 and amended in 1984,[26] 1988,[27] 2002[28] and by the Bipartisan Comprehensive Trade Priorities and Accountability Act of 2015, signed into law on 29 June 2015,[29] includes non-tariff measures (NTMs) and sets out overall objectives, principal objectives and other priorities to be achieved in international trade negotiations by the President. In return to negotiating powers on NTMs, it entails enhanced obligations to consult during negotiations with Congress and private sector committees. It entails ex ante bench marks by which treaties negotiated are assessed even prior to conclusion if special procedures to adopt a treaty are granted under the fast-track or today trade promotion authority. Section 8(c)(2) of the 2015 Act states under the heading of conditions:

[23]The Anti-dumping Agreement was subsequently implemented by through administrative action, Leebron (1997), p. 183, note 36.

[24]Cottier (2014).

[25]Trade Act of 1974, Pub. L. No. 93-618, 88 Stat. 1978 (1975), 19.U.S.C. paras. 22101-2487 (1976).

[26]Trade and Tariff Act of 1984, Pub. L. No. 98-573, 98 Stat. 2498 (1984).

[27]Omnibus Trade and Competitive Act of 1988, Pub. L. No. 100-418, 102 Stat. 1107 (1988), authorizing to negotiate and conclude the GATT Uruguay Round agreements.

[28]Bipartisan Trade Promotion Authority Act (BTPA) of 2002, Pub. L. No. 107-210, 116 Stat. 933 (2002), 19. U.S.C. paras. 3803–3805; U.S. Trade Promotion Authority Act, which was enacted as Title XXI of The Trade Act of 2002 (Pub. L. No. 107-210).

[29]The Bipartisan Comprehensive Trade Priorities and Accountability Act of 2015 (BCTPA). The proposed BCTPA was introduced on 16 April 2015, by Senators Hatch and Wyden and Representative Ryan (H.R. 1890), https://www.congress.gov/bill/114th-congress/senate-bill/995/text, and signed into law by the President on 29 June 2015 as a complex package deal including trade adjustment measures in the Trade Preferences Extension Act of 2015 (https://www.congress.gov/bill/114th-congress/house-bill/1295/text) as Title III of the Defending Public Safety Employées' Retirement Act, https://www.congress.gov/bill/114th-congress/house-bill/2146/text. The legislation was largely modelled on the Bipartisan Comprehensive Trade Priorities Act of 2014 (H.R. 3830, S. 1900), for a comparison see https://democrats-waysandmeans.house.gov/sites/democrats.waysandmeans.house.gov/files/documents/Side-by-side%20TPA%20Comparison.pdf (all last accessed 1 March 2017).

A trade agreement may be entered into under this subsection only if such agreement makes progress in meeting the applicable objectives described in subsections (a) and (b) of section 102 and the President satisfies the conditions set forth in sections 104 and 105.

Conditions thus take into account that trade negotiations are inherently bilateral or multilateral and results will include compromise. The conditions thus are not framed in absolute terms. They are of a programmatic nature and the benchmark is as to whether progress in meeting the goals and objectives in being made.

To the extent that the legislative objectives defined in the Trade Act are met in that way, resistance to the agreement is less likely in Congress. To the extent that goals remain unmet or new issues are being introduced, the President is subject to criticism and special efforts to defend the project need to be made. As the Trade Act is subject to revision, it allows Congress to regularly redefine procedures, objectives and goals of trade negotiations. It thus offers a reasonable framework and benchmark to structure political discussions prior to the engagement or at least final stages of international negotiations. Unlike in the European Union, major issues are not assessed ex post the process of negotiations, consent and approval of agreements reached. Changes to the Act take place outside and often prior to specific negotiations. They are public and also allow trading partners to making themselves familiar with US targets and expectations, priorities, benchmarks and red lines.

5.2 *Trade Promotion Authority (TPA)*

Under standard rules of US trade regulation, the President still is not in a position to secure full compliance and implementation of agreements concluded. Congress cannot unilaterally alter signed treaties; this is subject to agreement of the parties concerned. However, Congress could indirectly alter the terms of an agreement by deviating from treaty language in implementing legislation, or by filibuster and failure to implement the agreement in domestic law. Changes could be readily made ex post by means of the implementing legislation which in result could impair advantages and market access negotiated. To safeguard such powers, Congress turned, as discussed, to a dualist system in trade law, essentially banning direct effect and thus excluding non-application by courts of law of legislation inconsistent with international agreements entered into. Constant tensions and structural inability of the President to secure fully implemented results undermines the authority of the President and the United States and the willingness of trading partners to engage in serious talks and to address tariffs and non-tariffs measures on their part. Again, governments are not willing to engage in talks and to conclude agreements not knowing whether Congress will duly implement them at all, or in accordance with the terms of the treaty.

The unique trade policy prerogative of the US Congress eventually led to what first was called Fast-Track Procedures under the 1974 Trade Act and eventually termed Trade Promotion Authority (TPA) since the 2002 Trade Act. The decision to grant, or refuse, Trade Promotion Authority by Congress amounts to shaping trade policy in strategic terms and decided as to whether the Administration can successfully engage in international negotiations with important trading partners or not.

Under TPA, Congress agrees to, or refutes, consent by simple majority of both Houses to the agreement and to implementing legislation submitted by the President as a package deal. Under the 2015 Act, the President is obliged to inform Congress 90 days prior to the entering into a trade agreement. 60 days before, he is obliged to submit necessary changes in domestic law, and within 30 days before draft statements on administrative action planned. Draft legislation is submitted jointly to the House and Senate at the beginning of a session (when both houses are in session). Previous legislation provided that such decision needs to be taken within 45 days upon introducing the legislation for debate; no changes and amendments can be made at this stage. They needed to vote on it within 15 days after the bill is reported or discharged. These deadlines can no longer be found in the 2015 Act in light of more complex TPP and TTIP agreements impending. But implementing legislation will enter into force 30 days after the entry into force of the agreement, provided that the President is satisfied that partners are equally making progress in the process of implementation.

Upon completion of international negotiations or its very final stages, implementing legislation submitted by the President within 60 days prior to signature in reality is negotiated by the Administration, congressional Committees and staffers prior to introduction. It does not leave Congress without any influence while control over details largely rests with the President and USTR. Congress retains control over the adoption or rejection of the treaty package—take it or leave it—and thus can make strategic choices also based upon the legislation introduced. The configuration of congressional-executive agreement including implementing legislation allows rapid implementation largely in line with the agreements negotiated.

The implementation of NAFTA and the Uruguay Round results of multilateral Trade negotiations and successive trade agreements proved reasonably successful and by and large efficient while being more inclusive, despite the fact that a number of adopted rules have remained repeatedly contentious and were eventually addressed in WTO dispute settlement in particular relating to unilateral measures under the 1974 Trade Act[30] and the calculation of anti-dumping measures under US implementing regulations (zeroing).[31]

The Trade Promotion Authority (TPA) is not necessarily an inherent part of the Trade Act. It is merely granted for defined periods of time and then elapses. Thus, the 1974 fast track authority was set to expire in 1980, but was extended until 1979.

[30]Panel Report, *United States – Sections 301-310 of the Trade Act of 1974*, WT/DS152/R, adopted 22 December 1999.

[31]*United States – Measures Relating to Zeroing and Sunset Reviews*, WT/DS322, completed 18 August 2009, with a series of reports of the Panel and the Appellate Body under Articles 21(3)(c) and 21(5) DSU.

It was renewed from 1988 to 1993 and 1994, respectively. There was no fast track authority until adopted in a narrow vote in 2002 and expired in 2007. In 2015, after long battles and compromising in the context of a package deal, the Obama Administration was able to renew TPA known as the Bipartisan Congressional Trade Priorities and Accountability Act of 2015. It entailed powers to negotiate major trade agreements with Asia and Europe, thus the TPP and TTIP until 1 July 2018 and 1 July 2021 in case of extension.[32]

The granting of TPA in ordinary legislation is dependent upon approval by the House and the Senate and upon approval of amendments to the Trade Act and other legislation essentially setting binding goals for the Administration and for international treaty making and for domestic programmes. For example, renewal of TPA in 2015 was made dependent by the House of removing the trade adjustment programme from the bill which was eventually adopted as a separate Act. In other words, Congress, exercising its constitutional prerogative on international trade, is able to influence the course of negotiations ex ante not only by setting fairly detailed objectives, goals which should be promoted by the new agreements authorized to negotiate. It can also link the matter to other legislative projects and engage in cross-cutting package deals and political compromise. The control over TPA and extensions offers appropriate powers to strategically influence the process of treaty-making.

The condition for compliance in implementation, however, is that the President is able to comply with objectives and mandate inherent to the Trade Act, as repeatedly revised and updated. In other words, the major debate on trade policy takes place prior to the engagement of negotiations. Objectives and scope of trade policy are defined inclusively. Both houses and their respective committees participate. States and civil society are involved by representatives and lobbies in the process. The Presidency offers check and balance by means of the right to veto the Trade Act and to refuse to sign legislation into law.

5.3 Assessment

Critics maintain that TPA with its short delays and packages is not democratic as it undermines legislative powers of Congress and thus also reduces the possibility of lobbies and civil society to influence detailed outcomes of specific negotiations.[33] Democratic participation, however, fully takes place in shaping the Trade Act and TPA. It is at this stage and level that democracy can fully work while it inherently is difficult to achieve full participation in the stage of international negotiations with

[32]See fn. 29.

[33]E.g. Food safety concerns are out front as TPA "fast track" moves through Congress, Free Speech Ration News, 21 May 2015, https://fsrn.org/2015/05/food-safety-concerns-are-out-front-as-tpa-fast-track-moves-through-congress/ (last accessed 1 March 2017).

foreign powers. As trade policy is increasingly controversial, it is normal that debates are complex and compromise difficult to achieve. Moving into trade regulation issues are of broad interest and thus call for broad debate. From the point of view of negotiators, it is sometimes felt that seeking TPA is not advantageous for the President and USTR. It is argued that conditions and requirements to report and consult have become so cumbersome that achieving PTA is hardly worthwhile for the administration. Other critics complain the lack of transparency in TTIP negotiations as USTR—unlike the Commission—does not publish its negotiating proposals. This, however, is a matter legally unrelated to the Trade Act and TPA; in fact publication and enhanced transparency would be more consistent with the US system. Overall, it is felt that US Trade Act and TPA up to 2016 have been reasonably successful in combining inclusiveness and efficiency in international negotiations.[34] It remains to be seen whether this continues to be so as of 2017 under the administration of the Trump Presidency and the paradigm shifts contemplated.

It is important to reiterate that the US Trade Act and other related Acts entail specific instructions as what the Administration should seek to achieve in international negotiations. No additional mandate is formulated, and the initiative, agenda and speed of negotiations is essentially defined by the President, USTR and negotiating partners until a result is being achieved. It is interesting to observe that opposition to ongoing negotiations in the United States is less frequent on specific issues than in Europe despite the fact that trade policy in general is as contentious, if not more, than in Europe in particular in time of presidential elections. Candidates will pledge to support or oppose these projects in general; they are supporting an open trade policy or are critical of it.[35] They however do not seek to interfere with ongoing processes, such as demands to call them off or declare moot the talks in a dead-end street as it can be observed in Europe for local political gains.[36] It is submitted that this is due to the fact that US trade policy up to 2016 has been much more strongly front-loaded than in Europe where contentious issues evolve over time and during the negotiating process, destabilizing treaty-making powers.

[34]Assessment made based upon discussions with and by Steve Charnovitz and Michael Gadbaw on 25 October 2016 on the panel on Regulatory Coordination, held at Georgetown University in cooperation with the Swiss Embassy under the joint programme Law in Globalizing World, Washington DC, and informal discussions on the subject.

[35]Cf. The Guardian, Trump and Clinton's free trade retreat: a pivotal moment for the world's economic future, 20 August 2016; On the Issues: Hillary Clinton on Free Trade, http://www.ontheissues.org/2016/Hillary_Clinton_Free_Trade.htm (last accessed 1 March 2017).

[36]See fn. 7 and 8.

6 Towards an International Trade, Investment and Cooperation Regulation (ITICR)

It is not a matter of transposing the US Trade Act and TPA to the European Union. The constitutional frameworks differ substantially and cannot be readily compared. The difference between a federal state with comprehensive central foreign policy powers and the European confederation with enumerated central foreign policy powers looms large. However, the US model with its congressional prerogatives in trade policy encourages seeking appropriate ways and means to equally front-load domestic trade policy making and to think about instruments how this could be achieved under the TEU and TFEU. It is submitted to essentially work in two stages.

6.1 Defining Legal Objectives, Goals and Conditions

Based upon the broad precepts of primary law discussed above, it is submitted that the Union should enact general legislation (regulation) containing the contours, topics, objectives and principles of EU commercial policy, including trade and investment. Major issues such as the inclusion or exclusion of different sectors, such as audio-visuals, health, cultural and education, or the parameters for engaging in negotiations on agricultural in line with domestic policies, and some of those indicated above,[37] would be broadly debated in the process of enacting an appropriate regulation. The act would specify whether certain issues pertain to shared powers of the Union and thus to the domain of mixed agreements. Conditionalities to include items would be defined and hammered out. The act should not only define objectives and goals for negotiations, but should also define appropriate goals for safety nets in terms of flanking policies, such as adjustment programmes.

The Regulation could perhaps be termed International Trade, Investment and Cooperation Regulation, or International Trade Regulation (ITICR) or (informally) European Trade Act.[38] Article 207(2) TEFU can be interpreted to include not only implementing regulations, but also prospective instruments of this kind. The wording does not exclude such an understanding as it addresses commercial policy as whole and thus also the implementation of primary rules, not limited to international agreements.[39] Additional or different regulations could be passed for the

---

[37]See Section 4.2.

[38]The proposal was first made under the heading of International Trade, Cooperation and Investment Regulation, Cottier (2016), p. 38. The sequence is changed here to facilitate a readable abbreviation.

[39]Art 207(2) TFEU reads: The European Parliament and the Council, acting by means of regulations in accordance with the ordinary legislative procedure, shall adopt the measures defining the framework for implementing the common commercial policy.

purpose of associations and development cooperation agreements, or even specific policy areas, perhaps using a system of building blocks. Trade, investment and cooperation, in particular with developing countries, need not necessarily be concentrated in a single act. This issue would need further studies. The essential point, however, is that the process of elaborating and eventually amending ITICR follows standard procedures and thus also includes hearings and participation of industry and civil society, and also national and, and the case may be, of regional parliaments. It is subject to qualified majority approval by the Council and Parliament alike, thus clearly strengthening democratic representation in the field.

Major battles on trade and investment policy, its approach and scope, should be fought on this ground in the first place, independently from specific trade talks. Of course, the prospects of future negotiations will influence the debate. Yet, at this stage, it remains a matter of domestic policy making and home-work to define, in principle, the contours and objectives of trade policy vis-à-vis the rest of the World and to engage in and in-depth political discourse prior to taking up the matter in relation to a particular treaty project. Issues should be decided by majority in the Commission, qualified majority in the Council and majority in Parliament in accordance with Article 294 TEFU. For example, the debate on private state investment arbitration, or a basic debate on inclusion of tax issues and transparency in respective treaties and other international instruments would take place here and would be subject to qualified majority ruling, notwithstanding Article 207(4) TFEU. This provision, requiring unanimity in parallel to internal market powers, relate to negotiating mandates and directives for specific treaty negotiation projects and do not necessarily apply to general terms and conditions upon which these items are included in ITICR. It is submitted that basic debates independent of specific negotiations can be brought about even under the existing trade law framework of the TFEU and does not necessarily require treaty amendment at this stage.

The European Trade Act or ICTIR is a programmatic and procedural piece of legislation. It essentially defines the boundaries of trade policy and instructs the Commission and the Council in drafting more specific objectives and conditions in negotiating mandates, taking into account the priorities and the context of a particular negotiation. Other than domestic legislation, its operation takes place in negotiations with third parties. New topics may be introduced by trading partners in the negotiations and insisted upon. Results of negotiations, in other words, may not be fully compatible with the Act. This is in the nature of negotiations and agreements which take two to agree and conclude. In case results are likely to deviate from the framework, the Trade Act would not require blocking negotiations, but calls in time for internal information and consultations with its constituencies, in particular the Council, the European Parliament and national Parliaments. It structures the internal debate in accordance with developments in international negotiations, going back and forth and avoiding that critical issues will only be discussed in the final stages or upon signature of new agreements. These discussions may lead to amendments of specific negotiating mandates, or eventually the Trade Act in due course.

6.2 The Role of Parliaments of Member States

It is submitted that the draft ITICR would also be discussed by national Parliaments in accordance with Article 12 TEU and the 1st and 2nd Protocol to the TFEU.[40] The system of reasoned opinions, yellow and red cards would equally apply in accordance with the Protocol 2 on the application of the principles of subsidiarity and proportionality. National Parliaments (including regional ones in the case of Belgium) at this stage would be able to express their views on the inclusion or exclusion of new topics, objections and conditions of trade policy making in future trade, investment and cooperation agreements of the European Union. The instruments allows taking the temperatures of constituencies and to amend the draft should proposals do not reach the support of 2/3 of national Parliaments. Reasoned objections on subsidiarity and proportionality by 1/3 of all votes (each Member State having two) require reviewing and possibly amending or rejecting the draft proposal (Yellow Card). 18 votes of domestic parliaments (allocation depending upon domestic law) thus would again trigger a debate on the level of the European Union in addressing contentious issues and upon conditions upon which they could be included in a trade policy agenda. In case reasoned objections are mad by more than half of votes of national Parliaments, the draft needs to be resubmitted to the European Parliament and the Council (Orange Card).[41] Nothing in Protocols 1 and 2 prevents these instruments from being applied to regulations affecting foreign trade. Decisions to include issues in international negotiations often relate to issues of subsidiarity, i.e. as to whether the task could be better pursued autonomously by the EU or Member States or not. For example, the inclusion of cultural, educational or medical services in trade policy, or of certain health standards in food production, could be subject to such procedures and would allow assessing whether national constituencies see a benefit of doing so or whether fears of threatening European, regional or local production largely prevail.

In conclusion, the Union and Member States will benefit from a broader and large debate on the future of trade policy. It will deploy informational and educational effects and helps to reduce misinformation and misunderstandings but also deliberate lies in the heat of successive treaty negotiations. The international trade regulation or regulations, of course, are subject to periodical review and adjustment in line with international developments and outcomes in international negotiations.

---

[40] Protocol (no 1) on the Role of National Parliaments in the European Union, OJ 2010 C 83/203; Protocol (no 2) on the Application of the Principles of Subsidiarity and Proportionality the High Contracting Parties, OJ 2010 C 83/206.

[41] See House of Lords, EU Committee, The Role of National Parliaments in the European Union, 9th Report of Session 2013/2014, HL Paper 151; ERP Group: Relations with National Parliaments, The New role of National Parliaments in European Decision-Making: Implications of the Lisbon Treaty, Brussels 2009; Fabbrini and Granat (2013).

6.3 Negotiating Mandates

Specific directives in accordance with Article 218 TFEU for negotiations in relating to particular trading partners would rely upon the European Trade Act and take its objectives and provisions into account. The Act may constitute the substantive basis for authorizing negotiations in accordance with Article 218(2) TFEU. To the extent that goals and objectives are essentially in line with the ITICR, directives could be limited to defining trading partners and clearing powers to take up negotiations by the Commission. There is no need to repeat generalities and agreed objectives. Alternatively, they could contain additional and more specific instructions commensurate with the particularities of the relation and partner at hand and thus provide guidelines and special committees in accordance with Article 218(4) TFEU. Negotiating Directives continue to be proposed by the Commission, subject to discussion, amendment and approval by the Council. The Parliament is consulted, but its main focus would be on shaping the Trade Act. National Parliaments would not be involved at this stage as a matter of EU law, but may need to be consulted under domestic law.

6.4 Package Deal

The question arises whether Europe needs a fast-track or Trade Promotion Authority. There is no easy analogy, due to power sharing of the Council and Parliament in legislation. So far, the need has not materialised. The EU, however, potentially faces similar problems impairing treaty-making powers as the United States. Due to the exclusion of direct effect of trade agreements by the Court of the European Union, domestic implementation largely depends upon secondary legislation.[42] The breadth of modern treaties affects several regulatory areas, and implementation may be delayed or be inconsistent with treaty provisions adopted. To the extent that the role of Parliament is reinforced and enhanced in commercial policy by means of adopting ITICR, the idea of limiting powers of the Council and the Parliament to adopting a package deal of international agreements and implementing regulations—take it or leave it—should be contemplated. Appropriate procedures would be set out in the Trade Act, deviating from Article 194 TFEU, taking into account that these procedures accompany standards procedures of treaty-making under Articles 216–218 TFEU, thus retaining full powers in treaty-making of the Council upon consultation of the European Parliament, and of Member States in case of a mixed agreement. No changes of these provisions are required. The decision as to whether a specific negotiation should led under the package deal approach will be taken by the Negotiating Mandate, in accordance with rules set forth by the European Trade Act.

---

[42] See generally Cottier (2009b).

Under the package deal approach, all draft implementing legislation is prepared by the Commission and negotiated with the Trade Committees of the Council and the European Parliament in accordance with a specific time schedule defined in the Trade Act. The responsibility to submit lies with the Commission, leaving the Council and Parliament to adopt or reject the package within a reasonable period of time. Since Parliament is crucial in setting goals and objectives in the ITICR, and the Council instrumental in shaping directives of negotiations, it is appropriate to refrain from changing implementing legislation short of rejecting it if fundamentally in line with the agreement approved.

A package deal approach allows for well-defined time-lines and consistency with international agreements concluded. The configuration established an appropriate balance of power between the Council, Parliament and the Commission. It would greatly enhance European treaty making powers and reduces the risk of losing confidence due to potentially endless complications following the conclusion and adoption of a trade, cooperation and investment agreement.

6.5 Relationship to Mixed Agreements

It imports to assess the relationship to mixed agreements. A European Trade Act, as a matter of secondary legislation, cannot overrule the constitutional allocation of powers between Member States and the Union in primary law. It is not a tool to replace mixed agreements. As long as trade policy continues to deal with new issues pertaining domestically to mixed competences or exclusive competences of the Member States, mixed agreements and thus unanimous support by all Member States remain in operation. The European Trade Act, however, may politically prepare and ease tensions as it front-loads the debate and avoid contentious issues being discussed at the closing stages of international negotiations. To the extent that the Council, the European Parliaments and a two third majority of national Parliaments agree to the scope of the Trade Act, they are less likely to take issue with international agreements remaining within the scope of the Act. Procedures to inform and consult in case the scope cannot be maintained and new issues require to be addressed, equally see to it that the debate is front-loaded and assists in preventing show-downs recently witnessed with the Ukraine and CETA Agreements.[43] It may well work as an antidote to the recent experience of *vetocracy* and the extraction of special last-minute concessions for political ends.

Yet legally, Member States retain final decisions in mixed agreements. The requirement of unanimity could only be replaced by qualified majority ruling or elimination by changing the provisions of primary law, moving towards more comprehensive and federal powers of the Union in foreign affairs or at least in

[43]See fn. 3 and 5.

trade policy and regulatory convergence of non-tariff measures and other behind the border issues.

6.6 *The Role of the Judiciary*

The adoption of a Trade Act equally enhances the role of the Judiciary in external economic relations, thus reinforcing the rule of law and a rule-based trading system. A Trade Act will help in fine-tuning the horizontal balance of powers between different bodies involved in trade policy making. Current powers include advisory opinions of the European Court under Article 218(11) TFEU in assessing exclusive treaty-making powers of the Union and the need for mixed agreements, respectively. The Courts also address issues relating to the implementation of international agreement and implementing legislation, for example in the field of trade remedies or intellectual property rights. They are empowered to assess recourse to international arbitration, in particular WTO dispute settlement under the Trade Barriers Regulation. The Trade Act would add a new dimension. The Court of the European Union could be called upon to constitutionally assess whether the Trade Act is in line with the powers of the European Union, respecting the primary law, and respecting prerogatives of Members States requiring mixed agreements if included in an international agreement. It could be called upon to assess the legality of negotiating mandates issued by the Council. Finally, the Courts also would be eligible to assess procedural issues: whether internal procedures and treaty-making provisions are respected by the competent authorities.

7 Conclusions

It will be objected and argued that a European Trade Act will unduly restrain flexibility and treaty-making powers of the Union. It will be said that trade agreements evolve in negotiations, in a process of claims and responses. These cannot suitably prosper under a strait jacket of domestic regulation and objections fairly detailed in domestic law. These concerns are legitimate, but can be taken into account in defining the appropriate regulatory density of the European Trade Act. Much can be learned from studying the US experience. In reflects that international trade is not, and cannot, be a matter exclusively of the executive branch in the European tradition where foreign affairs historically often was a matter of the crown and ministers. Rather it shows that interfacing the field with processes comparable to those in domestic law is possible as the boundaries between domestic and foreign policy vane. The same applies to the European Union. The rule of law no longer is limited to domestic affairs; it extends today to international economic relations. Fundamental powers need to rest with the law-making bodies and thus Parliaments, while recognising that they themselves are not in a position to negotiate detailed agreements in due course. The present weaknesses inherent to broad negotiating mandates, the absence of effective powers of the Parliaments and political challenges to negotiations at a late stage based upon veto-powers inherent to mixed agreements, can be at least partly remedied by developing a Trade Act in the European Union. This Act will not dispose of mixed agreements. It needs to operate along them. Yet, as practical experience on inclusiveness, participation and front-loading of policy making increases over time, Member States may eventually be willing to leave the concept of mixed agreements behind in the field of commercial policy and accept and complete, formally exclusive powers of the Union which will be necessary to defend European interests and treaty making powers in the long run.

References

Cottier T (1993) Constitutional trade regulation in national and international law: structure-substance pairings in the EFTA experience. In: Hilf M, Petersmann EU (eds) National constitutions and international economic law. Kluwer International, Deventer, pp 409–442

Cottier T (2009a) The legitimacy of WTO law. In: Yueh L (ed) The law and economics of globalisation. New challenges for a world in flux. Edward Elgar, Cheltenham, pp 11–48

Cottier T (2009b) International trade law: the impact of Justiciability and separations of powers in EC law. Eur Const Law Rev 5(2):307–326

Cottier T (2014) International economic law in transition from trade liberalization to trade regulation. J Int Econ Law 17(3):671–677

Cottier T (2016) Gemischte Abkommen der Europäischen Union: Grundlagen und Alternativen. In: Bungenberg M, Herrmann C (eds) Die gemeinsame Handelspolitik der Europäischen Union: Fünf Jahre nach Lissabon – Quo Vadis? Nomos, Baden-Baden, pp 11–43

Cottier T, Trimberg L (2015) Articles 206 and 207 TFEU. In: von der Groeben H, Schwarze J, Hatje A (eds) Europäisches Unionsrecht, 7th edn. Nomos, Baden-Baden, pp 270–351

Fabbrini F, Granat K (2013) "Yellow card, but no foul": the role of the national parliaments under the subsidiarity protocol and the Commission proposal for an EU regulation on the right to strike. Common Mark Law Rev 50(1):115–143

Jackson JH (1967) The General Agreement on Tariffs and Trade in the Unites States Domestic Law. Mich Law Rev 66:249–316

Jackson JH (1984) United States law and implementation of the Tokyo Round negotiations. In: Jackson JH, Louis JV, Mathushita M (eds) Implementing the Tokyo Round: National constitutions and international economic rules. University of Michigan Press, Ann Arbor, pp 139–197

Jackson JH (1997) The great 1994 sovereignty debate: United States acceptance and implementation of the Uruguay Round results. Columbia J Int Law 36:137–188

Jackson JH (2000) The jurisprudence of GATT and the WTO: insights on treaty law and economic relations. Cambridge University Press, Cambridge

Leebron D (1997) Implementing of the Uruguay Round results in the United States. In: Jackson JH, Sykes A (eds) Implementing the Uruguay Round. Clarendon Press, Oxford, pp 175–242

Marmon B (2016) Dutch voters reject EU-Ukraine agreement. The European Institute, Washington

Rosas A (2010) The future of mixity. In: Hillion C, Kautrakos P (eds) Mixed agreements revisited: the EU and its member states in the world. Hart, Oxford, pp 367–374

International Trade Agreements and Democratic Participation

Mattias Wendel

Abstract The following contribution focuses on the question whether the negotiations on the two major transatlantic free trade agreements CETA (EU-Canada) and TTIP (EU-US) have so far corresponded to the principles of democratic participation, transparency, and public accessibility. Specific attention is drawn to the citizen's democratic participation through forms of participatory or direct democracy.

Contents

The author would like to thank Theresa Krampe for her extraordinary help in translating the original text into English. The text goes back to a presentation held in Berlin on 6 March 2015 during the conference "The EU's Common Commercial Policy five Years after Lisbon – Quo Vadis?". It was first published in German in Bungenberg M, Herrmann C (eds), Die gemeinsame Handelspolitik der Europäischen Union fünf Jahre nach Lissabon – Quo Vadis?, 2016, p. 92 et seqq.

M. Wendel (✉)
Department of Law, Freie Universität Berlin, Boltzmannstr. 3, 14195 Berlin, Germany
e-mail: mattias.wendel@jura.uni-freiburg.de

M. Bungenberg et al. (eds.), *European Yearbook of International Economic Law 2017*, European Yearbook of International Economic Law 8,
DOI 10.1007/978-3-319-58832-2_3

1 Introduction

Since its reformation by the Treaty of Lisbon,[1] the common commercial policy (CCP) has seldom attracted as much attention as in the course of the negotiations surrounding two major transatlantic free trade agreements: the Comprehensive Economic and Trade Agreement (CETA) with Canada[2] and the Transatlantic Trade and Investment Partnership (TTIP) with the United States.[3] Public protests against the evolving transatlantic free trade regimes were fairly heated at times. No doubt, many readers will recall the chlorine-washed chicken that, as a symbol, took on almost apocalyptic dimensions. "Heat does not always generate light". This popular proverb rings true for parts of the public discourse surrounding the free trade agreements. After all, the passionate advocacy of a cause does not always prove helpful but rather obscures the path to analytical clarity.[4]

However, pleading for a sober and rational attitude when approaching CETA and TTIP is not the same as unquestioningly endorsing the transatlantic international trade law as it is currently planned. Objective and constructive criticism can be formulated in many different ways, not least depending on the respective professional perspective from which the discussion is prompted. Two of the most controversial issues in legal scholarship are the treaty-making powers and the protection of investors through arbitration tribunals—in addition to the concrete design of market access rules, the regulatory regime, and the standards of protection.[5] The following contribution deliberately leaves untouched the substantial core of the agreements and the validity of their criticism.

Instead, it focuses on the question whether the progression of negotiations has so far corresponded to the principles of democratic participation, transparency, and public accessibility (Articles 1(2) and 10(3) TEU). What these boil down to is ultimately the relation between the principle of democracy and free trade which is examined with regard to the democratic accountability of the negotiation process. More specifically, this contribution does not primarily address the parliamentary

---

[1]Further analysis sees in Bungenberg and Hermann (2011). For the Federal Constitutional Court's critical analysis of the common commercial policy see Herrmann (2010).

[2]CETA negotiations have already been concluded. The agreement was signed in Brussels on 30 October 2016. The consolidated version is available under http://data.consilium.europa.eu/doc/document/ST-10973-2016-INIT/en/pdf (last accessed 1 March 2017).

[3]TTIP negotiations are still ongoing.

[4]With regard to the likewise emotionally charged European constitutional debate cf. Craig (2001), p. 125.

[5]For a discussion from the perspective of legal studies see Mayer and Ermes (2014), p. 237 et seqq.; Mayer F, Stellt das geplante Freihandelsabkommen der EU mit Kanada (Comprehensive Economic and Trade Agreement, CETA) ein gemischtes Abkommen dar?, legal opinion for the Federal Ministry for Economic Affairs and Energy, 28 August 2014, https://www.bmwi.de/BMWi/Redaktion/PDF/C-D/ceta-gutachten-einstufung-als-gemischtes-abkommen,property=pdf,bereich=bmwi2012,sprache=de,rwb=true.pdf (last accessed 1 March 2017); Cremona (2015), p. 351 et seqq.; Treier and Wernicke (2015), p. 334 et seqq.; Hoffmeister (2015), p. 35 et seqq.

legitimation of the common commercial policy,[6] but deals with the EU citizen's democratic participation through forms of *participatory* or *direct* democracy.[7] The mechanism of the European citizens' initiative (ECI) as well as the principle of transparency, an essential condition for democratic intervention, are of particular significance in this context.

A part of civil societies' rebellion against CETA and TTIP aimed to stop the negotiation process by forming a registered European citizens' initiative in accordance with Article 11(4) TEU. In concrete terms, the Commission as the EU's chief negotiator[8] was invited to recommend to the Council the non-completion of CETA and to annul the negotiation mandate[9] for TTIP. However, the Commission rejected the ECI's request for registration, arguing that an ECI can neither relate to purely preparatory acts nor aim for the non-proposal of a legislative measure.[10] Without adopting the (political) premises of the ECI, this contribution critically revisits the Commission's argument from the perspective of EU constitutional law and explores the extent of the competences of the EU citizens' initiative as an instrument of democratic participation in the field of the EU's external relations (see part 2).

These considerations then serve as a background for the discussion of the principle of transparency. From an individual rights perspective, this mainly concerns the access to documents while from an institutional perspective, the transparency of negotiations and the paths of dialogue mobilised for TTIP are of interest (part 3). The contribution will conclude with a brief outlook, pointing out potential future developments (part 4).

2 The Citizens' Initiative as a Means of Democratic Participation in External Relations?

Since November 2014, the lawsuit *Efler et al.*[11] was pending before the General Court (GC). In essence, it raises the question of the limits to the EU citizen's authority to shape the EU's External Relations with instruments of participatory or

---

[6]On this point of view see Streinz (2016).

[7]Participatory Democracy is here used as an umbrella term under which forms of direct democracy can be subsumed.

[8]Cf. Article 207(3), third subparagraph TFEU. Commission internally, this falls under the jurisdiction of the Directorate General for Trade (DG Trade). Until November 2014, Karel de Gucht acted as EU Trade Commissioner, since then the position is filled by Cecilia Malmström.

[9]Article 207(3) second subparagraph TFEU. The TTIP mandate is available under http://www.bmwi.de/BMWi/Redaktion/PDF/S-T/ttip-mandat,property=pdf,bereich=bmwi2012,sprache=de,rwb=true.pdf (last accessed 1 March 2017).

[10]European Commission, C(2014) 6501 final.

[11]The individual action was brought to the General Court on 19 November 2014. The lawsuit was pending for two and a half years as case T-754/14, *Efler and others v Commission*. The GC finally

direct democracy. The crux of the matter, therefore, is the scope of the European citizen's initiative in the context of the common commercial policy. In order to start delineating the scope of the ECI, it is useful to revisit the basic constitutional conditions before discussing the specificities of the lawsuit and its wider significance for the relationship between democracy and free trade.

2.1 *EU Constitutional Law Framework*

The relevant constitutional framework is primarily defined by the key provisions on democratic principles introduced by the Lisbon Treaty (Articles 9–12 TEU). For the context in question, the principle of democratic participation in the concrete form of the European citizens' initiative is of central importance.

2.1.1 The Principle of Democratic Participation

The principle of democratic participation is laid down in Article 10(3), first sentence TEU according to which every citizen has the right to participate in the democratic life of the Union. The second sentence furthermore specifies that decisions shall be taken as openly and as closely as possible to the citizen. While the first sentence substantiates a right to individual participation,[12] the second sentence[13] obliges especially the EU institutions to comply with the principles of transparency and proximity to the citizens.

In addition to the principles of democratic equality (Article 9, first sentence TEU) and representative democracy (Article 10(1) and (2) TEU), the principle of participatory democracy is one of the central pillars on which the EU is founded. In a general sense, this principle can be understood as a mechanism ensuring the citizens' influence on political decision-making, i.e. their *status activus*.[14] This *status activus* is ensured, at a first level, by individual rights exclusively reserved to EU citizens. These rights that also shape the status of EU citizenship as a legal concept[15] include the right to vote and to stand as candidates in elections to the

---

decided on 10 May 2017 - after the final version of this contribution has been submitted. The judgment, which could only be taken into account during the process of proof reading, is in line with the argument developped here. As suggested here, the GC concluded that the Commission infringed EU law by refusing to register the ECI proposal. The plaintiff's application can be accessed online (in German), https://stip-ttip.org/de/wp-content/uploads/sites/4/2014/11/EuGH-Klageschrift_Kempen_EBI.pdf, and in English, http://curia.europa.eu/juris/document/document.jsf?text=&docid=162026&pageIndex=0&doclang=EN&mode=lst&dir=&occ=first&part=1&cid=1435962 (both last accessed 21 July 2017).

[12]Ruffert (2016a), para. 11 et seq.

[13]Following Article 1(2) TEU.

[14]Cf. Huber (2012a), para. 42 et seq.

[15]More on this see Wendel (2014), p. 81 et seqq.

European Parliament and in municipal elections in the Member State of residence,[16] the right to petition the European Parliament,[17] and the formation of a citizens' initiative.[18] At a second level, the *status activus* is then completed and reinforced by legal positions which, in accordance with the principles of transparency and proximity to the citizen, are the rights of every person living within the Union. In particular, the right to good administration[19]—covering in and of itself a wide spectrum of guarantees[20]—as well as the right to access to documents,[21] and the right to apply to the European Ombudsman[22] are to be mentioned.

However, the principle laid down in Article 10(3) TEU can also be understood in a much more specific sense in that it may directly refer to particular instruments of participatory democracy.[23] By recognising certain forms of participatory democracy,[24] EU law opens up new resources of democratic legitimation[25] complementing the classical strands of legitimation.[26] With a view to the relation between participatory and direct democracy, it is important to note that the term participatory democracy is used in the present context as an umbrella term denoting various forms of citizens' participation including, but not limited to, instruments of direct democracy such as the European citizens' initiative.[27]

2.1.2 The European Citizens' Initiative

The legal basis of the European citizen's initiative is Article 11(4) TEU. Under this clause, EU citizens whose number is not less than one million and who are nationals

[16]Article 14(3) TEU, Articles 22 and 223 TFEU, Articles 39 and 40 CFR.

[17]Articles 24, second subparagraph and Article 227 TFEU, Article 44 CFR.

[18]Article 11(4) TEU, Article 24, first subparagraph TFEU.

[19]Article 41 CFR.

[20]Article 24, fourth subparagraph TFEU, Article 41(4) CFR.

[21]Article 15 TFEU, Article 42 CFR.

[22]Article 228 TFEU, Article 43 CFR.

[23]For an overview over the various theories on democratic participation see, from a political scientific perspective, Schmidt (2010), p. 236 et seqq.

[24]For the latter cf. the classification of Ruffert (2016b), paras. 3–5.

[25]Franzius and Preuß (2011), p. 24; Huber (1999), p. 27; Huber (2012a), para. 44, in opposition to BVerfGE 123, 267 – *Treaty of Lisbon*, para. 194 et seq. Which deconstructs the genuine value of this reservoir of legitimation.

[26]See also von Bogdandy (2009), p. 13.

[27]On terminology cf. the respective classification of Article 10(3) TEU and Article 11(4)TEU in Huber (2012a), para. 42: "*Grundsatz der partizipativen Demokratie*"; Huber (2012b), para. 33: "*direktdemokratische Komponente*"; Franzius and Preuß (2011), p. 24: "*partizipative Demokratie*", with reference to Article 10(3) TEU and p. 119: "*direkte Demokratie*", with reference toArticle 1(4) TEU; Ruffert (2016a), para. 10: "*Teilhabe*"; Ruffert (2016b), para. 14: "*Element direkter Demokratie*". Additionally, the citizen's initiative can be subsumed under participatory democracy, see for instance Kadelbach (2009), p. 611.

of a significant number of Member States[28] may invite the European Commission to take action. The norm's genesis goes back to the Convention on the Future of Europe[29] and, in its current wording, reflects the amount of participatory democracy for which a consensus could be found.[30] Article 11(4) TEU then became a binding part of EU primary law along with the Treaty of Lisbon. However, the norm was only concretised very recently by secondary law when the Regulation (EU) No 211/2011,[31] based on Article 24(1) TFEU, entered into force on 1 April 2012. The ECI is therefore a comparatively novel tool for which very little practical experience could be gathered yet.[32]

Article 11(4) TEU is an EU citizens' right which is, systematically speaking, strongly related to the right of petition and the right to apply to the European Ombudsman. Furthermore, as has been shown, the stipulation is part of the "provisions on democratic principles" of the TEU and thus a part of one of European constitutional law's most fundamental group of norms. It spells out the principle of democratic participation as laid down in Article 10(3), first sentence TEU[33] and serves, at the same time, the principle of proximity to the citizen in the sense of Article 10(3), second sentence TEU.

When taking into account the norm's *telos,* it becomes evident that Article 11(4) TEU aims for an—albeit limited—possibility of political agenda-setting on the part of the EU citizens.[34] As an instrument of democratic participation, the ECI empowers individuals to participate in the shaping of the political agenda at EU level, thereby creating a closer relation between the citizens and the EU institutions. In other words, the norm provides a right to initiate an initiative.[35] The greatest novelty inherent to the ECI is that it is an EU procedure which requires transnational civic mobilisation.[36] It is the first transnational instrument of citizen participation worldwide.[37]

---

[28]Specified in Article 7(1) of Regulation (EU) No 211/2011, according to which the signatories of a citizens' initiative must come from at least a quarter of the Member States. Additionally, according to Article 7(2), the signatories must in at least a quarter of the Member States reach a minimum number that differs from one Member State to the other as it is determined by multiplying the number of Members of the European Parliament "EP" elected in the respective Member State by 750 (sic).

[29]Cf. the expositions by Meyer, member of convention and known as *spiritus rector* of the ECI, in Meyer (2014), Präambel, para. 34. On the history of development see also Kaufmann (2011), p. 201 et seqq.

[30]Cf. Mayer (2013), p. 80 et seqq.

[31]For a general overview see Tiedemann (2012), p. 80 et seqq.

[32]In the meantime, the number of (registered) ECI's has risen significantly, cf. the list of ECI's at http://ec.europa.eu/citizens-initiative/public/initiatives/ongoing/details/2012/000003 (last accessed 1 March 2017).

[33]Cf. Nettesheim (2015a), para. 41; Huber (2012b), paras. 1–5; Ruffert (2016b), para. 6.

[34]Huber (2012b), para. 32.

[35]Mayer (2013), p. 147.

[36]Mayer (2013), p. 147.

[37]Franzius and Preuß (2011), p. 120.

The standard situation which is addressed by Article 11(4) TEU is the initiation of legislative procedures. However, the clause is by no means limited to secondary legislation under Article 289 TFEU. On the contrary, Article 11(4) TEU deliberately uses the broader expression "legal act of the Union" which, among others, also includes tertiary law.[38]

With view to the legal effects, citizens may, according to the wording of Article 11(4) TEU, only "take the initiative of inviting" the Commission to submit a proposal (German: "*die Initiative ergreifen*" *und die Kommission* "*auffordern*"; French: "*prendre l'initiative d'inviter*"). Accordingly, opinions on the scope of this right to participation differ significantly. In order to determine the scope of Article 11(4) TEU, it is useful to differentiate between different levels of intervention.

On the one hand it would be incompatible with the purpose of the ECI to assume that the citizens' invitation would be no more than a non-binding request.[39] Moreover, the EU legislator's procedural design of the ECI speaks against such a minimalistic interpretation: according to Article 10(1)(c) of the Regulation (EU) No 211/2011, the Commission is required, within three months after having received registered and certified ECI, to set out "in a communication its legal and political conclusions on the citizens' initiative, the action it intends to take, if any, and its reasons for taking or not taking that action". Against this backdrop, one has to conclude that the Commission is under the obligation to deal with the issue at hand that is to examine the citizens' initiative *au fond* and give reasons without (manifest) errors of assessment.

On the other hand, to assume that the Commission is also obliged to kick off a legislative proceeding by making a legislative proposal[40] is highly questionable.[41] After all, the EU legislator has explicitly stated in the Regulation that it is to be considered a valid reaction should the Commission decide *not* to take any further action. The decision to determine the procedures and conditions of the ECI remains within the EU legislator's powers, as laid down expressly in Article 24(1) TFEU and Article 11(4), second subparagraph TEU.[42] Even if one was to assume that the Commission was generally obliged to submit a proposal or that it could only refrain from doing so under exceptional and justified circumstances,[43] the citizen's concrete possibilities of intervention would nevertheless remain limited due to the Commission's considerable liberties and margins of appreciations within the

[38]Cf. Article 190(1), first subparagraph TFEU: "non-legislative acts of general application".

[39]See, however, the opinion of the Federal Constitutional Court, BVerfGE 123, 267 – *Treaty of Lisbon*, para. 290.

[40]In that sense Mader (2013), p. 358 et seq.; Epiney (2005), p. 49 et seq.; Huber (2012b), para. 42.

[41]See also Nettesheim (2015b), para. 27. With a more cautious outcome see also Biervert (2012), para. 3.

[42]Neither can the Regulation (EU) No 211/2011 be considered disproportionate when taking into account the open wording in Article 11(4) TEU and the legislator's similarly wide prerogative of evaluation.

[43]See Ruffert (2016b), para. 19; Franzius and Preuß (2011), p. 121.

framework of its right of initiative.[44] In short: Article 11(4) TEU *does not replace but precede* the Commission's right of initiative.

That the citizens' initiative nonetheless has a considerable political impact becomes evident when looking at the ECI "Right2Water".[45] In June 2013, the political pressure created by this ECI significantly influenced Commissioner *Barnier's* decision to exempt the water sector from the Commission's reform plans in the context of the concessions directive.[46]

2.2 *ECI and External Relations: The Case of "Stop TTIP"*

The citizens' initiative "Stop TTIP" raised the question as to how far the ECI extends to the field of external relations. In essence, "Stop TTIP" demanded that the negotiating mandate for TTIP should be repealed and that CETA should not be concluded. In its decision of 10 September 2014, the European Commission under leadership of the General Secretariat in coordination with the Directorate General for Trade (DG Trade) rejected the request for registration.[47] Notwithstanding the decision, the initiators continued to collect signatures, now under the label "self-organised" citizens' initiative, and brought an action for annulment before the General Court. The case involves two separate strands of argument.

2.2.1 "Legal Acts" in External Relations

With the ECI "Stop TTIP", the applicants in essence invite the Commission to submit a recommendation for a Council decision under Article 207(3), second subparagraph TFEU repealing the initial Council decision which authorised the opening of the TTIP negotiations, including the repeal of the negotiation mandate.

Preliminary Remarks

At this point, it is useful to recall the relevant provisions of primary and secondary law in their original wording.

Article 11(4) TEU:

> Not less than one million citizens who are nationals of a significant number of Member States may take the initiative of inviting the European Commission, within the framework

[44]Cf. Obwexer and Villotti (2010), p. 118; Guckelberger (2010) p. 753.

[45]ECI(2012)000003, otherwise known as "Water and sanitation are a human right! Water is a public good, not a commodity".

[46]For more details on effects of this ECI see Sule (2014), p. 727 et seqq.

[47]European Commission, C(2014) 6501 final.

of its powers, to submit any appropriate proposal on matters where citizens consider that a legal act of the Union is required for the purpose of implementing the Treaties. [...]

Article 4 Regulation (EU) No 211/2011:

[...]

2. Within two months from the receipt of the information set out in Annex II, the Commission shall register a proposed citizens' initiative under a unique registration number and send a confirmation to the organisers, provided that the following conditions are fulfilled:

[...]

(b) the proposed citizens' initiative does not manifestly fall outside the framework of the Commission's powers to submit a proposal for a legal act of the Union for the purpose of implementing the Treaties;

3. The Commission shall refuse the registration if the conditions laid down in paragraph 2 are not met.

In sum, for a successful registration the following four conditions[48] must be met: firstly, the Commission must be invited to submit a "proposal"; secondly, the proposal must be directed towards the adoption of a "legal act"; thirdly, this must serve the purpose of implementing the Treaties, and fourthly, the above must remain within the limits of the Commission's competences.

Decisions Authorising the Signature and Conclusion Only?

The Commission held the view that the requested recommendation did not constitute a "legal act" within the meaning of Article 11(4) TEU and Article 4(2) of the Regulation (EU) No. 211/2011 and consequently already failed to fulfil the second of the four conditions.[49] The Council decision authorising the opening of negotiations was, according to the Commission, only a preparatory act whose legal effects did not exceed the inter-institutional level.[50] Such a measure which solely paves the way for the opening of negotiations, however, could not be subject to an ECI. In the context of external relations the term "legal act" would refer only to the Council decisions to authorise the signature and the conclusion of an international agreement.[51]

The wording of Article 11(4) TEU—echoed in Article 4(2) Regulation (EU) No 211/2011—seems to support this interpretation in as far as both explicitly speak of a "proposal" (German *Vorschlag*, French *proposition*) of the Commission.

[48]Article 4(2) of the Regulation (EU) No 211/2011 additionally requires that the citizens' committee has been formed and the contact persons have been designated (lit. 1), that the proposed citizens' initiative is not manifestly abusive, frivolous or vexatious (lit. c) and that it is not manifestly contrary to the values of the Union (lit. d). However, the ECI in questions unproblematically fulfilled these requirements.

[49]European Commission, C(2014) 6501 final, p. 2.

[50]European Commission, C(2014) 6501 final, p. 2.

[51]European Commission, C(2014) 6501 final, p. 2.

A systematic comparison shows that the general rules on external relations—all of which, with the exception of the special requirements of Article 207 TFEU, also apply to the common commercial policy—indeed only speak of a Commission "proposal" where a Council decision to authorise the signature and the conclusion of an international agreement is concerned (Article 218(5) and (6) TFEU). By contrast, both the special requirements of the common commercial policy in the second subparagraph of Article 207(3) TFEU as well as the general rules on external relations in Article 218(3) TFEU speak of a "recommendation" with regard to the Council decision authorising the opening of negotiations.

The Negotiation Mandate as a "Legal Act" in the Sense of Article 11(4) TEU

However, the Commission's argument remains essentially limited to formal considerations and fails to convince in substance.[52] The main reason for the terminological differentiation between proposal and recommendation in the Treaties are the limitations to changes of proposals laid down in Article 293 TFEU. The fact that these limitations do not apply to recommendations within the meaning of Article 207(3), second subparagraph and Article 218(3) TFEU[53] does not change their basic nature: recommendations, too, are an expression of the Commission's constitutional prerogative of initiative which in the field of external relations specifically concerns the Council decision to authorise the opening of the negotiations and the related negotiation mandate.[54] Though not an act of legislation in the proper sense, this is still a case of law-making by way of a Council decision within the meaning of Article 288(4) TFEU.[55] Precisely because Article 11(4) TEU is not, as demonstrated above, limited to acts of legislation within the meaning of Article 289 TFEU, instead referring to "legal act[s] of the Union", it does not preclude a citizens' initiative in the present context.

Moreover, Article 11(4) TEU does not in any way require the citizens to be legally affected by the desired legal act and hence does not establish the requirement that the latter would necessarily have to produce legal effects outside the EU institutions. The term "legal act" only precludes purely factual acts without any legal relevance at all. Finally, the condition that the desired act must implement the Treaties only precludes ECIs that aim at a Treaty reform.[56]

---

[52]See now GC, judgment of 10 May 2017, case T-754/14, *Efler et al. v. Commission*, paras. 35 et seq. Cf. before Rathke H, Mehr Partizipation wagen!, JuWiss-Blog, 23 September 2014, https://www.juwiss.de/114-2014/ (last accessed 1 March 2017).

[53]Mögele (2012), para. 5.

[54]Cf. Lorenzmeier (2011), para. 25.

[55]Cf. again Rathke H, Mehr Partizipation wagen!, JuWiss-Blog, 23 September 2014.

[56]See Guckelberger (2010), p. 752. Huber (2012b), para. 39 is using the same starting point but excludes an ECI aiming at Commission activities outside the area of (secondary) legislation, for instance in the EU's external representation (para. 41).

What is indeed decisive is the purpose of the ECI. As has been shown, the ECI is an expression of the principle of democratic participation and serves the principle of proximity to the citizen. Obliging the EU institutions to take decisions "as closely as possible to the citizen", Article 10(3) establishes a constitutional principle or maxim which can be, from a methodological point of view, translated into an interpretive guideline aiming at optimising citizens' participation. Accordingly, a procedural provision intended to foster democratic participation shall be interpreted in a way that grants at least a minimum amount of efficiency and practicability. This understanding corresponds to the underlying considerations that guided the EU legislator when giving shape to the ECI.[57] The principles of democratic participation and proximity to the citizen, in turn, are of course normatively developed through the instruments and procedures established by primary law and given concrete form by secondary legislation. Naturally, a recourse to the *effet utile* of the abstract fundamental principle may neither override those instruments specifically designed for the realisation of the principles nor the legislator's choices and deliberations that find their expression in those instruments. However, the interpretative guideline to take decisions as closely as possible to the citizens means at any rate that the applicable procedural provision may not be interpreted in a restrictive manner at the expense of the citizen if the norm in question is of a general nature and open to interpretation. Hence, the general wording of Article 11(4) TEU and the regulation ("legal act of the Union") must not be restricted to Council decisions authorising the signature and the conclusion of international agreements to the detriment of citizens.

Furthermore, the constitutional function of the negotiation mandate in the context of external relations speaks in favour of including it within the scope of application of the ECI. As mentioned initially, the purpose of Article 11(4) TEU is to provide the EU citizens with a right to initiate an initiative and hence to participate in the political agenda-setting. However, the political agenda in the field of external relations is shaped, from the EU perspective, prior to the agreement's conclusion, namely during the negotiation process. Of course, due to the special dynamics inherent to the process of negotiations, EU citizens' participation can by definition only relate to the political guidelines on the part of the Union, especially since complete control over the negotiation process is already rendered impossible by the presence of participants from third countries. Setting the political guidelines for the EU starts with determining the negotiation mandate.[58] This, however, presupposes that the Commission exercises its right of initiative and submits a recommendation. After all, in the context of the CCP, it is the Commission's prerogative to formulate recommendations for a negotiation mandate and to

[57]Cf. the second recital of the Regulation (EU) No 211/2011: "The procedures and conditions required for the citizens' initiative should be clear, simple, user-friendly and proportionate to the nature of the citizens' initiative so as to encourage participation by citizens and to make the Union more accessible. They should strike a judicious balance between rights and obligations."

[58]Cf. the TTIP-mandate, http://data.consilium.europa.eu/doc/document/ST-11103-2013-DCL-1/en/pdf (last accessed 1 March 2017).

conduct these negotiations in consultation with a special committee.[59] A recent example of the Commission's political repositioning with regard to the field of investor-state dispute settlements (ISDS) helps to illustrate the importance of agenda-setting in the course of the negotiations. Under pressure from the European Parliament (EP) as well as the public,[60] the Commission initiated—while negotiations were still ongoing—a paradigm shift by suggesting the introduction of new "Investment Court System" for TTIP and other EU trade- and investment agreements.[61]

In sum, the EU's competences to politically and legally carry out the EU trade policy start with shaping the negotiation guidelines—an inner European process which is kicked off by recommendations submitted by the Commission. With a view to participation and political agenda-setting, the right to submit recommendations is functionally equivalent to the right to initiative in the classic EU legislative process; at least as far as political goals are to be specified. In terms of democratic participation it therefore cannot make a legally relevant difference whether an ECI aims at a Commission proposal on, say, the enactment of a directive concerning the freedom of services or whether it aims at a Commission recommendation on a negotiation mandate and the Council decision authorising the opening of negotiations on an international trade agreement relating to the service sector.

Not even the Commission, for that matter, argues that the ECI would be fully excluded from the domain of external relations. However, following the Commission's reasoning, citizens would only be entitled to invite the Commission to propose a Council decision authorising the signature and conclusion of an already negotiated agreement.[62] Obviously, this is not an expression of democratic participation in the sense of enabling the citizens to proactively influence the political agenda-setting but at best a way to involve citizens by letting them affirmatively invite the Commission to complete what has been negotiated on the basis of the political agenda-setting by the institutions. Reducing the citizens' democratic participation to affirming and acclaiming completed treaties[63] defies the key purpose of Article 11(4) TEU. Hence, when taking adequately into account the telos of Article 11(4) TEU, Commission "recommendations" cannot be regarded as falling outside the scope of application of the ECI.

[59]See on that committee Weiß (2015), para. 96.

[60]More detail see Sect. 3.2.

[61]The document in question is a draft text preparing the EU's position in its negotiations with the United States, see http://trade.ec.europa.eu/doclib/docs/2015/Sept./tradoc_153807.pdf (last accessed 1 March 2017).

[62]European Commission, C(2014) 6501 final, p. 2.

[63]See the written observations on behalf of the applicant, published 9 November 2014, https://stop-ttip.org/de/wp-content/uploads/sites/4/2014/11/EuGH-Klageschrift_Kempen_EBI.pdf (last accessed 1 March 2017), para. 43 et seq. The GC followed this line of argument in its judgment of 10 May 2017, case T-754/14, *Efler et al. v. Commission*,paras. 44 et seq.

2.2.2 The Citizens' Initiative and the Non-acceptance of an Agreement

The second goal of the planned citizens' initiative "Stop TTIP" was to invite the Commission *not* to propose a Council decision on the signature and the conclusion of CETA[64] and TTIP. Here, the problem does not lie with the quality of a "legal act" within the meaning of Article 11(4) TEU. As has already been mentioned, the Commission indeed considers a Council decision authorising the signature and the conclusion of negotiated international agreements to be a legal act falling within the scope of application of Article 11(4) TEU. Instead, the Commission rejected the registration of the ECI on the grounds that EU citizens could not invite the Commission to *not* submit a proposal or to propose a (Council) decision not to adopt a legal act. The reasons provided by the Commission are essentially limited to the wording of Article 11(4) TFEU and Regulation (EU) No 211/2011 as well as the consideration that a (Council) decision not to adopt a legal act "would not deploy any autonomous legal effect beyond the fact of the legal act at issue not being adopted."[65]

Ultimately, this argumentation is also defective. Here, too, it is important to keep in mind that the citizens' initiative serves the purpose of enabling the citizens to participate in the political agenda-setting. It necessarily follows that agenda-setting is by no means reserved for proposals to issue new legal acts or amend existing ones, but may also—and likewise legitimately—manifest itself in the repeal or the non-enactment of a legal act. In the end, positive and negative law-making are two sides of the same coin. There is no rational justification why a citizens' initiative, as a means of democratic participation, should only be authorised to initiate the creation of (further) regulation, but not its prevention.

In the context of external relations, the Commission's approach would lead to the result that a citizens' initiative could only aim at the acceptance of a fully negotiated contract. Neither the (positive) impulse to open negotiations and to influence the underlying negotiation mandate, nor the (negative) approach, not to conclude a negotiated agreement, would fall within the framework of the ECI. The result is a de facto exclusion of the ECI from the domain of external relations. The fact that the desired Council decision to refrain from signing or concluding the agreement does not create "autonomous" normative effects (beyond the mere statement that the agreement would not be signed or concluded) and could be revoked by a later decision is by no means an anomaly since even a newly issued legal act can be revoked later.

This being said, one has to conclude that the principle of *actus contrarius* must also apply in the context of external relations. It must be legally admissible to invite

[64]Regarding CETA the request for preliminary injunctions has been rejected in the meantime by the General Court and the Court of Justice, see GC, order of 23 May 2016, case T-754/14 R, *Efler et al. v Commission*, ECLI:EU:T:2016:306, and CJEU, order of 29 September 2016, case C-400/16 P(R), *Efler et al. v Commission*, ECLI:EU:C:2016:735.

[65]European Commission, C(2014) 6501 final, p. 2 et seq.

the Commission to propose a Council decision not to sign or conclude a negotiated international agreement, because this is the counterpart to the affirmative invitation (explicitly permitted also by the Commission).

2.2.3 Conclusion

Regardless of the question if the planned ECI "Stop TTIP" is to be seen as persuasive regarding its political goals (and there are a lot of reasons that it is not), it did hardly come as a surprise that the General Court annulled the Commission's decision not to register the ECI.[66] The European Commission was obliged under Article 11(4) TEU and Regulation (EU) No 211/2011 to register the ECI. The follow-up question then points to the potential effects of an approved ECI, given that the Commission would, with regard to its wider political margin of assessment, not be bound by the ECI. And yet the judicial annulment of the Commission's decision is not much ado about nothing, because the Commission will at least have to provide detailed reasons for the decision not to admit the ECI. This obligation to give reasons entail that the Commission cannot limit itself to formal considerations (as it has done in its decision on the non-registration), but needs to address the substance of the free trade agreements. This could be one out of many ways to disprove the myths dominating public discourse in this context.[67] If the citizens' critique was well-founded, however, the Commission could take these concerns seriously and provide redress by way of negotiations—as shown with regard to ISDS.

Undoubtedly, the ECI's range as an instrument for democratic input remains limited. The reasons why it functions solely as an additional element of democratic participation within the toolkit of European multilevel democracy are palpable. The central question of the democratic legitimation of the common commercial policy refers back to the parliaments at both EU and national levels. It is in parliament that social plurality is translated into a formalised process of deliberative dispute between the representatives of different ranges of opinion.[68] Parliamentary involvement is also particularly important when it comes to mechanisms of control. In the field of external relations, considerable rights to information are conferred on the European Parliament in general (Article 218(10) TFEU) and in the common commercial policy in particular (Article 207(3), third subparagraph, second sentence TFEU). Because of their characteristic structure and competences, parliaments are also particularly well-suited to provide for the necessary degree of

[66]GC, judgment of 10 May 2017, case T-754/14, *Efler et al. v. Commission*. The admissibility was not problematic with a view to Article 263(4) TFEU as the Commission's decision not to register the ECI directly addresses the organisers of the ECI.

[67]Cf. the Commission's online presence regarding TTIP, which has undergone considerable expansion in recent times, including a leaflet dealing with ten TTIP-myths, https://trade.ec.europa.eu/doclib/docs/2015/march/tradoc_153266.pdf (last accessed 1 March 2017).

[68]See Streinz (2016).

(public) openness. These considerations, then, lead over to questions of transparency and dialogue.[69]

3 Transparency and Dialogue

The principle of transparency[70] is laid down in Article 1(2) and Article 10(3), second sentence TEU. More specifically, it follows from the requirement that decisions must be taken as "openly" as possible. When assessing its scope and function within the context of the common commercial policy, special attention must be given to the specificities of the functioning of negotiations under international law. Heuristically, it might prove helpful to differentiate between two perspectives: the individual and the institutional.

3.1 *The Individual Rights Perspective*

Seen from the individual rights perspective, the principle of transparency finds its key expression in the right of access to documents.[71] As a basic condition for the formation of public opinion, this right is essential for exercising political rights in a most general sense. At the same time, it serves as a control mechanism, keeping a check on the executive.[72] The right of access to documents is thus rooted in the principle of democracy[73] on the one hand and the rule of law on the other. Its foundation is laid in Article 15(3) TFEU and Article 42 CFR.[74] Regulation (EC) No 1049/2001 then further concretises the modalities and limits of the right's exercise.[75] Article 4(1)(a), third alternative of the Regulation is central to the present context: where disclosure would undermine the protection of international relations, it reads, the institutions shall refuse access to documents.

[69]Cf. Pernice (2015), p. 521.

[70]In more detail on the principle of transparency see Sobotta (2001) as well as Riemann (2004), p. 29 et seqq.

[71]See the first recital of the Regulation (EC) No 1049/2001, OJ 2001 L 145/43.

[72]Appropriately Kadelbach (2015), para. 71.

[73]See opinion of AG Maduro to CJEU, case C-64/05 P, *Kingdom of Sweden v Commission*, ECLI: EU:C:2007:433, para. 41 et seqq.

[74]On the special quality of dual legal sources see Wendel (2014), para. 34 et seqq.

[75]Regulation (EC) No 1049/2001 of the European Parliament and of the Council of 30 May 2001 regarding public access to European Parliament, Council, and Commission documents. The regulation cannot be discussed in detail here. For further information see Meltzian (2004), p. 173 et seqq.; Marsch (2005), p. 639 et seqq.; Bartelt and Zeitler (2003), p. 489 et seqq.; Kranenborg (2008), p. 1083 et seqq.

This protective clause was recently elaborated by the General Court in the *Besselink* decision which was related to the negotiations concerning the EU's accession to the European Convention of Human Rights (ECHR). For the time being, accession plans have failed before the Court of Justice.[76] *Leonard Besselink*, professor of law at the University of Amsterdam, had unsuccessfully appealed to the Council to provide access to the negotiation mandate for the accession to the ECHR. Upon refusal, he introduced an action seeking annulment of the Council decision and achieved a partial victory before the General Court. Following the jurisprudence of the Court of Justice, the General Court principally chose a narrow interpretation of the exceptions granted in Article 4 of the Regulation as far as external relations are concerned.[77]

As a result, in the context of external relations, non-disclosure remains the exception to the rule, with transparency acting as the guiding principle. Again following the Court of Justice, the General Court granted a considerable margin of assessment to the Council which corresponds to a limitation of judicial control.[78] All in all, the General Court thought the Council's refusal to publish central parts of the mandate legitimate and only granted access to minor parts of the document.[79] Even though the document merely paves the way for the actual negotiations to follow, its publication could potentially weaken the EU's negotiating position.[80] The limitations discussed here go back to the special quality of external relations and are also applicable in the context of TTIP and CETA. In spite of these arguments, the Commission itself has announced the release of most of the requested documents.[81]

3.2 The Institutional Perspective

Seen from the institutional perspective, the principle of transparency translates into the requirement of transparent negotiations on the one hand and the inclusion of the public, for instance by means of consultations initiated by the Commission, on the other hand. Both points are of course inseparable from one another.

[76] CJEU, opinion 2/13, *Accession to the ECHR II*, ECLI:EU:C:2014:2454.

[77] GC, case T-331/11, *Besselink v Commission*, ECLI:EU:T:2013:419, para. 31. See also previously in the context of counter-terrorism CJEU, case C-266/05 P, *Sison*, ECLI:EU:C:2007:75, para. 63.

[78] GC, case T-331/11, *Besselink v Commission*, ECLI:EU:T:2013:419, paras. 32–34 and 51.

[79] GC, case T-331/11, *Besselink v Commission*, ECLI:EU:T:2013:419, paras. 73 and 108.

[80] GC, case T-331/11, *Besselink v Commission*, ECLI:EU:T:2013:419, para. 73.

[81] See http://trade.ec.europa.eu/doclib/press/index.cfm?id=1230 (last accessed 1 March 2017). As regards the significance of the documents, however, this does not allow for reliable conclusions.

3.2.1 Transparent Negotiations

What is important to note with a view to the conduct of the negotiations is that the negotiation rounds are not being held publicly. Following common international practice, this approach serves to create and secure a certain amount of leeway essential to all forms of negotiation aiming to dynamically balance different interests and ultimately achieve a compromise.[82] Disclosing the minimum goals beforehand would jeopardize the negotiation process or, in the case of a unilateral disclosure, the negotiation position of the party in question would be significantly weakened.

The authority to decide on the publication of a document is principally accessory to the decision-making authority in the case itself. Accordingly, the party responsible for the publication or non-publication in the case of the negotiation mandate was not the Commission but the Council (Article 207(3), third subparagraph and Article 218(4) TFEU). The TTIP mandate was initially declared confidential. However, after two requests by the Commission and the subsequent initiative of the Italian Council Presidency, the Council decided to publish after all.[83] The required decision was issued on 9 October 2014.[84] A detail worth noting is the Council's legal understanding—probably originating in Article 207(4), second and third subparagraph TFEU—that the decision must be taken unanimously. Politically, this majority was only possible due to the Italian Council Presidency's initiative. What remains unanswered is whether such a majority was strictly speaking necessary since it can convincingly be argued that the decision to publish is in fact a procedural decision which only requires a simple majority. Moreover, if the agreements are categorised as "mixed agreements" (as is at least the case for CETA[85]), increasing tensions with regard to competences and the authority to publish are to be expected.[86]

Particularly relevant to the Commission's publishing practice within the limits of its competences is EU Trade Commissioner *Cecilia Malmström's* communication concerning transparency in TTIP negotiations, published 15 November 2014.[87] Measures taken include firstly the systematic publication of all negotiation documents which the Commission shares with the European Parliament and the Council and which have already been communicated to the negotiation partners; secondly a revision of the previous practice of categorising documents; and thirdly the

[82]See Hoffmeister (2015), p. 38 et seq.

[83]Hoffmeister (2015), p. 40.

[84]The mandate had already been leaked by some members of the EP.

[85]See the text of the agreement as signed on 30 October 2016, http://data.consilium.europa.eu/doc/document/ST-10973-2016-INIT/en/pdf(last accessed 1 March 2017).

[86]This question cannot be dealt with in detail here. For the contrary positions on whether the free trade agreements are to be seen as mixed agreements see (affirmative) Meyer (2014) and (negative) Hoffmeister (2015), p. 54 et seqq.

[87]European Commission, C(2014) 9052 final.

increased consultation of the Parliamentarians, especially where documents classified as "restricted" or "limited" are concerned.[88] In the aftermath of the notification, the Commission published multiple documents, thereby greatly exceeding conventional measures of transparency. Among the documents published are even concrete text proposals that were actually used in the negotiations.[89]

3.2.2 Dialogue through Public Consultation

A dialogue between the Commission and the public has primarily been achieved through public consultations.[90] Furthermore, different formats of professional and political exchange with representatives of interest groups open up additional communicative channels. The legal basis of TTIP-related consultations is not Article 2 of the Protocol (no 2) on the application of the principles of subsidiarity and proportionality which only applies to legislative proposals. More relevant is Article 11(1) TEU which obliges EU institutions to, in a very general sense, promote communication.[91] However, this obligation is limited by the caveat "by appropriate means" which allows for a wide margin of assessment on the part of the institutions.[92] In spite of the lack of participatory elements, the provision only addresses the EU institutions and thus does not constitute any subjective rights.[93] The same holds true for paragraphs (2) and (3) of Article 11 TEU, both of which refer to the dialogue with representative organisations and civil society as well as to the hearing of the persons affected.

4 Conclusion

Ultimately, the legal framework of democratic participation in the context of the common commercial policy is rather soft. With regard to the principles of democratic participation and transparency, the EU institutions enjoy a considerable margin of assessment which can only be partially addressed or framed by legal norms. This corresponds to a limited judicial control. Bodies such as the European

---

[88]European Commission, C(2014) 9052 final.

[89]Another relevant question is in how far the Commission is entitled to publish documents from which indirect conclusions about the negotiation mandate may be drawn. This is still largely a grey area in positive law so that general duties of loyalty remain pretty much the only maxim still operable.

[90]More details see http://trade.ec.europa.eu/consultations/index.cfm#_tab_2015 and http://trade.ec.europa.eu/consultations/index.cfm#_tab_2016 (both last accessed 1 March 2017).

[91]Aptly put in Huber (2012b), para. 9.

[92]Nettesheim (2015b), para. 10.

[93]Ruffert (2016b), para. 8.

Ombudsman can at best fulfil a supplementary control function.[94] Where the creation of greater transparency and openness to the public are concerned, parliaments, namely the European Parliament,[95] remain of paramount importance.

Still, a public which is built on democratic participation and transparency can unfold considerable political power, as becomes evident in the example of the Commission's repositioning *in puncto* ISDS for which both public pressure and an EP resolution[96] served as catalysts. Most recently, the Commission suggested the replacement of the classic ISDS[97] with a new Investment Court System.[98]

May all this lead to a process in the course of which the focus of attention starts shifting towards truly substantial and decisive matters; a process which does not only generate heat but also a little light—perhaps even the light at the end of the tunnel.

References

Bartelt S, Zeitler H (2003) Zugang zu Dokumenten in der EU. Europarecht 38(3):487–503

Biervert B (2012) Art. 11 EUV. In: Schwarze J (ed) EU-Kommentar, 3rd edn. Nomos, Baden-Baden

Bungenberg M, Hermann C (2011) Die gemeinsame Handelspolitik der Europäischen Union nach Lissabon. Nomos, Baden-Baden

Craig P (2001) Constitutions, constitutionalism and the European Union. Eur Law J 7(2):125–150

Cremona M (2015) Negotiating the transatlantic trade and investment partnership (TTIP). Common Mark Law Rev 52(2):351–362

Epiney A (2005) Europäische Verfassung und Legitimation durch die Unionsbürger. In: Kadelbach S (ed) Europäische Verfassung und direkte Demokratie. Nomos, Baden-Baden, pp 33–56

Franzius C, Preuß K (2011) Die Zukunft der europäischen Demokratie. Nomos, Baden-Baden

Guckelberger A (2010) Die Europäische Bürgerinitiative. Die Öffentliche Verwaltung 63 (18):745–754

Herrmann C (2010) Die gemeinsame Handelspolitik der Europäischen Union im Lissabon-Urteil. Europarecht Beiheft 1:193–210

Hindelang S (2014) Study on Investor-State Dispute Settlement (ISDS) and Alternatives of Dispute Resolution in International Investment Law. In: European Parliament (ed) Investor-

[94]As a reply to the Commission's notification, she submitted a catalogue of no less than ten requests on the improvement of the transparency of TTIP negotiations, http://www.ombudsman.europa.eu/en/cases/decision.faces/en/58668/html.bookmark (last accessed 1 March 2017).

[95]See, as mentioned above, Article 207(3), third subparagraph, second sentence TFEU and Article 218(10) TFEU.

[96]European Parliament, resolution of 8 July 2015 containing the European Parliament's recommendations to the European Commission on the negotiations for the Transatlantic Trade and Investment Partnership (TTIP), 2014/2228(INI).

[97]For a detailed discussion of manifestations, meaning, and potential for reform see Hindelang (2014), p. 39 et seqq.

[98]See already as well as Pernice (2014), p. 161 and (regarding the former approach) Stöbener (2015), p. 372.

State Dispute Settlement (ISDS) Provisions in the EU's International Investment Agreements, vol 2. Studies, pp 39–131
Hoffmeister F (2015) Wider die German Angst – Ein Plädoyer für die transatlantische Handels- und Investitionspartnerschaft (TTIP). Archiv des Völkerrechts 53(1):35–67
Huber P (1999) Demokratie ohne Volk oder Demokratie der Völker. In: Drexl J, Kreuzer KF, Scheuing DH (eds) Europäische Demokratie. Nomos, Baden-Baden, pp 27–57
Huber P (2012a) Artikel 10 EUV. In: Streinz R (ed) EUV/AEUV, 2nd edn. Beck, München
Huber P (2012b) Artikel 11 EUV. In: Streinz R (ed) EUV/AEUV, 2nd edn. Beck, München
Kadelbach S (2009) Unionsbürgerschaft. In: von Bogdandy A, Bast J (eds) Europäisches Verfassungsrecht, 2nd edn. Springer, Berlin, pp 611–656
Kadelbach S (2015) Unionsbürgerrechte. In: Ehlers D (ed) Europäische Grundrechte und Grundfreiheiten, 4th edn. de Gruyter, Berlin, pp 797–838
Kaufmann B (2011) Direkte Demokratie auf transnationaler Ebene. Zur Entstehungsgeschichte der Europäischen Bürgerinitiative. In: Feld L, Huber PM, Jung O, Welzel C, Wittreck F (eds) Jahrbuch für direkte Demokratie 2010. Nomos, Baden-Baden, pp 201–222
Kranenborg H (2008) Access to documents and data protection in the European Union: on the public nature of personal data. Common Mark Law Rev 45(4):1079–1114
Lorenzmeier S (2011) Art. 218 AEUV. In: Grabitz E, Hilf M, Nettesheim M (eds) Das Recht der Europäischen Union. Beck, München, loose leaf
Mader O (2013) Bürgerinitiative, Petitionsrecht, Beschwerde zum Bürgerbeauftragten. Europarecht 48(3):348–371
Marsch N (2005) Das Recht auf Zugang zu EU-Dokumenten. Die Öffentliche Verwaltung 58 (15):639–644
Mayer F (2013) Direkte Demokratie und die Europäische Union. In: Efler M, Mörschel T (eds) Direkte Demokratie auf Bundesebene. Nomos, Baden-Baden, pp 147–160
Mayer F, Ermes M (2014) Rechtsfragen zu den Freihandelsabkommen CETA und TTIP. Zeitschrift für Rechtspolitik 47(8):237–240
Meltzian D (2004) Das Recht der Öffentlichkeit auf Zugang zu Dokumenten der Gemeinschaftsorgane. Duncker & Humblot, Berlin
Meyer J (2014) Charta der Grundrechte der Europäischen Union, 4th edn. Nomos, Baden-Baden
Mögele R (2012) Art. 218 AEUV. In: Streinz R (ed) EUV/AEUV, 2nd edn. Beck, München
Nettesheim M (2015a) Art. 10 EUV. In: Grabitz E, Hilf M, Nettesheim M (eds) Das Recht der Europäischen Union. Beck, München, loose leaf
Nettesheim M (2015b) Art. 11 EUV. In: Grabitz E, Hilf M, Nettesheim M (eds) Das Recht der Europäischen Union. Beck. München, loose leaf
Obwexer W, Villotti J (2010) Die Europäische Bürgerinitiative. Journal für Rechtspolitik 18 (3):108–121
Pernice I (2014) Study on International Investment Protection Agreements and EU Law. In: European Parliament (ed) Investor-State Dispute Settlement (ISDS) Provisions in the EU's International Investment Agreements, vol 2. Studies, pp 132–166
Pernice I (2015) Politisierung der EU nach der Europawahl – Politik zwischen TTIP und TTU. Europäische Zeitschrift für Wirtschaftsrecht 25(14):521–522
Riemann F (2004) Die Transparenz der Europäischen Union. Duncker & Humblot, Berlin
Ruffert M (2016a) Art. 10 EUV. In: Calliess C, Ruffert M (eds) EUV/AEUV, 5th edn. Beck, München
Ruffert M (2016b) Art. 11 EUV. In: Calliess C, Ruffert M (eds) EUV/AEUV, 5th edn. Beck, München
Schmidt M (2010) Demokratietheorien, 5th edn. VS Verlag, Wiesbaden
Sobotta C (2001) Transparenz in den Rechtssetzungsverfahren der Europäischen Union. Nomos, Baden-Baden
Stöbener P (2015) Investitionsschutzrecht: Neue Vorschläge der Kommission zu TTIP. Europäische Zeitschrift für Wirtschaftsrecht 26(10):372

Streinz R (2016) Repräsentative Demokratie und parlamentarische Kontrolle. In: Bungenberg M, Herrmann C (eds) Die gemeinsame Handelspolitik der Europäischen Union. Nomos, Baden-Baden, pp 71–92

Sule S (2014) "Recht auf Wasser" – Zur ersten der Europäischen Kommission vorgelegten Europäischen Bürgerinitiative nach dem Lissabonner Vertrag. Europäische Zeitschrift für Wirtschaftsrecht 25(19):725–729

Tiedemann M (2012) Die sekundärrechtliche Ausgestaltung der europäischen Bürgerinitiative durch die Verordnung (EU) Nr. 211/2011. Neue Zeitschrift für Verwaltungsrecht 31(2):80–85

Treier V, Wernicke S (2015) Die Transatlantische Handels- und Investitionspartnerschaft (TTIP) – Trojanisches Pferd oder steiniger Weg zum Olymp. Europäische Zeitschrift für Wirtschaftsrecht 25(9):334–339

von Bogdandy A (2009) Grundprinzipien. In: von Bogdandy A, Bast J (eds) Europäisches Verfassungsrecht, 2nd edn. Springer, Berlin, pp 13–71

Weiß W (2015) Art. 207 AEUV. In: Grabitz E, Hilf M, Nettesheim M (eds) Das Recht der Europäischen Union. Beck, München, loose leaf

Wendel M (2014) § 18 Unionsbürgerrechte, Freizügigkeit. In: Grabenwarter C (ed) Europäischer Grundrechteschutz. Enzyklopädie Europarecht, vol 2. Nomos, Baden-Baden

Sincere Cooperation in the Common Commercial Policy: Lisbon, a "Joined-Up" Union, and "Brexit"

Joris Larik

Abstract The article elaborates on the significance of the duty of sincere cooperation as a legal principle in the Common Commercial Policy (CCP) of the European Union (EU), in particular as regards the relationship between the Union and its Member States. It argues that while the duty of sincere cooperation is a judicially enforceable duty vis-à-vis the Member States, it is losing some of its relevance in the context of the CCP. This is due to the fact that the Lisbon Treaty, as confirmed by the case law of the Court of Justice of the EU, expanded the scope of the CCP and clearly identifies it as an exclusive competence of the Union. Loyalty in the CCP, therefore, is mainly covered by the obligation to respect the exclusivity of the Union's international powers in this area. While this does not equate to the disappearance of the Member States as actors in international economic governance, it does seriously constrain their leeway for autonomous action. In addition, the article applies this finding to a number of current developments surrounding the CCP. These include, firstly, the new Global Strategy for Foreign and Security Policy, which promotes the idea of a "joined-up" approach between different actors and policies; secondly, "Brexit" and the prospect of the United Kingdom negotiating new trade agreements of its own; thirdly, the position of the Member States in the WTO; and fourthly, the nature of the wave of new free trade agreements that the EU is negotiating and concluding.

Contents

J. Larik (✉)
Faculty of Governance and Global Affairs, Leiden University, Anna van Buerenplein 301, 3595 DG The Hague, The Netherlands
e-mail: j.e.larik@luc.leidenuniv.nl

M. Bungenberg et al. (eds.), *European Yearbook of International Economic Law 2017*, European Yearbook of International Economic Law 8,
DOI 10.1007/978-3-319-58832-2_4

1 Introduction

The Common Commercial Policy (CCP) of the European Union (EU) is arguably the most unequivocal manifestation of the Union as a power in international affairs and global governance.[1] Based on one of the world's largest markets, the Union pursues both trade-specific and other foreign policy goals on the global stage.[2] Inverting the order of the well-known quote by former Belgian Foreign Minister *Mark Eyskens*, next to the EU's "military worm" and "political dwarf", the "economic giant" still looms large.[3] Even "Brexit" will not change that, as without the United Kingdom (UK), the EU would still be the second largest economic bloc in the world, after the United States.[4]

In addition to pursuing traditional trade-related objectives that are enshrined in law since the Treaty of Rome,[5] which, among other things, call on the EU to contribute to "the harmonious development of world trade"[6] and "the progressive abolition of restrictions on international trade",[7] the CCP also serves as an instrument for pursuing a more ambitious, normative global agenda. This includes aspirations such as to "consolidate and support democracy, the rule of law, human rights and the principles of international law",[8] to promote "the sustainable development of the Earth",[9] and to bring about "an international system based on stronger multilateral cooperation and good global governance."[10] These objectives

[1]Meunier and Nicolaïdis (2011).

[2]Larik (2011), pp. 23–34.

[3]Minister Eyskens in 1990 noted that the European Community was "an economic giant, a political dwarf, and a military worm". Quoted in McCormick (2008), p. 192.

[4]See statistics on Gross Domestic Product (GDP) from the World Bank, GDP (current US$), http://data.worldbank.org/indicator/NY.GDP.MKTP.CD (last accessed 1 March 2017).

[5]Article 110 Treaty Establishing the European Economic Community (original version of 1957).

[6]Article 206 Treaty on the Functioning of the European Union (TFEU).

[7]Article 21(2) lit. e Treaty on European Union (TEU).

[8]Article 21(2) lit. b TEU.

[9]Article 3(5) TEU.

[10]Article 21(2) lit. h TEU.

serve as the substantive constitutional foundation for the CCP in the post-Lisbon era. They inform the implementation of trade and foreign policy of the EU, as expressed, for instance, in the Trade for All strategy of October 2015[11] and the Global Strategy for Foreign and Security Policy,[12] which was presented to the European Council in June 2016.[13]

Such an ambitious, codified mandate raises the question of which actors should realize all of this. Despite the CCP being an "exclusive" competence of the EU,[14] this does not only concern the EU institutions,[15] but also its 28 (or 27, post-"Brexit") Member States. These are represented, in addition to the Union, at the World Trade Organization (WTO) as full members,[16] and are, alongside the Union, parties to a range of comprehensive trade agreements with third countries around the world.[17] The Member States, and their respective parliaments, continue to stake their claim to exercise their rights in this external policy area.[18]

Therefore, in addition to economic power and ambitions in the area of global governance, the parallelism—or "polyphony"[19]—of EU institutions and Member States on the international stage remains one of the defining features of the CCP. To ensure that polyphony does not result in cacophony and that the EU's economic weight can be effectively leveraged in the pursuit of its aspirations, the duty of sincere cooperation plays a crucial role. This principle is enshrined in primary law as well. In relation to the Member States it is found in Article 4(3) TEU.

The duty of sincere cooperation has received sustained attention in the scholarly literature.[20] Precisely because of the "polyphony" in EU external relations, particular attention is paid to its importance in the external action of the Union and the collective implementation of mixed agreements (i.e. agreements with third countries or organizations to which both Union and Member States are parties).[21]

---

[11]European Commission, Trade for All: Towards a More Responsible Trade and Investment Policy, COM (2015) 497 final, Brussels, 14 October 2015; see previously European Commission, Global Europe: Competing in the World: A Contribution to the EU's Growth and Jobs Strategy, COM (2006) 567 final, Brussels, 4 October 2006.

[12]Shared Vision, Common Action: A Stronger Europe, A Global Strategy for the European Union's Foreign and Security Policy, June 2016.

[13]European Council, Conclusions, EUCO 26/16, Brussels, 28 June 2016, para. 20.

[14]Article 3(1) lit. e TFEU.

[15]See Dederer (2013).

[16]Article XI:1 Agreement Establishing the World Trade Organization.

[17]See, for instance, the Free trade Agreement between the European Union and its Member States, of the one part, and the Republic of Korea, of the other part, OJ 2011 L 127/6.

[18]See the reply of the European Commission to an opinion issued by 20 parliaments of the Member States, Maroš Šefčovič, Vice-President of the European Commission, Brussels, 16 October 2014, C (2014) 7557 final.

[19]Hillion (2010), p. 87.

[20]See De Baere and Roes (2015); Klamert (2014); Hatje (2001); Hyett (2000).

[21]Klamert (2014), p. 183 et seq.; Delgado Casteleiro and Larik (2011); Neframi (2010); Hillion (2010); Kaiser (2009), p. 47 et seq.; Heliskoski (2001), p. 46 et seq.

It is clear that both the orchestration of harmony among these actors and the surrounding "soundscape" are in transition, being drawn in different directions by six main legal and political developments. These are, firstly, the amendments introduced by the Lisbon Treaty, which entered into force in 2009 and which led to important changes to the CCP and the EU's system of external relations as a whole; secondly, the recent case law of the Court of Justice of the EU (CJEU), which is in the process of clarifying the new legal situation post-Lisbon; thirdly, the revamping of EU trade and foreign policy through the adoption of a new comprehensive strategy document; fourthly, the consequences of the EU membership referendum in the United Kingdom of June 2016 and the prospect of the UK leaving the Union over the next years; fifthly, the evolving external representation of the EU and its Member States at the WTO; and sixthly, the negotiation of a range of new, deep and comprehensive (and often controversial) trade agreements.

Against this backdrop, the objective of this article is to contribute to a better understanding of "harmony" in the complex interplay of actors and norms in the CCP in light of these developments. The argument put forward here affirms, on the one hand, the continuing importance of sincere cooperation as a legal principle in the external relations of the EU in general, and as regards the use of trade policy in implementing the Global Strategy and its "joined-up" approach in particular. On the other hand, it posits that in the area of the CCP proper, loyalty as a legal principle is losing some of its relevance due to both practical factors and the judicially sanctioned transfer of powers in favour of the Union. The article furthermore outlines the main consequences of "Brexit" in this area. Overall, "polyphony" and mixed agreements will continue to characterize the CCP. Therefore, the duty of sincere cooperation will remain an important legal principle also in the CCP—though not *the* most important one by any measure.

2 Sincere Cooperation in the EU's Primary Law

Sincere cooperation is not only a core legal principle within the EU legal order, but can be described more accurately as a principle of European composite constitutional law, as it applies not only to relations between the EU institutions,[22] but also in the mutual relations between the Union and its Member States. This application extends to the foreign relations of the Member States and the EU. It is this latter aspect which gives a special significance to it, since both the EU and the Member States remain active on the world stage. The principle is stipulated in Article 4(3) TEU, as amended by the Lisbon Treaty:

> Pursuant to the principle of sincere cooperation, the Union and the Member States shall, in full mutual respect, assist each other in carrying out tasks which flow from the Treaties.

[22] Article 13(2) TEU.

> The Member States shall take any appropriate measure, general or particular, to ensure fulfilment of the obligations arising out of the Treaties or resulting from the acts of the institutions of the Union.
>
> The Member States shall facilitate the achievement of the Union's tasks and refrain from any measure which could jeopardise the attainment of the Union's objectives.[23]

This provision follows directly after the call on the EU to respect the Member States' "national identities, inherent in their fundamental structures, political and constitutional".[24] Primacy of EU law and its full and effective implementation in the domestic legal order can be regarded as one of the foremost expressions of loyal cooperation.[25] However, as the recent case law of Member States' constitutional courts shows, loyalty can reach its limits where the core of constitutional identity starts.[26] Sincere cooperation is not to be understood as a duty of blind obedience for the Member States. At the same time, the structure of the TEU also suggests that the duty of sincere cooperation is fully applicable to any Member State actions that fall outside the narrow confines of "constitutional identity" to be guarded by national supreme or constitutional courts in the Member States.

Moreover, sincere cooperation is not to be understood as an end in itself, but as an inherently goal-oriented concept. This is clear from the obligations of Member States to "facilitate the achievement of the Union's tasks" and to "refrain from any measure which could jeopardise the attainment of the Union's objectives". These objectives are more extensive than ever in the EU Treaties post-Lisbon,[27] and represent a kaleidoscope of dimensions of the "common good" of the Union, rather than a catalogue of specific functions.[28]

In addition to this general formulation of the principle of sincere cooperation, it is also enshrined in other parts of the Treaties, applied to specific policies and actors. In the area of the Common Foreign and Security Policy (CFSP), it finds a rather eloquent expression. After evoking "the development of mutual political solidarity among Member States" and "the achievement of an ever-increasing degree of convergence of Member States' actions",[29] the following paragraph provides that:

---

[23] Article 4(3) TEU.

[24] Article 4(2) TEU; see seminally Millet (2013).

[25] See from the more recent case law of the CJEU, opinion 2/13, *ECHR*, ECLI:EU:C:2014:2454, para. 173; CJEU, case C-66/13, *Green Network*, ECLI:EU:C:2014:2399, para. 7; CJEU, case C-41/11, *Inter-Environnement Wallonie*, ECLI:EU:C:2012:103, para. 43.

[26] See the judgment of the German Federal Constitutional Court (Second Senate) of 15 December 2015, 2 BvR 2735/14, paras. 40–50, where explicit reference is made to Article 4(3) and Article 4(2) TEU.

[27] See first and foremost Article 3(1) TEU, which declares the promotion of peace, the Union's values and the well-being of its people to be objectives of the EU. Also with specific regard to the EU's external action, there is no shortage of broadly defined ambitions, see Articles 3(5) and 21 TEU.

[28] See Piris (2010), p. 73.

[29] Article 24(2) TEU.

> The Member States shall support the Union's external and security policy actively and unreservedly in a spirit of loyalty and mutual solidarity and shall comply with the Union's action in this area.
>
> The Member States shall work together to enhance and develop their mutual political solidarity. They shall refrain from any action which is contrary to the interests of the Union or likely to impair its effectiveness as a cohesive force in international relations.
>
> The Council and the High Representative shall ensure compliance with these principles.[30]

The same spirit is clearly present also in the EU's Global Strategy for Foreign and Security Policy, which notes that "EU foreign policy is not a solo performance: it is an orchestra which plays from the same score."[31]

This should not hide the fact that the justiciability of the principle of sincere cooperation in the area of the CFSP is highly restricted—if not denied—due to the limited jurisdiction of the CJEU.[32] The use of the word "political solidarity" suggests that in this case loyalty is not to be understood as a judicially enforceable duty. Lastly, also the mutual assistance clause in the event of armed aggression[33] and the solidarity clause in case of terrorist attacks and disasters[34] can be considered as manifestations of sincere cooperation laid down in the primary law. As part of the CCP, a duty of loyal cooperation is not specifically repeated. Here, therefore, the general principle enshrined in Article 4(3) TEU, which covers all policy areas, applies.

3 Case Law on Loyalty in EU External Action

The programmatic and open wording in the formulation of the principle of sincere cooperation in Article 4(3) TEU notwithstanding, it is a justiciable legal principle that applies both to internal and external action, and to the relationship both between the Member States *inter se* and in the relationship between the EU and

[30] Article 24(3) TEU.

[31] Shared Vision, Common Action: A Stronger Europe, A Global Strategy for the European Union's Foreign and Security Policy, June 2016, p. 46.

[32] Article 24(1) subpara. 2 TEU, read in conjunction with Article 40 TEU and Article 275(2) TFEU. See further on the "bipolarity" between CFSP and other EU policies, Dashwood (2014). But see, for an argument to extend the duty of sincere cooperation into the CFSP, Hillion (2014), p. 67.

[33] Article 42(7) TEU. This provision, and not the one on mutual solidarity enshrined in Article 222 TFEU, was invoked for the first time in December 2015 by the French government following the terrorist attacks in Paris, see Council of the European Union, Outcome of the Council Meeting, 3426th Council meeting, Foreign Affairs, Brussels, 16 and 17 November 2015, 14,120/15 (OR en), Presse 69, PR CO 61, p. 6.

[34] Article 222 TFEU.

Member States.[35] With regard to the case law of the CJEU in relation to Union loyalty in the external relations of the EU, one can distinguish a number of different legal effects. These effects, several of which can apply at the same time, become evident in four main situations. Firstly, in addition to a general interpretive component,[36] there exist both positive, optimizing duties to act as well as duties of abstention for the Member States when it comes to the negotiation of international agreements. Secondly, there are specific situations in which the Member States are obliged to act jointly in the Union's interest in international organizations. Thirdly, the duty of sincere cooperation plays a particularly important role in the implementation of mixed agreements. Fourthly, sincere cooperation can amount to a duty for Member States to refrain from acting altogether in international bodies if this undermines Union positions, both in areas of exclusive and shared competence.

As a preliminary observation, it should be noted that the CJEU derives from the principle of sincere cooperation also a "principle of unity in the international representation of the Union and its Member States".[37] However, rather than being an independent legal principle, it is to be understood as an expression of sincere cooperation on the international stage.[38]

3.1 *Sincere Cooperation in the Negotiation of International Agreements*

The negative and positive dimensions of sincere cooperation became clearly visible in CJEU judgments of 2005 on the signing and ratification of agreements between Member States and third countries concerning inland waterway transport. These actions were considered unlawful in light of the loyalty obligations towards the former European Community because the Commission was conducting negotiations on the same subject with the same third countries. In the judgment, the Court stated:

[35]From the recent case law in the context of internal EU policies see, for example, CJEU, case C-515/14, *Commission v. Cyprus*, ECLI:EU:C:2016:30; CJEU, case C-408/14, *Aliny Wojciechowski v. Office national des pensions (ONP)*, ECLI:EU:C:2015:591. See also the CJEU, opinion 2/13, *ECHR*, ECLI:EU:C:2014:2454, para. 173; CJEU, case C-66/13, *Green Network*, ECLI:EU:C:2014:2399, para. 7; CJEU, case C-41/11, *Inter-Environnement Wallonie*, ECLI:EU:C:2012:103, para. 43.

[36]See, for instance, CJEU, case C-308/06, *Intertanko*, ECLI:EU:C:2008:312, para. 52, where the CJEU found that in "view of the customary principle of good faith, which forms part of general international law, and of Article 10 EC [now Article 4(3) TEU], it is incumbent upon the Court to interpret" secondary Union legislation in a way that takes into account international legal rules which are binding on the Member States, but not the Union.

[37]CJEU, case C-246/07, *Commission v. Sweden (PFOS)*, ECLI:EU:C:2010:203, para. 104; and CJEU, opinion 2/91, *ILO*, ECLI:EU:C:1993:106, para. 36. See further Thies (2012), p. 721.

[38]See the Opinion of Advocate General Poiares Maduro, CJEU, case C-246/07, *Commission v. Sweden (PFOS)*, ECLI:EU:C:2009:589, para. 37.

> The adoption of a decision authorising the Commission to negotiate a multilateral agreement on behalf of the Community marks the start of a concerted Community action at international level and requires for that purpose, if not a duty of abstention on the part of the Member States, at the very least a duty of close cooperation between the latter and the Community institutions in order to facilitate the achievement of the Community tasks and to ensure the coherence and consistency of the action and its international representation [. . .].[39]

As one of the expressions of sincere cooperation, the CJEU admonished that the Member State governments should have coordinated better with the Commission. From that case it is evident that positive duties as part of sincere cooperation include an active information policy and regular consultations.[40]

The CJEU accords an independent status to the positive duty to provide information as an expression of Union loyalty in the external action of the Member States,[41] at least as long as this is not covered by specific requirements on information exchange in the Treaties.[42] This has to be distinguished from the question whether sharing information in a more timely and extensive fashion by Member States could justify certain, otherwise "disloyal" acts on the international scene. In the above case on inland waterway transport, while the Court noted information and consultation duties, the finding of unlawful conduct was based on the signature and ratification by the Member States of the agreements with third countries.[43] It remains doubtful that the Member States' infringement could have been remedied by them having more intensively consulted with the Commission in any way.

3.2 Member States Acting in the Union's Interest

In addition, the duty of sincere cooperation applies in situations in which the Union cannot represent itself in an international setting. The reason for this is that many international treaties and organizations allow only States—still considered the

[39] CJEU, case C-433/03, *Commission v. Germany (Inland Waterways)*, ECLI:EU:C:2005:462, para. 66; CJEU, case C-266/03, *Commission v. Luxembourg (Inland Waterways)*, ECLI:EU:C:2005:341, para. 60.

[40] CJEU, case C-433/03, *Commission v. Germany (Inland Waterways)*, ECLI:EU:C:2005:462, paras. 68–70; see also CJEU, case C-459/03, *Commission v. Ireland (Mox Plant)*, ECLI:EU:C:2006:345, paras. 179–181.

[41] CJEU, case C-459/03, *Commission v. Ireland (Mox Plant)*, ECLI:EU:C:2006:345, paras. 173–181.

[42] See CJEU, case C-658/11, *Parliament v. Council (Mauritius Pirate Transfer Agreement)*, ECLI:EU:C:2014:2025, in which the CJEU found the Council had violated the European Parliament's right to be informed, as enshrined in Article 218(10) TFEU, which is specifically about the negotiation and conclusion of international agreements, including those which fall primarily into the CFSP. Article 4(3) TEU was not mentioned in this case.

[43] CJEU, case C-433/03, *Commission v. Germany (Inland Waterways)*, ECLI:EU:C:2005:462, para. 73.

"normal" subjects of international law[44]—to acquire full party status or membership, including the right to vote.[45]

In such cases, the principle of sincere cooperation obliges the Member States to actively help the Union to ensure that its competences can nonetheless be exercised, and its objectives can be pursued internationally. In the words of the Court, the external competences of the EU should "be exercised through the medium of the Member States acting jointly in the [then] Community's interest."[46] The Member States thus become in these cases international "trustees" of the Union interest.[47] This can lead to situations in which a Member State has to defend a position in a multilateral forum, as soon as it is to be regarded as genuine Union position. This duty applies even if the agreement setting up that forum has not been concluded by the Union and even if the government of the Member State in question disagrees with the position and voted against its adoption within the Council.[48]

3.3 Sincere Cooperation in "Mixed" Agreements

Of particular importance with regard to sincere cooperation are so-called mixed agreements. Due to competences being shared between Union and Member States, which is also expressed externally by the parallel presence of Union and Member States on the international scene, the requirements of a "unity of international representation" and "close cooperation" between them become all the more relevant.[49] From this consideration, the Court later derived also an obligation of the Member States towards the Union to fully implement mixed agreements, including in areas not covered by EU competence.[50]

In more recent case law, the CJEU has noted, furthermore, that the adoption of so-called "hybrid decisions" to conclude an international agreement, i.e. decisions "by both the Council and the Representatives of the Governments of the Member

[44]Epping (2014), p. 49.

[45]See Wouters et al. (2016); Hoffmeister and Kuijper (2006); Govaere et al. (2004).

[46]CJEU, opinion 2/91, *ILO*, ECLI:EU:C:1993:106, para. 5; see also CJEU, case C-45/07, *Commission v Greece (IMO)*, ECLI:EU:C:2009:81, para. 31.

[47]Cremona (2011).

[48]CJEU, case C-399/12, *Germany v. Council (OIV)*, ECLI:EU:C:2014:2258. This case concerned the applicability of Article 218(9) TFEU to the establishment of a common EU position within the International Organisation of Vine and Wine (OIV). The CJEU confirmed the applicability of this provision, but did not make reference to Article 4(3) TEU. See further Govaere (2014).

[49]CJEU, opinion 1/94, *WTO*, ECLI:EU:C:1994:384, para. 108.

[50]CJEU, case C-13/00, *Commission v. Ireland (Berne Convention)*, ECLI:EU:C:2002:184; CJEU, case C-239/03, *Commission v. France (Étang de Berre)*, ECLI:EU:C:2004:598.

States meeting within the Council",[51] violates inter-institutional loyalty duties, even if the mixed nature of the agreement is not in dispute.[52]

3.4 Sincere Cooperation as a "Duty to Remain Silent" in International Bodies

Moreover, the duty of sincere cooperation may oblige Member States to refrain from certain autonomous actions within international bodies or fora, both in areas of exclusive and shared Union competence.

With regard to the former, a Member State is barred from autonomously submitting proposals to bodies of international organizations when their substance falls within the exclusive competence of the Union. The "ERTA doctrine"[53] hence applies also to these situations because a proposal unilaterally introduced by Member States can, in the eyes of the CJEU, set in motion "a procedure which could lead to the adoption" of new rules on the international plane with legal ramification for the Union.[54] Sincere cooperation in external action therefore starts for the Member States not only with unambiguous international legal acts, but much earlier, i.e. at the stage of discussing and preparing new rules within international fora.

The CJEU also notes that Member States must refrain from the above mentioned actions, even if they have previously tried in vain to put their concerns on the agenda within the EU institutions, and even if this was thwarted by possibly disloyal behaviour on the part of the European Commission. Although the Commission, when chairing the relevant committees, "may not prevent such an exchange of views on the sole ground that a proposal is of a national nature",[55] nonetheless any breach by the Commission of its loyalty obligations "cannot entitle a Member State to take initiatives likely to affect Community rules promulgated for the attainment of the objectives of the Treaty".[56] As it is unclear how this potentially disloyal Commission action could be addressed by the Member State, a certain asymmetry becomes apparent in the scope and the enforceability of the duty of sincere cooperation between Union institutions and Member States in the area of external relations.[57] In any event, it is reasonable to conclude that such a

---

[51]CJEU, case C-28/12, *Commission v. Council (U.S. Air Transport Agreement)*, ECLI: EU: C:2015:282, para. 6.

[52]CJEU, case C-28/12, *Commission v. Council (U.S. Air Transport Agreement)*, ECLI:EU: C:2015:282, para. 53, where the CJEU found a violation of Article 13(2) TEU.

[53]The doctrine originated in CJEU, case 22/70, *Commission v Council (ERTA)*, ECLI:EU: C:1971:32.

[54]CJEU, case C-45/07, *Commission v Greece (IMO)*, ECLI:EU:C:2009:81, para. 21.

[55]CJEU, case C-45/07, *Commission v Greece (IMO)*, ECLI:EU:C:2009:81, para. 25.

[56]CJEU, case C-45/07, *Commission v Greece (IMO)*, ECLI:EU:C:2009:81, para. 26.

[57]See Cremona (2009), p. 765 et seq.

breach of the duty by virtue of an external act could not be justified through (even) better communication or consultation with the Union institutions.

Such extensive loyalty obligations of the Member States at the international level do not only apply in areas of exclusive EU competence, but also where Union and Member States share competence in cases where a concerted, internally developed Union position is discernible. Hence, if a Member State departs from such positions in areas of shared competences, this amounts to a violation of its duty of sincere cooperation as well. The CJEU has emphasized that the "duty of genuine cooperation is of general application and does not depend either on whether the Community competence concerned is exclusive or on any right of the Member States to enter into obligations towards non-member countries".[58] Furthermore, a "point of departure for concerted Community action" can be assumed to exist as soon as the Commission has made a proposal to the Council, even if it has not been accepted (yet),[59] and regardless of the form it takes "provided that the content of that position can be established to the requisite legal standard".[60]

Hence, if a Member State submits certain proposals in international fora, which deviate from the Union's position and which can start processes that may lead to producing binding legal effects for the EU, a situation arises that is "likely to compromise the principle of unity in the international representation of the Union and its Member States and weaken their negotiating power with regard to" third parties.[61] Even when the adoption of certain decisions is postponed within the Union's institutions, the Court does not consider this a "decision-making vacuum", but still as a legitimate part a common strategy.[62]

The existence of shared competence does not diminish the negative obligation prohibiting Member States from undermining in any way such a "strategy" by acting internationally. Moreover, the Member States do not get back the freedom to become active internationally after a certain waiting period—even if such activities fall within their own competence. Advocate General *Poiares Maduro* had noted that the disloyally acting Member State should continue to try to participate in the Union's internal decision-making process "even if, politically, it felt that its efforts to achieve a common proposal [...] were as doomed as lemmings heading towards the edge of a cliff."[63] Also then, the Member States remain trustees of the Union interest.

In addition, further manifestations of disloyal external action become apparent from the CJEU's case law. Firstly, the Member States are prohibited from availing

---

[58]CJEU, case C-246/07, *Commission v. Sweden (PFOS)*, ECLI:EU:C:2010:203, para. 71; see also De Baere (2011).

[59]CJEU, case C-246/07, *Commission v. Sweden (PFOS)*, ECLI:EU:C:2010:203, para. 74.

[60]CJEU, case C-246/07, *Commission v. Sweden (PFOS)*, ECLI:EU:C:2010:203, para. 77.

[61]CJEU, case C-246/07, *Commission v. Sweden (PFOS)*, ECLI:EU:C:2010:203, para. 104.

[62]CJEU, case C-246/07, *Commission v. Sweden (PFOS)*, ECLI:EU:C:2010:203, para. 87.

[63]Opinion of AG Poiares Maduro to CJEU, case C-246/07, *Commission v. Sweden (PFOS)*, ECLI:EU:C:2009:589, para. 58.

themselves of international dispute settlement mechanisms, insofar as this endangers the exclusive jurisdiction of the CJEU.[64] When it comes to matters of EU law, the Member States can speak up at the Court of Justice in Luxembourg, but not at other venues.

In sum, two main points stand out from the CJEU's case law on the external action of the Union and the Member States. On the one hand, the Court has repeatedly stressed the importance of the duty of sincere cooperation in this context. Precisely because of the polyphony, complexity, and—from the perspective of traditional international law—peculiarity of the Union as an international actor, special efforts to maintain unity and ensure close cooperation are required. On the other hand, and without prejudice to the emphasis which the Treaties and the CJEU put on the general applicability of Union loyalty, the duty manifests itself as a justiciable principle—as far as it does not concern the CFSP or the core of national or constitutional identity—mainly as a "duty to remain silent"[65] incumbent upon the Member States on the international stage. The rationale of this manifestation of sincere cooperation is preventing Union strategies and positions from being undermined by autonomous national action taken outside of the EU framework.

4 Sincere Cooperation in the Common Commercial Policy

As regards the CCP in particular, sincere cooperation is certainly a legally significant duty also in this policy area. However, it is likely—though this may sound paradoxical—that precisely because of the expanded scope of the CCP after the Lisbon reform as an exclusive EU competence, sincere cooperation will lose some of its relevance as a legal principle.

4.1 The Widened Scope and Exclusive Nature of the Common Commercial Policy

The competences of the EU in the CCP have been expanded by the Lisbon Treaty, which now include also trade in services, trade-related aspects of intellectual property, and foreign direct investment as integral components.[66] Moreover, the

[64]Here, Article 344 TFEU (formerly Article 292 of the Treaty Establishing the European Community (TEC)) has to be "understood as a specific expression of Member States' more general duty of loyalty", CJEU, case C-459/03, *Commission v. Ireland (Mox Plant)*, ECLI:EU:C:2006:345, para. 169; see also CJEU, opinion 2/13, *ECHR*, ECLI:EU:C:2014:2454, para. 202.

[65]Delgado Casteleiro and Larik (2011).

[66]Article 207(1) TFEU. However, for these three areas special procedures apply, which deviate from qualified majority voting, according to Article 207(4) subpara. 2 TFEU.

Lisbon reform enshrined more clearly and extensively than before the pursuit of both trade-related and other objectives in the area of global governance through the CCP in the primary law.[67] In the TFEU, specific trade objectives are still present in the form of the call to "contribute, in the common interest, to the harmonious development of world trade, the progressive abolition of restrictions on international trade and on foreign direct investment, and the lowering of customs and other barriers."[68] In addition, trade policy objectives have been included in the catalogue of general objectives of EU external action, in the form of a commitment to "free and fair trade"[69] and the pledge to "encourage the integration of all countries into the world economy, including through the progressive abolition of restrictions on international trade".[70]

At the same time, a reference is made in the section on the CCP in the TFEU to the general canon of external relations objectives. Accordingly, the CCP "shall be conducted in the context of the principles and objectives of the Union's external action".[71] All objectives of the Union, also in the relationship between internal and external policies, are to be pursued in a coherent manner.[72] The codification in the primary law of the EU's geopolitical ambitions and the integration of the objectives of the CCP therein needs to be taken into account with regard to the interpretation and application of the duty of sincere cooperation. As shown above, it imposes on the Member States the obligation, which can be adjudged by the CJEU, to refrain from actions "which could jeopardise the attainment of the Union's objectives."[73]

Furthermore, the duty of sincere cooperation assumes an especially important position within the CCP since both the WTO agreements as well as the new generation of deep and comprehensive trade agreements following the "Global Europe" strategy[74] are mixed agreements.[75] Already in opinion 1/94, which concerned the extent of the competences of the former Community regarding the

[67] See Larik (2015a), p. 52 et seq.

[68] Article 206 TFEU.

[69] Article 3(5) TEU.

[70] Article 21(2) lit. e TEU.

[71] Article 207(1) TFEU; see Vedder (2013) and Dimopoulos (2010).

[72] Article 21(3) subpara. 2 TEU; as well as Article 13(1) TEU; see extensively on this issue Engbrink (2014); and also Larik (2016), p. 175 et seq.

[73] Article 4(3) subpara. 2 TEU.

[74] See European Commission, Global Europe: Competing in the World: A Contribution to the EU's Growth and Jobs Strategy, COM (2006) 567 final, Brussels, 4 October 2006, pp. 10–12 on trade agreements.

[75] See, for example, the Free trade Agreement between the European Union and its Member States, of the one part, and the Republic of Korea, of the other part, OJ 2011 L 127/6; the "mixed" Economic Partnerships Agreements with African, Caribbean and Pacific states, such as the Economic Partnership Agreement between the CARIFORUM States, of the one part, and the European Community and its Member States, of the other part, OJ 2008 L 289/3; and the Association Agreement between the European Union and the European Atomic Energy Community and their Member States, of the one part, and Georgia, of the other part, OJ 2014 L 261/4, especially Article 22 et seq. on the establishment of a free trade area.

conclusion of the WTO agreements, the CJEU stressed "the requirement of unity in the international representation" and the need for "close cooperation between the Member States and the Community institutions, both in the process of negotiation and conclusion and in the fulfilment of the commitments entered into"[76] in mixed agreements. Furthermore, the Court emphasized that specifically in the context of the WTO the "duty to cooperate is all the more imperative in the case of agreements such as those annexed to the Agreement establishing the World Trade Organization, which are inextricably interlinked, and in respect of which a dispute settlement system is established involving cross-retaliation measures."[77]

These findings certainly remain true today. However, with regard to the relevance of the duty of sincere cooperation as a legal principle in litigation and in the development of the law by the CJEU, some qualifications need to be borne in mind.

Traditionally, the CCP was not a shared but an exclusive competence of the former Community, which was interpreted to be broad in scope by the CJEU.[78] During a period that from today's perspective we need to understand as an interlude, starting with the creation of the WTO and the Treaty of Maastricht, the CCP became an intricately organized, shared competence.[79] During this period, the EU institutions repeatedly questioned the boundaries and nature of competences within the CCP in cases before the CJEU.[80] In a setting which is characterized by such complexity and fluidity, practicing sincere cooperation between the Union and Member States undoubtedly became all the more imperative.

However, with the entry into force of the Lisbon Treaty and seeing the recent CJEU case law, this interlude is coming to an end as today the CCP clearly falls within the exclusive competence of the EU as a whole again. In a catalogue of competences laid down in the TFEU, the CCP is explicitly listed as an exclusive Union competence.[81] This entails that "only the Union may legislate and adopt legally binding acts, the Member States being able to do so themselves only if so empowered by the Union or for the implementation of Union acts."[82]

The exclusive nature of the CCP was confirmed by the CJEU also concerning its scope as defined after the Lisbon reform, especially as regards former "grey areas" such as trade-related aspects of intellectual property rights and trade in services in

[76]CJEU, opinion 1/94, *WTO*, ECLI:EU:C:1994:384, para. 19.

[77]CJEU, opinion 1/94, *WTO*, ECLI:EU:C:1994:384, para. 19.

[78]CJEU, opinion 1/75, *Local Cost Standard*, ECLI:EU:C:1975:145; and CJEU, case 45/86, *Commission v. Council (Generalized Tariff Preferences)*, ECLI:EU:C:1987:163; see further Koutrakos (2015), pp. 17–74.

[79]Article 133 TEC; see also Herrmann (2002).

[80]CJEU, case C-53/96, *Hermès International*, ECLI:EU:C:1998:292; CJEU, joined cases C-300/98 and C-392/98, *Dior*, ECLI:EU:C:2000:688; CJEU, case C-431/05, *Merck Genéricos*, ECLI:EU:C:2007:496; CJEU, opinion 1/08, *GATS*, ECLI:EU:C:2009:739; see further Hoffmeister (2013), pp. 386–391.

[81]Article 3(1) lit. e TFEU.

[82]Article 2(1) TFEU.

the new generation of trade agreements with highly developed regulatory aspects.[83] In the CJEU's judgment in *Daiichi Sankyo*, it ruled that the CCP, as amended by the Lisbon Treaty, and in contrast to the pre-Lisbon case law, extends over the entire area substantively covered by the WTO's Agreement on Trade-Related Aspects of Intellectual Property Rights (TRIPS).[84] Furthermore, in the context of trade in services, the Court found in its judgment on the conclusion of the European Convention on the legal protection of services based on, or consisting of, conditional access that the proper legal basis for this is the CCP as defined in Article 207 TFEU,[85] and that therefore the Convention cannot become a mixed agreement. The underlying logic for this finding was concisely explained by Advocate General *Kokott* in her opinion:

> Article 207 TFEU can serve *a fortiori* as the legal basis for measures which do not lead to harmonisation of legislative provisions of the Member States within the Union (internal harmonisation) but, as in this case, contribute, in respect of external relations, to the approximation of the legislative provisions in the Union and in third countries (external harmonisation). The object of many modern trade agreements is precisely this kind of harmonisation: those agreements provide for the creation of uniform legal standards – if appropriate in the form of minimum standards – for certain products, activities or sectors with a view to facilitating cross-border trade.[86]

Hence, the Court has taken up again its approach to the CCP from before opinion 1/94 in terms of the congruence of the scope of WTO obligations and the extent of EU competence in the CCP,[87] but within a significantly enhanced framework, adapted to the realities of twenty-first century international trade policy.

4.2 *The Diminished Relevance of the Duty of Sincere Cooperation*

The preceding observations have an important consequence for the duty of sincere cooperation as a legal principle in the CCP. Infringing upon the EU's exclusive competence by a Member State represents in itself a violation of the Treaties, which

[83] See Ankersmit (2014). Also in the area of foreign direct investment, interesting legal development can be expected, though rather as part of a long-term process, see Dimopoulos (2012). After opinion 2/15, however, it is clear that non-direct investments and investor-state dispute settlement remain firmly within the domain of shared competences, CJEU, opinion 2/15, EU-Singapore FTA, ECLI:EU:C:2017:376.

[84] CJEU, case C-414/11, *Daiichi Sankyo and Sanofi-Aventis Deutschland*, ECLI:EU:C:2013:520.

[85] CJEU, case C-137/12, *Commission v. Council (Conditional Access Convention)*, ECLI:EU:C:2013:675.

[86] Opinion of Advocate General Kokott to CJEU, case C-137/12, *Commission v. Council (Conditional Access Convention)*, ECLI:EU:C:2013:441, para. 67.

[87] See Hahn and Danieli (2013), p. 49 et seq.

does not require an additional finding on disloyal behaviour.[88] It is still possible that the CJEU may address and admonish, *in addition*, violations of the duty of sincere cooperation by the Member States, such as providing information in an inadequate and untimely fashion to the Union institutions.[89] However, it is highly unlikely, in view of the case law to date, that the CJEU would find a violation in the area of the CCP *solely* on the basis on the duty of sincere cooperation according to Article 4(3) TEU.[90] It would in fact be a masterly feat in illegal behaviour if a Member State succeeded, given the current state of the primary law and CJEU case law, to manage to violate its duty of sincere cooperation within the CCP while, at the same time, fully respecting both the exclusive competence of the EU in this area and other specific EU law obligations.

Moreover, what distinguishes the CCP from the settings in opinion 2/91 and the *IMO* and *OIV* cases, is that the EU is represented prominently both within the WTO and at the negotiating table for trade agreements by the Commission. Hence, in both these cases the objectives and interests of the Union can be pursued without the assistance of Member States acting as "trustees". The EU is a founding member and fully-fledged party of the WTO.[91] It can look back on decades of active practice in the General Agreement on Tariffs and Trade (GATT) prior to the establishment of the WTO.[92]

Not least in WTO dispute settlement procedures, including when it comes to the use of retaliatory measures, regarding which the CJEU had emphasized the importance of loyal cooperation in opinion 1/94, one can observe that in practice it is

[88]By way of analogy, see CJEU, case C-114/12, *Commission v. Council (Convention on the Rights of Broadcasting Organizations)*, ECLI:EU:C:2014:2151, para. 103, where the CJEU found that the adoption of a "hybrid act" (para. 34) by the Council and the Member States to conclude the international agreement in question violated the exclusive competence of the Union according to Article 3(2) TFEU, resulting in the annulment of the decision. Following this finding, the Court refrained from going into the other pleas brought forward by the Commission, one of which claimed a violation of inter-institutional cooperation duties based on Article 13(2) TEU (para. 104). See also CJEU, case C-459/03, *Commission v. Ireland (Mox Plant)*, ECLI:EU:C:2006:345, para. 171, where the CJEU refrained from ruling on an alleged "failure to comply with the general obligations contained in Article 10 EC [now Article 4(3) TEU] that is distinct from the failure, already established, to comply with the more specific Community obligations devolving on Ireland pursuant to Article 292 EC [now Article 344 TFEU]" on the exclusive jurisdiction of the CJEU.

[89]It should be noted here that also in CJEU, case C-45/07, *Commission v Greece (IMO)*, ECLI:EU:C:2009:81, para. 26, the CJEU did not only find a violation of the duty of loyal cooperation by the Member States in question, but a "breach of that State's obligations, which, in a case such as the present, arise under Articles 10 EC, 71 EC and 80(2) [TEC]", which were "likely to affect Community rules promulgated for the attainment of the objectives of the Treaty".

[90]This occurred, by contrast, in the context of shared competences, see CJEU, case C-246/07, *Commission v. Sweden (PFOS)*, ECLI:EU:C:2010:203, where the CJEU found a violation the duty of loyal cooperation in Article 10 TEC (now Article 4(3) TEU), but did not detect any other breach of EU law obligations.

[91]Article XI:1 Agreement Establishing the World Trade Organization.

[92]CJEU, joined cases 21 to 24/72, *International Fruit*, ECLI:EU:C:1972:115, para. 18.

always the EU, represented by the Commission, which launches complaints and never the Member States. Moreover, the Commission takes on the defence whenever a third country starts a complaint against an EU Member State, even when it comes to issues that could not be clearly classified as belonging within the realm of exclusive Union competences at the time.[93] One can therefore assume that the Member States have by now been "socialized" or "Europeanized"[94] to such an extent that loyal (and therefore rather restrained) behaviour in the WTO has already become a common practice that requires little to no judicial intervention with reference to Article 4(3) TEU anymore.

Firstly, treaty reform and recent case law, and, secondly, decades of practice, hence point in the same direction with regard to the future relevance of the duty of sincere cooperation in the CCP: The less "mixed" the distribution of powers between Union and Member States in the WTO or in the negotiation of trade agreements, and the stronger the Union's external representation through the Commission, the less need there is legally and practically to make use of sincere cooperation as a justiciable legal obligation.

5 Outlook: The EU's Global Strategy, "Brexit", the WTO, and New Free Trade Agreements

Looking to the future, several relevant developments arise regarding the direction of the CCP and the relevance of sincere cooperation as a legal principle: firstly, the EU's new core foreign policy document, the Global Strategy on Foreign and Security Policy and its implementation; secondly, the UK's referendum on EU membership and the prospects of a "hard Brexit"; thirdly, the future representation of the Member States in the WTO; and fourthly, the current wave of new trade agreements that the EU is negotiating with third parties.

5.1 The Common Commercial Policy and the Global Strategy for Foreign and Security Policy

Since June 2016, the EU has a new, overarching policy document for its external action. The Global Strategy for Foreign and Security Policy, entitled "Shared

[93]See as examples for situations in which, despite a complaint launched against a Member State alone, it was the Union that acted as the party to the mutually agreed solution: Notification of Mutually Agreed Solution, *Belgium–Administration of Measures Establishing Customs Duties for Rice*, WT/DS210/6, 2 January 2002; and Notification of Mutually Agreed Solution, *Ireland–Measures Affecting the Grant of Copyright*, WT/DS82/3 and *European Communities–Measures Affecting the Grant of Copyright and Neighbouring Rights*, WT/DS115/3, 13 September 2002. See in detail Delgado Casteleiro and Larik (2013).

[94]See on this concept from political science in the context of EU external relations, Wong (2011).

Vision, Common Action: A Stronger Europe",[95] was presented to the European Council by High Representative *Federica Mogherini*.[96] The European Council noted in its subsequent Conclusions that it "welcomes the presentation of the Global Strategy for the European Union's Foreign and Security Policy by the High Representative and invites the High Representative, the Commission and the Council to take the work forward."[97] Unlike the 2003 European Security Strategy, or the Global Europe trade strategy for that matter, the Global Strategy is not policy-specific, but covers all areas of EU external relations, including trade. Consequently, even though not a legally binding act, the document is relevant for the embedding of the CCP within the overall direction of EU foreign policy and for the relationship between the Union and the Member States on the international stage.

In terms of substance, the Global Strategy stresses the concepts of "resilience" and a "joined-up approach" in terms of both policies and actors. Concerning the CCP, the Strategy refers to trade policy under the heading "Resilience in our Surrounding Regions":

> Echoing the Sustainable Development Goals, the EU will adopt a joined-up approach to its humanitarian, development, migration, trade, investment, infrastructure, education, health and research policies, as well as improve horizontal coherence between the EU and its Member States.[98]

The linkages between trade and other areas of external action are also highlighted elsewhere. For instance, the Strategy stresses that "trade and development – working in synergy – can underpin long-term peacebuilding".[99]

Trade agreements are mentioned in this context as instruments for a wider foreign policy agenda "to underpin sustainable development, human rights protection and rules-based governance."[100] This same idea is also expressed when the Strategy turns to "Cooperative Regional Orders". It mentions the series of Economic Partnership Agreements (EPAs) as a means to "spur African integration and mobility, and encourage Africa's full and equitable participation in global value chains".[101] Moreover, it portrays the Transatlantic Trade and Investment Partnership (TTIP) with the United States and the Comprehensive Economic and Trade

[95]Shared Vision, Common Action: A Stronger Europe, A Global Strategy for the European Union's Foreign and Security Policy, June 2016.

[96]For the background and process leading to the Global Strategy, see Tocci (2016).

[97]European Council, Conclusions, EUCO 26/16, Brussels, 28 June 2016, para. 20.

[98]Shared Vision, Common Action: A Stronger Europe, A Global Strategy for the European Union's Foreign and Security Policy, June 2016, p. 26.

[99]Shared Vision, Common Action: A Stronger Europe, A Global Strategy for the European Union's Foreign and Security Policy, June 2016, p. 31. See also p. 36, where it is noted that the EU "will build stronger links between our trade, development and security policies in Africa".

[100]Shared Vision, Common Action: A Stronger Europe, A Global Strategy for the European Union's Foreign and Security Policy, June 2016, pp. 26–27.

[101]Shared Vision, Common Action: A Stronger Europe, A Global Strategy for the European Union's Foreign and Security Policy, June 2016, p. 36.

Agreement (CETA) with Canada as means to strengthen "the transatlantic commitment to shared values and signals our willingness to pursue an ambitious rules-based trade agenda."[102] Lastly, trade features prominently in the section on "Global Governance in the 21st Century". There, the Strategy notes that "[a]mbitious agreements built on mutual benefits [...] can promote international regulatory standards, consumer protection, as well as labour, environmental, health and safety norms," serving "as building blocks of global free trade".[103]

Bringing this back to the law, and sincere cooperation as a legal principle in particular, the Global Strategy can be understood as an important step towards the translation into policy of the embedding of the CCP into EU external action in the post-Lisbon TEU. On the one hand, this speaks to the "hinge" included in Article 207 TFEU stating that the CCP "shall be conducted in the context of the principles and objectives of the Union's external action".[104] This entails a positive obligation on both the EU institutions and the Member States to pursue their foreign policies based on the objectives in the Treaties and as fleshed out further in the Global Strategy. On the other hand, as a policy document, the Strategy is of course not capable of changing in any way the division of competences between EU and Member States. The Strategy itself stresses that the EU's "diplomatic action must be fully grounded in the Lisbon Treaty".[105] Hence, when the Global Strategy states that "EU foreign policy is not a solo performance: it is an orchestra which plays from the same score",[106] this applies in the first place to areas which do not fall within the Union's exclusive competence. Given the extended scope of EU trade policy as an exclusive competence outlined above, the CCP is in fact very much a "solo performance" of the EU on the international stage, with the Member States not disappearing altogether, but rather acting as "backing vocals".

What the Global Strategy serves as a reminder of, in sum, is the need for sincere cooperation and coherence between different policies, which is especially relevant in areas of shared competence or when the EU and the Member States endeavor to implement a holistic approach vis-à-vis strategic partners. Such approaches will in most cases have a trade dimension, but also others, including security, development, human rights, and environmental aspects. Judicially, the duty of sincere cooperation will play continue to play a role in these cases—not least since it is of general application across all Union policies. However, the more trade-focused

[102]Shared Vision, Common Action: A Stronger Europe, A Global Strategy for the European Union's Foreign and Security Policy, June 2016, p. 37. See also p. 38, where the Strategy notes the ambition to work "towards ambitious free trade agreements with strategic partners such as Japan and India, as well as ASEAN member states".

[103]Shared Vision, Common Action: A Stronger Europe, A Global Strategy for the European Union's Foreign and Security Policy, June 2016, p. 41.

[104]Article 207(1) TFEU.

[105]Shared Vision, Common Action: A Stronger Europe, A Global Strategy for the European Union's Foreign and Security Policy, June 2016, p. 46.

[106]Shared Vision, Common Action: A Stronger Europe, A Global Strategy for the European Union's Foreign and Security Policy, June 2016, p. 46.

and "less mixed" a particular approach or agreement, the less need there will be to rely on loyalty due to the EU's exclusive competence.

5.2 "Brexit" and Sincere Cooperation of the EU27

As the Global Strategy acknowledges, the EU finds itself in a time of "existential crisis".[107] This is in the first place a reference to the referendum on EU membership in the UK, which was held on 23 June 2016—only a few days before the Global Strategy was launched—and resulted in a majority for leaving the European Union. In the turmoil that followed and is still ongoing, it is hard to say when and how the UK will leave. However, with the new British government being ostensibly committed to go through with the withdrawal,[108] "Brexit" seems increasingly a question of "when" rather than "if". This will lead to a myriad of legal intricacies, which will certainly not fail to garner scholarly attention. As far as the Common Commercial Policy and the duty of sincere cooperation are concerned, a number of legal observations can be made already now. These concern, on the one hand, the United Kingdom, and, on the other, the remaining 27 EU Member States, now referred to as the "EU27".[109] Overall, these confirm the findings above that the duty of sincere cooperation remains relevant, but is to a large extent overshadowed by the presence of a broadly defined exclusive Union competence in the area of trade.

As far as the UK is concerned, it did not cease to be a member when it triggered Article 50 TEU on 29 March 2017,[110] but will remain a member at least until "the date of entry into force of the withdrawal agreement or, failing that, two years" after triggering Article 50 TEU.[111] Time to negotiate the exit deal could even be

[107] Shared Vision, Common Action: A Stronger Europe, A Global Strategy for the European Union's Foreign and Security Policy, June 2016, p. 13.

[108] Prime Minister Theresa May seemed to even suggest a "hard Brexit", stating in her speech to the Conservative Party conference in October 2015: "I want it to give British companies the maximum freedom to trade with and operate within the Single Market – and let European businesses do the same here. But let's state one thing loud and clear: we are not leaving the European Union only to give up control of immigration all over again. And we are not leaving only to return to the jurisdiction of the European Court of Justice. That's not going to happen." As reproduced in: Theresa May's keynote speech at Tory conference in full, The Independent, 5 October 2016. See also Prime Minister's Office, The government's negotiating objectives for exiting the EU: PM speech, London, 17 January 2017, https://www.gov.uk/government/speeches/the-governments-negotiating-objectives-for-exiting-the-eu-pm-speech (last accessed 1 March 2017).

[109] See, e.g., Zalan, EU 27 meet for 'moment of truth', EUobserver, 16 September 2016, https://euobserver.com/political/135123 (last accessed 1 March 2017).

[110] More precisely Article 50(2) TEU.

[111] Article 50(3) TEU.

extended if all parties agree.[112] During that period, the UK remains bound by EU law, including the duty to respect the exclusive competence of the EU in trade policy as well as the duty of sincere cooperation in general. Under areas of exclusive competence, Member States can only act "if so empowered by the Union or for the implementation of Union acts."[113] For instance, authorizing the UK to start trade negotiations with third countries would be a possibility, especially for the period after triggering Article 50 TEU, but depends entirely on the goodwill of the EU institutions and the remaining Member States.

Apart from that, the obligations of still being an EU member stand in clear tension with any plans to start negotiations on trade agreements with third countries during this period. The latter would be a (basic) textbook example of a violation of the EU's exclusive competence under Article 3(2) TFEU. Thus far, the UK government brands its talks with non-EU partners on trade agreements as "preliminary discussions"[114] rather than negotiations—also arguably because there is little in terms of substance to negotiate about as long as the future relationship with the EU and its internal market is not clarified. However, looking at the existing body of CJEU case law, even such exploratory talks could be regarded as infringing upon the exercise of the EU's competence in combination with a violation of the duty of sincere cooperation incumbent on the UK vis-à-vis the EU institutions and the EU27.

As the CJEU pointed out in the *PFOS* judgment, which even concerned shared competences, if a Member State acts internationally in such a way that is "likely to compromise the principle of unity in the international representation of the Union and its Member States and weaken their negotiating power",[115] a violation of the duty of sincere cooperation can be detected. As the Court found in the earlier *Inland Waterways* cases, the Member States are barred from negotiating with third countries on matters which are covered already in ongoing negotiations by the EU.[116] This would be the situation as soon as "preliminary discussions" by the UK with countries such as the United States, Canada and others with which the EU is in the process of negotiating or concluding FTAs reach a minimum threshold of specificity and could be detrimental to the EU's own position in these negotiations. It would be up for the CJEU to determine this threshold, though the Commission might opt to refrain from bringing infringement proceedings against the UK for political reasons. Depending on how "hard" "Brexit" and the negotiations leading up to it

[112] Article 50(3) TEU. However, the period after triggering Article 50 TEU and before leaving would be legally even more "complex", Cremona, Negotiating Trade Deals Before Brexit?, Social Europe, 25 July 2016, https://www.socialeurope.eu/2016/07/negotiating-trade-deals-brexit/ (last accessed 1 March 2017).

[113] Article 2(1) TFEU.

[114] Theresa May: UK will lead world in free trade, BBC News, 7 September 2016, http://www.bbc.com/news/uk-politics-37291832 (last accessed 1 March 2017).

[115] CJEU, case C-246/07, *Commission v. Sweden (PFOS)*, ECLI:EU:C:2010:203, para. 104.

[116] CJEU, case C-433/03, *Commission v. Germany (Inland Waterways)*, ECLI:EU:C:2005:462; and CJEU, case C-266/03, *Commission v. Luxembourg (Inland Waterways)*, ECLI:EU:C:2005:341.

may become, the latter remains an option for the Commission and the remaining 27 Member States.[117]

Once "Brexit" would be complete, however, the "Treaties shall cease to apply"[118] to the UK, including its obligation to cooperate in the spirit of loyalty with the EU. Time will tell, to use the words of *Boris Johnson*, now the UK's Foreign Secretary, uttered shortly after the referendum, how Britain will fare in the world of international trade once it can "stand tall" and act "without being elbowed aside by a supranational body."[119] As a legal matter, it should be noted that also the EU institutions and the EU27 would have no obligations of loyalty against the UK anymore. Rather than "elbowing aside" the UK, the European Commission could simply sue the UK at the WTO and even impose trade sanctions, either under WTO dispute settlement or a possible future EU-UK trade agreement.

As regards the EU27 Member States, they would of course remain bound by their duty of sincere cooperation towards the EU, before, during and after "Brexit" negotiations. Internationally, they will continue to have to defend the common interest, uphold common positions and refrain from actions that could undermine the EU's negotiating position. Concerning the interaction with the departing UK, the exclusive competence of the EU in trade matters prohibits them from engaging in any separate negotiations with Britain. Hence, earlier suggestions by the UK's "Brexit" secretary *David Davis* "that Britain would negotiate individual trade deals with other EU countries"[120] are therefore manifestly at odds with the obligations of the EU27 under EU law both in terms of respecting the EU's competences and the duty of sincere cooperation. Here, it can be expected that the European Commission would not hesitate to bring infringement proceedings in the case of a Member State stepping out of line, given that this would question the cohesion of the Union as a whole. If any of the EU27 wanted to do that, they would have to first leave the EU themselves. This serves as another example of the overall argument of the article. The violation of the EU's exclusive competence would be both obvious and sufficient to declare such behaviour illegal. Sincere cooperation would only serve to confirm further what is already apparent.

[117]Article 258 and Article 259 TFEU, respectively.

[118]Article 50(3) TEU.

[119]See the transcript of his remarks in Boris Johnson: I will not be the next Tory leader, The Spectator, 30 June 2016, http://blogs.spectator.co.uk/2016/06/boris-johnson-will-not-next-tory-leader/ (last accessed 1 March 2017).

[120]Stone, Minister for Brexit David Davis appeared unaware of how EU trade deals actually work, The Independent, 14 July 2016, http://www.independent.co.uk/news/uk/politics/minister-for-brexit-davis-davis-eu-european-union-germany-single-market-trade-deals-unaware-mistake-a7136121.html (last accessed 1 March 2017).

5.3 Continued WTO Membership of the Member States

Regarding the future representation of the Member States in the WTO (possibly minus the UK), a simple truth prevails. The new division of competences, confirmed by the recent CJEU case law (see Sect. 4.1 above), does not herald the end of the membership of the Member States in the WTO.[121] This again underlines the future—albeit somewhat qualified—importance of the principle of sincere cooperation in the CCP.

The German Federal Constitutional Court noted already in its *Lisbon* judgment of 2009 that the "Treaty of Lisbon may at any rate not force the Member States to waive their [WTO] member status".[122] The Court also rejected the "idea that the Member States' own legal personality status in external relations gradually takes second place to a European Union which acts more and more clearly in analogy to a state" and stressed that the "development to date of a membership that is cooperatively mixed and is exercised in parallel" can be "a model for other international organisations and other associations of states".[123] However, the Court cautioned, "in so far as the development of the European Union in analogy to a state were to be continued on the basis of the Treaty of Lisbon, which is open to development in this context, this would come into conflict with constitutional foundations."[124]

Hence, also eight years after the entry into force of the Lisbon Treaty, including its explicit provision in the primary law on protecting the national identity of the Member States in Article 4(2) TEU, one has to conclude that sincere cooperation and the pursuit of common goals in the area of foreign policy and global governance cannot serve to deny the international legal personality and international actorness of the Member States. Union loyalty, including in the area of the CCP, is not to be understood as equating sole representation of the EU and all the Member States on the international stage. The substantive scope of the WTO, which is not set in stone despite the deadlocked Doha Round, remains from the legal point of view of the EU "mixed"—but "less mixed" due to the Lisbon reforms and in view of the recent case law confirming a much larger proportion now clearly falling within the exclusive competence of the Union. For Member States, this means that they will have to exercise their—at times rather nominal than substantial—international legal personality with even more self-restraint. It remains a matter of politics whether the parallel representation of Union and Member States at the WTO will continue to be seen as desirable against this background. Legally, the continued existence of the 28 (or 27 in the future) mostly taciturn Member State delegations at the WTO is not

[121]See also already Tietje (2006), p. 171 et seq.

[122]Judgment of the German Federal Constitutional Court (Second Senate) of 30 June 2009, 2 BvE 2/08, para. 375.

[123]Judgment of the German Federal Constitutional Court (Second Senate) of 30 June 2009, 2 BvE 2/08, para. 376.

[124]Judgment of the German Federal Constitutional Court (Second Senate) of 30 June 2009, 2 BvE 2/08, para. 376.

to be seen as an act of disloyalty in itself—rather perhaps as a matter of expense for the European taxpayer.

5.4 *Mixity and Cooperation in the New Free Trade Agreements*

A similar picture as with WTO membership emerges with regard to the new generation of deep and comprehensive free trade agreements. For instance, the "mixed" nature of CETA and TTIP remains disputed. More legal clarity was provided by the CJEU's opinion on the EU-Singapore FTA,[125] but this does not rule out that agreements might still be concluded as "mixed" for political reasons only,[126] even if the content is adapted to be exclusive from a legal point of view. Given the fact that there are still grey areas and that by inserting provisions on political dialogue agreements can be intentionally made "mixed",[127] it is unlikely that the Member States will abandon the practice of "mixed" trade agreements, including through insisting on it through litigation at the CJEU.

What is certain is that Article 4(3) TEU and other specific manifestations of sincere cooperation in the Treaties will require, as a judicially enforceable duty, from the Member States cooperative and loyal behaviour. This will apply regardless of the fact whether EU trade agreements with third countries—or other regional organizations such as ASEAN—will in the future be concluded with or without the Member States as parties. In situations where the Member States would not become parties, the agreements in their entirety will have to be regarded as part of EU law according to Article 216(2) TFEU and will have to be fully implemented by the EU and the Member States. By contrast, in situations where these agreements remain "mixed", the general duty of sincere cooperation assumes a more prominent role as it obliges the Member States to implement those parts of these agreements that fall within their own competence.[128] As regards the external actions of the Member States, ranging from the negotiation of trade agreements to acts in bodies created by

[125]CJEU, opinion 2/15, EU-Singapore FTA, ECLI:EU:C:2017:376.

[126]See European Commission, Press Release: European Commission proposes signature and conclusion of EU-Canada trade deal, IP-16-2371, Strasbourg, 5 July 2016, which includes the following quote from EU Trade Commissioner Cecilia Malmström: "Meanwhile, the open issue of competence for such trade agreements will be for the European Court of Justice to clarify, in the near future. From a strict legal standpoint, the Commission considers this agreement to fall under exclusive EU competence. However, the political situation in the Council is clear, and we understand the need for proposing it as a 'mixed' agreement, in order to allow for a speedy signature." After the delay caused by the region of Wallonia, however, the Commission may revisit the idea that mixity contributes to a more "speedy" process.

[127]Gstöhl and Hanf (2014), p. 739; Streinz (2015).

[128]CJEU, case C-13/00, *Commission v. Ireland (Berne Convention)*, ECLI:EU:C:2002:184; CJEU, case C-239/03, *Commission v. France (Étang de Berre)*, ECLI:EU:C:2004:598.

those agreements, the same applies as was mentioned above in the WTO context. In the now significantly expanded areas of exclusive Union competence, utmost restraint is required from the Member States. But even in areas of shared competence, the duty of sincere cooperation cautions the Member States against rash autonomous actions and obliges them to regularly consult and share information with the EU institutions.

Lastly, it should be noted that, on the one hand, the Union has to respect the identity, including the international legal personality, of the Member States according to Article 4(2) TEU. On the other hand, this does not amount to a requirement to facilitate and preserve "polyphony" in the external action of the Union and the Member States. If the latter decide to terminate a specific trade agreement or withdraw from an international organization, given the EU's extensive competences, expertise and ability to solely represent the common interest,[129] then the principle of sincere cooperation would require that the EU respect such a decision by the Member States concerned, rather than prompt them to maintain the "polyphony" in the EU's external representation.

6 Conclusion

The article availed itself of the opportunity to look back on more than half a decade of law and practice after the entry into force of the Lisbon Treaty as regards the CCP, in particular the relationship between the EU and its Member States. The contours of the consequences of the Lisbon reform of the primary law are now becoming more clearly visible. This also sets the stage for the conduct of the external action of the Union in the mid to long-term. The Common Commercial Policy, which has a relatively long history and is closely linked to the economic weight of the internal market, is now more than ever embedded in the overall foreign policy of the EU and its ambitions for shaping global governance. This finds its latest and most high-profile confirmation in the EU's Global Strategy for Foreign and Security Policy.

Implementing these ambitions is a constitutional mandate of the EU institutions and Member States alike, which all have to contribute and work together in the spirit of loyalty. Against this background, the preceding reflections on the importance of the duty of sincere cooperation in the CCP can be summarized in three main points. Firstly, the duty of sincere cooperation remains an important structural principle of constitutional rank for the external action of the Union, especially in the

[129]An example for such a development is the membership of the European Convention on the Legal Protection of Services based on, or consisting of, Conditional Access. Several Member States have withdrawn from this agreement after the EU became a party and following the CJEU ruling that the EU had exclusive competence in the area covered by the agreement, see CJEU, case C-137/12, *Commission v. Council (Conditional Access Convention)*, ECLI:EU:C:2013:675. See Larik (2015b), p. 795.

context of "polyphony" of the Member States and Union institutions at the international level. It also applies fully to Member States which may decide to withdraw from the Union until the moment they cease to be members. To paraphrase British Prime Minister *May*: Sincere cooperation means sincere cooperation. And the CJEU will enforce it. Secondly, the case law of the CJEU reveals the wide scope of application of the duty, also and especially in the area of shared external powers, which can at times take the form of a "duty to remain silent"[130] incumbent on the Member States in the international arena. Thirdly, in the specific context of the CCP, the duty of sincere cooperation will play a less significant role as a legal principle in the future. This shift is due, on the one hand, to the fact that the Lisbon Treaty, confirmed by the subsequent case law of the CJEU, extended the scope of the CCP significantly and confirmed its nature as an exclusive Union competence. On the other hand, its diminished legal relevance is due to the EU's strong presence at the WTO and in the negotiation of free trade agreements. This does not entail the abandonment of the missions of the Member States to the WTO or the end of mixed trade agreements in the future. Rather, this shift signifies a tangible contribution towards coherent and targeted cooperation in the day-to-day exercise of EU trade policy as part of its global outreach—in short, a contribution to more harmony in a changing soundscape in Europe and the world.

References

Ankersmit L (2014) The scope of the common commercial policy after Lisbon: the Daiichi Sankyo and conditional access services grand chamber judgments. Leg Issues Econ Integr 41 (2):193–209

Cremona M (2009) Extending the reach of the AETR principle: comment on Commission v Greece (C-45/07). Eur Law Rev 34(5):754–768

Cremona M (2011) Member States as Trustees of the union interest: participating in international agreements on behalf of the European Union. In: Arnull A, Bernard C, Dougan M, Spaventa E (eds) A constitutional order of states: essays in European Law in honour of Alan Dashwood. Hart Publishing, Oxford, pp 435–457

Dashwood A (2014) The continuing bipolarity of EU external action. In: Govaere I, Lannon E, Van Elsuwege P, Adam S (eds) The European Union in the world: essays in honour of Marc Maresceau. Martinus Nijhoff, Leiden, pp 3–16

De Baere G (2011) O, Where is Faith? O, Where is Loyalty? Some thoughts on the duty of loyal co-operation and the union's external environmental competences in the light of the PFOS case. Eur Law Rev 36(3):405–419

De Baere G, Roes T (2015) EU loyalty as good faith. Int Compar Law Q 64(4):829–874

Dederer HG (2013) The common commercial policy under the influence of commission, council, high representative and European external action service. In: Bungenberg M, Hermann C (eds) European yearbook of international economic law. Special issue: Common commercial policy after Lisbon. Springer, Heidelberg, pp 87–105

Delgado Casteleiro A, Larik J (2011) The duty to remain silent: limitless loyalty in EU external relations? Eur Law Rev 36(4):522–539

[130]Delgado Casteleiro and Larik (2011).

Delgado Casteleiro A, Larik J (2013) The "odd couple": the responsibility of the EU at the WTO. In: Evans M, Koutrakos P (eds) The international responsibility of the European Union. Hart Publishing, Oxford, pp 233–255

Dimopoulos A (2010) The effects of the Lisbon Treaty on the principles and objectives of the common commercial policy. Eur Foreign Aff Rev 15(2):153–170

Dimopoulos A (2012) The compatibility of future EU investment agreements with EU law. Leg Issues Econ Integr 39(4):447–471

Engbrink SD (2014) Die Kohärenz des auswärtigen Handelns der Europäischen Union. Mohr Siebeck, Tübingen

Epping V (2014) Völkerrechtssubjekte. In: Ipsen K (ed) Völkerrecht, 6th edn. C.H. Beck, Munich, pp 46–386

Govaere I (2014) Novel issues pertaining to EU Member States membership of other international organizations: the OIV case. In: Govaere I, Lannon E, Van Elsuwege P, Adam S (eds) The European Union in the world: essays in honour of Marc Maresceau. Martinus Nijhoff, Leiden, pp 225–243

Govaere I, Capiau J, Vermeersch A (2004) In-between seats: the participation of the European Union in international organizations. Eur Foreign Aff Rev 9(2):155–187

Gstöhl S, Hanf D (2014) The EU's post-Lisbon free trade agreements: commercial interests in a changing constitutional context. Eur Law J 20(6):733–748

Hahn M, Danieli L (2013) You'll never walk alone: the European Union and its member states in the WTO. In: Bungenberg M, Hermann C (eds) European yearbook of international economic law. Special issue: Common commercial policy after Lisbon. Springer, Heidelberg, pp 49–63

Hatje A (2001) Loyalität als Rechtsprinzip der Europäischen Union. Nomos, Baden-Baden

Heliskoski J (2001) Mixed agreements as a technique for organizing the international relations of the European Community and its member states. Kluwer, The Hague

Herrmann C (2002) Common commercial policy after nice: Sisyphus would have done a better job. Common Mark Law Rev 39(1):7–29

Hillion C (2010) Mixity and coherence in EU external relations: the significance of the "duty of cooperation". In: Hillion C, Koutrakos P (eds) Mixed agreements revisited: the EU and its member states in the world. Hart Publishing, Oxford, pp 87–115

Hillion C (2014) A powerless court? The European Court of Justice and the common foreign and security policy. In: Cremona C, Thies A (eds) The European Court of Justice and external relations law: constitutional challenges. Hart Publishing, Oxford, pp 47–70

Hoffmeister F (2013) Aktuelle Rechtsfragen in der Praxis der europäischen Außenhandelspolitik. Zeitschrift für Europarechtliche Studien 16(4):385–401

Hoffmeister F, Kuijper PJ (2006) The status of the European Union at the United Nations: institutional ambiguities and political realities. In: Wouters J, Hoffmeister F, Ruys T (eds) The United Nations and the European Union: an ever stronger partnership. T.M.C. Asser Press, The Hague, pp 9–34

Hyett I (2000) The duty of cooperation: a flexible concept. In: Dashwood A, Hillion C (eds) The general law of EC external relations. Sweet & Maxwell, London, pp 248–253

Kaiser F (2009) Gemischte Abkommen im Lichte bundesstaatlicher Erfahrungen. Mohr Siebeck, Tübingen

Klamert M (2014) The principle of loyalty in EU Law. Oxford University Press, Oxford

Koutrakos P (2015) EU international relations law, 2nd edn. Hart Publishing, Oxford

Larik J (2011) Much more than trade: the common commercial policy in a global context. In: Evans M, Koutrakos P (eds) Beyond the established legal orders: policy interconnections between the EU and the rest of the world. Hart Publishing, Oxford, pp 13–46

Larik J (2015a) Good global governance through trade: constitutional moorings. In: Wouters J, Marx A, Geraets D, Natens B (eds) Global governance through trade: EU policies and approaches. Edward Elgar, Cheltenham, pp 43–70

Larik J (2015b) No mixed feelings: the post-Lisbon common commercial policy in Daiichi Sankyo and Commission v. Council (conditional access convention). Common Mark Law Rev 52(3):779–799

Larik J (2016) Foreign policy objectives in European constitutional law. Oxford University Press, Oxford

McCormick J (2008) Understanding the European Union: a concise introduction, 4th edn. Palgrave Macmillan, Basingstoke

Meunier S, Nicolaïdis K (2011) The European Union as a trade power. In: Hill C, Smith M (eds) International relations and the European Union, 2nd edn. Oxford University Press, Oxford, pp 275–298

Millet FX (2013) L'Union européenne et l'identité constitutionnelle des États membres. L.G.D.J, Paris

Neframi E (2010) The duty of loyalty: rethinking its scope through its application in the field of EU external relations. Common Mark Law Rev 47(2):323–359

Piris JC (2010) The Lisbon Treaty: a legal and political analysis. Cambridge University Press, Cambridge

Streinz R (2015) Disputes on TTIP: does the agreement need the consent of the German Parliament? In: Herrmann C, Simma B, Streinz R (eds) European yearbook of international economic law. Special issue: Trade policy between law, diplomacy and scholarship. Springer, Heidelberg, pp 271–295

Thies A (2012) The PFOS decision of the ECJ: the member states' obligation to refrain from unilateral external action in areas of shared competence. In: Díez-Hochleitner J, Martinez Capdevila C, Blazquez Navarro I, Frutos Miranda J (eds) Recent trends in the case law of the Court of Justice of the European Union (2008–2011). La Ley, Madrid, pp 703–728

Tietje C (2006) Das Ende der parallelen Mitgliedschaft von EU und Mitgliedstaaten in der WTO? In: Herrmann C, Krenzler G, Streinz R (eds) Die Außenwirtschaftspolitik der Europäischen Union nach dem Verfassungsvertrag. Nomos, Baden-Baden, pp 161–173

Tocci N (2016) The making of the EU global strategy. Contemp Secur Policy 37(3):461–472

Vedder C (2013) Linkage of the common commercial policy to the general objectives for the union's external action. In: Bungenberg M, Hermann C (eds) European yearbook of international economic law. Special issue: Common commercial policy after Lisbon. Springer, Heidelberg, pp 115–144

Wong R (2011) The Europeanization of foreign policy. In: Hill C, Smith M (eds) International relations and the European Union, 2nd edn. Oxford University Press, Oxford, pp 149–171

Wouters J, Odermatt J, Ramopoulos T (2016) The EU in the world of international organizations: diplomatic aspirations, legal hurdles and political realities. In: Smith M, Keukeleire S, Vanhoonacker S (eds) The diplomatic system of the European Union: evolution, change and challenges. Routledge, London, pp 94–111

Article 21 TEU and the EU's Common Commercial Policy: A Test of Coherence

Alessandra Asteriti

Abstract This contribution investigates the role of Article 21 TEU in the context of the EU's common commercial policy (CCP), with specific reference to its new investment competence. Article 21, introducing non-commercial objectives in the CCP, has been both hailed for rebalancing and expanding the EU's foreign policy and criticised for needlessly politicising the external action of the EU. This article is an attempt to assess the true import of the changes introduced by the Lisbon Treaty in this area, for what is possible given the limited temporal extent of their application. Section 2 will briefly review the role of foreign investment in the CCP, while Section 3 will do the same for the non-commercial objectives pursued by the EU in the context of its CCP competences. Section 4 is dedicated to an analysis of Article 21 TEU and its legal value. In doing so, the section will consider issues such as to what extent Article 21 TEU constrains the foreign policy of the EU and its effect with specific reference to the CCP. Further, the article will consider the relationship between Article 21 TEU and other programmatic articles of the TEU, such as Article 3 TEU, and the incorporation of non-commercial objectives in the EU's Free Trade Agreements (FTAs) and Preferential Trade Arrangements (PTAs). In Section 5, there will be a review and implications of the recent *Front Polisario* case, in which the General Court determined the EU's scope of responsibility for what concern non-commercial objectives in a trade agreement, taking also into account the latest developments on the case in the Court of Justice of the EU's Judgment. Finally, Section 6 will offer some concluding remarks.

Contents

A. Asteriti (✉)
Competition and Regulation Institute, Leuphana University, Scharnhorststraße 1,
21335 Lüneburg, Germany
e-mail: alessandra.asteriti@leuphana.de

M. Bungenberg et al. (eds.), *European Yearbook of International Economic Law 2017*, European Yearbook of International Economic Law 8,
DOI 10.1007/978-3-319-58832-2_5

1 Introduction

The ratification of the Treaty of Lisbon in 2009 saw the incorporation of foreign direct investment (FDI) amongst the competences of the European Union (EU) in the area of the CCP in Article 207 TFEU. Contextually, Article 21 of the Treaty on the European Union (TEU) set forth the principles that should guide the external action of the EU, explicitly promoting the observance of these principles and objectives—at Article 2(3)—in the external action under Part Five of the TFEU, which covers the CCP and includes Article 207. This article will consider the legal and policy implications of the explicit linkage between the CCP and the non-commercial objective of the EU, with specific reference to its foreign investment policy.

Section 2 will briefly review the role of foreign investment in the CCP, while Section 3 will do the same for the non-commercial objectives pursued by the EU in the context of its CCP competences. Section 4 is dedicated to an analysis of Article 21 TEU and its legal value. In doing so, the section will consider issues such as to what extent Article 21 TEU constrains the foreign policy of the EU and its effect with specific reference to the CCP. Further, the article will consider the relationship between Article 21 TEU and other programmatic articles of the TEU, such as Article 3 TEU, and the incorporation of non-commercial objectives in the EU's Free Trade Agreements (FTAs) and Preferential Trade Arrangements (PTAs). In Section 5, there will be a review and implications of the recent *Front Polisario* case, in which the General Court determined the EU's scope of responsibility for what concern non-commercial objectives in a trade agreement, taking also into account the latest developments on the case in the Court of Justice of the EU's Judgment. Finally, Section 6 will offer some concluding remarks.

2 The EU's Investment Competence

Before 2009, the EU did not have competence to conclude bilateral investment treaties (BITs) or international investment agreements (IIAs), as they are now more commonly known[1]; all EU Member States are signatories to numerous BITs, either with third countries, mostly in the developing world, or with other EU countries, in

[1]By using the term BITs one more usually refers to the older style treaties, especially of the European model, very streamlined "political" instruments, with few if any references to other regimes of international law. It should also be recognised that at the time of this first generation of BITs, international investment law could hardly be described as a well-developed regime of international law.

particular the new accession countries in Eastern Europe.[2] In fact, modern BITs are a European development in international law, from the now famous first 1959 Treaty between Germany and Pakistan.[3]

The older, "first generation" BITs, mostly ratified between European and developing countries in Africa, Asia and South America are more aptly described as political tools than legally binding agreements (at least in terms of the intentions of the drafters) with few, general, substantive provisions and, from the late 1960s onwards, mixed arbitration clauses, with or without direct reference to the International Centre for the Settlement of Investment Disputes (ICSID) Convention.[4] Almost none of them contains any language expressly relating to non-commercial obligations of the host State of the investment, in particular other international obligations, for example in the area of environmental law or human rights.[5]

IIAs' subject-matter, the protection and promotion of FDI, puts them beyond the external competence of the EU in CCP, which was limited, until the Treaty of Amsterdam, to trade in goods, as per Article 133 TEC. The Treaties of Amsterdam and Nice included trade in services and TRIPs within the scope of the external competence of the EU. Additionally, the European Court of Justice (ECJ), now Court of Justice of the European Union (CJEU), progressively expanded the scope of the competence in matters of foreign trade, through a series of opinions and judgments, most significantly through the principle of pre-emption and the recognition of indirect implied competence.[6] For what concerns FDI, opinion 2/92 is crucial in recognising the indirect implied competence of the European Community in FDI issues.[7]

Before considering the findings of the Court in that opinion, it might be useful to remind ourselves of the contours of indirect implied competence to conclude international agreements, as first put forward by the Court in 1971 in the *AETR*[8] case and described in the 1977 opinion 1/76 in the following terms:

> Authority to enter into international commitments may not only arise from an express attribution by the Treaty but equally may flow implicitly from its provisions [. . .]. This is

[2]All IIAs are listed on the UNCTAD's website; see http://investmentpolicyhub.unctad.org/IIA (last accessed 1 March 2017).

[3]Treaty for the Promotion and Protection of Investments (with Protocol and exchange of notes), Germany and Pakistan, 25 November 1959, 457 UNTS 24, BGBl. 1961 II, 793 (entered into force 28 November 1962).

[4]1965 Convention on the Settlement of Investment Disputes Between States and Nationals of Other States, 575 UNTS 159.

[5]For an interesting comparison between the European and the North American approach to investment treaties, see Alschner (2013).

[6]See for a useful summary Waibel M, Competence Review: Trade and Investment, https://www.gov.uk/government/uploads/system/uploads/attachment_data/file/270992/bis-14-511-trade-and-investment-competence-review-independent-review-legal-research-by-michael-waibel.pdf (last accessed 1 March 2017).

[7]CJEU, opinion 2/92, *OECD*, ECLI:EU:C:1995:83.

[8]CJEU, case 22/70, *Commission/Council*, ECLI:EU:C:1971:32.

> particularly so in all cases in which internal power has already been used in order to adopt measures which come within the attainment of common policies [. . .][or] is necessary for the attainment of one of the objectives of the Community.[9]

Opinion 2/92 concerned the competence of the Community in the area of an OECD (of which the Community was not a Member) decision that dealt with the application of the national treatment standard to foreign undertakings. In its opinion, the Court acknowledged for the first time that the Community could have implied external competence in matters relating to foreign investment on the basis of its previous case law, and that this competence would be exercised jointly with the Member States.

Having established that investment was an area of shared competence, the EU nonetheless proceeded to develop its own Minimum Platform of FTAs, in order to foster two objectives: (a) additional market access in GATS modes one, three and four (i.e., cross border services, commercial presence and temporary entry for service providers); and (b) post-establishment standards for service suppliers, commercial presence and investors.[10] Amongst the instruments negotiated under the umbrella of the New Minimum Platform are the 2007 EU-Korea FTA[11] and the 2008 CARIFORUM-EU Economic Partnership Agreement (EPA).[12] This last one incorporates, in Article 2, the principles that underpin the 2000 Cotonou Agreement, as expressed in Articles 2 and 9, and more specifically, for what concerns the non-commercial principles contained in Article 21 TEU, "human rights, democratic principles and the rule of law".[13]

With the Treaty of Lisbon in 2009, FDI was expressly included in the exclusive competences of the EU in the context of the CCP. Article 207 TFEU lists FDI as part of the CCP, for which the EU has exclusive competence, as per Article 3(1)(e) TFEU. This is not the place to consider in detail the extent of the competence of investment and what it concerns, for example whether portfolio investments are included, as is the case in BITs and IIAs, or not (as the wording of Article 207 seems to imply) and whether protection and liberalisation of investments are both within the scope of the EU's competence.

---

[9]CJEU, opinion 1/76, *Draft Agreement establishing a European laying-up fund for inland waterway vessel*, ECLI:EU:C:1977:63, para. 3.

[10]Council of the EU, Minimum Platform on Investment for the EU FTAs, 5375/06, 27 November 2006 (unpublished) and revised version of 6 March 2009; for information on the content see especially Maydell (2007); also Bungenberg (2011), p. 29; Burgstaller (2009), p. 204 et seqq.; some background information also in Reinisch (2014), p. 115.

[11]OJ 2011 L 127/6.

[12]OJ 2008 L 289/1.

[13]The original agreement was signed in 2000; the text was revised in 2005 and in 2010 (still to be ratified), http://www.acp.int/content/acp-ec-partnership-agreement-cotonou-agreement-accord-de-partenariat-acp-ce-accord-de-cotono (last accessed 1 March 2017). The first mention of a human rights clause in an EU FTA is Article 5 of the 1989 Lomé IV Convention with African, Caribbean and Pacific (ACP) Countries, http://aei.pitt.edu/56901/1/THIRD.XIV.pdf (last accessed 1 March 2017).

Briefly, on the first issue, the EU Commission stated that

> Treaty provisions on capital payments complement the EU's exclusive competence under the CCP and provide for an implied exclusive competence. With reference to Article 3(2) TFEU, the EU has implied exclusive competence to regulate portfolio investment of EU investors in third countries to the extent that agreements on investment affect common rules set under the chapter on capital and payments (Articles 63–66 TFEU).[14]

On the second issue, the Member States argued strongly that, while liberalisation was within the competence of the EU, protection of investments (the traditional subject of BITs which normally do not cover pre-establishment rights, i.e. liberalisation) remained within the remit of Member States.[15] The EU Commission stressed that limiting the EU's competence to liberalisation would significantly impair the effectiveness of its FDI policy.[16] The acceptance of the position that the EU has competence post-entry still leaves an open question as to the extent of this competence, whether it includes all standards of treatment, or conversely whether it is limited to performance standards but not expropriation, on the basis of Article 345 TFEU, which preserves the sovereignty of the Member States on matters governing property ownership.[17] The ECJ/CJEU has confirmed that Article 345 does not prevent the introduction of harmonisation measures in the area of intellectual property.[18] Previous settled case law also confirms that Article 345 has to be construed as a restriction, and not an absolute bar to the exercise of competences in the area of property rights widely intended.[19] In short, while Member States retain the authority to determine whether expropriation occurs, this authority does not extend to define its conditions, which is a matter of international, and in this case EU, law. By way of analogy, BITs do not affect property rights, but only determine that expropriation of these property rights is subject to the conditions included in the treaty.

Issues of exclusive and shared competence, which are obviously relevant as a matter of future policy (as evidenced quite dramatically in the debate on the Transatlantic Trade and Investment Partnership—TTIP[20]) are also important in a

---

[14]European Commission, Towards a comprehensive European international investment policy, COM (2010) 343 final. But on this, see the recent Opinion 2/15 by the CJEU on the Singapore-EU FTA, where the Court established that non-direct foreign investment is not within the exclusive competence of the EU.

[15]Bungenberg (2011), p. 35 et seqq. See also, with considerable literature, Reinisch (2014).

[16]See European Commission, Towards a comprehensive European international investment policy, COM (2010) 343 final.

[17]For a review of the controversy, see Fina and Lentner (2016), p. 432.

[18]CJEU, case C-350/92, *Kingdom of Spain v Council*, ECLI:EU:C:1995:237, paras. 15–19.

[19]CJEU, case 182/83, *Fearon v Irish Land Commission*, ECLI:EU:C:1984:335.

[20]The debate on the TTIP centred mostly on the inclusion of the contested dispute settlement system, but also on the restriction of the Member States' regulatory powers; a lot of the debates took place in public fora, such as newspapers and social media (in itself indicative of the raised awareness about investment issues in the general public); for recent developments, the EU provides up-to-date news and commentary: see http://ec.europa.eu/trade/policy/in-focus/ttip/

historical sense, by which is intended the effect of the newly acquired competence on the status of BITs previously concluded by Member States both with third countries and with new EU Member States (intra-EU BITs).[21] Again, this is a complex debate that has had judicial repercussions both at the level of the CJEU[22] and in the context of arbitral awards in investment disputes.[23] In order to accommodate and "grandfather" these agreements within the body of EU law, Regulation No 1219/2012 was issued, "establishing transitional arrangements for bilateral investment agreements between Member States and third countries".[24] The regulation gives the Commission the authority to assess the compatibility of BITs with the *acquis communautaire* and whether they constitute an obstacle to the EU's FDI policy, at the same time enjoining Member States to remove the identified obstacles. Contextually the regulation allows Member States to maintain in force or conclude new BITs provided the Commission is notified and provided the EU is not planning to conclude IIAs with the relevant countries in the short term. The status of these agreements within EU law is relevant to issues of non-commercial obligations in the context of CCP policy to the extent that these agreements might contain non-commercial obligations. As already noted in the introduction, traditional European-style BITs are recognisable by their limited scope and consequent brevity—the standard structure will include only the main provisions on the protection of investors and their investment, inclusive of standards of treatment, expropriation, currency transfers and, in the more recent BITs, dispute settlement clauses. However, as already noted, Regulation No 1219/2012 also allows Member States to pursue the conclusion of BITs with third states. As a consequence, the adoption of the classic European BIT model in new treaties with third states would entail the

---

index_en.htm (last accessed 1 March 2017). The relative novelty of a trade and investment agreement attracting so much attention (for a similar phenomenon, we should probably have to go back to the negotiating history of the North American Free Trade Agreement (NAFTA) is proven by the wealth of literature, including volumes. See for example Morin et al. (2015). On the coherence of the EU's BITs policy, see also Lenk (2015).

[21]See Dimopoulos (2011), Burgstaller (2010), Hindelang (2011), Söderlund (2007) and Wierzbowski and Gubrynowicz (2009).

[22]CJEU, case C-118/07, *Commission v Finland*, ECLI:EU:C:2009:715; CJEU, case C-205/06, *Commission v Austria*, ECLI:EU:C:2009:118; CJEU, case C-249/06, *Commission v Sweden*, ECLI:EU:C:2009:119.

[23]There are several investment disputes in which the Commission sought to intervene by submitting *amicus curiae* briefs: amongst them are the following: *Eastern Sugar BV (Netherlands) v The Czech Republic*, UNCITRAL, SCC Case No 088/2004, Final Award 12 April 2007; *Electrabel SA v Republic of Hungary*, ICSID Case No ARB/07/19, Award 25 November 2015; *AES Summit Generation v Republic of Hungary*, ICSID Case No ARB/07/22, Award 23 September 2010; *Achmea BV v The Slovak Republic*, UNCITRAL, PCA Case No 2008–13 (formerly *Eureko BV v The Slovak Republic*); *European American Investment Bank AG (EURAM) v Slovak Republic*, UNCITRAL, Award on Jurisdiction 22 October 2012; *US Steel Global Holdings I BV v The Slovak Republic*, UNCITRAL, PCA Case No 2013–6 (discontinued—the Commission's brief was made available through IA Reporter).

[24]OJ 2012 L 351/40.

exclusion of any non-commercial provision from the body of the treaty. The current situation therefore results in two sets of issues:

1. For those BITs already concluded and that are grandfathered in the EU legal system, the incorporation of non-commercial obligations will have to happen by way of interpretation by the investment tribunals, in accordance to the general rules of interpretation as expressed in Article 30 of the Vienna Convention on the Law of Treaties (VCLT),[25] and application, in accordance of the provisions on applicable law in the BIT, when available.
2. For those BITs yet to be concluded, while the above approach is still pursuable, direct incorporation of specific provisions on non-commercial matters is also feasible. To this effect, the European Council Action Plan on Human Rights enjoins Member States

> to strive to include in new or revised Bilateral Investment Treaties (BITs) that they negotiate in the future with third countries provisions related to the respect and fulfilment of human rights, including provisions on Corporate Social Responsibility, in line with those inserted in agreements negotiated at EU level.[26]

A significant proviso to the first approach is that it is only applicable for non-commercial obligations (such as those derived from international human rights, environmental and labour law) that originate in international legal instruments and customary international law, and outwith the legal system of the EU. This is because these investment treaties will be interpreted and applied by investment tribunals, in accordance with the arbitration clause included in the treaty itself, the concession contract, or the domestic investment code. Therefore, arbitrators will be prevented from interpreting and applying EU law into the treaty, since the CJEU claims exclusive hermeneutic competence.[27] Additionally, since Article 344 TFEU could prevent Member States from submitting disputes that might fall under the competence of the CJEU to investment tribunals, which are prevented from interpreting and applying EU law—i.e., interpreting Article 21 TEU as applicable to the parties by way, for example, of Article 31(3)(c).

The well documented tension between intra-EU BITs and the EU legal space has repercussions that go well beyond the scope of this article and that have arisen from time to time both in investment disputes and in CJEU cases (as already noted). Several components of the arising conflicts are germane to the incorporation of non-commercial elements in investment law at EU level. The issue of exclusive

[25]On interpretation in international law see the recent Bianchi et al. (2015); on treaty interpretation in the investment regime see Wälde (2009).

[26]Council of the European Union, EU Action Plan on Human Rights and Democracy, December 2015, p. 39.

[27]Article 19(1) TEU: "The Court of Justice of the European Union [. . .] shall ensure that in the interpretation and application of the Treaties the law is observed." See also in general Rasmussen (2014).

hermeneutic competence of the CJEU, preventing the incorporation of the fundamental principles upheld in Article 21 TEU in BITs concluded by Member States, has already been mentioned. Amongst the arguments advanced by the Commission in investment arbitration that can be considered relevant, is the possibility of investment arbitrations settling issues of EU law that are linked to non-commercial matters—one can think for example of host State defences based on the application of EU legal obligations—thereby allowing the pursuance of investment policies in the EU legal space unmoored from the restraining influence of the foundational principles of EU law. Differential treatment of EU investors by different arbitration tribunals deciding under different instruments is undoubtedly problematic from the perspective of the non-discrimination obligation arising under EU law, and potentially triggers issues of non-compliance with equality obligations under Article 21 TEU. Finally, the principle of supremacy of EU law implies that non-conforming obligations arising from intra-EU BITs have to give way to EU legal obligations; neither do they constitute defences against a breach of EU law.

The linkage between investment competence and non-commercial objectives protected under Article 21 TEU is particularly poignant given the heavier footprint of investment activities compared with other commercial activities. While it is undoubtedly true that non-tariff barriers (regulatory barriers) loom large in trade discourse, the potential tension between the regulatory State (also in its international guise, where the principles underpinning Article 21 find their fullest realisation) and the interests and rights of foreign investors is potentially starker and more intractable to assuage and defuse.

This tension was not lost on the EU Parliament: In 2011 they passed a resolution on the future of European international investment policy in which they stressed the importance of the continued protection of the right to regulate and the necessity to include the appropriate social and environmental standards in EU-concluded IIAs.[28] The resolution exposes the disquiet in the Parliament about possible fetters to the regulatory power of Member States in the EU policy space; equally, commercial objectives pursued by the EU in its IIAs might conflict with its stated non-commercial objectives as defined in Article 21 TEU. In an economic, political and legal environment where IIAs are becoming more and more agreements between partners of equal status, the reciprocity of commitments is becoming a reality on the ground, and not anymore just a noble statement of political intent. All the same, the EU can wield considerable economic power, and weaker developing countries might find themselves unable to carve-out their own regulatory space. Article 21 TEU might well be the means for developing countries to vicariously protecting their own non-commercial objectives thanks to the umbrella of EU principles and standards.

[28]See European Parliament resolution of 6 April 2011 on the future European international investment policy (2010/2203(INI)), paras. 23–30.

3 The EU Non-Commercial Objectives in the Common Commercial Policy

The 2009 Lisbon Treaty provides a programmatic statement of intent for the Union that establishes it not only as a supranational community based on the common market, but as a constitutional community dedicated to the creation of a comprehensive legal space *sui generis* also capable of projecting its values internationally.[29]

This development ought to be seen in the context of a constitutionalization of similar values (the rule of law, democracy and human rights) at the international level.[30] This article is not the space to discuss whether this constitutionalization, to the extent that it is a real, measurable phenomenon, is problematic and whether it is the appropriate remedy for the issues of democratic deficit, legitimation crisis and political inability to tackle supranational problems that are recognised both at the European and international levels. Equally, the constitutionalization of values that accompanies the constitutionalization of economic policies (with the rule of law, democracy and human rights dove-tailing neatly with market capitalism, economic governance and protection of property rights) is not challenged here and is accepted as a given fact.[31]

Article 2 TEU establishes the fundamental values upon which the EU is founded:

> The Union is founded on the values of *respect for human dignity, freedom, democracy, equality, the rule of law and respect for human rights*, including the rights of persons belonging to minorities. These values are common to the Member States in a society in which pluralism, non-discrimination, tolerance, justice, solidarity and equality between women and men prevail.

Article 3(5) TEU situates the external action of the EU—in which one should also find its policy in respect to FDI—in the context of the objectives enumerated in Article 2 and referred to in the text and more specifically spelled out as follows:

> In its relations with the wider world, the Union shall uphold and promote its values and contribute to the protection if its citizens. It shall contribute to peace, security, the sustainable development of the Earth, solidarity and mutual respect among peoples, free and fair trade, eradication of poverty and the protection of human rights, in particular the rights of the child, as well as to the strict observance and the development of international law, including respect for the principles of the United Nations Charter.[32]

[29]The literature on the constitutionalization of the EU, both in its internal and external dimensions, is vast and pre-dates the Treaty of Lisbon. See for example Timmermans (2001), Rittberger and Schimmelfenning (2007), Christiansen and Reh (2009) and Habermas (2012).

[30]See for example Habermas (2008), Klabbers et al. (2009) and De Wet (2012).

[31]The literature on the constitutionalization of the world economy is equally rich; see for example Cass (2005), Cremona et al. (2013), Robé et al. (2016), Thompson (2012) and Schneiderman (2008).

[32]Article 3(5) TEU does not provide a legal basis for the EU's action in pursuance of these objectives, as clarified by Article 3(6): "The Union shall pursue its objectives by appropriate means commensurate with the competences which are conferred upon it in the Treaties."

At a further level of specification, Article 21 TEU establishes the principles governing the EU's external action, as follows:

> 1. The Union's action on the international scene shall be guided by the principles which have inspired its own creation, development and enlargement, and which it seeks to advance in the wider world: democracy, the rule of law, the universality and indivisibility of human rights and fundamental freedoms, respect for human dignity, the principles of equality and solidarity, and respect for the principles of the United Nations Charter and international law.
>
> The Union shall seek to develop relations and build partnerships with third countries, and international, regional or global organisations which share the principles referred to in the first subparagraph. It shall promote multilateral solutions to common problems, in particular in the framework of the United Nations.
>
> 2. The Union shall define and pursue common policies and actions, and shall work for a high degree of cooperation in all fields of international relations, in order to:
>
> (a) safeguard its values, fundamental interests, security, independence and integrity;
>
> (b) consolidate and support democracy, the rule of law, human rights and the principles of international law;
>
> (c) preserve peace, prevent conflicts and strengthen international security, in accordance with the purposes and principles of the United Nations Charter, with the principles of the Helsinki Final Act and with the aims of the Charter of Paris, including those relating to external borders;
>
> (d) foster the sustainable economic, social and environmental development of developing countries, with the primary aim of eradicating poverty;
>
> (e) encourage the integration of all countries into the world economy, including through the progressive abolition of restrictions on international trade;
>
> (f) help develop international measures to preserve and improve the quality of the environment and the sustainable management of global natural resources, in order to ensure sustainable development;
>
> (g) assist populations, countries and regions confronting natural or man-made disasters; and
>
> (h) promote an international system based on stronger multilateral cooperation and good global governance.
>
> 3. The Union shall respect the principles and pursue the objectives set out in paragraphs 1 and 2 in the development and implementation of the different areas of the Union's external action covered by this Title and by Part Five of the Treaty on the Functioning of the European Union, and of the external aspects of its other policies.
>
> The Union shall ensure consistency between the different areas of its external action and between these and its other policies. The Council and the Commission, assisted by the High Representative of the Union for Foreign Affairs and Security Policy, shall ensure that consistency and shall cooperate to that effect.[33]

[33]For a close analysis of Article 21 TEU, see Vedder (2013).

Finally, Article 207(1) TFEU contains a *renvoi* to the fundamental principles enumerated in the above articles and more closely in Article 21 TEU:

> The common commercial policy shall be based on uniform principles, particularly with regard to changes in tariff rates, the conclusion of tariff and trade agreements relating to trade in goods and services, and the commercial aspects of intellectual property, foreign direct investment, the achievement of uniformity in measures of liberalisation, export policy and measures to protect trade such as those to be taken in the event of dumping or subsidies. *The common commercial policy shall be conducted in the context of the principles and objectives of the Union's external action.*

As a matter of semantics, different articles articulate the obligations of the Union with respect to non-commercial objectives in different ways.[34] This terminological variety has repercussions—which cannot be fully explored in this contribution—both at the level of the Union's internal action and in terms of the relationship, and potential tension, with other regimes of international law as well as with the overarching structure of international law as expressed in the United Nations Charter.

Article 2 TEU enumerates the values upon which the Union is founded, and does not contain any practical obligation *per se* on the part of the Union to respect or promote these values; this obligation is spelled out in Article 3 TEU, which enjoins the Union to "uphold and promote" its values in its relations with the wider world. The obligation is worded as a "shall" duty on the part of the Union, but this has been clearly interpreted by the Commission as a "must".[35]

Article 3 TEU also provides a normative link and embeds Union law within the wider framework of international law, requiring the strict observance and the contribution to the development of international law by the Union—the first subordinating EU law to international law, the second one identifying the Union as an actor of international law, on par with States, and therefore as an active contributor to the development of international law itself.[36] The inclusion of the principles of the UN Charter, of which Article 103 forms part, more clearly establishes the obligation to respect the hierarchical primacy of the Charter with respect to any other treaty-based obligation, including those deriving from the Treaties.[37]

[34]For example, in Article 3(5) TEU, the Union "shall uphold, promote and contribute"; in Article 21(1) TEU the Union "shall be guided by the principles"; and in Article 207 TFEU "the CCP shall be based on uniform principles".

[35]European Commission, Trade for All: Towards a More Responsible Trade and Investment Policy, 14 October 2015, p. 7.

[36]For the duty to observe international law, see also CJEU, case C-366/10, *Air Transport Association of America and others*, ECLI:EU:C:2011:864, para. 101 and the case-law cited.

[37]On the sometimes problematic relationship between the law of the Charter and EU law, the seminal case is of course *Kadi*, see CJEU, joined cases C-402/05 P and C-415/05 P, *Kadi and Al Barakaat*, ECLI:EU:C:2008:461; GC, case T-85/09, *Kadi v Commission*, ECLI:EU:T:2010:418; CJEU, joined cases C-584/10 P, C-593/10 P and C-595/10 P, *European Commission and others v Yassin Abdullah Kadi*, ECLI:EU:C:2013:518.

This *renvoi* to the law of the Charter is not to be intended as frozen in amber, but as following the progressive development of UN law, including the work done in the business and human rights area.[38] The Commission has clearly linked the work of the EU in this area with the commitments of the UN-developed "Protect, respect and remedy" human rights and corporate social responsibility framework.[39]

Finally, Article 21 TEU more specifically concerns the "principles" that should guide the Union's international actions and not just the "values" that underpin its legal edifice; this is a more explicitly normative term of art,[40] where principles are intended to be an aid to interpretation and application of more specific rules and standards, or, as in this case, as a guide for the action of the Union internationally. In practice, Article 21 provides both a set of principles and a list of objectives: The first ones include the familiar principles underpinning the liberal democratic capitalist model, i.e. democracy, rule of law, human rights and fundamental freedoms. A more specific European flavour is provided by the reference to human dignity (the supreme value in the *Grundgesetz*) and solidarity,[41] while the embedding in the international system is guaranteed by the references to international law and the UN Charter. All the objectives are listed under the rubric of cooperation and multilateralism, both with third countries and other international organisations; they can be divided into four main areas of activity:

1. Democracy and rule of law objectives (political area);
2. Peace and security (international relations area);
3. Sustainable development, in its economic, social and environmental dimensions (social area);
4. Economic integration and free trade (economic area).

A crucial dimension of the coordination effort informing the set of objectives is the *normative coordination* between the diverse areas of intervention and the main EU policies with respect to the CCP and other fundamental areas of economic competence.[42] This normative coordination—defined in Article 21(3) as "consistency between the different areas of its [the Union's] external action and between

[38]Especially the work done by the Special Rapporteur John Ruggie; see Human Rights Council, 17th session, Report of the Special Representative of the Secretary-General on the issue of human rights and transnational corporations and other business enterprises; Ruggie J, Guiding Principles on Business and Human Rights: Implementing the United Nations "Protect, Respect and Remedy" Framework, A/HRC/17/31, 21 March 2011.

[39]European Commission, A renewed EU strategy 2011–14 for Corporate Social Responsibility, COM (2011) 681 final, 25 October 2011.

[40]On the distinction between rules and principles, see mainly Dworkin (1967) and Dworkin (1997).

[41]See Hilpold (2015).

[42]The attempt to improve the consistency and coherence of the EU actions, both in their internal and external policies, via application of Article 21 TEU is noted by the Commission in its Working document on implementing the UN guiding principles on business and human rights—state of play, SWD(2015)/144 final, p. 17.

these and its other policies"—is to be guaranteed by the Council and by the Commission assisted by the High Representative of the Union for Foreign Affairs and Security Policy.[43] This is a typical *ex ante* attempt at normative consistency and therefore more dependent on political and diplomatic negotiation rather than *ex post facto* conflict management and resolution by the courts, in this case the CJEU.[44] An example of the second approach, judicial conflict management, is the already mentioned jurisprudence of the CJEU in cases involving intra-EU BITs. It has already been noted how the new CCP competences as delineated in the Lisbon Treaty might result in its increased politicisation, not least by the inclusion of the European Parliament in the treaty-making processes of the EU, in accordance with Article 218(6) TFEU.[45] A further driver for this politicisation might be the inclusion of non-commercial objectives in Article 21 TEU, coupled with the mentioned principle of consistency included in Article 21(3), which requires the alignment of commercial and non-commercial objectives in pursuit of the CCP.[46] This widespread opinion[47] rests on the assumption that non-commercial objectives are inherently more "political" than the traditional commercial objectives pursued by the EU through its CCP. The author does not share this assumption, nor the simple binary distinction between political and apolitical objectives in the context of the EU external policy (and in many other areas besides). There is nothing inherently *apolitical* in the trade and investment liberalisation and promotion policy that underpins the CCP; consequently in this article politicisation is only adopted to signify the inclusion of non-commercial objectives and the consequent potential of conflict between commercial and non-commercial objectives in the external action of the EU.

---

[43]The English version of the article uses the term "consistency", while several other versions (e.g. German, French and Italian) use the term for "coherence". It has been argued that coherence and consistency are not identical, consistency requiring simply the absence of logical contradiction, while coherence demands the higher standard of consistency in principle; alternatively, consistency has to be considered the preliminary and necessary condition of coherence, but not the sufficient one; see Schiavello (2001). It seems that the non-English versions of the article better describe what is required of the EU in ensuring the coherence of its external action.

[44]Issues of normative conflicts have been recently discussed widely in the international community; the starting point is surely the Fragmentation Report produced by the International Law Commission (ILC), Fragmentation of International Law: Difficulties Arising from the Diversification and Expansion of International Law, Report of the Study Group of the International Law Commission, finalised by Koskenniemi M, A/CN4/L682, 13 April 2006; recently, a more integrationist approach has developed; see Andenas and Bjorge (2015) and Hindelang and Krajewski (2016).

[45]Krajewski (2013). The potential "intergovernmentalisation" of the CCP as a consequence of the mandatory compliance with the principles expressed in Article 21 has been noted as well; see Dederer (2013), p. 98; Bungenberg (2010), p. 99.

[46]Dederer (2013), p. 128 et seqq.

[47]See also Douma and van der Velde (2016), p. 106; Petersmann (2013). But see against Krajewski (2012), p. 297, on the different grounds that trade policy has never been exclusively about trade, and that trade liberalisation is not an end in itself.

Non-commercial principles and objectives that might have an effect on the CCP competence of the EU are therefore given different entry-points: they provide the normative values upon which the entire edifice of the EU legal system is built; they constitute the principles inspiring the EU's international action; and finally, they guide the normative production by the EU in compliance with coordination and multilateralism, from a political perspective, and regime awareness and conflict resolution, from a legal perspective.

4 The Legal Effects of Article 21 TEU

Non-commercial objectives were already included in the EU's CCP: issues such as democracy promotion, the rule of law, human rights and environmental protection were packaged in international instruments, as a consequence of the recognition that the EU could include such objectives for the areas in which it had competence[48]; trade and investment instruments, stabilisation and association agreements, and free trade agreements started including numerous references to non-commercial objectives in accordance with the General Systems of Preferences (GSPs) and GSP+ frameworks, originally agreed within the United Nations Conference on Trade and Development and incorporated in the EU's CCP by successive regulations.[49]

There remained however a lack of clarity, especially as to the extent of the EU's competence in this area and the exact legal basis for its action[50]; this lack of clarity has been remedied by the explicit incorporation of such objectives in Article 21 TEU, as considered in detail in Section 3.[51] Further, while the Court noted repeatedly that the EU could act to pursue non-commercial objectives in the

[48]Alston and Weiler (1998), with specific reference to human rights objectives: "It is instructive, by way of analogy, to consider some of the areas in which the Community has assumed exclusive competences, such as major aspects of the Common Commercial Policy, of the Common Agricultural Policy (which often implicate rights to property) or of the Single Market concerning the free movement of labour. It seems self-evident that in those areas it is only the Community which could reasonably be considered to be the custodian of human rights – in the same way that the Member States are custodians of human rights in the vast areas of state jurisdiction, like criminal law, which are largely outside Community jurisdiction."

[49]GSP Regulations 980/2005, 732/2008 and 878/2012; and EU Special Incentive Arrangement for Sustainable Development and Good Governance (GSP+) which makes access to the preferential system conditional on compliance with human rights, labour rights, environmental obligations and good governance.

[50]Kube (2016). In CJEU, opinion 2/94, *Accession to the ECHR*, ECLI:EU:C:1996:140, the Court stated that human rights could not provide a sufficient legal basis for external action, but only a constraining influence.

[51]See also Krajewski (2013), p. 83; Vedder (2013), p. 115.

context of its CCP policy to the extent of its competence to do so,[52] there remained a considerable level of ambiguity as to the *obligation* for the EU to abide by and pursue such non-commercial objectives.[53] In short, while there was an acknowledgement of the capacity for the EU to pursue such non-commercial objectives as development,[54] development aid[55] and foreign policy[56] there was ambiguity regarding the substantive value of the "objectives", the lack of legal basis for any specific action and the extent of the duty, as opposed to the capacity, to undertake any action.

From an institutional viewpoint, the already mentioned involvement of the EU Parliament post-Lisbon in the external action of the EU under the CCP has interesting repercussions, which can be grouped in two areas with reference to Article 21 objectives: one procedural, having to do with the democratic legitimacy—for the approval process for international agreements between the EU and third States, other international organisations or regional groupings—and transparency, and one substantive, related to the political input of the Parliament in the non-commercial objectives of the EU's external action.

The increased democratic legitimacy is guaranteed by the new role granted to the EU Parliament by Article 207(2) and (3) as well as Article 218 TFEU, which give the Parliament the right to be consulted in all cases, the right to give consent in certain cases (where the ordinary legislative procedure would apply in the CCP), and the right to obtain an opinion from the CJEU on the compatibility of the proposed agreement with the Treaties, therefore allowing them to be reviewed for compatibility with Article 21 TEU inclusive.[57] Equally, involving the Parliament in the negotiations through the right to be consulted improves the transparency of the process.[58] From a substantive point of view, the involvement of the Parliament allows non-commercial objectives to be given a more prominent role in the negotiations, as Parliament is more likely to express a variety of demands that go

[52]CJEU, opinion 1/78, *International Agreement on Natural Rubber*, ECLI:EU:C:1979:224; CJEU, case 45/86, *Tariff Preferences*, ECLI:EU:C:1987:163; CJEU, case C-70/94, *Werner*, ECLI:EU:C:1995:328, para. 10 et seqq.; CJEU, case C-83/94, *Leifer*, ECLI:EU:C:1995:329, para. 9; GC, case T-184/95, *Dorsch Consult*, ECLI:EU:C:2000:321; CJEU, case C-84/95, *Bosphorus*, ECLI:EU:C:1996:312; CJEU, opinion 2/00, *Cartagena Protocol*, ECLI:EU:C:2001:664, para. 23.

[53]Vedder (2013), p. 128.

[54]CJEU, opinion 1/78, *International Agreement on Natural Rubber*, ECLI:EU:C:1979:224.

[55]CJEU, case 45/86, *Tariff Preferences*, ECLI:EU:C:1987:163.

[56]CJEU, case C-70/94, *Werner*, ECLI:EU:C:1995:328, para. 10; CJEU, case C-83/94, *Leifer*, ECLI:EU:C:1995:329, para. 10 et seq.; CJEU, case C-124/95, *Centro-Com*, ECLI:EU:C:1997:8, para. 26.

[57]Article 207(3) enjoins the Commission to report on the progress of negotiations both to the Trade Policy Committee, a special body of the European Council, and to the Parliament, which are therefore put on equal footing for what concerns the reporting obligations—even if not for their capacity to process the information obtained, nor for having the same rights in consultation, see Krajewski (2013), p. 73.

[58]Whether transparency is to be interpreted here as a purely procedural right, or if it involves any substantive rights, is an open question.

beyond the limited trade and investment remit of the relevant agreements—or better, since new generation agreements tend to incorporate non-commercial objectives, to make sure that these objectives are given equal status with the traditional commercial ones, either by the provision of a normative space by way of carve-out, or by way of exception.

In fact, the procedural and substantive aspects of the new role given to the Parliament intersect precisely at the point where non-commercial objectives of the CCP are at issue. The recent cases of the Canada-EU Comprehensive Economic and Trade Agreement (CETA) and United States-EU TTIP and their difficult negotiation processes bring into focus the challenges of extending this sort of agreements beyond their more limited traditional remit. While the controversy cannot be imputed solely to the new role given to the Parliament in scrutinising these agreements, with equally important input being provided by civil society and domestic parliaments, undoubtedly the publicity of the negotiated drafts, including the leaking of crucial documents by Greenpeace Netherlands,[59] was enhanced by the relative transparency of the proceedings consequent to the involvement of the Parliament. Whether the politicisation of the negotiating process, and of the substantive outcome of the negotiations, will work to embed these agreements more strongly within the EU international action, or rather scupper the chances of ever reaching agreements on such a set of controversial issues, remains to be seen, but the trend does not so far seem positive.[60]

The negotiating history of agreements that have so far passed the hurdle of the EU Parliament's approval post-Lisbon might provide some insights. Specifically, the EU-Colombia and Peru Free Trade Agreement, ratified in 2013, includes specific provisions on human rights, therefore constitute an interesting case study both for the role of the EU Parliament post-Lisbon and the legal value of Article 21 in the conclusion of agreements under the CCP in the same timeframe.[61] In a policy document published in 2016 by the Directorate General for External Policies at the request of the Committee on International Trade of the EU Parliament, for example, the author notices that

> The Treaty of Lisbon enhanced the role of the European Parliament in trade agreements. This institution has been vocal in advocating a stronger position on labour and environmental standards in trade agreements. Recent EU trade agreements (South Korea, Singapore, Central America, Peru/Colombia, Canada) include a novel chapter on trade sustainability [...], which aims at ensuring states maintain their own labour and

---

[59]The documents were made available on Greenpeace's website, see https://ttip-leaks.org/ttip/ (last accessed 1 March 2017); further leaks were made available by a MEP of the German Green Party, http://www.euractiv.com/section/trade-society/news/green-party-leaks-confidential-ttip-paper/ (last accessed 1 March 2017).

[60]Negotiations on the TTIP have now stalled, although the 15th round of negotiations is scheduled for October 2016; see http://trade.ec.europa.eu/doclib/events/index.cfm?id=1544 (last accessed 1 March 2017).

[61]The complete text, together with annexes and declarations, see http://trade.ec.europa.eu/doclib/press/index.cfm?id=691 (last accessed 1 March 2017).

> environmental legislation, and ratify and comply with international standards as expressed in the International Labour Organisation (ILO) core conventions and international environmental treaties. The aims are to prevent liberalisation from affording firms an opportunity to engage in standards arbitrage, as well as following a normative commitment to social and environmental rights.[62]

These objectives are given "bite" by the insertion of the essential elements clause in the agreement, which makes the continuation of the preferential trade guarantees conditional on the respect of human rights.[63] Before proceeding in the discussion, it might be noteworthy to point out the considerable normative difference between the pursuance of non-commercial objectives under Article 21 TEU in wide-ranging development agreements, which include a trade and investment dimension coupled with human rights conditionalities, and the incorporation of those same objectives in agreements, such as the CETA and the TTIP, where there is no conditionality element, no essential elements clause and no development dimension.

In the EU-Colombia/Peru FTA, the essential elements clause is included in Article 1(1):

> [r]espect for democratic principles and fundamental human rights, as laid down in the Universal Declaration of Human Rights, and for the principle of the rule of law, underpins the internal and international policies of the Parties. Respect for these principles constitutes an essential element of this Agreement.

The history of these clauses evidences the absence of enforcement on the part of the EU even in the presence of repeated, serious and widespread human rights violations from the contracting parties to these agreements[64]; their value is therefore more correctly given as statements of principles, rather than enforceable provisions. The question remains whether the adoption of Article 21, embedding more forcefully non-commercial objectives in the CCP and mandating their inclusion in all international agreements, might not result in a more robust normative character to be vested into these clauses. Equally, a distinction will have to be made between the values that are included in the "essential elements" (human rights, rule of law, democracy) and the principles that are mandated by Article 21 but are not included in the essential elements clause (good governance, sustainable development, disarmament, etc.).

[62]Directorate General for External Policies, EU Trade Relations with Latin America: Results and Challenges in Implementing the EU-Colombia/Peru Trade Agreement, 2016, p. 14.

[63]See Hachez (2015) and Bartels (2005). The insertion of these clauses allowed the EU to condition compliance with the agreement on the respect of human rights (therefore providing a legitimate excuse for non-performance in the case of breach). The Commission clarified that the scope of these clauses in its Communication on the inclusion of respect for democratic principles and human rights in agreements between the community and third countries, COM (95) 216 final, 23 May 1995, p. 7 et seq. Amongst the most pointed criticisms of these clauses is of course the fact that both monitoring and enforcement are insufficient and potentially biased.

[64]See Hachez (2015), p. 20.

More specifically, what would be the difference as a matter of State responsibility (and countermeasures) between a breach of an essential elements clause and the breach of an Article 21 principle? The EU Commission clarified that an essential element clause

> [a]llows the parties to regard serious and persistent human rights violations and serious interruptions of democratic process as a "material breach" of the agreement in line with the Vienna Convention; constituting grounds for suspending the application of the agreement in whole or in part in line with the procedural conditions laid down in Article 65. The main condition involves allowing a period of three months between notification and suspension proper, except in "cases of special urgency", plus an additional period of race if an amicable solution is being sought.[65]

Much will depend on the wording of any other "Article 21" clause included in the agreement—including whether soft law language is adopted or hard law obligations are included. In any event, as a matter of practice, as we have seen, these essential elements clauses have been treated, for all intents and purposes, as soft law, hortatory clauses, rather than as hard law commitments, both in terms of compliance (or lack thereof) and enforcement. For example, the sustainability chapter of the EU-Colombia/Peru FTA, at Article 269(3) states:

> Each Party commits to the promotion and effective implementation in its laws and practice and in its whole territory of internationally recognised core labour standards as contained in the fundamental Conventions of the International Labour Organisation.

The provisions of this chapter are not subject to the FTA dispute settlement mechanism, including monetary compensation for breaches,[66] and neither has the normative strength of the essential elements clauses, with a language that is restricted to the soft law commitment to promotion and effective implementation, been linked to the compliance with international law standards, another objective of Article 21 TEU.

Given the relatively recent adoption of Article 21 TEU, there is still scant jurisprudence from the CJEU on its normative value. To date, it appears that the Court has referred to Article 21 TEU only on a few occasions.[67] In its 2014 judgment in *Commission v Council*,[68] resulting from a request of the Commission to annul Council Decision 2012/272/EU of 14 May 2012 on the signing, on behalf of the Union, of the Framework Agreement on Partnership and Cooperation between the European Union and its Member States, as one part, and the Republic

---

[65]COM (95) 216 final, p. 7 et seq.

[66]Directorate General for External Policies, EU Trade Relations with Latin America: Results and Challenges in Implementing the EU-Colombia/Peru Trade Agreement, 2016, p. 38. The chapter has its own dispute settlement regime and compliance is monitored by the Sub-Committee on Trade and Sustainable Development.

[67]GC, case T-85/09, *Kadi*, ECLI:EU:T:2010:418, para. 115 (the reference was not relevant to the decision).

[68]CJEU, case C-377/12, *Commission v Council*, ECLI:EU:C:2014:1903. For an analysis of the case, see Broberg and Holdgaard (2015).

of the Philippines, as the other part on the basis of additional, unnecessary and unlawful legal bases for certain provisions of the Framework Agreement,[69] the Court reiterated the well-known principle that, in the cases when an international agreement can be founded on more than one legal basis, the one upon which the main or predominant purpose is based shall be adopted. When the purposes cannot be distinguished between primary and secondary, the measure can be founded on multiple legal bases, provided their procedural aspects are not in conflict.[70] The Court in short based its reasoning on the *Portugal v Council* judgment, where a wide basis for the EU's action in the field of development was found in the Treaty title on development cooperation, therefore potentially empowering the EU to conclude wide-ranging agreements as a matter of exclusive competence.[71] At paras. 36 and 37, the Court went on to say:

> According to Article 208(1) TFEU, European Union policy in the field of development cooperation is to be conducted within the framework of the principles and objectives – as resulting from Article 21 TEU – of the European Union's external action. The primary objective of that policy is the reduction and, in the long term, the eradication of poverty and the European Union must take account of the objectives of development cooperation in the policies that it implements which are likely to affect developing countries. For implementation of that policy, Article 209 TFEU, upon which, inter alia, the contested decision is founded, provides in particular, in paragraph 2, that the European Union may conclude with third countries and competent international organisations any agreement helping to achieve the objectives referred to in Article 21 TEU and Article 208 TFEU.
>
> It follows that European Union policy in the field of development cooperation is not limited to measures directly aimed at the eradication of poverty, but also pursues the objectives referred to in Article 21(2) TEU, such as the objective, set out in Article 21(2) lit. d, of fostering the sustainable economic, social and environmental development of developing countries, with the primary aim of eradicating poverty.

In effect, the Court accepted Article 21 as providing the informing principles for the direct legal basis of the measures (in this case, the Framework Agreement); the Court also found support for a holistic reading of the EU's competence in the area in the so-called 2006 European Consensus, the joint statement by the three main institutions of the EU, Parliament, Commission and Council, and especially in its paragraph 12.[72] It should be noted however that the reliance on Article 21 as providing the underlying principles for action arose in the context of a discussion on the competence of the EU on the basis of Article 209 TFEU (the article providing the legal basis for development action, not CCP); nevertheless, the case brings to light the "constitutional" problems arising from an international action

---

[69]In addition to those proposed by the Commission, which were Articles 207, 209 and 218 (5) TFEU; the Council added Article 79(3) TFEU (on readmission of third-country nationals), Articles 91 TFEU and 100 TFEU (on transport), and Article 191(4) TFEU (on the environment).

[70]CJEU, case C-377/12, *Commission v Council*, ECLI:EU:C:2014:1903, para. 34.

[71]CJEU, case C-268/94, *Portugal* v *Council*, ECLI:EU:C:1996:461; for an analysis of the case with respect to the EU's development policy, see Peers (2000).

[72]The European Consensus on Development—The Development Challenge, OJ 2006 C 46/1.

that has taken the form of multifaceted, holistic instruments where trade, development, environment, human rights and investment are intertwined and co-dependent. Challenges on the proper legal basis for action are bound to result in increasingly complex analyses, always exposed to the risk of "distort[ing] the institutional balances and decision-making procedures set up in the Treaties".[73]

This is another way of posing the question of whether Article 21 enjoins the EU to respect its principles in implementing its CCP policy or whether it simply provides a Treaty based justification for the EU's action, rather than a jurisprudential one based on the case law of the Court. Furthermore, the margin of appreciation granted to the EU in applying Article 21 is said to be wide, given the vague and programmatic character of the objectives.[74] It seems altogether clear that Article 21 does not allow the extension of the competence of the EU per se beyond the already mentioned power to subject its international agreements concluded on the basis of Article 207 TFEU to human rights and other conditional fundamental values.[75]

From a substantive point of view, the potential for the non-commercial objectives contained in Article 21 TEU to be found to be in conflict with the traditional commercial objectives of the CCP has been noted. To the extent that non-commercial objectives are seen as potentially restrictive to the trade liberalisation objective of the CCP, appropriate balancing and the proportionate application in the context of the adopted trade policy have to be seen as the adequate response, especially in the absence of a GATT-style exception clause in Article 21 TEU or a carve-out clause to reserve the regulatory space necessary for these potentially restrictive measures.

5 Article 21 TEU and the Front Polisario Case

In the recent case *Front Polisario v Council*, Article 21 TEU was invoked by the applicants, the Front Polisario, the liberation movement for the independence of Western Sahara.[76] The applicants brought a case in the General Court against the European Council for the annulment of Council Decision 2012/497/EU for the Euro-Mediterranean Agreement between the EU and Morocco on the liberalisation of the agricultural and fisheries trade between the parties. The applicants argued that:

> the Front Polisario relies on Article 2 TEU, Article 3(5) TEU, Article 21 TEU and Article 205 TFEU. It claims that the contested decision is contrary to the European Union's

[73]Broberg and Holdgaard (2015), p. 560.

[74]Vedder (2013), p. 138; Dimopoulos (2010).

[75]Dimopoulos (2010), p. 165. One should note that the vague and programmatic tone of the fair and equitable standard in BITs has not impeded its strict application by investment tribunals.

[76]GC, case T-512/12, *Front Polisario v Council*, ECLI:EU:T:2015:953.

> fundamental values which govern its external action. It argues that, by approving the conclusion of the agreement referred to by the contested decision, the Council 'disregards the UN resolutions and the agreement between [the Kingdom of] Morocco and the Front Polisario for the organisation of the referendum on self-determination, encouraging the policy of unlawful annexation by [the Kingdom of] Morocco'. It takes the view that 'it was sufficient to suspend the agreement', since the Council '[was] perfectly aware that the economic development of [the Kingdom of] Morocco on the territory of Western Sahara [sought] to change the social structures and to subvert the very idea of the referendum'.[77]

The Court summarily dismissed this argument on the basis of the "wide discretion in the field of external economic relations" enjoyed by EU institutions, relying in part on a 1995 judgment,[78] a judgment made well before the entry into force of the Lisbon Treaty and with it, Article 21 TEU and its newly minted obligations in the field of external economic relations. However, the Court found separately that the Council had not satisfied itself that certain rights conferred on Morocco by the Agreement would not constitute a violation of the Charter of Fundamental Rights. Specifically, this concerned the exploitation of natural resources in the Western Sahara region that should have been conducted only for the advantage of the local population, also in acknowledgement of the fact that neither the EU, nor the UN, recognise Morocco's sovereignty over Western Sahara.[79]

The reliance of the Court on pre-Lisbon case law in assessing a situation that might have called for consideration of the import of Article 21 TEU on the facts of the case jars with the recognition by the same Court in a recent case of the necessity to have a critical attitude to such case law when, such as in the case of Article 207 TFEU, new competences are attributed to the EU. In that case, which concerned certain aspects of the CCP and intellectual property, the Court had the following to say:

> In view of that significant development of primary law, the question of the distribution of the competences of the European Union and the Member States must be examined on the basis of the Treaty now in force. Consequently, neither Opinion 1/94 ([1994] ECR I-5267), in which the Court established in relation to Article 113 of the EC Treaty which provisions of the TRIPs Agreement fell within the common commercial policy and hence the exclusive competence of the Community, nor the judgment in Merck Genéricos – Produtos Farmacêuticos, defining, at a date when Article 133 EC was in force, the dividing line between the obligations under the TRIPs Agreement assumed by the European Union and those remaining the responsibility of the Member States, is material for determining to what extent the TRIPs Agreement, as from the entry into force of the FEU Treaty, falls within the exclusive competence of the European Union in matters of the common commercial policy.[80]

---

[77]GC, case T-512/12, *Front Polisario v Council*, ECLI:EU:T:2015:953, para. 159.

[78]GC, case T-572/93, *Odigitria v Council and Commission*, ECLI:EU:T:1995:13, para. 38.

[79]GC, case T-572/93, *Odigitria v Council and Commission*, ECLI:EU:T:1995:13, paras. 226–248. The judgment of the GC was appealed by the Council, see CJEU, case C-104/16 P, *Council v Front Polisario*, ECLI:EU:C:2016:973.

[80]CJEU, case C-414/11, *Daiichi Sankyo and Sanofi-Aventis Deutschland*, ECLI:EU:C:2013:520, para. 48.

The *Polisario* case has been appealed by the Council, and the CJEU in its Grand Chamber judgment reversed the General Court's decision on jurisdictional grounds *ratione loci*, as they did not accept that Article 92 of the Agreement (on the territorial application of the Agreement) could be interpreted to include Western Sahara because of the principle of self-determination as expressed in Article 73 of the Charter of the United Nations and United Nations General Assembly Resolution 1514 (XV).[81] The Advocate General and the Court rejected the General Court's contention that the status of Western Sahara was contested, arguing instead that it was clearly a third party for the purpose of, amongst others, the Vienna Convention of the Law of Treaties. It should be noted that the *de facto* application of the Agreement to the territory of Western Sahara is acknowledged by the Council and as such recorded by the Court. However, the Court decided the focus exclusively on whether the Agreement applied to the territory as a matter of treaty interpretation, allowing the wilful ambiguity of the interpretative process to determine the behaviour of the parties. By accepting that international law prevents the applicability of the Agreement to Western Sahara, the Court sidestepped the substantive issue of obligations of the EU with respect to international human rights standards under EU law, at the same time raising the visibility of non-commercial standards in the conclusion of trade agreements.[82] All the same, the continued *de facto* application of the Agreement to Western Sahara seems now out of the question; equally, an amendment to the Agreement to explicitly include Western Sahara to the territory over which it applies would run counter both the CJEU's argument on the self-determination of the Sahrawi People, and the General Court's argument on the necessity to consider the human rights dimension of the Agreement.

6 Concluding Remarks

The constitutionalization of the EU legal space has been accompanied by a parallel constitutionalization of its external action. As an international actor, the EU is bound by a set of principles that provide the ethical framework for the harmonisation, liberalisation and promotion of trade and investment on the international plane. Democracy, the rule of law and fundamental human rights provide the basic constitutional framework; good governance, sustainability, environmental protection, human security and peaceful international relations are the objectives derived from the framework values of Article 21(1). Article 21 TEU binds the EU *qua* international actor and provides the legal basis for the incorporation of non-commercial objectives in international agreements entered with third parties under the CCP.

[81]CJEU, case C-104/16 P, *Council v Front Polisario*, ECLI:EU:C:2016:973.

[82]See Gehring M, EU Court Sidesteps Human Rights in Western Sahara, 26 December 2016, https://www.cigionline.org/articles/eu-court-sidesteps-human-rights-western-sahara (last accessed 1 March 2017).

The binding force of Article 21 on the one side (for the EU) and of the corresponding provisions in the international agreements, on the other side (for the parties to the agreement and in the second instance for the EU, given the practically non-reciprocal nature of many of these instruments) is distributed along a scale, in accordance with the language used (from soft law exhortations to hard law obligations) and the available remedies (from judicial resolution to arbitration, with or without damages).

The inclusion of Article 21 TEU, and its linkage with Article 3 TEU, has been heralded as signifier of a new, bolder role for the EU in the constitutionalization of fundamental principles at the EU level and their projection on the international plane, and also as a possible guarantee for increased policy coherence in the EU's external action.[83] At the same time, this development has been singled out as both not going far enough, in the absence of a clear distribution of competences in the matter of the EU's external action, and as presenting the risk of "politicisation" of the EU's CCP. I have already noted the reductionist meaning given to this term. To the extent that politics is about power and conflicts for the attribution of power,[84] it is obvious that there is nothing *apolitical* about the role granted to free trade, the market and private investment in the EU—these approaches can only be deemed apolitical insofar as conflicts on these decisions have been either excluded from the EU legal system or have already been settled.[85] The introduction of non-commercial objectives in the CCP does not mean its "politicisation" *tout-court*, but more simply, the re-opening of the political space, more clearly by the involvement of the European Parliament as co-legislator, where decisions on priorities and objectives are made. Equally, non-commercial objectives, and specifically human rights, have been seen as subordinated to the main, constitutional, objectives of trade liberalisation and (now) investment protection: their ancillary role makes them at least implicitly seen as exceptions to the norm (implicitly to the extent that they are not conceptualised as exceptions according to the Article XX GATT model), especially in the pre-Lisbon framework, but arguably with spill-over effects post-Lisbon.[86]

The inclusion of FDI in the competences of the EU post-Lisbon is bound to have repercussions in the pursuance of Article 21 TEU's objectives, given the heavier footprint that investment has, in comparison to trade, in the regulatory powers of the host State.[87] A common complaint in the investment community, and the cause of

[83]See Blockmans and Russack (2015), p. 2.

[84]The seminar work of Luhmann on social systems is here relevant, and his description of the political system's binary code power/no power, see Luhmann (1996) and more specifically Luhmann (1990), pp. 167–186.

[85]See Hoffmeister (2011).

[86]Kube (2016), p. 17.

[87]The potential conflict between the protection and promotion of foreign investment (especially in the context of environmental regulation) has generated considerable literature; see Mann H, Investment agreements and the regulatory state: can exception clauses create safe havens for governments? 2007, http://www.iisd.org/pdf/2007/inv_agreements_reg_state.pdf (last accessed

much reflection on its supposed legitimacy crisis, is precisely on the erosion of the regulatory powers in non-commercial matters, in itself the cause of a "backlash" against investment, and especially its much-maligned dispute settlement system.[88] Article 21 TEU, by introducing non-commercial objectives, presents the potential of aligning the objectives of investment agreements with the regulatory activity of the host State. Its harmonising potential is as yet untested and its coming into force has coincided with a crisis in the investment regime, the consequences of which still have to play out. To the extent that the harmonisation of objectives will not 'work its magic', and actual conflicts might materialise, the usual avenue of proportionality balancing, when the discretionary power granted to the Member States turned out to be insufficient to guarantee the harmonisation of the objectives, will be available to the Court. If the decision of the General Court in the *Front Polisario* case is followed for what concerns the merits, substantive review and application of proportionality will not be necessary, to the extent that the Court is satisfied with the procedural requirement of conducting an impact assessment of the trade agreement on the non-commercial objectives in question[89]—in that case, on the rights protected by the Charter of Fundamental Rights,[90] but one does not see why the Court would not be inclined to use similar reasoning where Article 21 TEU is concerned. The reversal of the judgment of the General Court on jurisdictional grounds is an unwelcome distraction in this regard. Whether the reasoning of the General Court will be followed in other cases where the application of the FTA in question is not controversial, remains to be seen.

References

Alschner W (2013) Americanization of the BIT universe: the influence of friendship, commerce and navigation (FCN) treaties on modern investment treaty law. Goettingen J Int Law 5(2):455–486

Alston P, Weiler JH (1998) An 'Ever Closer Union' in need of a human rights policy. Eur J Int Law 9(4):658–723

Andenas M, Bjorge E (2015) Farewell to fragmentation – reassertion and convergence in international law. Cambridge University Press, Cambridge

Bartels L (2005) Human rights conditionality in the EU's international agreements. Oxford University Press, Oxford

1 March 2017); Orrego Vicuña (2003); OECD, "Indirect expropriation" and the "right to regulate" in international investment law, OECD Working Papers on International Investment 2004/04; Wälde and Kolo (2001). See also Waincymer (2009), Schill (2011), Ortino (2013), Roberts (2013), Subedi (2012) and Sornarajah (2015).

[88]Waibel et al. (2010).

[89]The obligation to conduct impact assessment for trade and investment deals, more specifically in the area of human rights, has been recognised repeatedly; see for example, European Commission, Towards a comprehensive European international investment policy, COM (2010) 343 final.

[90]GC, case T-512/12, *Front Polisario v Council*, ECLI:EU:T:2015:953, paras. 242–247.

Bianchi A, Peat D, Windsor M (2015) Interpretation in international law. Oxford University Press, Oxford

Blockmans S, Russack S (2015) The commissioner's group on external action – key political facilitator. CEPS special report No. 125

Broberg M, Holdgaard R (2015) Demarcating the Union's development cooperation policy after Lisbon: Commission v Council (Philippines PCFA). Common Mark Law Rev 52(2):547–567

Bungenberg M (2010) Going global? The EU common commercial policy after Lisbon. In: Herrmann C, Terhechte J (eds) European yearbook of international economic law, vol 2. Springer, Heidelberg, pp 87–106

Bungenberg M (2011) The division of competences between the EU and its member states in the area of investment politics. In: Bungenberg M, Griebel J, Hindelang S (eds) European yearbook of international economic law. Special Issue: International investment law and eu law. Springer, Heidelberg, pp 29–42

Burgstaller M (2009) European law and investment treaties. J Int Arbitr 26(2):181–216

Burgstaller M (2010) The future of bilateral investment treaties of EU member states. In: Bungenberg M, Griebel J, Hindelang S (eds) Internationaler Investitionsschutz und Europarecht. Nomos, Baden-Baden, pp 113–138

Cass D (2005) The constitutionalization of the World Trade Organization. Oxford University Press, Oxford

Christiansen C, Reh C (2009) Constitutionalizing the European Union. Palgrave, London

Cremona M, Hilpold P, Lavranos N, Staiger Schneider S, Ziegler A (2013) Reflections on the constitutionalisation of international economic law. Brill, Leiden

De Wet E (2012) The constitutionalization of public international law. In: Rosenfeld M, Sajó A (eds) The Oxford handbook of comparative constitutional law. Oxford University Press, Oxford, pp 1209–1230

Dederer HG (2013) The common commercial policy under the influence of the commission, council, high representative and European external action service. In: Bungenberg M, Herrmann C (eds) European yearbook of international economic law. Special Issue: Common commercial policy after Lisbon, pp 87–106

Dimopoulos A (2010) The effects of the Lisbon treaty on the principles and objectives of the common commercial policy. Eur Foreign Aff Rev 15(2):153–170

Dimopoulos A (2011) EU foreign investment Law. Oxford University Press, Oxford

Douma WT, van der Velde S (2016) Protection of fundamental rights in third countries through EU external trade policy: the cases of conflict minerals and timber. In: Paulussen C et al (eds) Fundamental rights in international and European law: public and private law perspectives. Springer, The Hague, pp 101–122

Dworkin R (1967) The model of rules. Yale Law School, Faculty Scholarship Series Paper 3609

Dworkin R (1997) Taking rights seriously. Bloomsbury, London/New York

Fina S, Lentner GM (2016) The scope of the EU's investment competence. Santa Clara J Int Law 14:419–440

Habermas J (2008) The constitutionalization of international law and the legitimation problems of a constitution for a world society. Constellations 15(4):444–455

Habermas J (2012) The crisis of the European Union in the light of the constitutionalization of international law. Eur J Int Law 23(2):335–348

Hachez N (2015) Essential elements clauses in EU trade agreements making trade work in a way that helps human rights? Leuven Centre for Global Governance Studies, Working Paper 158

Hilpold P (2015) Understanding solidarity within EU law: an analysis of the "islands of solidarity" with particular regard to monetary union. Yearb Eur Law 34(1):257–285

Hindelang S (2011) Member state BITs – there's still (some) life in the old dog yet: incompatibility of existing member states BITs with EU law and possible remedies – a position paper. In: Sauvant K (ed) Yearbook of international investment law & policy 2010/2011. Oxford University Press, Oxford, pp 217–242

Hindelang S, Krajewski M (2016) Shifting paradigms in international investment law: more balanced, less isolated, increasingly diversified. Oxford University Press, Oxford
Hoffmeister F (2011) The European Union's common commercial policy a year after Lisbon - Sea change or business as usual? In: Koutrakos P (ed) The European Union's external relations a year after Lisbon. CLEER Working Paper 3
Klabbers J, Peters A, Ulfstein G (2009) The constitutionalization of international law. Oxford University Press, Oxford
Krajewski M (2012) The reform of the common commercial policy. In: Biondi A, Eeckhout P (eds) European Union law after the treaty of Lisbon. Oxford University Press, Oxford, pp 292–311
Krajewski M (2013) New functions and new powers for the European Parliament: assessing the changes of the common commercial policy from the perspective of democratic legitimacy. In: Bungenberg M, Herrmann C (eds) European yearbook of international economic law. Special Issue: Common commercial policy after Lisbon, pp 67–86
Kube V (2016) The European Union's external human rights commitment: what is the legal value of article 21 TEU?. European University Institute Working Papers 2016/10
Lenk H (2015) Challenging the notion of coherence in EU foreign investment policy. Eur J Leg Stud 8(2):6–20
Luhmann N (1990) Political theory in the welfare state. De Gruyter, Berlin/New York
Luhmann N (1996) Social systems. Stanford University Press, Stanford
Maydell N (2007) The European Community's minimum platform on investment or the Trojan horse of investment competence. In: Reinisch A, Knahr C (eds) International investment law in context. Eleven International Publishing, The Hague, pp 73–92
Morin JF, Novotná T, Ponjaert F, Telò M (2015) The politics of transatlantic trade negotiations: TTIP in a globalized world. Ashgate, Farnham
Orrego Vicuña F (2003) Regulatory authority and legitimate expectations: balancing the rights of the state and the individual under international law in a global Society. Int Law Forum du droit international 5(3):188–197
Ortino F (2013) The investment treaty system as judicial review. Am Rev Int Arbitr 24(3):437–468
Peers S (2000) Fragmentation or evasion in the Community's development policy? The impact of Portugal v. Council. In: Dashwood A, Hillion C (eds) The general law of E.C. external relations. Sweet & Maxwell, London, pp 100–112
Petersmann EU (2013) Integrating human rights into EU trade relations – the EU as a global role model?. In: Takács T, Ott A, Dimopoulos A (eds) Linking trade and non-commercial interests: the EU as a global role model? CLEER Working Paper 4, pp 15–26
Rasmussen M (2014) Revolutionizing European law: a history of the Van Gend en Loos judgment. Int J Constit Law 12(1):136–163
Reinisch A (2014) The EU on the investment path – Quo Vadis Europe? The future of EU BITs and other investment agreements. Santa Clara J Int Law 12(1):111–157
Rittberger B, Schimmelfenning F (2007) The constitutionalization of the European Union. Routledge, London/New York
Robé JP, Lyon-Caen A, Vernac S (2016) Multinationals and the constitutionalization of the world power system. Routledge, London/New York
Roberts A (2013) Clash of paradigms: actors and analogies shaping the investment treaty system. Am J Int Law 107:45–94
Schiavello A (2001) On "consistency" and "law": an analysis of different models. Ratio Juris 14(2):233–243
Schill S (2011) Enhancing international investment law's legitimacy: conceptual and methodological foundation of a new public law approach. Va J Int Law 52(1):57–102
Schneiderman D (2008) Constitutionalizing economic globalization: investment rules and democracy's premise. Cambridge University Press, Cambridge
Söderlund C (2007) Intra-EU BIT investment protection and the EC treaty. J Int Arbitr 24(5):455–468

Sornarajah M (2015) Resistance and change in the international law of foreign investment. Cambdrige University Press, Cambridge

Subedi S (2012) International investment law: reconciling policy and principle. Hart, Oxford/ Portland

Thompson GF (2012) The constitutionalizion of the global corporate sphere? Oxford University Press, Oxford

Timmermans C (2001) The constitutionalization of the European Union. Yearb Eur Law 21(1): 1–11

Vedder C (2013) Linkage of the common commercial policy to the general objectives for the Union's external action. In: Bungenberg M, Herrmann C (eds) European yearbook of international economic law. Special Issue: Common commercial policy after Lisbon. Springer, Heidelberg, pp 115–144

Waibel M, Kaushal A, Chung KH, Balchin C (2010) The backlash against investment arbitration: perceptions and reality. Kluwer Law International, Alphen aan den Rijn

Waincymer J (2009) Balancing property rights and human rights in expropriation. In: Dupuy M, Francioni F, Petersmann EU (eds) Human rights in international investment law and arbitration. Oxford University Press, Oxford, pp 275–309

Wälde T (2009) Interpreting investment treaties: experiences and examples. In: Binder C, Kriebaum U, Reinisch A, Wittich S (eds) International investment law for the 21st century: essays in honour of Christoph Schreuer. Oxford University Press, Oxford, pp 724–781

Wälde T, Kolo A (2001) Environmental regulation, investment protection and "regulatory taking" in international law. Int Compar Law Q 50(4):811–848

Wierzbowski M, Gubrynowicz A (2009) Conflict of norms stemming from intra-EU BITs and EU legal obligations: some remarks on possible solutions. In: Binder C, Kriebaum U, Reinisch A, Wittich S (eds) International investment law for the 21st century: essays in honour of Christoph Schreuer. Oxford University Press, Oxford, pp 544–560

The Perception of the EU Legal Order in International Law: An In- and Outside View

Christina Binder and Jane A. Hofbauer

Abstract The EU is a strange phenomenon, whether regarded from the perspective of international or domestic law. It evokes many questions on the relationship of its legal order with international law and domestic law, respectively. Despite the increasing trend by the CJEU to emphasize the EU's autonomy—both, internally and externally—, from an international law perspective, there is no reason to *per se* "detach" the EU from the international legal framework. This is in part also evident in how international dispute settlement bodies address questions touching upon the EU legal order and its relation to international law. This contribution focuses on the nature of the EU legal order as designated by international dispute settlement bodies, and particularly its relationship with the international legal order. On the basis of examples from four different fields—general international law, trade law, human rights law and investment law—, theoretical, jurisdictional and substantive reconciliatory techniques are identified. In particular, it is shown that the classification of the EU legal order as a subsystem of international law, as a *de facto* domestic order or as a *sui generis* legal order predetermines which conflict rules and reconciliatory techniques find application.

Contents

C. Binder • J.A. Hofbauer (✉)
Department of European, International and Comparative Law, University of Vienna, Wien, Austria
e-mail: christina.binder@univie.ac.at; jane.alice.hofbauer@univie.ac.at

M. Bungenberg et al. (eds.), *European Yearbook of International Economic Law 2017*, European Yearbook of International Economic Law 8,
DOI 10.1007/978-3-319-58832-2_6

1 Introduction

The EU[1] is a strange phenomenon, whether regarded from the perspective of international or domestic law, and evokes many questions on the relationship of its legal order with international law and domestic law, respectively.[2] Its placement in the spectrum of legal orders—i.e. as an international legal order, domestic legal order or as a *sui generis* legal order—determines the means and techniques of interaction available to judicial bodies. For the purpose of such determination, an inside and an outside view may be distinguished, i.e. the EU's self-perception and approaches of international dispute settlement bodies.

The EU's self-perception of its legal order is strongly influenced by the Court of Justice of the European Union (CJEU) which laid the basis early on in *van Gend en Loos*, stating that "the Community constitutes a *new legal order of international law*".[3] Similarly, in *Costa*, EU law is defined as "an independent source of law".[4] This (self-)understanding underscores the relationship of the EU legal order with regard to both, international law (external autonomy) and the legal orders of its member states (internal autonomy).[5] Though these two aspects of autonomy operate distinctly, they are also closely interlinked. Hence, the greater the EU's internal autonomy becomes (i.e. the more independent of its member states its decisions are taken), the more external autonomy will be sought (i.e. the EU will seek "to protect and preserve its institutional autonomy from *external* influences"[6]). This has become quite apparent in the case-law of the CJEU which has been termed "selfish"[7] or "rather unfriendly"[8] with regard to the manner in which it seeks to remain the sole instance for interpreting EU law.[9] Additionally, over the years, the

[1]In this contribution, the terms "EU"/"EU law" are also used when technically referring to the "European Community" or to "European Community law", except when quoting. "CJEU" is also used when referring to the "ECJ" (in its pre-Lisbon set-up).

[2]Cf. Klabbers (2015), pp. 52–71.

[3]CJEU, case 26/62, *van Gend en Loos*, ECLI:EU:C:1963:1 (emphasis added).

[4]CJEU, case 6/64, *Costa v E.N.E.L.*, ECLI:EU:C:1964:66.

[5]Odermatt (2016).

[6]Odermatt (2016), p. 5.

[7]De Witte (2014a), p. 33.

[8]De Witte (2010), p. 150.

[9]Hence, in this sense, Article 344 TFEU (exclusive jurisdiction) prevents international litigation between EU member states on matters that fall within the EU's (shared or exclusive) competence.

CJEU's standpoint on the interpretation of EU law has become very autonomist, extending its exclusive jurisdiction beyond the wording of its mandate.[10]

However, this internal viewpoint is not necessarily respected by international dispute settlement bodies,[11] raising concerns on the question of harmonious interpretation of EU provisions, and even being termed "the greatest threat to the autonomy of the EU legal order and of the Court of Justice itself".[12] From an international law perspective, there is no reason to *per se* "detach" the EU from the international legal framework. As *Simma* and *Pulkowski* point out,

> [t]he continuous assertion of the Community's *sui generis* character [. . .] does not by itself create an 'own legal order'. From a public international law perspective, the EC legal system remains a subsystem of international law.[13]

As will be shown, this is in part also evident in how international dispute settlement bodies address questions touching upon the EU legal order and its relation to international law.

Through the EU's participation in international dispute settlement mechanisms, either as a party or (non-disputing) third party, there is ample evidence to investigate the reach of these two diametrical positions, with the interrelationship between international law and EU law being far from settled. In light of this, this contribution will therefore focus on the nature of the EU legal order, and particularly its relationship with the international legal order.

In doing so, the contribution will begin with analysing the internal perspective of the EU, i.e. the (international) institutional framework of the EU and how the EU (especially the CJEU) presents itself and its legal order when engaging with other international regimes.[14] It will then contrast this with the manner in which international dispute settlement mechanisms in various fields treat the EU legal order. This is divided into four areas, each possessing distinct characteristics as to the role the EU plays within each field: first, general international law, where several rule-complexes overlap; second, the WTO/GATT system as exemplary of a setting where the EU is a party in its own right; third, the European human rights system,

---

See also CJEU, case C-459/03, *Commission v Ireland (MOX Plant)*, ECLI:EU:C:2006:345, paras. 93 and 123.

[10]See, inter alia, CJEU, case 181/73, *Haegeman v Belgium*, ECLI:EU:C:1974:41, para. 5.

[11]Parish (2012), p. 142.

[12]Eckes (2013), p. 86.

[13]Simma and Pulkowski (2006), p. 516. Similarly, also *Interpretation of the Agreement of 25 March 1951 Between the WHO and Egypt*, 1980 ICJ 73, Advisory Opinion (20 December 1980), para. 37: "[T]here is nothing in the character of international organizations to justify their being considered as some form of 'super-State' [. . .]. International organizations are subjects of international law and, as such, are bound by any obligations incumbent upon them under general rules of international law, under their constitutions or under international agreements to which they are parties."

[14]The EU's strive for greater autonomy primarily rests on two main features of EU law: the primacy of EU law and the exclusive jurisdiction of the CJEU. As shown, these also become apparent in the CJEU's case-law.

where all EU member states are party to the European Convention of Human Rights (ECHR), but the EU has so far not become a party; and fourth, the field of investment law (both in regards to the Energy Charter Treaty (ECT) and intra-EU BITs), where arbitral tribunals have shown different approaches in their treatment of the EU legal order.

The analysis of these four areas evidences that how international law and how specific fields of international law (specialized subsystems of international law[15]) interact with the EU legal order depends on a number of factors. In particular, the classification of the EU legal order as a subsystem of international law, as a *de facto* domestic order or as a *sui generis* legal order predetermines which conflict rules and reconciliatory techniques find application.

2 Regime Interaction: International Law and EU Law from a European Perspective

The interaction between international and EU law raises a number of questions which are not easily answered, particularly in relation to the multi-layered nature of the EU. The EU's position in international law has never definitely been settled and its position has arguably changed over the years. Most commonly, from an international law perspective, the EU is classified as a (supranational) international organization, i.e. an international organization which is embedded in international law by virtue of its founding instruments,[16] but in many aspects is more advanced or different than other international organizations.[17] The classification through the lens of international law as an international organization, based on treaties, strongly influences its relationship with other international law regimes.[18]

However, though European integration can be traced to a series of treaty amendments,[19] some merit must be given to the EU's self-perception as a *sui generis* entity. As the former CJEU judge *Federico Mancini* formulated it in 1998:

> [I]nsisting on defining it as an international organisation and describing all that does not fit well with this definition as 'frills and rhetorics' is much like trying to push the toothpaste back into the tube. Those who indulge in such an exercise are either die-hard acolytes of the neo-realist school in political science, eager to prove that any further progress on the part of the Union will falter in the face of unsurmountable barriers, or professors of international law anxious to maintain their hold on a luscious province increasingly coveted by constitutional lawyers.[20]

[15]For further reference see, inter alia, Simma and Pulkowski (2006).

[16]See Curtin and Dekker (2011), p. 163 et seqq.; Ziegler (2013), p. 3.

[17]Bengoetxea (2011), p. 449; Klabbers (2016), p. 3 et seq.; De Witte (2014b), p. 174; Wessel (2013), p. 134.

[18]In this regard see particularly Sect. 3 and the portrayal of the EU legal order by international judicial bodies.

[19]De Witte (2014b), p. 178 terms this the "treaty path towards European integration".

[20]Federico Mancini (1998), p. 31 (footnotes omitted).

The EU manifests its *sui generis* character especially in a strive for greater (internal and external) autonomy. This strive for greater autonomy directs attention to the question of whether the primacy of EU law and the CJEU's exclusive jurisdiction have any bearing on the qualification of the EU legal order. In its report on fragmentation of international law, the International Law Commission (ILC) Study Group—speaking about "regionalism"—references the EU as a "special kind of legal order between the Member States".[21] It points out the difficulties arising for third states in that the EU appears in a number of different roles on the international scene and that the division of competences is often difficult to grasp from an outside perspective.[22] Still, despite also containing "special secondary rules having to do with [. . .] [the] settlement of disputes", it concludes that the EU's legal system does not exist as an "isolated legal [system] on a regional basis."[23] Rather, as the report continues, the manner in which these legal systems interact must "be ascertained on a case-by-case basis [. . .] by bearing in mind the 'systemic' nature of the law of which they all form a part."

In this sense, the following briefly introduces the framework under which the EU operates within international law. This also pays special regard to the two distinct EU features fostering autonomy, i.e. the primacy of EU law and the role of the CJEU (Sect. 2.1). Based thereupon, a number of examples are portrayed from a European perspective (Sect. 2.2).[24] The examples are discussed both in light of arguments made by the European Commission in (self-)representation of the EU in the international legal order and by consideration of the CJEU's self-assessment of the EU legal order.

2.1 *The EU as an Object of International Law and the Nature of Its Legal Order*

The EU treaties are silent on the specific nature of the EU.[25] However, the broad competences of the EU, paired with an advanced decision-making and compliance

[21]ILC, Fragmentation of International Law: Difficulties Arising From the Diversification and Expansion of International Law—Report of the Study Group of the International Law Commission, 13 April 2006, UN Doc. A/CN.4/L.682, para. 218.

[22]ILC, Fragmentation of International Law: Difficulties Arising From the Diversification and Expansion of International Law—Report of the Study Group of the International Law Commission, 13 April 2006, UN Doc. A/CN.4/L.682, para. 219.

[23]ILC, Fragmentation of International Law: Difficulties Arising From the Diversification and Expansion of International Law—Report of the Study Group of the International Law Commission, 13 April 2006, UN Doc. A/CN.4/L.682, para. 221.

[24]Section 3 will provide examples from an international law perspective.

[25]Art. 1 TEU reads: "By the Treaty, the HIGH CONTRACTING PARTIES establishing among themselves a EUROPEAN UNION, hereinafter called 'the Union', on which the Member States confer competences to attain objectives they have in common." It does not clarify whether the EU

process, and in part the EU's state-like features (currency, citizenship) are some of the most obvious reasons for a distinct understanding of the EU legal order from an internal perspective.[26] One particularly important feature is the primacy of EU law in relation to national law,[27] i.e. those norms which have direct effect prevail over national law,[28] letting some scholars—and even the CJEU[29]—describe the EU as an "embryonic federation"[30] or constitutional system where the "Community [. . .] behaves as if its founding instrument were [. . .] a constitutional charter governed by a form of constitutional law".[31] Moreover, from an EU perspective, the principle of supremacy/primacy[32] also applies in regard to international law, i.e. international law that has become an integral part of the Community legal order is below primary EU law, but above secondary law.[33] This understanding "detaches" the EU legal order from the international legal system, and deviates from the horizontal structure

---

is an international organization or some other legal construct. Art. 47 TEU accords the EU legal personality ("The Union shall have legal personality"). On a similar line of argumentation see Wessel (2013), p. 132.

[26]See also De Witte (2014b), pp. 183–185; Wessel (2013), p. 135 et seqq.; von Bogdandy (2008), p. 399.

[27]On the normative quality of the EU's secondary law being the decisive "breaking point" from ordinary forms of international organizations see Schütze (2012), pp. 15 and 61 et seq.

[28]See in more detail also De Witte (2011).

[29]CJEU, opinion 1/91, *European Economic Area*, ECLI:EU:C:1991:490, para. 21: "[T]he [EU] Treaty, albeit concluded in the form of an international agreement, none the less constitutes the constitutional charter of a Community based on the rule of law. As the Court of Justice has consistently held, the Community treaties established a new legal order for the benefit of which the States have limited their sovereign rights, in ever wider fields, and the subjects of which comprise not only Member States but also their nationals [. . .]. The essential characteristics of the Community legal order which has thus been established are in particular its primacy over the law of the Member States and the direct effect of a whole series of provisions which are applicable to their nationals and to the Member States themselves."

[30]Hartley (1996), p. 109.

[31]Weiler (1997), p. 97. However, though EU law in part enjoys direct effect, this ultimately stems from treaty obligations entered into by the contracting parties of the EU treaty framework. De Witte (2014b), p. 187. In contrast, at the international level there is no specific method mandated how to give international law effect in national law and it is up to each and every state to ensure compliance of their national system with their international obligations. Crawford (2012), p. 48 et seq.; *Greco-Bulgarian Communities*, Advisory Opinion, 1930 PCIJ (ser. B) No. 17 (31 July 1930), para. 81.

[32]Though often a question of semantics, supremacy is understood as the further-reaching conceptual tool to describe the hierarchical relationship stemming from the EU legal order whereas primacy is a rule of conflict resolution applied in favour in the EU's legal system. See in more detail Avbelj (2011).

[33]Lavranos (2006a), p. 232. This stems from Art. 218(11) TFEU: "A Member State, the European Parliament, the Council or the Commission may obtain the opinion of the Court of Justice as to whether an agreement envisaged is compatible with the Treaties. Where the opinion of the Court is adverse, the agreement envisaged may not enter into force unless it is amended or the Treaties are revised."

generally applicable between different international tribunals operating at the same level without hierarchy.[34]

To ensure respect for this principle, the EU framework has resorted to particular instruments. For example, Article 351 TFEU (former Article 307 TEC) provides guidance to states which had entered into an international agreement with third states *prior* to their accession to the EU which was/is incompatible with their obligations arising from the EU Treaties. In such circumstances,—while the agreements with third states remain in force due to the principle of *pacta sunt servanda*—member states "shall take all appropriate steps to eliminate the incompatibilities established." The provision respects the confines of international law. Still, it has been argued that it "first and foremost aims to strike a balance between the protection of anterior treaties, and the integrity of Europe's integration process [...] based on the idea that the EC Treaty is somehow superior to the anterior treaty".[35]

Possible instruments exist also for conflicts between international agreements and the EU Treaties in cases where a state has concluded an international agreement *after* it has become an EU member state. Here, the EU's interest to carve out a special position for its legal order in part is evident in treaty practice, e.g., through the use of the so-called disconnection clause[36] or the "conditioned territorial application clause".[37] Both instruments aim at ensuring the primacy of EU law over international agreements on a substantive level. Nevertheless, they are in line with international law since they do so by explicit incorporation of the "carve-out position" into the agreement in question.

The second decisive feature of relevance in this regard is the exclusive jurisdiction of the CJEU, making the special nature of the EU legal order particularly palpable. In contrast to the abovementioned treaty mechanisms aimed at ensuring

---

[34]See also Sect. 4.1 in more detail.

[35]Cf. Klabbers (2009), pp. 118, 122. See, e.g., CJEU, case 10/61, *Commission v Italy*, ECLI:EU:C:1962:2, p. 10: "In fact, in matters governed by the EEC Treaty, that Treaty takes precedence over agreements concluded between Member States before its entry into force [...]." This approach shifts even clearer in favour of hierarchically superior EU law where an international agreement between two states is concerned which later both are EU member states. In such instances, Article 351 TFEU does not apply and the CJEU has held that the multilateral or bilateral agreement in question cannot be invoked in their *inter se* relations. Klabbers (2009), p. 125 et seqq., with references to case-law. Note, however, that this is an obligation of EU law—not international law—and that therefore international dispute settlement bodies located outside the EU framework are free to arrive at a different conclusion. See particularly the Sect. 3.4 on investment law in this context.

[36]A disconnection clause often provides that the treaty will only apply to relations between non-EU members or between an EU member and a non-EU member, but not between EU members *inter se*. In such a case, EU law will be applicable. See in more detail Klabbers (2009), pp. 219–223, also addressing the criticisms linked to the disconnection clause, particularly the risk of further fragmenting the international legal order.

[37]Typically, this clause specifies that, in relations with treaty partners, the treaty shall be applied for the European Union, under the conditions set out in EU law. As Klabbers observes, "[t]hat is a fairly innocuous-sounding statement, but still manages to disconnect Community law from the workings of such treaty." Klabbers (2009), p. 224.

the primacy of the EU legal order, the strong stand of the CJEU bears potential for (jurisdictional) conflicts with (other) international dispute settlement bodies. In fact, the EU has equipped the CJEU with extensive jurisdictional powers to ensure the consistent application and interpretation on matters of EU law throughout the EU.[38] In exercise of its mandate, the CJEU functions both as an inter-state (international) court exercising jurisdiction over EU law and international agreements entered into by the EU (particularly derived from Articles 259[39] and 344 TFEU[40]) and in a manner similar to a domestic supreme court (through the preliminary rulings procedure as contained in Article 267 TFEU[41]).[42] As will be shown below, the CJEU has interpreted Article 344 TFEU extensively and in a way as to create possible norm conflicts with other regimes. In particular, the CJEU—in order to safeguard the autonomy of the EU legal order—has considered its jurisdiction to be exclusive, also extending beyond Article 344 TFEU's wording ("the Treaties") to any interpretation/application of the EU legal order or international agreements entered into, even where mixed agreements are concerned.[43] Though it is not entirely settled whether this also covers those parts of mixed agreements which fall outside of the EU's competence, the CJEU has argued that in light of

[38]Article 19(1) TEU defines the CJEU's role as the EU's judiciary arm, stipulating that "[t]he Court of Justice of the European Union [. . .] shall ensure that in the interpretation and application of the Treaties the law is observed."

[39]Art. 259 TFEU: "A Member State which considers that another Member State has failed to fulfil an obligation under the Treaties may bring the matter before the Court of Justice of the European Union."

[40]Art. 344 TFEU: "Member States undertake not to submit a dispute concerning the interpretation or application of the Treaties to any method of settlement other than those provided for therein."

[41]Art. 267 TFEU: "The Court of Justice of the European Union shall have jurisdiction to give preliminary rulings concerning: (a) the interpretation of the Treaties; (b) the validity and interpretation of acts of the institutions, bodies, offices or agencies of the Union; Where such a question is raised before any court or tribunal of a Member State, that court or tribunal may, if it considers that a decision on the question is necessary to enable it to give judgment, request the Court to give a ruling thereon. Where any such question is raised in a case pending before a court or tribunal of a Member State against whose decisions there is no judicial remedy under national law, that court or tribunal shall bring the matter before the Court. [. . .]".

[42]Cf. Lock (2015), p. 75 et seq.

[43]In *Haegeman*, the CJEU explained that agreements become integral parts of EU law, CJEU, case 181/73, *Haegeman v Belgium*, ECLI:EU:C:1974:41, para. 5. The extent of its exclusive jurisdiction was moreover clarified in the *MOX Plant* case which equated the scope of jurisdiction of Art. 344 TFEU with the scope under Article 267 TFEU, holding that the provisions of the international agreement which had become an integral part of the Community legal order gave rise to "a dispute concerning the interpretation or application of the EC Treaty, within the terms of [Article 344 TFEU]." CJEU, case C-459/03, *Commission v Ireland (MOX Plant)*, ECLI:EU:C:2006:345, para. 126 et seq.

"Community interest" and the "duty of cooperation" (as expressed in Article 4(3) TEU) it possessed such exclusive jurisdiction.[44] In this sense, the CJEU has long established its authority to "determine its own jurisdiction"[45] (*Kompetenz-Kompetenz*).[46]

Hence, by virtue of this mandate, the CJEU has not only developed the autonomous character of the EU[47] but perceives itself as entitled to define the nature of the EU legal order, particularly in interaction with other legal orders.[48] In this regard, as addressed in more detail in the following section, the CJEU positions itself as the supreme arbiter of questions of EU law and interprets EU law functionally as a self-contained regime separate from other fields of international law.[49]

Both features—the primacy of EU and the exclusive jurisdiction of the CJEU—are prone to create possible conflicts of jurisdiction with other areas of international law. In cases of overlapping jurisdiction, the nature of the EU legal order and its relationship to the international legal order will be a decisive preliminary point which will have to be answered. In particular, it predetermines which means of reconciliation can be applied between two potentially conflicting provisions.[50]

2.2 *Looking In: The Relationship Between International Law and EU Law—A European Perspective*

A European perspective on the relationship of the EU legal order with regard to international law (external autonomy)[51] partly sharply deviates from the horizontal

[44]On the aspect of "Community interest" see CJEU, case C-53/96, *Hermès International v FHT Marketing Choice*, ECLI:EU:C:1998:292, para. 32. More weight was placed on the "duty of close cooperation" in CJEU, case C-300/98, *Dior and others*, ECLI:EU:C:2000:688, para. 36.

[45]Lock (2015), p. 102.

[46]See, e.g., CJEU, case C-431/05, *Merck Genéricos Produtos Farmacêuticos*, ECLI:EU:C:2007:496, para. 33.

[47]Regarding the internal aspect of autonomy see CJEU, case 6/64, *Costa v E.N.E.L.*, ECLI:EU:C:1964:66, where the CJEU speaks about the EU legal order as "an independent source of law"; Externally, the autonomous character of the EU legal order can be traced back to CJEU, opinion 1/91, *European Economic Area*, ECLI:EU:C:1991:490, para. 40.

[48]De Witte (2014b), p. 179.

[49]See, inter alia, CJEU, opinion 2/13, *EU Accession to the ECHR*, ECLI:EU:C:2014:2454; Lock (2015), p. 159.

[50]See in regard Sect. 4.

[51]Odermatt (2016). Note that the aspect of institutional autonomy also applies to other international organizations but it has been accorded particular importance by the CJEU on a continuous basis. Collins and White (2011). See particularly the case-law following CJEU, case 26/62, *van Gend en Loos*, ECLI:EU:C:1963:1 and CJEU, case 6/64, *Costa v E.N.E.L.*, ECLI:EU:C:1964:66; CJEU, case 28/67, *Molkerei Zentrale Westfalen-Lippe v Hauptzollamt Paderborn*, ECLI:EU:C:1968:17. See also below Sect. 2.2.2.

system between international judicial bodies under international law. The EU's institutional autonomy has not only led to increasing independence of the EU from its member states but has resulted in a more active EU at the international level. The more frequent interactions of the EU with international law, particularly when the EU itself engages in international fora, provide the opportunity for the EU to display its internal perspective on the interplay between the international legal order and its own to the international community.

2.2.1 The EU Legal Order in Self-Representation

When the EU is represented in international proceedings, this is done so through the European Commission.[52] There are different possibilities for the EU to act before an international or foreign dispute settlement mechanism. They depend in particular on the EU's position in the respective judicial *fora*. More generally, the way of action in a particular case of the European Commission depends on many factors. While the Commission follows no entirely coherent pattern, important factors include, however, whether the EU itself is a direct party to the proceedings[53] and whether it exercises exclusive competence.

[52]Article 17(1) sixth sentence TEU; as confirmed by the CJEU in case C-73/14, *Council v European Commission*, ECLI:EU:C:2015:663, this is also based on Article 335 TFEU, which is understood as an "expression of a general principle that the European Union has legal capacity and is to be represented, to that end, by the Commission" (para. 58). Note, however, that the Commission's authority as regards external representation must be distinguished from the internal decision-making process on which position to adopt. For example, in said judgment, the Council of the European Union initiated proceedings against the Commission regarding its submission of a written statement to the International Tribunal for the Law of the Sea (ITLOS). The Council alleged an infringement of the principle of conferral of powers, the principle of institutional balance (Article 13(2) TEU), and of the principle of sincere cooperation, both as the position of the European Union should have been predetermined by a "decision [...] establishing the positions to be adopted on the Union's behalf in a body set up by an agreement" as adopted by the Council (Article 218(9) TFEU) and as the Council was responsible to "carry out policy-making and coordinating functions" (Article 16(1) TEU). The CJEU held in this regard that Article 218(9) TFEU did not find application in this context as it concerned positions to be taken *in* a body set up by an agreement and not *before* such a body (paras. 63–67). Additionally, as the statement did not formulate a policy in relation to the subject matter but presented rather a set of legal observations (para. 71), also Article 16(1) TEU was not relevant in this instance (para. 73).

[53]In fact, there are different possibilities for the EU to act before an international or foreign dispute settlement mechanism, ranging from being the sole party (This is particularly the case in the WTO, see https://www.wto.org/english/tratop_e/dispu_e/dispu_by_country_e.htm (last accessed 1 March 2017), but also occurs in other bodies, see, e.g., *Case Concerning the Conservation and Sustainable Exploitation of Swordfish Stocks in the South-Eastern Pacific Ocean (Chile v European Union)*, ITLOS Case No. 7 (withdrawn and removed from the list of cases through Order 2009/1 of 16 December 2009)), to acting alongside one or some of its member states (at present, this is only the case in isolated instances, e.g. Panel Report, *European Communities—Customs Classification of Certain Computer Equipment*, WT/DS62/R, WT/DS67/R, WT/DS68/R, 5 February 1998; a co-respondent mechanism was, however, foreseen in the Draft Agreement on the EU's accession

Where the European Commission submits arguments in proceedings to which it is not a direct party or where it does not exercise exclusive competence, it generally refers to itself/the EU as an international organization, albeit with special features. For example, before the ECtHR in *Bosphorus*, the European Commission's submission focused on the question which responsibility remained with its member states after they "had ceded powers to an *international organization*".[54] Also in its *amicus curiae* submission before the US Supreme Court in *Kiobel*, the European Commission referred to itself/the EU as a "treaty-based international organization with the competence to develop and enforce Union-wide legislation in specified areas and policy".[55] From this perspective, the EU represents itself as an international organization albeit with special features.

In contrast, submissions to proceedings where the European Commission feels that the matter falls within the exclusive competence of the EU focus much stronger on the specific nature of the EU legal order. As mentioned, there is no absolute uniform line of argumentation though. In this context, a particularly interesting relationship can be observed between the World Trade Organization (WTO) and the EU.[56] Not only does the EU generally speak for the EU member states in disputes arising within the WTO,[57] but—deriving from its exclusive competence—

to the ECHR), to filing *amicus curiae* submissions or intervening in some other way (for example, the European Commission filed an *amicus curiae* submission in foreign jurisdictions (*Kiobel v Royal Dutch Petroleum*, Supreme Court of the United States of America, 13 June 2012), or in front of international dispute settlement mechanisms. It has done so, e.g., before the ECtHR as a third party (Article 36(2) ECHR, 4 November 1950, 213 UNTS 222) in *Bosphorus* (No. 45036/98) or *Senator Lines* (No. 56672/00), or as a non-disputing party in ICSID proceedings (Rule 37 (2) ICSID), e.g., in *Electrabel* (ICSID Case No. ARB/07/19) or *Micula* (ICSID Case No. ARB/05/20)). The EU may also delegate the representation to one of its member states in case of a dispute arising in an international organization where it does not have any formal status. See in this regard, e.g., the Statement of Ireland on Behalf of the European Union (30 January 2004) in *Legal Consequences of the Construction of a Wall in the Occupied Palestinian Territory*, 2004 ICJ 136, Advisory Opinion (9 July 2004).

[54]ECtHR, No. 45036/98, *Bosphorus v Ireland*, Judgment of 30 June 2005, para. 122 (emphasis added). A few lines later, the "special features" were taken as the basis for referring to the "equivalent protection approach" which it considered particularly important in the context of the EU "given its distinctive features of supranationality and the nature of Community law" (para. 124).

[55]*Kiobel v Royal Dutch Petroleum*, Supreme Court of the United States of America, 13 June 2012, 1.

[56]The common commercial policy constitutes one of the exclusive competences of the EU and "was originally the core of the EU's external relations powers". Kuijper et al. (2015), p. 295; Article 207 TFEU.

[57]For example, the EU has appeared in 97 cases as complainant, in 82 as respondent and in 158 as third party. See https://www.wto.org/english/tratop_e/dispu_e/dispu_by_country_e.htm (last accessed 1 March 2017). See also Hoffmeister (2012), pp. 88–90.

it has explicitly acknowledged its "responsibility in international law for the compliance by EC member States with the obligations of the EC under the WTO Agreements",[58] a construction which is also described as "executive federalism".[59] Hence, the functional understanding of the EU within the WTO results to a large degree in representation as a state-like construct with certain *sui generis* attributes.[60]

The EU's *sui generis* nature was also highlighted in the European Commission's recent *amicus curiae* submission to the US Court of Appeals regarding the enforcement of the *Micula* award.[61] Appearing before the US Court of Appeals, the Commission emphasized the EU being a "supranational organization" with a legal order which is characterized by "its primacy over the laws of the Member States [. . .]".[62] It also pointed out its strong interest in having the CJEU being the sole instance to decide on EU matters "and that other countries courts defer to these proceedings in the interests of comity."[63] It also drew parallels between intra-EU BITs and a scenario "in which New York and California conclude a bilateral investment treaty between themselves, which would be impermissible under federal law."[64] Thus, in front of a court of a foreign jurisdiction, the European Commission emphasized not only its specific characteristics (supranationality, primacy) but

[58]Panel Report, *European Communities—Selected Customs Matters*, WT/DS315/R, 16 June 2006, para. 4.708. This was accepted by the Panel, finding that "the European Communities may comply with its obligations [. . .] through organs in its member States" (para. 7.552 (referencing Article 4 of the Articles on Responsibility for States for Internationally Wrongful Acts)).

[59]See, inter alia, Delgado Casteleiro (2016), p. 178.

[60]This is particularly evident when viewing the manner how the European Commission has addressed the institutional nature of the CJEU. In *US-Zeroing Methodology*, when examining the principle of consistency and predictability of jurisprudence, the Commission addressed both, national and international legal systems, pointing out also the "sui generis character" of the EU's judicial system. Panel Report, *United States—Continued Existence and Application of Zeroing Methodology*, WT/DS350/R, 1 October 2008, para. 72, at fn. 67. In light thereof, it defined the CJEU as "a hybrid court—part constitutional court, part general national court of last instance" (para. 72). Its third party submission in *US-Final Anti-Dumping Measures on Stainless Steel from Mexico* addressed the same issue, again with a clear distinction between national and international legal systems. Here, the absence of its own jurisdiction among both categories is striking. Panel Report, *United States—Final Anti-Dumping Measures on Stainless Steel From Mexico*, WT/DS344/R, 20 December 2007, paras. 7.19–7.20.

[61]As dealt with extensively in Sect. 3.4 below, the question of intra-EU BITs is of special concern to the European Commission, and any implementation of an award obtained through proceedings initiated under such BITs would constitute state aid. (cf On 31 January 2014, the European Commission communicated to the Romanian authorities that the implementation or execution of the *Micula* award would constitute new state aid, see also Commission Decision (EU) 2015/1470 of 30 March 2015 on state aid SA.38617, OJ 2015 L 232/43.)

[62]*Micula v Romania*, US Court of Appeals (2nd Circ.), *Brief for Amicus Curiae the Commission of the European Union in Support of Defendant-Appellant*, 4 February 2016, p. 7.

[63]*Micula v Romania*, US Court of Appeals (2nd Circ.), *Brief for Amicus Curiae the Commission of the European Union in Support of Defendant-Appellant*, 4 February 2016, p. 11.

[64]*Micula v Romania*, US Court of Appeals (2nd Circ.), *Brief for Amicus Curiae the Commission of the European Union in Support of Defendant-Appellant*, 4 February 2016, p. 28.

correlated the EU with a federal system in an area where the EU exercises exclusive competence. This will be even further developed in CETA (and potentially TTIP), where EU law is considered as domestic law.[65]

Though not absolutely consistent, the arguments made by the European Commission in representation of the EU show its awareness of its international law background. Depending on the judicial *fora* concerned, or whether the European Commission considers a matter to fall within the EU's exclusive competences, special features of the EU legal order are emphasized.

2.2.2 The EU Legal Order in Self-Assessment/CJEU

The question of the relationship between the international and European legal order has likewise been addressed extensively by the CJEU, known for its broad powers and activism as regards the European process of integration. At first look, the case-law of the CJEU refrains from detaching the EU entirely from international law, acknowledging that the founding treaties are instruments of international law.[66] Though there have been instances where the CJEU has been confronted with arguments which would have moved it further from the realm of international law,[67] it has so far refrained from explicitly endorsing such opinions.

Still, the distinctness and autonomous nature of the EU legal order has been emphasized by the CJEU continuously, going back to its findings in *van Gend en Loos*, where the EU is described as "a new legal order of international law" and the EEC Treaty is held to be "more than an agreement which merely creates mutual obligations between the contracting states".[68] Additionally, as explained in *Costa*,

---

[65]Article 13(3) Commission draft text Transatlantic Trade and Investment Partnership—investment; Article 8.31(2) Comprehensive Economic and Trade Agreement (CETA) between Canada and the European Union.

[66]See, e.g., CJEU, case 6/64, *Costa v E.N.E.L.*, ECLI:EU:C:1964:66: "By contrast with ordinary international treaties, the EEC Treaty has created its own legal system [. . .]." See also CJEU, opinion 2/13, *EU Accession to the ECHR*, ECLI:EU:C:2014:2454, para. 157; cf. D'Aspremont and Dopagne (2008), p. 374.

[67]See, e.g., CJEU, case C-50/00 P, *Unión de Pequeños Agricultores v Council*, ECLI:EU:C:2002:462—opinion of AG Jacobs, ECLI:EU:C:2002:197, para. 78: "It may also be noted that although the European Communities originate in a set of Treaties concluded by the Member States in the context of public international law, the Community legal order has developed in such a way that it would no longer be accurate to describe it as a system of intergovernmental cooperation, nor would it be appropriate to describe the Court of Justice as an international tribunal."

[68]CJEU, case 26/62, *van Gend en Loos*, ECLI:EU:C:1963:1. Note, however, that the qualifier "of international law" was later dropped, see, e.g., CJEU, case 6/64, *Costa v E.N.E.L.*, ECLI:EU:C:1964:66; CJEU, case 28/67, *Molkerei Zentrale Westfalen-Lippe v Hauptzollamt Paderborn*, ECLI:EU:C:1968:17, p. 152.

the EU's legal order is one which is distinct both from international and national law.[69] Hence, following from the CJEU's conviction to be the sole instance to ensure the uniform application of EU law,[70] the CJEU has at times adopted "a strong constitutionalist approach"[71] on the relationship between EU law and international law, largely similar to the relationship between international law and national law.[72] For this purpose, it thus regularly refers to its treaties as the "constitutional charter",[73] a factor which has been interpreted to encompass a wider meaning than merely referencing the founding instrument of an international organization.[74]

The well-known *Kadi* cases demonstrate the at times autistic stance of the CJEU on the nature of the EU legal order in relation to international law. On the question of the lawfulness of EU Regulation No 881/2002, placing Kadi and the Al Barakaat International Foundation on the sanctions list as a consequence to Security Council Resolution 1267, the Court of First Instance (CFI) had first argued in a different manner on the delineation of the relationship between the EU and international law than later the Advocate General and Grand Chamber of the CJEU. Primarily, its line of reasoning focused on the hierarchical order existing within international law, stemming both from obligations under the United Nations Charter as well as *ius cogens* norms.[75] By doing so, the CFI not only positioned itself as an international court, but subordinated the EU legal order to an international value system (as also argued by the international constitutionalist approach[76]).[77] The Advocate General

[69]CJEU, case 6/64, *Costa v E.N.E.L.*, ECLI:EU:C:1964:66: "By creating a Community of unlimited duration, having its own institutions, its own legal capacity and capacity of representation on the international plan, and more particularly, real powers stemming from a limitation of sovereignty or a transfer of powers from the states to the Community, the Member States have limited their sovereign rights, albeit within limited fields [...]. [T]he law stemming from the Treaty, an independent source of law, could not because of its special and original nature, be overridden by domestic legal provisions [...]."

[70]CJEU, case C-459/03, *Commission v Ireland (MOX Plant)*, ECLI:EU:C:2006:345, para. 123.

[71]Ziegler (2013), p. 2 et seq.

[72]Ziegler (2013), p. 2 et seq.

[73]CJEU, case 294/83, *Les Verts v Parliament*, ECLI:EU:C:1986:166, para. 23; opinion of AG Maduro to CJEU, case C-402/05 P, *Kadi v Council and Commission*, ECLI:EU:C:2008:11, para. 21; CJEU, opinion 2/13, *EU Accession to the ECHR*, ECLI:EU:C:2014:2454, para. 158: "own constitutional framework".

[74]See, e.g., Krenzler and Landwehr (2011), p. 1006, fn. 10.

[75]CG, case T-315/01, *Kadi v Council and Commission*, ECLI:EU:T:2005:332, paras. 181–193 and 225–226. In particular, in reference to Articles 27 and 30 of the Vienna Convention on the Law of Treaties (VCLT) as well as Article 307 EC (now Article 351 TFEU) the CFI emphasized that obligations under the Charter of the United Nations (particularly also chapter VII Resolutions by the Security Council) were primary over domestic law, international treaty law and Community law. At the same time, however, the CFI found that while it could not review the Security Council Resolution in light of Community law, it was tasked to do so in light of potential *ius cogens* violations as *ius cogens* norms are "understood as a body of higher rules of public international law binding on all subjects of international law, including the bodies of the United Nations".

[76]See Sect. 4.1 in more detail.

[77]D'Aspremont and Dopagne (2008), p. 375.

rejected the CFI's argumentation—and its conception of hierarchically superior values stemming from outside the European legal order—firmly, denying that the Security Council Resolution could have any "supra-constitutional status".[78] On the relationship between the international legal order and the Community's legal order he expressed himself in the following manner:

> The Court [in *van Gend en Loos*] held that the Treaty is not merely an agreement between States, but an agreement between the *peoples* of Europe. It considered that the Treaty had established a 'new legal order', beholden to, but distinct from the existing legal order of public international law. In other words, the Treaty has created a *municipal legal order of transnational dimensions*[[79]], of which it forms the *'basic constitutional charter'*. This does not mean, however, that the Community's municipal legal order and the international legal order pass by each other like ships in the night. On the contrary, the Community has traditionally played an active and constructive part on the international stage. The application and interpretation of Community law is accordingly guided by the presumption that the Community wants to honour its international commitments. The Community Courts therefore carefully examine the obligations by which the Community is bound on the international stage and take judicial notice of those obligations.[80]

Particularly, in reference to the CJEU's case-law, the Advocate General emphasized that the "Community Courts determine the effect of international obligations within the Community legal order by reference to conditions set by Community law."[81] And though the Court strives to respect international obligations incumbent on the Community, "it seeks, first and foremost, to preserve the constitutional framework created by the Treaty."[82]

The CJEU approached the relationship between EU law and the international legal order from a similar constitutional perspective. After reasserting that the EU was based on the rule of law, it emphasized that "neither its Member States nor its institutions can avoid review of the conformity of their acts with the basic constitutional charter, the EC Treaty" and that "an international agreement cannot affect [...] the autonomy of the Community legal system".[83,84]

---

[78]Opinion of AG Maduro to CJEU, case C-402/05 P, *Kadi v Council and Commission*, ECLI:EU:C:2008:11, para. 28.

[79]The French version reads perhaps more accurately: "*un ordre juridique interne d'original internationale*".

[80]Opinion of AG Maduro to CJEU, case C-402/05 P, *Kadi v Council and Commission*, ECLI:EU:C:2008:11, para. 21 et seq. (footnotes omitted, emphasis added).

[81]Opinion of AG Maduro to CJEU, case C-402/05 P, *Kadi v Council and Commission*, ECLI:EU:C:2008:11, para. 23.

[82]Opinion of AG Maduro to CJEU, case C-402/05 P, *Kadi v Council and Commission o*, ECLI:EU:C:2008:11, para. 24.

[83]CJEU, case C-402/05 P, *Kadi v Council and Commission*, ECLI:EU:C:2008:461, para. 281 et seq. Referring, inter alia, to its previous *MOX Plant* judgment. It also states in para. 285 that "the obligations imposed by an international agreement cannot have the effect of prejudicing the constitutional principles of the EC Treaty".

[84]Additionally, the CJEU focused particularly on the internal regulation transposing the Security Council Resolution in question, reminding that "the Charter of the United Nations does not impose the choice of a particular model for the implementation of resolutions adopted by the Security Council under Chapter VII of the Charter, since they are to be given effect in accordance with the procedure applicable in that respect in the domestic legal order of each Member of the United

Hence, the CJEU demonstrated its perception of the EU legal order as a constitutional order which determined internally how to implement international legal obligations.[85] In doing so, the relationship between EU and international law was not guided by international law rules. Rather, it followed similar rules as apply to the implementation of international law in domestic law.[86]

A similar "self-contained" standpoint can be found in opinion 2/13 regarding the Draft Accession Agreement of the EU to the ECHR. In this regard, special emphasis is laid on the "autonomy enjoyed by EU law in relation to the laws of the Member States and in relation to international law".[87] To ensure said autonomy, the CJEU pointed out the need to also protect the judicial system established to ensure consistency and uniformity in the interpretation of EU law.[88] As the Draft Accession Agreement—from the viewpoint of the CJEU—did not respect this institutional set-up and autonomy of the EU legal order to a sufficient extent, the CJEU found that the Draft Agreement was not compatible with the EU Treaties.

Likewise, in opinion 1/91 on the Draft Agreement relating to the creation of the European Economic Area (EEA), the CJEU adopted an autonomist stand when deciding whether the envisaged width of jurisdiction of the EEA Court (which would have been called upon to interpret Community legislation) was acceptable in light of the CJEU's exclusive jurisdiction on the interpretation and application of EU law[89]; thus, it rejected it at first since the envisioned EEA Court would have been called to interpret Community legislation.[90]

Still, opinion 1/91 also evidences the CJEU's general acceptance of other tribunals' jurisdiction. After the criticized aspect was amended, and the CJEU was foreseen as the responsible authority regarding the interpretation of provisions

Nations." CJEU, case C-402/05 P, *Kadi v Council and Commission*, ECLI:EU:C:2008:461, para. 298.

[85]It does so through a primarily monist approach. For example, in *Racke* the CJEU stated in response to the Commission's doubts that the international rules referred were to be regarded as forming part of the Community legal order that "the [EU] must respect international law in the exercise of its powers [and that] the rules of customary international law [. . .] form part of the Community legal order". CJEU, case C-162/96, *Racke v Hauptzollamt Mainz*, ECLI:EU:C:1998:293, para. 45 et seq. Additionally, the absence in Article 218 TFEU on any particular requirement for the transformation of treaties into the EU legal order provides further indications of the monist system. However, particularly the *Kadi* judgment has let some speak of strong dualist tendencies emerging in the CJEU's more recent case-law, e.g., De Búrca (2010), p. 2 et seq. See also in more detail Krenzler and Landwehr (2011), pp. 1008–1015, who also argue that the origins of EU lie in international law, thus indicating monism as the more obvious choice.

[86]Cf. Cremona (2011), p. 267; D'Aspremont and Dopagne (2008), p. 374.

[87]CJEU, opinion 2/13, *EU Accession to the ECHR*, ECLI:EU:C:2014:2454, para. 170.

[88]CJEU, opinion 2/13, *EU Accession to the ECHR*, ECLI:EU:C:2014:2454, para. 174.

[89]As regards the question to which extent the EU can be subject to international dispute settlement mechanisms as established by international organizations or agreements and which nature is assigned to its legal order in such instances more generally, see Kuijper et al. (2015), p. 721; Van Vooren and Wessel (2014), p. 271.

[90]CJEU, opinion 1/91, *European Economic Area*, ECLI:EU:C:1992:189.

which were identical to the EU treaties and legislation, the CJEU had no further objections. It found that "the settlement of disputes by arbitration is not liable adversely to affect the autonomy of the Community order."[91] Accordingly, the compatibility between party-ship to such international agreements (with their own courts) and the CJEU's exclusive jurisdiction was answered favourably by the CJEU:

> An international agreement providing for such a system of courts is *in principle compatible* with Community law. The Community's competence in the field of international relations and its capacity to conclude international agreements necessarily entails the power to submit to the decisions of a court which is created or designated by such an agreement as regards the interpretation and application of its provisions.[92]

This statement also was more recently recalled in opinion 1/09 on the European and Community Patents Court.[93] Hence, notwithstanding its strongly autonomist standpoint, the CJEU accepted that the jurisdiction of other international courts and tribunals was "in principle compatible with Community law".

2.3 Conclusions on the European Perspective

The regime interaction between EU law and international law from a European perspective seems characterized by an emphasis on the internal and external autonomy of the EU, as evidenced in the principles of primacy/supremacy of EU law as well as the wide scope of jurisdiction of the CJEU. This has resulted in a partly autistic approach of the EU institutions towards international law, even though they recognize the EU's "international law origins" at least in principle. Especially the most recent case-law of the CJEU evidences an understanding of the EU legal order as a *sui generis* regime, which decides on its own how and which norms to incorporate from international law.[94]

From a European perspective, this serves to protect the unity of the EU legal order and the European institutional system. From an international law perspective, the EU's approach risks to undermine the effectiveness of international dispute settlement and may threaten the coherence of international law; in particular should other international tribunals adopt a deferent approach.[95] From a domestic perspective, this can also interfere with the sovereign right of EU member states to settle their international disputes in the most appropriate forum.[96] It potentially even

[91]CJEU, opinion 1/91, *European Economic Area*, ECLI:EU:C:1991:490.

[92]CJEU, opinion 1/91, *European Economic Area*, ECLI:EU:C:1991:490, para. 40 (emphasis added).

[93]CJEU, opinion 1/09, *European and Community Patents Court*, ECLI:EU:C:2011:123, para. 74.

[94]Cf. Koskenniemi (2007), p. 9.

[95]See respectively Sect. 3 below.

[96]Similarly Lavranos (2006b), p. 479.

undermines the effectiveness of international law in general, and international dispute settlement in particular,[97] especially with regard to the coherent development of international law.[98] At the same time, the CJEU accepts, in principle, the jurisdiction of other international tribunals.

Against this background, a look outside the EU seems warranted.

3 Looking Out: The EU Legal Order in International Proceedings

There are many examples of the EU's increasing role in international proceedings. Among others,[99] it has become established practice for the EU to engage in international relations as an active party.[100] This enhances the frictions caused by the differences between the in- and the outside view on the nature of the EU's legal order. In particular the CJEU's self-proclaimed exclusive jurisdiction in accordance with its understanding of Article 344 TFEU has caused tensions with the jurisdiction of other international tribunals in a number of cases.[101]

Respectively, two questions are of particular importance: how is the EU viewed by international dispute settlement bodies and which nature is assigned to its legal order? Second, to what extent do the different dispute settlement bodies defer to the jurisdiction of the CJEU?

The approaches opted for by international dispute settlement bodies have varied and are dependent on a number of factors. For example, the applicable

---

[97]This particularly, as demonstrated in Sects. 3 and 4, in light of the considerable deference exercised by other international courts and tribunals in their interaction with the EU legal order.

[98]See in this context also Shany's study on the effectiveness of international courts, listing as generic goals of international courts norm support, resolving international disputes and problems, regime support, and legitimizing public authority. Shany (2014), pp. 37–46. As is explained in a later chapter of the book, the CJEU also possesses two idiosyncratic goals, namely the constitutionalization of EU law and the advancement of market integration (p. 280).

[99]For example, despite the EU treaties remaining silent on whether the EU can become member to other international organizations, the EU has become a member to organisations such as the WTO. Van Vooren and Wessel (2014), p. 249. Implicitly this has been deduced, inter alia, from Article 211 TFEU ("Within their respective spheres of competence, the Union and the Member States shall cooperate with third countries and with the competent international organisations.") and the provisions providing the EU with the competence to conclude international agreements (Articles 216, 217 TFEU).

[100]See generally Hoffmeister (2012).

[101]As mentioned, Article 344 TFEU prohibits member states to submit a dispute to international litigation on matters that fall within the EU's (shared or exclusive) competence. This has generated quite some debate within the scholarly discussion on the proliferation of international courts and tribunals and a possible hierarchy among these bodies. See, e.g., Lavranos (2014) and Bennouna (2012).

legal framework is of relevance and whether the EU has become a party to the respective treaty.[102]

Moreover, since the respective treaty regimes generally also establish dispute settlement mechanisms, the treaties' jurisdictional clauses are of major importance. It simply is easier for an international tribunal to defer to the jurisdiction of the CJEU if it is provided with discretion whether to adjudicate are not.[103] A similar effect is achieved by means of a tribunal limiting its scope of jurisdiction to avoid jurisdictional conflicts with the CJEU.[104]

Finally, further factors are of importance such as the question of rights holders and whether the treaty regimes at stake confer rights to individuals or investors. In such cases, true jurisdictional conflicts between the CJEU and other international dispute settlement bodies (in the field of investment or human rights) are less likely as such disputes are not covered by Article 344 TFEU (which relates to inter-state disputes).[105]

The interplay between these factors will lead to different outcomes as to the international tribunals' assessment of the nature of EU law and the level of interaction. In part, the varying approaches can also be traced back to the respective institutional frameworks. Hence, in the following, four constellations will be

---

[102]For example, the EU is a contracting party of the Law of the Sea Convention (LOSC) (Council Decision of 23 March 1998 concerning the conclusion by the European Community of the United Nations Convention of 10 December 1982 on the Law of the Sea and the Agreement of 28 July 1994 relating to the implementation of Part XI thereof, OJ 1998 L 179/1), the WTO Agreement (Marrakesh Agreement Establishing the World Trade Organization, 15 April 1994, 1867 UNTS 154), and other bilateral agreements such as the 1963 Association Agreement with Turkey (Article 25(2) Agreement establishing an Association between the European Economic Community and Turkey, 12 September 1963, OJ 1977 L 361/29), as well as of the Energy Charter Treaty (ECT). It is thus directly bound by these treaties. In other constellations, the EU is not (yet) a party but (all) its member states are parties to the respective treaty regime (ECHR); in again other constellations, only some of the member states are treaty parties (e.g. as is the case with intra-EU BITs). The different constellations play a role for the qualification of EU law by the respective dispute settlement bodies.

[103]For example, the LOSC is provided with a weak jurisdictional clause. Article 282 LOSC: "If the States Parties which are parties to a dispute concerning the interpretation or application of this Convention have agreed, through a general, regional or bilateral agreement or otherwise, that such dispute shall, at the request of any party to the dispute, be submitted to a procedure that entails a binding decision, that procedure shall apply in lieu of the procedures provided for in this Part, unless the parties to the dispute otherwise agree." Conversely, the clauses of the GATT/WTO regime or the ECHR are "strong" and establish the exclusive jurisdiction of the respective bodies (in more detail see also below Sect. 4.2).

[104]For example, as dealt with below, in *Iron Rhine*, the tribunal's mandate and scope of review was formulated in a way as to pay respect to the EU legal order as a separate legal order. Also, some EU member states, when accepting the jurisdiction of the ICJ, limited the latter's jurisdiction in a way as to avoid conflicts of interests with other international tribunals, inter alia the CJEU (see below Sect. 3.1). This obviously had a bearing on the respective tribunals' scope jurisdiction *vis-à-vis* the CJEU.

[105]See, however, the contrary standpoint of the CJEU/the European Commission in investment cases. For details, below Sect. 3.4.

examined in turn: the EU and international dispute settlement proceedings on matters of general international law (International Court of Justice (ICJ), arbitral tribunals) (Sect. 3.1); the EU and the GATT/WTO regime (Sect. 3.2); the EU within the framework of the ECHR (Sect. 3.3); as well as the EU and investment tribunals (Sect. 3.4).

3.1 The EU and International Dispute Settlement Proceedings on Matters of General International Law

3.1.1 Introduction

To view the EU legal order through the lens of international judicial bodies' rulings on matters of general international law serves particularly well to examine the nature of the EU legal order as it demonstrates the clearest tensions between the CJEU's self-proclaimed exclusive jurisdiction and other jurisdictions.[106]

Both, international arbitral proceedings (*Mox Plant*, *Iron Rhine*) and the case-law of the ICJ evidence a potential the jurisdictional conflicts with the CJEU. One common feature of this jurisprudence is that the EU was not a direct party to the proceedings but that the outcome of the proceedings would potentially touch upon EU law. As will be shown, the respective tribunals referred to various techniques to accommodate their potentially overlapping jurisdictions with the jurisdiction of the CJEU.[107]

3.1.2 The MOX Plant Dispute

One of the best known examples on conflicting jurisdiction between separate rule-complexes is the *MOX Plant* dispute. Ireland commenced in total three sets of proceedings in relation to its authorization of the construction and operation of a mixed fuel (MOX) plant. It alleged that the information provided by the United Kingdom (UK) was incomplete. In this regard, the application of EU legislation was also an issue. Accordingly, the involved international tribunals were

[106]Note that these tensions are prime examples of the practical implications of the emergence of specialist rule-systems by the ILC. ILC, Fragmentation of International Law: Difficulties Arising From the Diversification and Expansion of International Law—Report of the Study Group of the International Law Commission, 13 April 2006, UN Doc. A/CN.4/L.682, para. 10.

[107]As will be shown in Sect. 4 in more detail, the tribunals referred to the principle of comity and to forms of judicial minimalism. In fact, at times, the principle of comity is made use of by one institution out of deference to another—more appropriate—forum for dispute resolution. De Búrca (2010), p. 10; Worster (2008), p. 120. Also judicial minimalism, i.e. a particular narrow understanding of the subject matter in dispute, has been a common occurrence to avoid interfering with the EU legal order or harmonious interpretation.

confronted quite clearly with the EU's action taken to underscore the reach of the EU's autonomous legal order and the exclusive jurisdiction of the CJEU.

The international legal instruments at stake were the OSPAR Convention and the LOSC. Both are mixed agreements.[108] In both cases, the dispute caused significant debate—particularly with regard to the LOSC proceedings[109]—on whether the tribunal was the appropriate forum to adjudicate the dispute or whether it was a matter of the CJEU. The respective arbitral tribunals approached the question quite differently (in relation to the agreements at stake but also on the basis of different jurisdictional clauses).

The OSPAR tribunal opted for a restrictive approach in the first of the three sets of proceedings against the UK which was commenced by Ireland in 2001. It delivered its final award on 2 July 2003,[110] paying no direct regard to EU legislation, and instead displayed a particularly narrow view of the scope of applicable law.[111]

The other tribunals (ITLOS and the Annex VII Tribunal) took a different approach in relation to the proceedings under LOSC which were initiated by Ireland a few months later: Ireland first brought the case before ITLOS to request provisional measures (which were denied in lack of urgency[112]), and then initiated proceedings before the Annex VII Tribunal.[113]

---

[108]On the effect of mixed agreements see, e.g., Kuijper et al. (2015), p. 101 et seqq.

[109]It has been assumed that a similar outcome before the CJEU would have also been reached regarding the OSPAR award. However, as the European Commission did not initiate infringement proceedings in that case—possibly to avoid a conflicting outcome—the question was not raised. See also Karaman (2012), p. 283. In any event, the OSPAR tribunal—*Dispute Concerning Access to Information under Article 9 of the OSPAR Convention between Ireland and the United Kingdom of Great Britain and Northern Ireland*, Final Award, XXIII RIAA 59, Decision (2 July 2003), para. 143—did state that the "OSPAR Convention contains a particular and self-contained dispute resolution mechanism [...] in accordance with which this Tribunal acts."

[110]*Dispute Concerning Access to Information under Article 9 of the OSPAR Convention between Ireland and the United Kingdom of Great Britain and Northern Ireland*, Final Award, XXIII RIAA 59, Decision (2 July 2003).

[111]The OSPAR Convention authorized the tribunal to decide on disputes "according to the rules of international law and, in particular, those of the Convention". Nevertheless, the tribunal restricted its analysis to the OSPAR Convention, warning that it "otherwise would transform [...] into an unqualified and comprehensive jurisdictional regime". *Dispute Concerning Access to Information under Article 9 of the OSPAR Convention between Ireland and the United Kingdom of Great Britain and Northern Ireland*, Final Award, XXIII RIAA 59, Decision (2 July 2003), para. 85. This prevented the tribunal from interpreting or applying EU law. As one consequence of the narrow understanding of applicable law, the tribunal in the end dismissed Ireland's claim for a violation of Article 9 of the OSPAR Convention.

[112]Note, however, that ITLOS dismissed arguments pertaining to its jurisdiction as it found that the dispute arose in regard to the interpretation or application of LOSC. *The MOX Plant Case*, ITLOS Case No. 10, Order of 3 December 2011, para. 52.

[113]This is an arbitral tribunal established when the parties have not chosen the same means of dispute settlement under Part XV LOSC.

The relevance of EU law and the scope of CJEU's jurisdiction is illustrated by the fact that shortly before the hearings were scheduled to commence before the Annex VII Tribunal, a written answer by the European Commission given to the European Parliament was brought to the Tribunal's attention, indicating that the Commission was deliberating whether to institute infringement proceedings against Ireland under Article 226 TEC (now Article 258 TFEU) as the matter concerned EU provisions and therefore fell within the scope of the CJEU's jurisdiction.[114] As a consequence, the Tribunal—despite affirming its *prima facie* jurisdiction[115]—pointed to the problems arising by a potentially competing procedure which could entail a binding decision (if only by virtue of Article 282 LOSC[116]). In this regard, it recognized that these matters:

> essentially concern[ed] the internal operation of a separate legal order (namely the legal order of the European Communities) to which both of the Parties to the present proceedings are subject and which [...] are to be determined within the institutional framework of the European Communities.[117]

Moreover, the Tribunal stated that even if not all invoked provisions were within the exclusive competence of the EU, there was no certainty that the remaining provisions "would in fact give rise to a self-contained and distinct dispute."[118] Hence, it concluded that:

> bearing in mind considerations of mutual respect and comity which should prevail between judicial institutions both of which may be called upon to determine rights and obligations as between two States, [...] it would be inappropriate for it to proceed further with hearing the Parties on the merits of the dispute in the absence of a resolution of the problems referred to. Moreover, a procedure that might result in two conflicting decisions on the same issue would not be helpful to the resolution of the dispute between the Parties.[119]

The Tribunal thus suspended the proceedings to await the developments at the EU level in application of the principles of "mutual respect and comity".

---

[114]*The MOX Plant Case (Ireland v United Kingdom)*, Annex VII Tribunal (PCA), Order No. 3, Suspension of Proceedings on Jurisdiction and Merits and Request for Further Provisional measures (24 June 2003), para. 21.

[115]*The MOX Plant Case (Ireland v United Kingdom)*, Annex VII Tribunal (PCA), Order No. 3, Suspension of Proceedings on Jurisdiction and Merits and Request for Further Provisional measures (24 June 2003), para. 14.

[116]Article 282 United Nations Convention on the Law of the Sea, 10 December 1982, 1833 UNTS 3.

[117]*The MOX Plant Case (Ireland v United Kingdom)*, Annex VII Tribunal (PCA), Order No. 3, Suspension of Proceedings on Jurisdiction and Merits and Request for Further Provisional measures (24 June 2003), para. 24.

[118]*The MOX Plant Case (Ireland v United Kingdom)*, Annex VII Tribunal (PCA), Order No. 3, Suspension of Proceedings on Jurisdiction and Merits and Request for Further Provisional measures (24 June 2003), para. 26.

[119]*The MOX Plant Case (Ireland v United Kingdom)*, Annex VII Tribunal (PCA), Order No. 3, Suspension of Proceedings on Jurisdiction and Merits and Request for Further Provisional measures (24 June 2003), para. 28.

Soon thereafter, in October 2003, the European Commission indeed initiated infringement proceedings against Ireland, claiming a violation of Article 10 TEC (principle of sincere cooperation, now Article 4(3) TEU) and Article 292 TEC (exclusive jurisdiction of the CJEU, now Article 344 TFEU).[120] The CJEU assessed, inter alia, whether its jurisdiction in this matter was exclusive, particularly as it concerned a matter of shared competence between the EU and its member states. It found in this regard that "mixed agreements have the same status in the Community legal order as purely Community agreements, as these are provisions coming within the scope of Community competence".[121] After recalling Article's 282 LOSC system of avoiding a breach of the CJEU's exclusive jurisdiction, it found that the LOSC provisions invoked by Ireland indeed formed "an integral part of the Community order" and therefore fell "within the terms of Article 292 TEC."[122] The CJEU's viewpoint was also accepted by the parties, with Ireland formally notifying the Annex VII Tribunal of the withdrawal of its claim against the UK. On this basis, the Tribunal subsequently terminated the proceedings.[123]

Thus, in the *MOX Plant* dispute, especially the Annex VII tribunal resorted to procedural means to ensure coordination within a horizontal system of dispute settlement bodies. The strength of the respective jurisdictional clauses (the subsidiary jurisdiction as deduced from the LOSC regime versus the CJEU's exclusive jurisdiction) tipped the scales in this instance in favour of the EU.[124] The Annex VII

[120] CJEU, case C-459/03, *Commission v Ireland (MOX Plant)*, ECLI:EU:C:2006:345.

[121] CJEU, case C-459/03, *Commission v Ireland (MOX Plant)*, ECLI:EU:C:2006:345, para. 84. The opinion of AG Maduro to CJEU, case C-459/03, *Commission v Ireland (MOX Plant)*, ECLI: EU:C:2006:42, para. 14, explained in this regard that "It may be that a dispute falls largely and perhaps predominantly outside the jurisdiction of the Court, and that only one or a few of the matters of contention come within its jurisdiction. However, in such circumstances Article 292 EC [. . .] nevertheless precludes that the entire dispute, including the elements falling within the scope of Community law, is submitted to a method of settlement other than those provided for in the Community Treaties. After all, there is no threshold in the rules establishing the Court's jurisdictional monopoly."

[122] CJEU, case C-459/03, *Commission v Ireland (MOX Plant)*, ECLI:EU:C:2006:345, para. 126 et seq. Within the decentralized judicial model contained in LOSC, Article 282 LOSC therefore constituted "a 'friendly' conflict rule" (Kuijper et al. (2015), p. 11), which the CJEU used to find the dispute settlement mechanism foreseen in the LOSC compatible with the EU's autonomous legal order. See also Schill (2013), p. 40. In this sense, the outcome before the CJEU reminds of its earlier argumentation/explanations in opinions 1/91 and 1/92, where it found membership of the EU and its member states in an international agreement with its own system of courts to be "in principle compatible" with EU law, but only where such procedure "is not liable adversely to affect the autonomy of the Community legal order." Hence, from a European perspective, where the international agreement enables deference in matters touching upon the interpretation and application of EU law, the CJEU's monopoly is not under threat. This, however, entails that an international tribunal called upon to adjudicate on matters touching upon European also acts accordingly.

[123] *The MOX Plant Case (Ireland v United Kingdom)*, Annex VII Tribunal (PCA), Order No. 6, Termination of Proceedings (6 June 2008).

[124] See also in more detail Sect. 4.

Tribunal pointed out that the question whether the CJEU would indeed possess exclusive jurisdiction was a matter dependent on the operation of a "separate legal order". Still, regardless of the *separateness* of the EU legal order, it applied the principles of "mutual respect and comity" between two judicial institutions. It relied thus on an international law means to resolve the potential jurisdictional conflict between two separate institutions.

3.1.3 The Iron Rhine Dispute

In contrast to the *MOX Plant* dispute, there are more defiant examples where arbitral tribunals or international courts have not directly ceded to the CJEU's exclusive jurisdiction. However, other methods of deference have been applied.[125]

In *Iron Rhine*, for example, the arbitral tribunal had no issue reaching a final award, albeit in consideration of EU law. The proceedings between the Netherlands and Belgium concerned the costs for the reactivation of an old railway line in an area which had been designated as a protected natural habitat by the Netherlands in accordance with the EU's Habitats Directive. The arbitral tribunal was requested to "render its decision on the basis of international law, including European law if necessary, while taking into account the Parties' obligations under Article 292 of the EC Treaty".[126] The tribunal's mandate and scope of review was thus formulated in a manner to pay respect to the Community's legal order as a separate legal order. Despite both states referring to EU law in their pleadings, they argued that the situation was different than in *MOX Plant* as neither party claimed that EU law had been violated, and the core of the issue concerned the interpretation of a bilateral treaty from 1839, as had also been communicated to the European Commission in advance.[127]

In the course of the proceedings, the arbitral tribunal analysed the role of European law in quite some detail, finding in connection with Article 292 TEC (now Article 344 TFEU) that

[125]As mentioned above, the OSPAR tribunal had emphasized that the OSPAR Convention contained a "self-contained dispute resolution mechanism" and in its findings paid no direct regard to EU legislation, thus side-stepping the issue. *Dispute Concerning Access to Information under Article 9 of the OSPAR Convention between Ireland and the United Kingdom of Great Britain and Northern Ireland*, Final Award, XXIII RIAA 59, Decision (2 July 2003), paras. 85 and 143; Lavranos (2006a), p. 227.

[126]Arbitration Agreement cited in para. 4 of the *Iron Rhine ("Ijzeren Rijn") Railway arbitration (Belgium v The Netherlands)*, Award, XXVII RIAA 35, Decision (24 May 2005).

[127]*Iron Rhine ("Ijzeren Rijn") Railway arbitration (Belgium v The Netherlands)*, Award, XXVII RIAA 35, Decision (24 May 2005), para. 14 et seq.

> within the EC legal system, following a division of competences among the courts of EC Member States and the European Court of Justice, only the European Court of Justice ultimately has the power to decide authoritatively questions of the interpretation or application of EC law.[128]

It found that the above-cited formulation chosen in the Arbitral Agreement placed it in a "position analogous to that of a domestic court within the EC"[129] with regard to whether or not to request a preliminary ruling whenever concerned with the interpretation or application of EU law. Thus, in reference to the CJEU's case-law, it explained that it was in its own discretion whether interpretation of EU law by the CJEU was needed. As a consequence to this conclusion, the tribunal had no issue with reviewing EU provisions, and concluded that "the points of EC law put forward by the parties [were] not conclusive for the task of the Tribunal [and thus] the obligation under Article 292 TEC does not come into play."[130]

Thus, while the arbitral tribunal's mandate and scope of review was formulated in a manner to pay respect to the Community's legal order as a separate legal order, the *Iron Rhine* tribunal engaged with EU law and considered itself competent to define as to when it should defer to the CJEU. The far-fetched (and creative) analogy comparing itself to domestic courts might stand in contrast to the CJEU's case-law on who constitutes a "court or and tribunal of a Member State" in the sense of Article 267 TFEU.[131] At the same time, however, it serves to demonstrate the tribunal's ultimate recognition of the EU's internal hierarchical rules.

3.1.4 The EU and the International Court of Justice

EU law was at stake also in proceedings before the ICJ. By virtue of Article 34 of the ICJ Statute,[132] only states may be parties in cases before the ICJ.[133] Depending on the subject matter,[134] the ICJ—as the principal judicial organ of the United

[128] *Iron Rhine ("Ijzeren Rijn") Railway arbitration (Belgium v The Netherlands)*, Award, XXVII RIAA 35, Decision (24 May 2005), para. 101.

[129] *Iron Rhine ("Ijzeren Rijn") Railway arbitration (Belgium v The Netherlands)*, Award, XXVII RIAA 35, Decision (24 May 2005), para. 103.

[130] *Iron Rhine ("Ijzeren Rijn") Railway arbitration* (Belgium v The Netherlands), Award, XXVII RIAA 35, Decision (24 May 2005), paras. 106 et seqq., 119 et seq., similarly 137.

[131] See also Lavranos (2006a), pp. 233–239.

[132] Statute of the International Court of Justice, 26 June 1945, 1 UNTS 993.

[133] Note, however, that the newly amended 2005 Rules of Court stipulate in Article 43(2) that "[w]henever the construction of a convention to which a public international organization is a party may be in question in a case before the Court, the Court shall consider whether the Registrar shall so notify the public international organization concerned. Every public international organization notified by the Registrar may submit its observations on the particular provisions of the convention the construction of which is in question in the case." In line with this provision, the EU has been invited in three cases to date to issue observations, but so far declined as it found that the subject matter did not fall within its competence, see also in more detail Hoffmeister (2012), p. 83 et seq.

[134] The CJEU's exclusive jurisdiction (Article 344 TFEU) does not generally pose a barrier since certain subject-matters are exempt from the CJEU's jurisdiction. For example, Article 275 TFEU

Nations[135]—has dealt with legal disputes involving member states of the EU.[136] Some also concerned (at least indirectly) questions of EU law. However, as can be seen in these few examples, they are characterized by restraint displayed by both, the ICJ and the EU's member states, on a jurisdictional as well as substantive level.

With regard to the ICJ's jurisdiction, half of the EU member states (14) have made declarations under Article 36 ICJ Statute. Some of them—when accepting the ICJ's compulsory jurisdiction—exempted disputes "which the Parties thereto have agreed or shall agree to have recourse to some other method of peaceful settlement or which is subject to another method of peaceful settlement chosen by all the Parties"[137] therefrom. This also applies to such instances where the CJEU would enjoy exclusive jurisdiction.

Thus, in *Jurisdictional Immunities*,[138] between the two EU member states Germany and Italy, Germany was keen to point out in its application to the ICJ that the matter did not fall within the jurisdictional clause of the CJEU. It stated that the dispute had "no direct link with the operation of the European market regime" and that the "general relationship between the European nations continues to be governed by general international law".[139] This was not disputed by Italy during the proceedings.

In contrast, there was some ambiguity in *Jurisdiction and Enforcement of Judgments in Civil and Commercial Matters*[140] on the question of the CJEU's

---

precludes the CJEU from exercising jurisdiction over matters relating to the common foreign and security policy. But also other matters where the EU does not possess competences escape the jurisdiction of the CJEU. See also Higgins (2003), p. 4.

[135]Jennings and Higgins (2012), p. 6.

[136]The following cases concerned legal disputes between two EU member states: *Sovereignty over Certain Frontier Lands (Belgium v Netherlands)*, 1959 ICJ 209 (Judgment, 20 June 1959); *North Sea Continental Shelf (Merits) (Federal Republic of Germany v Denmark; Federal Republic of Germany v Netherlands)*, 1969 ICJ 4 (Judgment, 20 February 1969), concerning maritime delimitation, thus escaping EU competences; *Jurisdictional Immunities of the State (Germany v Italy; Greece Intervening)*, 2012 ICJ 99 (Judgment, 3 February 2012).

[137]See Germany's Declaration Recognizing the Jurisdiction of the Court as Compulsory, 1 May 2008. See in a similar manner also Belgium (17 June 1958); Estonia (10 October 1991); Italy (25 November 2014); Lithuania (26 September 2012); Luxembourg (15 September 1930); Malta (6 December 1966); Netherlands (1 August 1956); Poland (25 March 1996); Portugal (25 February 2005); Romania (23 June 2015); Slovakia (28 May 2004); Spain (29 October 1990); United Kingdom (31 December 2014). Five EU member states have (currently) not issued any such declaration (Croatia, Czech Republic, France, Latvia, Slovenia), with the remaining nine not explicitly excluding such disputes from the ICJ's jurisdiction: Austria (19 May 1971); Bulgaria (24 June 1992); Cyprus (2 September 2002); Denmark (10 December 1956); Finland (25 June 1958): Greece (14 January 2015); Hungary (22 October 1992); Ireland (15 December 2011); Sweden (6 April 1957).

[138]*Jurisdictional Immunities of the State (Germany v Italy)*, 2008 ICJ, Application Instituting Proceedings (23 December 2008).

[139]*Jurisdictional Immunities of the State (Germany v Italy)*, 2008 ICJ, Application Instituting Proceedings (23 December 2008), para. 6.

[140]*Jurisdiction and Enforcement of Judgments in Civil and Commercial Matters (Belgium v Switzerland)*, 2009 ICJ, Application Instituting Proceedings (21 December 2009).

jurisdiction, namely on whether Belgium was entitled to initiate proceedings concerning the Lugano Convention.[141] Though Belgium maintained that the subject matter of the dispute did not concern the "new Lugano Convention" (from 2007) which the EU had concluded as a matter of it exclusive competence,[142] Switzerland questioned whether Belgium was entitled under EU law to initiate the proceedings regarding the 1988 Lugano Convention.[143] In the end, however, the case was withdrawn by Belgium "in concert with the Commission of the European Union",[144] though not with explicit reference to the question of EU competences. Hence, the ICJ did not have the opportunity to address the question of how the internal division of competences between the EU and its member states had an effect on their capability to initiate international proceedings. Consequently, it did not position itself as to the nature of the EU legal order.

Finally, a similar question was also implicit in the *Fisheries Jurisdiction* dispute between Spain and Canada.[145] Spain had initiated proceedings against Canada on questions relating to Canadian legislation and the interception of its fishing vessel. In this regard, however, Canada asserted that an agreement had already been reached between the EU and Canada on related questions regarding the legality of conduct undertaken by Canada under the North Atlantic Fisheries Convention. Canada maintained that the dispute had already been thereby settled as it saw no "distinction between a dispute with the European Community and a dispute with Spain".[146] The ICJ in this instance, as *Higgins* has noted "understandably",[147] side-stepped the issue.

Though the ICJ is the only judicial organ which possesses universal and general subject matter jurisdiction, the restraint afforded towards the EU is, inter alia, owed to the "friendly mutual respect" practiced by the ICJ in the interest of the "integrity of international law".[148] Thus, the ICJ's practice evidences a certain restraint when touching upon matters of EU law.

---

[141]The Lugano Convention on Jurisdiction and Enforcement of Judgements of Civil and Commercial Matters is identical to the Brussels Regulation, an instrument where the CJEU already clarified in 2006 that the EU had exclusive powers to conclude the revised Convention, see CJEU, opinion 1/03, *Lugano Convention*, ECLI:EU:C:2006:81.

[142]*Jurisdiction and Enforcement of Judgments in Civil and Commercial Matters (Belgium v Switzerland)*, 2009 ICJ, Application Instituting Proceedings (21 December 2009), para. 48.

[143]Jacobs (2013), p. 246 et seqq.

[144]*Jurisdiction and Enforcement of Judgments in Civil and Commercial Matters (Belgium v Switzerland)*, 2011 ICJ 341, 342, Order (5 April 2011).

[145]*Fisheries Jurisdiction (Spain v Canada)*, 1998 ICJ 432, Jurisdiction (4 December 1998).

[146]*Fisheries Jurisdiction (Spain v Canada)*, 1998 ICJ 432, Jurisdiction (4 December 1998), para. 27.

[147]See also Higgins (2003), p. 4 et seq.

[148]Higgins (2003), pp. 17–20; In fact, the ICJ will feel called upon to express itself on a matter another international court or tribunal has ruled only if it feels its monopoly over general issues of international law—such as state responsibility—stepped on. The classic example relates to the "scolding" of the ICTY expressing itself on "issues of general international law" which did not lie "within the specific purview of its jurisdiction" (on the matter of the effective/overall control test required in the context of attribution), *Application of the Convention on the Prevention and*

3.1.5 Evaluation: The EU and International Dispute Settlement Proceedings on Matters of General International Law

The international tribunals' approaches to the EU legal order in matters of general international law illustrates that, at the international level, generally no hierarchy among international judicial institutions is implemented.[149] Still, the tribunals used various techniques to reconcile overlapping jurisdictions, either when interpreting EU law or when ceding jurisdiction in favour of the CJEU. These techniques were in part predetermined by the jurisdictional clauses and the tribunals' mandates. Still, all techniques—ranging from the principle of comity (*MOX Plant* Annex VII Tribunal), a "disintegrated" understanding of one's mandate and jurisdictional scope (*MOX Plant* OSPAR tribunal), to a general display of judicial minimalism to avoid creating potentially conflicting interpretations of EU law (*Iron Rhine*, *Fisheries Jurisdiction*)[150]—demonstrate that international judicial bodies dealing with general aspects of international law do not cede jurisdiction to a hierarchically higher court but act in the interest of international coordination.[151] Guided by the objective to avoid conflicting outcomes, the tribunals generally displayed deference. They there by avoided jurisdictional conflicts. This approach, however, also resulted in the fact that the investigation of any *sui generis* elements of the EU legal order has so far remained minimal.

3.2 *The EU Within the WTO Regime*

3.2.1 Introduction

The relationship between the EU and the WTO regime is an entirely different case. The EU is a full member of the WTO. It thereby has accepted the (exclusive) jurisdiction of the WTO Dispute Settlement Body (DSB).[152] At the same time, the WTO dispute settlement mechanism is one of the few regimes where the EU can fully participate as an active party in the proceedings.[153] In numbers, it does so on

Punishment of the Crime of Genocide (Bosnia and Herzegovina v Serbia and Montenegro), 2007 ICJ 43, Judgment (26 February 2007), paras. 403–406.

[149]Leathley (2007).

[150]See particularly also Sect. 4.2 in more detail on these techniques.

[151]The discretionary choice on whether or not to apply these techniques stands in contrast to the CJEU which is eager to protect the "external dimension of supremacy", i.e. the autonomy of the EU legal order, from outside interference. Eckes (2012a), p. 232.

[152]As regards the exclusive jurisdiction, see Article 23(2) Understanding on Rules and Procedures Governing the Settlement of Disputes, 15 April 1994, 1869 UNTS 401.

[153]The WTO Agreement was concluded as a mixed agreement as some aspects fall within the competence of the member states, see CJEU, opinion 1/94, *Conclusion of the WTO Agreement*, ECLI:EU:C:1994:384.

an overwhelming basis: Of the 499 disputes which were initiated under the WTO dispute settlement system between 1995 and 2015, the EU participated in 316 of them as a complainant or defendant.[154] Moreover, in light of its exclusive competence with regard to the common commercial policy, the EU has generally taken over the role as a complainant or defendant in potential proceedings against EU member states.[155] This rests on the presumption that both the EU and its member states have assumed the same rights and obligations. It is also a necessary consequence of non-EU WTO members having limited insight into the division of competences between the EU and its member states.[156]

These aspects reflect on the case-law and how the EU legal order (and the CJEU) is considered by the WTO-DSB.

3.2.2 The EU Legal Order Through the Lens of the WTO Dispute Settlement Body

The position the Dispute Settlement Body (DSB Panel and Appellate Body (AB)) takes towards the EU and its common market is to a large extent similar to a state-like entity. In this sense, also the EU's legal order is generally treated in a similar manner to the domestic law of any other contracting party.[157] The analysis thereof serves a comparable purpose, i.e. evidence of fact, but also evidence of compliance

[154]Durán (2017), p. 10.

[155]Eckes (2013), p. 92; Durán (2017).

[156]Hoffmeister (2015), p. 124 et seq.

[157]The DSB regularly examines whether the alleged rights have been infringed by domestic measures, see also Matsushita et al. (2015), p. 32. The WTO's general treatment of domestic law can be discerned from cases investigated by the DSB, and was elaborated particularly clearly in *India-Patents (US)*: "In public international law, an international tribunal may treat municipal law in several ways. [. . .] Municipal law may serve as evidence of facts and may provide evidence of state practice. However, municipal law may also constitute evidence of compliance or non-compliance with international obligations. For example, in *Certain German Interests in Polish Upper Silesia*, the Permanent Court of International Justice observed: 'It might be asked whether a difficulty does not arise from the fact that the Court would have to deal with the Polish law of July 14th, 1920. This, however, does not appear to be the case. From the standpoint of International Law and of the Court which is its organ, municipal laws are merely facts which express the will and constitute the activities of States, in the same manner as do legal decisions and administrative measures. *The Court is certainly not called upon to interpret the Polish law as such; but there is nothing to prevent the Court's giving judgment on the question whether or not, in applying that law, Poland is acting in conformity with its obligations towards Germany under the Geneva Convention.*' [. . .] It is clear that an examination of the relevant aspects of Indian municipal law and, in particular, the relevant provisions of the Patents Act as they relate to the 'administrative instructions', is essential to determining whether India has complied with its obligations under Article 70.8(a). There was simply no way for the Panel to make this determination without engaging in an examination of Indian law. But, as in the case cited above before the Permanent Court of International Justice, in this case, the Panel was not interpreting Indian law 'as such'; rather, the Panel was examining Indian law solely for the purpose of determining whether India had met its obligations under the *TRIPS Agreement*. [. . .]" (Appellate Body Report,

or non-compliance of the EU with international obligations. Hence, EU law and judgments by the CJEU are referred to in order to establish whether the measures by the EU or its member states are in compliance with WTO regulations.[158]

Furthermore, there exist a number of examples which point to a position of the CJEU as a non-international judicial body.[159] In line with the attitude displayed by the EU itself,[160] non-EU WTO member states have utilized the CJEU's case-law as indicative of court rulings within a domestic legal order.[161] The DSB has also refrained from listing the CJEU among the "statutes of other international judicial bodies",[162] rather describing the CJEU as "the domestic court of 27 out of 153 Members of the WTO".[163] Moreover, in the latter instance, the DSB Panel continued to distinguish the CJEU's approach as one seeking "consistency [...] with [the EU's] [...] legal regime rather than applying the general rules of interpretation of public international law to determine the consistency of a measure with WTO obligations."[164]

Thus, also owed to the EU's position as a party in its own right, the EU legal order and the CJEU are treated in a similar manner to state-like entities or institutions.

However, at times, the *sui generis* character of the EU's legal framework is expressly acknowledged. For example, in *European Communities-Protection of Trademarks and Geographical Indications for Agricultural Products and Foodstuffs*, the legal framework and the division of competences regarding the implementation of EU law are categorized as "*sui generis* domestic constitutional

---

India—Patent Protection for Pharmaceutical and Agricultural Chemical Products, WT/DS50/AB/R, 19 December 1997, para. 65 et seq. (emphasis added by AB)).

[158]See, e.g., Panel Report, *European Communities—Measures Prohibiting the Importation and Marketing of Seal Products*, WT/DS401/R, 25 November 2013. For this purpose, judgments by the CJEU are treated similar to a domestic court, see, inter alia, Panel Report, *European Communities—Customs Classification of Frozen Boneless Chicken Cuts*, WT/DS269/R, 30 May 2005, para. 7.390 et seq. (equating CJEU judgments with EU legislation for the purpose of interpretation under Article 32 VCLT); cf. Fogdestam Agius (2014), p. 242.

[159]See, however, below as regards the distinct position of the CJEU.

[160]See, e.g., Panel Report, *United States—Continued Existence and Application of Zeroing Methodology*, WT/DS350/R, 1 October 2008, para. 72.

[161]See Marquet (2016), p. 11, with corresponding examples. The author argues that this might also be motivated by the disputing parties' intentions to keep the (moral) authority of the CJEU low or to weaken the consistency of the EU's position when pointing to cases conflicting with the EU's arguments as presented to the WTO DSB.

[162]Under this designation, the WTO Panel has, e.g., listed the ICJ, ITLOS, and the ICTY. Panel Report, *United States—Continued Suspension of Obligations in the EC—Hormones Disputes*, WT/DS320/R, 31 March 2008, para. 7.49.

[163]Panel Report, *European Communities and its Member States—Tariff Treatment of Certain Information Technology Products*, WT/DS375R, WT/DS376/R, WT/DS377/R, 16 August 2010, para. 7735, fn. 974; cf. Marquet (2016), p. 9.

[164]Panel Report, *European Communities and its Member States—Tariff Treatment of Certain Information Technology Products*, WT/DS375R, WT/DS376/R, WT/DS377/R, 16 August 2010, para. 7735, fn. 974.

arrangements",[165] whereby the member states of the EU become *de facto* organs to which certain functions are delegated.[166] However, despite recognizing the special institutional set-up, from an international law perspective, according to the WTO Dispute Settlement Body, this does not affect the individual status of EU member states as members of the WTO against whom non-EU member states have brought claims of violation.[167] Thus, whether or not EU member states choose to defend their own interests separate from the actions of the EU was considered as "entirely within their discretion".[168]

Additionally, the special position of EU institutions—particularly the CJEU—, floating between international and domestic law, is sometimes implicitly recognized. In fact, there are (albeit) isolated instances where the DSB deviates from the approach of treating the EU as a "mere" contracting party and instead cross-references the CJEU on an equal (international) level.[169] As pointed out in the *US-Anti-Dumping Act of 1916*, the DSB—where appropriate—develops its approach on questions of general international law "on the basis of that of international courts in similar circumstances."[170] In this sense, in *Korea-Taxes on Alcoholic Beverages*, the DSB pointed out the similarities between Article 95 of the TEC (now Article 114 TFEU) and Article III of the GATT, resorting to the CJEU's case-law on the understanding of the term "market".[171] In *US-Gambling*, the DSB Panel resorted to case-law of the CJEU on the question of limitations to

[165] See, e.g., Panel Report, *European Communities—Protection of Trademarks and Geographical Indications for Agricultural Products and Foodstuffs*, WT/DS174/R, 15 March 2005, para. 7.725. See also para. 7.450: "We recall the European Communities' explanation of its domestic constitutional arrangements [...] that Community laws are generally not executed through authorities at Community level but rather through recourse to the authorities of its member States which, in such a situation, 'act de facto as organs of the Community, for which the Community would be responsible under WTO law and international law in general'. [...] In accordance with its domestic law, the European Communities is entitled to delegate certain functions under its measure to the authorities of EC member States. [...]".

[166] See, e.g., Panel Report, *European Communities—Protection of Trademarks and Geographical Indications for Agricultural Products and Foodstuffs*, WT/DS174/R, 15 March 2005, para. 7.450.

[167] See particularly Panel Report, *European Communities and Certain Member States—Measures Affecting Trade in Large Civil Aircraft*, WT/DS316/R, 30 June 2010, para. 7.174.

[168] Panel Report, *European Communities and Certain Member States—Measures Affecting Trade in Large Civil Aircraft*, WT/DS316/R, 30 June 2010, para. 7.174.

[169] Cf. Qingzi Zang M, Shall We Talk? Judicial Communication Between the CJEU and the WTO Dispute Settlement, 2015, https://www.jus.uio.no/english/research/networks/european-law-network/events/european-law-forum/judicial-communication-cjeu-wto.pdf (last accessed 1 March 2017), p. 10.

[170] Panel Report, *United States—Anti-Dumping Act of 1916*, WT/DS136/R, 31 March 2000, para. 6.40.

[171] Panel Report, *Korea—Taxes on Alcoholic Beverages*, WT/DS84/R, 17 September 1998, para. 10.81. At the same time, however, the DSB Panel also pointed to the difference in scope and purpose of the EC Treaty and the General Agreement.

gambling activities in light of public policy considerations.[172] Finally, even more significant is the use of the CJEU's judgment *Racke*[173] in the Panel's report *Korea-Procurement* as support on the matter that Article 65 VCLT did not constitute customary international law,[174] evidencing the authority of the CJEU on a matter of general international law.[175] Notably, in the latter two instances, the EU was not party to the proceedings, underscoring the value designated to the CJEU as a parallel international adjudicatory body rather than a domestic court in support of evidence or state practice. These cases are, however, rather rare occasions and references to the CJEU's case-law appear to a significantly lesser degree than to the ICJ/PCIJ.[176]

3.2.3 Evaluation: The EU Within the WTO Regime

As a founding member of the WTO in its own right, the EU plays a dominant role within WTO proceedings, both as complainant and as defendant. On the basis of its (largely exclusive competences) it functionally represents itself—and is treated—as a state-like entity with a domestic market. As a consequence, its legal order is viewed similarly to the domestic orders of WTO member states, i.e. as a matter of fact, and in order to determine compliance/non-compliance with obligations deriving from the WTO regime. There are, however, few instances where the EU is viewed as an entity with *sui generis* characteristics. This relates particularly to its institutional design, i.e. the division of competences between the EU and its member states, and the special role of the CJEU. In dealing therewith, the DSB will in doubt resort to rules of international law—e.g. state responsibility[177]—to

---

[172]Panel Report, *United States—Measures Affecting the Cross-Border Supply of Gambling and Betting Services*, WT/DS285/R, 10 November 2004, para. 6.473: "Other jurisdictions have accepted that gambling activities could be limited or prohibited for public policy considerations, in derogation of general treaty or legislative rules." Supporting this statement with two CJEU cases, CJEU, case C-275/92, *H.M. Customs and Excise v Schindler*, ECLI:EU:C:1994:119; and CJEU, case C-6/01, *Anomar and others*, ECLI:EU:C:2003:446.

[173]CJEU, case C-162/96, *Racke v Hauptzollamt Mainz*, ECLI:EU:C:1998:293, note that the DSB Panel cites this case falsely with C-162/69, para. 59: "Even if such declarations do not satisfy the formal requirements laid down by Article 65 of the Vienna Convention, it should be noted that the specific procedural requirements there laid down do not form part of customary international law."

[174]Panel Report, *Korea—Measures Affecting Government Procurement*, WT/DS163/R, 1 May 2000, fn. 769.

[175]The ICJ formulated this slightly differently only a year prior to the *Racke* judgment in *Gabčikovo Nagymaros (Hungary v Slovakia)*, 1997 ICJ 7, Judgment (25 September 1997), para. 109: "Both Parties agree that Articles 65–67 of the Vienna Convention on the Law of Treaties, if not codifying customary law, at least generally reflect customary international law and contain certain procedural principles which are based on an obligation to act in good faith."

[176]See in this regard also Flett (2012), pp. 278–281, listing numerous examples.

[177]See, e.g., Panel Report, *European Communities—Selected Customs Matters*, WT/DS315/R, 16 June 2006, paras. 4.708 and 7.552, referencing Article 4 of the Articles on Responsibility for States for Internationally Wrongful Acts.

resolve open questions. Finally, in limited circumstances, the CJEU has also been used as an authoritative source to substantiate matters of international law.

3.3 The EU Within the ECHR Framework

3.3.1 Introduction

The EU in the system of the European Convention on Human Rights (ECHR) framework is dealt with differently again. The system of human rights protection is characterized by its vertical structure, with the rights of individuals being at stake. This also reflects on the relevant substantive law and the relation between the human rights regime and the EU.

So far, only EU member states are parties to the ECHR since the EU has not acceded to the Convention (yet). Consequently, to date, only states can be held accountable before the European Court of Human Rights (ECtHR) in accordance with Article 1 ECHR.[178] The EU legal order is merely indirectly at stake when acts of member states are examined by the European institutions (formerly the European Commission of Human Rights and, most importantly, the ECtHR) as to their human rights conformity.[179] While this will be changed in case of a future accession of the EU to the ECHR,[180] it is still uncertain when or whether this will take place, given the CJEU's rejection of the draft accession agreement.[181] The question of EU accession to the ECHR therefore still remains open.

---

[178]Article 1 ECHR: "The High Contracting parties shall secure to everyone within their jurisdiction the rights and freedoms defined in Section I of this Convention."; Acts directly against the EU or its institutions are inadmissible in Strasbourg ratione personae. See, e.g., European Commission, No. 8030/77, Confédération Francaise Démocratique du Travail v the European Communities, Decision of 10 July 1978, where the complaint was found inadmissible as being directed against a "person" not party to the Convention.

[179]As possible complaint avenues, the ECHR provides for individual and inter-state complaints (Articles 33, 34 ECHR).

[180]Note that a possible future accession of the EU to ECHR will considerably change the institutional setting. Once completed, the ECHR will become a mixed agreement and the acts of EU institutions may be examined as to their human rights conformity. The Treaty of Lisbon (Article 6(2) TEU) envisages the accession of the EU to the ECHR and states that the EU shall accede to the Convention under the conditions laid down in Protocol No. 8 to the Treaty. Accordingly, a draft agreement on the accession of the EU to the ECHR was negotiated early 2013. The very approach in the draft agreement was to generally treat the EU as a state and to give it a role identical to any other contracting party. See CJEU, Press release No 180/14 on Opinion 2/13, 18 December 2014, p. 2.

[181]While the CJEU was given a possibility to ensure, via the preliminary ruling procedure, a consistent interpretation and application of EU law, this was criticized by the CJEU as, inter alia, undermining the autonomy of EU law and, thus, not being compatible with EU law. (CJEU, opinion 2/13, *EU Accession to the ECHR*, ECLI:EU:C:2014:2454, para. 170 et seq.) See above, Sect. 2.2.2.

The relation between the ECHR and EU law is primarily at stake in the context of substantive obligations, i.e. alleged violations of the ECHR through (primary and secondary) EU law as applied by EU member states. In contrast, so far, no clear jurisdictional conflicts between the ECtHR and the CJEU have arisen. Individual applications do not concern the same subject matter and thus do not run the risk to encroach upon the exclusive jurisdiction of the CJEU (Article 344 TFEU). However, there is a possibility of such conflicts in case of inter-state complaints.[182] A possible example therefor has only recently (September 2016) been lodged with the ECtHR in form of the first EU inter-state complaint between Slovenia and Croatia.[183] Still, so far, the main issues concerning the EU's position within the ECHR framework have been substantive.

3.3.2 The EU Legal Order Through the Lens of ECHR Institutions

The ECtHR (and the European Commission of Human Rights) have mainly indirectly addressed the nature of the EU and its legal order. Questions have primarily concerned the responsibility of EU member states when applying (primary or secondary) EU law.[184] In these instances, the European Commission has also sometimes intervened through *amicus curiae* submissions.[185] Dependent on the

---

[182]Article 55 ECHR.

[183]On 15 September 2016, *Slovenia v Croatia* was lodged at the ECtHR, concerning claims of Ljubljanska banka towards Croatian companies. See also Hojnik J, Slovenia v Croatia: The first EU inter-state case before the ECtHR, EJIL:Talk!, 17 October 2016, for further reference. Although current EU member states have in the past been involved in mutual disputes before the ECtHR, at least one of them was not an EU member state at the time of those proceedings. See the inter-state complaints *Austria v Italy*, lodged in 1960 (No. 788/60), *Ireland v UK*, lodged in 1971 and 1972 (Nos. 5310/71 and 5451/72), and *Denmark and Sweden against Greece*, lodged in 1967 (Nos. 3321/67 and 3323/67), respectively.

[184]Aside from the instances addressed below under the equivalent protection doctrine, other constellations include interactions as regards admissibility/jurisdiction and whether infringement proceedings could be considered "another procedure of international investigation or settlement" in the meaning of Article 35(2)(b) ECHR. The ECtHR denied this, given the lack of similarity between the procedures, see ECtHR, No. 23205/08, *Karoussiotis v Portugal*, Judgment of 1 February 2011. Furthermore, non-compliance with EU law by EU member states was examined as to whether it amounted to a violation of the ECHR. Concerning the question whether a lack of reliance on the preliminary ruling procedure amounted to violation of Article 6(1) ECHR, the ECtHR's findings depended on the circumstances of the case. For example, in ECtHR, Nos. 3989/07, 38,353/07, *Ullens de Schooten and Rezabek v Belgium*, Judgment of 20 September 2011, the ECtHR, having regard to the proceedings as a whole, stated that there had been no violation of the Convention. Conversely, in ECtHR, No. 17120/09, *Dhahbi v Italy*, Judgment of 8 April 2014, non-compliance with the preliminary ruling procedure was (inter alia) found to be a violation of Article 6(1) ECHR because of the deficiencies in the procedure before the Italian court which had not given reasons for refusing to submit a preliminary question to the CJEU.

[185]See, inter alia, ECtHR, No. 45036/98, *Bosphorus v Ireland*, Judgment of 30 June 2005; ECtHR, No. 56672/00, *Senator Lines v Austria and others*, Judgment of 10 March 2004; ECtHR, No. 62023/00, *Emesa Sugar v the Netherlands*, Decision of 13 January 2005; ECtHR, No. 17502/07, *Avotiņš v Latvia*, Judgment of 23 May 2016.

respective constellations, the ECHR institutions' approaches to EU law and their perception of the EU have varied. Two typical constellations shall be demonstrated below. Firstly, situations concerning the transfer of competences on the EU as an international organization, i.e. the ECHR institutions' treatment of violations of the Convention through primary EU law; as well as the emergence of the equivalent protection doctrine when the ECtHR assesses the conduct of EU member states applying secondary EU law without any margin of discretion afforded. Secondly, other constellations, i.e. situations where the ECtHR scrutinizes the manner in which EU member states have implemented EU law as to its human rights conformity in cases where the member states are granted discretion.

The Classic Constellation: The EU as an International Organization

Violations of Member States' Human Rights Obligations Through Primary EU Law

The first set of cases concern violations of the ECHR through primary EU law. In these constellations, EU member states are held accountable for violations of human rights under the Convention through the adoption of the EU treaties. In those constellations, in so far possible, the ECtHR dealt with the EU as a "classic international organisation" and EU law was viewed as "normal" international law.

The point of departure and general framework of Strasbourg institutions was the continuous application of the ECHR on the basis of the *res inter alios acta* rule (Article 30(4)(b) VCLT). Accordingly, in case of successive treaties relating to the same subject matter, when not all parties to the first treaty—the 1950 ECHR—are parties to the later treaty or treaties (the EU treaties), the rules of the prior treaty apply between the states which are not parties to both treaties. Already in 1958, the European Commission of Human Rights ruled that

> if a State contracts treaty obligations and subsequently concludes another international agreement which disables it from performing its obligations under the first treaty, it will be answerable for any resulting breach of its obligations under the earlier treaty.[186]

This was particularly so, according to the (then) European Commission of Human Rights, as the obligation in question had been assumed in a treaty, the ECHR, whose guarantees affected "the public order of Europe".[187]

Also, the ECtHR referred to the well-established rule[188] that states cannot circumvent their obligations under the ECHR through the establishment of an international organization. In *Matthews v UK*[189] the ECtHR dealt with the interrelationship between the ECHR and the EU treaties accordingly. A UK resident in Gibraltar had alleged a breach of her right to free elections on account of the fact that the UK had not organized elections to the European Parliament in Gibraltar. The violation of

[186]European Commission, No. 236/56, *X v Germany*, Decision of 10 June 1958.

[187]European Commission, No. 788/60, *Austria v Italy*, Decision of 11 January 1961.

[188]See generally on this also Ryngaert (2011), p. 997 et seqq.

[189]ECtHR, No. 24833/94, *Matthews v UK*, Judgment of 18 February 1999.

the ECHR originated in primary EU law. The ECtHR stated that a state could not absolve itself from its human rights obligations through a transfer of competences to international organizations as the state retained the responsibility for a treaty it had been involved in adopting. While the ECtHR pointed out that the ECHR did not exclude the transfer of competences to international organizations, it stated that Convention rights would need to remain "secured".[190] The responsibility of member states therefore continued after such transfer.[191] As regards the "nature" of the EU, the ECtHR thus clearly perceived it as a "classic" international organization.

In relation to primary EU law and the direct responsibility of member states in its adoption, the approach of Strasbourg institutions is thus relatively straight forward.

The Equivalent Protection Doctrine

The question is more complex in situations where EU member states are to be held accountable for the application of secondary EU law. This, especially, if there is no discretion as regards its application. When states have only limited possibility to influence EU acts and those of EU institutions, they may be "torn" between their obligations under the ECHR and those arising from their membership in the EU with little means to correct this.

This constellation underscores the ECtHR's prevailing approach to the EU and gave rise to the development of the equivalent protection doctrine. The leading case in this regard is *Bosphorus Airways v Ireland*,[192] a Grand Chamber judgment of 2005. It was the first time that the ECtHR accepted to examine a complaint on the merits concerning measures adopted to give effect to Community law where the state had no discretion as regards the application.[193] The ECtHR thus had to assess the compatibility of EU law with the ECHR and the responsibility of states for EU acts. The ECtHR found that Ireland had merely complied with its obligations as a result of its membership of the EU and "the presumption [arose] that Ireland did not depart from the requirements of the Convention when it implemented legal obligations flowing from its membership of the European Community".[194] Still, according to the ECtHR, the presumption could also be rebutted in situations where the protection of Convention rights was manifestly deficient.[195]

---

[190] ECtHR, No. 24833/94, *Matthews v UK*, Judgment of 18 February 1999, para. 32.

[191] On that basis, the Court established a violation of Article 3 of Protocol No. 1 to the ECHR.

[192] ECtHR, No. 45036/98, *Bosphorus v Ireland*, Judgment of 30 June 2005.

[193] Irish authorities had seized and impounded an aircraft leased by the applicant company to a Yugoslavian company under a Community Regulation giving effect to UN sanctions against the Federal Republic of Yugoslavia. The ECtHR, No. 45036/98, *Bosphorus v Ireland*, Judgment of 30 June 2005, para. 154, stated that "absolving Contracting States completely from their Convention responsibility in the areas covered by such a transfer would be incompatible with the purpose and object of the Convention; the guarantees of the Convention could be limited or excluded at will, thereby depriving it of its peremptory character and undermining the practical and effective nature of its safeguards."

[194] ECtHR, No. 45036/98, *Bosphorus v Ireland*, Judgment of 30 June 2005, para. 165.

[195] ECtHR, No. 45036/98, *Bosphorus v Ireland*, Judgment of 30 June 2005, paras. 156 and 158.

The equivalent protection doctrine was further developed in later cases.[196] In *Kokkelvisserij v the Netherlands*,[197] the ECtHR referred to the doctrine in relation to the system of preliminary rulings to the CJEU and alleged violations of Article 6 ECHR. It found—again—that the applicant (organisation) had failed to show that the protection afforded was manifestly deficient and thus had been unable to rebut the presumption that the procedure before the CJEU provided equivalent protection of its rights. The application was thus rejected as manifestly ill-founded.

The equivalent protection doctrine shows the ECtHR's cautious approach towards the EU and its lenient level of scrutiny. The Court does not apply a strict standard of review. It does not examine the proportionality of the measures adopted[198] but restricts itself to examining whether the protection has been

[196]In addition to *Kokkelvisserij* see, inter alia, ECtHR, No. 12323/11, *Michaud v France*, Judgment of 6 December 2012; ECtHR, No. 3890/11, *Povse v Austria*, Judgment of 18 June 2013. Most recently, in *Avotiņš v Latvia* (2016), the ECtHR referred to the equivalent protection doctrine in relation to the enforcement in Latvia of a judgment delivered in 2004 in Cyprus with regard to the repayment of a debt. Although relevant EU law had not left any discretion to Latvia as to the enforcement of a judgment of another member state, the applicant had filed a complaint against Latvia claiming that the Latvian courts had authorized the enforcement of the Cypriot judgment which, in his opinion, had been delivered in violation of his defence rights. (See also the observations by the Commission of the European Union in ECtHR, No. 17502/07, *Avotiņš v Latvia*, Judgment of 23 May 2016, para. 89: "Hence, the courts of the Member States could not exercise any discretion in ordering the enforcement of a judgment given in another Member State. Such an act fell strictly within the scope of the international legal obligations of the Member State in which enforcement was sought, arising out of its membership of the European Union.") In application of the equivalent protection doctrine, the ECtHR did not find that the protection of fundamental rights had been manifestly deficient to such an extent that the presumption of equivalent protection was rebutted and thus there had been no violation of Article 6(1) ECHR. ECtHR, No. 17502/07, *Avotiņš v Latvia*, Judgment of 23 May 2016, was the first case upholding the *Bosphorus* presumption after opinion 2/13 by the CJEU.

[197]ECtHR, No. 13645/05, *Kokkelvisserij v the Netherlands*, Decision of 20 January 2009, B.3.: "The nexus between a preliminary ruling by the ECJ under Article 234 of the EC Treaty and the domestic proceedings which give rise to it is obvious. [. . .] However, as already noted, there is a presumption that a Contracting Party has not departed from the requirements of the Convention where it has taken action in compliance with legal obligations flowing from its membership of an international organisation to which it has transferred part of its sovereignty, as long as the relevant organisation is considered to protect fundamental rights, as regards both the substantive guarantees offered and the mechanisms controlling their observance, in a manner which can be considered at least equivalent to that for which the Convention provides. As a corollary, this presumption applies not only to actions taken by a Contracting Party but also to the procedures followed within such an international organisation and hence to the procedures of the ECJ. In that connection the Court also reiterates that such protection need not be identical to that provided by Article 6 of the Convention; the presumption can be rebutted only if, in the circumstances of a particular case, it is considered that the protection of Convention rights was manifestly deficient. Consequently, the Court must examine whether, in the present case, the procedure before the ECJ was accompanied by guarantees which ensured equivalent protection of the applicant association's rights."

[198]See ECtHR, No. 45036/98, *Bosphorus v Ireland*, Judgment of 30 June 2005, para. 165, where the ECtHR held that it was not necessary to examine whether the measure had been proportionate to the aims pursued, given that "the protection of fundamental rights by Community law [is] [. . .] 'equivalent' to that of the Convention system".

"manifestly deficient". In doing so, the Court exercises deference *vis-à-vis* the EU and carves out space for the EU's radius of action. The ECtHR's deference is also evidenced by the fact that so far, it seems to have never established that the human rights protection in the EU was "manifestly deficient" at a point as to rebut the presumption of an equivalent protection of rights within the organization. The general rule that a state must not circumvent its human rights violations through the transfer of competences to an international organization remains applicable; however, the equivalent protection doctrine somehow softens the approach by creating a presumption of human rights compliance. Also, despite the absence of close human rights scrutiny with regard to EU action, the ECtHR retains the final word (*Kompetenz-Kompetenz*) as regards the human rights conformity of EU acts. The rebuttable presumption under the equivalent protection doctrine and the implementation of the "manifestly deficient" standard empower the ECtHR to install certain "outer limits" for EU action from a human rights perspective.[199]

Overall, the equivalent protection doctrine is a prudent approach to deal with the EU as an international organization in relation to compliance with Convention guarantees.[200] All by upholding the ECHR as the constitutional instrument of the European public order (*Loizidou*), the ECtHR spares EU member states the "Catch 22" situation of being found in violation of Convention guarantees in situations which they have limited possibility to change at the EU level (whether in light of CJEU rulings or the adoption of EU decisions by majority rule). In a multilevel system of law, the ECtHR creates room for action by the EU and its member states, however, within a constitutional order which is governed by human rights.[201]

[199]This was shown, e.g., in ECtHR's discussion of the preliminary rulings procedure in *Kokkelvisserij* where the Court examined whether the procedure was accompanied by guarantees which ensured the equivalent protection of the applicant's rights. ECtHR, No. 13645/05, *Kokkelvisserij v the Netherlands*, Decision of 20 January 2009, see quote in fn. 197. Still, the ECtHR generally accepts the EU division of competences on which it bases its judgments. In ECtHR, No. 3890/11, *Povse v Austria*, Judgment of 18 June 2013, the ECtHR declared a complaint in reliance on Article 8 ECHR inadmissible in a situation where Austrian courts had limited themselves to comply with their obligations under EU law in relation to the Austrian ordering of the enforcement an Italian judgment without examining the argument that the child's return to Italy would be against her interest.

[200]See again ECtHR, No. 13645/05, *Kokkelvisserij v the Netherlands*, Decision of 20 January 2009, quote in fn 197.

[201]See Tietje's similar suggestion for investment law, Tietje (2013), p. 22 et seq. The ECtHR's case-law may also be compared to the *Solange II* jurisprudence of the German Federal Constitutional Court. In BVerfGE 73, 339—*Solange II*, the German Federal Constitutional Court stated that the standard of human rights protection ensured by the (then) European Community could be considered as in substance, content and effect, substantially equal to the one provided by the German Basic Law. Therefore, the German Federal Constitutional Court would no longer carry out a review of secondary Community legislation as long as the human rights protection by the European Community and in particular the CJEU could be considered as basically equal to the one provided by the German Basic Law.

Further Constellations: Discretion of EU Member States in the Implementation of EU Law

The ECtHR also assessed its relationship with the EU and its legal order in situations where EU member states were afforded discretion in the implementation of EU law. A cautious approach by the ECtHR can be discerned in this constellation as well.[202] The ECtHR reviews how the state filled the room for manoeuvre left by EU law.[203] This review, however, is limited to the action of the state parties since—as explained above—the ECtHR does not directly subject EU acts and the EU system as such to its jurisdiction. For example, in *MSS v Belgium and Greece*,[204] the ECtHR found, inter alia, that Belgium had violated the ECHR by acting in compliance with rules of EU asylum law (Dublin II Regulation). Belgium had sent an Afghan asylum seeker back to Greece, his first point of entry in the EU, in line with the Dublin II system. Still, EU law had not required Belgium to act this way and rather left certain leeway in implementation.[205] Hence, while the ECtHR found Belgium in violation of the ECHR, it did not take a direct position as regards the human rights conformity of the EU system as such. As stated by *Eckes*:

> [. . .] even though the MSS ruling questioned the blind mutual trust on which EU asylum law is built (see e.g. the presumption that all EU Member States are safe), it did not entail a judgment that the Dublin II system as such is unlawful.[206]

Accordingly, the way how EU member states implement EU law may be subject to review. However, the ECtHR refrains also in this context from assessing the human rights conformity of the EU legal order properly speaking. As a result, the

[202]See, e.g., ECtHR, No. 45036/98, *Bosphorus v Ireland*, Judgment of 30 June 2005, para. 157 et seq., distinguishing between cases with and without states' discretion in the implementation of EU law. "It remains the case that a State would be fully responsible under the Convention for all acts falling outside its strict international legal obligations. The numerous Convention cases cited by the applicant company in paragraph 117 above confirm this. Each case (in particular, Cantoni, p. 1626, para. 26) concerned a review by this Court of the exercise of State discretion for which Community law provided. [. . .] 158. Since the impugned measure constituted solely compliance by Ireland with its legal obligations flowing from membership of the European Community [. . .], the Court will now examine whether a presumption arises that Ireland complied with the requirements of the Convention in fulfilling such obligations and whether any such presumption has been rebutted in the circumstances of the present case".

[203]Already in 1996, in ECtHR, No. 17862/91, *Cantoni v France*, Judgment of 11 November 1996, a state's (France's) accountability for the application of EU law was at stake.

[204]ECtHR, No. 30696/09, *MSS v Belgium and Greece*, Judgment of 21 January 2011.

[205]See the general "first entry" rule in Council Regulation (EC) No 343/2003 (OJ 2003 L 50/1), Article 3(1) and the possibility for Belgium to derogate from that rule and take charge of the application in Article 3(2) thereof. Cf. Eckes (2012b), p. 261. A similar conclusion can be drawn from ECtHR, No. 29217/12, *Tarakhel v Switzerland*, Judgment of 4 November 2014, where the ECtHR's scrutiny focused on how the Swiss authorities exercised their discretion in applying the Dublin Regulation.

[206]Eckes (2012b), p. 261 et seq. (footnote omitted).

ECtHR again only indirectly examines the status of EU law: namely *via* its impact in the domestic legal orders of states under its scrutiny.

3.3.3 Evaluation: The EU Within the ECHR Framework

The Strasbourg institutions do not acknowledge the *sui generis* character of the EU. Rather, the EU is approached as a "classic" international organization. Nor do the ECtHR (and the European Commission of Human Rights) accept the primacy/supremacy of EU law. To arrive at this conclusion, they relied on classic rules of international law as regards the resolution of norm conflicts, such as the *res inter alios acta* rule. At the same time, the ECtHR exercises certain (limited) deference towards the EU and EU law. The ECtHR will, in principle, refrain from taking a direct position on the conformity of EU law with the ECHR. Rather, it will hold states accountable in relation to how they use their remaining discretion when applying EU law without directly positioning itself in relation to the "conventionality" of the latter (see *MSS*). Where member states have no discretion, the ECtHR will defer to EU acts in application of the equivalent protection doctrine. However, the deference is not unlimited: the presumption of equivalent protection is rebuttable where the protection under EU law has proved to be "manifestly deficient" in the specific case at hand (which has so far never been the case). As a result of this approach, the EU is perceived as an international organization which is given space for its functioning. This, however, in an international order which is ultimately determined by human rights.[207]

An even more direct human rights scrutiny of the EU and EU law will be exercised after the EU's accession to the ECHR. In accordance with the draft accession agreement, EU acts and laws will be directly examined as to their human rights conformity: Complaints can then be lodged directly against the EU. Furthermore, the EU should be given a role identical in every respect to that of any other contracting party.[208] EU law should accordingly be treated as any other domestic law.[209] Still, it will take some time for this option to materialize given the CJEU's strong position that the draft accession of the EU to the ECHR was not compatible with EU law.

[207] In fact, the ECtHR's approach to the EU seems generally characterized by its aim to maintain the ECHR as the "constitutional instrument of the European public order". ECtHR, No. 15318/89, *Loizidou v Turkey*, Judgment of 23 March 1995, para. 75.

[208] CJEU, Press release No 180/14 on opinion 2/13, 18 December 2014.

[209] Cf. Odermatt (2014), p. 42 citing De Schutter: "It would be neither legally justified nor politically opportune to maintain the Bosphorus doctrine in its current form, as a doctrine that places the European Union in a privileged position, and that, instead of treating the Court of Justice of the European Union as a constitutional court comparable to any other, somehow inexplicably defers to its assessments more generously than to similar assessments made by its national counterparts."

3.4 The EU Within the Investment Law Regime

3.4.1 Introduction

The jurisprudence of international investment tribunals is another example of how the EU and EU law may be approached. Of most interest with regard to the interaction of the EU legal order with the investment law regime are challenges of the jurisdiction of investment tribunals as well as alleged violations of investment treaties—mainly of bilateral investment treaties which have been concluded between EU member states (intra-EU BITs) and of the Energy Charter Treaty (ECT) as a mixed agreement where the EU and its member states are parties. In all these situations, investment tribunals had to take a clear position as to the status of EU law. This even more, since especially intra-EU BITs are strongly opposed by the European Commission, inter alia because, according to the Commission, there exists a potential and actual conflict between EU law and the substantive standards contained in BITs; and investment arbitration constitutes a parallel system of adjudication which is removed from CJEU supervision and control.[210] Against this background, the European Commission has started infringement proceedings against several member states, inter alia, Austria, Sweden, Romania, Slovakia and the Netherlands.[211] The European Commission also opposes claims by investors of EU member states against other EU member states under the ECT.[212] It is thus of particular interest how the investment tribunals dealt with the EU and EU law.

3.4.2 The EU Legal Order Through the Lens of Investment Tribunals

The investment tribunals' approaches to the EU legal order were at stake in several cases which have been brought before investment tribunals under intra-EU BITs. Most of these were brought in the context of the accession of new member states to the EU which had previously concluded investment treaties and where measures adopted as required by EU law impacted negatively on investors. From the question

---

[210]See, inter alia, the arguments brought in *Electrabel v Hungary*, ICSID Case No. ARB/07/19, Decision on Jurisdiction, Applicable law and Liability (30 November 2012); Letter of the European Commission, Internal Market and Services of 13 January 2006 quoted in *Eastern Sugar*, UNCITRAL, Partial Award (27 March 2007), paras. 24–26; European Commission Observations, 7 July 2010, paras. 30 and 38, cited in *Eureko/Achmea*, UNCITRAL, Decision on Jurisdiction (26 October 2010), paras. 180 and 182; see generally Kriebaum (2015).

[211]See European Commission, Commission asks member states to terminate their intra-EU bilateral investment treaties, Press release IP-15-5198, 18 June 2015.

[212]See generally Roe et al. (2011), p. 93 et seq.

of the investment tribunals' dealing with EU law and EU institutions, the most interesting are *Eastern Sugar v Czech Republic*, *Eureko v Slovakia*, *Oostergetel v Slovakia* and *Micula v Romania*.[213] Under the ECT, *Electrabel v Hungary*, *AES v Hungary* and *RREEF Infrastructure v Spain* are of relevance.[214]

One may distinguish between the approaches by investment tribunals at the stage of jurisdiction (first, in application of the techniques for the resolution of norm conflicts under general international law; and second, in cases of potential jurisdictional conflict with the CJEU (Article 344 TFEU)) and the question of applicable law as a predominantly substantive question.

Jurisdiction of Investment Tribunals and the EU Legal Order

Techniques for the Resolution of Norm Conflicts Under General International Law

The investment tribunals' position on the EU and EU law was influenced by the arguments brought in relation to challenges of their jurisdiction by respondent states (formally or informally supported by the European Commission). Respectively, as regards intra-EU BITs, investment tribunals in *Eastern Sugar*, *Eureko*, *Oostergetel* and *Micula* were confronted with the argument that the investment treaties would have automatically terminated upon accession of the new member states to the EU and deprive investment tribunals of their jurisdiction. This either on the basis of the primacy of EU law or because the investment treaties had

[213] *Eastern Sugar*, UNCITRAL, Partial Award (27 March 2007); *Eureko/Achmea*, UNCITRAL, Decision on Jurisdiction (26 October 2010); *Oostergetel v The Slovak Republic*, UNCITRAL, Decision on Jurisdiction (30 April 2010); *Micula v Romania*, ICSID Case No. ARB/05/20, Final Award (11 December 2013); see also *Binder v Czech Republic*, UNCITRAL, Final Award (15 July 2011); *European American Investment Bank AG (EURAM) v Slovak Republic*, UNCITRAL, Award on Jurisdiction (22 October 2012). The latter are of reduced relevance in view of their only indirect dealing with EU law.

[214] *Electrabel v Hungary*, ICSID Case No. ARB/07/19, Decision on Jurisdiction, Applicable law and Liability (30 November 2012); *AES v Hungary*, ICSID Case No. ARB/07/22, Award (23 September 2010); *RREEF Infrastructure v Spain*, ICSID Case No. ARB/13/30, Decision on Jurisdiction (6 June 2016).

automatically terminated upon the date of accession to the EU in application of Articles 59(1)[215] and 30(3) VCLT.[216,217] As regards the ECT, similar objections to jurisdiction were brought forward. For example, in *Electrabel* the European Commission submitted in its *amicus curiae* brief that EU law had superseded the ECT, changed the scope of Hungary's consent or rendered the arbitration agreement invalid or inapplicable.[218] Also in *RREEF v Spain*, related arguments ("intra-EU objections") were made.[219]

In relation to these submissions, the investment tribunals' approach was relatively firm. They declined to assign any specific status to the EU and EU law and did not accept the latter's primacy/supremacy.[220] Rather, they generally relied on the treaties on the basis of which they had been established—the intra-EU BIT or the ECT—to uphold their jurisdiction and discarded EU law. For example, the *Eureko* tribunal did not consider EU law of importance when determining its jurisdiction by stating that "[i]t considers that its jurisdiction is fixed by laws"[221] and that "the Tribunal cannot derive any part of its jurisdiction or authority from EU law as such: its jurisdiction is derived from the consent of the Parties to the dispute, in accordance with the BIT and German law".[222] On this basis, the tribunal set aside the application of relevant EU law.

---

[215] Article 59 VCLT reads as follows: "Termination or suspension of the operation of a treaty implied by conclusion of a later treaty. (1) A treaty shall be considered as terminated if all the parties to it conclude a later treaty relating to the same subject matter and: a) it appears from the later treaty or is otherwise established that the parties intended that the matter should be governed by that treaty; or b) the provisions of the later treaty are so far incompatible with those of the earlier one that the two treaties are not capable of being applied at the same time. [...]".

[216] Article 30 VCLT reads as follows: "Application of successive treaties relating to the same subject matter: [...] (3) When all the parties to the earlier treaty are parties to the later treaty but the earlier treaty is not terminated or suspended in operation under Article 59, the earlier treaty applies only to the extent that its provisions are compatible with those of the later treaty."

[217] See, for example, the position of the European Commission (letter of the DG Internal Market) in a letter submitted in *Eastern Sugar*, UNCITRAL, Partial Award (27 March 2007). See for further reference Reinisch (2012), p. 161. For a position which supports the supremacy of EU law see Eilmansberger (2009), p. 426. The latter was, however, unanimously rejected by investment tribunals. See also *Micula v Romania,* ICSID Case No. ARB/05/20, Final Award (11 December 2013), para. 179 et seq. For further references, where the Commission took the position that the treaties had automatically lapsed by operation of Article 59(1) VCLT, also upheld in *Micula v Romania*, ICSID Case No. ARB/05/20, Decision on Annulment (26 February 2016), para. 331 et seq.

[218] See arguments of European Commission as cited in *Electrabel v Hungary*, ICSID Case No. ARB/07/19, Decision on Jurisdiction, Applicable law and Liability (30 November 2012), para. 4.102 et seqq.

[219] *RREEF Infrastructure v Spain*, ICSID Case No. ARB/13/30, Decision on Jurisdiction (6 June 2016), para. 35.

[220] In fact, the position which confers primacy/supremacy to EU law is strongest. To presume a *sui generis* nature and to assign an according primacy to EU law over other treaties (see Article 218(11) TFEU) would imply that BIT provisions contrary to (primary or secondary) EU law can no longer be applied. See Tietje (2013), p. 8.

[221] *Eureko/Achmea*, UNCITRAL, Decision on Jurisdiction (26 October 2010), para. 219.

[222] *Eureko/Achmea*, UNCITRAL, Decision on Jurisdiction (26 October 2010), para. 225.

Also the *RREEF* tribunal stated that "EU law as a whole [. . .] must be considered as being part of international law outside the EU legal order."[223] On this basis the Tribunal held:

> [. . .] in case of any contradiction between the ECT and EU law, the Tribunal would have to insure the full application of its 'constitutional' instrument, upon which its jurisdiction is founded. [. . .] [I]f there must be a 'hierarchy' between the norms to be applied by the Tribunal, it must be determined from the perspective of public international law, not of EU law. Therefore, the ECT prevails over any other norm (apart from those of *ius cogens* – but this is not an issue in the present case).[224]

As regards the status of EU law, when upholding their jurisdiction, investment tribunals generally adopted a public international law approach and applied the techniques for the resolution of conflicts of norms, i.e. Articles 59(1) and 30(3) VCLT (all parties to the earlier treaty are party to the later treaty), in relation to intra-EU BITs.[225] On this basis, the "automatic termination" argument, i.e. that the intra-EU BITs had automatically terminated upon accession of the new member states to the EU was generally rejected by tribunals.[226] The tribunals found the intra-EU BITs to be fully applicable and affirmed their jurisdiction.

A similar "general international law approach" was adopted in ECT arbitrations.[227] On the basis of the *res inter alios acta* rule (Article 30(4)(b)

[223] *RREEF Infrastructure v Spain*, ICSID Case No. ARB/13/30, Decision on Jurisdiction (6 June 2016), para. 73.

[224] *RREEF Infrastructure v Spain*, ICSID Case No. ARB/13/30, Decision on Jurisdiction (6 June 2016), para. 75.

[225] Articles 59(1) and 30(3) VCLT.

[226] Inter alia, it was argued that the treaties did not cover the "same subject matter" since the substantive guarantees in the BITs were more specific than those available under EU law. See for further reference *Eureko/Achmea*, UNCITRAL, Decision on Jurisdiction (26 October 2010), paras. 69 et seq., 235, 244 et seq., 262 and 283; *Eastern Sugar*, UNCITRAL, Partial Award (27 March 2007), paras. 101, 167, 172 and 180; *Oostergetel v The Slovak Republic*, UNCITRAL, Decision on Jurisdiction (30 April 2010), paras. 66, 80 and 104. See for further reference Kriebaum (2015), p. 31. See also Reinisch (2012), p. 165 et seqq. Also the *Micula* tribunal found that there was no real conflict under the law of treaties, see *Micula v Romania*, ICSID Case No. ARB/05/20, Final Award (11 December 2013), para. 319. See generally Binder (2016).

[227] The *Electrabel* tribunal affirmed its jurisdiction. In fact, the jurisdictional issue had not been raised by a party but the EU which suggested in its *amicus* submission that the tribunal lacked jurisdiction to hear the PPA Termination claim. The tribunal highlighted that the EU had accepted jurisdiction of the tribunal and the possibility of investment arbitration with private parties, including EU nationals, by ratifying the ECT. *Electrabel v Hungary*, ICSID Case No. ARB/07/19, Decision on Jurisdiction, Applicable law and Liability (30 November 2012), para. 4.158.

VCLT)—when not all parties to the earlier treaty (the ECT) were parties to the later treaty[228]—both the *Electrabel*[229] and the *RREEF*[230] tribunals considered that the ECT was to be applied.

Accordingly, the investment tribunals' classic international law approach viewed EU law as "normal" international law. This led the investment tribunals in intra-EU BIT as well as in ECT proceedings to generally uphold their jurisdiction, mainly in reliance on the techniques for the resolution of norm conflicts under general international law. Any reference to the primacy/supremacy of EU law was rejected.

Possible Conflicts with the CJEU's Exclusive Jurisdiction (Article 344 TFEU)

Likewise, the CJEU's exclusive jurisdiction was declined by the investment tribunals, when considering the relevance of Article 344 TFEU in investor-state dispute settlement proceedings. It had been argued by the European Commission or respondent states, inter alia, in reliance on the *MOX Plant* proceedings, that Article 344 TFEU (and the principle of loyalty) would imply that the CJEU had exclusive jurisdiction over disputes between two member states.[231]

Investment tribunals, however, have consistently rejected the argument. They generally found that Article 344 TFEU was inapplicable since it referred to inter-state—rather than to investor-state—disputes. Accordingly, the fields of dispute were different. For example, the *Eureko* tribunal held in this regard:

> There is, however, no rule of EU law that prohibits investor-State arbitration. Far from it: transnational arbitration is a commonplace throughout the EU, including arbitrations between legal persons and States; and the European Court of Justice has given several indications of how questions of EU law should be handled in the course of arbitrations, including important questions of public policy. It cannot be asserted that all arbitrations that involve any question of EU law are conducted in violation of EU law.[232]

[228]The 1994 ECT (entry into force 1998) is the earlier treaty; still it has 54 treaty parties, see http://www.energycharter.org/who-we-are/members-observers/ (last accessed 1 March 2017). In relation to previous agreements, Article 16 ECT applies.

[229]*Electrabel v Hungary*, ICSID Case No. ARB/07/19, Decision on Jurisdiction, Applicable law and Liability (30 November 2012), para. 4.112. See also *AES v Hungary*, ICSID Case No. ARB/07/22, Award (23 September 2010), para. 7.6.4.

[230]*RREEF Infrastructure v Spain*, ICSID Case No. ARB/13/30, Decision on Jurisdiction (6 June 2016), para. 74: "[. . .] this Tribunal has been established by a specific treaty, the ECT, which binds both, the EU and its Member States on the one hand and non-EU States on the other hand. As for the latter, EU law is *res inter alios acta* and it cannot be upheld that, by ratifying the ECT, those non-EU States have accepted the EU law as prevailing over the ECT".

[231]See, e.g., *Eureko/Achmea*, UNCITRAL, Decision on Jurisdiction (26 October 2010), para. 276. As stated above, the object and purpose of Article 344 TFEU is to avoid arrangements that would deprive the CJEU of its jurisdiction to settle disputes concerning EU law. See also *Binder v Czech Republic*, UNCITRAL, Award on Jurisdiction (6 June 2007), para. 44.

[232]*Eureko/Achmea*, UNCITRAL, Decision on Jurisdiction (26 October 2010), para. 274.

The tribunal also expressly distinguished the case before it from the abovementioned *MOX Plant* dispute where the tribunal's approach had been characterized by comity and deference *vis-à-vis* the CJEU's jurisdiction:

> Reference was made to the ruling of the ECJ in the MOX Plant case [...]. Whatever the implications of that ruling might be for Article 10 of the BIT, which is concerned with disputes between the BIT Contracting Parties, the ruling is not applicable to disputes under Article 8 which are not disputes between the BIT Contracting Parties but investor-State disputes. There is no suggestion here that every dispute that arises between a Member State and an individual must be put before the ECJ; nor would the ECJ have the jurisdiction (let alone the capacity) to decide all such cases.[233]

Accordingly, on the basis of the difference of the disputes, the tribunal upheld its jurisdiction.

Appreciation

Investment tribunals thus generally considered the respective intra-EU BITs and the ECT to be applicable, discarded EU law and affirmed their jurisdiction. This does not equal the same level of deference as portrayed by other international tribunals (e.g. in the *MOX Plant* dispute) or the ECtHR. Investment tribunals have neither resorted to jurisdictional means of coordination (e.g. the principle of comity) nor carved out space for the functioning of the EU by techniques such as the ECtHR's equivalent protection doctrine. Rather, investment tribunals affirmed their jurisdiction in application of the rules for the resolution of norm conflict of general international law, expressly stating or inferring thereby that the EU Treaties—at least insofar as their jurisdiction was concerned—remained classified as general international law instruments.

The EU Legal Order and the Question of Applicable Law

The question of the nature of the EU legal order likewise arose in relation to the applicable law.[234] The qualification of EU law was in part predetermined by the respective applicable law provisions in investment treaties, which establish which law

[233] *Eureko/Achmea*, UNCITRAL, Decision on Jurisdiction (26 October 2010), para. 276.

[234] As a general rule, the law in force at the time of the relevant events has to be applied to the merits of the case. This principle is reflected in Article 13 ARSIWA—Articles on Responsibility of States for Internationally Wrongful Acts, UNGA Res 56/83 (2001) UN Doc. A/56/10. See also Article 28 VCLT concerning the non-retroactivity of treaties. This rule is also firmly established in arbitral practice. Already Judge Huber in *Island of Palmas (United States of America v Netherlands)*, 2 RIAA 829, Award (4 April 1928), p. 845, stated: "[...] a juridical fact must be appreciated in the light of the law contemporary with it, and not of the law in force at the time when a dispute in regard to it arises or falls to be settled." Accordingly, EU law can only be part of the "applicable law" if the relevant events occurred after the accession of the respective states to the EU (or are judged by reference to earlier treaties such as the 1995 Europe Agreement in *Micula*).

is to be applied to a case. These clauses vary. For example, while Article 26(6) ECT refers to international law as applicable law[235] other applicable law-provisions in investment treaties are broader. For ICSID proceedings, the ICSID Convention establishes in Article 42(1):

> The Tribunal shall decide a dispute in accordance with such rule of law as may be agreed by the parties. In the absence of such agreement, the Tribunal shall apply the law of the contracting party to the dispute [. . .] and such rules of international law as may be applicable.[236]

Many intra-EU BITs contain similar provisions and (also) refer to domestic law as law which is applicable to the dispute.[237]

On the basis of such varying clauses, distinct approaches by investment tribunals can be identified. In certain intra-EU BIT proceedings, EU law was considered as part of the applicable domestic law of one of the parties. In *Oostergetel*, the tribunal held that the applicable law included domestic law which in turn included EU law following Slovakia's accession to the EU. On how to deal with the resulting interaction between the two legal orders, the tribunal stated "if EU law must be applied, this Tribunal will seek to interpret both the BIT and applicable EU law in a manner that minimizes conflict and enhances consistency."[238] In *Eureko*, the arbitral tribunal distinguished between two successive stages regarding the consent of the parties (first, the conclusion of the BIT; and second, the initiation of proceedings). It continued by clarifying in relation to the second stage its understanding of the "nature" of EU law as part of domestic law by stating that "EU law operates [. . .] as part of German law as the *lex loci arbitri*".[239] On this basis, the tribunals applied relevant EU law insofar pertinent.

[235]Article 26(6) ECT, see also Article 16 ECT (conflict of norms provision); cf. Tietje (2013), p. 5.

[236]Convention on the Settlement of Investment Disputes Between States and Nationals of Other States, 18 March 1965, 575 UNTS 159.

[237]For example, Article 8(6) applicable to the *Eureko* UNCITRAL arbitration of the 1991 Netherlands-Czech and Slovak Republic BIT states: "The arbitral Tribunal shall decide on the basis of the law, taking into account in particular though not exclusively: the law in force of the Contracting Party concerned; the provisions of this Agreement, and other relevant Agreements between the Contracting Parties; the provisions of special agreements relating to the investment; the general principles of international law."

[238]*Oostergetel v The Slovak Republic*, UNCITRAL, Decision on Jurisdiction (30 April 2010), para. 100.

[239]*Eureko/Achmea*, UNCITRAL, Decision on Jurisdiction (26 October 2010), paras. 223–225: "The second stage originates from the offer's acceptance by Claimant, as an investor and national of the Netherlands, here effected through the initiation of arbitral proceedings under Article 8 of the BIT. [. . .] This second stage operates both under international law and, here, also under German law as the *lex loci arbitri* applying to UNCITRAL arbitration proceedings where the agreed place of arbitration is Frankfurt in the Federal Republic of Germany. [...] As a result, this is a German arbitration; and this Tribunal is an *ad hoc* German arbitration tribunal subject to German law and not an international tribunal (such as an ICSID tribunal under the 1965 Washington Convention). Germany is a founding member of the EU; and German law includes, of course, EU law. The Tribunal cannot derive any part of its jurisdiction or authority from EU law as such: its

In other proceedings the investment tribunals did not take any explicit position on the qualification of EU law. For example, in *Micula*, the tribunal held that the primary source of law applicable to the case at hand was the BIT and found that there was no conflict of treaty norms.[240] Still, the tribunal took the factual context of EU law into account when interpreting the BIT.[241] Accordingly, treaty interpretation somehow mediated between investment law and EU law.

The treatment of the EU legal order was approached differently in ECT proceedings as well. As the ECT only provides for international law as applicable law (Article 26(6) ECT) the qualification of EU law has direct consequences for its applicability to a case. On this matter, the *AES* and *Electrabel* tribunals reached exactly opposite conclusions. Thus, in *AES*, the qualification of EU law as domestic law led the tribunal to consider EU law merely as fact:

> [EU law] has a dual nature: on the one hand, it is an international law regime, on the other hand, once introduced in the national legal orders, it is part of these legal orders. It is common ground that in an international arbitration, national laws are to be considered as facts. [The EU competition law] will be considered by this Tribunal as a fact, always taking into account that a state may not invoke its domestic law as an excuse for alleged breaches of international obligations.[242]

In contrast, the tribunal in *Electrabel* pointed to the multiple nature of EU law. According to the tribunal, depending on the perspective from which it was regarded, EU law could be considered as international law, as it was created by international instruments; as part of Hungary's domestic legal order (by virtue of being an EU member state); or from the perspective of EU institutions, as a distinct legal order.[243] However, as the *Electrabel* tribunal held that it was a body constituted under public international law, it concluded that it should treat EU law as (applicable) *international law*[244]:

---

jurisdiction is derived from the consent of the Parties to the dispute, in accordance with the BIT and German law. Although EU law, as between the EU and member States of the EU (including Respondent and the Netherlands, but not Claimant), operates at the level of international law, EU law operates, as between the Parties, as part of German law as the *lex loci arbitri*."

[240] *Micula v Romania*, ICSID Case No. ARB/05/20, Final Award (11 December 2013), para. 318 et seq. In fact, EU law was not directly applicable since the accession treaty entered into force only on 1 January 2007 which was after the interferences with the investment had occurred.

[241] *Micula v Romania,* ICSID Case No. ARB/05/20, Final Award (11 December 2013), para. 327.

[242] *AES v Hungary*, ICSID Case No. ARB/07/22, Award (23 September 2010), para. 7.6.6. See in this regard also the WTO DSB's treatment of EU law as fact as addressed above in Sect. 3.2.2.

[243] See *Electrabel v Hungary*, ICSID Case No. ARB/07/19, Decision on Jurisdiction, Applicable law and Liability (30 November 2012), paras. 4.117 et seq. This was summarized in para. 4.20: "EU law is operating at three possible levels: (i) as international law, (ii) as distinct legal order within the European Union, separate from both from national laws of EU Members States, and international law and (iii) as part of Hungary's national law."

[244] Also the *RREEF* tribunal considered EU law as a subset of international law. Similarly, in the intra-EU BIT arbitration *Eastern Sugar*, the tribunal dealt with EU law as "normal" international law and applied relevant techniques for the resolution of conflicts of norms (Articles 59, 65 VCLT). *Eastern Sugar*, UNCITRAL, Partial Award (27 March 2007), para. 159.

> [...] the international setting in which this Tribunal is situated and from which it necessarily derives its perspective, EU law has to be classified first as international law.[245]

Moreover, according to the *Electrabel* tribunal, not only primary but also secondary EU law had the character of public international law: "it [the Tribunal] does not draw a material distinction [...] between the EU Treaties [...] and the '*droit derivé*'".[246] In support of its finding, the tribunal held that "all EU legal rules are part of a regional system of international law and therefore have an international legal character".[247]

As a bottom line, the investment tribunals generally declined to confer primacy/supremacy to EU law. This set aside, the tribunals' approaches to EU law as applicable law (as well as more generally) varied. Some investment tribunals considered EU law as international law (*Electrabel*) other tribunals as domestic law (*AES*, *Oostergetel*). Other tribunals took again a different approach: for example, the *Eureko* tribunal held that EU law was part of the German domestic legal system, as part of the *lex loci arbitri*.[248] Overall, this evidences the multi-faceted nature of the EU legal order.[249]

3.4.3 Evaluation: The EU Within the Investment Law Regime

Investment tribunals, as a rule, took a strong stand in relation to EU law and generally did not pay deference to the EU. While the tribunals did not accept the primacy/supremacy of EU law and rejected to align themselves with the exclusive jurisdiction of the CJEU (Article 344 TFEU), their approaches varied. They considered EU law either as international law or as domestic law. In any case, investment tribunals generally found that the relevant investment law framework was fully applicable (the respective intra-EU BIT or the ECT).

---

[245] *Electrabel v Hungary*, ICSID Case No. ARB/07/19, Decision on Jurisdiction, Applicable law and Liability (30 November 2012), para. 4.119.

[246] *Electrabel v Hungary*, ICSID Case No. ARB/07/19, Decision on Jurisdiction, Applicable law and Liability (30 November 2012), para. 4.122.

[247] See also *Electrabel v Hungary*, ICSID Case No. ARB/07/19, Decision on Jurisdiction, Applicable law and Liability (30 November 2012), para. 4.122, citing *Van Gend & Loos*. "The community constitutes a new legal order of international law for the benefit of which the states have limited their sovereign rights."

[248] Note, however, that in the respective investment proceedings the qualification of EU law is of secondary importance. Rather, it is of prevailing relevance whether EU law is qualified in a way as to be applicable law to the dispute in line with the "applicable law clause". Whether EU law is viewed as national or international law seems secondary as long as the applicable law clause allows for its application.

[249] The multifaceted nature of EU law was also explicitly recognized by some tribunals (e.g. *AES*, *Electrabel*). The different approaches in part must be seen in the context of the varying "applicable law" clauses. In fact, also the submissions of the parties play a role as regards the qualification of EU law since the investment tribunals generally decide on the basis of the submissions.

Respectively, regarding the classification of EU law by the investment tribunals, it was not decisive as to whether only member states were parties to the treaty (intra-EU BIT) or whether also the EU was party (ECT). This may be explained by the fact that the EU has not been the respondent party to the proceedings under the ECT. It will be different when the EU is the only treaty party and thus becomes the logical respondent in investment arbitrations.[250] The latter would be the "standard" constellation in the CETA (and draft TTIP agreement) which were/are negotiated by the EU on behalf of its member states and where EU law is viewed as domestic law.[251]

Finally, in dealing with the EU legal order, investment tribunals resorted to a number of techniques to deal with the in part conflicting sets of rules. In particular, tribunals—regardless of their classification of the EU legal order—were keen to nevertheless ensure a harmonious interpretation of the applicable investment treaty and EU law by virtue of Articles 31 et seq. VCLT.[252]

---

[250]With the Treaty of Lisbon, FDI is explicitly mentioned as part of the EU common commercial policy (Article 207(1) para. 4 TFEU). The common commercial policy is one of the Union's exclusive competences (Article 3(1)(e) TFEU). Thus, investment, after the treaty of Lisbon, gives the EU full exclusive competence. Accordingly, in treaties such as the CETA, draft TTIP and the Singapore agreement, the EU is the negotiating party. While CETA was concluded as a mixed agreement between Canada and the EU and its member states, this was due to growing political pressure within a number of EU member states. It was, however, solely negotiated by the EU. See also Briefing of the European Parliament, January 2016, http://www.europarl.europa.eu/RegData/etudes/BRIE/2016/573929/EPRS_BRI%282016%29573929_EN.pdf (last accessed 1 March 2017).

[251]See the respective provisions in the TTIP and CETA agreements where domestic law is excluded from the scope of jurisdiction and EU law is seen as domestic law. Article 13(3) Applicable law and rules of interpretation of the Commission draft text Transatlantic Trade and Investment Partnership—investment: "For greater certainty, pursuant to paragraph 1, the domestic law of the Parties shall not be part of the applicable law. Where the Tribunal is required to ascertain the meaning of a provision of the domestic law of one of the Parties as a matter of fact, it shall follow the prevailing interpretation of that provision made by the courts or authorities of that Party." Article 8.31(2) Applicable law and interpretation of the Comprehensive Economic and Trade Agreement (CETA) Between Canada and the European Union: "The Tribunal shall not have jurisdiction to determine the legality of a measure, alleged to constitute a breach of this Agreement, under the domestic law of the disputing Party. For greater certainty, in determining the consistency of a measure with this Agreement, the Tribunal may consider, as appropriate, the domestic law of the disputing Party as a matter of fact. In doing so, the Tribunal shall follow the prevailing interpretation given to the domestic law by the courts or authorities of that Party and any meaning given to domestic law by the Tribunal shall not be binding upon the courts or the authorities of that Party."

[252]*Oostergetel v The Slovak Republic*, UNCITRAL, Decision on Jurisdiction (30 April 2010), para. 100 (but no explicit reference to Article 31 VCLT); *Micula v Romania*, ICSID Case No. ARB/05/20, Final Award (11 December 2013); *RREEF Infrastructure v Spain*, ICSID Case No. ARB/13/30, Decision on Jurisdiction (6 June 2016), para. 76.

4 Techniques Applying to Regime Interaction with the EU Legal Order

As mentioned earlier, the manner in which legal systems interact will depend on the systemic position from which they operate. The examples discussed throughout this contribution highlight the distinct approaches of international courts and tribunals in their interaction with the EU legal order. In determining the priority of applicable rules—either in relation to jurisdictional clauses or substantive provisions—general conflict rules (*lex specialis*, *lex posterior*) will not always work, particularly when two or more branches of international law are concerned.[253] Which additional techniques of reconciliation are resorted to will, inter alia, depend on factors such as the status of the EU as treaty party, the respective jurisdictional clauses, and last but not least, the classification of the EU legal order as international law, domestic law or as a *sui generis* legal order. In this sense, the following sketches out theoretical (Sect. 4.1), jurisdictional (Sect. 4.2) and substantive (Sect. 4.3) approaches which have guided the relationship between international law and the EU legal order in the abovementioned examples.

4.1 Interaction Through Subordination to a Hierarchical Order in International Law (Theoretical Approach)

On a theoretical level, the CJEU's positioning of the EU legal order as regards the international legal order and the approach by international dispute settlement bodies towards the interaction of general international law and EU law deviate.

The international legal order is generally classified as a horizontal system where its sources and principles are in no hierarchical relationship with each other and which, consequently, "does not exclude rule conflict."[254] Accordingly, conflicts of norms may occur. In overcoming such conflict situations, various techniques may be discerned, most of them being "systemic", i.e. stemming directly from the international legal system (see below Sects. 4.2 and 4.3). They function as tools

[253]From the perspective of the European Commission, this is clearly the case in the field of investment law. The difficulties are more generally discussed in Michaels and Pauwelyn (2011), p. 35. Moreover, the conflict rules contained in Articles 59 and 30 VCLT both require the "same subject-matter", which is generally interpreted narrowly, and will thus prevent treaty regimes with overlapping jurisdictional mandates. See, e.g., ILC, Fragmentation of International Law: Difficulties Arising From the Diversification and Expansion of International Law—Report of the Study Group of the International Law Commission, 13 April 2006, UN Doc. A/CN.4/L.682, para. 116 et seqq.; Tietje (2013), p. 14.

[254]Crawford and Nevill (2012), p. 236; ILC, Fragmentation of International Law: Difficulties Arising From the Diversification and Expansion of International Law—Report of the Study Group of the International Law Commission, 13 April 2006, UN Doc. A/CN.4/L.682, para. 324. On *ius cogens* or other forms of normative hierarchy, see below.

for regime interaction of juxtaposed regimes engaging on a horizontal level. Additionally, however, there is a growing debate on the "constitutionalization" of international law, which attempts to discern a normative global order.[255] This installs a hierarchical relationship—based on international values—within the global legal order, and extends also to its subsystems,[256] hence also to the European legal order.[257]

Whether or not to indeed follow the theoretical vocabulary and theory of international constitutionalism exceeds the scope of this paper,[258] but general tendencies of accepting an international value system and a therefrom flowing normative hierarchy can be made out clearly in judicial practice.[259] In most simple terms, the content of such a system is put together on the basis of *ius cogens* norms, obligations *erga omnes* and—by virtue of its universal membership and functioning—obligations under the United Nations Charter, particularly binding Security Council decisions (Article 103 UN Charter).[260] Where the EU subordinates itself to this system, it acknowledges itself as part of the international legal system.[261] In contrast, where the EU chooses to protect the autonomy of its legal order, it moves its legal order closer to an enclosed constitutional regime, resembling the relationship between international and domestic law.[262] The results thereof are evident in the abovementioned *Kadi* saga. While the CFI placed itself—and thereby the EU legal order—within the international legal system, conducting a review of Security Council resolutions in light of *ius cogens* norms, the Advocate General and the CJEU expressly rejected the possibility of hierarchically superior values stemming from outside the EU legal order.[263] This understanding of its legal order as being

[255]De Wet (2006).

[256]For further reference on subsystems of international law see, inter alia, Simma and Pulkowski (2006).

[257]D'Aspremont and Dopagne (2009), p. 951.

[258]On the debate of international constitutionalization see for many Klabbers et al. (2009) and D'Aspremont and Dopagne (2009).

[259]See, inter alia, *Barcelona Traction, Light and Power Company, Limited (Second Phase) (Belgium v Spain)*, 1970 ICJ 3, Judgment (5 February 1970), para. 33 et seq.; *East Timor (Portugal v Australia)*, 1995 ICJ 90, Judgment (30 June 1995), para. 29; *Legal Consequences of the Construction of a Wall in the Occupied Palestinian Territory*, 2004 ICJ 136, Advisory Opinion (9 July 2004), paras. 88 and 156; *Application of the Convention and Punishment of the Crime of Genocide (Bosnia and Herzegovina v Yugoslavia)*, 1996 ICJ 595, Preliminary Objections (11 July 1996), Dissenting Opinion by *ad hoc* Judge Kreca, para. 68.

[260]ILC, Fragmentation of International Law: Difficulties Arising From the Diversification and Expansion of International Law—Report of the Study Group of the International Law Commission, 13 April 2006, UN Doc. A/CN.4/L.682, para. 327 et seqq.

[261]D'Aspremont and Dopagne (2009), p. 951.

[262]Shirlow (2014), p. 8.

[263]CFI, case T-315/01, *Kadi v Council and Commission*, ECLI:EU:T:2005:332; Opinion of AG Maduro to CJEU, case C-402/05 P, *Kadi v Council and Commission*, ECLI:EU:C:2008:11; CJEU, case C-402/05 P, *Kadi v Council and Commission*, ECLI:EU:C:2008:461.

"separate" and of a "constitutional nature" in light of its "coherent and structured 'system'"[264] underscores a series of cases decided by the CJEU.[265] Hence, by approaching international legal obligations in a similar manner to a domestic order incorporating international law, the CJEU reserves the right to impose the outer "constitutional" limits to the application of international law within the European system,[266] thus creating its own European hierarchical order.

Thus, the EU's internal perspective—as portrayed through the CJEU's case-law—in this regard deviates from the international law perspective. As is discernible in a number of cases discussed above (inter alia *Mox Plant* (Annex VII Tribunal), *Korea-Procurement* (WTO DSB), *Electrabel* (ICSID tribunal)), international judicial bodies approach the EU legal order and the CJEU primarily on a horizontal level. This becomes apparent when paying special regard to the jurisdictional and substantive techniques resorted to by these bodies in their interaction with the EU, as addressed in the following.

4.2 Reconciliation Through Jurisdictional Techniques

Though each sector analysed—general international law, trade law, human rights law, investment law—is marked by specific characteristics, similar techniques can be identified which guide the respective international dispute settlement bodies in their approach towards the EU legal order. This can be placed in the larger context of how to deal with the proliferation of international courts and tribunals and the overlap of different treaty regimes. One aspect to consider in this regard is which judicial body is the more appropriate forum to adjudicate arising disputes. This also applies in relation to the CJEU, which asserts exclusive jurisdiction over all matters pertaining to the interpretation and application of EU law. In certain instances, as mentioned previously, this approach has even prevented the EU from becoming party to certain international agreements where this exclusive jurisdiction might have been under threat.[267]

[264] D'Aspremont and Dopagne (2009), p. 947.

[265] See, e.g., CJEU, case C-459/03, *Commission v Ireland (MOX Plant)*, ECLI:EU:C:2006:345; CJEU, case 294/83, *Les Verts v Parliament*, ECLI:EU:C:1986:166; CJEU, opinion 2/13, *EU Accession to the ECHR*, ECLI:EU:C:2014:2454.

[266] Cf. Lenaerts (2015), p. 263.

[267] CJEU, opinion 1/91, *European Economic Area*, ECLI:EU:C:1991:490; CJEU, opinion 2/13, *EU Accession to the ECHR*, ECLI:EU:C:2014:2454, para. 194: "In so far as the ECHR would, in requiring the EU and the Member States to be considered Contracting Parties not only in their relations with Contracting Parties which are not Member States of the EU but also in their relations with each other, including where such relations are governed by EU law, require a Member State to check that another Member State has observed fundamental rights, even though EU law imposes an obligation of mutual trust between those Member States, accession is liable to upset the underlying balance of the EU and undermine the autonomy of EU law."

At a second glance, however, the risk of potentially conflicting outcomes of proceedings is somewhat subdued when considered in light of instruments which were developed to avoid jurisdictional conflicts. Hence, even though there is no hierarchy among international courts and tribunals, a number of jurisdictional techniques can be discerned which function to avoid jurisdictional—and in a wider sense—regime conflicts.[268] When these techniques are applied, the "systemic interest"[269] in international law functioning as *one* international legal order operates to prevent conflicting outcomes in parallel proceedings (this under the presumption that the CJEU's self-proclaimed exclusive jurisdiction does not in itself constitute a barrier to the exercise of jurisdiction by other courts and tribunals).

On a procedural level, the respective jurisdictional clauses determine to which extent an international "regime" will exert a stronger or weaker position on when to exercise jurisdiction.[270] Paired with a variety of jurisdictional principles, the judicial institutions are equipped with a certain manoeuvring space to avoid regime conflict. In this context, the International Law Commission pointed out that when and how to apply these judicial techniques is in principle "best dealt with by the institutions themselves".[271]

The examples discussed throughout this contribution demonstrate the wide discretion available to international judicial bodies: Operating to achieve the abovementioned "systemic interest", especially international dispute settlement mechanisms designed with weaker jurisdictional clauses have employed a variety of techniques to avoid judicial conflict. Thus, there are certain treaty regimes which are equipped with a type of fall-back/subsidiary jurisdiction. The Law of the Sea Convention (LOSC) is often named as the archetypical example for a system which fosters the fragmentation of dispute settlement regarding law of the sea matters[272]

[268]For an exemplary listing of a number of such techniques see, e.g., Crawford and Nevill (2012). As explained by *Shany*, these techniques can be divided into two different "narratives of international law": disintegrationism (limiting the dispute to specific claims for the purpose of jurisdiction) and integrationism (resolving the dispute by coordinating—as far as possible—the application of substantive and procedural sub-sets of international law). Shany (2007), p. 108 et seq.

[269]See also Shany (2007), p. 109.

[270]See above Sect. 3.1.

[271]ILC, Fragmentation of International Law: Difficulties Arising From the Diversification and Expansion of International Law—Report of the Study Group of the International Law Commission, 13 April 2006, UN Doc. A/CN.4/L.682, para. 13.

[272]See, e.g., the criticism voiced by the former ICJ Vice-President Shigeru Oda in Oda (1995). Article 282 of the LOSC provides the framework for this attitude: "If the States Parties which are parties to a dispute concerning the interpretation or application of this Convention have agreed, through a general, regional or bilateral agreement or otherwise, that such dispute shall, at the request of any party to the dispute, be submitted to a procedure that entails a binding decision, that procedure shall apply in lieu of the procedures provided for in this Part, unless the parties to the dispute otherwise agree."

and—when confronted with a stronger jurisdictional clause—will give way to alternative dispute settlement forums.[273] This was also an underlying motive of the *MOX Plant* Annex VII Tribunal, suspending its proceedings as it "would not be helpful to the resolution of the dispute" to reach two conflicting decisions, but also in light of Article 282 LOSC.[274] In contrast, Article 23(2) of the WTO's Dispute Settlement Understanding (DSU) provides for exclusive jurisdiction of the DSB to interpret the agreements, a passage which was even suggested by the EU during the Uruguay Round.[275] However, the effect thereof is partly attenuated in practice. For example, where the WTO's subject matter overlaps with the subject matter of other free trade agreements or when its disputes may be linked on a broader level to other non-trade-related dispute settlement fora, there have been cases where parallel proceedings were conducted before another dispute settlement body[276] or where the WTO DSB has been asked to take a position on matters which would fall within the exclusive jurisdiction of another judicial organ. Still, by displaying considerable deference regarding the subject matter of the disputes, the threat of directly conflicting outcomes has so far been avoided. Thus, in *European Communities-Selected Customs Matters*, the WTO DSB (and later also the AB) was careful to avoid entering into the discussion regarding the coherence of the set-up of the entire EU customs system.[277]

A similar approach, i.e. deference on a substantive level,[278] may be discerned within the ECHR regime. As within the WTO, also Article 55 ECHR excludes means of dispute settlement between states parties regarding disputes "arising out of the interpretation or application of [the ECHR] [. . .] other than those provided for in this Convention."[279] As explained by the ECtHR, this establishes a "monopoly of the Convention institutions for deciding disputes arising out of the interpretation and application of the Convention."[280] Thus, depending on the facts of the

[273]See, e.g., *Southern Bluefin Tuna (New Zealand v Japan, Australia v Japan)*, Award on Jurisdiction and Admissibility, XXIII RIAA 59, Decision (4 August 2000), para. 54; *The MOX Plant Case (Ireland v United Kingdom)*, Annex VII Tribunal (PCA), Order No. 3, Suspension of Proceedings on Jurisdiction and Merits and Request for Further Provisional measures (24 June 2003).

[274]*The MOX Plant Case (Ireland v United Kingdom)*, Annex VII Tribunal (PCA), Order No. 3, Suspension of Proceedings on Jurisdiction and Merits and Request for Further Provisional measures (24 June 2003), para. 28.

[275]Hoekman and Mavroidis (2014), p. 246.

[276]See for examples Henckels (2008), p. 573.

[277]Panel Report, *European Communities—Selected Customs Matters*, WT/DS315/R, 16 June 2006, paras. 2.2–2.31; Eckes (2013), p. 95.

[278]Note that deference on a substantive level (as practiced by the WTO DSB or the ECtHR) could also be seen as a substantive means for reconciliation. As it is, however, also an instrument used to reconcile competing jurisdictional mandates, it has been included in this section.

[279]Article 55 ECHR.

[280]European Commission, No. 25781/94, *Cyprus v Turkey*, Decision of 28 June 1996. In CJEU, opinion 2/13, *EU Accession to the ECHR*, ECLI:EU:C:2014:2454, para. 179, the CJEU acknowledged that inter-state applications between two EU member states were in principle compatible with its exclusive jurisdictional mandate under Article 344 TFEU as the ECHR had not been

case—concurrent jurisdiction may be an issue between the ECtHR and the CJEU as regards inter-state disputes. While a possible example has been pending before the ECtHR since September 2016,[281] so far, this has not been an issue. Moreover, in individual complaints proceedings, the ECtHR has developed the doctrine of equivalent protection—as discussed above in *Bosphorus* and *Kokkelvisserij*[282]—to defer on a substantive level from a close scrutiny of EU law. It thus presumes that in absence of "manifest deficiency", the protection of fundamental rights afforded by the EU is "in principle equivalent" to that under the ECHR.[283] By carving out this space for the EU, potential normative conflicts arising between the two orders are avoided,[284] thus also not competing with the CJEU's exclusive jurisdiction (in the broad sense).

In other instances, jurisdictional conflicts between an international court or tribunal and the CJEU may be resolved by resorting to jurisdictional techniques or principles—sometimes also called "meta-principles"[285]—such as judicial comity/coordination, judicial minimalism or the principle of cooperation between international jurisdictions. For example, again in *MOX Plant*, the Annex VII Tribunal exercised its discretion to suspend proceedings also while "bearing in mind considerations of mutual respect and comity".[286] The *MOX Plant* OSPAR tribunal limited the scope of applicable law to avoid any conflict with the CJEU's exclusive jurisdiction.[287] In *Fisheries Jurisdiction*, the ICJ avoided voicing an opinion on the internal division of competences within the EU, practicing a type of judicial minimalism.[288] Similarly, the tribunal in *Iron Rhine* was keen to emphasize that EU law was "not conclusive" for settling the dispute.[289]

"formally incorporated into the legal order of the EU" yet. This notwithstanding the fact that the CJEU found the scrutinized Draft Accession Agreement incompatible in its present form.

[281] See, e.g., the most recent inter-state case lodged at the ECtHR, the first between two EU member states, ECtHR, *Slovenia v Croatia*, Application lodged 15 September 2016.

[282] ECtHR, No. 45036/98, *Bosphorus v Ireland*, Judgment of 30 June 2005; ECtHR, No. 13645/05, *Kokkelvisserij v the Netherlands*, Decision of 20 January 2009.

[283] See, inter alia, ECtHR, No. 12323/11, *Michaud v France*, Judgment of 6 December 2012, para. 105.

[284] See particularly also Sect. 3.2.2; cf. Korenica (2015), p. 55.

[285] Crawford and Nevill (2012), p. 243 et seq.

[286] *The MOX Plant Case (Ireland v United Kingdom)*, Annex VII Tribunal (PCA), Order No. 3, Suspension of Proceedings on Jurisdiction and Merits and Request for Further Provisional measures (24 June 2003), para. 28.

[287] *Dispute Concerning Access to Information under Article 9 of the OSPAR Convention between Ireland and the United Kingdom of Great Britain and Northern Ireland*, Final Award, XXIII RIAA 59, Decision (2 July 2003), para. 85.

[288] *Fisheries Jurisdiction (Spain v Canada)*, 1998 ICJ 432, Jurisdiction (4 December 1998); cf. Higgins (2003), p. 4 et seq.

[289] *Iron Rhine ("Ijzeren Rijn") Railway arbitration (Belgium v The Netherlands)*, Award, XXVII RIAA 35, Decision (24 May 2005), paras. 106 et seqq., 119 et seq., similarly 137.

Application of these techniques and principles fall within the inherent powers of international courts and tribunals,[290] namely to ensure the "administration of justice"[291] and the "orderly settlement of all matters in dispute"[292] to ensure the observance of its judicial function. Resorting to these judicial techniques enables a dispute settlement body to "waive" its right to exercise jurisdiction or to limit its jurisdiction to specific aspects of the issue and is based on the mutual respect for the "other" dispute settlement body, by virtue of the "common membership in the international system".[293] It does not, however, introduce a hierarchy among international courts and tribunals—also not placing the CJEU at a higher rank[294]—, and lays mainly in the discretion of the applying judicial body.[295]

4.3 The Use of Substantive Means for Reconciliation

In addition to jurisdictional techniques, the examples listed above demonstrate that reconciliation between competing regimes is also achieved through other instruments. As formulated by the ILC, "the task of legal reasoning" should establish a meaningful relationship between legal systems and work towards either applying these in a "mutually supportive way" or determine some form of priority of one regime over the other.[296] It is in this instance that the nature of the respective legal orders will play out strongest as the interaction between two international legal orders will follow other rules than the interaction between an international and a domestic legal order or between an international and a *sui generis* legal order, possessing characteristics such as the EU asserts for itself (particularly the primacy of EU law).

A primary means to achieve reconciliation between two *international* legal regimes is through means of interpretation, particularly through the principle of systematic integration (Article 31(3)(c) VCLT) which establishes that account

[290] Cf. Henckels (2008), p. 583.

[291] *Northern Cameroons (Cameroon v United Kingdom)*, 1963 ICJ 15, Judgment (2 December 1963), p. 29.

[292] *Nuclear Tests (Australia v France)*, 1974 ICJ 253, Judgment (20 December 1974), p. 258, para. 23.

[293] Slaughter (2003), p. 205.

[294] Note in this regard also the approach by investment tribunals with regard to arguments pertaining to Article 344 TFEU (as discussed above in Sect. 3.4.2.1), which leave the question of its effect on possible inter-state complaints arising under a BIT open. Moreover, in distinguishing their approach from *MOX Plant*, tribunals refer to the distinct nature of investor-state relations in contrast to inter-state disputes.

[295] Henckels (2008), p. 585.

[296] ILC, Fragmentation of International Law: Difficulties Arising From the Diversification and Expansion of International Law—Report of the Study Group of the International Law Commission, 13 April 2006, UN Doc. A/CN.4/L.682, para. 220.

should be taken also of "any relevant rules of international law applicable in the relations between the parties".[297] The relevance thereof is particularly evident in the interaction of the EU legal order and the investment law regime.[298] As detailed in Sect. 3.4, investment tribunals adopted a firm stand regarding their jurisdiction and generally rejected the special status claimed by the EU. Still, in certain instances the respective tribunals also avoided outright confrontation of the two distinct regimes by resorting to techniques of treaty interpretation. While the application of abovementioned conflict rules (*lex posterior* or *lex specialis*) implies an "either or" and entails that one norm is applied to the exclusion of the other, the reliance on the techniques of treaty interpretation enables a harmonious reading of different norms.[299] On this basis, investment tribunals, when interpreting relevant provisions of intra-EU BITs, also relied on pertinent EU law and interpreted the BIT provisions accordingly.[300] This approach was used, for example, in *Micula*, drawing on Article 31(1) and (2) VCLT for a harmonious reading of the pertinent BIT and the Europe Agreement.[301] The *RREEF* likewise placed emphasis on the objective to interpret the treaties as far as possible "in such a way as not to contradict each other".[302] It seems promising to further draw on these interpretation techniques to achieve a reconciliation between intra-EU BITs and EU law in the future.[303] However, while a harmonious interpretation can do some good, it has its

[297]As to the relevance of the principle of systemic integration see Simma and Kill (2009); see also the reference to Article 31(3)(c) VCLT in ILC, Fragmentation of International Law: Difficulties Arising From the Diversification and Expansion of International Law—Report of the Study Group of the International Law Commission, 13 April 2006, UN Doc. A/CN.4/L.682, para. 423; Gardiner (2015), p. 304 et seq.; McLachlan (2005), for further reference; see also the respondent's arguments on the application of Art. 31(1)(c) VCLT in *Micula v Romania*, ICSID Case No. ARB/05/20, Final Award (11 December 2013), paras. 305–308.

[298]Note that reference to the techniques of interpretation has also been made in other regimes, such as human rights. Hence, Article 31(3)(c) VCLT has also been resorted to by the ECtHR to reconcile ECHR obligations with obligations flowing from EU membership. See, e.g., ECtHR, No. 45036/98, *Bosphorus v Ireland*, Judgment of 30 June 2005, para. 150.

[299]For further reference on the VCLT's rules concerning treaty interpretation see Gardiner (2015); in the investment law context, see Dolzer and Schreuer (2012), p. 28 et seqq.

[300]As stated above, this applies under the caveat of assuming that (primary and) also secondary EU law is considered as "international law" and not as law *sui generis*.

[301]*Micula v Romania*, ICSID Case No. ARB/05/20, Final Award (11 December 2013), para. 326: "the Tribunal will interpret each of the various applicable treaties having due regard to the other applicable treaties assuming that the parties entered in to each of those treaties in full awareness of their legal obligations under all of them". It also found that "factually, the general context of EU accession must be taken into account when interpreting the BIT. In particular, the overall circumstances of EU accession may play a role in determining whether the Respondent has breached some of its obligations under the BIT" (para. 327).

[302]*RREEF Infrastructure v Spain*, ICSID Case No. ARB/13/30, Decision on Jurisdiction (6 June 2016), para. 76.

[303]The latter, of course, only in case of acceptance of a reconciling treaty interpretation approach (Article 31(3)(c) VCLT). See for positive examples ECtHR, No. 10593/08, *Nada v Switzerland*, Judgment of 12 September 2012, para. 169; *Oil Platforms (Islamic Republic of Iran v United*

obvious limits as regards reconciliation/harmonization between different norms, i.e. the text of the relevant provisions, and will moreover not find application in instances where the tribunal classifies the EU legal order as "non-international".

Thus, the qualification of EU law as *domestic law* will—in accordance with the general principle regarding the interaction between international and domestic law[304]—result in its treatment as a matter of fact.[305] This is evident firstly with regard to some investment tribunals that have viewed EU law as domestic law (inter alia *Eureko*, *AES*)—thus as evidence of fact—particularly in light of its incorporation into the respective national legal orders. Secondly, this also can be seen in the WTO regime where the EU is a party in its own right and its legal order is drawn upon to determine the EU's compliance/non-compliance with WTO obligations.[306] Thus, where the EU is a party to a treaty and proceeding in its own right (as it will become with regard to the ECHR, but also is in the process of becoming as regards CETA (and TTIP)), a similar treatment—EU law as domestic law—will mostly likely be the result. In such instances, it is also not to be expected that EU law enjoys precedence.[307]

It follows that EU law will only be accorded primacy at a material level in instances where special regard is paid to the *sui generis* nature of the EU legal order. So far, despite the European Commission arguing along such lines particularly in the field of investment law,[308] there are only limited indications that this might be the case. Though the various regimes do not shy away from pointing to the specific characteristics of the EU and the CJEU, placing its legal order at a hierarchically higher level would exude considerable influence on the functioning of international law as it stands. This would, on the one hand, require creative solutions to ensure that the effectiveness of international courts and tribunals—established on the basis of state consent—is not undermined and, on the other hand, that the harmonious development of EU law is not endangered. A possible avenue in this regard was demonstrated by the *Iron Rhine's* arbitral tribunal which placed itself in a "position

States of America), 2003 ICJ 161, Judgment (6 November 2003), para. 41. For the potential of Article 31(3)(c) VCLT to reconcile, for example, international investment law and human rights law see Kriebaum (2009), p. 668. Conversely, the *Electrabel* case, based on an intra-EU application of the ECT, illustrates the risks and rejection of the technique, see *Electrabel v Hungary*, ICSID Case No. ARB/07/19, Decision on Jurisdiction, Applicable law and Liability (30 November 2012), para. 4.130. See for further reference, Paparinskis (2014), p. 56.

[304] *Certain German Interests in Polish Upper Silesia*, Judgment, 1926 PCIJ 5, 19 (ser. A) No. 7 (25 May 1926).

[305] *AES v Hungary*, ICSID Case No. ARB/07/22, Award (23 September 2010), para. 7.6.6.

[306] See, e.g., Panel Report, *European Communities—Measures Prohibiting the Importation and Marketing of Seal Products*, WT/DS401/R, 25 November 2013. For this purpose, judgments by the CJEU are treated similar to a domestic court, see, inter alia, Panel Report, *European Communities—Customs Classification of Frozen Boneless Chicken Cuts*, WT/DS269/R, 30 May 2005, para. 7.390 et seq., equating CJEU judgments with EU legislation for the purpose of interpretation under Article 32 VCLT.

[307] Article 27 VCLT.

[308] See, inter alia, *Eastern Sugar*, UNCITRAL, Partial Award (27 March 2007).

analogous to that of a domestic court within the EC",[309] suggesting that in case a question of EU law arose where it felt that the matter was not sufficiently settled, it could request a preliminary ruling from the CJEU. Similar suggestions have also been proposed by respondent states in regard to intra-EU investment proceedings. They have, so far, however been rejected.[310]

5 Conclusions

The EU's interactions with a plurality of international courts and tribunals provides fertile ground for the investigation of the interaction of international law's subsystems with one another and with other legal orders. As a preliminary question, international dispute settlement bodies will have to determine which reconciliatory techniques may be resorted to. That this is not an easy or obvious exercise becomes apparent in regard to the interaction with the EU legal order. From an international law perspective, tensions between international law and the EU legal order arise primarily in two aspects: through jurisdictional conflicts in light of the CJEU's self-proclaimed exclusive jurisdiction; and with regard to the question of applicable law and which legal framework should enjoy precedence.

As demonstrated in four distinct fields—general international law, the WTO regime, the ECHR framework, and investment law—the manner in which international bodies interact with the EU/EU law is dependent on the nature assigned to the EU's legal order, i.e. whether the respective legal orders engage at a horizontal level, thus as (potentially conflicting) subsystems of international law, or whether the EU legal order is classified as a *de facto* domestic or as a *sui generis* legal order. This classification predetermines whether conflicts will be settled with international law techniques, whether EU law will be treated as a matter of fact, similar to domestic law, or whether some priority is assigned to the EU and its institutions in recognition of its *sui generis* position.

Among the courts and tribunals constituted under public international law, there are certain discernible efforts traceable in the case-law of international dispute settlement bodies to engage in a "system-building" exercise while concomitantly respecting the autonomy of the EU legal order. Depending on the respective bodies' mandate, the involved parties and the level of intensity of the interaction, different jurisdictional and substantive means are used to work towards an outcome in the interest of international coordination instead of risking conflicting outcomes.

[309] *Iron Rhine ("Ijzeren Rijn") Railway arbitration (Belgium v The Netherlands)*, Award, XXVII RIAA 35, Decision of 24 May 2005, para. 103.

[310] On the promise of preliminary rulings in the context of intra-EU BITs, see Schreuer, European law and investment arbitration, Vienna Arbitration Days 18 February 2012; see also the suggestions by the Czech Republic in *Binder v Czech Republic*, UNCITRAL, Award on Jurisdiction (6 June 2007), para. 7; and by Slovakia in *Oostergetel v The Slovak Republic*, UNCITRAL, Decision on Jurisdiction (30 April 2010), para. 68 (rejected in para. 105).

Which instruments are applied specifically is dependent on the respective regime's relationship with the EU. Under general international law, the EU has so far not been a direct party to the proceedings. The nature of its legal order and the therefrom stemming characteristics have therefore only indirectly been subject to the scrutiny of the respective international dispute settlement bodies. In exercise of their judicial function (inter alia regime support), these bodies have so far taken the EU's international law "heritage" as a point of departure, while simultaneously paying respect to the EU's internal perspective and *sui generis* understanding of its own legal order through exercising judicial minimalism or procedural deference (particularly through the principle of comity) to avoid jurisdictional conflicts.

A deeper level of integration can be found within the WTO regime, with the EU being one of the founding members and, hence, a direct party to the proceedings. Functionally, the WTO DSB generally treats the EU as a state-like entity with a domestic market. As a consequence, the EU legal order is largely equated with domestic legal orders, and assessed as a matter of fact. However, at times the special nature of the EU is recognized in regard to the EU's institutions (i.e. the CJEU floating between international and domestic law) and design (particularly concerning the EU's internal division of competences).

Eventually, this might also be the case under the ECHR framework. However, as currently the EU has not yet become party to the ECHR, the ECtHR treats it as an international organization which is given space for its functioning. In light of all EU member states being party to the ECHR, a number of constellations have arisen where the ECtHR has had to develop an approach to, on the one hand, ensure the ECHR as a "constitutional instrument"[311] within Europe and, on the other hand, carve out a space for the EU's autonomous order. For this purpose, the ECtHR exercises considerable deference towards the EU and its legal system in application of the equivalent protection doctrine. The ECtHR thus generally avoids a precise content analysis of the EU legal order, and will—in theory—only engage more closely where it has been proven that the human rights protection under EU law is "manifestly deficient". So far, however, this has never been the case.

The complexities arising from the interaction with the EU legal order become particularly evident in the field of investment law. Investment tribunals have displayed different approaches and—as a general rule—not recognized any primacy/supremacy stemming from the EU legal order. Inter alia dependent on the applicable law clauses, EU law is thus treated as international or domestic law. Still, efforts can be witnessed also in this field to ensure consistency and coherence between investment law and EU law, particularly through means of treaty interpretation.

In conclusion, and as phrased perhaps most aptly by the *Electrabel* tribunal, "EU law has a multiple nature"[312] and its treatment/classification will therefore most

[311]ECtHR, No. 15318/89, *Loizidou v Turkey*, Judgment of 23 March 1995, para. 75.

[312]*Electrabel v Hungary*, ICSID Case No. ARB/07/19, Decision on Jurisdiction, Applicable law and Liability (30 November 2012), para. 4.118.

often be dependent on the international institution undertaking the analysis. As demonstrated throughout this contribution, the EU legal order (still *and* albeit its special features) firmly remains placed within international law. Though the EU's internal perspective is further-reaching and the CJEU pursues idiosyncratic goals,[313] the EU's international law origins and operation sustain its international character unless otherwise foreseen or the consequence of a particular international law instrument (especially a treaty).

References

Avbelj M (2011) Supremacy or primacy of EU law – (why) does it matter? Eur Law J 17 (6):744–763

Bengoetxea J (2011) The EU as (more than) an international organization. In: Klabbers J, Wallendahl A (eds) Research handbook on the law of international organizations. Edward Elgar, Cheltenham, pp 448–465

Bennouna M (2012) How to cope with the proliferation of international courts and coordinate their action. In: Cassese A (ed) Realizing utopia – the future of international law. Oxford University Press, Oxford, pp 287–294

Binder C (2016) A treaty law perspective on intra-EU BITs. J World Invest Trade 17:964–983

Casteleiro D (2016) The international responsibility of the European Union – from competence to normative control. Cambridge University Press, Cambridge

Collins R, White ND (2011) International organizations and the idea of autonomy – institutional independence in the international legal order. Routledge, Abingdon

Crawford J (2012) Brownlie's principles of public international law, 8th edn. Oxford University Press, Oxford

Crawford J, Nevill P (2012) Relations between international courts and tribunals: the "regime problem". In: Young MA (ed) Regime interaction in international law – facing fragmentation. Cambridge University Press, Cambridge, pp 235–260

Cremona M (2011) External relations and external competence of the European Union: the emergence of an integrated policy. In: Craig P, De Búrca G (eds) The evolution of EU law. Oxford University Press, Oxford, pp 217–268

Curtin DM, Dekker IF (2011) The European Union from Maastricht to Lisbon: institutional and legal unity out of the shadows. In: Craig P, De Búrca G (eds) The evolution of EU law. Oxford University Press, Oxford, pp 155–185

D'Aspremont J, Dopagne F (2008) Kadi: the ECJ's reminder of the elementary divide between legal orders. Int Organ Law Rev 5:371–379

D'Aspremont J, Dopagne F (2009) Two constitutionalisms in Europe: pursuing an articulation of the European and international legal orders. Heidelb J Int Law 69:939–978

De Búrca G (2010) The European Court of Justice and the international legal order after Kadi. Harv Int Law J 51(1):1–49

De Wet E (2006) The emergence of international and regional value systems as a manifestation of the emerging international constitutional order. Leiden J Int Law 19:611–632

De Witte B (2010) European Union law: how autonomous is its legal order? Zeitschrift für öffentliches Recht 65:141–155

[313]As analysed by Shany (2014), p. 280, these are the constitutionalization of EU law and the advancement of market integration.

De Witte B (2011) Direct effect, primacy, and the nature of the legal order. In: Craig P, De Búrca G (eds) The evolution of EU law. Oxford University Press, Oxford, pp 323–362

De Witte B (2014a) A selfish Court? The Court of Justice and the design of international dispute settlement beyond the European Union. In: Cremona M, Thies A (eds) The European Court of Justice and external relations law: constitutional challenges. Hart Publishing, Oxford/Portland, pp 33–46

De Witte B (2014b) EU law: is it international law? In: Barnard C, Peers S (eds) European Union law. Oxford University Press, Oxford, pp 174–195

Dolzer R, Schreuer C (2012) Principles of international investment law. Oxford University Press, Oxford

Durán GM (2017) The EU and its member states in WTO dispute settlement: a "competence model", or a case apart, for managing international responsibility? In: Cremona A, Thies A, Wessel R (eds) The EU and international dispute settlement. Hart Publishing (forthcoming)

Eckes C (2012a) Protecting supremacy from external influences: a precondition for a European constitutional legal order? Eur Law J 18(2):230–250

Eckes C (2012b) EU accession to the ECHR: between autonomy and adaptation. Mod Law Rev 76(2):254–285

Eckes C (2013) The European Court of Justice and (quasi-)judicial bodies of international organisations. In: Wessel RA, Blockmans S (eds) Between autonomy and dependence. T.M.C. Asser Press, The Hague, pp 85–109

Eilmansberger T (2009) Bilateral Investment Treaties and EU law. Common Mark Law Rev 46:383–429

Flett J (2012) Importing other international regimes into World Trade Organization litigation. In: Young MA (ed) Regime interaction in international law – facing fragmentation. Cambridge University Press, Cambridge, pp 261–304

Fogdestam Agius A (2014) Interaction and delimitation of international legal orders. Brill Nijhoff, Leiden/Boston

Gardiner R (2015) Treaty interpretation. Oxford University Press, Oxford

Hartley TC (1996) The European Court, judicial objectivity and the constitution of the European Union. Law Q Rev 112:95–109

Henckels C (2008) Overcoming jurisdictional isolationism at the WTO-FTA nexus: a potential approach for the WTO. Eur J Int Law 19(3):571–599

Higgins R (2003) The ICJ, the ECJ, and the integrity of international law. Int Compar Law Q 52:1–20

Hoekman BM, Mavroidis PC (2014) Luxembourg or Strasbourg: improvising the distributional impacts of trade conflicts. In: Kosta V, Skoutaris N, Tzevelekos V (eds) The EU accession to the ECHR. Hart Publishing, Oxford/Portland, pp 237–254

Hoffmeister F (2012) The European Union and the peaceful settlement of international disputes. Chinese J Int Law 11:77–105

Hoffmeister F (2015) The European Union in the World Trade Organization – a model for the EU's status in international organisations. In: Kaddous C (ed) The European Union in international organisations and global governance. Hart Publishing, Oxford/Portland, pp 121–137

Jacobs FG (2013) Member states of the European Union before the International Court of Justice. In: Govaere I, Lannon E, Van Elsuwege P, Stanislas A (eds) The European Union in the world – essays in honour of Marc Maresceau. Brill Nijhoff, Leiden, pp 245–258

Jennings R, Higgins R (2012) General introduction. In: Zimmermann A, Tomuschat C, Oellers-Frahm K, Tams CJ (eds) The Statute of the International Court of Justice. Oxford University Press, Oxford, pp 3–46

Karaman IV (2012) Dispute resolution in the law of the sea. Brill Nijhoff, Leiden

Klabbers J (2009) Treaty conflict and the European Union. Cambridge University Press, Cambridge

Klabbers J (2015) Straddling the fence – the EU and international law. In: Arnull A, Chalmers D (eds) The Oxford handbook of European Union law. Oxford University Press, Oxford, pp 52–71

Klabbers J (2016) Sui generis? The European Union as an international organization. In: Patterson D, Södersten A (eds) A companion to European Union law and international law. Wiley-Blackwell, Chichester, pp 3–15

Klabbers J, Peters A, Ulfstein G (2009) The constitutionalization of international law. Oxford University Press, Oxford

Korenica F (2015) The EU accession to the ECHR: between Luxembourg's search for autonomy and Strasbourg's credibility on human rights protection. Springer, Heidelberg

Koskenniemi M (2007) International law: constitutionalism, managerialism and the ethos of legal education. Eur J Leg Stud 1(1):8–24

Krenzler HG, Landwehr O (2011) 'A new legal order of international law': on the relationship between public international law and European Union law after Kadi. In: Fastenrath U, Geiger R, Khan DE, Paulus A, von Schorlem S, Vedder C (eds) From bilaterism to community interest – essays in honour of Judge Bruno Simma. Oxford University Press, Oxford, pp 1004–1023

Kriebaum U (2009) Human rights of the population of the host state in international investment arbitration. J World Invest Trade 10:653–677

Kriebaum U (2015) The fate of intra-EU BITs from an investment law and public international law perspective. ELTE Law J 2015(1):27–35

Kuijper PJ, Wouters J, Hoffmeister F, Ramopoulos T, De Baere G (2015) The law of EU external relations – cases, materials, and commentary on the EU as an international legal actor, 2nd edn. Oxford University Press, Oxford

Lavranos N (2006a) The MOX Plant and IJzeren Rijn disputes: which court is the supreme arbiter? Leiden J Int Law 19:223–246

Lavranos N (2006b) Protecting its exclusive jurisdiction: the MOX Plant judgment of the ECJ. Law Pract Int Courts Tribunals 5:479–493

Lavranos N (2014) The systemic responsibility of the ECJ for judicial comity towards international courts and tribunals. In: Cremona M et al (eds) Reflections on the constitutionalisation of international economic law. Nijhoff, Leiden/Boston, pp 51–63

Leathley C (2007) An institutional hierarchy to combat the fragmentation of international law: has the ILC missed an opportunity? NY Univ J Int Law Polit 40(1):259–306

Lenaerts K (2015) The Court of Justice as the guarantor of the rule of law within the European Union. In: De Baere G, Wouters J (eds) The contribution of international and supranational courts to the rule of law. Edward Elgar Publishing, Cheltenham/Northampton

Lock T (2015) The European Court of Justice and international courts. Oxford University Press, Oxford

Mancini DG (1998) Europe: the case for statehood. Eur Law J 4:29–42

Marquet C (2016) A forbidden fruit? The European Court of Justice's case law before the World Trade Organization. Geneva Jean Monnet Working Papers 21/2016

Matsushita M, Schoenbaum T, Mavroidis P (2015) The World Trade Organization: law, practice, and policy. Oxford University Press, Oxford

McLachlan C (2005) The principle of systemic integration and Article 31(1)(c) of the Vienna Convention. Int Compar Law Q 54:279–320

Michaels R, Pauwelyn J (2011) Conflict of norms or conflict of laws? Different techniques in the fragmentation of international law. In: Broude T, Shany Y (eds) Multi-sourced equivalent norms in International law. Hart Publishing, Oxford/Portland

Oda S (1995) Dispute settlement prospects in the law of the sea. Int Compar Law Q 44:863–872

Odermatt J (2014) The EU's accession to the European Convention on human rights: an international law perspective. KU Leuven Working Paper No. 136

Odermatt J (2016) When a fence becomes a cage: the principle of autonomy in EU external relations law. EUI Working Paper MWP 2016/07

Paparinskis M (2014) Regulating treaties: a comparative perspective. In: Tams CJ, Tzanakopoulos A, Zimmermann A (eds) Research handbook on the law of treaties. Edward Elgar, Cheltenham/Northampton, pp 39–73

Parish M (2012) International courts and the European legal order. Eur J Int Law 23:141–153

Reinisch A (2012) Articles 30 and 59 of the Vienna Convention on the law of treaties in action: the decisions on jurisdiction in the Eastern Sugar and Eureko investment arbitrations. Leg Issue Econ Integr 39(2):157–177

Roe T, Happold M, Dingemans J (2011) Settlement of investment disputes under the Energy Charter Treaty. Cambridge University Press, Cambridge

Ryngaert C (2011) The European Court of Human Rights' approach to the responsibility of member states in connection with acts of international organizations. Int Compar Law Q 60:997–1016

Schill S (2013) Luxembourg limits: conditions for investor-state dispute settlement under future EU investment agreements. In: Bungenberg M, Reinisch R, Tietje C (eds) EU and investment agreements – open questions and remaining challenges. Nomos, Baden-Baden, pp 37–57

Schütze R (2012) European constitutional law. Cambridge University Press, Cambridge

Shany Y (2007) Regulating jurisdictional relations between national and international courts. Oxford University Press, Oxford

Shany Y (2014) Assessing the effectiveness of international courts. Oxford University Press, Oxford

Shirlow E (2014) Taking stock: assessing the implications of the Kadi saga for international law and the law of the European Union. Melb J Int Law 15(2):1–26

Simma B, Kill T (2009) Harmonizing investment protection and international human rights: first steps towards a methodology. In: Binder B, Kriebaum U, Reinisch A, Wittich S (eds) International investment law for the 21st century. Oxford University Press, Oxford, pp 678–707

Simma B, Pulkowski D (2006) Of planets and the universe: self-contained regimes in international law. Eur J Int Law 17(3):483–529

Slaughter AM (2003) A global community of courts. Harv Int Law J 44(1):191–219

Tietje C (2013) Bilateral investment treaties between EU member states (intra-EU-BITs) – challenges in the multilevel system of law. TDM 2:1–24

Van Vooren B, Wessel RA (2014) EU external relations law. Cambridge University Press, Cambridge

Von Bogdandy A (2008) Pluralism, direct effect, and the ultimate say: on the relationship between international and domestic constitutional law. Int J Constitut Law 6:397–413

Weiler JHH (1997) The reformation of constitutionalism. J Common Mark Stud 35(1):97–131

Wessel RA (2013) Can the EU replace its member states in international affairs? An international law perspective. In: Govaere I, Lannon E, Van Elsuwege P, Adam S (eds) The European Union in the world – essays in honour of Marc Maresceau. Brill Nijhoff, Leiden/Boston, pp 129–148

Worster WT (2008) Competition and comity in the fragmentation of international law. Brook J Int Law 34(1):119–149

Ziegler KS (2013) The relationship between EU law and international law. University of Leicester School of Law Research Paper No. 13–17

The EU's Trade Defence Instruments: Recent Judicial and Policy Developments

Wolfgang Müller

Abstract The European Union's Trade Defence Instruments consist of the Basic Anti-Dumping Regulation (Regulation (EU) 2016/1036, OJ 2016 L 176/21.), the Basic Anti-Subsidy Regulation (Regulation (EU) 2016/1037, OJ 2016 L 176/55.) as well as the safeguard instruments (Regulation (EU) 2015/478 of the European Parliament and of the Council of 11 March 2015 on common rules for imports, OJ 2015 L 83/16; Regulation (EU) 2015/755 of the European Parliament and of the Council of 29 April 2015 on common rules for imports from certain countries, OJ 2015 L 123/33.). In particular the anti-dumping instrument is currently very much in the public focus because of the steel crisis and the widely discussed question of how to treat exports from China in anti-dumping investigations. The latter issue is usually (and somewhat misleadingly) referred to as China's market economy status. However, the issue is only about the calculation of the normal value in anti-dumping investigations against imports from China, see in detail Annex S of the Staff Working Document, SWD(2016) 330 final, that is published together with the Commission's Annual Report on the EU's Anti-Dumping, Anti-Subsidy and Safeguard Activities. This contribution describes recent salient developments in the EU's trade defence instruments in the light of rulings by the Courts in Luxembourg and in relation to possible changes of the Basic Anti-Dumping and Anti-Subsidy Regulations.

Contents

The views expressed in this article are personal and cannot be attributed to the European Commission.

W. Müller (✉)
European Commission, DG Trade, Brussels, Belgium
e-mail: wolfgang.mueller@ec.europa.eu

M. Bungenberg et al. (eds.), *European Yearbook of International Economic Law 2017*, European Yearbook of International Economic Law 8,
DOI 10.1007/978-3-319-58832-2_7

1 Jurisprudence

The measures taken by the institutions in the field of trade defence are increasingly subject to intensive judicial review by the Courts in Luxembourg. The body of jurisprudence has considerably clarified many concepts contained in the basic regulations and the institutions' practice.[1] The following two recent judgments merit to be described in more detail.

1.1 Grünwald Judgment

If the General Court or the European Court of Justice annuls a regulation imposing an anti-dumping duty, this is not necessarily the end of the matter for the applicants. Rather, in the area of trade defence the Institutions have developed a practice to "repair" the shortcomings of the challenged legal act that had been identified by the Courts in Luxembourg. The *Grünwald* ruling[2] has now confirmed this practice.

The facts of the case are quickly recounted. In December 2008, the Council imposed by Regulation No 1355/2008 a definitive anti-dumping duty on imports of certain prepared or preserved citrus fruits (canned mandarins) originating in China.[3] The German importer Grünwald Logistik Service challenged the collection of anti-dumping duties on imports of these citrus fruits by the *Hauptzollamt Hamburg-Stadt*. By its judgment, the Court of Justice declared the regulation imposing definitive anti-dumping measures invalid. The definitive anti-dumping duty regulation established the normal value for the imports from China on the basis of prices paid in the EU to EU producers. While this approach is a possibility foreseen under Article 2(7)(a) of the Basic Anti-Dumping Regulation, the Court held that this method could only be resorted to once it is established that the conditions for the application of the primary method, i.e. to base the normal value on costs and prices in an analogue third country, could not be used. The Court noted that the regulation imposing definitive anti-dumping duties referred to imports of canned mandarins from Israel, Swaziland, Turkey and Thailand and that the Commission should have

[1] A complete list of rulings concerning trade defence instruments handed down each year by the courts can be found in Annex S of the Staff Working Document, SWD(2016) 330 final, that is published together with the Commission's Annual Report on the EU's Anti-Dumping, Anti-Subsidy and Safeguard Activities.

[2] CJEU, joined cases C-283/14 and C-284/14, *Grünwald*, ECLI:EU:C:2016:000.

[3] OJ 2008 L 350/35.

examined whether one of those market economy countries could have served as an analogue country.[4]

In June 2012, the Commission published a notice stating that it decided to reopen the investigation and that the reopening is limited in scope to the implementation of the afore-mentioned judgment by the Court of Justice. The notice also stated that the imports of canned mandarins where no longer subject to anti-dumping duties and that the duties collected previously had to be repaid.[5] During the re-investigation, the Commission contacted the missions of these four countries in Brussels as well as the Commission delegations in these countries in order to find out whether during the original investigation period (October 2006–September 2007) that was used for the purposes of Regulation No 1355/2008 there was indeed production of canned mandarins and, if so, whether a producer in these countries would be willing to cooperate as an analogue third country producer. No replies were received from the missions of Swaziland and Thailand, although they were contacted twice. Israel informed that it did not produce canned mandarins while the Turkish authorities provided a list of six potential producers of this product. However, none of these six companies was willing to cooperate with the Commission. The Commission delegation in Thailand also identified two potential producers but also they were not willing to cooperate. The reopened investigation was concluded in February 2013 by the publication of Council Regulation No 158/2013 re-imposing the anti-dumping duty on canned mandarins from China.[6]

Grünwald and CM Eurologistik challenged the collection of anti-dumping duties based on the February 2013 regulation before the *Finanzgericht Hamburg* and the *Finanzgericht Düsseldorf* respectively. The two courts asked whether Regulation No 158/2013 is valid. The *Finanzgericht Hamburg* referred to the absence of provisions in the Basic Anti-Dumping Regulation expressly providing for the possibility of reopening the procedure after a regulation imposing anti-dumping duties has been declared invalid. According to the Court of Justice, the absence of such provisions does not prevent the Institutions from re-opening the investigation. The Court recalled that Article 266 TFEU requires the institution which adopted the annulled act to take the necessary measures to comply with the judgment. Moreover, the annulment of a Union act does not necessarily affect the preparatory acts thereof. The Court of Justice pointed out that the irregularity found (the Commission's failure to examine on its own motion whether Israel, Swaziland, Turkey or Thailand could constitute an analogue third country) did not affect the

[4] CJEU, case C-338/10, *Grünwald Logistik Service GmbH (GLS) v Hauptzollamt Hamburg-Stadt*, ECLI:EU:C:2012:158.

[5] OJ 2012 C 175/19.

[6] OJ 2013 L 49/29. This regulation also implemented a judgment rendered by the GG, case T-122/09, *Zhejiang Xinshiji Foods and Hubei Xinshiji Foods v Council*, ECLI:EU:T:2011:46. These two Chinese exporters also challenged the definitive anti-dumping duty on canned mandarins and the General Court upheld their applications, finding that their rights of defence had been infringed as well as the Institutions' duty to state reasons. For details see recitals 8–15 and 64–111 of Council Regulation No 158/2013.

anti-dumping procedure in its entirety but only the determination of the normal value. Both referring courts also questioned whether the Commission's reopening could be reconciled with Article 6(9) of the Basic Anti-Dumping Regulation. That provision provides that an investigation must be closed within 15 months following its initiation, at the latest. The Court of Justice pointed out that Article 6 (9) covers only initial procedures and not those investigations that have been reopened following a judgment of annulment or invalidity.

Furthermore, the referring courts wondered whether Regulation No 158/2013 could be reconciled with Article 6(1) of the Basic Anti-Dumping Regulation. This provision states *inter alia* that for "the purpose of a representative finding, an investigation period shall be selected which, in the case of dumping shall, normally, cover a period of not less than *six months immediately prior to the initiation of the proceeding*" (emphasis added). However, the Commission in its reinvestigation relied on data relating to the original investigation period (October 2006–September 2007) that was used for the purposes of Regulation No 1355/2008. It did not use updated information relating to a period prior to the release of Regulation No 158/2013. The Court of Justice was not impressed by this argument. It pointed out that the rules for determining the reference period in Article 6(1) are a guide and not mandatory. According to Article 11(2) of the Basic Anti-Dumping Regulation, anti-dumping measures may remain in force for 5 years. The duration of Regulation No 158/2013 was limited to reinstating the anti-dumping duties for the remainder of the original 5-year period (that is until December 2013), Therefore, the data collected during the reinvestigation but relating to the original investigation period were considered as "sufficiently recent".

In short, the *Grünwald* judgment confirms that the Commission can resume an investigation following a judgment unfavourable to it and repair the mistakes identified by the Courts. The European Court of Justice had already recognized in *Industrie de Poudres Sphériques* the possibility of such a resumption of the investigation.[7] However, a different legal framework was applicable to that case, i.e. Basic Regulation No 2423/88 which did not provide yet for mandatory time limits of the duration of the investigation as does Article 6(9) of the current Basic Anti-Dumping Regulation. Second, in *Industrie de Poudres Sphériques* the Commission established in its reinvestigation new facts based on a different investigation period (see Article 6(1) of the Basic Anti-Dumping Regulation) while in the *Grünwald* judgment, the reinvestigation was conducted on the basis of the investigation period used in the original investigation. Therefore, *Grünwald* constitutes a welcome clarification of the law, all the more so because as mentioned at the beginning of this chapter, judicial review of each and every measure adopted by the Commission now seems to be the rule.

[7] CJEU, case C-458/98 P, *Industrie de Poudres Sphériques v. Council*, ECLI:EU:C:2000:531, para. 79 et seq.

1.2 Einhell Judgment

Once an anti-dumping duty has been imposed it has normally a shelf life of 5 years. The duty level will be varied if it is found in an interim review pursuant to Article 11(3) of the Basic Anti-Dumping Regulation that the level of dumping or injury is different as compared to that established in the original investigation, if that change is of a lasting nature and if that change has an effect on the level of the applicable anti-dumping duty. Such a change in the duty (or even its repeal) will only apply to those subject imports that are made after the regulation publishing the results of the interim review has entered into force. However, importers also have a possibility to get back any anti-dumping duties already paid on imports. This is called a refund pursuant to Article 11(8) of the Basic Anti-Dumping Regulation.[8]

Refund investigations are an increasingly common occurrence in the Union's anti-dumping practice.[9] The basic features of a refund investigation can be summarised as follows. The essential question of such investigation is whether the dumping margin of an exporter is lower than the duty level paid. In other words, the refund investigation will not only focus on those export transactions for which an exporter claims a refund but it will take into consideration all exports to the Union of a particular exporter during a representative period (usually 1 year) which covers all the dates of export transactions for which a refund is sought. By using a representative period, a pick and choose approach is excluded. In other words, an exporter cannot—in coordination with its importers—limit the refund request to export transactions with high export prices (and hence less dumping) while leaving aside export transactions where the duty level might even be higher than the one originally established. The refund can only be claimed by the importer because this company has paid the anti-dumping duty. However, the successful outcome of such an investigation depends entirely on the cooperation of the exporter. Only if the exporter cooperates with the Commission by answering a questionnaire and accepting a verification visit of Commission officials can it be established whether the actual dumping margin is lower than the duty level paid. In a nutshell, a refund investigation looks at the dumping situation of a particular exporter during a representative period with a view to determine whether the duty paid was higher than the actual degree of dumping. Issues related to injury of the Union industry or Union interest are outside the scope of a refund investigation. Note finally that for a refund claim to be admissible it must be introduced within 6 months of the date when the competent customs authorities determined the customs debt.[10]

[8]Article 21 of the Basic Anti-Subsidy Regulation contains similar provisions. The equivalent provisions of the WTO Anti-Dumping Agreement can be found in its Article 9.3.2.

[9]European Commission, Refund Investigations, http://trade.ec.europa.eu/tdi/refunds.cfm (last accessed 1 March 2017).

[10]The details of refund procedures are set out in the Commission Notice concerning the reimbursement of anti-dumping duties, OJ 2016 C 184/9.

There is one particular challenge when calculating the dumping margin in a refund investigation especially when the importer seeking a refund is related to the exporter in question. This issue is referred to as "duty as a cost" and is linked to the construction of the export price. The *Einhell* judgment[11] has now largely settled this issue which was before fraught with considerable uncertainty. This issue is rooted in Article 11(10) in combination with Article 2(9) of the Basic Anti-Dumping Regulation. Article 11(10) reads as follows:

> In any investigation carried out pursuant to this Article, the Commission shall examine the reliability of export prices in accordance with Article 2. However, where it is decided to construct the export price in accordance with Article 2(9), it shall calculate it with no deduction for the amount of the anti-dumping duties paid when conclusive evidence is provided that the duty is duly reflected in resale prices and subsequent selling prices in the Community.

Article 2(9) reads in relevant part:

> [When constructing the export price,] adjustment for all costs, including duties and taxes, incurred between importation and resale, and for profits accruing, shall be made so as to establish a reliable export price, at the Community frontier level.

In case of a transaction between an exporter and its related importer, the export price (which is then compared to the normal value; if such export price is inferior to the normal value there is dumping) is usually constructed pursuant to Article 2(9). The reason for constructing the export price—instead of taking the price agreed between the exporter and its related importer—is that prices between related parties are normally not at arm's length. When the export price is constructed, the importer's resale price is used as a starting point and costs incurred by the importer are deducted. The question at issue in the *Einhell* judgment was how to establish pursuant to Article 11(10) of the Basic Anti-Dumping Regulation that the related importer's resale prices reflected the duty. This has a direct impact on the level of the dumping margin. If the resale price does not reflect the anti-dumping duty paid by the related importer, that duty will be deducted in order to construct the export price. However, if the duty is reflected, no deduction of an anti-dumping duty will be made. As the export price at Union frontier level is in this second scenario higher than in the first one, less or even no dumping will be found in the second scenario. In the case at hand the Commission carried out an analysis which established for each product type or PCN[12] whether the duty was reflected in the resale price. It found that for five of the best-selling models the duties were duly reflected but not for the other five best-selling models. Therefore, the Commission deducted all anti-dumping duties paid by the importer when constructing the export price pursuant to

[11]GC, case T-73/12, *Einhell Germany et al. v Commission*, ECLI:EU:T:2015:000.

[12]Product types are usually defined by PCNs. PCN stands for "product control number" and they are used for each unique type and possible combination of product characteristics. For instance in a case against imports of TVs, the different screen sizes would usually be attributed to different PCNs.

Article 2(9) of the Basic Anti-Dumping Regulation, including for the five models where it found that the duty was reflected in the resale price.

Einhell challenged this decision arguing that the Commission should have carried out an aggregate analysis, i.e. for the product concerned and not for each product type or model of which the product concerned is composed, when examining whether the resale prices reflected the duties paid. They pointed out, amongst others, that the total turnover relating to the product concerned—imported air compressors—exceeded the purchasing price including the duties paid and that the Commission treated all product types of air compressors as one single product for the purposes of the investigation. The Court rejected the request for an aggregate analysis based on an increase of turnover *inter alia* on the following grounds:

The Commission enjoys a broad discretion in the field of measures to protect trade.[13] The Basic Anti-Dumping Regulation does not specify a particular method in order to examine this issue while not only one but several methods exist by which to determine whether the requirements of Article 11(10) are met.[14] The Court concluded, based on an interpretation of the relevant provisions of the WTO Anti-Dumping Agreement, that the deduction of any anti-dumping duties paid ("duty as a cost") for the purposes of constructing the export price is the general rule. Like any exception to a general rule, the non-deduction of anti-dumping duties from the constructed export price must be interpreted strictly. As the PCN-by-PCN method leads to a stricter assessment than the aggregate method, it is more consistent with a literal purposive interpretation of Article 11(10).[15]

However, the Court took issue with the Commission's approach to deduct the anti-dumping duty paid for all models including for the five models where the resale price reflected the anti-dumping duty. It criticized that (a) the Commission used the PCN-by-PCN method to determine whether the resale prices of individual models reflected the duty but (b) when it came to the question of deducting the duty as a cost, the Commission applied an aggregate approach and deducted the duties for all models. In short, the Court accepted a partial non-deduction of duties.[16] This is an important clarification. Following the *Einhell* judgment, the focus of the analysis is now simply on whether for the product type or model in question ("PCN") the resale price went up by an amount corresponding to the anti-dumping duty. If that question is answered affirmatively, no deduction for duty as a cost should be made. There should be a full parallelism between the analysis and the refund. Both must be made at PCN level while the Commission made the latter at an aggregate level. Note however that in the refund decision, subsequent selling prices beyond the resale prices charged by the related importer were not at issue.

---

[13]GC, case T-73/12, *Einhell Germany et al. v Commission*, ECLI:EU:T:2015:000, paras. 56 and 69.

[14]GC, case T-73/12, *Einhell Germany et al. v Commission*, ECLI:EU:T:2015:000, para. 67.

[15]GC, case T-73/12, *Einhell Germany et al. v Commission*, ECLI:EU:T:2015:000, paras. 83–93.

[16]GC, case T-73/12, *Einhell Germany et al. v Commission*, ECLI:EU:T:2015:000, paras. 132–159.

The decision underlying the *Einhell* ruling also settles a further issue. This issue predates the existing Basic Anti-Dumping Regulation and the WTO Anti-Dumping Agreement. Before 1994 it was generally believed (and confirmed by the Courts in the NMB judgments)[17] that a related importer could only claim that anti-dumping duties should not be deducted from the resale price if they demonstrated that their resale price reflected twice the amount of the anti-dumping duty paid ("double jump"). The reason for this was that by giving a full refund to a related importer in case of a single jump, i.e. the resale price reflects only the anti-dumping duty, there would be a discrimination between related and unrelated importers. The alleged discrimination resulted from differences at the level of the actual export price after the imposition of anti-dumping duties (as opposed to the resale price). In the case of export sales between related parties, no change of the actual export price was necessary—it sufficed that the resale price went up by the amount of the duty paid. By contrast, in case of transactions between the exporter and an unrelated importer the resale price of the latter would normally have reflected a higher (non-dumped) export price (i.e. its purchasing price) plus the anti-dumping duty paid. In other words, an unrelated importer adopting normal commercial behaviour would also have attempted a double jump.[18] This distinction and thus the double jump no longer seem to be relevant.[19]

2 Modernization of the EU's Trade Defence Instruments

2.1 Background and Content of the Commission Proposal

The design of the EU's current trade defence instruments dates back to 1994. At that time the EU transposed the results of the Uruguay Round into Union law. All the subsequent changes concerned narrowly circumscribed areas, notably the removal of Russia and Ukraine from the scope of the non-market economy rules as set out in Article 2(7) of the Basic Anti-Dumping Regulation, the introduction of the possibility of market economy treatment for exporters in economies in transition to a market economy, a change in the decision making rules prior to enlargement of the EU from 15 to 25 members[20] and finally the application of the Post Lisbon comitology regulation to the trade defence instruments.[21]

---

[17]CJEU, case C-188/88, *NMB (Deutschland) GmbH and others v Commission*, ECLI:EU:C:1992:114; GC, case T-162/94, *NMB France SARL, NMB-Minebea-GmbH, NMB (UK) Ltd. and NMB Italia Sarl v Commission*, ECLI:EU:T:1996:71.

[18]See the numerical example in Müller et al. (2009), para. 11.101.

[19]GC, case T-73/12, *Einhell Germany et al. v Commission*, ECLI:EU:T:2015:000, paras. 95–104.

[20]See Müller et al. (2009), para. 1.37.

[21]Regulation (EU) No 37/2014 of 15 January 2014, OJ 2014 L 18/1.

In 2013, the Commission released the so-called modernisation package which aimed at a broader change of the existing rules.[22] This was the second attempt to change a broader set of provisions of the Union's trade defence instruments. A first attempt was undertaken at the end of 2006 under Commissioner *Mandelson* by releasing the so-called Green Paper.[23] This paper launched a public consultation and the vast majority of responses received were not favourable to this initiative,[24] as were a significant number of Member States. The ideas expressed in the Green Paper were considered as favouring more importing interests as opposed to the interests of EU manufacturers. The Commission ultimately abandoned the Green Paper initiative and did not even make a legislative proposal.

The 2013 modernisation package was different. The selection of the various proposals contained therein was based on two guiding principles. First, in order to avoid the pitfalls of the Green Paper, that is to favour the interests of one group of stakeholders over the others, it attempted to prepare a package that would be interesting for both sides of stakeholders, i.e. those normally supporting the adoption of trade defence measures and those traditionally opposed to such measures. Second, and linked to the preceding point, the modernisation package tried to find pragmatic solutions to a number of problems that were increasingly encountered in the administration of the instruments.

The package proposes a number of changes to the Basic Anti-Dumping Regulation and the Basic Anti-Subsidy Regulation as well as some non-legislative changes including four draft guidelines. The legislative proposal was released together with a Commission communication that pulls the various ideas together and puts them in context.

The package proposes changes in six areas. The first group of proposals aims at improving transparency and predictability in trade defence investigations. The Commission put forward the ideas in this context: (a) a better information of interested parties about the imposition of provisional duties and (b) the release of Commission guidelines covering key concepts of substantive trade defence rules. The better information about provisional measures is often labelled as a "shipping clause". However, the mechanism proposed in the modernisation package is conceptually different from a real shipping clause as contained in the Basic Safeguard Regulation which allows goods already in transit at the time of the entry into force of measures to enter the Union market without payment of duties.[25] The problem is that provisional anti-dumping and anti-subsidy duties come to economic operators

[22]European Commission, Modernisation of Trade Defence Instruments—Adapting trade defence instruments to the current needs of the European economy, COM (2013) 191 final.

[23]European Commission, Global Europe—Europe's trade defence instruments in a changing global economy—A Green Paper for public consultation, COM (2006) 763 final.

[24]European Commission, Evaluation of the responses to the public consultation on Europe's trade defence instruments in a changing economy, http://trade.ec.europa.eu/doclib/docs/2007/november/tradoc_136846.pdf (last accessed 1 March 2017).

[25]See Article 15(5) of Regulation (EU) 2015/478 of the European Parliament and of the Council of 11 March 2015 on common rules for imports, OJ 2015 L 83/16. The mechanism provided for in

often as a surprise. While the time table of the Commission's investigation of a case is generally well known as well as the content of possible definitive measures, there is some uncertainty as far as provisional measures are concerned. These uncertainties relate to the precise timing as well as to the level of measures. Therefore, the Commission proposed to inform interested parties 2 weeks in advance of its intention to impose provisional duties as well as the level of such duties. Moreover, exporters would receive the possibility to review the Commission's dumping and subsidy calculations prior to the adoption of provisional measures in order to further reduce the risk that such calculations contain clerical errors. The proposed guidelines cover Union interest,[26] the selection of the analogue country for the purposes of establishing the normal value of exporters in non-market economy countries,[27] the determination of the target profit when calculating the injury margin as well as expiry reviews.[28] With regard to all of these areas the institutions have developed a coherent practice. However, the relevant text of the Basic Regulations is only cursory.[29]

The second area covered by the modernisation package addresses the problem of retaliation. Occasionally, Union operators wishing to file an application for the initiation of a trade defence investigation are exposed to pressure from their customers, suppliers or foreign governments. The purpose of this pressure is to prevent Union producers from the exercise of their rights under WTO rules and Union legislation that are designed to protect manufacturers from unfair trade. Such pressure can result in that Union producers do not submit a complaint, or do not support the complaint when it comes to establishing standing,[30] or do not cooperate as Union producers. Note that *de lega lata* Union law does not contain any obligation of Union producers to cooperate. The way forward suggested in the Commission proposal was two-pronged. The Commission announced that it could use so called *ex officio* investigations. This is a vehicle already existing today in the Basic Regulations and means that the Commission opens on its own motion the investigation instead of waiting for a complaint by the Union industry.[31] However,

---

Article 15(5) in fact delays the application of the measures which would be in contradiction to one of the purposes of the modernisation packages, i.e. to have earlier provisional measures.

[26]See Article 21 of the Basic Anti-Dumping Regulation and Article 32 of the Basic Anti-Subsidy Regulation.

[27]See Article 2(7) of the Basic Anti-Dumping Regulation.

[28]See Article 11(2) of the Basic Anti-Dumping Regulation and Article 18 of the Basic Anti-Subsidy Regulation.

[29]The draft guidelines were subject to a public consultation. The results of this consultation are available in European Commission, Replies of interested parties on Commission draft guidelines, Summary, http://trade.ec.europa.eu/doclib/docs/2013/december/tradoc_151968.pdf (last accessed 1 March 2017).

[30]See Article 5(4) of the Basic Anti-Dumping Regulation and Article 10(6) of the Basic Anti-Subsidy Regulation.

[31]See Article 5(6) of the Basic Anti-Dumping Regulation and Article 10(8) of the Basic Anti-Subsidy Regulation.

as no investigation could ever be successfully concluded without cooperation by the Union industry (otherwise no injury findings could be made), the Commission proposal suggested as a second prong the introduction into the Basic Regulations of an obligation of the Union industry to cooperate in case of an *ex officio* initiation.

The third area of the Commission proposal covered the effectiveness of the instruments and better enforcement of existing anti-dumping and anti-subsidy measures. One proposal under this heading is fairly straightforward and does not require a legislative change, i.e. that the Commission would in future open more on its own initiative circumvention investigations pursuant to Article 13 of the Basic Anti-Dumping Regulation and Article 23 of the Basic Anti-Subsidy Regulation. The second element falling under this heading proved in the subsequent discussions with the co-legislators as highly contentious, i.e. not to apply at all the lesser duty rule in anti-subsidy investigations and to suspend its application in anti-dumping investigations if the exporting country maintains structural distortions on upstream raw materials. The rationale underlying this proposal was not to give a benefit to exporters if they benefit from major distortions of the level playing field. This was also in line with the Commission's raw material initiative.[32] The Commission communication on the modernisation of trade defence instruments also mentions that the Commission seeks to reduce in general the time needed for deciding provisional measures by 2 months without however giving any details how this would be implemented.

The fourth area aimed at facilitating cooperation of interested parties. Again, it contained two proposals. The first one provided for an upgrade of the helpdesk for small and medium sized enterprises well as initiatives designed to improve awareness of trade defence instruments. Both Union producers but also those negatively affected by the imposition of measures would benefit from action (which does not require any legislative changes) in this area. The second proposal falling under this heading is to prolong the deadlines for responding to questionnaires addressed to importers and generally questionnaires aimed at the Union interest investigation. The implementation of this proposal would give more time to those parties that are potentially negatively affected by any measures to defend themselves without compromising the quality of the investigation. Indeed, information relating to Union interest considerations is typically needed after dumping and injury are established.

The purpose of the fifth area of intervention was to optimize the review practice. Anti-dumping and anti-subsidy measures are normally adopted for a period of 5 years. They can be renewed for another 5-year period if an expiry review establishes that there is a likelihood of a continuation or recurrence of injurious dumping or subsidisation. Such expiry reviews are initiated at the end of the 5 year period and last between 12 and a maximum of 15 months. The anti-dumping and anti-subsidy measures remain in force during the review investigation. It was felt

[32]European Commission, The raw materials initiative—meeting our critical needs for growth and jobs in Europe, COM (2008) 699 final.

that the status quo is not optimal if the expiry review concludes that measures should not be renewed as this implies that the Union industry benefitted 6 years from protection although—with hindsight—only 5 years were warranted. The way forward was to provide for the possibility to pay any duties back which have been collected during the expiry review investigation.

Last but not least the Commission's modernisation proposal contains a number of very technical changes to the Basic Regulations that reflect WTO rulings and jurisprudence by the Courts in Luxembourg. Most of the proposed changes would not affect current Commission practice as these rulings are already consistently followed today but the legal texts became obsolete in these respects. It would go beyond the scope of this contribution to describe them here in detail.

In terms of procedure, the Commission proposal respected the Commission's "better regulation rules". Hence, the Commission commissioned a study,[33] conducted a public consultation and carried out an impact assessment before drawing up its proposal.

2.2 *European Parliament*

The European Parliament adopted a legislative resolution on 16 April 2014, i.e. within an exceptionally short time frame, and thus closed its first reading.[34] This would have in principle allowed for sufficient time to conduct the trilogue with Commission and Council before the Parliament went into recess for re-election in 2014. The position adopted by the European Parliament tilted the balance of the Commission proposal clearly in favour of traditional producer interests in the Union. It provided for significant exceptions to the lesser duty rule. According to the first reading position, the lesser duty rule should not be applied if the exporting country has not accepted or not applied international treaties concerning labour rights and environmental protection, where it interferes in exchange rates and where the Union industry consists of small and medium-sized enterprises. The Parliament also proposed not to sign into law those parts of the Commission proposal that are of interest to importers, i.e. the proposal for reimbursement of collected duties in case an expiry review does not lead to a renewal of measures and the pre-information of importers and exporters with regard to forthcoming provisional measures. While

[33]Bkp Development Research & Consulting, Evaluation of the European Union's Trade Defence Instruments—Final Evaluation Study, 2 volumes, 27 February 2012, http://trade.ec.europa.eu/doclib/docs/2012/august/tradoc_149882.pdf (last accessed 1 March 2017).

[34]European Parliament, Protection against dumped and subsidised imports from countries not members of the EU, resolution of 16 April 2014, P7_TA(2014)0420. The European Parliament also organized on 7 November 2013 a workshop on this initiative, http://www.europarl.europa.eu/RegData/etudes/workshop/join/2014/433842/EXPO-INTA_AT(2014)433842_EN.pdf (last accessed 1 March 2017). A detailed account of the decision making process within the European Parliament can be found in Hoffmeister (2015), pp. 371–374.

recognizing the need to act against retaliation, the European Parliament proposed not to adopt a duty to cooperate. The underlying argument was that Union producers that are exposed to retaliation should not in addition be made subject to an obligation to cooperate, i.e. to come under pressure from the Commission and their customers as well as third country authorities.[35]

2.3 *Council*

The Council could up to now not agree on a position that would have allowed to the presidency to enter into trilogues. The partial removal of the lesser duty rule proved to be the main obstacle in this respect. After intensive efforts under the Italian Presidency in the second of semester 2014 to achieve a mandate for trilogues, work in the Council on this file came temporarily to a halt by the end of that year. However, in the wake of the steel crisis activities resumed in 2016 because the European steel industry could have been much better shielded from the effects of unfair international competition had the modernisation package already entered into force. It was precisely the lesser duty rule that was at the origin of criticism expressed by the European industry and some Member States in relation to an allegedly insufficient low level of anti-dumping duties, all the more so because other jurisdictions imposed considerably higher duties on the same or similar products.

Therefore, the European Commission in its Steel Communication of March 2016[36] recalled its proposal made back in 2013 and that in order to further improve the efficiency and the effectiveness of EU action, the EU's trade defence instruments needed to be modernised. It pointed out that additional reforms need to be considered, for example the rationale for the removal of the lesser-duty rule should apply also to the steel sector and more generally to situations where the market of the exporting country is subject to significant distortions. According to the Steel Communication, it might also be appropriate with regard to the calculation of the injury margin to better define the target profit to ensure that the injury is adequately removed.[37] Finally, the Steel Communication pointed out that intermediary deadlines set out in the Basic Regulations with regard to investigations such as the one on sampling[38] should be reviewed in order to accelerate the adoption of provisional measures (currently usually after slightly less than 9 months) and thus providing

[35]On the development of the modernisation file in the European Parliament see in detail Hoffmeister (2015), pp. 371–374.

[36]European Commission, Steel: Preserving sustainable jobs and growth in Europe, COM (2016) 155 final, p. 5 et seq.

[37]The mechanics of the lesser-duty-rule are explained in Müller et al. (2009), paras. 14.03–14.48.

[38]See Article 17 of the Basic Anti-Dumping Regulation and Article 27 of the Basic Anti-Subsidy Regulation.

quicker relief to the Union industry. The primary purpose of these points was to broaden the basis of discussions to ultimately help the Council to find a common basis for a mandate to the Presidency to start trilogues.

The European Council in its meeting on 20 and 21 October 2016 noted the crucial importance of effective EU trade defence instruments in the face of global challenges. This requires "an urgent and balanced agreement on the Council position on the comprehensive modernisation of all trade defence instruments by the end of 2016."[39] Subsequently on 13 December 2016, the Coreper agreed on the Council's negotiating position. The compromise found within the Council included to inform parties about the intended course of action in relation to provisional measures about 4 weeks before such measures are actually adopted and to change the methodology for applying the lesser-duty rule in cases of significant raw material distortions. In this context, the compromise stipulates the minimum percentages that distorted raw materials must individually and collectively account for in the total cost of production in order to be relevant.[40] Trilogues between the three institutions started in March 2017 and were not concluded yet when this contribution went into print. The March 2017 European Council called for a quick adoption of the proposal.[41]

3 China's Accession Protocol and EU Anti-Dumping law

When China joined the WTO in 2001, it concluded with the US an agreement that set out, *inter alia*, the special rules applicable in relation to anti-dumping actions against exports from China. This agreement was multi-lateralized and is now included in paragraphs (a) and (d) of section 15 of the Protocol annexed to the decision concerning China's accession to the WTO.[42] The relevant text is reproduced in the annex to this contribution. Section 15(a)(ii) expires on 11 December 2016 but no expiry date is foreseen for the remaining text.

The discussion about the consequences of this expiration if often referred to as "China's market economy status". While it is true that section 15 refers five times to the term "market economy" the implications of this discussion are fairly well circumscribed. This issue is only relevant for the very technical determination of normal value in anti-dumping investigations concerning imports from China: should Chinese costs and prices be used for that purpose or non-Chinese data.

[39]EUCO 31/16 of 21 October 2016, Conclusions adopted by the European Council at the above meeting.

[40]See http://www.consilium.europa.eu/en/press/press-releases/2016/12/13-trade-defence-instruments-general-approach/ (last accessed 1 March 2017).

[41]Conclusions by the President of the European Council, 9 March 2017, point 4.

[42]Protocol on the Accession of the People's Republic of China, WT/L/432 of 23 November 2001. See also paragraph 151 of the Working Party Report on China's Accession, WT/ACC/CHN/49 (Oct. 2001).

The issue does not imply any wider classification of the Chinese economy as a whole.

The anti-dumping rules in section 15 are not a model of clarity. However, what is known about the negotiation history makes it clear that the structure which found its way in the Accession Protocol is not an "accident de parcours" but a deliberate choice made by the negotiators.[43]

To put section 15 in context, it is useful to recall the general rules. Article 2.1 of the WTO Anti-Dumping Agreement defines a product as being dumped if it is introduced into the commerce of another country at less than its normal value. The term "normal value" refers to the comparable price, sold in sufficient quantities and in the ordinary course of trade, for the like product (a product that is comparable to the one exported) when destined for consumption in the exporting country. In short, there is dumping if the export price is lower than the normal value, and the selling price in the home market of the exporter can constitute the normal value. There are two further possibilities of determining the normal value, i.e. a constructed normal (based on the costs incurred in producing the like product plus a reasonable margin of profit) and a normal value based on export prices to third countries. It is obvious that these general rules governing the determination of the normal value are not suitable if the exporting country operates a planned economy run by the State. That was the reason why the GATT contracting parties added 1955 an interpretative note to Article VI of GATT 1947 that stipulates in its second paragraph:

> It is recognized that, in the case of imports from a country which has a complete or substantially complete monopoly of its trade and where all domestic prices are fixed by the State, special difficulties may exist in determining price comparability for the purposes of paragraph 1 [of Article VI of the GATT 1947], and in such cases importing contracting parties may find it necessary to take into account the possibility that a strict comparison with domestic prices in such a country may not always be appropriate.[44]

This second *Ad* note to Article VI is the legal basis for using third country proxies when a normal value has to be established for exports from a non-market economy country. Under EU practice, which is based on Article 2(7)(a) of the Basic Anti-Dumping Regulation, the third country is usually referred to as "analogue country" while in the USA the term "surrogate country" is used. As a consequence, in order to determine dumping the export price from a non-market economy country is not compared to the normal value in the country of origin of the exports but to a normal value in an appropriate analogue country. The non-market economy provisions were originally applied to exports from the USSR and the other COMECON

[43]The US released a negotiation document of their bilateral Agreement on Market Access with China where the current architecture of paras. (a) and (d) of section 15 was essentially introduced, see https://archive.org/stream/AgreementOnMarketAccess/Us-chinaBilateralAgreementProtocols#page/n3/mode/2up (last accessed 1 March 2017). The text of section 15 has essentially been reproduced in Vietnam's accession to the WTO, see the Working Party report, WT/ACC/VNM/48, 27 October 2006, para. 255.

[44]Article 2.7 of the WTO Anti-Dumping Agreement sets out that Article 2 is without prejudice to this second *Ad* note. Miranda (2014), p. 95 describes the negotiation history of this second *Ad* note.

countries as well as China. When China joined the WTO in 2001 after lengthy accession negotiations, there was a common understanding that the Chinese economic model did no longer correspond to the one envisaged by the *Ad* note. However, the Chinese State continued to play a very important role in the economy. Hence the specific rules for establishing normal value in section 15 of China's WTO accession protocol.

These rules did not generate much interest until 2011. In that year *Bernard O'Connor* sparked off a discussion about the consequences of the expiration of section 15(a)(ii) by publishing his article "The Myth of China and Market Economy Status in 2016".[45] Since then numerous articles have been published about this topic. There is no consensus amongst practitioners and scholars about the consequences of the expiration of section 15(a)(ii). A discussion about the precise implications of this expiration is beyond the scope of this contribution. Some believe that the expiration of section 15(a)(ii) will effectively end the possibility of using out of country benchmarks in order to determine whether or not imports from China are dumped.[46] This interpretation is however strongly disputed by many. In the latter camp, the prevailing view is that the consequence of the expiration of section 15(a)(ii) is that the presumption that China and its industrial sectors have not evolved yet into market economy becomes inoperative.[47] As to what precisely this means in the light of the section 15(a)(i) is subject to debate. One contributor has expressed the view that as of 11 December 2016 individual Chinese exporters (as opposed to an entire sector or industry of the Chinese economy)[48] must be given the possibility to demonstrate that they work under market economy conditions. If that demonstration is successful, the exporter's own data should be used and not those from an analogue country.[49] Others consider that the burden of proof concerning the existence of non-market economy conditions in China shifts to the investigating authority and the domestic industry of the importing country.[50] That view is however difficult to reconcile with the wording of the surviving section 15(a)(i).

Whether or not Chinese costs and prices are used for establishing normal value has direct economic consequences. It is generally thought that normal values based on Chinese data and hence dumping margins would be considerably lower. Therefore, those associated with producing interests in the EU fear that the anti-dumping

[45]See http://worldtradelaw.typepad.com/files/oconnorresponse.pdf (last accessed 1 March 2017).

[46]See e.g. Graafsma and Kumushova (2014), Nicely (2014), p. 161 et seq.; Watson (2014), Tietje and Nowrot (2011).

[47]Miranda (2014), p. 102; Posner (2014), p. 148 et seq.; Ruessmann and Beck (2014), pp. 458–460; Rosenthal and Beckington (2014), p. 353 et seq.; Stewart et al. (2014), p. 278 et seq.

[48]This possibility to demonstrate that market economy conditions prevail in a particular industry or sector exists already since China's accession back in 2001, based on the third sentence of section 15(d). The latter provision is not subject to a sunset date.

[49]See Ruessmann and Beck (2014), p. 460 et seq.

[50]Miranda (2014), p. 103; Posner (2014), pp. 151–153; Rosenthal and Beckington (2014), p. 354. Similar Gatta (2014).

instrument would lose its effectiveness in assessing unfair competition from imports from China. A number of industry associations (many of whom typically rely on trade defence measures) have formed a pressure group called AEGIS Europe that follows this matter very closely. Note that about 60% of all anti-dumping measures currently in force are directed against imports from China. The European Commission itself estimates that the level of anti-dumping measures would be 27 percentage points lower than today if Chinese cost and price data were to be used without further adjustment. This in turn could put around 200,000 jobs at risk according to an independent study.[51]

The Commission discussed for the first time this topic in an orientation debate on 13 January 2016.[52] This was followed by a presentation of this issue to European trade ministers and to the European Parliament at the beginning of February 2016.[53] Essentially three options were identified: (1) leaving the EU legislation unchanged; (2) removing China from the list of "non-market economies" and applying the standard methodology for dumping calculations; (3) changing the antidumping methodology with a new approach which would maintain a strong trade defence system, while giving effect to the EU's WTO obligations. Following these discussions, and the release of the Inception Impact Assessment,[54] a comprehensive impact assessment was conducted which included a public consultation launched on 10 February 2016[55] and also a public hearing on 17 March 2016. A second Orientation Debate followed on 20 July 2016. In that second debate the Commission endorsed in principle the third option and stressed the need that Europe has trade defence instruments that can deal with the current realities—notably existing overcapacities—in the international trading environment.[56]

---

[51]The Commission has released the above-mentioned figures in an information note, http://trade.ec.europa.eu/doclib/docs/2016/february/tradoc_154241.pdf (last accessed 1 March 2017). The study itself was subsequently published on 9 November 2016 together with the legislative proposal and the Impact Assessment, http://trade.ec.europa.eu/doclib/press/index.cfm?id=1573&title=Commission-proposes-changes-to-the-EUs-anti-dumping-and-anti-subsidy-legislation (last accessed 1 March 2017). A good summary of the politics of this issue can be found in Huotari M, Gaspers J, Böhnke O, Asserting European interests – How Brussels should deal with the question of China's Market Economy status. Merics policy brief, January 2016, http://www.merics.org/fileadmin/user_upload/downloads/China_Policy_Brief/China_Policy_Brief_January_2016.pdf (last accessed 1 March 2017).

[52]European Commission, College orientation debate on the treatment of China in anti-dumping investigations, MEMO/16/61.

[53]European Commission, Change in the methodology for anti-dumping investigations concerning China, http://trade.ec.europa.eu/doclib/docs/2016/february/tradoc_154241.pdf (last accessed 1 March 2017).

[54]European Commission, Inception Impact Assessment, http://ec.europa.eu/smart-regulation/roadmaps/docs/2016_trade_002_dumping_investigations_china_en.pdf (last accessed 1 March 2017).

[55]European Commission, Commission opens a public consultation on future measures to prevent dumped imports from China, http://trade.ec.europa.eu/doclib/press/index.cfm?id=1455 (last accessed 1 March 2017).

[56]European Commission, Press release IP/16/2567, 20 July 2016.

The European Parliament adopted on 12 May 2016 a resolution on China's market economy status. In its resolution, it stressed that China is not a market economy and that the five criteria established by the EU to define market economies have not yet been fulfilled. Moreover, it urged the Commission to coordinate with the EU's major trading partners including in the context of G7 and G20 summits, on how best to ensure that all provisions of section 15 that remain in force after 2016 are given full legal meaning and to oppose any unilateral granting of market economy status to China. The European Parliament also expressed its conviction that until China meets all five EU criteria required to qualify as a market economy, the EU should use a non-standard methodology in anti-dumping and anti-subsidy investigations into Chinese imports in determining price comparability.[57]

The discussion of a change of the calculation methodology of the normal value for imports from China was overshadowed by the steel crisis. The steel crisis is essentially an issue of overcapacities and many point the finger to Chinese excess production capacities. The slowing down of the Chinese economy in 2015/2016 has also brought to the fore the concern that overcapacities in that country not only exist in the steel sector but also in other sectors of the economy.[58] Note that overcapacity is a typical root cause of dumping practices. A company with significant spare production capacities is economically better off if it increases production and sales, provided that the additional output can be sold at price levels which cover the variable costs of such additional out and in addition contribute to the company's block of fixed costs. Such sales will be dumped because they are made in significant quantities and below the full cost of production. Hence, the normal value would not be based on prices but constructed covering the full cost of production plus a reasonable profit margin.[59]

On 18 October 2016, the Commission has in its Communication "Towards a robust trade policy for the EU in the interest of jobs and growth"[60] reiterated its choice of the third option by saying that it will propose a new anti-dumping methodology to capture market distortions linked to state intervention in third countries.

The Communication also deplored the lack of transparency in many third countries regarding subsidies. Given that subsidies contribute to distortions and overcapacities the Communication concluded that the rules should be strengthened by allowing the Commission to take action on new subsidies which are only discovered in the course of an anti-subsidy investigation. It also announced that

[57]European Parliament, China's market economy status, P8_TA(2016)0233, resolution of 12 May 2016 (2016/2667(RSP)).

[58]European Union Chamber of Commerce, Overcapacity in China: An Impediment to the Party's Reform Agenda, 22 February 2016, http://www.europeanchamber.com.cn/en/publications-overcapacity-in-china (last accessed on 1 March 2017).

[59]See Articles 2(3) and (4) of the Basic Anti-Dumping Regulation.

[60]European Commission, Towards a robust trade policy for the EU in the interest of jobs and growth, COM (2016) 690 final, p. 4 et seq.

there will be an orderly and transparent transition to the new system ("grandfathering").

On 9 November 2016, the Commission finally released its proposal that was entirely in line with the announcements made in the Communication.[61] According to the proposal, a new paragraph 6a is to be inserted in Article 2 of the Basic Anti-Dumping Regulation. This paragraph sets out a new methodology for calculating normal value in case of government induced distortions in the exporting country. Point (a) of the new paragraph 6a stipulates that if

> it is not appropriate to use domestic prices and costs in the exporting country due to the existence of significant distortions, the normal value shall be constructed on the basis of costs of production and sale reflecting undistorted prices or benchmarks. For this purpose, the sources that may be used include undistorted international prices, costs, or benchmarks, or corresponding costs of production and sale in an appropriate representative country with a similar level of economic development as the exporting country, provided the relevant cost data are readily available.

Subparagraph (b) further explains the trigger for using the new methodology:

> Significant distortions for the product concerned within the meaning of point (a) may be deemed to exist, inter alia, when reported prices or costs, including the costs of raw materials, are not the result of free market forces as they are affected by government intervention. In considering whether or not significant distortions exist regard may be had, inter alia, to the potential impact of the following: the market in question is to a significant extent served by enterprises which operate under the ownership, control or policy supervision or guidance of the authorities of the exporting country; state presence in firms allowing the state to interfere with respect to prices or costs; public policies or measures discriminating in favour of domestic suppliers or otherwise influencing free market forces; and access to finance granted by institutions implementing public policy objectives.

Many stakeholders in the EU expressed the concern that the new methodology would make it very difficult if not impossible to launch in future applications for the initiation of an anti-dumping case, if this new methodology has to be relied on. The proposal has responded to these concerns by providing in point (c) for the possibility to issue reports that describe the distortions in a certain country or a certain sector. According to point (d) the Union industry can rely on such a report for the calculation of the normal value when filing a complaint to launch an investigation. Such a report and the evidence on which it is based will also be placed on the file of any investigation relating to that country or sector. Interested parties will have ample opportunity to supplement, comment or rely on the report and the evidence on which it is based in each investigation in which such report or evidence is used. The determinations made shall take into account all of the relevant evidence on the file (point (c)). In other words, as it is the case today, it will be for the Union

[61] European Commission, Proposal for a Regulation of the European Parliament and of the Council amending Regulation (EU) 2016/1036 on protection against dumped imports from countries not members of the European Union and Regulation (EU) 2016/1037 on protection against subsidised imports from countries not members of the European Union, COM (2016) 721 final. See further http://trade.ec.europa.eu/doclib/press/index.cfm?id=1573&title=Commission-proposes-changes-to-the-EUs-anti-dumping-and-anti-subsidy-legislation (last accessed 1 March 2017).

industry to file complaints, but they can rely on such reports by the Commission to make their case.

Note that that it is not a precondition for the use of the new calculation methodology that a report has been issued previously. Indeed, provided that there is sufficient relevant evidence of the existence distortions in the exporting country, the new calculation methodology can be applied without such a report.

It should be pointed out that the application of the new methodology is country neutral. While recital 2 *in fine* of the Commission proposal clarifies that it should be without prejudice to establishing whether or not any WTO Member is a market economy the new text of Article 2(7) has a substantially reduced scope. WTO Members would no longer be subject to this provision that is the basis for using the analogue country methodology. Last but not least, the proposal makes it clear that the new system will only apply to investigations initiated after the legislative change enters into force.

The file is now dealt with by the two co-legislators under the ordinary legislative procedure pursuant to Article 294 of the TFEU. The Council agreed on its negotiation position on 3 May 2017 and the INTA Committee on 19 June 2017. Trilogues started in July.

4 Conclusion

Jurisprudence by the Courts in Luxembourg has clarified significantly important aspects of European anti-dumping law. However, 2017 is likely to see a rise in legislative activity in this area of Union law. Given the commitment by the European Council to move forward the modernisation package, a successful solution of this file is now within reach. 2017 will also see intensive debate by the co-legislators on a Commission proposal designed to respond to recent changes in the economic and legal environment, notably the expiration of section 15(a)(ii) of China's WTO Accession Protocol.

5 Annex: Paragraph 15 of China's WTO Accession Protocol

15. Price Comparability in Determining Subsidies and Dumping.

Article VI of the GATT 1994, the Agreement on Implementation of Article VI of the General Agreement on Tariffs and Trade 1994 ("Anti-Dumping Agreement") and the SCM Agreement shall apply in proceedings involving imports of Chinese origin into a WTO Member consistent with the following:

(a) In determining price comparability under Article VI of the GATT 1994 and the Anti-Dumping Agreement, the importing WTO Member shall use either Chinese prices or costs for the industry under investigation or a methodology that is not based on a strict comparison with domestic prices or costs in China based on the following rules:

(i) If the producers under investigation can clearly show that market economy conditions prevail in the industry producing the like product with regard to the manufacture, production and sale of that product, the importing WTO Member shall use Chinese prices or costs for the industry under investigation in determining price comparability;

(ii) The importing WTO Member may use a methodology that is not based on a strict comparison with domestic prices or costs in China if the producers under investigation cannot clearly show that market economy conditions prevail in the industry producing the like product with regard to manufacture, production and sale of that product.

[...]

(d) Once China has established, under the national law of the importing WTO Member, that it is a market economy, the provisions of subparagraph (a) shall be terminated provided that the importing Member's national law contains market economy criteria as of the date of accession. In any event, the provisions of subparagraph (a)(ii) shall expire 15 years after the date of accession. In addition, should China establish, pursuant to the national law of the importing WTO Member, that market economy conditions prevail in a particular industry or sector, the non-market economy provisions of subparagraph (a) shall no longer apply to that industry or sector.

References

Gatta B (2014) Between "automatic market economy status" and "status quo": a commentary on "interpreting paragraph 15 of China's protocol of accession". Global Trade Customs J 9 (10):165–172

Graafsma F, Kumushova E (2014) In re China's protocol of accession and the anti-dumping agreement: temporary derogation or permanent modification? Global Trade Customs J 9 (10):154–159

Hoffmeister F (2015) Modernising the EU's trade Defence instruments: mission impossible. In: Herrmann C, Simma B, Streinz R (eds) Trade policy between law, diplomacy and scholarship – Liber amicorum in Memoriam Horst G. Krenzler. Springer, New York, pp 365–376

Miranda J (2014) Interpreting paragraph 15 of China's protocol of accession. Global Trade Customs J 9(10):94–103

Müller W, Khan N, Scharf T (2009) EC and WTO anti-dumping law – a handbook, 2nd edn. Oxford University Press, Oxford

Nicely MR (2014) Time to eliminate outdated non-market economy methodologies. Global Trade Customs J 9(10):160–164

Posner TR (2014) A comment on Interpreting paragraph 15 of China's protocol of accession by Jorge Miranda. Global Trade Customs J 9(10):146–153

Rosenthal PC, Beckington JS (2014) The People's Republic of China: a market economy or a non-market economy in anti-dumping proceedings starting on December 12, 2016? Global Trade Customs J 9(10):352–355

Ruessmann L, Beck J (2014) 2016 and the application of an NME methodology to Chinese producers in anti-dumping investigations. Global Trade Customs J 9(10):457–463

Stewart TP, Fennell WA, Bell SM, Birch NJ (2014) The special case of China; why the use of a special methodology remains applicable to China after 2016. Global Trade Customs J 9 (10):272–279

Tietje C, Nowrot K (2011) Myth or Reality? China's Market Economy Status under WTO Anti-Dumping Law after 2016. Policy Papers in Transnational Economic Law No 34

Watson W (2014) Will Nonmarket Economy Methodology Go Quietly into the Night? U.S. Antidumping Policy toward China after 2016. Cato Institute Policy Analysis No 763

Democratic Legitimacy and the Rule of Law in Investor-State Dispute Settlement under CETA

Christoph Ohler

Abstract In recent years only, investor-state dispute settlement has come into the focus of public debate. In particular in Germany and Austria, but also in other EU Member States its democratic legitimacy is questioned. Arbitral tribunals, the argument goes, would intrude into the exercise of sovereign powers by democratically elected parliaments while the tribunals themselves would not possess a similar level of legitimacy. As a consequence, the European Parliament adopted a resolution on 8 July 2015 that it would not approve of an investment treaty which is based on the traditional model of international investment arbitration. This article analyses the fundamentals of legal legitimacy and applies them to the mechanics of investor-state dispute settlement. It argues that issues of legality and legitimacy must be seen in their interdependency. Insofar, the most outstanding deficits of investor-state dispute settlement are not of procedural but of substantive nature. Arbitral tribunals interpret and apply substantive standards under bilateral investment treaties which in most cases are too vague and, therefore, translate into too much power of the tribunals. In contrast thereto, the Comprehensive Economic and Trade Agreement between Canada and the European Union and its Member States will considerably change the standards of international investment protection. It strengthens the rule of law in substantive and procedural terms which also translates into a higher level of democratic legitimacy.

Contents

C. Ohler (✉)
Friedrich-Schiller-University Jena, Carl-Zeiss-Strasse 3, 07743 Jena, Germany
e-mail: christoph.ohler@uni-jena.de

M. Bungenberg et al. (eds.), *European Yearbook of International Economic Law 2017*, European Yearbook of International Economic Law 8,
DOI 10.1007/978-3-319-58832-2_8

1 Introduction

On 6 July 2016 the European Commission released its proposals for two Council decisions to sign and conclude the Comprehensive Economic and Trade Agreement between the European Union and Canada (CETA).[1] This was the most recent step in a long negotiation history aiming, as far as the European Union is concerned, at a new generation of free trade agreements. While the results of other negotiations, in particular on the Transatlantic Trade and Investment Partnership with the US (TTIP), remain uncertain, CETA is still considered a milestone for future agreements with other trading partners. Less than half a year ago, in the wake of massive public criticism, the European Commission and Canada had fully reversed the original version of the investment chapter. Both partners officially labelled this step a "legal review"[2] which in effect changes the patterns of investor-state dispute settlement (ISDS) drastically. It denies the right of investors to appoint arbitrators and, insofar, re-nationalises ISDS. In political terms, this reversal was a reaction particularly to a resolution of the European Parliament which had been adopted on 8 July 2015. Even if its wording applies to TTIP only, there can be no doubt that it was adopted also with a view to CETA and other agreements. The European Parliament declared that it will not approve of an investment treaty which is based on the traditional model of international investment arbitration. Instead, it recommended,

> to replace the ISDS-system with a new system for resolving disputes between investors and states which is subject to democratic principles and scrutiny, where potential cases are treated in a transparent manner by publicly appointed, independent professional judges in public hearings and which includes an appellate mechanism, where consistency of judicial decisions is ensured, the jurisdiction of courts of the EU and of the Member States is respected, and where private interests cannot undermine public policy objectives.[3]

The discussion on democratic legitimacy of international institutions is older[4] than the one on ISDS which surfaced only a few years ago. But this time it is, contrary to earlier academic debates, a highly controversial public discussion which

---

[1]COM (2016) 443 final; COM (2016) 444 final.

[2]European Commission, Joint statement: Canada-EU Comprehensive Economic and Trade Agreement (CETA), STATEMENT/16/446, 29 February 2016.

[3]European Parliament resolution of 8 July 2015 containing the European Parliament's recommendations to the European Commission on the negotiations for the Transatlantic Trade and Investment Partnership (TTIP) (2014/2228(INI)), para. 2(d)(xv).

[4]See e.g. with respect to the WTO Benvenisti (2004), p. 343 et seq.; Krajewski (2001), p. 167 et seq.; Wouters et al. (2003), p. 182 et seq.

demonstrates a vastly spread dissatisfaction about what is conceived as the power of internationally operating firms and the weakness of states in the age of globalisation. Insofar, the ongoing debate is not one about the economic relationship between Canada and the EU, if one takes into account that in 2015 Canada was the EU's 12th most important trading partner, accounting for only 1.8% of the EU's total external trade.[5] Rather, CETA, and more particularly its investment chapter, is considered a symbol for a loss of national sovereignty, or, in other terms, of democratic self-determination in favour of "faceless" international investors. In this discussion, ISDS is flagged as "obscure legal system"[6] whose procedures suffer from insufficient transparency and whose case law tends to promote foreign investors for the detriment of national public interests.[7] It is also claimed that arbitrators in classical ISDS, mainly lawyers from multinational law firms, lack structural independence since their professional interest would be maintaining a profitable "arbitration boom" for a small club of beneficiaries. Others, including academics and practitioners, criticised the missing appellate body under the Convention on the Settlement of Investment Disputes between States and Nationals of Other States (ICSID Convention).[8] As a result, the issue of democratic legitimacy played a crucial role also in national court proceedings against CETA.[9]

2 Framing Democratic Legitimacy

2.1 Lead Questions

The concept of legitimacy in international law is as unclear as it is its qualification "democratic legitimacy". Unravelling the numerous theoretical and normative approaches requires distinguishing between several lead questions. First, who or what requires legitimacy? The need for legitimacy can refer to persons or institutions as well as to measures adopted by these persons or institutions. Underlying is the fundamental question why somebody or something requires legitimacy at all. In the realm of domestic government the classical answer is that the exercise of command (or at least control) over human beings requires a justification.[10] Also in the case of the EU where primary and secondary law may have direct effect on the

[5]Figures available under http://ec.europa.eu/trade/policy/countries-and-regions/countries/canada/ (last accessed 1 March 2017).

[6]See e.g. the contribution by Provost C and Kennard M, The obscure legal system that lets corporations sue countries, The Guardian, 10 June 2015.

[7]Cf. the contributions in Waibel et al. (2010) and van Harten (2015). For a positive view Böckstiegel (2015), p. 1871, para. 41 et seq.

[8]Griebel (2008), p. 144 et seq.; for a broad analysis see Tams (2007).

[9]Cf. Federal Constitutional Court, 2 BvR 1368/16, *CETA – Preliminary Injunction*, judgment of 13 October 2016.

[10]This classical insight is provided by Jellinek (1922), p. 184 et seq.; Kelsen (1925), p. 27 et seq.

citizens, creating rights and obligations for them, the exercise of supranational authority is "founded on representative democracy" as Article 10(1) TEU provides. For other international institutions the need for justification is not fundamentally different, even if they do not exercise direct authority over human beings but control the behaviour of their sovereign members.[11] This is so because they enjoy the right to restrict the sovereignty of the states on the basis of powers delegated to them. As far as the quest for legitimacy refers to measures adopted by the international institution, the question must be addressed whether legally binding measures only[12] or also other measures require being legitimated. It is clear that the concept of legitimacy is considerably expanded once it applies not only to binding measures but to all acts with some kind of authoritative or at least compelling character.[13] The need for legitimacy does not only depend on the authoritative character of a measure but also on the room for deviation or discretion it leaves for the party addressed by it.[14]

The second lead question is who provides legitimacy? In most social contexts, legitimacy is attributed by someone to the institution or measure in need of legitimacy. Defining this "someone", the subject of legitimacy, the "sovereign", is one of the core problems in constitutional history and political thinking. A quite helpful description is provided by the concept of a principal-agent relationship. The principal has mandated an agent or delegated powers to him and, on this basis, is affected by the measures taken by the agent. Where the principal is a state, its competent organs authorise the agent or express their consent to a measure adopted by the agent. In a system of representative democracy these authorisations or consents will normally find their basis, directly or indirectly, in a decision of the parliament, as it is the case in the EU under Article 218(6) TFEU.

The third lead question refers to the relationship between subject and object of legitimacy. Does providing legitimacy translate into the observance of certain ("right") processes only,[15] be they of parliamentary, participatory[16] or deliberative nature,[17] or does it also require the observance of material elements, like e.g. the conformity with human rights or certain community values?[18]

---

[11]Cf. Bodansky (1999), p. 601 et seq.; Stein (2004), p. 565.

[12]Wolfrum (2011), para. 1.

[13]Krajewski (2008), para. 12; for an even broader approach see Goldmann (2015), p. 359 et seq.

[14]Krajewski (2008), para. 12.

[15]See e.g. Franck (1988), p. 705 et seqq.

[16]For this view see e.g. Benvenisti (2004), p. 348 et seq.

[17]See Habermas (1998), p. 166 et seq.; Wheatley (2011), p. 535 et seq.

[18]For the latter approach see e.g. Krajewski (2001), p. 169 et seq.; Bogdandy and Venzke (2012) p. 24.

2.2 Legitimacy and Legality

Framing the concept of legitimacy inevitably leads to an analysis of the relationship between legitimacy and legality. First, it must be stressed that public international law as it is in force today does only provide a narrow basis to determine the legitimacy of international institutions. If measures of an international organisation shall be deemed to be binding on the state parties, this requires the existence of an international treaty forming the legal basis of the organisation. The international treaty defines the mandate of the organisation, its organs and their powers towards the state parties and, if intended by the parties, the effect of the treaty and of secondary law adopted thereunder in the domestic legal orders. Accordingly, consent by the state parties is still the most important tool to create legitimacy,[19] out-weighing by far other factors where legally binding consent is not the basis, as in the case of standard setting bodies or the various international clubs like G7, G8 and G20.

In the international community there is no uniform understanding of what "democratic" legitimacy means in a given situation.[20] Whether an international treaty requires parliamentary approval prior to entering into force is not an issue for international law but for the domestic (constitutional) law of the parties. The democratic concepts as expressed in domestic constitutional norms differ considerably between the various jurisdictions. Accordingly, while in some countries or with respect to some types of international treaties democratic legitimacy is accomplished by consent given by the government only, in other cases the parliament or even the electorate is called upon to vote on the treaty prior to its ratification. These constitutional processes enable democratic legitimacy on the domestic level and legitimate the national act of delegation of powers to the international institution. In addition, national constitutions may provide that an international institution must meet certain qualitative criteria for the exercise of its delegated powers being lawful. The German *Grundgesetz*, e.g., requires the European Union itself being democratic, adhering to the rule of law and respecting fundamental rights as prerequisites for each conferral of competences by the German legislator.[21] The fulfilment of these criteria is an essential element of the legitimacy of the European Union. The rationale behind this concept is one of functional equivalence: whenever state measures require the compliance with the rule of law and the democratic principle, then equivalent measures taken by an international organisation must respect similar requirements. Accordingly, the decision to confer competences to the EU is based on the expectation that its organs act in conformity with provisions of primary law ascertaining these standards. But it should be also mentioned that

[19]This basis is still to be found in Permanent Court of International Justice, *S.S. "Lotus" (France v. Turkey)*, PCIJ Reports Series A, No. 10 (1927), p. 18. Cf. also Bodansky (1999), p. 596 et seq.; Wolfrum (2011), para. 6.

[20]For a theoretical account see Bogdandy (2004), p. 889 et seq.

[21]Article 23(1) German *Grundgesetz*.

particularly in cases where the decision to delegate power to an international organisation is highly controversial, there will always remain the problem of broader political acceptance beside the legal act of delegation. This is the ground on which claims for additional participation of and deliberation by the "civil society" grow.

Yet, this narrow concept of legitimacy by consent is more meaningful as it seems at first glance.[22] Its key element is the mandate[23] of the international institution, i.e. the sum of its legal powers as attributed by the founding treaty. The more precise the mandate was drafted the more legally certain the powers of the institution and, vice-versa, the obligations of the parties under the treaty will be. This has immediate effects for the quality of the consent given and accordingly also for the parliamentary approval. Under a precise mandate, the impact of the international institution on the domestic legal order can be more easily assessed by the national legislator. It leaves less leeway to the international institution and reduces the uncertainties surrounding its future operation. Contrary to that, in cases where the mandate is vague and burdened with legal uncertainties, the parties take a bigger risk that the outcome of the institutions' operations will contradict the general expectations on the day the treaty was concluded.

In this respect, a distinction should be drawn between the various international institutions and the radically different types of mandates. It would make little sense to restrict, e.g., the mandate of an international peace organisation like the UN too much. Highly political tasks may require a much broader leeway than merely technical tasks. Yet, it is exactly this vast power which commonly raises concerns over the legitimacy of the organ and its measures.[24] But also in these cases legality forms the basis for legitimacy.[25] The legal framework of an international institution and its compliance with the provisions of the mandate legitimate the measures adopted by the international institution.[26]

2.3 *Legitimacy of Judicial Functions*

What does all of that mean for the judicial functions of an international institution? There is no doubt that international courts and tribunals exercise public authority on the basis of powers conferred upon them by the states.[27] This authority requires

[22]For a critical account cf. Wheatley (2011), p. 537: "not sufficient to explain the legitimacy and authority of political power"; also Bogdandy and Venzke (2012), p. 20: "static perspective"; Schill (2012), p. 144: "loss of control".

[23]From a legal point of view, the commonly used term "mandate" is not correct, as an international organization normally acts on its behalf and in its own name.

[24]Cf. Bodansky (1999), p. 596 et seq.; Wolfrum (2011), para. 18; both with respect to the Security Council.

[25]Cf. Kumm (2004), p. 918 et seq.

[26]Wolfrum (2011), para. 23.

[27]Lauterpacht (1933, 2011), p. 213.

justification beyond the mere consent of state parties,[28] as the legitimacy of the judiciary depends on a number of factors. These include institutional safeguards for the independence and impartiality of the judges or arbitrators, procedural guarantees for the parties, the definition of applicable law, its content and objectives as well as the nature of the powers of the respective court or tribunal. Independence and impartiality of a judge or arbitrator are essential conditions for the exercise of judicial authority and without them any judiciary would fall short of its functions.[29] Judicial legitimacy also translates into effective procedural guarantees of the parties, in particular rights of defence and other due process rights.[30] Where the applicable law is vague, the powers of the judiciary will be bigger as there is more room for interpretation and application of the law in each case. A more precisely constructed law, however, will reduce this margin and make the outcome of a dispute less unforeseeable for the parties. Putting these elements together, one can argue that at least from the point of view of the state parties, an international court or tribunal enjoys a higher degree of legitimacy once its mandate, including the applicable law, is drafted more precisely.[31] However, it must be added that also an opposite view is possible once international human rights come into play. In this case, it is often argued that the restrictions imposed by international human rights create legitimacy in a substantive meaning.[32] It is one of the mysteries of the ongoing public discussion that this argument is rarely applied in the case of investment protection—which underlines the special status of property as an international human right.

As far as the powers of a particular international judiciary are concerned, a clear distinction must be made between courts and tribunals the decisions of which have primacy over and direct legal effect in the domestic legal orders and those with more limited powers. One of the few courts with supranational powers is the Court of Justice of the European Union. In contrast to that, the decisions of most international courts and tribunals have legally binding effect only in the sphere of international law and not directly in domestic law. In practice, this means that international courts and tribunals do not possess the power to annul measures of the state parties under domestic law. The obligations resulting from a judgement or award are binding for the state parties and their organs,[33] yet implementation and enforcement are a matter of national law.[34] Non-compliance mechanisms under international law, as provided by Article 94(2) of the UN Charter, Article 46 of the

[28]Bogdandy and Venzke (2012), p. 17 et seq.

[29]Cf. Lauterpacht (1933, 2011), p. 211: "The problem of the impartiality of the international judge is the Cape Horn of international judicial settlement". See also Bogdandy and Venzke (2012), p. 32 et seq.

[30]Bodansky (1999), p. 612.

[31]For similar view Classen (2014), p. 615.

[32]See e.g. Moravcsik (2000).

[33]With respect to decisions of the ICJ see Oellers-Frahm (2012), para. 14.

[34]Oellers-Frahm (2012), para. 8; cf. also Article 54(3) ICSID Convention.

European Convention of Human Rights (ECHR) or Articles 21 and 22 of the WTO Dispute Settlement Understanding, complement national procedures but do not replace them. Also the New York Convention on the Recognition and Enforcement of Foreign Arbitral Awards of 10 June 1958 leaves the responsibility for enforcement with the state parties.

3 Legitimacy of ISDS

Investor-state arbitral tribunals are international institutions established by states in order to resolve disputes on the basis of investment treaties under international law. Also the ICSID tribunals, to which such treaties refer in most instances, are established on the basis of international law, namely the ICSID Convention of 18 March 1965.[35] From an institutional perspective they are not private arbitral tribunals because their existence and operation are built on a convention under public international law and not on a private law contract.[36] Yet the tribunals could also be described as a hybrid phenomenon since their individual composition in a given dispute is based on decisions of both the private claimant and the public respondent.[37] Under the ICSID Convention, the arbitral tribunal consists of one or any uneven number of arbitrators appointed according to an agreement of the parties.[38] Where the parties do not agree upon the number of arbitrators and the method of their appointment, the tribunal consists of three arbitrators, whereby each party appoints one arbitrator and the third and presiding arbitrator is appointed by agreement of the parties.[39] Insofar it should be noted that also the act of appointment by the private claimant derives its legitimacy from the sphere of public international law because it is based on an investment treaty and the ICSID Convention.

These tribunals exercise public authority because they decide on the legality of sovereign acts of national institutions under international investment law.[40] Even if their awards do not have a direct legal effect on the domestic legal order of the respondent host state,[41] they may restrict its sovereign rights considerably. The scope of measures under scrutiny covers nearly every aspect of public regulation.[42] If a national measure violates an investment treaty, the tribunal's decision is

[35] Available under https://icsid.worldbank.org/ICSID/StaticFiles/basicdoc/basic-en.htm (last accessed 1 March 2017).

[36] Ohler (2016), p. 18 et seq.

[37] Cf. Tietje (2015), p. 3.

[38] Article 37(2)(a) ICSID Convention.

[39] Article 37(2)(b) ICSID Convention.

[40] Schill (2012), p. 136 et seq.

[41] Ohler (2015), p. 344; Schill (2012), p. 137; see also Classen (2014), p. 615.

[42] Kleinheisterkamp (2015), p. 794 et seq.; Schill (2012), p. 137.

normally limited to awarding monetary damages. In cases of an unlawful expropriation, CETA goes a little step further by providing the possibility that the tribunal awards the restitution of property.[43] Insofar the subject-matter of the dispute and the award of the tribunal relate directly to the exercise of sovereign powers of states. When the respondent host state is organized as a representative democracy, the award may have an indirect impact on the competences of the national parliament. Grave monetary sanctions imposed by an award exercise considerable pressure on the legislator to bring its laws into conformity with the investment treaty as interpreted by the tribunal.[44] The assumption is not far-fetched that the apprehension about future disputes with a potentially negative outcome for the state party has a chilling effect on the activities of the legislator.[45]

Is the exercise of these powers legitimate? The answer clearly depends on the requirements under national constitutional law of the respondent state. This is the relevant legal order that defines whether the parliamentary consent to the investment treaty and the ICSID Convention are the sole basis for creating a sufficient level of legitimacy for the arbitral tribunal or whether additional requirements must be fulfilled. Additional criteria can refer to the personal legitimacy of the arbitrators and to the substantive powers of the tribunal as will be discussed below.

3.1 *Personal Legitimacy of Arbitrators*

Under existing appointment procedures, the respondent appoints one half of the tribunal's members. From his perspective only these members are directly legitimated by consent of the sovereign. The second half of the members who are appointed by the investor enjoy only an indirect form of legitimacy via the prior consent to the investment treaty by the state party. The problem is that a higher level of legitimacy can be hardly conceived. The alternative model where the respondent appoints 100% of the arbitrators would fundamentally contradict the concept of an international judiciary which is separate and detached from the national judicial system. If, however, the right to appoint the arbitrators is vested in the home state of the investor,[46] the effective level of democratic legitimacy would not be higher from the point of view of the respondent host state. For measures taken by another state do not increase the level of legitimacy under the constitutional order of the host state. At least from the point of view of a representative democracy, sovereignty is vested in the people (or the citizens) of a state—and considered as being separate from the sovereignty of another people. Accordingly, the decisions of

[43] Article 8.39(1)(b) CETA.

[44] Schill (2012), p. 137.

[45] Jaeger (2016), p. 209.

[46] Under Article 8.27(2) CETA, the CETA Joint Committee comprising representatives of both parties appoint the 15 members of the Tribunal.

other states and their citizens remain outside the chain of legitimacy which exists between a state and an international institution. Insofar, any arbitral tribunal with members from various international parties has only limited personal legitimacy.[47] This analysis would only change once the relevant constitutional order for determining legitimacy would not be a national one but the constitutional system of the international community with the international community being the final sovereign.

Further aspects of the personal legitimacy of an arbitrator are his independence and impartiality. The ICSID Convention clarifies that arbitrators shall be persons of high moral character and recognized competence in the fields of law, commerce, industry or finance, who may be relied upon to exercise independent judgement.[48] In practice, the main aspects for the selection of arbitrators are their professional expertise, legal knowledge and language skills as well as their availability in the arbitral proceedings. As the nationality of arbitrators is traditionally being considered as a threat to their impartiality,[49] the ICSID Convention provides that the majority of arbitrators shall be nationals of states other than the home and the host state of the investor, unless the parties appoint the arbitrators by mutual agreement.[50] The ICSID Convention protects their personal independence by providing that after the tribunal has been constituted and proceedings have begun, its composition shall remain unchanged.[51] However, it also permits to disqualify an arbitrator on account of any fact indicating a manifest lack of the qualities required for his appointment.[52] The independence of the arbitral tribunal also rests on Article 42 of the ICSID Convention which provides that the dispute will be decided solely on the basis of the applicable law. Rule 6 of the Arbitration Rules clarifies that arbitrators may not take instructions or benefits from the parties. Extensive rules on the independence and impartiality exist also under CETA.[53]

In the recent debate about ISDS the apprehension was expressed that the arbitrators might structurally be neither independent nor impartial. For a majority of them works as lawyers in international law firms and therefore are believed to have primarily a private economic interest in the disputes. It can hardly be doubted that there is some truth in this assumption. But does this allow the conclusion that arbitrators would in any dispute at hand tend to decide in favour of the private claimant and disregard the public interest of the respondent? Solid evidence for a structural lack of impartiality has yet to be presented.[54] As far as the criticism refers

[47]Cf. Classen (2014), p. 615.

[48]Article 14(1) ICSID Convention.

[49]Lauterpacht (1933, 2011), p. 212.

[50]Article 39 ICSID Convention.

[51]Article 56(1) ICSID Convention.

[52]Articles 57 and 58 ICSID Convention.

[53]Article 8.30 CETA.

[54]For an insightful comparison between WTO and ICSID see Pauwelyn (2015) who assumes an ideologically polarized pool of ICSID arbitrators.

to the high daily fees which the arbitrators are entitled to receive under the ICSID rules,[55] the conclusion cannot be drawn that these amounts lead to a structural bias in favour of one of the parties to a dispute. Accordingly, it was rather a political decision by Canada and the EU in CETA to give up the existing arbitral model and introduce a completely new model where representatives of the state parties appoint the tribunal's members for a 5-year term.

3.2 *Legitimacy of the Tribunal's Powers*

In international investment law, arbitral tribunals have the right to scrutinise the conformity of a national measure with an investment treaty. Once the arbitral tribunal finds that the measure is incompatible with the treaty, it can determine a financial damage in favour of the investor. Under most investment treaties, the powers of the tribunals are vast since relevant standards of protection like "indirect expropriation", "fair and equitable treatment" and "full protection and security" are framed in an extremely broad and vague language. This is exacerbated by the fact that exemptions and justification for the regulation of public interest objectives are missing in many treaties. The vagueness and incompleteness of the legal texts leave a large room for interpretation and application to the tribunals[56] and create a considerable degree of legal uncertainty for the state parties.[57] It is this fairly unlimited "law-making" power that constitutes the greatest problem for the legitimacy of arbitral tribunals. Contrary to constitutional courts on the domestic level which enjoy a similar leeway, the members of arbitral tribunals do not enjoy the same level of personal legitimacy insofar as they are appointed by the private claimant.

As far as the arbitral tribunal's power to award damages to the claimant is concerned, it seems that this competence is Janus-faced. On the one hand, it protects the respondent host state from the arbitral tribunal intruding directly into the domestic legal order. On the other hand, it privileges the investor, in particular when the applicable investment treaty does not oblige the foreign investor to exhaust legal remedies in the host state prior to submitting his claim. The privilege stems from the fact that domestic legal orders normally build on the primacy of primary legal protection and attribute monetary damages against the state on a secondary basis only when all available legal remedies against the measure have been exhausted.[58] Also in a fundamental rights perspective the investor is privileged. Contrary to the pre-constitutional model of "*dulde und liquidiere* – forbear

[55] According to No 3 Schedule of Fees (as of 1 July 2016) the daily rate per arbitrator is USD 3000.

[56] Cf. Schill (2012), p. 150: "significant law-making powers".

[57] Cf. Henckels (2016); Kleinheisterkamp (2015), p. 794 et seq.; Miles (2016), p. 281 et seq.

[58] Cf. CJEU, joined cases C-46/93 and C-48/93, *Brasserie de Pêcheur*, ECLI:EU:C:1996:79, para. 85. See also Kleinheisterkamp (2014), p. 460.

and liquidate" a citizen may enforce fundamental rights primarily by challenging the legal or administrative act before the competent courts and not by claiming monetary damages. For this purpose, Article 13 ECHR and national constitutional laws[59] guarantee the right to an effective judicial remedy—but for the main purpose of primary legal protection. However, on a broader basis, the legal analysis is not that clear. In particular in EU law, the relationship between primary and secondary legal protection under Articles 263(4) and 340(2) TFEU is more detached. The Court of Justice of the European Union (CJEU) holds that the action for damages under Article 340(2) TFEU was "introduced as an autonomous form of action", since "it differs from an application for annulment in that its end is not the abolition of a particular measure, but compensation for damages caused by an institution in the performance of its duties".[60] Accordingly, "a party may take action by means of a claim for compensation without being obliged by any provision of law to seek the annulment of the illegal measure which causes him damage", unless this action circumvents "the inadmissibility of an application which concerns the same illegality and which has the same financial end in view."[61]

What does this mean for the legitimacy of ISDS? Is the introduction of a liability system which is different from the one in the Member States (and partly the EU) a policy choice[62] or does it require a substantive justification?[63] The latter seems to be correct since the liability of the state party established by an investment treaty has a direct impact on the budgetary responsibility of the government and, in a representative democracy, of the parliament. These effects can still be justified by the legitimate objective to protect nationals of the home state when they operate as investors in foreign host states. ISDS forms part of this protection as it substitutes ineffective domestic judicial systems in states the courts of which are not independent and impartial or lack the necessary qualifications to decide disputes between investor and host state in an adequate manner.

If one applies this justification on CETA, there would be hardly any convincing reason why foreign investors should be privileged in terms of judicial protection. To the contrary, as the judicial systems in Canada, the EU and the Member States operate fairly well and effective, there are better reasons to assume that investors should seek judicial protection before national courts under rules applicable for everybody.[64] But does this mean that the scope of ISDS should be reduced to problematic jurisdictions whereas developed jurisdictions would exclude it in their bilateral relations?[65] For several reasons, this selective approach does not seem to

[59]Cf. Article 19(4) German *Grundgesetz*.

[60]CJEU, case 5/71, *Schöppenstedt/Council*, ECLI:EU:C:1971:116, para. 3.

[61]CJEU, case 543/79, *Birke/Commission and Council*, ECLI:EU:C:1981:265, para. 28.

[62]Kleinheisterkamp (2014), p. 460.

[63]See Jaeger (2016), p. 208 et seq.

[64]For a different view see Bronckers (2015), p. 658 who argues in favor of a fail-safe system also amongst developed jurisdictions.

[65]Cf. Kleinheisterkamp and Poulsen (2016), p. 533 referring to the Australia-US BIT of 2005; see also Jaeger (2016), p. 210.

be viable. A reduced scope of application of ISDS only for states with a failed judicial system would automatically mean an obvious stigma for this state. Even if a selective application could be enforced on a case-by-case basis, this approach would only work as long as these states consider ISDS as a necessary trade-off for capital imports, i.e. as the political price that has to be paid in order to attract direct investment. In particular with strong economies, bilateral negotiations do not take place in clinical isolation, but in a broader political context where the parties refer to the general international practice[66] and accept isolated solutions only when they seem to be advantageous for them. Insofar, CETA and other bilateral investment treaties must be seen as part of a global approach in EU trade policy and cannot reasonably be considered as isolated measures.[67] Accordingly, it is reasonable to assume that CETA could contribute to the coherence of the international system of investment treaties and operate as a blueprint for the negotiations with other states.

4 New Features of ISDS Under CETA

4.1 Substantive Standards

Contrary to earlier generations of BITs, CETA creates a better balanced relationship between investors' rights and states powers. First of all, CETA reaffirms the right of the contracting parties to regulate within their territories to achieve legitimate policy objectives such as the protection of public health, safety, the environment or public morals, social or consumer protection or the promotion and protection of cultural diversity.[68] The provision is not conclusive which means that also other public policy objectives must be taken into consideration in resolving an investment dispute. As regards investors' rights, the common international standards of "fair and equitable treatment" and "full protection and security" are narrowly defined and bring these standards closer to fundamental rights.[69] This is also reflected in a narrower understanding of state measures that potentially could restrict these rights. Article 8.9(2) expressly provides that

> the mere fact that a Party regulates [. . .] in a manner which negatively affects an investment or interferes with an investor's expectations, [. . .] does not amount to a breach of obligation under this Section.

[66] Cf. Bronckers (2015), p. 658; for a different view see Kleinheisterkamp and Poulsen (2016), p. 538.

[67] Cf. Federal Constitutional Court, 2 BvR 1368/16, *CETA – Preliminary Injunction*, judgment of 13 October 2016, para. 48.

[68] Cf. Article 8.9(1) CETA.

[69] Article 8.10 CETA.

A further important consequence of this new approach is that broadly understood public welfare objectives can serve as carve-out for the prohibition of indirect expropriations.[70] All these reforms create a new balance between investors and host states and strengthen the rule of law in investment protection.

4.2 Permanent Tribunal and Appellate Tribunal

For the first time in the not so long history of ISDS, the CETA investment chapter establishes a court-like judicial system. The members of the "Tribunal", as CETA terms the new institution, are appointed for a 5-year term, renewable once.[71] The permanent character of the Tribunal distinguishes it most clearly from usual arbitral tribunals the members of which are appointed on an ad-hoc basis for each individual dispute. Altogether 15 members will serve on the bench, five of them being nationals of EU Member States, five members being nationals of Canada and five members being nationals of third countries.[72] They are appointed by the CETA Joint Committee which comprises representatives of both the EU and Canada.[73] The CETA Joint Committee also draws by lot the President and the Vice-President of the Tribunal from the group of third country nationals and appoints them for a 2-year term. This means that investors bringing a claim to the Tribunal face a bench that was selected exclusively by the contracting parties of the CETA. Hence, in comparison to ICSID rules the right to appoint the arbitrators is fully re-nationalized.[74]

To be eligible, the members of the Tribunal must possess the qualifications required in their respective countries for appointment to judicial office, or be jurists of recognized competence. They shall have demonstrated expertise in public international law and, preferably, also in international investment law, in international trade law and dispute resolution.[75] All these elements taken together, the CETA provisions aim at pushing lawyers from private law firms out of business as arbitrators. So far, it is not clear who will replace them. In some jurisdictions, judges from domestic courts with a sufficient level of international qualifications will be found. Choosing jurists from national administrations or the European Commission will hardly be possible since Article 8.30(1) of the CETA provides that the members of the Tribunal shall not be affiliated with any government.

As far as the procedural rules of the tribunal are concerned, CETA provides that the Tribunal hears cases in divisions consisting of three members of the Tribunal,

[70]Annex 8-A(3) CETA.

[71]Article 8.27(5) CETA.

[72]Article 8.27(1) CETA.

[73]Article 26.1 CETA.

[74]A minor exemption is provided by Articles 8.23(5) and 8.27(9) CETA.

[75]Article 8.27(4) CETA.

chaired by a member who is a national of a third country.[76] The President of the Tribunal appoints the members of the division hearing the case on a rotation basis, ensuring that the composition of the division is random and unpredictable, while giving equal opportunity to all members of the Tribunal to serve.[77] The Tribunal may draw up its own working procedure,[78] yet this applies mainly to the internal sphere of the Tribunal. All other procedural rules which have a direct bearing on the claimant are submitted together with the claim under Article 8.23(2) of the CETA by the claimant himself. Insofar, the claimant may choose between ICSID, UNCITRAL and, on the agreement of the disputing parties, any other rules. Irrespective of the applicable procedural rules it should be noted that the Tribunal exercises public authority and, accordingly, must respect fundamental human rights. The applicable standards are reflected in Article 6(1) ECHR and Article 47 of the EU Charter of Fundamental Rights and comprise the right to be heard, the right to a fair trial and the procedural equality of the parties to the dispute. As regards transparency of the proceedings, CETA refers to UNCITRAL Transparency Rules.[79] They go considerably further than similar requirements under national law, e.g. when Article 3(1) of the UNCITRAL Transparency Rules provides that all written statements of the disputing parties have to be published.

Another new feature of the CETA is the Appellate Tribunal which reviews awards rendered by a division of the Tribunal.[80] Its members are eligible under the same conditions as the members of the Tribunal and will be appointed by the CETA Joint Committee. The Appellate Tribunal may uphold, modify or reverse an award based on (a) errors in the application or interpretation of applicable law, (b) manifest errors of fact, including the appreciation of relevant domestic law, and (c) the grounds under Article 52 of the ICSID Convention. Insofar, the powers of the Appellate Tribunal are considerably broader than the ones of the Committee under Article 52 of the ICSID Convention. This closes a lacuna in judicial protection that often has been deplored.[81]

5 Applicable Law Under the CETA Investment Chapter

Under Article 42(1) of the ICSID Convention, the tribunal shall decide a dispute in accordance with such rules of law as may be agreed by the parties. In the absence of such agreement, the tribunal shall apply the law of the host state and applicable rule

[76] Article 8.27(6) CETA.

[77] Article 8.27(7) CETA.

[78] Article 8.27(10) CETA.

[79] Article 8.36(1) CETA.

[80] Article 8.28 CETA.

[81] Cf. e.g. Miles (2016) p. 289.

of international law. In contrast thereto, Article 8.31(1) of the CETA provides that the Tribunal applies

> this Agreement as interpreted in accordance with the Vienna Convention on the Law of Treaties, and other rules and principles of international law applicable between the Parties.

Article 8.31(2) of the CETA reads:

> The Tribunal shall not have jurisdiction to determine the legality of a measure, alleged to constitute a breach of this Agreement, under the domestic law of a Party. For greater certainty, in determining the consistency of a measure with this Agreement, the Tribunal may consider, as appropriate, the domestic law of a Party as a matter of fact. In doing so, the Tribunal shall follow the prevailing interpretation given to the domestic law by the courts or authorities of that Party and any meaning given to domestic law by the Tribunal shall not be binding upon the courts or the authorities of that Party.

Where serious concerns arise as regards matters of interpretation, the CETA Joint Committee may adopt an interpretation that is binding on the Tribunal.[82]

These provisions aim at reducing the risk that the CETA Investment Chapter, in particular the powers of the Tribunal thereunder, could not be in conformity with EU primary law. Such concerns have arisen in the wake of opinion 2/13 of the CJEU on the accession agreement of the EU to the ECHR.[83] In this Opinion, the CJEU emphasized again the specific characteristics and the autonomy of the EU legal order which it is called upon to protect.[84] It also expressed the necessity of retaining control over the interpretation and application of EU fundamental rights (and other Union law) which, in his eyes, excluded an external control by the European Court of Human Rights under the ECHR.[85] As a result, the CJEU held that the accession agreement to the ECHR violated the primary law of the EU. However, this line of reasoning cannot be transferred automatically to investment treaties and ISDS thereunder.[86] The CJEU already stated that international agreements providing for the creation of a court responsible for the interpretation of its provisions and whose decisions are binding on the institutions are not, in principle, incompatible with EU law.[87] This applies at least as long as the decision-making of these international courts has no adverse effect on the autonomy of the EU legal order and does not bind the EU and its institutions, in the exercise of their internal powers, to a particular interpretation of the rules of EU law.[88] It seems that under Article 8.31 of the CETA these conditions are fulfilled as long as the Tribunal actually applies international law only and considers EU law as

---

[82]Article 8.31(3) CETA.

[83]Hindelang (2015), Ohler (2015), Schill (2015).

[84]CJEU, opinion 2/13, *Accession to the ECHR*, ECLI:EU:C:2014:2454, para. 174 et seq.; see also CJEU, opinion 1/09, *European Patent Court*, ECLI:EU:C:2011:123, paras. 67, 76 et seq.

[85]CJEU, opinion 2/13, *Accession to the ECHR*, ECLI:EU:C:2014:2454, para. 179 et seq.

[86]Hindelang (2015), p. 73; Ohler (2015), p. 345; Schill (2015), p. 382 et seq.

[87]CJEU, opinion 2/13, *Accession to the ECHR*, ECLI:EU:C:2014:2454, para. 182; CJEU, opinion 1/91, *European Economic Area*, ECLI:EU:C:1991:490, paras. 40, 70; CJEU, opinion 1/09, *European Patent Court*, ECLI:EU:C:2011:123, para. 74.

[88]CJEU, opinion 2/13, *Accession to the ECHR*, ECLI:EU:C:2014:2454, para. 183 et seq.

matter of fact.[89] In addition, it is worth noticing that the standards of investment protection under CETA are not directly reflected in EU primary law, thereby reducing the risk of divergent interpretations of international and EU law by the CETA courts and the CJEU respectively.[90]

6 Prospects

Difficult questions arise if CETA should actually be used as a blueprint for other bilateral investment agreements to be concluded by the EU. Does this system work with respect to those countries whose judicial systems are defective in terms of European standards? Host states which do not meet the minimum requirements for an impartial and independent administration of justice would then be able to send their national judges to the permanent tribunal, although the original function of ISDS was to circumvent these legal systems. Another question would be whether a high number of permanent tribunals and appellate tribunals augments the fragmentation of the international judiciary[91] or contributes to a higher degree of legal coherence in international investment law. The answer, it is suggested, will not only depend on the number of institutions but on the clarity, precision and coherence of the underlying substantive law. It is, in practical terms, therefore hard to imagine that one day the world will be covered with a net of permanent tribunals operating on a bilateral basis.[92] If the CETA model would actually set new, universally accepted standards, then the political conclusion should be to multilateralize it and amend the ICSID Convention accordingly. The contracting parties of the CETA had that option in mind when agreeing on an obligation to "pursue with other trading partners the establishment of a multilateral investment tribunal and appellate mechanism for the resolution of investment disputes".[93]

References

Benvenisti E (2004) Welfare and democracy on a global level: the WTO as a case study. In: Benvenisti E, Nolte G (eds) The welfare state, globalization, and international law. Springer, Berlin, pp 343–369

[89]Critically about the factual pressure created by awards Hindelang (2015), p. 74 et seq.; Kerkemeyer (2016), p. 15.

[90]Cf. Kokott and Sobotta (2016), p. 19.

[91]On the problem of "proliferation of international courts and tribunals" see e.g. Buergenthal (2001); Kingsbury (1999).

[92]Critically also Tietje (2015), p. 7.

[93]Article 8.29 CETA.

Böckstiegel KH (2015) The future of international investment law – substantive protection and dispute settlement. In: Bungenberg M, Griebel J, Hobe S, Reinisch A (eds) International investment law. C.H. Beck, München, pp 1863–1872
Bodansky D (1999) The legitimacy of international governance: a coming challenge for international environmental law? Am J Int L 93(3):596–624
Bogdandy A (2004) Globalization and Europe: how to square democracy, globalization, and international law. Eur J Int Law 15(5):885–906
Bogdandy A, Venzke I (2012) In whose name? An investigation of international courts' public authority and its democratic justification. Eur J Int Law 23(1):7–41
Bronckers M (2015) Is investor-state dispute settlement (ISDS) superior to litigation before domestic courts?: an EU view on bilateral trade agreements. J Int Econ Law 18(3):655–677
Buergenthal T (2001) Proliferation of international courts and tribunals: is it good or bad? Leiden J Int Law 14(2):267–275
Classen CD (2014) Die Unterwerfung demokratischer Hoheitsgewalt unter eine Schiedsgerichtsbarkeit. Europäische Zeitschrift für Wirtschaftsrecht 25(16):611–616
Franck T (1988) Legitimacy in the international system. Am J Int Law 82(4):705–759
Goldmann M (2015) Internationale Öffentliche Gewalt. Springer, Berlin
Griebel J (2008) Internationales Investitionsrecht. C.H. Beck, München
Habermas J (1998) Die postnationale Konstellation. Suhrkamp, Frankfurt/Main
Henckels C (2016) Protecting regulatory autonomy through greater precision in investment treaties: the TPP, CETA, and TTIP. J Int Econ Law 19(1):27–50
Hindelang S (2015) Repellent forces: the CJEU and investor-state dispute settlement. Archiv des Völkerrechts 53(1):68–89
Jaeger T (2016) Zum Vorschlag einer permanenten Investitionsschiedsgerichtsbarkeit. Eur Secur 51(2):203–228
Jellinek G (1922) Allgemeine Staatslehre, 3rd edn. Springer, Berlin
Kelsen H (1925) Allgemeine Staatslehre. Springer, Berlin
Kerkemeyer A (2016) Unionsrecht und internationales Investitionsschutzrecht auf Kollisionskurs. Europäische Zeitschrift für Wirtschaftsrecht 27(1):10–16
Kingsbury B (1999) Is the proliferation of international courts and tribunals a systematic problem? N Y Univ J Int Law Polit 31(4):679–696
Kleinheisterkamp J (2014) Financial responsibility in European international investment policy. Int Comp Law Q 63(2):449–476
Kleinheisterkamp J (2015) Investment treaty law and the fear for sovereignty: transnational challenges and solutions. Mod Law Rev 78(5):793–825
Kleinheisterkamp J, Poulsen L (2016) Investment protection in TTIP: three feasible proposals. In: Bungenberg M, Hermann C, Krajewski M, Terchechte JP (eds) European yearbook of international economic law, vol 7. Springer, Heidelberg, pp 527–541
Kokott J, Sobotta C (2016) Investment arbitration and EU law. Camb Yearb Eur Leg Stud 18:3–19
Krajewski M (2001) Democratic legitimacy and constitutional perspective of WTO law. J World Trade 35(1):167–186
Krajewski M (2008) International organizations or institutions, democratic legitimacy. In: Wolfrum (ed) Max Planck encyclopedia of public international law, online edition
Kumm M (2004) The legitimacy of international law: a constitutional framework of analysis. Eur J Int Law 15(5):907–931
Lauterpacht H (1933, 2011) The function of law in the international community. Oxford University Press, Oxford
Miles K (2016) Investor-state dispute settlement: conflict, convergence, and future directions. In: Bungenberg M, Hermann C, Krajewski M, Terchechte JP (eds) European yearbook of international economic law, vol 7. Springer, Heidelberg, pp 273–308
Moravcsik A (2000) The origins of human rights regimes: democratic delegation in postwar Europe. Int Organ 54(2):217–252

Oellers-Frahm K (2012) Article 94. In: Simma B, Khan DE, Nolte G, Paulus A (eds) The charter of the United Nations, 3rd edn. Oxford University Press, Oxford

Ohler C (2015) Die Vereinbarkeit von Investor-Staat-Schiedsverfahren mit deutschem und europäischem Verfassungsrecht. JuristenZeitung 70(7):337–346

Ohler C (2016) Demokratische Legitimation und rechtsstaatliche Bindung von Investor-Staats-Schiedsverfahren. In: Herrmann C, Bungenberg M (eds) Die gemeinsame Handelspolitik der Europäischen Union. Nomos, Baden-Baden, pp 118–134

Pauwelyn J (2015) The rule of law without the rule of lawyers? Why investment arbitrators are from Mars and trade adjudicators from Venus. Am J Int Law 109(4):761–805

Schill S (2012) System-building in investment treaty arbitration and lawmaking. In: Bogdandy A, Venzke I (eds) International judicial lawmaking. Springer, Heidelberg, pp 133–177

Schill S (2015) Editorial: opinion 2/13 – the end for dispute settlement in EU trade and investment agreements? J World Invest Trade 16(3):379–388

Stein T (2004) Demokratische Legitimierung auf supranationaler und internationaler Ebene. Zeitschrift für ausländisches öffentliches Recht und Völkerrecht 64(3):563–570

Tams C (2007) Is there a need for an ICSID appellate structure? In: Hofmann R, Tams C (eds) The international convention for the settlement of investment disputes: taking stock after 40 years. Nomos, Baden-Baden

Tietje C (2015) Ein internationales Handels- und Schiedsgericht für CETA (und TTIP)?. Policy Papers on Transnational Economic Law, No. 42

Van Harten G (2015) A parade of reforms: The European Commission's latest proposals for ISDS. Osgoode Legal Studies Research Paper No. 21/2015

Waibel M, Kaushal A, Chung L, Balchin C (eds) (2010) The backlash against investment arbitration. Kluwer Law International, The Hague

Wheatley S (2011) A democratic rule of international law. Eur J Int Law 22(2):525–548

Wolfrum R (2011) Legitimacy in international law. In: Wolfrum R (ed) Max Planck encyclopedia of public international law, online edition

Wouters J, De Meester B, Ryngaert C (2003) Democracy and international law. Neth Yearb Int Law XXXIV:137–198

The EU and Investor-State Dispute Settlement: WTO Litigators Going "Investor-State Arbitration" and Back to a Permanent "Investment Court"

August Reinisch

Abstract With acquiring powers to conclude investment treaties in the field of the common commercial policy, the EU has entered the scene as a regional actor in investment treaty law-making. Since the Commission, the EU's trade negotiating arm, has refrained from adopting a Model BIT or Model IIA, the contours of investment agreements and investment chapters in the EU's trade agreements remained vague and uncertain for a while. Meanwhile the first finalized texts of such investment standards have emerged. Most prominent are the 2015 draft TTIP investment chapter and the 2016 CETA text. This contribution focuses on the role of investor-State dispute settlement in the negotiation of these agreements. It shows that the Commission initially adopted the traditional European view that an effective investment protection required the enforcement mechanism of investor-State arbitration. With the increasing public criticism of this form of investor-State dispute settlement, however, various attempts have been made to correct the perceived deficiencies of investor-State arbitration. In addition to fine-tuning and limiting the scope of the substantive investment protection standards in the new EU treaties, the Commission has equally inserted a number of changes to investor-State arbitration, such as broad transparency rules, the possibility of *amicus curiae* submissions, strict rules on arbitrator independence and impartiality, the power to dismiss frivolous claims, etc. Then, in a September 2015 TTIP text, the Commission proposed to the US-side the adoption of an investment court system with standing judges on two levels.

This is a slightly amended and updated version of "The European Union and Investor-State Dispute Settlement: From Investor-State Arbitration to a Permanent Investment Court", published by the Centre for International Governance Innovation in Second Thoughts: Investor-State Arbitration between Developed Democracies, edited by Armand de Mestral, and republished here with permission.

A. Reinisch (✉)
Department for European, International and Comparative Law, University of Vienna, Schottenbastei 10-16, 1010 Vienna, Austria
e-mail: august.reinisch@univie.ac.at

M. Bungenberg et al. (eds.), *European Yearbook of International Economic Law 2017*, European Yearbook of International Economic Law 8,
DOI 10.1007/978-3-319-58832-2_9

Contents

1 Introduction

A few years ago, Investor-State Arbitration (ISA) was hardly taken note of in EU external trade circles. With the Treaty of Lisbon and the EU's new powers in the field of foreign direct investment that has considerably changed. The EU Commission, the Union's main external trade actor, asserted its newly-won competence to negotiate investment agreements containing both substantive protection standards as well as the enforcement mechanism in case of disputes, ISA being the most prominent form of Investor-State Dispute Settlement (ISDS).

When EU trade negotiations started to include investment chapters, as in the negotiations with Canada on a Comprehensive Economic and Trade Agreement (CETA),[1] with Singapore on an enlarged free trade agreement,[2] and with the US on

[1]Consolidated Comprehensive Economic and Trade Agreement Text, published on 26 September 2014 (Consolidated 2014 CETA text), http://trade.ec.europa.eu/doclib/docs/2014/september/tradoc_152806.pdf; see also Revised CETA text of 29 February 2016 (Revised 2016 CETA text), http://trade.ec.europa.eu/doclib/docs/2016/february/tradoc_154329.pdf (both last accessed 1 March 2017).

[2]EU-Singapore Free Trade Agreement, authentic text as of May 2015, published on 29 June 2015, http://trade.ec.europa.eu/doclib/press/index.cfm?id=961 (last accessed 1 March 2017).

a Transatlantic Trade and Investment Partnership (TTIP),[3] public interest and opposition to what is sometimes portrayed as a secret parallel justice for big multinational firms circumventing legitimate domestic courts intensified. Suddenly, the hitherto technical questions of designing a cost-efficient, depoliticized and effective settlement mechanism for investment disputes became a major political issue in a number of EU Member States. Growing opposition by grass-roots movements and an alliance of various, often rather divergent political groupings threatened to halt trade deals the EU Commission was negotiating. In a rare move, the Commission interrupted its trade talks with the US in order to conduct a public consultation in early 2014, focusing on the investment part of TTIP. Ever since ISA has remained the most controversial part of the planned trade agreements.

It is against this background that this contribution tries to analyse the position of the EU towards the use of ISA as a means for settling investor-State disputes.

2 The First Steps of the EU Towards Investor-State Arbitration

In spite of the preeminent practical importance of ISA after the EU has gained an explicit external power to negotiate investment agreements through the Lisbon Treaty, the use of ISA by the EU is not an entirely new phenomenon. In fact, already in the Energy Charter Treaty (ECT)[4] of the mid-1990s, the EU as contracting party of this "mixed agreement"[5] for the first time assumed specific obligations regarding the treatment of foreign investment and, in this context, accepted ISA as a tool for settling investment disputes.

While the ECT has led to a number of investor-State arbitrations, among them the *Yukos*-related cases against the Russian Federation[6] and most recently a wave of cases involving cut-backs on solar energy subsidy programs by EU Member States,

[3]European Union's proposal for Investment Protection and Resolution of Investment Disputes of 12 November 2015 (TTIP), http://trade.ec.europa.eu/doclib/docs/2015/november/tradoc_153955.pdf (last accessed 1 March 2017).

[4]Energy Charter Treaty (ECT), opened for signature 17 December 1994, entered into force 1 April 1998.

[5]When the subject-areas covered by an international agreement negotiated by the EU are not entirely covered by the EU's external powers, such agreements are entered into by the EU plus at least some of its Member States. Because of the joint participation as treaty parties on the EU side, they are referred to as "mixed" agreements. See, e.g. Bischoff (2011), p. 1527 et seq. Generally on the issue of mixed agreements, see Craig and De Burca (2011), p. 334 et seq.; Eeckhout (2011), p. 213 et seq.; Hillion and Koutrakos (2010).

[6]*Hulley Enterprises Limited (Cyprus) v The Russian Federation*, PCA Case No. AA 226, Award 18 July 2014; *Yukos Universal Limited (Isle of Man) v The Russian Federation*, PCA Case No. AA 227, Award 18 July 2014; *Veteran Petroleum Limited (Cyprus) v The Russian Federation*, PCA Case No. AA 228, Award 18 July 2014.

like the Czech Republic,[7] Italy,[8] and Spain,[9] no case has been instituted against the EU so far.

[7]See *Antaris Solar and Dr. Michael Göde v Czech Republic*, PCA Case No. 2014-01; *Natland Investment Group NV, Natland Group Limited, G.I.H.G. Limited, and Radiance Energy Holding S.à r.l. v Czech Republic*, registered 8 May 2013; *Voltaic Network GmbH v Czech Republic*, registered 8 May 2013; *ICW Europe Investments Limited v Czech Republic*, registered 8 May 2013; *Photovoltaik Knopf Betriebs-GmbH v Czech Republic*, registered 8 May 2013; *WA Investments-Europa Nova Limited v Czech Republic*, registered 8 May 2013; *Mr. Jürgen Wirtgen, Mr. Stefan Wirtgen, and JSW Solar (zwei) v Czech Republic*, registered June 2013.

[8]*See Blusun S.A., Jean-Pierre Lecorcier and Michael Stein v Italian Republic*, ICSID Case No. ARB/14/3, registered 21 February 2014; *Greentech Energy Systems and Novenergia v Italy*, SCC, registered 7 July 2015; *Silver Ridge Power BV v Italian Republic*, ICSID Case No. ARB/15/37; *Belenergia S.A. v Italian Republic*, ICSID Case No. ARB/15/40; *Eskosol S.p.A. in liquidazione v Italian Republic*, ICSID Case No. ARB/15/50; *ESPF Beteiligungs GmbH, ESPF Nr. 2 Austria Beteiligungs GmbH, and InfraClass Energie 5 GmbH & Co. KG v Italian Republic*, ICSID Case No. ARB/16/5.

[9]The following proceedings have been instituted under the auspices of ICSID: *RREEF Infrastructure (G.P.) Limited and RREEF Pan-European Infrastructure Two Lux S.à r.l. v Kingdom of Spain*, ICSID Case No. ARB/13/30, Decision on Jurisdiction 6 June 2016; *Antin Infrastructure Services Luxembourg S.à r.l. v Kingdom of Spain*, ICSID Case No. ARB/13/31; *Eiser Infrastructure Limited v Kingdom of Spain*, ICSID Case No. ARB/13/36; *Masdar Solar & Wind Cooperatief UA v Kingdom of Spain*, ICSID Case No. ARB/14/1; *NextEra Energy Global Holdings BV v Kingdom of Spain*, ICSID Case No. ARB/14/11; *InfraRed Environmental Infrastructure GP Limited v Kingdom of Spain*, ICSID Case No. ARB/14/12; *RENERGY S.à r.l. v Kingdom of Spain*, ICSID Case No. ARB/14/18; *RWE Innogy GmbH and RWE Innogy Aersa S.A.U. v Kingdom of Spain*, ICSID Case No. ARB/14/34; *Stadtwerke München GmbH, RWE Innogy GmbH, and others v Kingdom of Spain*, ICSID Case No. ARB/15/1; *STEAG GmbH v Kingdom of Spain*, ICSID Case No. ARB/15/4; *9REN Holding S.à r.l v. Kingdom of Spain*, ICSID Case No. ARB/15/15; *BayWa r.e. renewable energy GmbH and BayWa r.e. Asset Holding GmbH v Kingdom of Spain*, ICSID Case No. ARB/15/16; *Cube Infrastructure Fund SICAV and others v Kingdom of Spain*, ICSID Case No. ARB/15/20; *Mathias Kruck and others v Kingdom of Spain*, ICSID Case No. ARB/15/23; *KS Invest GmbH and TLS Invest GmbH v Kingdom of Spain*, ICSID Case No. ARB/15/25; *JGC Corporation v Kingdom of Spain*, ICSID Case No. ARB/15/27; *Cavalum SGPS, S.A. v Kingdom of Spain*, ICSID Case No. ARB/15/34; *E.ON SE, E.ON Finanzanlagen GmbH and E.ON Iberia Holding GmbH v Kingdom of Spain*, ICSID Case No. ARB/15/35; *OperaFund Eco-Invest SICAV PLC and Schwab Holding AG v Kingdom of Spain*, ICSID Case No. ARB/15/36; *SolEs Badajoz GmbH v Kingdom of Spain*, ICSID Case No. ARB/15/38; *Hydro Energy 1 S.à r.l. and Hydroxana Sweden AB v Kingdom of Spain*, ICSID Case No. ARB/15/42; *Watkins Holdings S.à r.l. and others v Kingdom of Spain*, ICSID Case No. ARB/15/44; *Landesbank Baden-Württemberg and others v Kingdom of Spain*, ICSID Case No. ARB/15/45; *Eurus Energy Holdings Corporation and Eurus Energy Europe B.V. v Kingdom of Spain*, ICSID Case No. ARB/16/4; *Sun-Flower Olmeda GmbH & Co KG and others v Kingdom of Spain*, ICSID Case No. ARB/16/17; *Infracapital F1 S.à r.l. and Infracapital Solar B.V. v Kingdom of Spain*, ICSID Case No. ARB/16/18; *Sevilla Beheer B.V. and others v Kingdom of Spain*, ICSID Case No. ARB/16/27. Four cases have been registered at the Arbitration Institute of the SCC: *Isolux Infrastructure Netherlands B.V. v Spain*, registered 2013; *CSP Equity Investment S.à r.l.. v. Spain*, registered June 2013; *Charanne and Construction Investments v Spain*, SCC Arbitration No. 062/2012, Award 21 January 2016; *Alten Renewable Energy Developments BV v Spain*, registered March 2015. At least one ECT claim-based tribunal has been constituted under the UNCITRAL Arbitration Rules, see *AES Solar and others v Spain*, registered November 2011.

Nevertheless, the ISA provisions in the ECT provide a useful template for current ISA negotiations, in particular in situations where both EU and EU Member State action may be challenged, and it has inspired EU internal legislation on the allocation of financial burdens arising from ISA awards.[10]

Under the ECT's dispute settlement provisions, an investor alleging a breach of the treaty's protection standards can either resort to domestic courts and administrative tribunals or institute arbitral proceedings before ICSID, before a tribunal constituted under UNCITRAL Arbitration Rules or before the Arbitration Institute of the Stockholm Chamber of Commerce (SCC).[11] As an overlap between the EU's internal market freedoms and the ECT's substantive protection standards is not unlikely to occur, the determination of the proper respondent is in some cases of particular importance. In this regard, the (then) European Communities issued a statement pursuant to which the "Communities and the Member States will, if necessary, determine among them who is the respondent party [. . .]"[12] upon request of the investor within a period of 30 days. CETA contains a similar but more elaborated provision on the determination of the respondent for disputes with the European Union or its Member States.[13]

3 The EU's New Lisbon Powers in the Field of Investment

With the Lisbon Treaty, entering into force in 2009,[14] the EU's external trade powers were significantly enlarged. They now include "foreign direct investment" as part of the Common Commercial Policy.[15]

[10]See Regulation No 912/2014 of the European Parliament and of the Council establishing a framework for managing financial responsibility linked to investor-to-state dispute settlement tribunals established by international agreements to which the European Union is party, OJ 2014 L 257/121.

[11]Article 26 ECT.

[12]Statement submitted by the European Communities to the Secretariat of the Energy Charter pursuant to Article 26(3)(b)(ii) ECT, OJ 1998 L 69/115. This notwithstanding, the statement further clarifies in a footnote that this does not exclude the right of an investor to institute proceedings against both the (then) Communities and their Member States.

[13]Pursuant to Article 8.21 Revised 2016 CETA Text. Determination of the respondent for disputes with the European Union or its Member States, the EU is primarily competent for the determination of the proper respondent before the institution of arbitral proceedings. If the investor has not been informed of the determination within 50 days, the Member State shall be respondent in cases where the measure allegedly breaching CETA's protection standards is exclusively a measures of a Member State. If the dispute at stake includes measures of the European Union, the European Union shall be respondent.

[14]Treaty of Lisbon Amending the Treaty on European Union and the Treaty Establishing the European Community, signed 13 December 2007, OJ 2007 C 306/1.

[15]Article 207(1) TFEU: "The common commercial policy shall be based on uniform principles, particularly with regard to changes in tariff rates, the conclusion of tariff and trade agreements

Since the Treaty explicitly speaks of "foreign direct investment" and not generally of "foreign investment", a controversy arose as to whether this new competence in the external trade field was indeed limited to "foreign direct investment", or could be regarded as a full "investment" power. Not surprisingly, the EU Commission came out in favour of the latter, arguing that portfolio investments were implicitly covered as a result of parallel internal powers under the *ERTA* doctrine,[16] while some Member States remained adamant in limiting the EU's powers strictly to direct investments.[17] Given this controversy, the scope of the EU's competence on "foreign direct investment" under Article 207(1) remains to be clarified by the CJEU in an opinion requested by the European Commission pursuant to Article 218(11) TFEU.[18]

---

relating to trade in goods and services, and the commercial aspects of intellectual property, foreign direct investment, the achievement of uniformity in measures of liberalisation, export policy and measures to protect trade such as those to be taken in the event of dumping or subsidies. The common commercial policy shall be conducted in the context of the principles and objectives of the Union's external action." See also Bungenberg (2010), Chaisse (2012), Dimopoulos (2011), Hoffmeister and Ünüvar (2013), Bungenberg and Hobe (2015).

[16]See European Commission, Towards a comprehensive European international investment policy, COM (2010) 343 final, p. 8: "[T]he articulation of investment policy should be consistent with the Treaty's Chapter on capital and payments (Articles 63–66 TFEU) [. . .]. That chapter does not expressly provide for the possibility to conclude international agreements on investment, including portfolio investment. However, to the extent that international agreements on investment affect the scope of the common rules set by the Treaty's Chapter on capitals and payments, the exclusive Union competence to conclude agreements in this area would be implied [. . .]." Hoffmeister and Ünüvar (2013), p. 65 et seq.

[17]See Reinisch (2014b), p. 136. The German Federal Constitutional Court stressed this in its Lisbon Treaty judgment, 2 BvE 2/08, 30 June 2009, para. 379: "The extension of the common commercial policy to 'foreign direct investment' (Article 207(1) TFEU) confers exclusive competence on the European Union also in this area. Much, however, argues in favour of assuming that the term 'foreign direct investment' only encompasses investment which serves to obtain a controlling interest in an enterprise [. . .]. The consequence of this would be that exclusive competence only exists for investment of this type whereas investment protection agreements that go beyond this would have to be concluded as mixed agreements." See also Bungenberg et al. (2011), Tietje (2009), p. 16; Reinisch (2010b), p. 107; Meyer, Stellt das geplante Freihandelsabkommen der EU mit Kanada (Comprehensive Economic and Trade Agreement, CETA) ein gemischtes Abkommen dar?, Rechtsgutachten für das Bundesministerium für Wirtschaft und Energie, 22 September 2014, https://www.bmwi.de/Redaktion/DE/Downloads/C-D/ceta-gutachten-einstufung-als-gemischtes-abkommen.pdf?__blob=publicationFile&v=4 (last accessed 1 March 2017), p. 10 et seq.

[18]Article 218(11) TFEU: "Member State, the European Parliament, the Council or the Commission may obtain the opinion of the Court of Justice as to whether an agreement envisaged is compatible with the Treaties." The Commission made use of this provision in the context of the envisaged EU-Singapore FTA. See Commission Decision of 30 October 2014 requesting an opinion of the Court of Justice pursuant to article 218(11)TFEU on the competence of the Union to sign and conclude a Free Trade Agreement with Singapore, C(2014) 8218 final.

This seemingly academic question has, of course, important political implications. Mixed agreements require adherence of the (as of 2016) 28 individual EU Member States which would imply a kind of *de facto* unanimity requirement,[19] while agreements falling under the exclusive competence of the EU are solely negotiated by the EU Commission and just require majority approval of the Council of Ministers and the EU Parliament.

A further competence issue regarding the scope of investment protection to be negotiated seems to have been tacitly resolved in favour of EU powers. One could question though whether the EU has external powers to agree on expropriation clauses, typically contained in International Investment Agreements (IIAs), since the TFEU expressly reserves the question of property ownership to the Member States.[20]

Finally, and most importantly in the present context, doubts have been voiced whether the Lisbon Treaty powers concerning "foreign direct investment" also encompass ISA.[21] It seems, however, that procedural mechanisms to enforce substantive protection standards are seen as being implicitly covered by the latter power.[22]

The events surrounding the planned conclusion of CETA in autumn 2016 have demonstrated that the issue of the distribution of powers between the EU and its Member States are not only unsolved as a matter of EU law scholarship, but have also led to fierce political debates. While the Commission initially announced that its exclusive power to conclude CETA comprised also the latter's investment

[19]Based on a proposal made by the Commission after the finalization of negotiations and subsequent to the consultation or consent of the European Parliament according to Article 218(6) TFEU, the Council adopts a decision to conclude the agreement pursuant to Article 218(2) and (6) TFEU. Additionally, in the case of mixed agreements the Members States' consent pursuant to domestic law is warranted. It has been the practice of the EU that the Council will only conclude an agreement once all Member States have given their consent. The effect of abstention of individual Member States remains unclear. In particular, it is questionable whether such conduct would be in breach of the duty of co-operation under Article 4 TEU and whether the non-approving Member States would be bound by the parts of the respective agreement covered by exclusive competences of the EU by virtue of Article 116(2) TFEU. In this context, one has to take into account Article 218(5) TFEU as well which expressively provides for the possibility of provisional application of an envisaged agreement in the sense of Article 25 Vienna Convention on the Law of Treaties and thus for a means of circumventing the Member State acceptance requirement. For more detail see, e.g., Eeckhout (2011), p. 258 et seq.

[20]See Article 345 TFEU: "The Treaties shall in no way prejudice the rules in Member States governing the system of property ownership." On this issue, see, e.g., Dimopoulos (2008), p. 115 et seq.; Akkermans and Ramaekers (2010), p. 292; Dimopoulos (2011), p. 108 et seq.; Hindelang (2011), p. 163; Bungenberg (2011), p. 36 et seq.

[21]See Meyer, Stellt das geplante Freihandelsabkommen der EU mit Kanada (Comprehensive Economic and Trade Agreement, CETA) ein gemischtes Abkommen dar?, Rechtsgutachten für das Bundesministerium für Wirtschaft und Energie, 22 September 2014, p. 15 et seq.; Shan and Zhang (2011), p. 1070; Kläger (2014), p. 69.

[22]See, e.g., Schill (2013), p. 40.

chapter, it had to give in to the Member States' political protests and announced that it would proceed on the basis of concluding a mixed agreement.[23]

While the EU is asserting its powers concerning investment, it is also clear that—with the exception of the Energy Charter Treaty—to date no EU IIA has entered into force. Thus, the roughly 1.400 bilateral investment treaties (BITs) of the EU's Member States[24] still form the basis for international investment protection of EU investors abroad and of investors in the EU. Recognizing that the full transition to EU IIAs will require substantial time, the EU has adopted a regulation establishing transitional arrangements for Member States' BITs with third States, which basically permit the continued validity of such IIAs as well as even the negotiation and conclusion of new ones.[25]

Once the competence issues had been overcome, or at least pragmatically left open, the issue arose how the EU would position itself toward ISA and other forms of investor-State dispute settlement (ISDS) such as conciliation or mediation, as alternatives to recourse to domestic courts of the host States only.[26]

Since the 1990s with the increase of ISA under the ICSID Convention[27] and other arbitration systems, investment arbitration has been viewed as a crucial form of effective investment protection,[28] rendering the need for an espousal of claims under the traditional diplomatic protection paradigm unnecessary. Simultaneously, avoiding the political harassment factor of such espoused inter-State claims[29] has been regarded an important de-politicization of investment disputes.[30]

[23]See Proposal for a Council Decision on the signing on behalf of the European Union of the Comprehensive Economic and Trade Agreement between Canada of the one part, and the European Union and its Member States, of the other part, European Commission, COM (2016) 444 final.

[24]European Commission, Fact sheet, Investment Protection and Investor-to-State Dispute Settlement in EU Agreements, November 2013, p. 4.

[25]Regulation (EU) No 1219/2012 of the European Parliament and of the Council of 12 December 2012 establishing transitional arrangements for bilateral investment agreements between Member States and third countries, OJ 2012 L 351/40.

[26]See also Brown and Naglis (2013).

[27]Convention on the Settlement of Investment Disputes between States and Nationals of Other States (ICSID Convention), 18 March 1965.

[28]See e.g. *Eastern Sugar B.V. v Czech Republic*, SCC Case No. 088/2004, Partial Award, 27 March 2007, para. 165: "Whereas general principles such as fair and equitable treatment or full security and protection of the investment are found in many international, regional or national legal systems, the investor's right arising from the BIT's dispute settlement clause to address an international arbitral tribunal independent from the host state is the best guarantee that the investment will be protected against potential undue infringements by the host state." *National Grid plc v Argentina*, Decision on Jurisdiction, 20 June 2006, para. 49: "assurance of independent international arbitration is an important – perhaps the most important – element in investor protection."

[29]On the so called "gun boat diplomacy", see Wallace (2005), p. 674; Johnson and Gimblett (2012), p. 649.

[30]See already Shihata (1986), p. 1; Paulsson J, Keynote Address: Confronting Global Challenges: From Gunboat Diplomacy to Investor-State Arbitration, PCA Peace Palace Centenary Seminar, 11 October 2013.

According to recent statistics, more than 90% of all (approximately 3.200) IIAs contain ISA.[31] With regard to the actual use of ISA, UNCTAD lists 696 initiated cases until the end of 2015.[32] More than 70% of all ISA cases decided in 2011–2015 and won by investors were initiated against States in Latin America and Central and Eastern European States.[33]

4 An Emerging EU Investment Policy

In spite of the general recognition of these advantages, it was unclear after the entry into force of the Lisbon Treaty's new investment powers of the EU whether the EU would strive for ISA or rather settle for other forms of dispute settlement, possibly limited to the inter-State level, e.g. along the trade law paradigm to which the Commission has become accustomed over years of GATT and WTO experience. One should also not forget that shortly before the EU started to think about ISA, Australia and the US had found it unnecessary to include ISA in a bilateral free trade agreement concluded between two developed OECD States.[34]

After an initial orientation phase, however, the EU institutions finally came out in favour of adopting ISA,[35] though the European Parliament, in particular, voiced concern about this form of ISDS.[36] This latter concern together with increased pressure from various NGOs, lobbying against ISDS in 2013, gained such political

[31] See Pohl et al. (2012), p. 11; Gaukroder and Gordon (2012), pp. 10 and 64.

[32] For the complete list of investor-state disputes including those on the basis of Intra-EU BITs, see http://unctad.org/en/Pages/DIAE/ISDS.aspx (last accessed 1 March 2017).

[33] UNCTAD, IIA Issue Notes, Latest Development in Investor-State Dispute Settlement, No. 1 April 2012, p. 19; UNCTAD, IIA Issue Notes, Recent Development in Investor-State Dispute Settlement (ISDS), No. 1 May 2013, p. 31; UNCTAD, IIA Issue Notes, Recent Development in Investor-State Dispute Settlement (ISDS), No. 1 April 2014, pp. 2–33; UNCTAD, IIA Issue Notes, Investor-State Dispute Settlement: Review of Developments in 2014, No. 2 May 2015, p. 29 et seq.; UNCTAD, IIA Issue Notes, Investor-State Dispute Settlement: Review of Developments in 2015, No. 2 June 2016, p. 29 et seq.

[34] See Australia-United States FTA (2005), ATS 1, HR Doc No 108-199. See also Australian Government, Department of Foreign Affairs and Trade, Gillard Government Trade Policy Statement: Trading Our Way to More Jobs and Prosperity, April 2011, http://blogs.usyd.edu.au/japaneselaw/2011_Gillard%20Govt%20Trade%20Policy%20Statement.pdf (last accessed 1 March 2017), p. 14; Nottage (2011), Trakman (2012), p. 83; Dodge (2006).

[35] COM (2010) 343 final, p. 10: "ISDS is such an established feature of investment agreements that its absence would in fact discourage investors and make a host economy less attractive than others."

[36] European Parliament, resolution of 6 April 2011 on the future European international investment policy, 2010/2203(INI), para. 24: "Expresses its deep concern regarding the level of discretion of international arbitrators to make a broad interpretation of investor protection clauses, thereby leading to the ruling out of legitimate public regulations; calls on the Commission to produce clear definitions of investor protection standards in order to avoid such problems in the new investment agreements."

momentum that in early 2014 the EU Commissioner in charge of trade and investment negotiations called for a reflection period to consult the European public on investment and ISDS.[37]

Since the EU Commission chose not to adopt a Model BIT/IIA,[38] the actual position of the EU towards ISA can only be deduced from policy papers and treaty negotiations.[39] Most important in this context is the September 2014 draft CETA text which comprises a full investment chapter including ISA.[40]

In addition, some documents emanating from the EU policy-making institutions provide guidance toward the EU's stance on issues of ISA. In this context it is important to keep in mind certain basic division of powers principles of the EU with regard to the negotiation and conclusion of trade (and now also investment) agreements. While the Council of Ministers (representing the Member States) in the format of the External Trade Council has the final say in actually concluding trade agreements with a qualified majority, it also provides initial guidance to the Commission in formulating negotiating directives. On the basis of the latter, the Commission (as the Union's supranational trade executive) is tasked with negotiating the agreements which have to gain final approval by the EU Parliament as well.

Already in July 2010, the Commission adopted a Policy Communication, entitled "Towards a comprehensive European international investment policy",[41] in which ISDS is referred to as an "established feature of investment agreements" that should be included in future EU IIAs.[42]

---

[37]European Commission, Press Release, Commission to consult European public on provisions in EU-US trade deal on investment and investor-state dispute settlement, 21 January 2014.

[38]COM (2010) 343 final, p. 6.

[39]See also Reinisch (2014a), p. 679; Lentner (2014), p. 156.

[40]See on the negotiations with Canada also Lévesque (2013).

[41]COM (2010) 343 final.

[42]COM(2010) 343 final, p. 9 et seq.: "In order to ensure effective enforcement, investment agreements also feature investor-to-state dispute settlement, which permits an investor to take a claim against a government directly to binding international arbitration [footnote: The Energy Charter Treaty, to which the EU is a party, equally contains investor-state dispute settlement.]. Investor-state dispute settlement, which forms a key part of the inheritance that the Union receives from Member State BITs, is important as an investment involves the establishment of a long-term relationship with the host state which cannot be easily diverted to another market in the event of a problem with the investment. Investor-state is such an established feature of investment agreements that its absence would in fact discourage investors and make a host economy less attractive than others. For these reasons, future EU agreements including investment protection should include investor-state dispute settlement. This raises challenges relating, in part, to the uniqueness of investor-state dispute settlement in international economic law and in part to the fact that the Union has not historically been a significant actor in this field. Current structures are to some extent ill-adapted to the advent of the Union. To take one example, the Convention on the Settlement of Investment Disputes between States and Nationals of Other States (the ICSID Convention), is open to signature and ratification by states members of the World Bank or party to the Statute of the International Court of Justice. The European Union qualifies under neither. In approaching investor-state dispute settlement mechanisms, the Union should build on Member State practices to arrive at state-of-the art investor-state dispute settlement mechanisms."

This Communication received comments by the other EU institutions; most importantly among them were the Council Conclusions of 25 October 2010[43] and the European Parliament's Resolution of 6 April 2011.[44] Though containing language of a rather high level of generality, they both displayed a positive attitude towards ISA. While the Council emphasized the importance of an "effective investor-to-state dispute settlement mechanism"[45] in EU IIAs, the Parliament more cautiously expressed its view that "in addition to state-to-state dispute settlement procedures, investor-state procedures must also be applicable in order to secure comprehensive investment protection."[46]

More details emanated from the Council Negotiating Directives of 12 September 2011[47] concerning the negotiations with Canada, India and Singapore which—though confidential—were leaked at some stage and which contained valuable information on the EU's official position with regard to a number of investment related issues. They suggested that an investment chapter should include fair and equitable treatment (FET), full protection and security, national treatment and most-favoured-nation (MFN) treatment as well as guarantees against uncompensated expropriation and probably an umbrella clause. As regards the level of detail, the instructions appear to favour the traditional European approach by adhering to a rather concise treaty text, without clarifications limiting the scope of FET and indirect expropriation as they are known from US and Canadian BITs as well as the North American Free Trade Agreement (NAFTA).[48] With regard to dispute settlement, the need for direct ISA seemed to be unquestioned, though the precise contours were still open given the difficulty of access to ICSID (and ICSID Additional Facility) dispute settlement by the EU as an international actor not being a State and the ICSID Convention being open to States only.[49]

[43]Council of the EU, Conclusions on a comprehensive European international investment policy, 3041st Foreign Affairs Council Meeting, 25 October 2010.

[44]European Parliament resolution of 6 April 2011 on the future European international investment policy, 2010/2203(INI).

[45]Council, Conclusions on a comprehensive European international investment policy, 3041st Foreign Affairs Council Meeting, Luxembourg, 25 October 2010: "[. . .] stresses, in particular, the need for an effective investor-to-state dispute settlement mechanism in the EU investment agreements".

[46]European Parliament, European Parliament resolution of 6 April 2011 on the future European international investment policy, 2010/2203 (INI), para. 32: "Takes the view that, in addition to state-to-state dispute settlement procedures, investor-state procedures must also be applicable in order to secure comprehensive investment protection".

[47]Council Negotiating Directives (Canada, India and Singapore), 12 September 2011, http://www.bilaterals.org/spip.php?article20272&lang=en (last accessed 1 March 2017).

[48]North American Free Trade Agreement, ILM 32 (1993) 289.

[49]See the leaked negotiating mandate "EU-Canada (CETA), India and Singapore FTAs – European Commission negotiating mandate on investment (2011)", http://www.bilaterals.org/spip.php?article20272&lang=en (last accessed 1 March 2017): "Enforcement: the agreement shall aim to provide for an effective investor-to state-dispute settlement mechanism. State-to-state dispute settlement will be included, but will not interfere with the right of investors to have

Also the subsequent 2013 Council Negotiating Directives for TTIP called for the inclusion of "an effective and state-of-the-art investor-to-state dispute settlement mechanism."[50] The qualifications what should be understood as a modern state-of-the-art ISA reflect already on a number of the publicly criticized features of ISA and also take into account US practice in shaping ISA provisions. The EU is currently negotiating BITs with China and Myanmar, as well as investment chapters as part of FTAs with India, Japan, the US, Libya, Egypt, Jordan, Morocco and Tunisia, Malaysia and Thailand.[51] The negotiations with Canada,[52] Vietnam[53] and Singapore[54] have already been concluded in substance. By mid-2015, the most advanced negotiating draft reflecting the EU Commission's position on ISA was contained in the above-mentioned September 2014 CETA draft.

Before analysing this 2015 Commission approach to ISA in detail, it is useful, however, to reflect on the public debate that has reached a remarkable intensity in

recourse to the investor-to-state dispute settlement mechanism. It should provide for investors a wide range of arbitration fora as currently available under the Member States' bilateral investment agreements (BIT's)." Pursuant to Article 67 ICSID Convention, the convention is only accessible for Member States of the International Bank for Reconstruction and Development or to any other State which is a party to the ICJ Statute. See already Burgstaller (2014), p. 557. Notably, Article X.22(4) Consolidated 2014 CETA Text makes reference to the ICSID Convention, to the ICSID Additional Facility Rules and to the UNCITRAL Arbitration Rules. See also, Reinisch A, Stifter L, European Investment Policy and ISDS, 13 November 2014, http://papers.ssrn.com/sol3/papers.cfm?abstract_id=2564018 (last accessed 1 March 2017), p. 11 et seq.

[50]Council, Directives for the negotiation on the Transatlantic Trade and Investment Partnership between the European Union and the United States of America, 11103/13 DCL 1, 9 October 2014, p. 9: "Enforcement: the Agreement should aim to provide for an effective and state-of-the-art investor-to-state dispute settlement mechanism, providing for transparency, independence of arbitrators and predictability of the Agreement, including through the possibility of binding interpretation of the Agreement by the Parties. State-to-state dispute settlement should be included, but should not interfere with the right of investors to have recourse to the investor-to-state dispute settlement mechanisms. It should provide for investors as wide a range of arbitration fora as is currently available under the Member States' bilateral investment agreements. The investor-to-state dispute settlement mechanism should contain safeguards against manifestly unjustified or frivolous claims. Consideration should be given to the possibility of creating an appellate mechanism applicable to investor-to-state dispute settlement under the Agreement, and to the appropriate relationship between ISDS and domestic remedies."

[51]The Overview of FTA and other Trade Negotiations of the Commission shows the current state of negotiations of international agreements currently negotiated by the EU, http://trade.ec.europa.eu/doclib/docs/2006/december/tradoc_118238.pdf (last accessed 1 March 2017).

[52]Consolidated 2014 CETA text and Revised 2016 CETA text.

[53]EU-Vietnam Free Trade Agreement: Agreed text as of January 2016, published on 1 March 2016, http://trade.ec.europa.eu/doclib/press/index.cfm?id=1437 (last accessed 1 March 2017).

[54]On 20 September 2013, the EU and Singapore have initialled the text of a comprehensive FTA. The authentic text as of May 2015 of the EU-Singapore Free Trade Agreement, was published on 29 June 2015, http://trade.ec.europa.eu/doclib/press/index.cfm?id=961 (last accessed 1 March 2017).

some EU Member States and that has even led to an interruption of the investment negotiations of the EU, in particular those with the US on TTIP. In this contribution's final section, the September 2015 suggestions of the EU Commission on a future TTIP investment chapter,[55] which contained already a proposal for a permanent Investment Court System (ICS), will be analysed below. It was this template, not accepted by the US, which was successfully integrated into the February 2016 CETA text.[56]

5 The Public Debate on Investor-State Arbitration in EU Member States

While already the CETA negotiations triggered some questions and critical comments on investor protection and in particular ISA,[57] the TTIP negotiations led to a major public debate in several EU Member States. It is interesting to note that this debate was sparked in some EU Member States and has reached a very high level of intensity there, while in others it seems to be a non-issue. In particular, in Germany and Austria, NGOs and also a number of politicians have questioned the need for ISA. Given the fact that both countries have a long-standing practice of concluding BITs this may appear surprising.[58]

The underlying reasons for this scepticism are complex and can undoubtedly be better examined by political scientists. This notwithstanding, one could argue that the negative stance towards TTIP mirrors the widespread phenomenon of euroscepticism and thus a certain degree of mistrust towards EU institutions, linking up with the anti-globalization movement of the 1990s that had already led to the demise of the multilateral agreement on investment (MAI) in 1998.[59] Furthermore,

[55]Commission draft text TTIP – investment, 16 September 2015, http://trade.ec.europa.eu/doclib/docs/2015/september/tradoc_153807.pdf (last accessed 1 March 2017).

[56]Revised 2016 CETA text, http://trade.ec.europa.eu/doclib/docs/2016/february/tradoc_154329.pdf (last accessed 1 March 2017).

[57]See, e.g., Barlow M, CETA: A Threat to Local Democracy. Huffington Post Canada, 22 October 2011, http://www.huffingtonpost.ca/maude-barlow/ceta_b_1021782.html (last accessed 1 March 2017); see Trew S, Down with human rights! The Harper government's peculiar objection to European trade deal, rabble.ca blogs, 22 November 2012, http://rabble.ca/blogs/bloggers/council-canadians/2012/11/down-human-rights-harper-governments-unfathomable-objection (last accessed 1 March 2017).

[58]UNCTAD lists 65 BITs concluded by Austria (60 in force) and 134 BITs concluded by Germany (127 in force), http://investmentpolicyhub.unctad.org/IIA (last accessed 1 March 2017).

[59]See OECD Negotiating Group On The Multilateral Agreement On Investment (MAI), The Multilateral Agreement On Investment Draft Consolidated Text 6, OECD Doc. DAFFE/MAI (98)7/REV1 (22 April 1998); see also Muchlinski (2011).

it is interesting to note that the general TTIP criticism coincided with NSA/WikiLeaks revelations about spying activities of the US in Europe,[60] feeding into the notion of the US as an overwhelmingly powerful trade partner that would outwit the Europeans on all fronts,[61] including forcing their (in European public perception) low health, safety, environmental, labour, etc. standards for goods[62] on European consumers as well as empowering US corporations to prevent legitimate European regulation via ISA.

From an institutional perspective, one can observe on the EU level that the Council seemed to be in favour of the inclusion of an ISA-mechanism in TTIP.[63] While the European Commission initially used to strongly advocate this option,[64] the new cabinet under *Jean-Claude Juncker* adopted a softer stance towards this issue.[65]

From a Member State perspective, it is worth mentioning that in mid-2014 the German Federal Council expressly rejected the inclusion of a specific ISDS-mechanism in TTIP.[66] In the following months, the public debate especially in Germany and Austria became increasingly hostile to the idea of including ISA in an investment chapter of the TTIP. ISA was portrayed as a special right of large

---

[60]The beginning of the negotiations in mid-2013 were already politically overshadowed by waves of new revelations concerning US spying activities directed against EU Member State governments.

[61]See e.g. Mason R, 'Corporate Wolves' will exploit TTIP trade deal, MPs warned, The Guardian, 15 January 2015, http://www.theguardian.com/business/2015/jan/15/corporate-wolves-warning-ttip--trade-deal (last accessed 1 March 2017).

[62]See e.g. Faiola A, Free trade with U.S.? Europe balks at chlorine chicken, hormone beef, The Washington Post, 4 December 2014, https://www.washingtonpost.com/world/europe/free-trade-with-us-europe-balks-at-chlorine-chicken-hormone-beef/2014/12/04/e9aa131c-6c3f-11e4-bafd-6598192a448d_story.html (last accessed 1 March 2017); Traynor I, Rice-Oxley M, US-EU trade deal—the Guardian briefing, The Guardian, 5 February 2015, http://www.theguardian.com/business/2015/feb/05/us-eu-trade-deal-the-guardian-briefing (last accessed 1 March 2017).

[63]Council, Directives for the negotiation on the Transatlantic Trade and Investment Partnership between the European Union and the United States of America, 11103/13 DCL 1, 9 October 2014, p. 9.

[64]COM (2010) 343 final.

[65]See President Juncker's political guidelines of 15 July 2014 addressed to the next Commission and entitled "A New Start for Europe: My Agenda for Jobs, Growth, Fairness and Democratic Change", http://ec.europa.eu/priorities/docs/pg_en.pdf (last accessed 1 March 2017), p. 25: "The negotiating mandate foresees a number of conditions that have to be respected by such a regime [ISDS] as well as an assessment of its relationship with domestic courts. There is thus no obligation in this regard: the mandate leaves it open and serves as a guide."

[66]German Federal Council Resolution of 11 July 2014, BR-Drs. 295/14: "9. Der Bundesrat hält spezielle Investitionsschutzvorschriften und Streitbeilegungsmechanismen im Verhältnis Investor und Staat zwischen der EU und den USA für verzichtbar und mit hohen Risiken verbunden. Gründe dafür sind insbesondere: – Beide Partner gewährleisten für Investoren einen hinreichenden Rechtsschutz vor unabhängigen nationalen Gerichten. – Durch Investor-Staat-Schiedsverfahren können allgemeine und angemessene Regelungen zum Schutz von Gemeinwohlzielen, die in demokratischen Entscheidungen rechtsstaatlich zustande gekommen und rechtmäßig angewandt wurden, ausgehebelt oder umgangen werden."

transnational corporations to circumvent domestic courts.[67] In early 2015, the Socialists and Democrats in the EU Parliament, led by their German branch, proposed the establishment of a permanent investment court instead of the traditional *ad hoc* tribunals.[68]

In May 2015, the EU Commission published a concept paper entitled "Investment in TTIP and beyond – the path for reform"[69] in which it highlighted the ideas of "strengthening governments' right to regulate, making arbitral tribunals operate more like traditional court systems with a clear code of conduct for arbitrators, and guaranteeing access to an appeals system."[70]

Then in summer 2015, the European Parliament adopted a resolution containing recommendations to the European Commission on the negotiations for TTIP pledging for a

> new system for resolving disputes between investors and states which is subject to democratic principles and scrutiny, where potential cases are treated in a transparent manner by publicly appointed, independent professional judges in public hearings and which includes an appellate mechanism, where consistency of judicial decisions is ensured the jurisdiction of courts of the EU and of the Member States is respected, and where private interests cannot undermine public policy objectives.[71]

In mid-September 2015, the next move was taken by the EU Commission when it went public with a draft text of the TTIP investment chapter which in addition to some adaptations of the investment chapter already found in CETA, contained a very detailed section on investment dispute resolution, proposing an "Investment Court System" (ICS).[72] This ICS was then successfully integrated into the February 2016 CETA text.[73]

---

[67]Liebrich S, Diese Verträge werden das Leben unserer Kinder beeinflussen, Süddeutsche Zeitung, 5 May 2015, http://www.sueddeutsche.de/wirtschaft/kritik-an-freihandelsabkommen-diese-vertraege-werden-das-leben-unserer-kinder-beeinflussen-1.2465023 (last accessed 1 March 2017); Gerstetter C, Meyer-Ohlendorf N, Investor-state dispute settlement under TTIP – a risk for environmental regulation?, Heinrich Böll Stiftung, 31 December 2013, p. 4; see also the Internet campaign "Stop TTIP", https://stop-ttip.org/de/wo-liegt-das-problem/ (last accessed 1 March 2017); Greenpeace, TTIP: Scharfe Kritik am "Ja" zu ISDS, 8 July 2015, http://www.greenpeace.org/austria/de/News/Aktuelle-Meldungen/Gentechnik-News/2015/Scharfe-Kritik-am-Ja-zu-ISDS/ (last accessed 1 March 2017).

[68]S&D Position Paper on Investor-state dispute settlement mechanisms in ongoing trade negotiations, 4 March 2015.

[69]European Commission, Concept Paper, Investment in TTIP and beyond – the path for reform, 6 May 2015.

[70]See European Commission, Press Release, Commissioner Malmström consulted the European Parliament on reforms of investment dispute resolution in TTIP and beyond, 6 May 2015, http://trade.ec.europa.eu/doclib/press/index.cfm?id=1303 (last accessed 1 March 2017).

[71]European Parliament, resolution of 8 July 2015 containing the European Parliament's recommendations to the European Commission on the negotiations for the Transatlantic Trade and Investment Partnership (TTIP), 2014/2228(INI).

[72]Commission draft text TTIP – investment, 16 September 2015, http://trade.ec.europa.eu/doclib/docs/2015/september/tradoc_153807.pdf (last accessed 1 March 2017).

[73]Revised CETA text, 29 February 2016, http://trade.ec.europa.eu/doclib/docs/2016/february/tradoc_154329.pdf (last accessed 1 March 2017).

5.1 Major Points of Criticism

The arguments brought forward against ISA were not wholly new, partly rehashing the NAFTA debate's topics familiar to the Canadian and US public, and well-epitomized in the 2001 New York Times article, which notoriously likened NAFTA panels to secret tribunals.[74] The anti-investment groups relied on a number of serious concerns about the actual practice of ISA combined with fears and anti-globalization rhetoric familiar from the Seattle anti-WTO campaigns of the 1990s. Recently, with the US negotiating not only TTIP with the EU, but also a Trans-Pacific Partnership (TPP) with Asian countries opposition to ISA has grown in the US as well. This is illustrated by two rounds of open letters from law professors, one urging congressional leaders to omit ISA from TPP and TTIP[75] and a reply advocating a reformed inclusion of ISA.[76]

Among the most prominent areas criticised by NGOs and increasingly by the media in a number of EU Member States were the lack of transparency of the dispute settlement procedure, the impossibility to appeal against investment decisions, the alleged pro-investor bias of tribunals, and too broad investor rights which would lead to a "chilling effect" on legitimate regulation by sovereign

[74]See DePalma A, Nafta's Powerful Little Secret: Obscure Tribunals Settle Disputes, but Go Too Far, Critics Say, New York Times, 11 March 2001, http://www.nytimes.com/2001/03/11/business/nafta-s-powerful-little-secret-obscure-tribunals-settle-disputes-but-go-too-far.html (last accessed 1 March 2017): "THEIR meetings are secret. Their members are generally unknown. The decisions they reach need not be fully disclosed. Yet the way a small group of international tribunals handles disputes between investors and foreign governments has led to national laws being revoked, justice systems questioned and environmental regulations challenged. And it is all in the name of protecting the rights of foreign investors under the North American Free Trade Agreement." See also Brower (2001), p. 43, mentioning the concern that the ISDS under NAFTA could have a "chilling effect" on regulation.

[75]Open Letter by the "Alliance for Justice" from March 2015 to Majority Leader McConnell, Minority Leader Reid, Speaker Boehner, Minority Leader Pelosi, and Ambassador Froman, http://www.afj.org/wp-content/uploads/2015/03/ISDS-Letter-3.11.pdf (last accessed 1 March 2017), p. 1: "[...] we urge you to protect the rule of law and our nation's sovereignty by ensuring ISDS is not included."

[76]Open letter by law professors, 7 April 2015, to Majority Leader McConnell, Minority Leader Reid, Speaker Boehner, Minority Leader Pelosi, and Ambassador Froman, https://www.mcgill.ca/fortier-chair/files/fortier-chair/isds_letter-april_20_final.docx (last accessed 1 March 2017): "We the undersigned – professors and scholars of international law, arbitration, and dispute settlement – strongly support a robust, even-handed, and careful discussion about investment treaty arbitration (ITA), which is sometimes referred to as investor-state dispute settlement (ISDS). We believe, however, that the discussion should be based on facts and balanced representations, rather than on errors or skewed information." and on p. 5 "Contrary to the assertions contained in the "Alliance for Justice" letter, investment treaty arbitration does not undermine the rule of law. It ensures that, where a right is given, a remedy is also provided. It permits foreign investors to hold host states to the obligations they have undertaken in their treaties by means of a quasi-judicial process; and it also offers a forum for states to vindicate their policy choices."

States.[77] With regard to the latter point, critics of TTIP and CETA allege that ISA would lead to an overly-broad investment protection entailing a "regulatory chill".[78] They refer to cases like *Vattenfall v Germany*,[79] *Philip Morris v Australia*[80] and *Philip Morris v Uruguay*[81] or *Lone Pine v Canada*[82]—none of which had been decided on the merits at the time—in order to argue that sovereign States will be deprived of their right to exit nuclear power generation, to protect against the risks of smoking or to prohibit "fracking".[83] Meanwhile, *Philip Morris*

[77]See e.g., Monbiot G, This transatlantic trade deal is a full-frontal assault on democracy, The Guardian, 4 November 2013, http://www.theguardian.com/commentisfree/2013/nov/04/us-trade-deal-full-frontal-assault-on-democracy (last accessed 1 March 2017); Brühl J, Unbekannte Kläger, geheime Dokumente, Süddeutsche Zeitung, 12 August 2014, http://www.sueddeutsche.de/wirtschaft/ttip-faktencheck-investorenschutz-unbekannte-klaeger-geheime-dokumente-1.2085316 (last accessed 1 March 2017); Pinzler P, Uchatius W, Kohlenberg K, Schattenjustiz: Im Namen des Geldes, Die Zeit, 27 February 2014, http://www.zeit.de/2014/10/investitionsschutz-schiedsgericht-icsid-schattenjustiz (last accessed 1 March 2017).

[78]In this vein, see, e.g., the Seattle to Brussels Network in a brief from January 2014, entitled "Seattle to Brussels Network refutes European Commission's defense of controversial investor-to-state dispute settlement", http://www.tni.org/sites/www.tni.org/files/download/s2b_response_to_dgtrade_long.pdf (last accessed 1 March 2017): "There is clear evidence that proposed and even adopted laws on public health and environmental protection have been abandoned or watered down because of the threat of corporate claims for damages. [...] Through regulatory chill effects and the cost of arbitration and awards, ISDS provisions constitute a considerable and growing policy and financial risk. The exponential growth in the number of ISDS cases spurred on by international trade lawyers; frivolous claims; and pressures to shelve regulation under threat of investment claims are systemic flaws." Further on this issue, see Neumayer (2001), p. 231; Schill (2007), p. 469; Tienhaara (2011), p. 607.

[79]*Vattenfall AB and others v Federal Republic of Germany*, ICSID Case No. ARB/12/12, registered 31 May 2012.

[80]*Philip Morris Asia Limited v The Commonwealth of Australia*, PCA Case No. 2012-12, Notice of Arbitration dated 21 November 2011.

[81]*Philip Morris Brands S.à r.l., Philip Morris Products S.A. and Abal Hermanos S.A. v Oriental Republic of Uruguay*, ICSID Case No. ARB/10/7, registered 26 March 2010.

[82]*Lone Pine Resources Inc. v The Government of Canada,* NAFTA, Notice of Arbitration dated 6 September 2013.

[83]See, e.g., a report released on 6 March 2015 by the Sierra Club, Issue Brief, No fracking way: how the EU-US trade agreement risks expanding fracking, March 2014, http://action.sierraclub.org/site/DocServer/FoEE_TTIP-ISDS-fracking-060314.pdf?docID=15241 (last accessed 1 March 2017), p. 5: "The proposed investment chapter in the TTIP is expected to include far-reaching rights for foreign investors that could undermine government decisions to ban and regulate fracking. US companies investing in Europe could directly challenge fracking bans or regulations at private international tribunals – potentially paving the way for millions of euro in compensation, paid by European taxpayers." Further on this issue, see The Council of Canadians, The CETA Deception: The right to regulate—health and environmental standards, http://www.canadians.org/ceta-deception-2 (last accessed 1 March 2017): "Free trade, whether in Canada's agreements with other countries or at the World Trade Organization, is absolutely designed to limit when, where and how governments regulate. [...] These deals also contain investment chapters that give corporations tools to enforce their rights to be free from what they consider overly burdensome regulation. [...] The investor-to-state dispute settlement process [...] fundamentally undermines health and environmental regulation. Governments may continue to regulate where a policy has been found to

v Australia[84] was dismissed on jurisdictional grounds and *Philip Morris v Uruguay*[85] was won by the host State on the merits, affirming Uruguay's right to regulate for public health. In general, the regulatory chill debate is not new but largely resembles similar discussions concerning NAFTA's investment chapter more than a decade ago.[86]

Interestingly, the public debate about investment law also turned to more technical aspects of the specific nature of ISA. The traditional confidentiality of arbitral proceedings was portrayed as a lack of transparency and threat to public, democratic decision-making because anonymous arbitrators could "force" sovereign States to undo their policy decisions.[87]

While a number of ISA specific issues did indeed raise concern and had been discussed in investment arbitration and policy-making circles for quite a while, the anti-ISA campaign of the 2010s appeared to overlook, or chose to ignore, the multiple developments in investment arbitration over the last decade. In fact, many of these developments addressed core aspects of the criticism raised against ISA.

The perceived secrecy or lack of transparency of ISA, resulting from the confidentiality prevalent in commercial arbitration—though never as pervasive in ISA, has been significantly reduced mostly through the work of institutions active in the role of administering ISA, but also by policy makers negotiating IIAs. In 2006, the ICSID Arbitration Rules were amended with a view to more transparency, now permitting amicus curiae participation as well as more general publication of awards.[88] In a similar effort, UNCITRAL adopted Rules on Transparency in Investor-State Arbitration in 2013.[89] Pursuant to the 2015 Mauritius Convention

---

violate investment rights, but only after paying fines of tens and even hundreds of millions of dollars." See also Eberhardt P, Feodoroff T, Lui E, Olivet C and Trew S, The right to say no: EU-Canada trade agreement threatens fracking bans, May 2013, http://corporateeurope.org/sites/default/files/publications/ceta-fracking-briefing.pdf (last accessed 1 March 2017).

[84] *Philip Morris Asia Limited v The Commonwealth of Australia*, PCA Case No. 2012-12, Award on Jurisdiction and Admissibility, 17 December 2015.

[85] *Philip Morris Brands S.à r.l., Philip Morris Products S.A. and Abal Hermanos S.A. v Oriental Republic of Uruguay*, ICSID Case No. ARB/10/7, Award, 8 July 2016.

[86] See Jenkins (2007), Tienhaara (2011).

[87] See, e.g., Open letter by the Alliance for Justice, http://www.afj.org/wp-content/uploads/2015/03/ISDS-Letter-3.11.pdf (last accessed 1 March 2017): "Essentially, corporations use ISDS to challenge government policies, actions, or decisions that they allege reduce the value of their investments. These challenges are not heard in a normal court but instead before a tribunal of private lawyers."

[88] Amendments to the ICSID Rules and Regulations and the Additional Facility Rules, effective 10 April 2006, http://www.worldbank.org/icsid/basicdoc/CRR_English-final.pdf (last accessed 1 March 2017). See also Antonietti (2006).

[89] UNCITRAL Rules on Transparency in Treaty-based Investor-State Arbitration, adopted by A/RES/68/109, 16 December 2013, http://www.uncitral.org/pdf/english/texts/arbitration/rules-on-transparency/Rules-on-Transparency-E.pdf (last accessed 1 March 2017).

these transparency rules can even be made to apply retroactively to existing investment treaties concluded before 1 April 2014.[90]

At the same time treaty negotiators have increasingly provided for transparency in the ISA chapters of IIAs. These range from publication obligations of awards and even submissions to permitting access to ISA to third-parties through amicus briefs and the possibility of public hearings.[91] As a result ISA is often more transparent and its outcome more easily accessible to the public than the normal domestic court system.[92]

[90]Article 1(1) United Nations Convention on Transparency in Treaty-based Investor-State Arbitration, adopted by A/RES/69/116, 18 December 2014, opened for signature on 17 March 2015, not yet in force, as of 28 October 2016, 16 countries have signed and only Mauritius has ratified – Article 1: "This Convention applies to arbitration between an investor and a State or a regional economic integration organization conducted on the basis of an investment treaty concluded before 1 April 2014". See also Arbitration Institute of the Stockholm Chamber of Commerce, Mauritius Convention and UNCITRAL Rules on Transparency in SCC case, 22 May 2015, http://sccinstitute.com/media/72819/mauritius-convention-and-uncitral-rules-on-transparency-in-scc-cases.pdf (last accessed 1 March 2017); Schill S, The Mauritius Convention on Transparency: A Model for Investment Law Reform?, EJIL:Talk 8 April 2015.

[91]As for the publication of awards under NAFTA's chapter 11, see NAFTA, Annex 1137.4: Publication of an Award, pursuant to which either the investor or the respondent may make an award public in cases where Canada or the U.S. is/are disputing parties. No similar allowance is contained for Mexico. However, the publication of documents submitted to arbitral tribunal constituted under NAFTA chapter 11 became mandatory by virtue of a binding interpretation of the NAFTA Free Trade Commission. See Notes of Interpretation of Certain Chapter 11 Provisions, 31 July 2001, http://www.state.gov/documents/organization/38790.pdf (last accessed 1 March 2017). While the possibility for amicus briefs has not been formally provided for in NAFTA itself, it has been, first of all, permitted within arbitral practice—see *Methanex Corporation v United States of America*, UNCITRAL, Decision of the Tribunal on Petitions from Third Persons to Intervene as "amici curiae" of 15 January 2001, para. 53—and subsequently confirmed by the Statement of the NAFTA Free Trade Commission on Non-Disputing Party Participation (7 October 2003), http://www.state.gov/documents/organization/38791.pdf (last accessed 1 March 2017). Similarly, NAFTA does not regulate public access to hearings. This issue had, however, been addressed by a joint statement of the Governments of Canada and the United States guaranteeing public hearings in NAFTA proceedings to which they are a disputing party. See Office of the U.S. Trade Representative, NAFTA Commission Announces New Transparency Measures of 7 October 2003, https://ustr.gov/archive/Document_Library/Press_Releases/2003/October/NAFTA_Commission_Announces_New_Transparency_Measures.html (last accessed 1 March 2017). This step was subsequently followed by Mexico, see NAFTA Free Trade Commission Joint Statement – A Decade of Achievement, 16 July 2004, https://ustr.gov/archive/Document_Library/Press_Releases/2004/July/NAFTA_Free_Trade_Commission_Joint_Statement_-_A_Decade_of_Achievement.html (last accessed 1 March 2017). See also Calamita (2014), p. 653 et seq. Generally on transparency, see, e.g., Veeder (2006), Mann (2008), Delaney and Magraw (2008), Maupin (2013).

[92]See Open letter by law professors, 7 April 2015, https://www.mcgill.ca/fortier-chair/files/fortier-chair/isds_letter-april_20_final.docx (last accessed 1 March 2017), p. 5: "The United States and Canada have been champions of transparency in investment treaty arbitration. Each has, since 2001, maintained a website where they post the awards rendered in the cases they defend. They also post pleadings, memorials, and procedural decisions. Mexico has followed the same practice in NAFTA Chapter 11 proceedings. These materials are available for free. In that respect they are more easily and widely available than documents in most U.S. courts. The U.S. federal government maintains an electronic records system for domestic litigation, but users must pay for access ($.10 per page)."

Similarly, the notion that investors enjoy too broad rights by being able to invoke unpredictably vague standards whenever their profits may be threatened[93] has been recognized by host States as inherently against their own interest and led to a number of treaty changes, leading to ever-more detailed formulations of the substantive standards of investment protection.[94] In parallel, IIA treaty-negotiators have started to include express clauses recognizing the host State's right to regulate.[95]

At the same time, it should not be overlooked that also investment tribunals have refined their jurisprudence over the years, clarifying that investment standards are not intended to limit the legitimate regulatory space ("right to regulate") of host countries.[96] Further, IIA treaty-makers have increasingly resorted to the use of joint

---

[93]See, e.g., Open letter by the Alliance for Justice: "ISDS grants foreign corporations a special legal privilege, the right to initiate dispute settlement proceedings against a government for actions that allegedly cause a loss of profit for the corporation. Essentially, corporations use ISDS to challenge government policies, actions, or decisions that they allege reduce the value of their investments."

[94]See also the examples given *infra* in the text at n. 110.

[95]See, e.g., Article [12] Norwegian Draft Model BIT (2007), https://www.regjeringen.no/contentassets/e47326b61f424d4c9c3d470896492623/draft-model-agreement-english.pdf (last accessed 1 March 2017): "Nothing in this Agreement shall be construed to prevent a Party from adopting, maintaining or enforcing any measure otherwise consistent with this Agreement that it considers appropriate to ensure that investment activity is undertaken in a manner sensitive to health, safety or environmental concerns." Article 6(6) Finland-China BIT (2004), http://investmentpolicyhub.unctad.org/Download/TreatyFile/733 (last accessed 1 March 2017): "Provided that such measures are not applied in a manner which would constitute a means of arbitrary or unjustifiable discrimination by a Contracting Party, or a disguised investment restrict, nothing in this Agreement shall be construed as preventing the Contracting Parties from taking any measure necessary for the maintenance of public order." See also Article 43 EFTA-Singapore FTA (2002), http://www.efta.int/media/documents/legal-texts/free-trade-relations/singapore/EFTA-Singapore%20Free%20Trade%20Agreement.pdf (last accessed 1 March 2017): "Nothing in this Chapter shall be construed to prevent a Party from adopting, maintaining or enforcing any measure consistent with this Chapter that is in the public interest, such as measures to meet health, safety or environmental concerns". Preamble Consolidated CETA Text: "Recognizing that the provisions of this Agreement preserve the right to regulate within their territories and resolving to preserve their flexibility to achieve legitimate policy objectives, such as public health, safety, environment, public morals and the promotion and protection of cultural diversity".

[96]See, e.g., *Parkerings v Lithuania*, ICSID Case No. ARB/05/8, Award, 11 September 2007, para. 332: "It is each State's undeniable right and privilege to exercise its sovereign legislative power. A State has the right to enact, modify or cancel a law at its own discretion. Save for the existence of an agreement, in the form of a *stabilisation* clause or otherwise, there is nothing objectionable about the amendment brought to the regulatory framework existing at the time an investor made its investment. As a matter of fact, any businessman or investor knows that laws will evolve over time. What is prohibited however is for a State to act unfairly, unreasonably or inequitably in the exercise of its legislative power." *Plama v Bulgaria*, ICSID Case No. ARB/03/24, Award, 27 August 2008, para. 177: "The stability of the legal framework has been identified as *'an emerging standard of fair and equitable treatment in international law.'* However, the State maintains its legitimate right to regulate, and this right should also be considered when assessing the compliance with the standard of fair and equitable treatment." *Impregilo v Argentina*, ICSID Case No. ARB/07/17, Award, 21 June 2011, para. 290: "In the Tribunal's understanding, fair and

commissions or committees consisting of representatives of the Contracting Parties empowered to give authoritative interpretations of IIAs.[97]

Much time and effort has also been spent by various arbitration institutions and treaty-makers to consider how appellate structures could be inserted into ISA. This started with proposals for amending the ICSID Convention a decade ago,[98] and also led to the inclusion of possible appellate mechanisms in individual IIAs.[99]

With regard to the perceived dominance of self-interested, unaccountable lawyers as arbitrators, who "rotate between being arbitrators and bringing cases for corporations against governments",[100] various arbitration institutions have adopted

---

equitable treatment cannot be designed to ensure the immutability of the legal order, the economic world and the social universe and play the role assumed by stabilization clauses specifically granted to foreign investors with whom the State has signed investment agreements." *Mobil Investments Canada Inc. & Murphy Oil Corporation v Canada*, ICSID Case No. ARB(AF)/07/4, Decision on Liability and on Principles of Quantum, 22 May 2012, para. 153: "This applicable [FET] standard does not require a State to maintain a stable legal and business environment for investments, if this is intended to suggest that the rules governing an investment are not permitted to change, whether to a significant or modest extent. Article 1105 may protect an investor from changes that give rise to an unstable legal and business environment, but only if those changes may be characterized as arbitrary or grossly unfair or discriminatory, or otherwise inconsistent with the customary international law standard. In a complex international and domestic environment, there is nothing in Article 1105 to prevent a public authority from changing the regulatory environment to take account of new policies and needs, even if some of those changes may have far-reaching consequences and effects, and even if they impose significant additional burdens on an investor. Article 1105 is not, and was never intended to amount to, a guarantee against regulatory change, or to reflect a requirement that an investor is entitled to expect no material changes to the regulatory framework within which an investment is made." *Suez, Sociedad General de Aguas de Barcelona S.A. and Interagua Servicios Integrales de Agua S.A. v Argentina*, ICSID Case No. ARB/03/17, Decision on Liability, 30 July 2010, para. 216: "In interpreting the meaning of 'just' or 'fair and equitable treatment' to be accorded to investors, the Tribunal must balance the legitimate and reasonable expectations of the Claimants with [the] right to regulate the provision of a vital public service." See also Yannaca-Small (2005), Titi (2014), Henckels (2012).

[97]See, e.g., Article 1131 NAFTA or Article 31 of the 2012 US Model BIT.

[98]See ICSID Secretariat, Possible Improvements of the Framework for ICSID Arbitration, Discussion Paper, 22 October 2004; Sauvant and Chiswick-Patterson (2008).

[99]Article 28(10) of the 2012 US Model BIT; Article 28(10) Annex D US-Rwanda BIT (2012), http://www.state.gov/documents/organization/101735.pdf (last accessed 1 March 2017); Article 28(10) Annex E US-Uruguay BIT (2006), https://ustr.gov/sites/default/files/uploads/agreements/bit/asset_upload_file748_9005.pdf (last accessed 1 March 2017).

[100]See Open letter by the Alliance for Justice: "ISDS proceedings lack many of the basic protections and procedures of the justice system normally available in a court of law. There is no appeals process. There is no oversight or accountability of the private lawyers who serve as arbitrators, many of whom rotate between being arbitrators and bringing cases for corporations against governments. The system is also a one-way ratchet because corporations can sue, forcing governments to spend significant resources, while governments impacted by foreign corporations cannot bring any claims." Weisman J, Trans-Pacific Partnership seen as Door for Foreign Suits against U.S., New York Times, 25 March 2015, http://www.nytimes.com/2015/03/26/business/trans-pacific-partnership-seen-as-door-for-foreign-suits-against-us.html? (last accessed 1 March 2017).

and revised their conflict of interest rules which subject arbitrators to strict ethical rules concerning their independence and impartiality.[101] Failure to comply with these demands leads to disqualification from sitting on a tribunal. Furthermore, investment arbitration practice since around the year 2000 demonstrates that tribunals have become more sensitive to allegations of actual or perceived lack of independence or impartiality of arbitrators, resulting in a number of successful arbitrator challenges.[102]

Further, and linked to the argument that ISA merely serves big corporate interests, it is sometimes asserted that investors often resort to abusive litigation by bringing highly expensive proceedings before investment tribunals which force host States into costly settlements. Finally, critics argue that ISA circumvents the national judiciary and is thus a form of "privatized" dispute settlement lacking democratic legitimacy[103] and offering a preferential procedural treatment not enjoyed by domestic investors.

5.2 *The EU Commission's Reflection Period and Consultations on Investor-State Arbitration*

Towards the end of 2013, public criticism of investment protection and, in particular, of ISA gained such momentum that the Commission interrupted the TTIP negotiations and pronounced a "reflection period" in late January 2014.[104] This led to a public consultation, whereby the Commission invited the public to comment on

[101]See, *inter alia*, Article 6(7) UNCITRAL Arbitration Rules 2010: "The appointing authority shall have regard to such considerations as are likely to secure the appointment of an independent and impartial arbitrator and shall take into account the advisability of appointing an arbitrator of a nationality other than the nationalities of the parties." Article 14(1) ICSID Convention: "Persons designated to serve on the Panels shall be persons of high moral character and recognized competence in the fields of law, commerce, industry or finance, who may be relied upon to exercise independent judgment. Competence in the field of law shall be of particular importance in the case of persons on the Panel of Arbitrators." See also IBA Guidelines on Conflicts of Interest in International Arbitration, approved on 22 May 2004 by the Council of the International Bar Association, http://www.ibanet.org/Publications/publications_IBA_guides_and_free_materials.aspx (last accessed 1 March 2017).

[102]See Reinisch and Knahr (2012), Sheppard (2009).

[103]See e.g., Open letter by the Alliance for Justice: "This practice [of ISA] threatens domestic sovereignty and weakens the rule of law by giving corporations special legal rights, allowing them to ignore domestic courts, and subjecting the United States to extrajudicial private arbitration." See also Broß (2015).

[104]EU Trade Commissioner de Gucht launched a public consultation on the EU's investment chapter within the EU-US Free Trade negotiations. See European Commission, Press Release of 21 January 2014, Commission to consult European public on provisions in EU-US trade deal on investment and investor-state dispute settlement.

various issues of its trade policy. The questions posed included specific sections dealing with ISA.[105]

In the course of this public consultation, the Commission received a total of 149,399 online contributions. The largest number of replies was received from the United Kingdom (52,008), followed by Austria (33,753) and Germany (32,513).[106] Depending on the specific interests of the respective participants of this survey, the opinions submitted to the Commission have been divided. However, the general outcome of the consultation fairly unambiguously reflected a broad opposition to ISA in TTIP or in general and, in some cases, even to TTIP as such.[107] As the Commission's assessment noted, out of nearly 150,000 responses almost 145,000 were more or less identical answers sent in a copy/paste fashion by individuals on the basis of answers prepared by NGOs.[108] Nevertheless, some 3000 individuals as well as 450 organizations representing EU civil society (business organizations, trade unions, consumer organizations, law firms, academics, etc.) participated in the consultation with individual responses.

6 The Main Features of Investor-State Arbitration in the 2014 CETA Text

While ISA was negotiated together with the substantive investment protection provisions in the agreement with Canada the public debate did not only call for various reforms with regard to the perceived deficiencies of ISA, as contained in most of the traditional EU Member State IIAs, it also led to an increased opposition towards ISA in general.[109]

Since much of the specific criticism voiced against traditional ISA coincided with the ISA scepticism debated within NAFTA countries, the EU Commission

[105]Among them: Question 6: Transparency in ISDS; Question 7: Multiple claims and relationship to domestic courts; Question 8: Arbitrator ethics, conduct and qualification; Question 9: Reducing the risk of frivolous and unfounded cases; Question 10: Allowing claims to proceed (filter); Question 11: Guidance by the Parties (the EU and the US) on the interpretation of the agreement; Question 12: Appellate Mechanism and consistency of rulings.

[106]For further details, see European Commission, Preliminary report (statistical overview), Online public consultation on investment protection and investor-to-state dispute settlement (ISDS) in the Transatlantic Trade and Investment Partnership Agreement (TTIP), July 2014, http://trade.ec.europa.eu/doclib/docs/2014/july/tradoc_152693.pdf (last accessed 1 March 2017), p. 2.

[107]European Commission, Report Online public consultation on investment protection and investor-to-state dispute settlement (ISDS) in the Transatlantic Trade and Investment Partnership Agreement, SWD(2015) 3 final.

[108]European Commission, SWD(2015) 3 final, p. 3.

[109]In this regard, it is telling that according to the European Commission a significant number of the questions on specific issues regarding ISA posed by the EU Commission in its public consultation on ISDS were frequently answered with phrases such as "no comment – I don't think that ISDS should be part of TTIP", see European Commission, SWD(2015) 3 final, p. 10.

found a ready interlocutor on the Canadian side to negotiate a number of new features reacting to ISA criticism.

In fact, a number of issues raised by critics of ISA related not only to the dispute settlement method of ISA, but were in fact a result of the scope of protection under IIAs and the scope of rights granted to investors under typical IIA substantive protection standards. Thus, these issues and the way how the treaty negotiators tried to cope with them will be addressed as well. As can be seen in the following analysis, the 2014 draft CETA text contained a number of novel features that reflected the negotiators' attempt to limit investor rights quite considerably compared to traditional IIAs and BITs.

6.1 Limits to Investor Rights in Order to Secure the Right to Regulate of Host States

As already mentioned above, many of the points of criticism voiced against ISA in the most recent anti-ISA debate in some EU Member States were not entirely new and have already been addressed on various levels.

The 2014 CETA text similarly demonstrated that EU negotiators attempted to seriously react to perceived pro-investor bias in traditional IIAs. The resulting investment chapter of the CETA clearly limited investor rights compared to the texts of previous IIAs and it specifically used language aimed at improving ISA.

6.1.1 More Precise and More Limited Protection Standards

In particular, the concern that investment protection standards would be too vague and imprecise, potentially leading to an investor protection level that could threaten the regulatory freedom of host States and the legitimate exercise of their right to regulate,[110] was addressed by incorporating very limiting language, making clear that host State rights should not be unduly limited.

The traditional IIA or BIT concluded by EU Member States in the past contained rather similarly phrased substantive treatment standards: Typically, the twin obligations of fair and equitable treatment (FET) as well as full protection and security (FPS)—often even contained in a single provision—and the two non-discrimination obligations of national treatment and MFN, frequently supplemented by prohibitions of arbitrary or discriminatory treatment. A further cornerstone of European BITs had always been the guarantee that investors would not be expropriated—directly or indirectly—except in the public interest, in a non-discriminatory way, according to due process and—most important in practice—under the condition that they receive adequate, prompt and effective compensation. Less uniformly

[110]See also the discussion *supra* text at fn. 94.

contained in BITs were so-called umbrella clauses, while "free transfer of funds" guarantees were regularly found in IIAs.

The often laconic language of such protection standards has increasingly been regarded as a potential threat to the regulatory sovereignty of host States. Thus, a number of BITs, in particular the Canadian and US Model BITs of 2004[111] and subsequent treaty practice started to adopt more elaborate restrictive language aimed at ensuring that investor rights are not interpreted too broadly. In parallel, investment arbitration decisions have become increasingly cautious and tribunals very explicitly started to balance investor and host State rights.

A Specific Restriction of the Fair and Equitable Treatment Standard

The most critically viewed investment protection standard is FET which is also the most often invoked one. The detailed wording of the CETA FET standard can be regarded as a "codification" of the more restrictive elements of FET jurisprudence by investment tribunals which have emphasized the sovereign right to regulate of host States and held that mere changes in the regulatory environment or legitimate regulatory actions as such do not normally constitute violations of FET.[112]

---

[111] Canada Model FIPA 2004; US Model BIT 2004.

[112] See, e.g., *Parkerings v Lithuania*, ICSID Case No. ARB/05/8, Award, 11 September 2007, para. 332: "It is each State's undeniable right and privilege to exercise its sovereign legislative power. A State has the right to enact, modify or cancel a law at its own discretion. Save for the existence of an agreement, in the form of a *stabilisation* clause or otherwise, there is nothing objectionable about the amendment brought to the regulatory framework existing at the time an investor made its investment. As a matter of fact, any businessman or investor knows that laws will evolve over time. What is prohibited however is for a State to act unfairly, unreasonably or inequitably in the exercise of its legislative power." *Plama v Bulgaria*, ICSID Case No. ARB/03/24, Award, 27 August 2008, para. 177: "The stability of the legal framework has been identified as *'an emerging standard of fair and equitable treatment in international law.'* However, the State maintains its legitimate right to regulate, and this right should also be considered when assessing the compliance with the standard of fair and equitable treatment." *Impregilo v Argentina*, ICSID Case No. ARB/07/17, Award, 21 June 2011, para. 290: "In the Tribunal's understanding, fair and equitable treatment cannot be designed to ensure the immutability of the legal order, the economic world and the social universe and play the role assumed by stabilization clauses specifically granted to foreign investors with whom the State has signed investment agreements." *Mobil Investments Canada Inc. & Murphy Oil Corporation v Canada*, ICSID Case No. ARB(AF)/07/4, Decision on Liability and on Principles of Quantum, 22 May 2012, para. 153: "This applicable [FET] standard does not require a State to maintain a stable legal and business environment for investments, if this is intended to suggest that the rules governing an investment are not permitted to change, whether to a significant or modest extent. Article 1105 may protect an investor from changes that give rise to an unstable legal and business environment, but only if those changes may be characterized as arbitrary or grossly unfair or discriminatory, or otherwise inconsistent with the customary international law standard. In a complex international and domestic environment, there is nothing in Article 1105 to prevent a public authority from changing the regulatory environment to take account of new policies and needs, even if some of those changes may have far-reaching consequences and effects, and even if they impose significant additional burdens on an investor. Article 1105 is not, and was never intended to amount to, a guarantee against regulatory change, or to reflect a requirement that an investor is entitled to expect no material changes to the regulatory framework

In fact, the usual short FET clause stipulating that "[e]ach Party shall accord in its territory to investors and to covered investments of the other Party fair and equitable treatment"[113] is accompanied by a paragraph defining a breach of the FET obligation as a

> Measure or series of measures constitut[ing]:
>
> Denial of justice in criminal, civil or administrative proceedings;
>
> Fundamental breach of due process, including a fundamental breach of transparency, in judicial and administrative proceedings;
>
> Manifest arbitrariness;
>
> Targeted discrimination on manifestly wrongful grounds, such as gender, race or religious belief;
>
> Abusive treatment of investors, such as coercion, duress and harassment; or
>
> A breach of any further elements of the fair and equitable treatment obligation adopted by the Parties in accordance with paragraph 3 of this Article.[114]

Apparently, the CETA drafters incorporated many elements found in arbitration practice, though, presumably intentionally, not all of them. For instance, "stability", an element usually identified by investment tribunals in attempts to define the content of FET[115] and normally serving investor interests, is clearly missing in

---

within which an investment is made." *Suez, Sociedad General de Aguas de Barcelona S.A. and Interagua Servicios Integrales de Agua S.A. v Argentina*, ICSID Case No. ARB/03/17, Decision on Liability, 30 July 2010, para. 216: "In interpreting the meaning of 'just' or 'fair and equitable treatment' to be accorded to investors, the Tribunal must balance the legitimate and reasonable expectations of the Claimants with [the] right to regulate the provision of a vital public service." See also Yannaca-Small (2005), Titi (2014), Henckels (2012).

[113] Article X.9(1) Consolidated 2014 CETA text and Article 8.10(1) Revised 2016 CETA text.

[114] Article X.9(2) Consolidated 2014 CETA text and Article 8.10(2) Revised 2016 CETA text.

[115] See e.g. *Occidental Exploration and Petroleum Company v The Republic of Ecuador*, UNCITRAL, Award, 1 July 2004, para. 183: "Although fair and equitable treatment is not defined in the Treaty, the Preamble clearly records the agreement of the parties that such treatment 'is desirable in order to maintain a stable framework for investment and maximum effective utilization of economic resources'. The stability of the legal and business framework is thus an essential element of fair and equitable treatment." See also *CMS Gas Transmission Company v The Republic of Argentina*, ICSID Case No. ARB/01/8, Award, 12 May 2005, para. 276 et seq.: "276. In addition to the specific terms of the Treaty, the significant number of treaties, both bilateral and multilateral, that have dealt with this standard also unequivocally shows that fair and equitable treatment is inseperable (sic!) from stability and predictability. [...] 277. It is not a question of whether the legal framework might need to be frozen as it can always evolve and be adapted to changing circumstances, but neither is it a question of whether the framework can be dispensed with altogether when specific commitments to the contrary have been made. The law of foreign investment and its protection has been developed with the specific objective of avoiding such adverse legal effects." Dolzer and Schreuer (2012), p. 145 et seq.

the draft CETA text. This indicates that the negotiating parties intended not to make the CETA's FET version too "investor-friendly". It seems to underline the intention, expressed in the November 2013 Commission Fact sheet, to "reaffirm the right of the Parties to regulate to pursue legitimate public policy objectives" and to "set out precisely what elements are covered and thus prohibited" by FET in EU investment agreements.[116]

Full Protection and Security Limited to Physical Security

The overall limiting tendency underlying CETA's substantive treatment provisions is also evident in the context of full protection and security (FPS). However, it is not in the sense that FPS would be limited by the customary international law minimum standard, as one might have expected given the NAFTA heritage of such an approach.[117] Rather, the limiting element derives from another strand of FPS jurisprudence. While the CETA article containing FPS, combined with FET, merely requires that "[e]ach Party shall accord in its territory to investors and to covered investments of the other Party [fair and equitable treatment and] full protection and security [...]", paragraph 6 of this article clarifies that "full protection and security" is limited to "physical security".[118] This limitation must be understood against the background of a jurisprudential divide according to which some investment tribunals have held that FPS would be limited to prevent actual physical security of investors and investments,[119] whereas others have considered that the standard would go "beyond physical security."[120]

---

[116]European Commission, Fact sheet, Investment Protection and Investor-to-State Dispute Settlement in EU agreements, November 2013, pp. 2 and 7 et seq.

[117]NAFTA Free Trade Commission, Notes of Interpretation of Certain Chapter 11 Provisions: "The concepts of 'fair and equitable treatment' and 'full protection and security' do not require treatment in addition to or beyond that which is required by the customary international law minimum standard of treatment of aliens." See also, e.g., Salacuse (2010), p. 216; Lorz (2015), p. 766 et seq.

[118]Article X.9(6) Consolidated 2014 CETA text and Article 8.10(5) Revised 2016 CETA text: "For greater certainty, 'full protection and security' refers to the Party's obligations relating to physical security of investors and covered investments."

[119]See, e.g., *Saluka Investments BV (The Netherlands) v The Czech Republic,* Partial Award, 17 March 2006, para. 484: "The practice of arbitral tribunals seems to indicate, however, that the 'full security and protection' clause is not meant to cover just any kind of impairment of an investor's investment, but to protect more specifically the physical integrity of an investment against interference by use of force." *Suez, Sociedad General de Aguas de Barcelona S.A., and InterAgua Servicios Integrales del Agua S.A. v The Argentine Republic*, ICSID Case No. ARB/03/17, Decision on Liability, 30 July 2010, para. 169: "the absence of the word 'full' or 'fully' in the full protection and security provisions [...] supports this view of an obligation limited to providing physical protection and related legal remedies for the Spanish Claimants and their assets."

[120]See, e.g., *Siemens A.G. v Argentina*, ICSID Case No. ARB/02/08, Award, 6 February 2007, para. 303: "the obligation to provide full protection and security [was] wider than 'physical' protection and security" because it was "difficult to understand how the physical security of an intangible asset would be achieved." *Compañiá de Aguas del Aconquija S.A. and Vivendi Universal v Argentine Republic*, ICSID Case No. ARB/97/3, Award, 20 August 2007, para. 7.4.15: "If the

While the clarification in the draft CETA text will ensure that FPS can be invoked only in cases concerning physical interferences with investments, it is questionable whether this will imply a significant reduction of protection for investors since most non-physical interferences often constitute violations of the FET standard.

Expropriation and the Right to Regulate

Similarly, the expropriation provision of CETA, which resembles the typical expropriation clause found in many European BITs,[121] is expressly made subject to clarifications in an annex on expropriation which basically reproduces the shared understandings already expressed in the Canadian[122] Model BIT 2004 and the US Model BITs of 2004 and 2012.[123]

This CETA understanding sets out that a finding of indirect expropriation requires a case-by-case, fact-based inquiry and provides a number of relevant factors, such as the economic impact of the measure, its duration, the extent to which it interferes with "distinct, reasonable investment-backed expectations", and the character of the measure or series of measures, notably their object, context and intent, in order to determine whether specific measures constitute indirect expropriation. Finally, the understanding contains police powers doctrine[124]-inspired language aiming at ensuring that bona fide regulation in the public interest should not be considered expropriatory[125] which in turn is reflective of investment arbitration jurisprudence on the limits of indirect expropriation.[126] While such language

parties to the BIT had intended to limit the obligation to 'physical interferences', they could have done so by including words to that effect in the section. In the absence of such words of limitation, the scope of the Article 5(1) protection should be interpreted to apply to reach any act or measure which deprives an investor's investment of protection and full security, providing, in accordance with the Treaty's specific wording, the act or measure also constitutes unfair and inequitable treatment. Such actions or measures need not threaten physical possession or the legally protected terms of operation of the investment."

[121] Article X.11 Consolidated 2014 CETA text and Article 8.12 Revised 2016 CETA text.

[122] Annex B.13(1) Canada Model BIT 2004.

[123] Annex B US Model BIT 2012.

[124] Mostafa (2008), Bungenberg (2015), p. 28; see also UNCTAD, Expropriation: UNCTAD Series on Issues in International Investment Agreements II, 2012, http://unctad.org/en/Docs/unctaddiaeia2011d7_en.pdf (last accessed 1 March 2017), p. 79.

[125] Annex X.11(3) Consolidated 2014 CETA text and Annex 8-A(3) Revised 2016 CETA text: "For greater certainty, except in the rare circumstance where the impact of the measure or series of measures is so severe in light of its purpose that it appears manifestly excessive, non-discriminatory measures by a Party that are designed and applied to protect legitimate public welfare objectives, such as health, safety and the environment, do not constitute indirect expropriations."

[126] See, e.g., *Telenor v Hungary*, ICSID Case No. ARB/04/15, Award, 13 September 2006, para. 64: "It is well established that the mere exercise by government of regulatory powers that create

will not be able to solve all issues it clearly constitutes helpful guidance to investment tribunals.

The approach also is in line with the November 2013 Commission Factsheet on "Investment Protection and Investor-to-State Dispute Settlement in EU agreements" which specifically stated "that future EU agreements will provide a detailed set of provisions giving guidance to arbitrators on how to decide whether or not a government measure constitutes indirect expropriation. In particular, when the state is protecting the public interest in a non-discriminatory way, the right of the state to regulate should prevail over the economic impact of those measures on the investor."[127] It seems that the Commission thereby adopted not only the Canadian approach, but also followed the wishes of the European Parliament to find a "clear and fair balance between public welfare objectives and private interests" in defining indirect expropriation.[128]

MFN Treatment Excluding Maffezini

Also with regard to the non-discrimination standard of MFN treatment, the CETA text contains two significant limitations, which contrasts with the considerable extension of the national treatment obligation to the pre-investment phase.[129]

Reacting to the uncertainty created by investment tribunals in the aftermath of the *Maffezini* case,[130] whether an MFN clause should permit claimants to invoke more favourable procedural, maybe even jurisdictional,[131] provisions in third

impediments to business or entail the payment of taxes and other levies does not of itself constitute expropriation."

[127]European Commission, Fact sheet, Investment Protection and Investor-to-State Dispute Settlement in EU agreements, November 2013, p. 2.

[128]European Parliament, resolution of 6 April 2011 on the future European international investment policy 2010/2203(INI), para. 19 calling for "protection against direct and indirect expropriation, giving a definition that establishes a clear and fair balance between public welfare objectives and private interests."

[129]Article X.6(1) National Treatment Consolidated 2014 CETA text and Article 8.6(1) Revised 2016 CETA text: "Each Party shall accord to investors of the other Party and to covered investments, treatment no less favourable than the treatment it accords, in like situations to its own investors and to their investments with respect to the establishment, acquisition, expansion, conduct, operation, management, maintenance, use, enjoyment and sale or disposal of their investments in its territory." This follows the Canada/US approach to ensure market access/admission obligations by extending national treatment to the establishment phase. See, e.g., Article 3(1) US Model BIT 2012. See also Dolzer and Schreuer (2012), p. 89; Reinisch (2015), p. 816.

[130]*Emilio Agustín Maffezini v Spain*, ICSID Case No. ARB/97/7, Decision on Jurisdiction, 25 January 2000.

[131]*RosInvestCo UK Ltd. v The Russian Federation*, SCC Case No. Arb. V079/2005, Award on Jurisdiction 2007.

country BITs or at least to overcome procedural obstacles, such as waiting periods,[132] or whether it would not permit them to do so,[133] the MFN clause of the CETA expressly excludes ISA.[134]

Secondly, the CETA MFN clause contains innovative language aimed at preventing not only the "importation" of more favourable dispute settlement provisions, but also more generally of better treatment standards contained in third country IIAs,[135] something routinely allowed in investment arbitration.[136] Thereby, CETA will ensure that the specifically negotiated limitations of the scope of FET, FPS and indirect expropriation cannot be circumvented by reliance on more favourable provisions in third country IIAs.

Overall, the substantive treatment provisions in CETA demonstrate a very cautious approach to investment protection, which has led commentators to conclude that they will provide only a low level of protection and a large freedom of host States to regulate.[137]

---

[132]See, e.g., *Siemens A.G. v The Argentine Republic,* ICSID Case No. ARB/02/8, Decision on Jurisdiction, 3 August 2004; *Impreglio S.p.A. v Argentine Republic*, ICSID Case No. ARB/07/17, Award, 21 June 2011; *Hochtief AG v Argentina,* ICSID Case No. ARB/07/31, Decision on Jurisdiction, 24 October 2011; *Gas Natural SDG, S.A. v The Argentine Republic*, ICSID Case No. ARB/03/10, Decision of the Tribunal on Preliminary Questions on Jurisdiction, 17 June 2005; *Camuzzi International S.A. v The Argentine Republic,* ICSID Case No. ARB/03/2, Decision on Objection to Jurisdiction, 11 May 2005; *National Grid plc v The Argentine Republic*, Decision on Jurisdiction, 20 June 2006; *AWG Group Ltd. v The Argentine Republic*, Decision on Jurisdiction, 3 August 2006; *Teinver S.A., Transportes de Cercanías S.A. and Autobuses Urbanos del Sur S.A.* v *The Argentine Republic*, ICSID Case No. ARB/09/1, Decision on Jurisdiction, 21 December 2012.

[133]In *Plama Consortium Limited v Republic of Bulgaria*, ICSID Case No. ARB/03/24, Decision on Jurisdiction, 8 February 2005, para. 223, the tribunal held that "an MFN provision in a basic treaty does not incorporate by reference dispute settlement provisions in whole or in part set forth in another treaty, unless the MFN provision in the basic treaty leaves no doubt that the Contracting Parties intended to incorporate them." See also *Daimler Financial Services AG v The Argentine Republic*, ICSID Case No. ARB/05/1, Decision on Jurisdiction, 22 August 2012. The tribunal in *Wintershall Aktiengesellschaft v Argentine Republic*, ICSID Case No. ARB/04/14, Award, 8 December 2008, even denied the avoidance of waiting periods.

[134]Article X.7(4) Consolidated 2014 CETA text and Article 8.7(4) Revised 2016 CETA text: "For greater certainty, the 'treatment' referred to in Paragraph 1 and 2 does not include investor-to-state dispute settlement procedures provided for in other international investment treaties and other trade agreements."

[135]Article X.7(4) Consolidated 2014 CETA text and Article 8.7(4) Revised 2016 CETA text: "Substantive obligations in other international investment treaties and other trade agreements do not in themselves constitute 'treatment', and thus cannot give rise to a breach of this article, absent measures adopted by a Party pursuant to such obligations."

[136]See e.g. *Berschader v Russian Federation*, SCC Case No. 080/2004, Award, 21 April 2006, para. 179: "It is universally agreed that the very essence of an MFN provision in a BIT is to afford to investors all material protection provided by subsequent treaties [...]." *MTD Equity v Chile*, ICSID Case No. ARB/01/7, Award, 25 May 2004, para. 100: "[T]he Tribunal considers it appropriate to examine the MFN clause in the BIT and satisfy itself that its terms permit the use of the provisions of the Denmark BIT and Croatia BIT as a legal basis for the claims submitted to its decision."

[137]See Schill S, Auswirkungen der Bestimmungen zum Investitionsschutz und zu den Investor-Staat-Schiedsverfahren im Entwurf des Freihandelsabkommens zwischen der EU und Kanada

6.1.2 Treaty Interpretation by the Contracting Parties

While the more detailed formulation of the precise scope of the substantive protection standards is guided by the idea to secure the "right to regulate" of host States, the same purpose is intended to be served by a legal device allowing the parties to the CETA to amend the treaty in a flexible way through a joint committee without the need to resort to formal renegotiation.

CETA will set up a Trade Committee empowered to adopt interpretations and amendments of some of the CETA provisions.[138] With regard to the investment chapter, CETA also envisages a Committee on Services and Investment which is intended to serve as a forum for consultations between the parties on "possible improvements of this Chapter, in particular in the light of experience and developments in other international fora."[139] In addition to its various advisory functions in the field of the planned appellate structure of CETA,[140] the Committee on Services and Investment should have the power to recommend to the Trade Committee interpretations and clarifications of substantive investment protection standards of the CETA.

This emphasizes the mutual interdependence of treaty-makers and investment tribunals in particular in regard to the FET clause by offering the Contracting Parties (through the Trade and the Committee on Services and Investment) a possibility to review and clarify the specific content of FET by adding further elements.[141] This is an interesting alternative to the authoritative interpretation approach pursued by Article 1131 NAFTA which has led to a number of sometimes controversial interpretations, including the one that stipulated that NAFTA's FET does not go beyond the customary international law minimum standard.[142]

(CETA) auf den Handlungsspielraum des Gesetzgebers (Kurzgutachten), 22 September 2014, http://www.bmwi.de/Redaktion/DE/Downloads/C-D/ceta-gutachten-investitionsschutz.html (last accessed 1 March 2017), p. 32. Similarly, Tietje C and Baetens F, The Impact of Investor-State-Dispute Settlement (ISDS) in the Transatlantic Trade and Investment Partnerships, 24 June 2014, http://www.rijksoverheid.nl/bestanden/documenten-en-publicaties/rapporten/2014/06/24/the-impact-of-investor-state-dispute-settlement-isds-in-the-ttip/the-impact-of-investor-state-dispute-settlement-isds-in-the-ttip.pdf (last accessed 1 March 2017), paras. 108, 111, 115 and 116.

[138]Pursuant to Article X.02 of the final provisions of the Consolidated 2014 CETA text, while the Parties may amend the agreement itself, the "Trade Committee may decide to amend the Annexes, Appendices, Protocols and Notes of this Agreement. The Parties may approve the decision subject to their respective applicable internal requirements and procedures. The decision shall enter into force on such date as the Parties may agree."

[139]Article X.42 Consolidated 2014 CETA text and Article 8.44(1) Revised 2016 CETA text.

[140]Article X.42 Consolidated 2014 CETA text.

[141]Article X.9(3) Consolidated 2014 CETA text and Article 8.10(3) Revised 2016 CETA text: "The Parties shall regularly, or upon request of a Party, review the content of the obligation to provide fair and equitable treatment. The Committee on Services and Investment may develop recommendations in this regard and submit them to the Trade Committee for decision."

[142]NAFTA Free Trade Commission Clarifications Related to NAFTA chapter 11, Decisions of 31 July 2001, http://www.worldtradelaw.net/nafta/chap11interp.pdf (lasst accessed 1 March

But the CETA text also follows the NAFTA experience which allows for authoritative treaty interpretation by the Contracting Parties,[143] in providing that

> [w]here serious concerns arise as regards matters of interpretation that may affect investment, the Committee on Services and Investment may, pursuant to Article X.42(3)(a), recommend to the Trade Committee the adoption of interpretations of the Agreement. An interpretation adopted by the Trade Committee shall be binding on a Tribunal established under this Chapter. The Trade Committee may decide that an interpretation shall have binding effect from a specific date.[144]

Thereby the parties will be able to correct "unexpected" and/or otherwise "unwelcome" interpretations of substantive treaty provisions by investment tribunals.

6.2 *Specific Investor-State Arbitration—Relevant Aspects of the 2014 CETA*

In addition to spelling out very clearly in regard to the applicable substantive investment protection standards that investment tribunals should not limit the policy space of host States, the Consolidated 2014 CETA Text also specifically addressed a number of the major points of criticisms raised against the system of ISA itself, ranging from the perceived or actual lack of transparency, of appellate review, of arbitrator independence or pro-investor or pro-State bias, etc.

6.2.1 The Relationship to the National Judiciary/Avoidance of Parallel Proceedings

The argument that ISA allows investors to by-pass or circumvent domestic adjudication is often an over-simplification. While ISA is frequently portrayed as a

2017): "B.1. Article 1105(1) prescribes the customary international law minimum standard of treatment of aliens as the minimum standard of treatment to be afforded to investments of investors of another Party. 2. The concepts of "fair and equitable treatment" and "full protection and security" do not require treatment in addition to or beyond that which is required by the customary international law minimum standard of treatment of aliens."

[143] Article 2001 NAFTA established the Free Trade Commission. According to Article 1131(2) NAFTA, interpretations adopted by the Free Trade Commission shall be binding upon arbitral tribunals constituted under NAFTA chapter 11. See also Matiation (2003), Brower (2006), Brower (2003), Roberts (2010), Kaufmann-Kohler (2011).

[144] Article X.27(2) Consolidated 2014 CETA text and Article 8.31(3) Revised 2016 CETA text, referring to the "CETA Joint Committee" instead of the "Trade Committee".

dangerous avoidance of domestic courts,[145] one should not forget that one of the initial purposes of ISA was exactly to have access to a more neutral international forum instead of the local courts of the host State that is a party to the dispute and, of course, to serve as an alternative to diplomatic protection.

A related issue is the question whether investors should have both domestic and international recourse. Traditional rules of diplomatic protection in fact required the exhaustion of local remedies before international dispute settlement options could be accessed. While this requirement is expressly dispensed with in the ICSID Convention in general,[146] also most other investment tribunals have permitted investors to sue without requiring them to exhaust local remedies. Some IIAs expressly address the issue of parallel litigation and try to design rules to avoid such duplication, which range from fork-in-the-road to exhaustion of local remedies clauses.[147]

Also the CETA text contains language to this effect. It neither requires nor prohibits investors to first litigate their claims in domestic fora; rather, it merely seeks to prevent parallel proceedings by permitting access to ISA only when a final determination has been made or the investor claims have been effectively withdrawn.[148]

---

[145]See e.g., Open letter by the Alliance for Justice: "This practice [of ISA] threatens domestic sovereignty and weakens the rule of law by giving corporations special legal rights, allowing them to ignore domestic courts, and subjecting the United States to extrajudicial private arbitration." See also Broß (2015).

[146]Article 26 ICSID Convention: "Consent of the parties to arbitration under this Convention shall, unless otherwise stated, be deemed consent to such arbitration to the exclusion of any other remedy. A Contracting State may require the exhaustion of local administrative or judicial remedies as a condition of its consent to arbitration under this Convention".

[147]See Schreuer (2005), Schreuer (2004), Douglas (2009), p. 152. See also Article 26 ICSID Convention: "A Contracting State may require the exhaustion of local administrative or judicial remedies as a condition of its consent to arbitration under this Convention."

[148]Article X.21 Procedural and Other Requirements for the Submission of a Claim to Arbitration, Consolidated 2014 CETA text: "An investor may submit a claim to arbitration under Article X.22 (Submission of a Claim to Arbitration) only if the investor: [...] where it has initiated a claim or proceeding seeking compensation or damages before a tribunal or court under domestic or international law with respect to any measure alleged to constitute a breach referred to in its claim to arbitration, provides a declaration that: a final award, judgment or decision has been made; or it has withdrawn any such claim or proceeding; [...]." And see the stricter requirement in Article 8.22(1) Revised 2016 CETA text: "An investor may only submit a claim pursuant to Article 8.23 if the investor: [...] (f) withdraws or discontinues any existing proceeding before a tribunal or court under domestic or international law with respect to a measure alleged to constitute a breach referred to in its claim; and (g) waives its right to initiate any claim or proceeding before a tribunal or court under domestic or international law with respect to a measure alleged to constitute a breach referred to in its claim."

A related issue is the fear that ISA may be used to circumvent the domestic judiciary for purely contractual claims against host States is often voiced.[149] In fact, this is a complex problem that needs careful attention.

The main tool to raise claims that are usually settled by domestic courts before investment tribunals are so-called umbrella or observance of obligations clauses which require States to respect the obligations they entered into with regard to a specific investment.[150] A good example is found in the ECT to which the EU is a party. It provides that host States shall observe "any obligations" they have "entered into with an Investor".[151] In other words, umbrella clauses potentially bring contractual and other individual obligations within the ambit of an IIA and thus make them enforceable under ISA.

In this context, it is important to note that Canada has traditionally resisted umbrella clauses and that while the "Draft CETA Investment Text of 21 November 2013" contained an EU suggestion for an umbrella clause,[152] the final draft agreement does not contain such a clause.[153] This implies that contractual disagreements and disputes can also not be brought under the protection of CETA.

Further, the CETA is fairly unambiguous in permitting only so-called treaty claims.[154] Hence, this provision excludes investment disputes concerning contractual issues from being litigated under the ISDS chapter of the treaty. This is evident

---

[149]See e.g., Open letter by the Alliance for Justice: "This practice [of ISA] threatens domestic sovereignty and weakens the rule of law by giving corporations special legal rights, allowing them to ignore domestic courts, and subjecting the United States to extrajudicial private arbitration." See also Broß (2015).

[150]See Dolzer and Schreuer (2012), p. 166 et seq. With regard to the question whether an umbrella clause transforms the applicable law to the underlying obligation, there has been a controversial discussion; on this issue see Sasson (2010), p. 180 et seq.

[151]See e.g. Article 10(1) last sentence ECT: "Each Contracting Party shall observe any obligations it has entered into with an Investor or an Investment of an Investor of any other Contracting Party."

[152]In November 2013, the Trade Justice Network leaked draft texts on CETA at http://www.tradejustice.ca/leakeddocs (accessed in early 2014—those documents have been removed from the internet since). The "Draft CETA Investment Chapter" contained the following suggestion on p. 13: "[EU: Article X Each Party shall observe any specific written obligation it has entered into with regard to an investor of the other Party or an investment of such an investor.]" This would have been in accordance with the EU Commission's initial position on this issue, see European Commission, COM (2010) 343 final, p. 8.

[153]See Lévesque and Newcombe (2013), p. 60 et seq. Also, NAFTA's chapter 11 on investments does not contain such a clause.

[154]Article X.17 Consolidated 2014 CETA text: "Without prejudice to the rights and obligations of the Parties under Chapter [XY](Dispute Settlement), an investor of a Party may submit to arbitration under this Section a claim that the respondent has breached an obligation under: Section 3 (Non-Discriminatory Treatment) of this Chapter, with respect to the expansion, conduct, operation, management, maintenance, use, enjoyment and sale or disposal of its covered investment; or Section 4 (Investment Protection) of this Chapter; and where the investor claims to have suffered loss or damage as a result of the alleged breach." So similar in Article 8.18(1) Revised 2016 CETA text.

when comparing the current formulation with broader dispute settlement clauses in other IIAs.[155]

6.2.2 An Appellate Mechanism

The 2014 CETA draft also reacted to a political demand countering the threat of an unpredictable and inconsistent jurisprudence, by envisaging the creation of an appellate mechanism, similar to some of the new US IIAs and the US Model BIT.[156] The 2014 CETA draft specifically entrusted the Committee on Services and Investment to provide a consultation forum for the CETA parties to consider whether such a mechanism "to review, on points of law, awards rendered by a tribunal" pursuant to the ISDS chapter should be created in the future.[157]

This idea relates to a long-standing debate in investment law circles about the feasibility and usefulness of the creation of a "second instance" in this form of dispute settlement.[158] Though clearly prolonging proceedings and leading to higher litigation costs, it is often asserted that an appellate mechanism would foster the uniformity and predictability of the outcomes of investment disputes. In this context, the WTO dispute settlement system which provides for an appellate mechanism in the form of the Appellate Body since 1995[159] is frequently invoked as a reference point.[160]

Nevertheless, the 2014 draft CETA text fell short of establishing an appellate mechanism. Rather, it merely outlined some of the main features mentioned in the treaty mandate given to the Committee on Services and Investment to be taken into account when designing such a system, such as:

[155] E.g. Article 139 of the 2009 China-Peru Free Trade Agreement which empowers the arbitral tribunal to decide on "[a]ny dispute between an investor of one Party and the other Party in connection with an investment in the territory of the other Party". Some treaties opt for an median approach by providing for an exhaustive list of causes of actions covered by the ISDS mechanism and by defining the breaches listed therein, see e.g. Article 15.15 of the 2003 Singapore-United States FTA: "(a) the claimant, on its own behalf, may submit to arbitration under this Section a claim: (i) that the respondent has breached (A) an obligation under Section B, (B) an investment authorization, or (C) an investment agreement; and (ii) that the claimant has incurred loss or damage by reason of, or arising out of, that breach."

[156] Article 28(10) US Model BIT 2012; United States—Singapore Free Trade Agreement, signed 6 May 2003, entry into force 1 January 2004; see also United States—Morocco Free Trade Agreement, signed 15 June 2004, entry into force 1 January 2006.

[157] Article X.42 Consolidated 2014 CETA text.

[158] See, e.g., Tams (2006), Tams (2007), Sauvant and Chiswick-Patterson (2008), Platt (2013).

[159] WTO Dispute Settlement Understanding, 33 ILM 1226 (1994).

[160] The identical or at least similar composition of the actual decision-makers should enhance the likelihood of a consistent case-law. Apparently, the major advantage expected from introducing an appellate mechanism lies in securing more coherence and consistency of investment awards. Clearly, appeals to be decided by a limited number of largely identical decision-makers are likely to be consistent.

the nature and composition of an appellate mechanism;

the applicable scope and standard of review; transparency of proceedings of an appellate mechanism;

the effect of decisions by an appellate mechanism;

the relationship of review by an appellate mechanism to the arbitration rules that may be selected under Article X.22 (Submission of a Claim to Arbitration); and

the relationship of review by an appellate mechanism to domestic laws and international law on the enforcement of arbitral awards.[161]

As discussed below, it is this appellate mechanism that forms a core aspect of the proposed "Investment Court System" in the 2016 revised CETA text, based on the TTIP proposal.

6.2.3 Arbitration Made More Transparent

One of the main public concerns about ISA is its perceived lack of transparency. ISA is often portrayed as secret justice by private arbitrators taking place behind closed doors and leaving the public affected by its outcome in the dark.[162] This criticism ignores major changes in investment arbitration over the last 10–15 years which have developed the commercial arbitration hallmark of confidentiality into far-reaching transparency demands. Today all ICSID cases, the primary ISA venue, are publicly registered with basic information about the parties, the claims, etc. A large majority of ICSID awards and annulment committee decisions are available on the ICSID homepage as well as on other publicly accessible internet sites.[163] Further, many ISDS institutions have adopted new rules on transparency such as the 2006 Amendments to the ICSID Rules[164] or the 2013 UNCITRAL Transparency

[161] Article X.42 Consolidated 2014 CETA text.

[162] See DePalma A, Nafta's Powerful Little Secret: Obscure Tribunals Settle Disputes, but Go Too Far, Critics Say, New York Times, 11 March 2001, http://www.nytimes.com/2001/03/11/business/nafta-s-powerful-little-secret-obscure-tribunals-settle-disputes-but-go-too-far.html (last accessed 1 March 2017).

[163] See, e.g., "investment treaty arbitration law", http://www.italaw.com/ (last accessed 1 March 2017); "investment claims", http://oxia.ouplaw.com/ (last accessed 1 March 2017).

[164] Amendments to the ICSID Rules and Regulations and the Additional Facility Rules, effective 10 April 2006, http://www.worldbank.org/icsid/basic doc/CRR_English-final.pdf (last accessed 1 March 2017).

Rules.[165] CETA declares these UNCITRAL Transparency Rules applicable to CETA dispute settlement[166]; it even foresees the possibility of open hearings.[167]

6.2.4 Arbitrator Independence and Ethics

Linked to a perceived lack of transparency, critics of ISA also often call for "ethical requirements for arbitrators". Such demands seem to be inspired by concerns about private justice operating in secrecy and thus beyond scrutiny, as it was first formulated in the context of the NAFTA anti-ISDS discussion.[168] The lack of oversight of private lawyers deciding ISA claims is meanwhile equally deplored in the European debate.[169] As already mentioned, many of these concerns have been taken into account by a number of amendments to the arbitrator ethics rules.[170] To further strengthen this development it should be noted that, for instance, in the EU-Singapore FTA, negotiated in parallel to CETA, a code of conduct for arbitrators has been included.[171] In substance, however, this code does not add much to the existing obligations under most arbitration rules demanding independence and impartiality of arbitrators.[172]

---

[165]UNCITRAL Rules on Transparency in Treaty-based Investor-State Arbitration, adopted by A/RES/68/109, 16 December 2013, http://www.uncitral.org/pdf/english/texts/arbitration/rules-on-transparency/Rules-on-Transparency-E.pdf (last accessed 1 March 2017).

[166]Article X.33(1) Consolidated 2014 CETA text and Article 8.36(1) Revised 2016 CETA text.

[167]See Article X.33(5) Consolidated CETA text and Article 8.36(5) Revised 2016 CETA text: "Hearings shall be open to the public. The Tribunal shall determine, in consultation with the disputing parties, the appropriate logistical arrangements to facilitate public access to such hearings. Where the tribunal determines that there is a need to protect confidential or protected information, it shall make the appropriate arrangements to hold in private that part of the hearing requiring such protection."

[168]See DePalma, Nafta's Powerful Little Secret: Obscure Tribunals Settle Disputes, but Go Too Far, Critics Say. New York Times, 11 March 2001, http://www.nytimes.com/2001/03/11/business/nafta-s-powerful-little-secret-obscure-tribunals-settle-disputes-but-go-too-far.html (last accessed 1 March 2017).

[169]See e.g. Monbiot G, This transatlantic trade deal is a full-frontal assault on democracy, The Guardian, 4 November 2013, http://www.theguardian.com/commentisfree/2013/nov/04/us-trade-deal-full-frontal-assault-on-democracy (last accessed 1 March 2017); Muchlinski P, Muir Watt H, Schepel H and Van Harten G, Statement of Concern about Planned Provisions on Investment Protection and Investor-State Dispute Settlement (ISDS) in the Transatlantic Trade and Investment Partnership (TTIP), 2014, http://www.kent.ac.uk/law/downloads/ttip_isds_public_consultation_final.pdf (last accessed 1 March 2017), p. 20.

[170]See, *inter alia*, Article 6(7) UNCITRAL Arbitration Rules 2010; Article 14(1) ICSID Convention; see also IBA Guidelines on Conflicts of Interest in International Arbitration, approved on 22 May 2004 by the Council of the International Bar Association, http://www.ibanet.org/Publications/publications_IBA_guides_and_free_materials.aspx (last accessed 1 March 2017).

[171]Annex 9-F to the ISDS Section of the EU-Singapore Free Trade Agreement.

[172]Annex 9-F to the ISDS Section of the EU-Singapore Free Trade Agreement, 2. Responsibilities to the process: "Throughout the proceedings, every candidate and arbitrator shall avoid

6.2.5 Limitation of Claims to Lawfully Made Investments/Avoidance of Frivolous and Harassing Claims

ISA critics often deplore the harassment factor of investment claims forcing host States to take out expensive legal representation. Thus, various demands have been made to ensure that unmeritorious, frivolous as well as claims based on unlawfully made investments should be excluded from benefiting from ISA.

A number of legal devices have already been developed both in IIA treaty-making as well as in arbitral practice. So-called “in accordance with host State law” clauses in IIAs as well as an inherent legality requirement of the notion of an “investment” under Article 25 ICSID Convention have been used to extend ISA protection only to lawfully made investments and tribunals have used their discretionary powers to allocate costs in order to “punish” “frivolous” or “harassing” litigants.

CETA incorporates some of these developments and makes them mandatory for ISA pursuant to its rules. An interesting provision thus limiting the scope of potential arbitration claims states:

> For greater certainty, an investor may not submit a claim to arbitration under this Section where the investment has been made through fraudulent misrepresentation, concealment, corruption, or conduct amounting to an abuse of process.[173]

What this novel provision aims at is the exclusion of claims such as those made by investors in cases like *Inceysa v. El Salvador*[174] and *Phoenix v. Czech Republic* where it has been argued that the investments had been made in an unlawful way.[175] In those cases the claims were held inadmissible because they were considered to be contrary to an “in accordance with host State law” clause. However, a closer analysis of, in particular, the *Inceysa* case demonstrates that such reasoning was a bit complicated and not wholly convincing.[176] Also the *Phoenix* award, with its

---

impropriety and the appearance of impropriety, shall be independent and impartial, shall avoid direct and indirect conflicts of interests and shall observe high standards of conduct so that the integrity and impartiality of the dispute settlement mechanism is preserved. Arbitrators shall not take instructions from any organisation or government with regard to matters before a tribunal. Former arbitrators must comply with the obligations established in paragraphs 15, 16, 17 and 18 of this Code of Conduct.”

[173] Article X.17(3) Consolidated 2014 CETA text and Article 8.18(3) Revised 2016 CETA text.

[174] *Inceysa Vallisoletana S.L. v Republic of El Salvador*, ICSID Case No. ARB/03/26, Award, 2 August 2006.

[175] *Phoenix Action, Ltd. v Czech Republic*, ICSID Case No. ARB/06/5, Award, 15 April 2009.

[176] In its scrutiny whether the investment had been made in accordance with the law of the host State, the tribunal did not restrict itself to a consideration of the law of El Salvador. Instead, it reasoned that—because treaties formed part of the law of El Salvador—the BIT with its reference to generally recognized rules and principles of international law allowed it to look at these sources in order to establish the legality or illegality of the investment. Relying on a number of general principles of law, such as *Nemo Auditur Propriam Turpitudinem Allegans*, the tribunal found, *inter alia*, “that the foreign investor cannot seek to benefit from an investment effectuated by means of

enlargement of the *Salini* criteria[177] by an "in accordance with host State law" and a bona fide requirement[178] has remained controversial.[179]

The above-quoted CETA language avoids these uncertainties by clearly establishing that fraud, concealment, corruption, or other abusive conduct deprive investors of access to ISA. In addition, CETA requires an investment, more generally, to be "made in accordance with the applicable law at that time" in order to constitute a "covered investment" for the purpose of the investment chapter.[180] The draft CETA text furthers aims at excluding or at least limiting unfounded claims or abusive litigation by investors by adopting the "loser pays" principle.[181] Further, the CETA text contains two provisions which are intended to allow ISA tribunals to dismiss claims which are "manifestly without legal merit"[182] or otherwise unsuitable to lead to a finding of liability.[183] Practice under the

one or several illegal acts and, consequently, enjoy the protection granted by the host State, such as access to international arbitration to resolve disputes, because it is evident that its act had a fraudulent origin and, as provided by the legal maxim, nobody can benefit from his own fraud". *Inceysa Vallisoletana S.L. v Republic of El Salvador*, ICSID Case No. ARB/03/26, Award, 2 August 2006, para. 242.

[177] *Salini Costruttori S.p.A. and Italstrade S.p.A. v Kingdom of Morocco*, ICSID Case No. ARB/00/4, Decision on Jurisdiction, 23 July 2001, para. 52.

[178] *Phoenix Action, Ltd. v Czech Republic*, ICSID Case No. ARB/06/5, Award, 15 April 2009, para. 114: "1 – a contribution in money or other assets; 2 – a certain duration; 3 – an element of risk; 4 – an operation made in order to develop an economic activity in the host State; 5 – assets invested in accordance with the laws of the host State; 6 – assets invested *bona fide*."

[179] See *Saba Fakes v Republic of Turkey*, ICSID Case No. ARB/07/20, Award, 14 July 2010, para. 110: "the criteria of (i) a contribution, (ii) a certain duration, and (iii) an element of risk, are both necessary and sufficient to define an investment within the framework of the ICSID Convention. In the Tribunal's opinion, this approach reflects an objective definition of 'investment' that embodies specific criteria corresponding to the ordinary meaning of the term 'investment', without doing violence either to the text or the object and purpose of the ICSID Convention." *Deutsche Bank AG v Democratic Socialist Republic of Sri Lanka*, ICSID Case No. ARB/09/2, Award, 31 October 2012, para. 295: "The development of ICSID case law suggests that only three of the above criteria, namely contribution, risk and duration should be used as the benchmarks of investment, without a separate criterion of contribution to the economic development of the host State and without reference to a regularity of profit and return. It should also be recalled that the existence of an investment must be assessed at its inception and not with hindsight."

[180] Article X.3 Consolidated 2014 CETA text and Article 8.1 Revised 2016 CETA text.

[181] Article X.36(5) CETA Consolidated 2014 CETA text and Article 8.39(5) Revised 2016 CETA text, provide that an ISDS tribunal "shall" order that the costs of arbitration be borne by the unsuccessful disputing party.

[182] Article X.29(1) Consolidated 2014 CETA text and Article 8.32(1) Revised 2016 CETA text: "The respondent may, no later than 30 days after the constitution of the tribunal, and in any event before the first session of the Tribunal, file an objection that a claim is manifestly without legal merit."

[183] Article X.30(1) Consolidated 2014 CETA text and Article 8.33(1) Revised 2016 CETA text: "Without prejudice to a tribunal's authority to address other objections as a preliminary question or to a respondent's right to raise any such objections at any appropriate time, the Tribunal shall address and decide as a preliminary question any objection by the respondent that, as a matter of

comparable ICSID standard, introduced by the 2006 amendments to the ICSID Arbitration Rules,[184] shows that investment tribunals are using this rule to screen out manifestly ill-founded claims prior at an early stage.[185]

6.2.6 Other Procedural Investor-State Arbitration Innovations

Further, the CETA negotiators included alternative dispute resolution mechanisms like mediation or non-disputing party participation through amicus curiae briefs. Most interesting in this context is probably the idea of an obligatory alternative dispute settlement procedure preceding recourse to ISA. The overarching goal seems to be the prevention of arbitral proceedings by way of amicable settlement of disputes. In this connection, the CETA contains elaborate provisions on "Consultations"[186] as well as on "Mediation".[187] CETA includes an innovative provision on alternative dispute settlement by providing for a permanent option of mediation,[188] clearly inspired by the WTO conciliation/mediation possibilities which are also available during the entire process of settling trade disputes.[189] Additionally, Annex III to CETA entitled "Mediation Procedure" provides detailed procedural guidelines for the finding of mutually agreed solutions through mediation. While the extremely short time-period of 60 days[190] does not appear to provide a realistic option for the resolution of often highly technical and complex investment disputes,

law, a claim, or any part thereof, submitted pursuant to Article X.22 (Submission of a Claim to Arbitration) is not a claim for which an award in favour of the claimant may be made under this Section, even if the facts alleged were assumed to be true."

[184]2006 Amendments to the ICSID Rules and Regulations and the Additional Facility Rules – Rule 41(5) permits parties within 30 days after the constitution of the tribunal to object to claims that are "manifestly without legal merit". See also Parra (2004), Antonietti (2006).

[185]See *Trans-Global Petroleum, Inc. v Jordan*, ICSID Case No. ARB/07/25, Decision on the Respondent's Objection under Rule 41(5) of the ICSID Arbitration Rules, 12 May 2008, in which some claims were dismissed as "manifestly without legal merit".

[186]Article X.18 Consolidated 2014 CETA text and Article 8.19 Revised 2016 CETA text: "Any dispute should as far as possible be settled amicably. Such a settlement may be agreed at any time, including after the arbitration has been commenced. Unless the disputing parties agree to a longer period, consultations shall be held within 60 days of the submission of the request for consultations pursuant to paragraph 3."

[187]Article 8.20(1) Revised 2016 CETA text.

[188]Article X.19 Consolidated CETA text and Article 8.20 Revised 2016 CETA text: "The disputing parties may at any time agree to have recourse to mediation."

[189]See Article 5.1 WTO Dispute Settlement Understanding: "Good offices, conciliation and mediation are procedures that are undertaken voluntarily if the parties to the dispute so agree."

[190]Article X.19(4) Consolidated 2014 CETA text and Article 8.20(4) Revised 2016 CETA text: "The disputing parties shall endeavour to reach a resolution to the dispute within 60 days from the appointment of the mediator."

this language is clearly hortatory only and will not prevent disputing parties from continuing to engage in mediation.

7 The September 2015 TTIP Proposal

Many of the ISA ideas formulated in the draft CETA and the EU-Singapore agreement were taken up and further refined in the mid-September 2015 "Commission draft text TTIP – investment".[191] Apparently without any prior consultation with the US negotiating partner,[192] the EU Commission integrated the demands for a permanent investment court raised by the Socialists and Democrats in the European Parliament as well as by many TTIP critical voices in Europe into a new proposal for an investment chapter of TTIP. The most remarkable part of that proposal which reinforces the idea of "taming" the unpredictable outcomes of ISA is the idea of an investment court to handle future investment disputes.

But the 2015 TTIP draft text on investment also contains a few additions on substantive issues aiming at preserving the right to regulate and at clarifying that investor protection should not be too high. For instance, a new article specifically states that all protection standards in the investment chapter shall not affect the sovereign "right to regulate" of host States and to pursue legitimate policy objectives.[193] Countering the frequently heard,[194] but erroneous[195] criticism that ISA would offer a right of investors to sue when they consider their profits reduced, the proposal clarifies that none of the investment protection standards should be interpreted as an implied stabilization clause that would trigger a right to recover

[191]Commission draft text TTIP – investment, 16 September 2015, http://trade.ec.europa.eu/doclib/docs/2015/september/tradoc_153807.pdf (last accessed 1 March 2017).

[192]According to the Commission the document "is not a formal text proposal to the United States in the TTIP negotiations but an internal document of the European Union. The Commission will consult the EU's Member States in the Council and will discuss the proposal with the European Parliament before presenting a formal text proposal to the United States." Commission draft text TTIP – investment, p. 1.

[193]Article 2(1) Commission draft text TTIP – investment: "The provisions of this section shall not affect the right of the Parties to regulate within their territories through measures necessary to achieve legitimate policy objectives, such as the protection of public health, safety, environment or public morals, social or consumer protection or promotion and protection of cultural diversity."

[194]Open letter by the Alliance for Justice, http://www.afj.org/wp-content/uploads/2015/03/ISDS-Letter-3.11.pdf (last accessed 1 March 2017).

[195]Open letter by law professors, 7 April 2015, https://www.mcgill.ca/fortier-chair/files/fortier-chair/isds_letter-april_20_final.docx (last accessed 1 March 2017), p. 2: "It is not correct that investment treaty arbitration permits corporations to initiate dispute settlement against governments 'for actions that allegedly cause a loss of profit for the corporation'. 'Lost profits' is merely a measure of damages, not a cause of action, which must be predicated on allegedly wrongful government acts, such as discriminating against foreigners or failing to provide them with due process, that violate the express terms of a treaty."

expected lost profits if breached.[196] It even contains a *Micula*-inspired[197] clause pursuant to which State aid should become insulated from investment law to the effect that the latter cannot lead to an obligation to compensate for the discontinuance of the granting of subsidies.[198]

The investment court ideas are found in Section 3 of the September 2015 draft text TTIP.[199] It contains a number of further procedural details aiming at embedding the new "Investment Court System" into the broader system of investment dispute settlement and at further eliminating the risk of too many claims.

7.1 The New Two-Tier Permanent "Investment Court System"

The major novelty of the Commission proposal is the idea to set up both a Tribunal of First Instance and an Appeal Tribunal to hear investment claims brought under the TTIP. These tribunals are in fact hybrids between courts and arbitral tribunals. They consist of appointed "judges" serving for renewable 6-year terms, but they render "awards" in order to make them enforceable under the rules of the ICSID Convention or, more likely, under the New York Convention.[200]

Qualifications for appointment resemble that of other international courts and tribunals by requiring specific knowledge in the field.[201] Interestingly, the demand to limit it to judges and academics (apparently in order to exclude practising

[196]Article 2(2) Commission draft text TTIP – investment: "For greater certainty, the provisions of this section shall not be interpreted as a commitment from a Party that it will not change the legal and regulatory framework, including in a manner that may negatively affect the operation of covered investments or the investor's expectations of profits."

[197]In *Ioan Micula, Viorel Micula, S.C. European Food S.A, S.C. Starmill S.R.L. and S.C. Multipack S.R.L. v Romania*, ICSID Case No. ARB/05/20, Final Award, 11 December 2013, an ICSID tribunal came to the conclusion that the termination of a state aid program constituted a violation of FET. When the investors tried to enforce their award the Commission took various steps to prevent this; Chevry (2015), p. 114 et seq.

[198]Article 2(4) Commission draft text TTIP – investment: "For greater certainty, nothing in this Section shall be construed as preventing a Party from discontinuing the granting of a subsidy and/or requesting its reimbursement, or as requiring that Party to compensate the investor therefor, where such action has been ordered by one of its competent authorities listed in Annex III."

[199]Section 3—Resolution of Investment Disputes and Investment Court System, Commission draft text TTIP – investment.

[200]As to potential problems concerning the envisaged enforcement regime see *infra* text starting at fn. 219.

[201]Section 3, Article 9(4) Commission draft text TTIP – investment: "The Judges shall possess the qualifications required in their respective countries for appointment to judicial office, or be jurists of recognised competence. They shall have demonstrated expertise in public international law. It is desirable that they have expertise in particular, in international investment law, international trade law and the resolution of disputes arising under international investment or international trade agreements."

lawyers)[202] has not been adopted. Rather, the office is open to all "jurists of recognised competence". In order to prevent that the new "investment court" bench is filled by lawyers, wearing two hats, i.e. serving as adjudicators and also advising clients in other, but sometimes similar cases,[203] the rules provide for judges that "upon appointment, they shall refrain from acting as counsel in any pending or new investment protection dispute under this or any other agreement or domestic law."[204] Further incompatibility provisions, aimed at excluding governmental or other influence and a separate Code of Conduct seek to minimize the risk of adjudicator bias. In practice, it may, of course, limit the pool of experienced adjudicators available, also because the envisaged retainer fee, in the equivalent of a third of the one for WTO Appellate Body Members,[205] and the planned fee schedule along the rather low ICSID figures[206] may not attract many investment specialists. Also an increase of academics, instead of corporate lawyers, on the bench of a new "investment court" will not be feasible given the strict prohibition of any other occupation in case the tribunal is converted into a permanent court.[207]

A major organizational step away from traditional ISA where the disputing parties have a right to select their arbitrators lies in the idea of a random allocation of cases to chambers of three Tribunal and Appeal Tribunal judges each.[208] The

---

[202]See S&D Position Paper on Investor-state dispute settlement mechanisms in ongoing trade negotiations, 4 March 2015.

[203]See, *inter alia*, Article 6(7) UNCITRAL Arbitration Rules 2010: "The appointing authority shall have regard to such considerations as are likely to secure the appointment of an independent and impartial arbitrator and shall take into account the advisability of appointing an arbitrator of a nationality other than the nationalities of the parties." Article 14(1) ICSID Convention: "Persons designated to serve on the Panels shall be persons of high moral character and recognized competence in the fields of law, commerce, industry or finance, who may be relied upon to exercise independent judgment. Competence in the field of law shall be of particular importance in the case of persons on the Panel of Arbitrators." See also IBA Guidelines on Conflicts of Interest in International Arbitration, approved on 22 May 2004 by the Council of the International Bar Association, http://www.ibanet.org/Publications/publications_IBA_guides_and_free_materials.aspx (last accessed 1 March 2017).

[204]Section 3, Article 11(1) last sentence Commission draft text TTIP – investment.

[205]Section 3, Article 9(12) Commission draft text TTIP – investment: "In order to ensure their availability, the Judges shall be paid a monthly retainer fee to be fixed by decision of the [...] Committee. [Note: the retainer fee suggested by the EU would be around 1/3rd of the retainer fee for WTO Appellate Body members (i.e. around €2000 per month)] [...]".

[206]Section 3, Article 9(14) Commission draft text TTIP – investment.

[207]Section 3, Article 9(15) Commission draft text TTIP – investment: "In that event, the Judges shall not be permitted to engage in any occupation, whether gainful or not, unless exemption is exceptionally granted by the President of the Tribunal."

[208]Section 3, Article 9(6)(7) Commission draft text TTIP – investment: "6. The Tribunal shall hear cases in divisions consisting of three Judges, of whom one shall be a national of a Member State of the European Union, one a national of the United States and one a national of a third country. The division shall be chaired by the Judge who is a national of a third country. 7. Within 90 days of the submission of a claim pursuant to Article 6, the President of the Tribunal shall appoint the Judges composing the division of the Tribunal hearing the case on a rotation basis, ensuring that the composition of the divisions is random and unpredictable, while giving equal opportunity to all

only "influence" of the parties remains with making the initial selection. Here the proposal departs again from traditional ISA practice which avoids that nationals of disputing parties hear individual claims[209] and resembles more the structure of the Iran-US Claims Tribunal. It suggests that an equal number of EU, US and third country nationals shall be appointed as judges.[210]

7.2 *The Appellate Option*

Clearly the most interesting aspect of the new permanent structure is the appeals possibility. It combines the limited annulment grounds of the ICSID Convention,[211] also reflected in the set-aside reasons pursuant to the New York Convention,[212] with

---

Judges to serve." See also Section 3, Article 10(8)(9) Commission draft text TTIP – investment, for the Appeal Tribunal.

[209] See e.g. Articles 38 and 39 ICSID Convention.

[210] Section 3, Article 9(2) Commission draft text TTIP – investment: "The [. . .] Committee shall, upon the entry into force of this Agreement, appoint fifteen Judges to the Tribunal. Five of the Judges shall be nationals of a Member State of the European Union, five shall be nationals of the United States and five shall be nationals of third countries." See also Section 3, Article 10(2) Commission draft text TTIP – investment, for the Appeal Tribunal: "The Appeal Tribunal shall be composed of six Members, of whom two shall be nationals of a Member State of the European Union, two shall be nationals of the United States and two shall be nationals of third countries."

[211] Article 52(1) ICSID Convention: "Either party may request annulment of the award by an application in writing addressed to the Secretary-General on one or more of the following grounds: (a) that the Tribunal was not properly constituted; (b) that the Tribunal has manifestly exceeded its powers; (c) that there was corruption on the part of a member of the Tribunal; (d) that there has been a serious departure from a fundamental rule of procedure; or (e) that the award has failed to state the reasons on which it is based."

[212] See Article V(1) Convention on the Recognition and Enforcement of Foreign Arbitral Awards: "Recognition and enforcement of the award may be refused, at the request of the party against whom it is invoked, only if that party furnishes to the competent authority where the recognition and enforcement is sought, proof that: (a) The parties to the agreement referred to in article II were, under the law applicable to them, under some incapacity, or the said agreement is not valid under the law to which the parties have subjected it or, failing any indication thereon, under the law of the country where the award was made; or (b) The party against whom the award is invoked was not given proper notice of the appointment of the arbitrator or of the arbitration proceedings or was otherwise unable to present his case; or (c) The award deals with a difference not contemplated by or not falling within the terms of the submission to arbitration, or it contains decisions on matters beyond the scope of the submission to arbitration, provided that, if the decisions on matters submitted to arbitration can be separated from those not so submitted, that part of the award which contains decisions on matters submitted to arbitration may be recognized and enforced; or (d) The composition of the arbitral authority or the arbitral procedure was not in accordance with the agreement of the parties, or, failing such agreement, was not in accordance with the law of the country where the arbitration took place; or (e) The award has not yet become binding, on the parties, or has been set aside or suspended by a competent authority of the country in which, or under the law of which, that award was made."

not only the power to review errors of law, but also manifest errors in the appreciation of facts.

Pursuant to draft Article 29(1) of the Commission proposal:

> Either disputing party may appeal before the Appeal Tribunal a provisional award, within 90 days of its issuance. The grounds for appeal are:
>
> (a) that the Tribunal has erred in the interpretation or application of the applicable law;
>
> (b) that the Tribunal has manifestly erred in the appreciation of the facts, including the appreciation of relevant domestic law; or,
>
> (c) those provided for in Article 52 of the ICSID Convention, in so far as they are not covered by (a) and (b).[213]

Distinct from an ICSID annulment committee, the Appeal Tribunal will decide the dispute finally, modifying the award in whole or in part.[214] Subsequently, the First Instance Tribunal has to issue a revised award within 90 days of receiving the report of the Appeal Tribunal.[215] Combined with the mandate to decide appeal cases within 6 months[216] this should lead to an acceleration of investment dispute settlement. Whether this acceleration idea, inspired again by the WTO DSU, will work in practice needs to be seen.[217]

7.3 *The Enforcement of Awards*

The Commission's draft TTIP text also elaborates on the enforcement of the new "investment court" decisions. These provisions are largely shaped along the template of the ICSID Convention's rules. They provide for the final and binding nature of "final awards", i.e. awards of the Appeal Tribunal or non-appealed awards of the Tribunal of First Instance.[218] Further Article 30(2) provides:

---

[213]Section 3, Article 29(1) Commission draft text TTIP – investment.

[214]Section 3, Article 29(2) Commission draft text TTIP – investment: "If the Appeal Tribunal rejects the appeal, the provisional award shall become final. If the appeal is well founded, the Appeal Tribunal shall modify or reverse the legal findings and conclusions in the provisional award in whole or part."

[215]Section 3, Article 28(7) Commission draft text TTIP – investment.

[216]Section 3, Article 29(3) Commission draft text TTIP – investment.

[217]In particular, whether the limited extension possibility to a total of 9 months, provided for in Section 3, Article 29(3) Commission draft text TTIP – investment, will be sufficient.

[218]Section 3, Article 30(1) Commission draft text TTIP – investment: "Final awards issued pursuant to this Chapter by the Tribunal or the Appeal Tribunal shall be binding between the disputing parties and shall not be subject to appeal, review, set aside, annulment or any other remedy." Compare with Article 53(1) ICSID Convention: "The award shall be binding on the parties and shall not be subject to any appeal or to any other remedy except those provided for in this Convention."

> Each Party shall recognize an award rendered pursuant to this Agreement as binding [and] enforce the pecuniary obligation within its territory as if it were a final judgement of a court in that Party.[219]

This provision mirrors Article 54(1) ICSID Convention.[220] However, the strength of the ICSID provision lies in the fact that it imposes an enforcement obligation on all contracting parties of the ICSID Convention and thus considerably broadens the possibility of enforcement measures against assets found in third States. Since the ICSID Convention will not be applicable to EU IIAs, as long as the problem of an EU accession to it is not solved,[221] the duty of all ICSID Parties to enforce ICSID awards will not apply to the awards of any TTIP tribunal awards. Thus, the obligation to comply with final awards is limited to the parties to the TTIP, i.e. the US, the EU and probably its Member States.[222] Equally, the obligation to enforce pecuniary obligations which is usually sought in third States, is limited to the parties of the TTIP. Given recent experiences with Commission opposition to the enforcement of ICSID awards, it remains at least open to question to what extent an enforcement obligation will add to the principal obligation to accept TTIP final awards as binding pursuant to Article 30(1).[223]

Finally, the suggested enforcement rules leave the State immunity provisions regarding enforcement measures intact, additionally limiting the chances of enforcing TTIP awards.[224] Experience under the similar provisions of the ICSID Convention[225] has demonstrated that this constitutes the major legal hurdle in case an award is not voluntarily complied with and enforcement measures against host State assets located in third countries have to be resorted to.[226] Where in the future

[219]Section 3, Article 30(2) Commission draft text TTIP – investment.

[220]Article 54(1) ICSID Convention: "Each Contracting State shall recognize an award rendered pursuant to this Convention as binding and enforce the pecuniary obligations imposed by that award within its territories as if it were a final judgment of a court in that State."

[221]Pursuant to Article 67 ICSID Convention, the convention is only accessible for Member States of the International Bank for Reconstruction and Development or to any other State which is a party to the ICJ Statute.

[222]See Reinisch (2016).

[223]Section 3, Article 30(1) Commission draft text TTIP – investment: "Final awards issued pursuant to this Chapter by the Tribunal or the Appeal Tribunal shall be binding between the disputing parties and shall not be subject to appeal, review, set aside, annulment or any other remedy."

[224]Section 3, Article 30(3) Commission draft text TTIP – investment: "Execution of the award shall be governed by the laws concerning the execution of judgments in force where such execution is sought."

[225]Article 55 ICSID Convention: "Nothing in Article 54 shall be construed as derogating from the law in force in any Contracting State relating to immunity of that State or of any foreign State from execution."

[226]See Reinisch (2010a).

such attempts will be made in either the US or the EU with regard to assets of the other party, this is likely to lead to major political friction—a development that may run counter the idea of depoliticizing investment disputes.[227]

7.4 *Other Procedural Safeguards to Ensure a Speedy and Transparent Settlement of Investment Disputes*

The September 2015 draft TTIP text also incorporates many of procedural innovations already found in the CETA chapter on investor-state arbitration. It incorporates the UNCITRAL Transparency Rules.[228] It provides for an expedited dismissal of claims which are "unfounded as a matter of law".[229] It also offers the option of mediation and even contains a separate annex[230] which does no longer contain the strict 60 day time limit of the Consolidated 2014 CETA Text.[231]

8 The "Investment Court System" in the Revised 2016 CETA

An investment court system, modelled upon the September 2015 draft TTIP text, was then successfully integrated into the final February 2016 CETA text. It contains provisions that largely correspond to the ones outlined above in regard to the TTIP proposal. This demonstrates that the EU Commission has now fully embraced the idea of an ICS.

---

[227]See Shihata (1986).

[228]Section 3, Article 18(1) Commission draft text TTIP – investment: "The "UNCITRAL Transparency Rules" shall apply to disputes under this Section, with the following additional obligations."

[229]Section 3, Article 17(1) Commission draft text TTIP – investment: "Without prejudice to the Tribunal's authority to address other objections as a preliminary question or to a respondent's right to raise any such objections at any appropriate time, the Tribunal shall address and decide as a preliminary question any objection by the respondent that, as a matter of law, a claim, or any part thereof, submitted under this section is not a claim for which an award in favour of the claimant may be made under Article 6, even if the facts alleged were assumed to be true. The Tribunal may also consider any relevant facts not in dispute."

[230]Annex I Mediation Mechanism for investor-to-state disputes, Commission draft text TTIP – investment.

[231]Article X.19(4) Consolidated 2014 CETA text and Article 8.20(4) Revised 2016 CETA text: "The disputing parties shall endeavour to reach a resolution to the dispute within 60 days from the appointment of the mediator."

9 The New "Investment Court System" and EU Law from a CJEU Perspective

When analysing the "investment court system" plans of the Commission one should not forget another powerful player, the CJEU. In particular after the Court's Opinion on the EU's accession to the ECHR,[232] it appears questionable whether it will accept a permanent international investment tribunal as a competing judicial means of dispute resolution.[233] While the Luxembourg Court has not generally ruled out the possibility of the EU submitting to international dispute settlement with binding outcomes on the EU,[234] it has clearly drawn a line in favour of the autonomy of the Union's legal order by insisting that EU law should ultimately be interpreted and determined by EU organs only, preferably by the Court itself. This demand already voiced in the opinions on the European Patent Court[235] and, most recently, the relationship to the ECtHR,[236] has obviously been taken into consideration by the Commission in its 2015 draft TTIP text and the February 2016 CETA text.

While this problem is not expressly addressed in the draft text, a number of specific provisions indicate the Commission's awareness of the sensitivities of the Court. Both texts explicitly allow only treaty disputes. Technically, this is ensured by providing for the Tribunals' power not to broadly decide "any dispute relating to an investment" as found in other IIAs,[237] but rather by limiting claims to violations of the substantive standards of the investment chapter.[238] The draft dispute settlement provisions clearly permit treaty claims only.[239] In addition, the provisions on

---

[232] CJEU, opinion 2/13, *Accession to the ECHR*, ECLI:EU:C:2014:2454.

[233] See also Burgstaller (2012), Parish (2012), Dimopoulos (2012), Hindelang (2013), Hindelang (2015), Schill (2013).

[234] CJEU, opinion 1/91, *European Economic Area I*, ECLI:EU:C:1991:490.

[235] CJEU, opinion 1/09, *European and Community Patent Court*, ECLI:EU:C:2011:123.

[236] CJEU, opinion 2/13, *Accession to the ECHR*, ECLI:EU:C:2014:2454.

[237] See e.g. Article 9(1) Austrian 2008 Model BIT: "Any dispute arising out of an investment, between a Contracting Party and an investor of the other Contracting Party shall, as far as possible, be settled amicably between the parties to the dispute." Article 2(4) Austria-Chile BIT 1997: "In the event of a dispute between a Party and an investor of the other Party relating to an investment, the parties to the dispute shall initially seek to resolve the dispute by consultations and negotiations." Article 8 Argentina-France BIT 1991: "1. Any dispute relating to investments made under this Agreement between one Contracting Party and an investor of the other Contracting Party shall, as far as possible, be settled amicably between the two parties concerned."

[238] See, e.g., Article 1116(1) NAFTA: "An investor of a Party may submit to arbitration under this Section a claim that another Party has breached an obligation under: (a) Section A or Article 1503(2) (State Enterprises), or (b) Article 1502(3)(a) (Monopolies and State Enterprises) where the monopoly has acted in a manner inconsistent with the Party's obligations under Section A, and that the investor has incurred loss or damage by reason of, or arising out of, that breach." Section A only mentions treaty standards of the NAFTA, not domestic legislation.

[239] Section 3, Article 13(1) Applicable law and rules of interpretation, Commission draft text TTIP – investment: "The Tribunal shall determine whether the treatment subject to the claim is

applicable law expressly remove EU law from the interpretation and to a certain extent even from the application by the Tribunals. It does so by declaring domestic law not to form part of the applicable law[240] and by stressing that any meaning given to EU law by the Tribunals shall not be binding on EU institutions and by insisting that the Tribunals do not have to power to exercise judicial review of EU acts.[241] Clearly all these form elements of the core power of the CJEU's exclusive "interpretative monopoly" as asserted in its above-mentioned decisions. By removing EU law from "investment court" scrutiny the Commission obviously intends to make the latter EU-compatible. Whether the CJEU will concur remains to be seen.

10 Conclusion

Over the last years, the position of the EU towards ISA has gradually evolved. Since the EU is a complex entity comprising often diverging Member States as well as organs, it is not possible to identify "the" EU position on any current issue. Rather, the institutions, the Member States and different political groups within the EU may have diverging views. The question of ISA is a perfect example of a seemingly technical legal problem that has attracted unexpected public interest. While some groups want to stop TTIP and CETA altogether, others aim at a reform of ISA and again others may want to maintain the status quo of effective investor protection. Thus, the position of the Commission, the main external trade negotiating actor of the EU, is shaped by constant and sometimes conflicting demands. The Commission itself has tried to react to this by gradually adopting a position that has shifted from reluctance to endorsing ISA as a meaningful mechanism to enforce investment protection standards to reforming the system by proposing the substitution of ISA by a permanent "Investment Court System". Thereby the Commission has reacted to many of the concerns and criticism voiced against ISA, and ISDS more

inconsistent with any of the provisions referred to in Article 1(1) alleged by the claimant." Section 3, Article 1(1): "This Section shall apply to a dispute between, on the one hand, a claimant of one Party and, on the other hand, the other Party concerning treatment alleged to breach [investment protection provisions, i.e. the investment protection section and the national treatment and the most-favoured nation treatment provisions concerning post-establishment], which breach allegedly causes loss or damage to the claimant or its locally established company."

[240]Section 3, Article 13(3) Applicable law and rules of interpretation, Commission draft text TTIP – investment: "For greater certainty, pursuant to paragraph 1, the domestic law of the Parties shall not be part of the applicable law. Where the Tribunal is required to ascertain the meaning of a provision of the domestic law of one of the Parties as a matter of fact, it shall follow the prevailing interpretation of that provision made by the courts or authorities of that Party."

[241]Section 3, Article 13(4) Applicable law and rules of interpretation, Commission draft text TTIP – investment: "For greater certainty, the meaning given to the relevant domestic law made by the Tribunal shall not be binding upon the courts or the authorities of either Party. The Tribunal shall not have jurisdiction to determine the legality of a measure, alleged to constitute a breach of this Agreement, under the domestic law of the disputing Party."

broadly, without depriving investment protection of its major procedural guarantee to effectively enforce the (already lowered) standards promised by the contracting parties.

This development of the EU's position towards ISA is reflected by numerous internal documents of the Union's law-making institutions as well as the Commission's negotiating outcomes, in particular the Canada-EU draft CETA text of September 2014 and the EU-Singapore free trade agreement. These texts provide useful hints not only with regard to the EU's position on ISA, but also on what is feasible to negotiate with third parties. In addition, the September 2015 proposals by the Commission, calling for an "investment court system", further elaborated on by the February 2016 CETA text, provide useful insights. With its appellate structure and a number of other features the "investment court system" draws inspiration from the WTO. Thereby, the Commission, the EU's external trade actor, which does not only negotiate agreements, but also litigates disputes before the WTO's DSU institutions, has re-introduced WTO features into ISDS. From its initial preference for State-to-State dispute settlement along the WTO paradigm, the Commission has endorsed ISA and is now re-installing WTO features into ISDS. Whether this will be acceptable to the EU's negotiating partners is unclear.

Even if it may, it leaves the CJEU out of the present picture. As already mentioned, however, one should not underestimate this organ's power, in particular when it comes to vetoing the Unions' submission to external dispute settlement systems. As so often, the Court will have the final say.

References

Akkermans B, Ramaekers E (2010) Article 345 TFEU (ex Article 295 EC), its meanings and interpretations. Eur Law J 16(3):292–314

Antonietti A (2006) The 2006 amendments to the ICSID rules and regulations and the additional Facility rules. ICSID Rev Foreign Invest Law J 21(2):427–448

Bischoff J (2011) Just a little bit of "mixity"? The EU's role in the field of international investment protection law. Common Mark Law Rev 48(5):1527–1569

Broß S (2015) Freihandelsabkommen, einige Anmerkungen zur Problematik der privaten Schiedsgerichtsbarkeit. Hans Böckler Stiftung Report Nr 4

Brower CH (2001–2002) Investor-state disputes under NAFTA: the empire strikes back. Columbia J Transnational Law 40:43–88

Brower CH (2003) Structure, legitimacy, and NAFTA's investment chapter. Vanderbilt J Transnlational Law 36:37–94

Brower CH (2006) Why the FTC notes of interpretation constitute a partial amendment of NAFTA article 1105. Va J Int Law 46(2):347–363

Brown C, Naglis I (2013) Dispute settlement in future EU investment agreements. In: Bungenberg M, Reinisch A, Tietje C (eds) EU and investment agreements – open questions and remaining challenges. Nomos, Baden-Baden, pp 17–36

Bungenberg M (2010) Going global? The EU common commercial policy after Lisbon. In: Hermann C, Terhechte JP (eds) European yearbook of international economic law, vol 1. Springer, Heidelberg, pp 23–151

Bungenberg M (2011) The division of competences between the EU and its member states in the area of investment politics. In: Bungenberg M, Griebel J, Hindelang S (eds) European yearbook of international economic law, special issue: international investment law and EU law – special issue. Springer, Baden-Baden, pp 29–42
Bungenberg M, Griebel J, Hindelang S (eds) (2011) European yearbook of international economic law, special issue: international investment law and EU law – special issue. Springer, Baden-Baden
Bungenberg M (2015) Towards a more balanced international investment law 2.0? In: Herrmann C, Simma B, Streinz R (eds) Trade policy between law, diplomacy and scholarship – Liber amicorum in memoriam Horst G Krenzler. Springer International Publishing, New York, pp 15–38
Bungenberg M, Hobe S (2015) The relationship of international investment law and European Union law. In: Bungenberg M, Griebel J, Hobe S, Reinisch A (eds) International investment law. Nomos/Hart, Baden-Baden/Oxford, pp 1602–1628
Burgstaller M (2012) Investor-state arbitration in EU international investment agreements with third states. Leg Issues Econ Integr 39(2):207–221
Burgstaller M (2014) Dispute settlement in EU international investment agreements with third states: three salient problems. In: Bungenberg M, Reinisch A (eds) The anatomy of the (invisible) EU model BIT. J World Invest Trade 15:551–569
Calamita NJ (2014) Dispute settlement transparency in Europe's evolving investment treaty policy. In: Bungenberg M, Reinisch A (eds) The anatomy of the (invisible) EU model BIT. J World Invest Trade 15:645–678
Chaisse J (2012) Promises and pitfalls of the European Union policy on foreign investment – how will the new EU competence on FDI affect the emerging global regime? J Int Econ Law 15 (1):51–84
Chevry J (2015) Micula v Romania. World Trade Rev 14:540
Craig P, De Burca G (2011) EU law: text, cases, and materials, 5th edn. Oxford University Press, Oxford
Delaney J, Magraw D (2008) Procedural transparency. In: Muchlinski P, Ortino F, Schreuer S (eds) The Oxford handbook of international investment law. Oxford University Press, Oxford, pp 721–788
Dimopoulos A (2008) The common commercial policy after Lisbon: establishing parallelism between internal and external economic relations? Croat Yearb Eur Law Policy 4(4):101–116
Dimopoulos A (2011) EU foreign investment law. Oxford University Press, Oxford
Dimopoulos A (2012) The compatibility of future EU investment agreements with EU law. Leg Issues Econ Integr 39(4):447–471
Dodge WS (2006) Investor-state dispute settlement between developed countries: reflection on the Australia-United States free trade agreement. Vanderbilt J Transnational Law 39(1):1–37
Dolzer R, Schreuer C (2012) Principles of international investment law, 2nd edn. Oxford University Press, Oxford
Douglas Z (2009) The international law of investment claims. Cambridge University Press, Cambridge
Eeckhout P (2011) External relations law, 2nd edn. Oxford University Press, Oxford
Gaukroder D, Gordon K (2012) Investor-state dispute settlement: a scoping paper for the investment policy community. OECD Working Papers on International Investment No. 2012/3
Henckels C (2012) Indirect expropriation and the right to regulate: revisiting proportionality analysis and the standard of review in investor-state arbitration. J Int Econ Law 15(1):223–255
Hillion C, Koutrakos P (2010) Mixed agreements revisited. Hart, Oxford
Hindelang S (2011) Der primärrechtliche Rahmen einer EU-Investitionsschutzpolitik: Zulässigkeit und Grenzen von Investor-Staat-Schiedsverfahren aufgrund künftiger EU Abkommen. In: Bungenberg M, Herrmann C (eds) Die Gemeinsame Handelspolitik der Europäischen Union nach Lissabon. Nomos, Baden-Baden, pp 157–184

Hindelang S (2013) The autonomy of the European legal order – EU constitutional limits to investor-state arbitration on the basis of future EU investment-related agreements. In: Bungenberg M, Hermann C (eds) European yearbook of international economic law, Special Issue Common Commercial Policy after Lisbon. Springer, Heidelberg, pp 187–198
Hindelang S (2015) Repellent forces: the CJEU and investor-state dispute settlement. Archiv des Völkerrechts 53(1):68–89
Hoffmeister F, Ünüvar G (2013) From BITS and pieces towards European investment agreements. In: Bungenberg M, Reinisch A, Tietje C (eds) EU and investment agreements – open questions and remaining challenges. Nomos/Hart, Baden-Baden/Oxford, pp 57–86
Jenkins BW (2007) The next generation of chilling uncertainty: indirect expropriation under CAFTA and its potential impact on environmental protection. Ocean Coast Law J 12 (2):269–304
Johnson OT, Gimblett J (2012) From gunboats to BITs: the evolution of modern international investment law. In: Sauvant K (ed) Yearbook on international investment law and policy 2010–2011. Oxford University Press, Oxford, pp 649–692
Kaufmann-Kohler G (2011) Interpretive powers of the free trade commission and the rule of law. In: Gaillard E, Bachand F (eds) Fifteen years of NAFTA chapter 11 arbitration. IAI Series on International Arbitration 7:175–194
Kläger R (2014) The impact of the TTIP on Europe's investment arbitration architecture. Zeitschrift für Deutsches und Amerikanisches Recht 39(2):68–73
Lentner G (2014) A uniform European investment policy?: The unwritten EU model BIT. J Law Adm Sci 2:156–165
Lévesque C (2013) The challenges of 'marrying' investment liberalisation and protection in the Canada-EU CETA. In: Bungenberg M, Reinisch A, Tietje C (eds) EU and investment agreements – open questions and remaining challenges. Nomos/Hart, Baden-Baden/Oxford, pp 121–146
Lévesque C, Newcombe A (2013) Canada. In: Brown C (ed) Commentaries on selected model investment treaties. Oxford University Press, Oxford, pp 53–129
Lorz RA (2015) Protection and security (including the NAFTA approach). In: Bungenberg M, Griebel J, Hobe S, Reinisch A (eds) International investment law. Nomos, Baden-Baden, pp 764–789
Mann H (2008) Transparency and consistency in international investment law: can the problem be fixed by tinkering? In: Sauvant K (ed) Appeals mechanism in international investment disputes. Oxford University Press, Oxford, pp 213–222
Matiation S (2003) Arbitration with two twists: Loewen v. United States and free trade commission intervention in NAFTA chapter 11 disputes. Univ Pa J Int Econ Law 24(2):451–507
Maupin J (2013) Transparency in international investment law: the good, the bad, and the murky. In: Bianchi A, Peters A (eds) Transparency in international law. Oxford University Press, Oxford, pp 142–171
Mostafa B (2008) The sole effects doctrine, police powers and indirect expropriation under international law. Aust Int Law J 15(1):267–296
Muchlinski P (2011) The rise and fall of the MAI: lessons for the regulation of international business. In: Fletcher I, Mistelis L, Cremona M (eds) Foundations and perspectives in international trade law, pp 114–134
Neumayer E (2001) Do countries fail to raise environmental standards? An evaluation of policy options addressing "regulatory chill". Int J Sustain Dev 4(3):231–241
Nottage L (2011) The rise and possible fall of investor-state arbitration in Asia: a Skeptic's view of Australia's Gillard government trade policy statement. Transnational Dispute Manage 8 (5):1–25
Parish M (2012) International courts and the European legal order. Eur J Int Law 23(1):141–153
Parra A (2004) The new amendments to the ICSID regulations and rules and additional facility rules. Law Pract Int Courts Tribunals 3:181–188

Platt R (2013) The appeal of appeal mechanisms in international arbitration: fairness over finality? J Int Arbitr 30(5):531–560

Pohl J, Mashigo K, Nohen A (2012) Dispute settlement provisions in international investment agreements: a large sample survey. OECD Working Papers on International Investment No. 2012/2

Reinisch A (2010a) The division of powers between the EU and its member states "after Lisbon". In: Bungenberg M, Griebel J, Hindelang S (eds) Internationaler Investitionsschutz und Europarecht. Nomos, Baden-Baden, pp 99–112

Reinisch A (2010b) Enforcement of investment awards. In: Yannaca-Small C (ed) Arbitration under international investment agreements: a guide to the key issues. Oxford University Press, Oxford, pp 671–697

Reinisch A (2014a) The EU on the investment path – quo Vadis Europe? The future of EU BITs and other investment agreements. Santa Clara J Int Law 12(1):111–156

Reinisch A (2014b) Putting the pieces together . . . an EU model BIT. In: Bungenberg M, Reinisch A (eds) The anatomy of the (invisible) EU model BIT. J World Invest Trade 15:679–704

Reinisch A (2015) Most favoured nation treatment. In: Bungenberg M, Griebel J, Hobe S, Reinisch A (eds) International investment law. Nomos, Baden-Baden, pp 807–845

Reinisch A (2016) Will the EU's proposal concerning an investment court system for CETA and TTIP lead to enforceable awards? – the limits of modifying the ICSID convention and the nature of investment arbitration. J Int Econ Law 19(4):761–786

Reinisch A, Knahr C (2012) Conflict of interest in international investment arbitration. In: Peters A, Handschin L, Hoegger D (eds) Conflict of interest in governance – an interdisciplinary outlook on the global, public, corporate and financial sphere. Cambridge University Press, Cambridge, pp 103–124

Roberts A (2010) Power and persuasion in investment treaty interpretation: the dual role of states. Am J Int Law 104(2):179–225

Salacuse J (2010) The law of investment treaties. Oxford University Press, Oxford

Sasson M (2010) Substantive law in investment treaty arbitration: the unsettled relationship between international and municipal law. Kluwer Law, Alphen aan den Rijn

Sauvant K, Chiswick-Patterson M (2008) Appeals mechanism in international investment disputes. Oxford University Press, Oxford

Schill S (2007) Do investment treaties chill unilateral state regulation to mitigate climate change? J Int Arbitr 24(5):469–477

Schill S (2013) Luxembourg limits: conditions for investor-state dispute settlement under future EU investment agreements. In: Bungenberg M, Reinisch A, Tietje C (eds) EU and investment agreements – open questions and remaining challenges. Nomos, Baden-Baden, pp 37–56

Schreuer C (2004) Travelling the BIT route: of waiting periods, umbrella clauses and forks in the road. J World Invest and Trade 5(2):231–256

Schreuer C (2005) Calvo's grandchildren: the return of local remedies in investment arbitration. Law Pract Int Courts Tribunals 4:1–17

Shan W, Zhang S (2011) The treaty of Lisbon: half way toward a common investment policy. Eur J Int Law 21(4):1049–1073

Sheppard A (2009) Arbitrator independence in ICSID arbitration. In: Binder C, Kriebaum U, Reinisch A, Wittich S (eds) International investment law for the 21st century. Essays in Honour of Christoph Schreuer. Oxford University Press, Oxford, pp 131–156

Shihata I (1986) Towards a greater depoliticization of investment disputes: the roles of ICSID and MIGA. ICSID Rev Foreign Invest Law J 1:1–32

Tams C (2006) An appealing option? The Debate about an ICSID Appellate Mechanism. Beiträge zum Transnationalen Wirtschaftsrecht Heft 57

Tams C (2007) Is there a need for an ICSID appellate structure? In: Hofmann R, Tams C (eds) The international convention for the settlement of investment disputes: taking stock after 40 years. Nomos, Baden-Baden, pp 223–250

Tienhaara K (2011) Regulatory chill and the threat of arbitration: a view from political science. In: Brown C, Miles K (eds) Evolution in investment treaty law and arbitration. Cambridge University Press, Cambridge, pp 606–627

Tietje C (2009) Die Außenwirtschaftsverfassung der EU nach dem Vertrag von Lissabon. Beiträge zum Transnationalen Beiträge zum transnationalen Wirtschaftsrecht Heft 83

Titi A (2014) The right to regulate in international investment law. Nomos, Baden-Baden

Trakman LE (2012) Investor state arbitration or local courts: will Australia set a new trend? J World Trade 46(1):83–120

Veeder V (2006) The transparency of international arbitration: process and substance. In: Mistelis L, Lew J (eds) Pervasive problems in international arbitration. Kluwer Law International, New York, pp 89–102

Wallace D (2005) Fair and equitable treatment and denial of justice: from Chattin v. Mexico to Loewen v. USA. In: Weiler T (ed) International investment law and arbitration: leading cases from the ICSID. Cameron May, London, pp 669–700

Yannaca-Small C (2005) Indirect expropriation and the "Right to Regulate" in international investment law. In: OECD (ed) International investment law. A changing landscape. OECD, pp 43–72

Competition Law in EU Free Trade and Cooperation Agreements (and What the UK Can Expect After Brexit)

Florian Wagner-von Papp

Abstract Free trade and competition law, for the most part, mutually reinforce each other by breaking up entrenched positions of market power and creating competitive constraints on any entities with market power. Competition law enforcement still adheres mostly to the nineteenth century paradigm of enforcement by sovereign nation states, albeit with extended extraterritorial prescriptive jurisdiction. At the same time national competition law enforcers face an increasingly transnational economy. The increase in free trade and competition advocacy has resulted in a proliferation of national competition law regimes. The patchwork of multiple national enforcement leads to enforcement gaps and enforcement overlaps (Guzman). While some call for global solutions to global problems and advocate a global competition agency (or appointing a lead jurisdiction), it is questionable if such centralisation would be desirable and at any rate it does not seem politically feasible. The intermediate path between pure unilateral enforcement and a centralised global enforcer consists in unilateral enforcement tempered by cooperation and coordination of enforcement activities. Regional cooperation leads to internally relatively homogeneous clusters, and reduces complexity on the global scale. The extremely close cooperation in such regional cooperation agreements is supplemented by a second layer of reciprocal cooperation links, which are characterised by a slightly lower but still high degree of internal homogeneity, and accordingly cooperation that does not go quite as far as the one in the central region. As we move in concentric circles further away from the centre, heterogeneity of competitive conditions or interests increases and the depth of cooperation decreases. This results in regional clusters. Within each cluster, issues of gaps and overlaps can be reduced to the greatest possible extent. Some of the clusters are interconnected among each other by bilateral links (such as CETA between the EU and Canada). Between clusters, the weaker cooperation and coordination may not resolve all gaps and overlaps, but as global heterogeneity of views on competition policy decreases through the work of international organisations (such as the OECD, the ICN or APEC), gradual progress is made here as well.

F. Wagner-von Papp (✉)
UCL Faculty of Laws, Bidborough House, 38–50 Bidborough Street, London WC1H 9BT, UK
e-mail: f.wagner-von-papp@ucl.ac.uk

M. Bungenberg et al. (eds.), *European Yearbook of International Economic Law 2017*, European Yearbook of International Economic Law 8,
DOI 10.1007/978-3-319-58832-2_10

This contribution exemplifies the concentric circles of cooperation around the EU by examining the intergovernmental and inter-agency agreements concluded by the EU to face the complexities of the transnational economy of the twenty-first century. It then turns to a development that does not fit this neat picture of ever-increasing cooperation at all: Brexit and its implications.

Contents

1 Introduction

This is, for two reasons, a curious time for an academic in the United Kingdom (UK) to write about free trade and competition law.

First, the global enchantment with free trade, and especially multi- and pluri-lateral Free Trade Agreements (FTAs), seems to be coming to an end.[1] There had been a surge of FTAs in recent years, both of the bilateral and of the pluri-lateral variety.[2] However, the backlash against FTAs—in particular the Trans-Pacific Partnership (TPP),[3] the Comprehensive Economic and Trade Agreement

[1]See Evenett and Fritz (2015); see also European Commission, Reflection paper on harnessing globalisation, COM(2017) 240 of 10 May 2017, https://ec.europa.eu/commission/sites/beta-political/files/reflection-paper-globalisation_en.pdf (last accessed 16 July 2017).

[2]Bi- and pluri-lateral FTAs proliferated especially after it had become clear in the Doha Round that substantial progress in multilateral agreements on the World Trade Organisation (WTO) level would be difficult. The same trend was observable for antitrust cooperation agreements. See Gerber (2010), p. 108 et seq.

[3]US President-Elect Trump has vowed to withdraw from the TPP "from day one"—Woolf N, McCurry J, Haas B, Trump to Withdraw from Trans-Pacific Partnership on Day One in Office, The

(CETA),[4] the Trans-Atlantic Trade and Investment Partnership (TTIP), and, in the wake of the criticism against all these, the EU-Ukraine Deep and Comprehensive Free Trade Agreement (DCFTA)—have cast doubt on the future of trade deals.[5] The 2016 presidential race and the outcome of the elections in the United States signal a retreat from the free trade paradigm.[6]

Secondly, and closer to home, an uneasy alliance of free traders and protectionists has won the EU Referendum on "Brexit" in the UK.[7] More than a year after the referendum and some four months after notifying the EU of its withdrawal, it is still not clear in which direction the UK is headed. Options range, at least in theory, from trading under WTO rules (with schedules yet to be teased out from the schedules negotiated for the EU), to tailored bilateral agreements with the EU—which in themselves could range from a mere traditional FTA to modern versions à la EU-South Korea or CETA to a near-replication of the rights and obligations in

Guardian, 22 November 2016—and ordered withdrawal by executive order on 23 January 2017, https://www.whitehouse.gov/the-press-office/2017/01/23/presidential-memorandum-regarding-withdrawal-united-states-trans-pacific (last accessed 16 July 2017).

[4]CETA was narrowly saved after being pulled back from the brink of extinction in Wallonia—cf. Donnan S, Canada and EU reach finishing line over trade deal, Financial Times, 29 September 2016. The Council decided to sign CETA on 28 October 2016, see Council Decision (EU) 2017/37 of 28 October 2016 on the signing on behalf of the European Union of the Comprehensive Economic and Trade Agreement (CETA) between Canada, of the one part, and the European Union and its Member States, of the other part, OJ 2017 L 11/1. CETA was signed on the EU-Canada summit on 30 October 2016 and the European Parliament approved CETA by a vote of 408–254, with 33 abstentions on 15 February 2017. As a mixed agreement, it will have to be approved by the (national and in some cases regional) parliaments of the Member States.

[5]See, e.g., Goodman PS, More jobs, but not for everyone, The New York Times, 29 September 2016, p. A1; Barber T, Free trade sceptics on the rise in European Parliament, Financial Times, 21 September 2016, reporting on the voting pattern analysis conducted by VoteWatch Europe, see Frantescu DP, Who is for and against free trade in the European Parliament?, 19 September 2016, http://www.votewatch.eu/blog/who-is-for-and-against-free-trade-in-the-european-parliament/ (last accessed 16 July 2017); Donnan S, Free trade v populism: The fight for America's economy, Financial Times, 22 September 2016.

[6]For an analysis of the US presidential candidates' positions on free trade, see Noland et al. (2016). Since President Trump's inauguration, he has withdrawn from the Trans-Pacific Partnership by executive order on 23 January 2017, https://www.whitehouse.gov/the-press-office/2017/01/23/presidential-memorandum-regarding-withdrawal-united-states-trans-pacific (last accessed 16 July 2017), and is reportedly investigating the possibility to bypass the WTO in order to impose unilateral trade sanctions, Donnan S, Trump's trade shake-up: why has the US taken aim at the WTO, Financial Times, 2 March 2017, linking to an internal draft paper that had considered this option in a passage omitted from the final paper (for the draft, see http://im.ft-static.com/content/images/1dd70b12-fe25-11e6-96f8-3700c5664d30.pdf (last accessed 16 July 2017)).

[7]Nixon S, Britain's Post-Brexit Trade Ambitions Run Up Against Protectionist Forces, Wall Street Journal, 14 September 2016; see also Thomas N, May: Britain Wants to be Free Trade "Leader", Financial Times, Fast FT Comment, 5 September 2016, on the Prime Minister's assurances to the G20 that there would not be any "retreat to protectionism"; Pickard J, Parker G, Plimmer G, Hinkley Point Deal Prompts Tougher Line on Infrastructure Sales, Financial Times, 15 September 2016, on considerations by the British Government to introduce a "tougher approach to the rules governing mergers and acquisitions by examining whether the sale of 'critical infrastructure' should be overseen by ministers".

the European Economic Area (EEA) à la Switzerland—or even full membership in the EEA.[8] The UK government has set out its position in a White Paper, according to which the UK will not seek to stay within the Single Market or the Customs Union, but will instead seek to negotiate a custom-made "ambitious and comprehensive FTA".[9] Once the UK has made up its mind what precisely it wants to ask for, it remains to be seen how its advances are received by the EU (and possibly all EEA) Member States. Whatever form Brexit will take, one of the issues that will have to be dealt with is what UK competition law will look like and to what extent there will be cooperation between the UK authorities and courts with their counterparts in the EU, EEA, Switzerland, and the rest of the world.

This essay gives a short overview of the relationship between free trade and competition law (Sect. 2) and the extent to which the expansion of unilateral extraterritorial competition law enforcement may render international cooperation less necessary, and conversely the extent to which gaps and overlaps due to the unilateral enforcement regime requires international cooperation (Sect. 3). Uncoordinated unilateral enforcement by the approximately 130 competition law regimes in the world[10] would result in enforcement gaps and overlaps in enforcement.[11] The EU has reduced the complexity on the global level by staggering the intensity of cooperation in concentric circles according to the degree of homogeneity of competitive conditions and interests: extremely intensive regional cooperation between the competition authorities within the EU at the core, very intensive cooperation with the EFTA Surveillance Authority in the EEA, intensive bilateral cooperation with Switzerland, close cooperation with various potential candidates and candidates for accession and certain Euro-Mediterranean and other neighbouring states, and generally less detailed cooperation with states further away, albeit with selectively deeper cooperation with important trading partners such as Canada, Japan, Singapore and South Korea. Section 4 examines how the EU has integrated competition law into FTAs, Association Agreements and intergovernmental and inter-agency cooperation agreements. If other regions followed this example of concentric circles with intense cooperation at the centre that eliminates internal gaps and overlaps to the greatest possible degree, and gradually decreasing cooperation with other areas in which the competitive conditions and interests are not as homogeneous, then this global network of nodes and links would, while not eliminating gaps and overlaps, arguably reduce them to a manageable level. Section 5 turns to a development that does not fit this view of the world, namely Brexit and its implications for the relationship in competition law enforcement between the UK and the EU as well as between the UK and the rest of the world. Section 6 concludes.

---

[8]For an overview of the options and some of the arising issues see Lehmann and Zetzsche (2016).

[9]HM Government, The United Kingdom's exit from and new partnership with the European Union, February 2017, CM 9417, https://www.gov.uk/government/uploads/system/uploads/attachment_data/file/589191/The_United_Kingdoms_exit_from_and_partnership_with_the_EU_Web.pdf (last accessed 16 July 2017), section 8, pp. 35–49.

[10]Cf. Capobianco and Nagy (2016), p. 2, figure 1.

[11]For the costs of gaps and overlaps see in particular Guzman (2004, 2010).

2 Free Trade and Competition Law

Free trade interacts with competition law on many levels.[12] In many ways, free trade and competition law have common objectives and mutually reinforce each other (below Sects. 2.1 and 2.2). Nevertheless, the goals of trade law and competition law are, at least in the prevailing views in the respective disciplines, not identical, and the diverging goals mean that trade and competition law may come into conflict with each other (below Sect. 2.3).

2.1 Mutual Reinforcement Part 1: Free Trade Invigorates Competition

The added competition from foreign competitors that comes with free trade undermines domestic market power. Where free trade results in a substantial reduction of entry barriers, the geographic scope of relevant markets may expand. Even if foreign undertakings should not quite be included in the relevant market, they may at least become a competitive constraint on the fringes. This increased competition from foreign competitors may be even more invigorating than mere market shares would indicate: a different mind-set of foreign mavericks may undermine collusive practices that were established, explicitly or tacitly, among domestic competitors, and disrupt their complacency. The self-correcting mechanisms of markets are therefore boosted by the entry of foreign competitors made possible through free trade. Ceteris paribus, this would seem to indicate that competition law has a lesser role to play where there is free trade.

2.2 Mutual Reinforcement Part 2: Competition Law to Address Blowback Against Free Trade

However, if one changes one variable in a dynamic and homeostatic system such as a market, things will not remain "*ceteris paribus*". Domestic market participants

---

[12]For more detail, see in particular Bradford and Chilton (2017), a statistical analysis based on a new extensive data set, whose (for the time being: provisional) finding is a positive correlation between "trade openness and the specificity and stringency of countries' law antitrust regimes" (p. 4 of the manuscript). Bradford and Chilton's paper would have deserved much greater attention here, but their draft could only be worked into the proofs of this contribution. Their paper is strongly recommended to anyone interested in the relationship between trade and competition law. My account that follows in the text below is only a rough sketch, and the Bradford and Chilton paper provides much more detail on the empirics and the relevant literature. I am glad to say, however, that my intuitive account that follows in the text below is not contradicted by their empirical findings. See also Bradford and Büthe (2015), Trebilcock and Iacobucci (2004) and Trebilcock (1996).

may, individually or collectively, respond to the increased competitive pressure by resorting to exclusionary practices against foreign competitors. Private barriers to entry may be erected and replace the state barriers to entry that existed before free trade agreements removed them. Trade is impaired by these private barriers, unless competition law intervenes. Alternatively, or cumulatively, domestic and foreign competitors may agree to reduce the mutual competitive pressures by allocating markets or by fixing prices amongst themselves—following the motto "if you can't beat 'em, join 'em". At the same time, free trade allows supply chains to become truly international.[13] This combination of longer (and more international) supply chains and the greater incentive to enter into cartels to escape competitive pressure means that more cartels acquire an international dimension, with collusion often occurring higher up in the supply chain, far removed from the eventual end consumers.[14] The need for effective competition law and the difficulties for its enforcement are increased.

It was these interactions that motivated the founders of the Rome Treaties in Europe to include competition rules to complement the fundamental free movement rights when the European Communities were established. This interaction between the integration of markets and competition law still shapes the EU's approach to substantive competition law. Exclusionary measures will often consist in (a network of) vertical agreements by domestic companies or exclusionary practices by dominant undertakings. The more aggressive approach in the EU to vertical agreements and abuses of dominant positions may be explicable, at least in part, with this market integration objective of the EU competition rules. Within the European Union, the supranational character of EU competition law allows the EU to address such private practices that impede trade by prohibiting them, in much the same way as a federal state, such as the US, would address such issues internally.

When it comes to external relations, however, the situation becomes more complicated. Assume a third country has foreclosed its market by a comprehensive network of vertical and conglomerate relationships (similar to the accusation which the US levelled against Japan's *keireitsu* system in the Structural Impediments Initiative[15]). Similar to the reasoning in intra-EU cases, such anti-competitive conduct can impair market access and so—as the CETA puts it—"undermine the

[13]See, e.g., the 2014 OECD-WTO-World Bank Report to the G20, Global Value Chains: Challenges, Opportunities, and Implications for Policy, Sydney, Australia, 19 July 2014, https://www.oecd.org/tad/gvc_report_g20_july_2014.pdf (last accessed 16 July 2017).

[14]See the discussion below in Sect. 3.1 on the "component cases", such as *Minn-Chem v Agrium*, 683 F.3d 845, 856–858 (7th Cir. 2012), *cert. Den.*, 134 S.Ct. 23 (2013); *Motorola Mobility LLC v AU Optronics Corp*, 775 F.3d 816 (7th Cir. 26 November 2014, amended 12 January 2015), *cert. den.* docket number 14–1122, 15 June 2015; *United States v Hsiung*, 758 F.3d 1074 (9th Cir. 2014), amended by 778 F.3d 738 (9th Cir. 2015), *cert den.* docket number 14–1121, 15 June 2015; *Lotes Co. v. Hon Hai Precision Industry Co.*, 753 F.3d 395, 409–413 (2d Cir. 2014).

[15]Cf. the description in Morita (1991).

benefits of trade liberalisation".[16] Where the anticompetitive practices in the third country have a direct, foreseeable and substantial effect on competition within the EU, and if this affects, directly or indirectly, actually or potentially, trade between Member States, EU competition law may apply to these practices. In other words, the unilateral extraterritorial application of EU competition law may address some of the issues in this scenario. However, even where the substantive EU competition prohibitions apply extraterritorially, there remains a need for international cooperation because *enforcement jurisdiction* remains strictly territorial. This need is partly addressed by measures that incentivise the foreign state to establish its own domestic competition law (such as requirements to introduce competition laws and authorities contained in FTAs[17] and Association Agreements), and to enforce these laws (such as requirements in FTAs[18] and positive comity agreements), and partly by entering into mutual legal assistance treaties (MLATs) and extradition treaties.[19]

Where such qualified effects cannot be shown to exist in this scenario, public international law prevents the application of EU competition law.[20] In these instances, there may well be an EU *trade* interest in opening up the foreign market for exporters, which is foreclosed due to private anticompetitive practices, an interest that cannot be addressed by the unilateral application of EU competition law. Accordingly, trade agreements and bilateral intergovernmental or inter-agency agreements may be, and are, used to urge the foreign state to adopt and enforce its own domestic competition law provisions against the anticompetitive practices on its territory.[21] As will be explained below, the US purports to be more aggressive in this latter group of cases, both as a matter of the unilateral extraterritorial

[16]Article 17.2(1) of CETA, Council Decision (EU) 2017/37 of 28 October 2016 on the signing on behalf of the European Union of the Comprehensive Economic and Trade Agreement (CETA) between Canada, of the one part, and the European Union and its Member States, of the other part, OJ 2017 L 11/1; similarly Article 12.1.1 of the EU-Singapore FTA. See also Article 11.1.1 of the EU-South Korea FTA, Council Decision of 16 September 2010 on the signing, on behalf of the European Union, and provisional application of the Free Trade Agreement between the European Union and its Member States, of the one part, and the Republic of Korea, of the other part, OJ 2011 L 127/1 ("to prevent the benefits of the trade liberalisation process in goods, services and establishment from being removed or eliminated by anti-competitive business conduct or anti-competitive transactions").

[17]See, e.g., Article 16.1(1) and (3) of the TPP. For similar requirements in EU agreements see below Sect. 4.

[18]See, e.g., Article 16.1(2) of the TPP.

[19]See below Sect. 3 for the scope of unilateral extraterritorial application of EU competition law (and US antitrust law), and the remaining need for international cooperation when it comes to enforcement.

[20]See, e.g., opinion by AG Wahl to CJEU, case C-413/14 P, *Intel v Commission*, ECLI:EU:C:2016:788, paras. 294–305. Where there are qualified effects on competition in one of the Member States, but no sufficient effect on trade between Member States can be shown, public international law would permit the application of EU competition law, but the conflicts and substantive law clauses on effects on trade contained in Articles 101 and 102 TFEU prevent the application of EU competition law (although the Member States' national competition laws may still apply extraterritorially).

[21]See below Sect. 4.

application of its antitrust laws and as a matter of international trade law. However, even these more aggressive US instruments are primarily used as a bargaining tool to open up markets by way of trade agreements.[22]

2.3 *The Relationship Between Trade and Competition Law: Frictions*

Despite these mutually reinforcing effects that free trade and competition law often have, they can come into conflict as well. On an abstract level, the goals pursued by (and mind-sets of) trade lawyers and competition lawyers are different. Trade lawyers are generally primarily focussed on protecting the interests and welfare of their home jurisdiction's domestic industry, that is, its producers and exporters. For public choice and collective action reasons, they are generally less focussed on their home jurisdiction's consumers, and consumers abroad do not figure in their calculation at all. The focus of competition lawyers tends to be total welfare and the process of competition, at least in their home jurisdictions, but potentially also, though to a lesser extent, abroad. On the margin, competition lawyers therefore give greater weight to consumer and total welfare than trade lawyers, who have a greater focus on domestic producer welfare.

This difference on the abstract level becomes clearer when comparing the trade concept of dumping and the competition law concept of predatory pricing.[23] From a trade perspective, dumping exists where an exporter charges prices that are lower than those normally charged on the exporter's home market, causing injury to the domestic industry in the export market.[24] From a competition perspective, the

[22]See below Sect. 3.2.2.

[23]See, e.g., Hoekman and Mavroidis (1996).

[24]See Agreement on Implementation of Article VI of the General Agreement on Tariffs and Trade 1994, in particular Article 2, which defines dumping; Article 3, which sets out how "injury" is determined; Article 4, which defines "domestic industry"; and Article 9 on the imposition and collection of dumping duties. In the EU, see Regulation (EU) 2016/1036 of the European Parliament and of the Council of 8 June 2016 on protection against dumped imports from countries not members of the European Union, OJ 2016 L 176/21 (the "Anti-Dumping Regulation"); see in particular Articles 1, 2, which set out the principles and what constitutes dumping; Article 3, which defines injury; Article 4, which defines who must be injured, namely the "Union industry" consisting of Union *producers*; and Article 9 on the imposition of definitive duties. It should, however, be mentioned that in the EU a final prong, which is *not* required by WTO law, is added, namely the requirement that anti-dumping measures are not against the Union's interest (Article 21 of the Anti-Dumping Regulation). This test takes the welfare not only of the industry, but also of consumers into account (Article 21(1) of the Anti-Dumping Regulation). However, first, the test shall be "based on an appreciation" of all the interests; this is less than saying that the measures should not be taken where the net welfare effect would be negative. Secondly, this prong is formulated as an exception to the rule: measures may not be applied only where "the authorities can clearly conclude that it is not in the Union's interest". Thirdly, as a matter of practice and public choice, one may expect producers' interests to be much more coordinated and better represented in the procedure than consumers' interests.

relationship between prices in the exporter's home market and the export market is irrelevant. Indeed, unless the competitor in question has a dominant position (or unless competitors collude), competition lawyers would not worry about low prices at all. Competition lawyers would be concerned only where there is collusion, or where the cumulative criteria of the undertaking being in a dominant position *and* prices being below an appropriate cost measure (and, depending on the jurisdiction, a dangerous probability or reasonable likelihood of recoupment) are fulfilled.

The different mind-sets of trade and competition lawyers also came to the fore in the Structural Impediment Initiative (SII): while Chicago-inspired competition lawyers argued (rightly or wrongly) that the largely vertical and conglomerate relationships making up the *keiretsu* system in Japan were unproblematic from a competition perspective,[25] the US Trade Representative focussed alone on the interests of the US exporters who felt that market entry was made more difficult.[26] This is sending mixed signals.

Yet another emanation of the different focus of trade law and competition law is crystallised in legislation exempting exporters from antitrust scrutiny. While the empirical magnitude of the effect of such (explicit or implicit[27]) exemptions for export cartels is controversial,[28] conceptually there is little question that they are an attempt to implement beggar-thy-neighbour strategies.[29] One could object that the preferential treatment of export cartels actually follows from the consumer welfare orientation of competition law: it lies in the effects test's nature, with its focus on domestic effects, to exempt pure[30] export cartels from scrutiny implicitly. Pure export cartels by definition do not have any substantial effects in their home jurisdiction. Unless the law additionally provides for enforcement based on the territoriality or nationality principle, pure export cartels are automatically (implicitly) exempt, even without explicit legislative exemptions.[31] From a competition

[25] Melamed (1998), p. 441 et seq. See also Trebilcock (1996), p. 99; Marsden (2010), p. 306; Wagner-von Papp (2012), p. 37 et seq.

[26] Supporting the arguments made in the SII by the USTR e.g. Morita (1991).

[27] Levenstein and Suslow (2005).

[28] Sokol (2008), p. 970 et seq.; Sweeney (2007), pp. 91–96.

[29] Wagner-von Papp (2012), pp. 49–51; Martyniszyn (2012b); Becker (2007); Guzman (2004), p. 373; Immenga (1995); Hoekman and Mavroidis (2003), p. 11; Scherer (1994), p. 93; Jenny (2012).

[30] As opposed to "mixed" export cartels, that is, export cartels where it is reasonably foreseeable that there will be substantial domestic effects, for example because of a realistic possibility of reimports, cf. CJEU, case C-306/96, *Javico v YSLP*, ECLI:EU:C:1998:173. A difficult question, but one that is beyond the scope of this overview, is to what extent the indirect effects resulting from the distortions in the pattern of trade caused by *any* cartel are to be taken into account when determining domestic effects (e.g., where an export cartel raises export prices, some of the domestic supply may shift to the export markets, thereby reducing domestic supply and raising domestic prices; or the raised export prices may lead to reduced demand in the export market, reducing production by domestic producers, which may result in reduced economies of scale, raising domestic prices).

[31] Wagner-von Papp (2012), pp. 49–51.

policy point, however, export cartels are nearly universally condemned, and it is possible to prohibit export cartels: There are examples of legislation that subject cartel activity of pure export cartels to the home jurisdiction's scrutiny. From a public international law perspective, such legislation can be justified on the basis of the territoriality (or possibly the active nationality) principle: it is not, after all, the exercise of *extra*-territorial jurisdiction where an export cartel is established on domestic territory. Nevertheless, one could raise the question what the home jurisdiction's legitimate interest is in prohibiting activity that will not have any substantial effects on its own territory. In other words, one may ask whether it does not follow from the logic of the effects test that it *limits territorial jurisdiction as well as expands extraterritorial jurisdiction*. While such an interest-based genuine-link requirement has its attractions, it certainly departs from the orthodoxy in public international law that a sovereign state can prohibit conduct on its own territory and conduct by its own citizens. Even those who would reject territorial enforcement against conduct without foreseeable substantial domestic effects may be willing to let it suffice that collusive practices in the export sector may have spill-over effects on domestic competition, or that non-enforcement may result in negative reputational effects on the international level for the enforcing jurisdiction.

This leads to a further possible conflict between the trade lawyer's focus on domestic industry and the competition lawyer's focus on total welfare in the context of export cartels. Competition lawyers in the target state, where the negative welfare effects of the cartels on consumers are felt, will be in favour of enforcing the target state's competition laws against the export cartel. However, there have been cases where the target state's trade lawyers have tolerated or even actively encouraged foreign export cartels that raised prices, because this attenuated the competitive pressure on the target state's domestic industry (even where this came at the expense of domestic consumers), occasionally resulting in formalised voluntary export restraint agreements.[32] This is just another emanation of the trade lawyer's aversion to low prices by foreign competitors that we already encountered in relation to dumping. In essence, the target state in voluntary export restraint agreements delegates the task of imposing an anti-dumping tariff to the cartel, without regard to whether or not even the relaxed preconditions for dumping would have been fulfilled, never mind the strict conditions of predatory pricing.

These different goals and mind-sets between trade and competition lawyers have arguably contributed to the relative neglect with which competition law has been treated in FTAs. Another factor why FTAs and other international agreements have not featured competition concerns more prominently is that many of these concerns can be addressed by unilateral extraterritorial enforcement. The scope and limits of this extraterritorial enforcement will be summarised in Sect. 3, before turning to competition law in international agreements in Sect. 4.

[32]Immenga (1995). These Voluntary Export Restraints (VERs) have been phased out under the WTO agreement on safeguards, but as the *In re Vitamins Antitrust Litigation* case shows (discussed in Sect. 3.2.1 below), they continue to have restrictive effects under a different name. For other continuing effects of VERs see Kagitani and Harimaya (2015).

3 Unilateral Extraterritorial Enforcement

This is not the place to elaborate on the development and exact scope of unilateral extraterritorial enforcement.[33] Nevertheless, a brief overview is necessary to identify which competition issues can be addressed by unilateral extraterritorial enforcement (below Sect. 3.1) and the gaps that a pure unilateral extraterritorial enforcement scheme cannot fill (below Sects. 3.2, 3.3, and 3.4), and the overlaps that are created (below Sect. 3.5). For these gaps and overlaps international cooperation is required.

3.1 Qualified Effects Doctrine (in particular: "Component Cases")

The qualified effects doctrine has won the day in the US and the EU. For the US, this is an old hat.[34] The EU has famously taken its time, and the Court of Justice of the European Union (CJEU) has yet to adopt the qualified effects test explicitly. However, for all intents and purposes, EU institutions have always applied EU competition law extraterritorially *as if* a qualified effects test were the law of the land, either by explicitly applying the effects test, as the Commission, the General Court and various Advocates General at the CJEU have done,[35] or by using crutches, as the CJEU has done so far, like finding domestic conduct by employing

[33]See e.g. Geradin et al. (2010) and Wagner-von Papp (2012).

[34]*United States v Aluminum Co of America*, 148 F.2d 416 (2d Cir. 1945) ("Alcoa"); *Hartford Fire v California*, 509 U.S. 764, 795–796 (1993); *Hoffmann-La Roche v Empagran*, 542 U.S. 155, 165 (2004); US Department of Justice & Federal Trade Commission Antitrust Guidelines for International Enforcement and Cooperation, 13 January 2017, https://www.ftc.gov/public-statements/2017/01/antitrust-guidelines-international-enforcement-cooperation-issued-us (last accessed 16 July 2017), section 3. More precisely, the qualifications under *Alcoa* and *Hartford Fire* are that US law is applicable as soon as there are "intended and substantial effects". For foreign commerce other than import commerce, the more stringent criteria of the FTAIA of "direct, substantial and foreseeable effects" have to be fulfilled.

[35]GC, case T-286/09, *Intel v Commission*, ECLI:EU:T:2014:547, paras. 231–258; on appeal: Opinion by AG Wahl in CJEU, case C-413/14 P, *Intel v Commission*, ECLI:EU:C:2016:788, paras. 294–305; see previously already Commission Decision 69/243/EEC, *Dyestuffs*, OJ 1969 L 195/11; AG Mayras's Opinion to CJEU, case 48/69, *ICI v Commission*, ECLI:EU:C:1972:32, paras. 688–691; Commission Decision 85/202/EC, *Woodpulp*, OJ 1985 L 85/1, para. 79; AG Darmon's Opinion to CJEU, joined cases 89/85, 104/85, 114/85, 116/85, 117/85 and 125/85 to 129/85, *Ahlström v Commission*, ECLI:EU:C:1988:258, para. 7 et seq.; obiter in GC, case T-91/11, *InnoLux v Commission*, ECLI:EU:T:2014:92, para. 62, finding that the implementation test was satisfied in the case at bar; see also Opinion of AG Wathelet to CJEU, case C-231/14 P, *InnoLux v Commission*, ECLI:EU:C:2015:292, who, however, considered the effects not sufficiently direct in the component case in question; the Court eventually did not consider the question to be relevant.

the single economic entity principle[36] and an expansive implementation test,[37] which, while notionally based on the territoriality principle and theoretically narrower than the effects doctrine, has never in its practical application been more restrictive than the effects doctrine would have been.

The qualifications of the effects test—effects must be "direct, substantial and foreseeable"—have so far not usually proved to be a high hurdle, either.[38] "Substantiality" is generally interpreted as a de minimis standard, and would more accurately be described as "appreciability"; even potential effects are sufficient.[39] "Foreseeability" is the normative filter by which conduct is excluded from scrutiny in which the actors could not reasonably have been aware that there would be anticompetitive effects in the jurisdiction in question. Where it is clear from the supply or distribution chains that semi-final or end products will reach a particular jurisdiction, it is unlikely that the foreseeability test would not be met.

The qualification creating the greatest difficulties is arguably the "directness" criterion. On a literal reading, it would seem to exclude any "indirect" effect, that is, any effect that is caused by way of some intermediate causal step. Taken literally, practically all economic effects are indirect, because markets are complex phenomena. Neither excluding all indirect effects nor including remote indirect ripple effects can be the correct interpretation of the "directness" criterion. The latter would subject all anticompetitive conduct to universal jurisdiction; the former would eliminate extraterritoriality entirely. Directness is therefore not a black-or-white question, but rather a question of which of the 50 shades of grey still deserve antitrust scrutiny. This has led to the problem how to treat the so-called "component cases". In these cases, which are getting more frequent because of global supply chains enabled by free trade,[40] the cartel is between producers of components that are sold and delivered to (innocent) assemblers in a foreign jurisdiction, who may or may not be subsidiaries of the cartelist or the eventual victim, where they are assembled into a final product, before this finished product is exported to the end consumers' jurisdiction. Some argue that here the end consumer market is only

[36]CJEU, case 48/69, *Imperial Chemical Industries Ltd. v Commission*, ECLI:EU:C:1972:70.

[37]CJEU, joined cases 89/85, 104/85, 114/85, 116/85, 117/85 and 125/85 to 129/85, *Ahlström v Commission ("Wood Pulp I")*, ECLI:EU:C:1988:447, paras. 16–18.

[38]Wagner-von Papp (2012), pp. 28–32, for the qualifiers in the FTAIA.

[39]However, see opinion by AG Wahl to CJEU, case C-413/14 P, *Intel v Commission*, ECLI:EU:C:2016:788, paras. 318–327, considering that the General Court's assessment that the effects were substantial is vitiated by error, that the relevant facts were not assessed by the General Court, and that the case should be referred back to the General Court.

[40]See the 2014 OECD-WTO-World Bank Report to the G20, Global Value Chains: Challenges, Opportunities, and Implications for Policy, Sydney, Australia, 19 July 2014, https://www.oecd.org/tad/gvc_report_g20_july_2014.pdf (last accessed 16 July 2017).

indirectly affected by the upstream cartel. Despite some prevarication,[41] US courts have decided that the US antitrust laws extend to these cases and the directness criterion is satisfied as long as there is a "reasonably proximate causal nexus".[42] This is also the position taken in the 2017 Antitrust Guidelines for International Enforcement and Cooperation.[43] However, *private* enforcement in these cases is constrained because of the lack of standing for indirect purchasers under federal antitrust law.[44] This normative and nuanced understanding of the "directness" criterion is by far the preferable approach.

In EU law, the issues arising from component cases are not yet settled. They had first been raised in a case concerning the very same LCD cartel underlying the US case *Motorola v. AU Optronics*: the *InnoLux* case.[45] In this case, Advocate General *Wathelet* argued that the Court of Justice of the European Union should consider sales of the cartelised good (LCD screens) to the vertically integrated appellants' subsidiaries, who then integrated the screens into the end product, as extra-territorial sales that did not have a direct effect in the EU.[46] In making his argument he pointed to the "similar" decision in *Motorola v. AU Optronics*, apparently

---

[41]See the decision *Motorola Mobility LLC v AU Optronics Corp*, 746 F.3d 842 (7th Cir. 27 March 2014)—Judge Posner arguing that the sale from the defendants to the plaintiff's foreign subsidiaries who then imported finished products into the US did not create a "direct" effect in the US, and additionally did not give rise to a claim in the US because these were indirect purchases (vacated and rehearing granted 1 July 2014); see also *Minn-Chem v Agrium*, 657 F.3d 650, 661–662 (7th Cir. 2011) (vacated and rehearing en banc granted). For the decisions after rehearing, see the references in the next footnote.

[42]*Motorola Mobility LLC v AU Optronics Corp*, 775 F.3d 816 (7th Cir. 26 November 2014, amended 12 January 2015)—Judge Posner, now conceding that the effects may have been "direct" and assuming this for the appeal; however, rejecting that this gave rise to a claim in the US, because these were indirect purchases, *cert. den.* 15 June 2015; *Lotes Co. v. Hon Hai Precision Industry Co.*, 753 F.3d 395, 409–413 (2d Cir. 2014); *Minn-Chem v Agrium*, 683 F.3d 845, 856–858 (7th Cir. 2012)—Chief Justice Diane Wood, considering that the "directness" criterion only requires a "reasonably proximate causal nexus", *cert. den.*, 134 S.Ct. 23 (2013). The three-judge panel in *United States v. Hui Hsiung*, 778 F.3d 738 (9th Cir. 2014, amended 30 January 2015) did not have to decide whether the majority opinion in *United States v. LSL Biotechnologies*, 379 F.3d 672 (9th Cir. 2004) should be reversed; that majority opinion had given a stricter interpretation to the directness criterion than the 2nd and 7th Circuit in the aforementioned cases. See also Wagner-von Papp (2012), pp. 29–31.

[43]US Department of Justice & Federal Trade Commission Antitrust Guidelines for International Enforcement and Cooperation, 13 January 2017, https://www.ftc.gov/public-statements/2017/01/antitrust-guidelines-international-enforcement-cooperation-issued-us (last accessed 16 July 2017), section 3.2.

[44]See the *Empagran* and *Motorola Mobility* cases, as well as US Department of Justice & Federal Trade Commission Antitrust Guidelines for International Enforcement and Cooperation, 13 January 2017, https://www.ftc.gov/public-statements/2017/01/antitrust-guidelines-international-enforcement-cooperation-issued-us (last accessed 16 July 2017), section 3.2, p. 25 et seq.

[45]For an analysis of *InnoLux* see, e.g., Martyniszyn (2016).

[46]Opinion of AG Wathelet to CJEU, case C-231/14 P, *InnoLux v Commission*, ECLI:EU:C:2015:292, paras. 23–62.

referring to the decision which the Seventh Circuit had later vacated[47] and not the revised November 2014 decision[48] which had eventually assumed the effects to be sufficiently direct.[49] The Advocate General accordingly recommended that the Court set aside the General Court's judgment and annul the Commission decision on the fine to the extent it was based on the sale of imported finished end products that merely incorporated the cartelised goods. The CJEU in *InnoLux* did *not* follow the Advocate General's recommendation and dismissed the appeal.[50] This, however, was not based on an acceptance of the Commission's and General Court's argument that the effects of the sales of finished end products containing the cartelised goods were sufficiently direct, substantial and foreseeable, but based on the argument that the question simply did not arise in the case: the cartel agreement undoubtedly had qualified effects and was implemented in the EU, and the only question raised by the case was the question whether the sales of the end products incorporating the cartelised goods could be used in determining the fine.[51] In the *Intel* case, Advocate General *Wahl* indicated that he, in contrast to Advocate General *Wathelet*, would not exclude the possibility that indirect sales could be considered an implementation of the infringement in the EU.[52] For reasons I have explained elsewhere, I would hope that the CJEU will follow the Second and Seventh Circuits in the US in determining whether or not the effects in the component cases are sufficiently "direct" by applying a purposive interpretation to this qualifier of the qualified effects test.[53]

There is no question that the long arm of unilateral extraterritorial competition law enforcement reaches far. Nevertheless, some gaps remain. In terms of

---

[47]*Motorola Mobility LLC v AU Optronics Corp*, 746 F.3d 842 (7th Cir. 27 March 2014) (vacated 1 July 2014).

[48]*Motorola Mobility LLC v AU Optronics Corp*, 775 F.3d 816 (7th Cir. 26 November 2014, amended 12 January 2015), *cert. Den.* 15 June 2015.

[49]Opinion of AG Wathelet to CJEU, case C-231/14 P, *InnoLux v Commission*, ECLI:EU:C:2015:292, paras. 39–41.

[50]CJEU, case C-231/14 P, *InnoLux v Commission*, ECLI:EU:C:2015:451.

[51]CJEU, case C-231/14 P, *InnoLux v Commission*, ECLI:EU:C:2015:451, paras. 71–76.

[52]Opinion by AG Wahl to CJEU, case C-413/14 P, *Intel v Commission,* ECLI:EU:C:2016:788, para. 292 with fn. 180, giving as an example the situation in which the two foreign companies are part of a single economic entity, as had been the case in *InnoLux*. As I have explained elsewhere (Wagner-von Papp (2012), p. 46), I agree that the implementation test can reach cases where the foreign cartelist sell to foreign subsidiaries which then export into the EU when cartelist and the subsidiary form a single economic entity; where this is not the case (as, for example, in the US case *Motorola Mobility v AU Optronics*), the qualified effects test would apply. Whether the effects are sufficiently direct in that case depends, in my view, on whether there is a "reasonably proximate causal nexus" (as the Second and Seventh Circuits put it in *Motorola Mobility LLC v AU Optronics Corp*, 775 F.3d 816 (7th Cir. 26 November 2014, amended 12 January 2015); *Lotes Co. v. Hon Hai Precision Industry Co.*, 753 F.3d 395, 409–413 (2d Cir. 2014); *Minn-Chem v Agrium*, 683 F.3d 845, 856–858 (7th Cir. 2012)); and whether this nexus is reasonably proximate is, in my view, synonymous with the question whether the effects in the jurisdiction in question were reasonably foreseeable (Wagner-von Papp (2012), p. 31).

[53]Wagner-von Papp (2012), pp. 29–31 and 46.

prescriptive jurisdiction or substantive reach of the competition laws, gaps remain in so far as there is state involvement and in "outbound" cases (below Sect. 3.2). Arguably even more frequent are problems that result from limits to the enforcement jurisdiction, which, in contrast to prescriptive jurisdiction, is strictly territorial (below Sect. 3.3).

3.2 Gaps in the Prescriptive Jurisdiction or Substantive Reach

In terms of prescriptive jurisdiction, there are relatively few constraints on extraterritoriality. Remaining gaps in the extraterritorial coverage regarding prescriptive jurisdiction or the substantive requirements of competition law mostly concern the involvement of state action in one form or another (below Sect. 3.2.1). Also, access-restricting exclusionary measures implemented exclusively in a foreign jurisdiction are outside the reach of an effects test in combination with the territoriality principle; justifying exercising prescriptive jurisdiction in these cases hinges on the more doubtful combination of the effects principle with a passive personality principle (below Sect. 3.2.2).

3.2.1 An Example of State Involvement: In re Vitamin C Antitrust Litigation

With regard to prescriptive jurisdiction and substantive reach of the competition laws, nearly all gaps are due to state involvement in the infringement. Unproblematic are those cases in which one jurisdiction allows what the other prohibits—for example: export cartels from one jurisdiction, which are prohibited as import cartels by the other. In these cases, there is a way to conform with all legal obligations by refraining from the conduct, and courts both in the US and the EU have made clear that they will not accept the mere legality of conduct in one jurisdiction, or even encouragement by that state, as an excuse if the conduct infringes the law of the other jurisdiction.[54]

More problematic are cases in which one jurisdiction prescribes what the other proscribes (true conflict cases). Traditionally, cases in this category mostly had a procedural flavour: they often concerned cases in which one jurisdiction (most often the US) sought to compel the production of evidence in the discovery

[54] *Hartford Fire Insurance v California*, 509 U.S. 764, 798–799 (1993); *Continental Ore v Union Carbide*, 370 U.S. 690, 706–707 (1962); CJEU, joined cases 89/85, 104/85, 114/85, 116/85, 117/85 and 125/85 to 129/85, *Ahlström v Commission*, ECLI:EU:C:1988:447, para. 19 et seq.; GC, case T-102/96, *Gencor v Commission*, ECLI:EU:T:1999:65, para. 103.

procedure, while the foreign jurisdiction had a blocking statute.[55] In cases concerning substantive competition law, defendants often plead true conflicts, but it is rare that courts find sufficient state compulsion to accept that there is a true conflict.

Recently, however, there has been an interesting case in the US in which a substantive competition law infringement was considered to be subject to a true conflict, and which demonstrates the interaction between competition and trade law. In *In re Vitamins Antitrust Litigation*, the defendants had not denied their participation in a price-fixing cartel, but instead argued that they had been compelled by Chinese law to enter into the cartel. Defendants argued that a "Chamber" determined prices, and that only exports based on these "industry-wide negotiated" Chamber-coordinated prices would receive the Ministry's seal of approval (so-called "price-verification-chop", or PVC system). In contrast to previous cases in which a true conflict had been claimed, the Chinese government filed an *amicus curiae* brief supporting the defendants' interpretation of Chinese law. Interestingly for our purposes, the Ministry had introduced this PVC system in 2002 in lieu of the previous system of export quote licences "in order to accommodate the new situations since China's entry into [the World Trade Organization], maintain the order of market competition, *make active efforts to avoid anti-dumping sanctions imposed by foreign countries on China's exports*, promote industry self-discipline and facilitate the healthy development of exports".[56] The cartel was, in other words, a reaction to the phasing out of VERs under the WTO agreement on safeguards.

The District Court had denied defendants' motions to dismiss and for summary judgment, because it considered the Ministry's submission that Chinese law compelled the cartel to be contradicted by other evidence, showing, among other things, that the defendants had occasionally undercut the PVC prices without any repercussions. Essentially, the District Court treated the Chamber merely as a cartel that was encouraged and facilitated, but not compelled, by the Chinese government. After the jury had returned its verdict, the District Court entered judgment for plaintiffs and awarded $147 million in damages. On 20 September 2016, the Court of Appeals for the Second Circuit vacated the judgment for plaintiffs, reversed the District Court's decision to reject defendants' motion to dismiss and remanded with the instruction to dismiss the complaint with prejudice. The Court of Appeals applied principles of international comity and found that it was an abuse of

---

[55]See, e.g., *Société Nationale Industrielle Aérospatiale v US District Court*, 482 U.S. 522, 544 f. 29 (1987); *Richmark Corp. v Timber Falling Consultants*, 959 F.2d 1468, 1474–1475 (9th Cir. 1992); *In re Honda American Motor Dealership Relations Lit.*, 168 FRD 535 (D. Md. 1996). For a case in the EU see, e.g., Commission Decision 76/593/EEC, *CSV*, OJ 1976 L 192/27 (duty to comply with a request for information despite assumed applicability of Article 273 of the Swiss Criminal Code).

[56]*In re Vitamin C Antitrust Litigation, Animal Science Products Inc. et al. v Hebei Welcome Pharmaceutical Co. et al.*, Docket No. 13–4791–cv (2nd Cir., 20 September 2016), slip opinion, p. 10 (emphasis added).

discretion for the District Court not to defer to the Chinese government's interpretation of its domestic laws, and that, pursuant to the *Timberlane Lumber* and *Mannington Mills* comity balancing test,[57] subject matter jurisdiction over the extraterritorial conduct should not be exercised. The Second Circuit interpreted the *Hartford Fire* decision narrowly: in that decision, the Supreme Court had held that because there was no true conflict, there was "no need in this litigation to consider other considerations that might inform the decision to refrain from the exercise of jurisdiction on the ground of international comity".[58] This left unclear whether the "other considerations" would have to be considered where there was a true conflict. The Second Circuit was of the view that these other comity balancing factors would have to be considered where there was a true conflict.[59] In applying these other factors, and finding comity to require refraining from exercising jurisdiction, the Second Circuit noted, among other things,[60] that

> complaints as to China's export policies can adequately be addressed through diplomatic channels and the World Trade Organization's processes. Both the U.S. and China are members of the World Trade Organization and are subject to the same rules on export restrictions[61]

and that

> the Plaintiffs are not without recourse to the executive branch, which is best suited to deal with foreign policy, sanctions, treaties, and bi-lateral negotiations.[62]

The Second Circuit did not reach the act of state, foreign sovereign compulsion and political question issues because it considered that the District Court's judgment should be reversed on comity grounds. The US Supreme Court is currently considering the certiorari petition (sub nomine *Animal Science Products, Inc.*

---

[57]*Timberlane Lumber v Bank of America*, 549 F.2d 597, 610 et seq. (9th Cir. 1976); *Mannington Mills v Congoleum Corp*, 595 F2d 1287, 1297–1298 (3d Cir. 1979). Also cf. § 403 Restatement (Third) of Foreign Relations Law and Justice Scalia's dissenting opinion in *Hartford Fire Insurance v California*, 509 U.S. 764, 800 et seq. (1993).

[58]*Hartford Fire Insurance v California*, 509 U.S. 764, 798 (1993).

[59]*In re Vitamin C Antitrust Litigation, Animal Science Products Inc. et al. v Hebei Welcome Pharmaceutical Co. et al.*, Docket No. 13–4791–cv (2nd Cir., 20 September 2016), slip opinion, p. 21 et seq. The Second Circuit left open whether, as some lower courts had held even after *Hartford Fire*, a comity balancing test might even apply in the absence of a true conflict.

[60]Other factors mentioned were that the conduct took place between Chinese defendants on Chinese soil, that the case had led to strained relations to the Chinese Government, that the conduct was not targeted specifically at the US, that the defendants would otherwise be subject to contradicting obligations under US and Chinese law, and that injunctive relief would almost certainly not be obtainable in China.

[61]*In re Vitamin C Antitrust Litigation, Animal Science Products Inc. et al. v Hebei Welcome Pharmaceutical Co. et al.*, Docket No. 13–4791–cv (2nd Cir., 20 September 2016), slip opinion, p. 41.

[62]*In re Vitamin C Antitrust Litigation, Animal Science Products Inc. et al. v Hebei Welcome Pharmaceutical Co. et al.*, Docket No. 13–4791–cv (2nd Cir., 20 September 2016), slip opinion, p. 44.

v. Hebei Welcome Pharmaceutical Co. Ltd., Docket No. 16-1220), and on 26 June 2017, the Court requested the Acting Solicitor General to file a brief for the United States, indicating that the Court is minded to consider granting certiorari.

In the EU, anticompetitive conduct *compelled* by foreign law would arguably not be subject to competition law, although it is less clear that European Courts would have found this to be the case on the facts of *In re Vitamin C Litigation*. The Chinese scheme in *In re Vitamins C Litigation* does not seem to amount to state compulsion that would prevent the undertakings from engaging in autonomous economic activity "on their own initiative" in the meaning of the EU state action cases.[63] While the legislative requirement of ministerial approval (the "chop") could be seen to remove the "possibility of competitive conduct", the Chinese legislative scheme seems merely to delegate price-setting authority to the market participants without obliging them to consider the public interest, and the ministerial procedure does not seem to give the minister room for independent control over the "industry-wide negotiated" prices.

Wood Pulp and *Gencor* at least indicate that the public international law principles of non-interference or proportionality could prevent exercise of international jurisdiction in the case of a true conflict, although these cases stopped short of endorsing such a principle.[64] It seems likely that in cases of true conflict, the EU Court would not apply EU competition law, although there are policy reasons both for and against the application. On the one hand, the only way in which the undertakings could conform to both legal orders where the foreign state genuinely *requires* exports at a cartelised price, would be to refrain entirely from importing into the EU. This would dampen instead of invigorate competition in the EU. On the other hand, of course, refraining from applying competition law in true conflict cases provides an incentive to foreign undertakings and foreign governments to enact requirements compelling anti-competitive conduct.

It appears unlikely, however, that European courts would have accorded the Chinese Government's intervention the absolute deference that the Second Circuit

---

[63]This assumes that the intra-EU state action jurisprudence would be applied by analogy to non-Member States as well. For a discussion whether the standards of the US state action docrine (that is, the *Midcal* test of clear articulation and active supervision, rather than strict compulsion) should be applied to foreign nations, see Baker and Rushkoff (1990), p. 425 et seq. For a comparison of the US Foreign Sovereign Compulsion Doctrine (which is separate from both the state action doctrine and the comity test applied in *In re Vitamins C Antitrust Litigation*) and the EU case law on state action see Martyniszyn (2012a), correctly pointing to the unclear status of state compulsion in EU law as either exempting from the substantive provisions in Articles 101, 102 TFEU (as is usually argued in cases involving compulsion) or as providing the undertakings (but not the compelling state) with a defence based on legal certainty while leaving the infringement of Articles 101 or 102 TFEU untouched, CJEU, case C-198/01, *Consorzio Industrie Fiammiferi (CIF) v Autorità Garante della Concorrenza e del Mercato*, ECLI:EU:C:2003:430, para. 53 et seq.

[64]CJEU, joined cases 89/85, 104/85, 114/85, 116/85, 117/85 and 125/85 to 129/85, *Ahlström v Commission*, ECLI:EU:C:1988:447, para. 19 et seq.; GC, case T-102/96, *Gencor v Commission*, ECLI:EU:T:1999:65, para. 103.

required, and the findings of the District Court in the case arguably indicate that the system of voluntary self-restraint did not in practice amount to an irresolvable conflict between compliance with Chinese law and foreign competition law. In the past, claims of state compulsion have been treated with deep scepticism in the EU when raised outside a clear regulatory framework, and there is little reason to suspect that this will change.

Nevertheless, to the extent prescriptive jurisdiction or the legality of its exercise is denied in true conflict cases, this produces some gaps in the unilateral enforcement of competition law.

3.2.2 "Outbound" Cases: Effects on Exporters

The extraterritorial reach of EU competition law may also exclude cases in which private conduct on foreign soil prevents competition in that foreign jurisdiction. In particular, where a foreign market forecloses access by exclusionary private agreements which have no substantial, direct and reasonably foreseeable effect on competition in the EU, not even the qualified effects doctrine in combination with the territoriality principle (much less the implementation test) can justify international jurisdiction. Why should the EU be permitted to export its competition law along with its goods?[65] From a European perspective, such issues of market access would have to be resolved by domestic competition law of the importing foreign state, possibly incentivised by FTAs or enforcement cooperation agreements.

The US is, or at least purports to be, more aggressive in these cases. The Foreign Trade Antitrust Improvement Act 1982 (FTAIA) provides that the Sherman and FTC Acts are applicable not only when import commerce is restrained (in which case the FTAIA does not limit the extraterritorial application at all[66]), or when there are direct, substantial and reasonably foreseeable effects on trade and commerce "which is not trade or commerce with foreign nations, or on import trade or import commerce with foreign nations" (that is, when there are effects on any trade and commerce that is not purely foreign or pure export),[67] but also where there are direct, substantial and reasonably foreseeable effects "*on export trade or export commerce with foreign nations, of a person engaged in such trade or commerce in the United States*".[68] Until 1992, the Department of Justice's (DOJ) 1988 International Guidelines made clear that the DOJ did not intend to make use of this provision. Footnote 159 of these 1988 Guidelines provided:

> Although the [FTAIA] extends jurisdiction under the Sherman Act to conduct that has a direct, substantial, and reasonably foreseeable effect on the export trade or export commerce of a person engaged in such commerce in the United States, *the Division is*

[65]Trebilcock (1996).

[66]15 U.S.C. § 6a *principium*. In these cases, where import commerce or trade is restrained directly, the *Hartford Fire* standard (intended and actual effects) applies.

[67]15 U.S.C. § 6a(1)(A).

[68]15 U.S.C. § 6a(1)(B).

> *concerned only with adverse effects on competition that would harm U.S. consumers by reducing output or raising prices.*[69]

In 1992, the DOJ famously withdrew this footnote 159, and declared that it would

> in appropriate cases, take antitrust enforcement action against conduct occurring overseas that restrains United States exports, whether or not there is direct harm to US consumers, where it is clear that: (1) the conduct has a direct, substantial, and reasonably foreseeable effect on exports of goods or services from the United States; (2) the conduct involves anticompetitive activities which violate the US antitrust laws – in most cases, group boycotts, collusive pricing, and other exclusionary activities; and (3) US courts have jurisdiction over foreign persons or corporations engaged in such conduct.[70]

The subsequent 1995 DOJ/FTC International Guidelines included examples of market foreclosure to the detriment of US exporters in which the DOJ and FTC would consider application of US law justified.[71] The new 2017 DOJ/FTC International Guidelines do not mention this "outbound" category any longer.[72]

In theory, this extension of the unilateral extraterritorial reach of competition laws would seem to reduce the need for international cooperation. In practice, however, the US appears to use the *threat* of exercising this kind of "outbound" jurisdiction as leverage for negotiating a solution instead of actually enforcing their antitrust laws in this category of cases. The 1992 statement that superseded footnote 159 already hinted at this use. It stated that "[i]f the conduct is also unlawful under the importing country's antitrust laws, the [DOJ] is prepared to work with that country if that country is better situated to remedy the conduct and is prepared to take action against such conduct pursuant to its antitrust laws",[73] a statement that was included nearly verbatim in the 1995 DOJ/FTC International Guidelines.[74] An alternative way for the US to address these cases, and one which is

[69]1988 U.S. Department of Justice Antitrust Enforcement Guidelines for International Operations, reprinted in Department of Justice, World Competition 12 (1988), pp. 105–207, note 159 (emphasis added).

[70]Department of Justice, Press Release, Justice Department will challenge foreign restraints on US exports under antitrust laws, 3 April 1992, https://www.justice.gov/archive/atr/public/press_releases/1992/211137.htm (last accessed 16 July 2017).

[71]US Department of Justice and Federal Trade Commission, Antitrust Enforcement Guidelines for International Operations, April 1995, https://www.justice.gov/atr/antitrust-enforcement-guidelines-international-operations (last accessed 16 July 2017), section 3.122, illustrative examples D and E.

[72]US Department of Justice & Federal Trade Commission Antitrust Guidelines for International Enforcement and Cooperation, 13 January 2017, https://www.ftc.gov/public-statements/2017/01/antitrust-guidelines-international-enforcement-cooperation-issued-us (last accessed 16 July 2017).

[73]Department of Justice, Press Release, Justice Department will challenge foreign restraints on US exports under antitrust laws, 3 April 1992, https://www.justice.gov/archive/atr/public/press_releases/1992/211137.htm (last accessed 16 July 2017).

[74]US Department of Justice and Federal Trade Commission, Antitrust Enforcement Guidelines for International Operations, April 1995, https://www.justice.gov/atr/antitrust-enforcement-guidelines-international-operations (last accessed 16 July 2017), section 3.122. The differences were

arguably more consistent with the delimitation between antitrust and trade law than the application of antitrust law,[75] would be directly by trade remedies under section 301 of the 1974 Trade Act.[76]

3.3 Enforcement Jurisdiction

While prescriptive jurisdiction is far-reaching and subject to relatively few constraints (above Sects. 3.1 and 3.2), the same cannot be said about enforcement jurisdiction. Enforcement jurisdiction has always been and remains strictly territorial. The EU and US can prohibit import cartels as much as they want, but this does not allow them to take investigatory (or sanctioning) measures on foreign soil.

In some cases, domestic enforcement may be used to overcome this gap. For example, requests for information from, or inspections of, a domestic subsidiary may yield the required evidence; and where the infringers directly import into the EU or US, imposing and enforcing pecuniary sanctions (and, by way of periodic penalty orders, injunctive relief) is usually unproblematic.

In many cases, however, it will be difficult to uncover evidence of competition law infringements committed entirely abroad, in particular where the infringers do not have any direct sales into the enforcing jurisdiction, as is the case in the "component cases" with upstream cartels in global value chains. In these cases, it may also be difficult to impose sanctions on the infringers. Even where infringers import directly into the EU or US, sanctions other than pecuniary sanctions on the undertakings, such as criminal sanctions against individuals, are difficult to enforce due to the territorial limits of enforcement jurisdiction.

To fill these gaps in jurisdiction for investigations and sanctioning, the cooperation of the foreign state is required. The cooperation may take the form of the foreign state enforcing its own domestic competition laws, or of assisting the state in which the anticompetitive effects materialise with extraterritorial enforcement. Section 4 will discuss ways to achieve such cooperation.

3.4 De Facto Gaps

The previous sections have argued that unilateral extraterritorial enforcement cannot reach all competition law infringements for *legal* reasons. It should not be

minuscule ("as well" instead of "also", "Agencies" instead of "DOJ" to include the FTC as well; "country's authorities" instead of "country"). The 2017 Guidelines no longer refer to the category of "outbound" cases.

[75]Trebilcock and Iacobucci (2004), pp. 158–161.

[76]19 U.S.C. § 2411.

forgotten, however, that there is also a critical de facto reasons for the emergence of gaps in a pure unilateral enforcement system.

First, there is the obvious problem that not all antitrust jurisdictions and authorities have the capacity to apply their laws extraterritorially. For example, even though *theoretically* export cartels should not lead to gaps, because every export cartel is an import cartel in another jurisdiction, it seems clear that despite the fact that some 130 jurisdictions have antitrust laws, and most are able to reach extraterritorial conduct *de iure*, not all of them will be able to enforce them effectively extraterritorially. In some cases, competition law infringements of multinationals may not be prosecuted for fear of deterring foreign investment.

Second, there is a difference in perception by market participants between extraterritorial enforcement by a foreign state and domestic competition law enforcement. Consider an export cartel, initiated in Europe or Asia, into the United States. Theoretically, the criminal sanctions under US law should deter such cartels. The goal of competition law enforcement is not primarily to uncover and sanction competition law infringements; the primary goal is to deter from infringements in the first place. The effectiveness of deterrence is mediated by the market participants' understanding of the content of the law. Market participants tend to be more familiar with the laws of their own jurisdiction than with foreign laws. This means that even where there are no legal obstacles to unilateral extraterritorial enforcement, it may still be preferable to bolster domestic competition law regimes and their enforcement.

To illustrate the point and that it does not only affect unsophisticated actors, one may look at the debate about criminalisation of competition law in European jurisdictions. Opponents of criminalisation in jurisdictions that have not yet criminalised (any or all) horizontal hardcore cartels often argue that the introduction of criminal sanctions could lead to chilling effects for permissible horizontal cooperation. While this is in principle a legitimate argument, I have yet to see an acknowledgement that if there were such a chilling effect, we should already observe it for all undertakings that export to the United States (or to other jurisdictions enforcing criminal sanctions). Cartels with qualified effects in the United States are already criminalised, even though actors in other jurisdictions may not be aware of this fact.[77]

3.5 Overlaps

In addition to the enforcement gaps (above Sects. 3.2, 3.3 and 3.4), a system of uncoordinated unilateral extraterritorial enforcement would also lead to overlaps.[78] While the gaps are perhaps more exciting from a theoretical perspective, in practice

[77] Wagner-von Papp (2016), pp. 179–181.

[78] Guzman (2004, 2010).

the overlaps are arguably the greater problem. Many mergers require multijurisdictional merger filings, whether or not they pose a serious competition problem. These have to be adapted to the legal and factual differences of the various jurisdictions. The timeline may present problems for securing financing. In some cases, mergers have reportedly not been notified to all jurisdiction whose notification thresholds were exceeded to prevent one jurisdiction from derailing the deal, in the hope that the gun jumping would not be noticed in that jurisdiction. More often, the costs are in the form of a Type I error from one of several jurisdictions. Since the clearing of a merger in all affected jurisdictions is usually a sine qua non for proceeding with the transaction, the most restrictive jurisdiction will set the tone.[79]

Cartels are prosecuted and sanctioned in several jurisdictions,[80] and leniency applicants have to comply with multiple leniency regimes, which are broadly similar to each other but differ ever so slightly with regard to details such as the rules on markers, finalising the marker, the information required etc. Conflicting leniency conditions may mean that the overall expected sanctions have to be considered before a decision on the leniency application can be made—should a leniency application be submitted where the applicant would be the first in all affected jurisdictions and would receive full immunity from fines, but where the directors involved would still be criminally liable in one or two jurisdictions?

Both in the merger context and the leniency context "one-stop shop" solutions are regularly requested.[81] With regard to mergers, only very integrated systems such as the EU have been able to provide such a one-stop shop (Article 21 EU Merger Regulation 139/2004). With regard to leniency, so far not even the EU has been able to find a one-stop shop solution, even though the European Competition Network (ECN) recognises that

> [m]aking multiple parallel applications across the ECN is a complex exercise given the existing discrepancies between the different leniency regimes. Certain discrepancies may have adverse effects on the effectiveness of individual programmes.[82]

Without greater cooperation and possibly a one-stop shop, costly mistakes can and do happen.[83] While the costs in individual cases where these mistakes happen are regrettable enough, the greater cost is arguably the social cost associated with the loss of attractiveness of leniency programmes more generally.

[79]See, e.g., Guzman (2004, 2010); Wagner-von Papp (2015b), p. 620 et seq.

[80]See, e.g., the *Marine Hose Cartel*—Capobianco and Nagy (2016), p. 7 et seq. with fn. 52–57.

[81]See, e.g., Taladay (2012), global one-stop shop for markers; Pereira (2016), for a European solution modifying the current ECN Model Leniency Programme approach and making it binding; see also Capobianco and Nagy (2016), pp. 12–14.

[82]ECN, ECN Model Leniency Programme, explanatory notes, as revised November 2012, http://ec.europa.eu/competition/ecn/mlp_revised_2012_en.pdf (last accessed 16 July 2017), p. 10, para. 6.

[83]Cf. CJEU, case C-428/14, *DHL Express (Italy) v AGCM*, ECLI:EU:C:2016:27.

4 Competition Law in Trade and Cooperation Agreements

The legal and de facto limits to the exercise of extraterritorial prescriptive and enforcement jurisdiction and the overlaps created by the proliferation of regimes that are enforced unilaterally result in a need for international cooperation. This cooperation could theoretically result in a multilateral competition law regime in which the current externalities between jurisdictions are internalised by agreeing on international standards and/or enforcement institutions—similar to the internalisation of such externalities between the Member States by applying EU law. Yet such moves towards a global competition law have, with the exception of some isolated and mostly sector-specific provisions, largely failed, from the Havana Charter to the Draft International Antitrust Code and the WTO Doha Round. Nor is it clear that a more centralised approach would be desirable. Among other things, a centralised regime could lead to an ossification of the law, which would be problematic in particular in an area of law as dynamic as competition law, and it could take less account of local circumstances or preferences. Some have suggested a lead jurisdiction approach.[84] This would eliminate overlaps and would avoid many of the drawbacks of centralisation. However, at least on the global level the political feasibility of this approach seems minuscule. Sovereign nations are not going to defer to the assessment by another nation's authority, especially given that both the legal and the factual conditions may differ starkly from jurisdiction to jurisdiction even where the same conduct or concentration is in question.

Realistically, then, international cooperation is largely based on bilateral and plurilateral agreements, either between states or between competition authorities. Agreements of this sort have two aims: first, the enactment and enforcement of domestic competition law in the jurisdiction in which the conduct occurs, and, second, the provision of assistance with the extraterritorial enforcement of the laws of the jurisdiction in which there are substantial, direct and reasonably foreseeable effects.

While the proliferation of bilateral and plurilateral agreements may at first glance look like a messy second-best solution, it can nevertheless result in a system of international cooperation that combines the advantages of a decentralised approach with the benefits of reducing overall complexity and gaps as well as overlaps. This part will describe from an EU-centric perspective how this is achieved. According to the prevailing gravity model of trade, the intensity of trade between two economies depends on the geographic distance and the size of the economies. The closer other states are geographically to the EU, the more intensive is the cooperation, and the closer their "orbit" is to the centre. This system of concentric circles, in which cooperation gets weaker as one moves away from the centre, establishes one node (or centre of gravity) of the international network. Other centres of gravity may develop similar systems of concentric circles of regional trade and cooperation agreements to make up other nodes in the network (for example, the US and NAFTA). The network is completed by establishing links

[84] Budzinski (2008); see also Capobianco and Nagy (2016), p. 14 et seq.

between different nodes (or centres of gravity), such as the links between the EU and geographically distant but larger economies, such as the United States, Canada, Japan, Singapore and South Korea. This network of regional nodes and links between the nodes, combined with soft cooperation in organisations such as the International Competition Network or the OECD, may lead to a system of international coordination that reduces complexity, gaps and overlaps while avoiding the pitfalls of a centralised system.

4.1 Competition Law in Trade Agreements

FTAs concluded by the US and EU typically include a requirement to enact or maintain competition laws and specify some of the modalities of their enforcement and of cooperation between the parties. Famously, the US and the EU take a slightly different approach to the formulation of such requirements in FTAs.[85]

4.1.1 US Free Trade Agreements

FTAs concluded between the US and other states tend to establish a general requirement that the parties introduce or maintain competition laws (usually without further definition of the content of these laws) and enforcement authorities,[86] and relatively detailed provisions on due process rights,[87] cooperation,[88] and the principles of transparency[89] and non-discrimination.[90] The TPP, though now abandoned by the current US government,[91] even includes a provision that parties "should adopt or maintain [...] measures that provide an independent right of

[85]See Solano and Sennekamp (2006); see also the typology in Laprévote FC et al., Competition policy within the context of Free Trade Agreements, E15 Initiative, September 2015, http://e15initiative.org/wp-content/uploads/2015/07/E15-Competition-Laprevote-Frisch-Can-FINAL.pdf (last accessed 16 July 2017), pp. 2–14; Papadopoulos (2013), p. 99; Tschaeni and Engammare (2013) p. 44 et seq.

[86]See, for example, Article 16.1 of the TPP, https://ustr.gov/sites/default/files/TPP-Final-Text-Competition.pdf (last accessed 16 July 2017). This provision does, however, specify that the objective of the laws is to be the promotion of "economic efficiency and consumer welfare".

[87]See, e.g., Article 16.2 of the TPP.

[88]See, e.g., Articles 16.4 and 16.5 of the TPP.

[89]See, e.g., Article 16.7 of the TPP.

[90]See the reference in Article 16.1 of the TPP to the APEC Principles to Enhance Competition and Regulatory Reform, done at Auckland, 13 September 1999, http://www.apec.org/Meeting-Papers/Leaders-Declarations/1999/1999_aelm/attachment_apec.aspx (last accessed 16 July 2017), which contain non-discrimination as the first principle.

[91]Executive Order of 23 January 2017, https://www.whitehouse.gov/the-press-office/2017/01/23/presidential-memorandum-regarding-withdrawal-united-states-trans-pacific (last accessed 16 July 2017).

action", or, failing that, at least the right for individuals to request that a competition authority investigate, and, where a violation is found, a right to a follow-on action.[92]

4.1.2 EU Trade Agreements

In contrast to the FTAs between the US and third countries, the EU's agreements tend to have a greater focus on requiring substantive competition law provisions that are similar to the competition rules in the TFEU. International agreements concluded between the EU and other states tend to fall into different categories, depending on the closeness of the association between the EU and the other state.[93]

The following sections will outline the system of concentric circles that determines the depth of the cooperation in competition matters, starting from the centre—cooperation within the EU itself—moving to the inner orbit of close cooperation between the EU Commission and the EFTA Surveillance Authority and via Stabilisation and Accession Agreements (SAAs) to Euro-Mediterranean Agreements (EMAs) and Partnership and Cooperation Agreements (PCAs). These agreements describe the various "orbits" around the EU that together with the EU make up one of several clusters on the global scale. The last section in this part will look at several links interconnecting the cluster around the EU with other clusters—such as CETA, the EU-South Korea FTA, the EU-Singapore FTA and TTIP.

European Union

The centre of this system of concentric circles is made up of the supranational law of the European Union, which consists of a substantive harmonisation of national competition laws as well as close cooperation of the national competition authorities (NCAs) among themselves and between the NCAs and the Commission as *primus inter pares* in the ECN.

The control of illegal state aid is largely centralised. Outside the state aid procedure, the substantive and procedural cooperation is closest with regard to merger control. EU law provides for a one-stop shop for concentrations with a Union dimension (Article 21(3) EU Merger Regulation 139/2004), thus avoiding overlaps altogether which could result from the applicability of several national competition laws of different Member States and ultimately in divergent outcomes. This desire to avoid overlaps is also apparent in the possibility to refer a concentration without a Union dimension to the Commission if it would otherwise be controlled under the laws of at least three Member States, Article 4(5) EU Merger Regulation 139/2004. The close cooperation in merger cases between the Commission and the NCAs, which aim at allocating jurisdiction to the appropriate level in

[92]Article 16.3 of the TPP.

[93]For greater analytical depth than the overview in this section can provide, see Papadopoulos (2010), pp. 93–144.

the multilevel governance structure and at avoiding gaps and overlaps, can further be seen in the other possibilities for referral (Articles 4(4), 9 and 22 EU Merger Regulation 139/2004). This does not completely exclude the possibility of overlaps, for example, where a merger is controlled under the laws of several Members States' laws and not referred. Nevertheless, it reduces the danger of gaps and overlaps to the greatest possible extent. If concerns arise from concentrations in third countries, Article 24 with recital 44 of the EU Merger Regulation 139/2004 provide for a feedback mechanism to enable the EU to address such concerns by negotiating for non-discriminatory treatment.

With regard to the competition rules on conduct ("antitrust"), the supranational competition rules in the Treaty have to be applied by the national competition authorities (Article 3(1) Regulation 1/2003[94]) where trade between Member States may be affected. In the area of restrictive agreements, the convergence rule in Article 3(2) Regulation 1/2003 provides that national law may not lead to diverging results. Only in the area of unilateral conduct is there a significant danger of overlaps with diverging substantive standards.

The information flow within the European Competition Network (ECN) is governed in antitrust cases by Regulation 1/2003—in particular Articles 11–16—, the Network Notice,[95] and the Notice on cooperation between the Commission and the courts of the Member States.[96] Crucially, these provisions allow the exchange of confidential information within the ECN. In merger cases, the Commission liaises with the NCAs and consults the Advisory Committee under Article 19 of the EU Merger Regulation 139/2004.

European Economic Area

The closest cooperation with non-EU Member States exists between the Surveillance Authorities within the European Economic Area (EEA). The EEA Agreement's substantive competition law provisions are practically identical to those of the EU anyway. Protocol 23 concerning the Cooperation between the Surveillance Authorities (Article 58) provides for the closest possible cooperation between the EFTA Surveillance Authority and the European Commission, including administrative assistance (Article 8) and the exchange of confidential information (Article 9). Protocol 24 provides for similarly close cooperation in the area of merger control.

[94]Council Regulation (EC) No 1/2003 of 16 December 2002 on the implementation of the rules on competition laid down in Articles 81 and 82 of the Treaty, OJ 2003 L 1/1.

[95]Commission Notice on cooperation within the Network of Competition Authorities, OJ 2004 C 101/43.

[96]Commission Notice on the co-operation between the Commission and the courts of the EU Member States in the application of Articles 81 and 82 EC, OJ 2004 C 101/54.

Stabilisation and Accession Agreements and Turkey Customs Union

Moving from the centre via the "first orbit" made up of EEA states (and disregarding, for the time being, the special status of Switzerland), the next closest cooperation is afforded to candidate countries for accession and potential candidate countries for accession. The EU has entered into "Stabilisation and Accession Agreements" (SAAs) with the Western Balkan candidate countries for accession to the European Union (Albania, the former Yugoslav Republic of Macedonia [fYRoM], Montenegro, and Serbia) and potential candidate countries (Bosnia and Herzegovina, Kosovo). These agreements contain prohibitions that mirror (in greater or lesser detail) the competition provisions in the Treaty on the Functioning of the European Union (TFEU), in particular on state monopolies,[97] horizontal and vertical anticompetitive agreements,[98] abuses of dominant positions,[99] public undertakings and undertakings with special and exclusive rights,[100] as well as state aid.[101] With the candidate country Turkey, the Turkey Customs Union Decision 1/95, based on the Ankara Agreement, provides for a nearly verbatim rendering of Articles 101, 102 and 107 TFEU as far as trade between the EU and Turkey may be affected,[102] includes the content of Article 106 TFEU by reference,[103] and provides for an approximation of Turkey's competition laws to the EU's competition rules.[104] Of course, even identical "law in the books" does not necessarily result in similar "law in action", especially where the provisions are as

[97]Compare Article 37 TFEU with Article 40 in the Albania SAA, Article 39 in the fYRoM SAA, Article 43 in the Montenegro and Serbia SAAs, Article 41 in the Bosnia and Herzegovina SAA, Article 45 in the Kosovo SAA.

[98]Compare Article 101 TFEU with Article 71(1)(i) in the Albania SAA, Article 69(1)(i) in the fYRoM SAA, Article 73(1)(i) in the Montenegro and Serbia SAAs, Article 71(1)(a) in the Bosnia and Herzegovina SAA, Article 75(1)(a) in the Kosovo SAA.

[99]Compare Article 102 TFEU with Article 71(1)(ii) in the Albania SAA, Article 69(1)(ii) in the fYRoM SAA, Article 73(1)(ii) in the Montenegro and Serbia SAAs, Article 71(1)(b) in the Bosnia and Herzegovina SAA, Article 75(1)(b) in the Kosovo SAA.

[100]Compare Article 106 TFEU with Article 72 in the Albania SAA; see also Article 70 in the fYRoM SAA, Article 74 in the Montenegro and Serbia SAAs, and Article 76 in the Kosovo SAA which directly reference Article 86 TEC or Article 106 TFEU.

[101]Compare Article 107 TFEU with Article 71(1)(iii) in the Albania SAA, Article 69(1)(iii) in the fYRoM SAA, Article 73(1)(iii) in the Montenegro and Serbia SAAs; Article 71(1)(c) in the Bosnia and Herzegovina SAA, Article 75(1)(c) in the Kosovo SAA.

[102]Compare Article 32 of Decision No 1/95 of the EC-Turkey Association Council of 22 December 1995 on implementing the final phase of the Customs Union, OJ 1996 L 35/1, with Article 101 TFEU; Article 33 of Decision 1/95 with Article 102 TFEU; Article 34 of Decision 1/95 with Article 107 TFEU. See also Article 42 of Decision 1/95 and compare it to Article 37(1) TFEU.

[103]Article 41 Decision 1/95 directly references Article 90 TEC (now Article 106 TFEU).

[104]Article 39 of the Turkey Customs Union Decision 1/95.

abstract as competition provisions. The SAAs and the Turkey Customs Union Decision 1/95 seek to address this point by requiring interpretation of the competition rules in accordance with the EU's practice.[105]

In comparison to US FTAs, the institutional, procedural and cooperation issues seem at first glance to be treated superficially in the SAAs and the Turkey Customs Union Decision 1/95.[106] However, it should be borne in mind that there are separate communication channels for notifications available in the form of the Stabilisation and Association Council and the EU-Turkey Association Council.[107]

Euro-Mediterranean Agreements

Similarly, but in a slightly less detailed fashion, agreements between the EU and various Mediterranean countries provide for the adoption of rules similar to the substantive EU competition rules in so-called "Euro-Mediterranean Agreements" (EMAs). These form the next "orbit" of the system of concentric circles of cooperation. The scope varies slightly from EMA to EMA. Provisions similar to Articles 101 and 102 TFEU are always included,[108] as are rules on state monopolies

---

[105]For example, the Albania SAA provides in Article 71(3): "Any practices contrary to this Article shall be assessed on the basis of criteria arising from the application of the competition rules applicable in the Community, in particular from Articles 81, 82, 86 and 87 of the Treaty establishing the European Community [that is, Articles 101, 102, 106 and 107 TFEU] and interpretative instruments adopted by the Community institutions." See, identically, Article 73 (2) in the Montenegro and Serbia SAAs, Article 71(2) in the Bosnia and Herzegovina SAA, and (using the TFEU numbering) Article 75(2) in the Kosovo SAA. See, similarly (but leaving out Article 86 TEC/Article 106 TFEU, which is directly referenced elsewhere in those agreements), Article 69(2) in the fYRoM SAA, Article 35 of the Turkey Customs Union Decision 1/95.

[106]The SAAs require the establishment of an operationally independent competition authority (see SAA Article 71(3), (4) in the Albania SAA; Article 73(3), (4) in the Montenegro and Serbia SAAs; Article 71(3), (4) in the Bosnia and Herzegovina SAA; Article 75(3), (4) in the Kosovo SAA) and some provide for information exchange in a rather desultory fashion (see Article 69(6) in the fYRoM SAA; see also Article 36 of the Turkey Customs Union Decision 1/95). More detailed transparency requirements apply to state aids (see Article 71(5) of the Albania SAA, Article 69(3) (b) in the fYRoM SAA, Article 73(5), (6) in the Montenegro and Serbia SAAs, Article 71(5), (6) in the Bosnia and Herzegovina SAA, Article 75(5), (6) in the Kosovo SAA). The Turkey Customs Union Decision 1/95 provides for notifications (Articles 39(3) and 40) and positive comity (Article 43); where one of the parties objects to the state aid granted by the other, conflicts not settled consensually will be resolved by arbitration or litigation before the CJEU (Article 39(4), (5)).

[107]See Article 71(9) in the Albania SAA, Article 69(5) in the fYRoM SAA, Article 73(10) in the Montenegro SAA, Article 73(8), (9) Serbia SAA, Article 71(10) in the Bosnia and Herzegovina SAA, Article 75(9) in the Kosovo SAA.

[108]See Article 41(1) Algeria EMA; Article 34(1)(i), (ii) Egypt EMA; Article 36(1)(i), (ii) Israel EMA; Article 53(1)(a), (b) Jordan EMA; Article 35(1)(a), (b) Lebanon EMA; Article 36(1)(a), (b) Morocco EMA; Article 36(1)(a), (b) Tunisia EMA; Article 30(1)(i), (ii) West Bank and Gaza Strip EMA.

similar to Article 37 TFEU[109] and public undertakings and undertakings with special and exclusive rights similar to Article 106 TFEU.[110] Not all, but some, EMAs contain rules on public (state/official) aid similar to Article 107 TFEU,[111] and/or public procurement.[112] A few of the EMAs provide, similar to the SAAs, for the application of these rules in accordance with the criteria applied to the EU rules.[113] Some of these agreements are supplemented by detailed cooperation agreements similar to (and affected by the same weaknesses as) the dedicated intergovernmental cooperation agreements between the EU and the US,[114] providing for notification, exchange of information, and negative and positive comity.[115] Others only contain a cursory rule on information exchange.[116] The EMAs also provide that appropriate measures may be taken, after giving an opportunity for consultation between the parties, where anticompetitive agreements or abuses of a dominant position "cause or threaten to cause serious prejudice" to the other party.[117]

Partnership and Cooperation Agreements and Subsequent Association Agreements

The next orbital ring is formed of Partnership and Cooperation Agreements (PCAs) between the EU and a number of East European and Asian countries. In contrast to the SAAs and EMAs described above, some PCAs merely provide on an abstract

[109] Article 42 Algeria EMA; Article 35 Egypt EMA; Article 37 of the Israel EMA; Article 54 Jordan EMA; Article 36 Lebanon EMA; Article 37 of the Morocco EMA; Article 37 of the Tunisia EMA; Article 31 West Bank and Gaza Strip EMA.

[110] Article 43 of the Algeria EMA; Article 36 Egypt EMA; Article 38 of the Israel EMA; Article 55 Jordan EMA; Article 37 Lebanon EMA; Article 38 Morocco EMA; Article 38 Tunisia EMA; Article 32 West Bank and Gaza Strip EMA.

[111] Article 34(1)(iii) Egypt EMA, Article 36(1)(iii) Israel EMA, Article 53(1)(c) Jordan EMA; Article 36(1)(iii) Morocco EMA; Article 36(1)(iii) Tunisia EMA; Article 30(1)(iii) West Bank and Gaza Strip EMA (each supplemented by transparency requirements).

[112] Article 38 Egypt EMA; Article 58 Jordan EMA; Article 34 West Bank and Gaza Strip EMA.

[113] Article 53(2) Jordan EMA: Article 36(2) Morocco EMA; Article 36(2) Tunisia EMA; Article 30(2) West Bank and Gaza Strip EMA.

[114] See below Sect. 4.2.2.

[115] Article 41(2) of the Algeria EMA, with Annex 5 to that agreement; Decision No. 1/2004 of the EU-Morocco Association Council of 19 April 2004 adopting the necessary rules for the implementation of the competition rules, OJ 2005 L 165/10, with the Annex Mechanism of cooperation between the Parties' competition authorities responsible for the implementation of competition rules.

[116] Article 34(6) of the Egypt EMA; Article 53(7) Jordan EMA; Article 36(7) Morocco EMA; Article 36(7) Tunisia EMA; Article 30(8) West Bank and Gaza Strip EMA (all subject to the possibility of more detailed implementing rules).

[117] Article 41(3) of the Algeria EMA; Article 34(5) Egypt EMA; Article 36(5) Israel EMA; Article 53(6) Jordan EMA; Article 36(6) Morocco EMA; Article 36(6) Tunisia EMA; Article 30(7) West Bank and Gaza Strip EMA.

level that the parties endeavour to approximate their competition laws gradually, and that the parties "examine ways" to coordinate the application of their competition laws in cases where trade between them is affected.[118] Some of the PCAs, however, go further and approach the level of detail contained in EMAs.[119] Action plans adopted under the European Neighbourhood Policy have added a few more specific obligations, for example with regard to transparency in state aids.[120] The cooperation with these states is further strengthened, for example, by the contacts in the Cooperation Council and the Twinning Instrument, which allows for secondments of civil servants between the parties. Nevertheless, the obligations in the PCAs by themselves remain relatively open textured.

Some of the parties to PCAs have since entered into more detailed Association Agreements. These provide for an obligation to maintain a competition authority,[121] and maintain comprehensive competition laws "which effectively address anti-competitive agreements, concerted practices and anti-competitive unilateral conduct of enterprises with dominant market power and which provide effective control of concentrations to avoid significant impediment to effective competition and abuse of dominant position."[122] Noteworthy is in particular the inclusion of a requirement to maintain a merger control regime, which is not usually included even in the more elaborate (but older) SAAs and EMAs. Similar to these agreements, the Association Agreements also provide for rules on state monopolies and undertakings with exclusive and special rights[123] and state aids.[124] The 2014 Ukraine Association Agreement goes further by obliging the Ukraine to

[118]Article 43 Armenia PCA; Article 43 Azerbaijan PCA; Article 43, 44(2) Georgia PCA.

[119]Cf. Article 48(2) Moldova PCA; Article 49(2) Ukraine PCA; more tentatively Articles 53, 55 Russian Federation PCA.

[120]See, e.g., section 4.5.5. of the Proposal for a Council Decision on the position to be adopted by the Communities and its Member States within the Cooperation Council established by the Partnership and Cooperation Agreement establishing a partnership between the European Communities and its Member States, of the one part, and the Republic of Azerbaijan, of the other part, with regard to the adoption of a Recommendation on the implementation of the EU-Azerbaijan Action Plan, COM (2006) 637 final, adopted by the Council for submission to the EU-Azerbaijan Cooperation Council, 8 November 2006, CS/2006/14416, and which was adopted in the same year by that Cooperation Council.

[121]Article 204(2) of the 2014 EU-Georgia Association Agreement; Article 335(2) of the 2014 EU-Moldova Association Agreement; Article 255(2) of the 2014 EU-Ukraine Association Agreement.

[122]Article 204(1) of the 2014 EU-Georgia Association Agreement; similarly Article 335(1) of the 2014 EU-Moldova Association Agreement; Article 254 of the 2014 EU-Ukraine Association Agreement.

[123]Article 205 of the 2014 EU-Georgia Association Agreement; Article 336 of the 2014 EU-Moldova Association Agreement; Articles 257 and 258 of the 2014 EU-Ukraine Association Agreement.

[124]Article 206 of the 2014 EU-Georgia Association Agreement; in more detail Articles 339–342 of the 2014 EU-Moldova Association Agreement; in even more detail, and subject to the dispute settlement mechanism, Articles 262–267 of the 2014 EU-Ukraine Association Agreement, which even requires interpretation in accordance to the EU rules (Article 264).

approximate its laws to very specific instruments, including Regulation 1/2003, the EU Merger Regulation 139/2004, and the vertical Block Exemption Regulation 330/2010.[125]

The EU-Moldova and EU-Ukraine Agreements additionally contain rudimentary cooperation provisions that do not, however, approach the level of detail seen in the cooperation agreements discussed below.[126]

Similar to the US-style FTAs, but in less detail, the Association Agreements also state that the parties "recognise the importance of applying their respective competition laws in a transparent and non-discriminatory manner, respecting the principles of procedural fairness and rights of defence of the enterprises concerned."[127]

However, in a feature that is common to practically all FTAs with competition provisions, the competition rules (with the exception of the state aids provisions) are excluded from the dispute settlement mechanism of the Association Agreements.[128]

Links Between Nodes: CETA, Singapore and South Korea (and TTIP, Japan...?)

The sections above deal with trade agreements on different orbitals with the EU at their centre. The international network is completed by links between the nodes, namely by trade agreements between the EU and geographically distant states that are on a similar level of economic development. Recent examples of such trade agreements are the Comprehensive Economic and Trade Agreement (CETA) between the EU and Canada,[129] the (nearly certainly stillborn) Transatlantic Trade and Investment Partnership (TTIP), [130] and the FTAs with Singapore and

[125]Article 256 of the 2014 EU-Ukraine Association Agreement.

[126]Articles 337 and 343 of the 2014 EU-Moldova Association Agreement; Articles 259 and 260 of the 2014 EU-Ukraine Association Agreement.

[127]Article 204(3) of the 2014 EU-Georgia Association Agreement; Article 335(1) of the 2014 EU-Moldova Association Agreement; going into a little more detail Article 255(3) of the 2014 EU-Ukraine Association Agreement.

[128]Article 207 of the 2014 EU-Georgia Association Agreement; Article 338 of the 2014 EU-Moldova Association Agreement; see also Article 261 of the 2014 EU-Ukraine Association Agreement, which, however, excludes the duty to approximate to the various competition Regulations in Article 256.

[129]Council Decision (EU) 2017/37 of 28 October 2016 on the signing on behalf of the European Union of the Comprehensive Economic and Trade Agreement (CETA) between Canada, of the one part, and the European Union and its Member States, of the other part, OJ 2017 L 11/1. CETA was approved by the European Parliament on 15 February 2017.

[130]For the EU negotiating position, see EU negotiating texts in TTIP, http://trade.ec.europa.eu/doclib/press/index.cfm?id=1230#regulatory-cooperation (last accessed 16 July 2017). Specifically for the EU negotiating position with regard to competition matters see below.

South Korea.[131] A number of further FTAs are in the pipeline: the negotiations of the EU-Japan FTA are at an advanced stage,[132] the EU-India FTA[133] has been held up primarily because of reservations on part of the UK, and negotiations with a number of Mercosur nations are planned.[134]

For the most part, these agreements do not contain great detail on competition law. At first glance, this may seem surprising, because at least Canada, the United States and South Korea have been especially vigorous enforcers of competition law in recent years, so that the elimination of overlaps and gaps with these jurisdictions would seem to be a particularly pressing concern. The explanation lies arguably not so much in the uneasy relationship between trade law and competition law described above in Sect. 2.3. Instead, the very importance of cooperation with these active enforcers of competition law has led to competition-law specific cooperation agreements that predate the trade agreements, and which will be described below in Sect. 4.2.1.

CETA refers to competition law primarily in chapter 17. Article 17.2.1 provides that the parties "recognise the importance of free and undistorted competition" and the potential of anti-competitive business conduct to "distort the proper functioning of markets and undermine the benefits of trade liberalisation." The parties "shall take appropriate measures to proscribe anti-competitive business conduct" (Article 17.2.2). These measures "shall be consistent with the principles of transparency, non-discrimination, and procedural fairness", and in particular exclusions from the application of competition law are to be transparent (Article 17.2.4). The measures are to be applied to public entities according to Canadian and EU law respectively (Article 17.3). In terms of cooperation, Article 17.3 refers to and incorporates into the CETA by reference the terms of the 1999 Agreement between the European Communities and the Government of Canada Regarding the Application of their Competition Laws. In keeping with other trade and association agreements,[135] the provisions on competition policy in chapter 17 are not subject to the dispute settlement mechanism (Article 17.4).

Chapter 18 of the CETA deals specifically with state enterprises, monopolies, and enterprises granted special rights or privileges ("covered entities" as defined in Article 18.1). While the parties are not prevented "from designing or maintaining

[131]Council Decision of 16 September 2010 on the signing, on behalf of the European Union, and provisional application of the Free Trade Agreement between the European Union and its Member States, of the one part, and the Republic of Korea, of the other part, OJ 2011 L 127/1.

[132]On 6 July 2017, the EU and Japan announced the agreement in principle of the Economic Partnership Agreement and the Strategic Partnership Agreement at political level (EU Commission, 24th EU-Japan Summit Joint Statement, Statement/17/1920, http://europa.eu/rapid/press-release_STATEMENT-17-1920_en.htm (last accessed 16 July 2017)).

[133]See http://ec.europa.eu/trade/policy/countries-and-regions/countries/india/index_en.htm (last accessed 16 July 2017).

[134]See Mercosur-EU joint communiqué 28th negotiating round, Brussels, 7 July 2017, http://trade.ec.europa.eu/doclib/press/index.cfm?id=1688 (last accessed 16 July 2017); Barber T, Brexit and Trump push world trade deals up EU priority list, Financial Times, 28 February 2017.

[135]Article 207 of the 2014 EU-Georgia Association Agreement; Article 338 of the 2014 EU-Moldova Association Agreement; Article 261 of the 2014 EU-Ukraine Association Agreement.

state enterprises or monopolies or from granting special rights or privileges", they are under a duty not to "require or encourage such a covered entity to act in a manner inconsistent with [the CETA]" (Article 18.3), and to ensure that such covered entities accord non-discriminatory treatment to covered investments, goods and service suppliers (Article 18.4). Covered entities generally have to "act in accordance with commercial considerations" when purchasing or selling goods or purchasing or supplying services, unless non-commercial considerations are required to fulfil the purpose of the monopoly, special right, privilege or public mandate (Article 18.5). Chapter 19 goes into much more detail with regard to public procurement. In other sections of CETA, competition law is mentioned in order to ensure that CETA provisions do not prevent the application of competition law. For example, obligations to separate ownership or to prevent a concentration of market power under competition law are not inconsistent with the obligation to guarantee unimpeded market access through establishment (Article 8.4.2), and the forced transfer of technology or proprietary knowledge is permissible where it is imposed as a remedy of a competition law infringement (Article 8.5.4).

The EU-South Korea FTA addresses competition law specifically in chapter 11.[136] Prior to the FTA, the EU had already entered into an agreement with South Korea on cooperation on anti-competitive activities (although one would hope that what is meant is cooperation on *fighting* anti-competitive activities).[137] The FTA refers to this agreement in Article 11.6.2 and adds a general obligation to enter into consultations regarding the other Party's representations and to provide relevant non-confidential information (Article 11.7). Most of the other competition provisions in the EU-South Korea FTA are similar to the ones described for CETA. An interesting aspect is that the EU-South Korea FTA does not only oblige the parties to maintain their own competition rules against restrictive agreements, concerted practices and abuse of dominance by one or more enterprises as well as effective merger control (Article 11.1.2) and to maintain appropriately equipped competition authorities that apply the law in a transparent, timely and non-discriminatory manner, respecting the principles of procedural fairness and rights of defence (Article 11.3.). In addition, Article 11.1.3 essentially replicates the operative text of Articles 101 and 102 TFEU and the substantive merger control test (SIEC test) from Article 2 of the EU Merger Regulation 139/2004, substituting "trade between [the Parties]" for "trade between Member States" to define activities that are "incompatible with the proper functioning of" the FTA. These rules are

[136] Council Decision of 16 September 2010 on the signing, on behalf of the European Union, and provisional application of the Free Trade Agreement between the European Union and its Member States, of the one part, and the Republic of Korea, of the other part, OJ 2011 L 127/1.

[137] Council Decision 2009/586/EC of 16 February 2009 relating to the conclusion of the Agreement between the European Community and the Government of the Republic of Korea concerning cooperation on anti-competitive activities, OJ 2009 L 202/35. This agreement covers the "usual" content of such cooperation agreements as outlined below in Sect. 4.2, such as notifications and consultation, positive and negative comity, and assistance in and coordination of enforcement activities.

supplemented by rules on public enterprises, enterprises with special or exclusive rights, and state monopolies (Articles 11.4 and 11.5). The dispute settlement mechanism in the EU-South Korea FTA does not apply to disputes arising under any of the aforementioned rules (Article 11.8). This is a difference to the CETA, in which the application of the dispute settlement mechanism is excluded only for the general competition rules in chapter 17, but not for disputes arising under chapter 18 on state enterprises, monopolies, and enterprises granted special rights or privileges. In the competition chapter, only the rules on specific subsidies in the EU-South Korea FTA (Articles 11.9–11.15) are subject to the dispute settlement mechanism.

The EU-Singapore FTA, negotiations for which were concluded on 17 October 2014, considers competition and related matters in chapter 12 similarly to the EU-South Korea FTA.[138] What is separated in the EU-South Korea FTA into two separate provisions (the maintenance of effective competition rules on their own territory on the one hand, and the practices prohibited to the extent they affect trade between the parties), is conflated in the EU-Singapore agreement: the parties agree to maintain specified competition rules, which are here essentially an adapted replication of Articles 101, 102 and the substantive SIEC/SLC merger test, only to the extent they affect trade between the parties (Article 12.1). Similar to the EU-South Korea FTA, the EU-Singapore Agreement obliges the parties to maintain appropriately equipped competition authorities that apply the rules in a "transparent and non-discriminatory manner, respecting the principles of procedural fairness and rights of defence"; in the EU-Singapore FTA, the right of the parties to be heard is specifically mentioned. Again the general competition rules are supplemented by rules on public undertakings, undertakings entrusted with special or exclusive rights and state monopolies (Articles 12.3 and 12.4); Article 12.3.4 imposes an obligation on Singapore to ensure that its public undertakings and undertakings entrusted with special or exclusive rights act in accordance with commercial principles. Articles 12.5–12.10 cover specific subsidies similar to the equivalent rules in the EU-South Korea FTA. Articles 12.11–12.13 outline generic cooperation and confidentiality obligations. Only Article 12.7 on Prohibited Subsidies is subject to the dispute and mediation mechanisms under the EU-Singapore FTA.

As mentioned above, the EU has a number of other free trade agreements in the pipeline, including those with Japan, India and South American states. With regard to the US-EU Trans-Atlantic Trade and Investment Partnership, only the EU's negotiating position is known.[139] The negotiating position covers, first, general competition rules—which do not go beyond the existing competition rules on the two sides of the Atlantic or the 1995/98 Cooperation Agreements described below Sect. 4.2.1. Secondly, they cover rules on state enterprises, monopolies and

[138]See the authentic text as of May 2015 under http://trade.ec.europa.eu/doclib/press/index.cfm?id=961 (last accessed 16 July 2017).

[139]See the EU negotiating texts at http://trade.ec.europa.eu/doclib/press/index.cfm?id=1230#regulatory-cooperation (last accessed 16 July 2017).

enterprises with special or exclusive rights, which includes the principle of non-discrimination, mutual obligations to act in accordance to commercial considerations unless the fulfilment of the purpose requires otherwise (clarifying that differential pricing in different markets is not precluded by these obligations), and imposes on the parties an obligation to ensure that such enterprises conform to high standards of transparency and corporate governance, and to enable the parties to request from the other party information on such enterprises, although confidential information is excluded from such disclosures. Finally, a chapter on subsidies was also envisaged. While the EU negotiating position in this regard is not very detailed and largely refers to the obligations under the WTO Agreement on Subsidies and Countervailing Measures, adding obligations of transparency and consultations on request, this chapter would likely have been one where the negotiations would have been interesting to watch. However, the TTIP negotiations appear to have stalled due to resistance both in the US and in Europe, and it seems politically unlikely that this Agreement is going to progress much in 2017.[140]

4.2 Cooperation Agreements

The common denominator of the SAAs, EMAs, and PCAs described above is that they are primarily (but, as noted above, not exclusively) aimed at incentivising the counterparties to adopt and maintain their own domestic competition laws.

A complementary way to address the gaps in the international enforcement scheme is to strengthen the unilateral extraterritorial enforcement mechanisms. This is the primary aim of various competition cooperation agreements (below Sect. 4.2.1), mutual legal assistance treaties (below Sect. 4.2.2), and extradition treaties (below Sect. 4.2.3).

4.2.1 Competition Cooperation Agreements

Following an OECD 1967 Recommendation,[141] and its latest revision in 2014,[142] states (in inter-governmental agreements) and their competition authorities (in - inter-agency agreements) started to enter into cooperation agreements.[143]

[140]But see the U.S.-EU Joint Report on TTIP Progress to Date, 17 January 2017, http://trade.ec.europa.eu/doclib/docs/2017/january/tradoc_155242.pdf (last accessed 16 July 2017).

[141]OECD C(67)53 final.

[142]OECD C(2014)108 final.

[143]For an early example, see the 1976 US-Germany Antitrust Accord.

US-EU Comity Agreements

In 1991, the European Commission entered into an agreement with the US.[144] This agreement provides for duties of notification (Article II) and encourages the exchange of information (Article III) as well as cooperation and coordination between the authorities (Article IV). The so-called "positive comity" Article V allows a party that believes that conduct in the second party's territory affects the first party's interests to request the second party to take enforcement action. The "negative comity" Article VI tells the parties to consider the other party's important interests when enforcing their laws.

The conclusion of this agreement was celebrated as a milestone in transatlantic cooperation. The actual legal content, however, is rather disappointing. Most "duties" are not duties at all, because they are contingent on "potestative conditions", that is, conditions that depend solely on the will of the "obligated" party. If they were contained in a private agreement, they would arguably be considered illusory promises. In the article on cooperation and coordination, it is said that the parties "*may agree that it is in their mutual interest to coordinate their enforcement activities*". The negative comity article "requires" the parties, when enforcing their respective laws, to "*seek* [...] *to take into account*"(!) the other party's interests. The positive comity article disclaims any binding or even discretion-limiting effects on either of the parties in its final paragraph. The exchange-of-information article, which looks at first glance as if it contained substantive duties, is rendered largely ineffective by Article VIII, which excludes information that is either confidential under the laws of the requested party or whose exchange would be incompatible with that party's important interests.[145] The only duties that are relatively unqualified are those providing for notification.

In 1998, the "Positive Comity" Agreement between the US and the EU supplemented the 1991/95 agreement. The Positive Comity Agreement clarifies that a party may request the other party to look into practices in the requested party's territory even if the practice does not infringe the requesting party's laws. Article IV of the Positive Comity Agreement establishes something coming close to a real duty by specifying circumstances in which the requesting party "*will normally defer or suspend*" its own investigations. But even if the numerous criteria of Article IV are fulfilled, the requesting party may still continue its parallel enforcement, provided it informs the requested party of this decision and its reasons; and in

[144] International Legal Materials 30 (1991), p. 1491. Although the CJEU later declared this Treaty a nullity, because only the European *Community*, and not the *Commission* could be party to such an agreement—CJEU, case C-327/91, *France/Commission*, ECLI:EU:C:1994:305, the 1991 Treaty was ratified ex post in 1995 by the competent bodies with *ex tunc* effect, OJ 1995 L 95/45, corrigendum OJ 1995 L 131/38. Despite this complication, the 20th birthday was celebrated in 2011.

[145] See additionally the Exchange of Interpretative Letters between the EEC/ECSC and Government of the United States of America in the Corrigendum, OJ 1995 L 131/38.

any case the requesting party may "later" initiate or resume its enforcement. Although introduced with much fanfare, the positive comity provision was virtually never used.[146]

Even though the legal content of the two US-EU cooperation agreements is negligible, they were certainly a symbolic success, and have probably contributed to the enhanced spirit of cooperation between US and EU authorities, as reflected in the Administrative Arrangement on Attendance and the (updated) "Best Practices on Cooperation in Merger Investigations".[147] However, this is probably at least as much a result of the interaction at the International Competition Network and the OECD as of the bilateral cooperation agreements. A more direct consequence is that they have also served as a template for numerous other cooperation agreements (Sect. 4.2.1 below).

Other EU Intergovernmental Cooperation Agreements and Inter-Agency Memoranda of Understanding

Agreements similar to the cooperation agreements between the EU and the US have been concluded with several other countries. Some of these have taken the form of inter-governmental agreements, such as the agreements with Canada,[148] Japan,[149] the Republic of Korea,[150] and Switzerland.[151] In other cases, the Directorate-General Competition of the EU Commission (DG Competition) has entered into Memoranda of Understanding (MOU) directly with the competition authorities of

[146] *Amadeus/SABRE* being the notable exception, see Commission press releases IP/99/171 and IP/00/835. In other cases, such as *AC Nielsen*, requests to look into anticompetitive practices were made informally. For the reasons why the positive comity provisions largely remained a dead letter see Marsden (2010).

[147] Dabbah (2010), p. 289 et seq. Attributing the use of the word "*dominance*" in US merger decisions such as the *Staples* decision to the transatlantic cooperation (as does Dabbah (2010), p. 290) is falling prey to a *faux ami*, however. Proving a "dominant position" to show a substantial lessening of competition preceded the comity agreements, and indeed the EUMR, by several decades, see, e.g., *United States v Continental Can*, 378 U.S. 441, 458, 459 (1964).

[148] Agreement between the European Communities and the Government of Canada regarding the application of their competition laws, OJ 1999 L 175/49.

[149] Agreement between the European Community and the Government of Japan concerning cooperation on anti-competitive activities, OJ 2003 L 183/12.

[150] See Council Decision 2009/586/EC of 16 February 2009 relating to the conclusion of the Agreement between the European Community and the Government of the Republic of Korea concerning cooperation on anti-competitive activities, OJ 2009 L 202/35.

[151] See Agreement between the European Union and the Swiss Confederation concerning cooperation on the application of their competition laws, OJ 2014 L 347/3.

other countries, for example Brazil,[152] China,[153] India,[154] the Russian Federation,[155] and South Africa.[156]

While these cooperation agreements differ from each other, nearly all of them provide for a common core of the elements contained in the US-EU Comity Agreements, that is, notification requirements, exchange of information, and negative and positive comity provisions. Confidential information may be exchanged if and to the extent the persons concerned consent to the exchange (the notable exception being the Agreement with Switzerland, which allows the exchange of confidential information even without consent under certain conditions).[157] Some agreements provide for a framework of meetings.

The inter-agency MOU differ from the agreements between the EU and other countries in that they are generally less detailed and formal,[158] and in that they do not provide for notification duties. On the other hand, they often provide for additional cooperation, in particular technical assistance.

While most of the agreements and MOU differ only in the details with respect to their coverage, there are "outliers" in both directions. At one end of the spectrum is the MOU with the Chinese authorities. The MOU with the Chinese authorities is markedly less specific than the other cooperation agreements and MOU, and only provides for an exchange of views, experiences and non-confidential information; it does not deal with notifications, negative or positive comity. However, the EU-China Competition Policy Dialogue provides for an institutional forum for the exchange of views and experiences, and also for technical assistance and capacity building[159]; in the area of merger control, the Practical Guidance for Cooperation on Reviewing Merger Cases provides for closer cooperation in individual merger cases, including an exchange on the "definition of relevant markets,

---

[152]See the Memorandum of Understanding on cooperation between DG Competition and CADE and SEAE of the Government of the Federative Republic of Brazil, signed 8 October 2009.

[153]Memorandum of Understanding on cooperation in the area of anti-monopoly law between DG Competition and NDRC and SAIC, signed 20 September 2012.

[154]Memorandum of Understanding between DG Competition and the Competition Commission of India on cooperation in the field of competition laws, signed 21 November 2013.

[155]Memorandum of Understanding on cooperation between the DG Competition and the Federal Antimonopoly Service (FAS Russia), signed 10 March 2011.

[156]Memorandum of Understanding between DG Competition and the Competition Commission of South Africa, signed 22 June 2016.

[157]Article 7(4) of the Agreement between the European Union and the Swiss Confederation concerning cooperation on the application of their competition laws, OJ 2014 L 347/3.

[158]While the agreements often allow notifications and exchanges between the competition authorities directly, these have to be followed by communications through diplomatic channels.

[159]See Agreement between the Ministry of Commerce of China and the Directorate-General for Competition of European Commission on a structured dialogue on competition, 6 May 2004, and the terms of reference of the EU-China competition policy dialogue.

theory of harm, competitive impact assessment and the design of remedies" and coordination of information requests to the merging and third parties.[160]

The outlier at the other end of the spectrum is the 2014 EU-Switzerland Agreement. While this agreement mirrors for the most part the other cooperation agreements, with its provisions on notification, exchange of information, and positive as well as negative comity, the crucial difference is that Article 7(4) of the 2014 EU-Switzerland Agreement allows the parties' competition authorities under certain conditions to exchange *confidential* information even where the undertakings concerned have not consented to such an exchange. Such an exchange of confidential information without consent of the persons concerned is not completely unprecedented, as it can be found in a few other "second-generation" cooperation agreements, but is still exceedingly rare.[161]

4.2.2 Mutual Legal Assistance Treaties

Apart from these competition-law specific agreements, general mutual legal assistance treaties, such as the ones entered by EU Member States and the US on the basis of the EU-US Mutual Legal Assistance Agreement[162] and extradition treaties can become relevant for antitrust investigations, and frequently these more general agreements have more "bite". While they also include clauses according to which legal assistance may be denied, such a denial is usually possible only in narrowly defined exceptions, e.g. where "*execution of the request would prejudice the sovereignty, security, or other essential interests of the Requested State*." Mutual legal assistance treaties frequently require dual criminality at least for some forms of legal assistance. Their significance for competition cases therefore often depends on the extent to which competition law is criminalized in the jurisdictions in question. A notable exception is the Mutual Legal Assistance Treaty between the US and Germany,[163] according to which "[*c*]*riminal investigations or proceedings*

---

[160] Practical guidance for cooperation on reviewing merger cases between DG Competition and Ministry of Commerce of PR China, signed 15 October 2015.

[161] See the Agreement on Mutual Antitrust Enforcement Assistance between the US and Australia, in force since 5 November 1999, based on the authorisation in the 1994 International Antitrust Enforcement Assistance Act (IAEAA, or informally the "vowel Act"), 15 U.S.C. §§ 6201–6212. Table 3 of OECD, Inventory of Co-Operation Agreements, 2015, https://www.oecd.org/daf/competition/competition-inventory-list-of-cooperation-agreements.pdf (last accessed 16 July 2017), lists the following second-generation agreements in addition to the EU-Switzerland and US-Australia agreements: Australia-Japan (2015); New Zealand-Australia on compulsorily-acquired information and investigative assistance (2013); and the Nordic Co-Operation Agreement between Denmark, Iceland, Norway and Sweden (2001). To these one could add the cooperation agreements between the EFTA Surveillance Authority and the EU Commission in Protocols 23, 24 to the EEA Agreement.

[162] Signed at Washington on 25 June 2003, entered into force 1 February 2010, https://www.state.gov/documents/organization/180815.pdf (last accessed 16 July 2017).

[163] In force since 18 October 2009.

for the purpose of this Treaty include investigations or proceedings relating to regulatory offenses (Ordnungswidrigkeiten) under German antitrust law."

4.2.3 Extradition Treaties

One of the limitations of criminal antitrust enforcement has traditionally been the difficulty to get hold of individuals located abroad. The only jurisdiction that has a sufficiently robust system of criminal enforcement to care about extraterritorial criminal enforcement is, so far, the United States. For a long time, the United States relied on a carrot-and-stick policy to incentivise defendants located abroad to submit voluntarily to prosecution in the United States: as a carrot, the Department of Justice promised plea agreements with "no jail time" to foreign defendants (and often facilitated future entry to the United States for "cooperating aliens"[164]), and, as a stick, it impeded international travel by placing non-cooperating foreign infringers on border watches and, since 2001, on the Interpol Red Notice list. The days of "no jail time" agreements are gone. The conclusion of extradition treaties has made them unnecessary. Of course, extradition treaties require dual criminality, and there are few countries in the world in which there is active criminal antitrust enforcement. However, many jurisdictions have adopted criminal antitrust statutes at least as law in the books over the past two decades, and while law in the books may not be a good deterrent as such, it is sufficient to meet the dual criminality requirement. This means that a participant in a criminal antitrust infringement with effects in the United States may not be able to travel to any jurisdiction which has criminal statutes applicable to the conduct and an extradition treaty with the United States.

The *Ian Norris* case concerned conduct that preceded the introduction of the cartel offence in the United Kingdom, so that the extradition was effectuated only after a lengthy court battle and not on the basis of the actual cartel conduct.[165] In contrast, the extradition in the *Pisciotti* case went relatively smoothly: Mr. *Pisciotti*, an Italian allegedly participating in the *Marine Hose* cartel, was arrested during a stop-over at the Frankfurt International Airport and extradited to the United States. Given that the Marine Hose cartel was a bid-rigging cartel and bid rigging is a criminal offence in Germany, the dual criminality requirement was fulfilled without question.[166]

[164]See the Memorandum of Understanding between the Antitrust Division, United States Department of Justice, and the Immigration and Naturalization Service, United States Department Of Justice, 15 March 1996, https://www.justice.gov/atr/memorandum-understanding-between-antitrust-division-united-states-department-justice-and (last accessed 16 July 2017).

[165]*Ian Norris v Government of the United States of America* [2008] UKHL 16, [2008] 1 A.C. 920.

[166]The litigation in the *Pisciotti* case concerned the question whether Mr. Pisciotti, as an EU citizen, could rely on Article 16 of the German Constitution which prohibits the extradition of German citizens from Germany. The Higher Regional Court in Frankfurt denied this, as did the German Federal Constitutional Court (BVerfG of 17 February 2014, case 2 BvQ 4/14). Mr. Pisciotti sought help from the EU Commission, which decided not to intervene, and

5 EU and UK Relations After Brexit

The story in this contribution so far has been one of increasing cooperation to decrease complexity and overcome the gaps and overlaps created by uncoordinated unilateral enforcement. The EU is a paragon in this regard. Regional supranational integration in the EU enables, for example, the approximation of substantive competition law under Article 3 Regulation 1/2003, the close cooperation within the ECN under Regulation 1/2003 and the Network Notice, and the one-stop shop for concentrations with an EU dimension under Article 21(3) of the EU Merger Regulation 139/2004.[167] Outside of this core of integration of the Member States in the supranational organisation itself, which in the area of competition law comes close to the integration in a federal state, the EU has established external links of varying intensity to neighbouring jurisdictions and jurisdictions with active competition law enforcement (Sect. 4).

The Brexit Referendum, which ended with a majority for leaving the European Union (51.9%:48.1%), and the decision by Her Majesty's Government to act on the result of this advisory referendum[168] will have various and as yet unknown implications for competition law in the United Kingdom.

What is clear, however, is that Brexit turns the development towards greater cooperation described above on its head. The UK will exit the integrated EU, a geographically proximate and large economy, and lose the benefits of the information exchange and close cooperation within the ECN. Undertakings will lose the benefit of a one-stop shop for concentrations. The UK will lose the indirect benefits of the close cooperation that the European Union has with Switzerland through the 2014 Agreement[169] and the European Commission has with the EFTA Surveillance Authority through the EEA-Agreement. It will also lose the indirect benefits from all the other intergovernmental cooperation agreements and the inter-agency MOUs

---

Mr. Pisciotti's attempts to force the European Commission to intervene by applying to the General Court and the CJEU were unsuccessful—GC, case T-403/14, *Romano Pisciotti v Commission*, ECLI:EU:T:2014:692; CJEU, case C-411/14 P, *Romano Pisciotti v Commission*, ECLI:EU:C:2015:48. Mr. Pisciotti was extradited in 2014. He has since initiated an action against the Federal Republic of Germany for compensation, and the civil court in Berlin has made a preliminary reference to the CJEU, case C-191/16, pending.

[167] See above Sect. 4.1.2 (EU).

[168] See Uberoi, E, European Union Referendum Bill 2015-16, House of Commons Library Briefing Paper Number 07212, 3 June 2015, p 25, http://researchbriefings.parliament.uk/ResearchBriefing/Summary/CBP-7212#fullreport (last accessed 16 July 2017) ("It does not contain any requirement for the UK Government to implement the results of the referendum"); see also *R (on the application of Miller and another) (Respondents) v Secretary of State for Exiting the European Union (Appellant) and Reference by the Attorney General for Northern Ireland—In the matter of an application by Agnew and others for Judicial Review, and Reference by the Court of Appeal (Northern Ireland)—In the matter of an application by Raymond McCord for Judicial Review*, [2017] UKSC 5 [124], stating that the referendum result was politically but not legally binding.

[169] Agreement between the European Union and the Swiss Confederation concerning cooperation on the application of their competition laws, OJ 2014 L 347/3.

which the EU and the Commission have entered into and which have been described in Sect. 4 above. It is a return to largey unshared sovereignty in the sense of the nineteenth century nation state. Time will tell if this is a sustainable model in the integrated world economy in the twenty-first century.

5.1 A Brief Overview of the State of Brexit

As indicated in the introduction, it is still unclear what form Brexit will eventually take. The only firm announcement that has been made by the UK Government is that "Brexit means Brexit". The UK government submitted the notification under Article 50 Treaty on European Union (TEU) on 29 March 2017. Given that the negotiating position of the UK Government is still not yet determined, that the Government's majority in Parliament after the recent general election is thin and depends on support from the DUP, and that the policy statements that have been published by the Government so far seem rather flimsy, it is likely that the 2-year period provided for in Article 50(3) TEU will expire and the United Kingdom will cease to be a member of the European Union without any negotiated trade agreement with the EU, unless an extension of the negotiation period can be arranged.

Article 50(1) TEU requires the decision to leave the EU to be made in accordance with the Member State's constitutional requirements. Initially, Her Majesty's Government believed and argued that it could decide to leave the EU and notify the EU Council of its intention based on the Crown's Prerogative powers without Parliament's involvement. The High Court, sitting in a panel including the Lord Chief Justice of England and Wales, the Master of the Rolls, and Lord Justice Sales, rejected this view and held that UK constitutional law, in particular the principle of parliamentary sovereignty, does not allow the Government to notify the Council under Article 50 TEU under the Crown's Prerogative powers but instead requires an Act of Parliament.[170] The Government appealed to the Supreme Court of the United Kingdom. The Supreme Court, sitting in a panel consisting of all eleven Justices, dismissed the appeal in a decision of eight to three and upheld the High Court's decision that an Act of Parliament was required.[171]

The case before the Supreme Court concerned only the procedural path to notification. Subsequent to the UK Supreme Court's decision, the Government submitted a very brief bill (the European Union (Notification of Withdrawal) Bill 2016–17) which provided only that the Prime Minister had the power to notify the

[170] *The Queen on the application of Gina Miller & Deir Tozetti Dos Santos v The Secretary of State for Exiting the European Union* [2016] EWHC 2768 (Admin).

[171] *R (on the application of Miller and another) (Respondents) v Secretary of State for Exiting the European Union (Appellant) and Reference by the Attorney General for Northern Ireland—In the matter of an application by Agnew and others for Judicial Review, and Reference by the Court of Appeal (Northern Ireland)—In the matter of an application by Raymond McCord for Judicial Review*, [2017] UKSC 5 [101], [123] (holding that the mere resolution in the House of Commons of 7 December 2016 was insufficient because an Act of Parliament was required), [152].

United Kingdom's intention to withdraw from the EU under Article 50 TEU.[172] This bill was passed by the House of Commons without amendments, and amendments adopted in the House of Lords were voted down in the Commons.[173] The UK Government submitted its notification of the UK's withdrawal from the EU on 29 March 2017, and unexpectedly called for a snap election on 18 April 2017, scheduled for 8 June 2017; in this election, the Conservative party lost its majority, but negotiated an agreement (falling short of a coalition agreement) with the ten Members of Parliament belonging to the DUP.[174]

The argument "du jour" by those who seek to limit the consequences of Brexit is that notification under Article 50 TEU and the following exit from the EU would not automatically end membership in the EEA, because Article 127 of the EEA Agreement provides that ending membership in the EEA requires giving notice to the other Contracting Parties. The issue arises because the United Kingdom is a Contracting Party of the EEA Agreement, but is so by virtue of its EU membership. While EU membership was clearly the *motivation* for accessing the EEA, it would seem that the UK is an EEA Contracting Party in its own right. There is no explicit provision that would automatically end EEA membership where an EEA Contracting Party leaves the EU. If one followed this argument, this would allow the UK Government to trigger Article 50 TEU and leave the EU without leaving the EEA. Against this line of argument, one could point to numerous provisions in the EEA Agreement that indicate that EEA members are either EU Member States or EFTA Member States. Even assuming, arguendo, that the argument from Article 127 EEA Agreement is correct, it would merely *allow* the UK to stay within the EEA. It is unclear at best whether the UK Government has the intention of doing so, and the "White Paper on the United Kingdom's exit from and new partnership with the European Union" (the "Brexit White Paper") indicates that the UK does not seek EEA membership and the Government has since repeated multiple times that the UK seeks to leave both the Single Market and the Customs Union (while somehow retaining seamless trade).[175] The members of the Cabinet had appeared divided on whether to prioritise staying within the Single Market, a position which the Chancellor *Philip Hammond* initially appeared to favour, or whether to prioritise "taking back control" with regard to immigration, an option the so-called "Three Brexiteers", the Foreign Secretary *Boris Johnson*, the Secretary

[172]For the text of the original bill, see https://www.publications.parliament.uk/pa/bills/cbill/2016-2017/0132/17132.pdf (last accessed 16 July 2017).

[173]For the progress of the bill see http://services.parliament.uk/bills/2016-17/europeanunionnotificationofwithdrawal.html (last accessed 16 July 2017).

[174]For the notification, see EU Commission, Taskforce on Article 50 negotiations with the United Kingdom, Notification of Article 50 TEU by the United Kingdom, 29 March 2017, https://ec.europa.eu/info/news/notification-article-50-teu-united-kingdom-2017-mar-29_en (last accessed 16 July 2017). For the results of the general election see http://www.bbc.co.uk/news/election/2017/results (last accessed 16 July 2017).

[175]White Paper on the United Kingdom's exit from and new partnership with the European Union, February 2017, CM 9417, https://www.gov.uk/government/uploads/system/uploads/attachment_data/file/589191/The_United_Kingdoms_exit_from_and_partnership_with_the_EU_Web.pdf (last accessed 16 July 2017).

for Exiting the European Union *David Davis* and the Secretary for International Trade *Liam Fox*, appeared to prefer. The latter approach was set on ending freedom of movement of workers, and this would be incompatible with Article 28 et seq. of the EEA Agreement.[176]

In the Brexit White Paper, Her Majesty's Government outlined its plans, albeit in highly simplistic and less than clear terms. It seems that the limitation of freedom of movement takes priority over membership in the Single Market, and that the UK also seeks to leave the Customs Union.[177] This means that the Government would, even if the notification under Article 50 TEU and the subsequent leaving of the EU did not automatically end the UK's membership in the EEA, give the required notice under Article 127 EEA Agreement as well. In other words, even if the argument from Article 127 EEA Agreement should be considered persuasive, this may give the UK Government a unilateral option to leave the EU and stay within the EEA even without positive consent from the other EEA Member States, but at the moment it seems highly unlikely that the current Government would exercise any such option.

Thus, while continued membership in the EEA may still be a remote possibility, it appears much more likely that the United Kingdom will leave the EU in a so-called "hard Brexit" in 2019, unless all Member States agree to an extension of the 2-year period.

5.2 *Implications of Brexit for Competition Law*

If the UK stayed within the EEA, UK competition law would not change dramatically. For the reasons outlined above, this section considers the implications of a "hard" Brexit, that is, of leaving both the EU and the EEA (and likely the customs union).

5.2.1 Substantive Competition Law in the UK Post Brexit

UK Competition Law

The substantive provisions of UK Competition Law would continue to apply even after a hard Brexit. Nor does it seem likely that the main prohibitions (the chapter I

[176]While the Government's preferred policy seems to be to "have their cake and eat it", in other words to keep access to the Single Market without free movement (sometimes pointing to the restrictions on taking residence in Liechtenstein provided for in Annex VIII to the EEA Agreement), it seems exceedingly unlikely that the other EEA Contracting Parties would be willing to grant the UK an exemption from the free movement provisions, given that the provisions for Liechtenstein are based on its "specific geographic situation".

[177]White Paper on the United Kingdom's exit from and new partnership with the European Union, February 2017, CM 9417, section 8.

and chapter II prohibitions of the Competition Act 1998) would necessarily be changed.

Unless the Competition Act 1998 is modified, even section 60 of the Competition Act 1998 would continue to apply, a provision which requires courts and the Competition and Markets Authority (CMA) to avoid inconsistency between, on the one hand, the principles they apply and the decisions they reach, and, on the other hand, the principles laid down by the TFEU and the Court of Justice, and by the decisions reached by the Court of Justice, as well as decisions reached and statements made by the Commission. In principle, this provision could continue to apply after Brexit, and especially considering the dearth of decision practice in the UK,[178] it may even make sense to continue to aspire to continued harmony between the more active decision-making practice on the EU level and in the UK. Not being a Member State of the EU would not preclude this aspiration. In Switzerland, for example, there is an active debate to what extent Swiss courts should and already do follow precedent of the Court of Justice and interpret laws in accordance with the interpretation of equivalent laws in the EU.[179] Nevertheless, as *Richard Whish* has pointed out, it appears unlikely that section 60 of the Competition Act 1998 would survive the UK's striving for "taking back control", given that one of the reasons often cited for leaving the EU was being subject to the Court of Justice's jurisdiction.[180] On 13 July 2017, the UK Government introduced the "European Union (Withdrawal) Bill" (informally known as the "Great Repeal Bill").[181] This Bill provides that a court or tribunal "is not bound by any principles laid down, or any decisions made, on or after exit day by the European Court" and "need not have regard to anything done on or after exit day by the European Court, another EU entity or the EU but may do so if it considers it appropriate to do so".[182]

[178]National Audit Office, The UK competition regime, HC 737, Session 2015–16, 5 February 2016, https://www.nao.org.uk/wp-content/uploads/2016/02/The-UK-Competition-regime.pdf (last accessed 16 July 2017), noting that "the low caseflow we identified in 2010 has continued, with the Office of Fair Trading and the CMA making 24 decisions and the regulators just eight since 2010. The UK competition authorities issued only £65 million of competition enforcement fines between 2012 and 2014 (in 2015 prices), compared to almost £1.4 billion of fines imposed by their German counterparts. The CMA faces significant barriers in increasing its flow of competition cases, although recent activity means it now has 12 ongoing cases." Wils (2013).

[179]Baudenbacher (2012), pp. 626–645; Lehmann and Zetzsche (2016); see also Zeiler H, Auswirkungen des EU-Rechts auf Nicht-EU-Mitglieder ("de facto Mitgliedschaft" der Schweiz und Liechtensteins?), XVI Meeting of the Highest Administrative Courts of Austria, Germany, Liechtenstein and Switzerland, 18/19 September 2008, http://www.bger.ch/landesbericht_schweiz_auswirkungen_eu-recht.pdf (last accessed 16 July 2017).

[180]Whish (2016), p. 297. See now White Paper on the United Kingdom's exit from and new partnership with the European Union, February 2017, CM 9417, section 2, which has the title "Taking control of our laws" and stating in the abstract: "We will take control of our own affairs, as those who voted in their millions to leave the EU demanded we must, and bring an end to the jurisdiction in the UK of the Court of Justice of the European Union (CJEU)."

[181]For the progress of this bill see http://services.parliament.uk/bills/2017-19/europeanunionwithdrawal/documents.html (last accessed 16 July 2017).

[182]Clause 6(1)(a) and 6(2) of the Bill, respectively.

Accordingly, if these provisions become law, they will replace the slightly stricter obligations of section 60 of the Competition Act 1998 with a mere possibility to have regard to the practice of the European institutions.[183] The same provisions in clause 6 will also immediately destroy, as of exit day, the binding effect of EU Commission decisions under Article 16 of Regulation (EC) No. 1/2003 for follow-on actions, and the corresponding prima facie effect of infringement decisions of foreign NCAs required by Article 9 of the Damages Directive 2014/104/EU, which was implemented into UK law only in March 2017, and will so render British courts and tribunal a much less attractive venue for damages actions.[184]

Clause 2 of the European Union (Withdrawal) Bill would ensure that the various European Block Exemption Regulations continue to apply, in the version in force on the day before exit day, under UK law (even though it is unclear, for example, who would have the competence to withdraw the benefit of the Block Exemption Regulations until provision for this deficiency is made under the "Henry VIII" power provided for in clause 7 of the Bill).

There are, of course, many other implications for substantive competition law post Brexit: How should the independent UK deal with merger control, given that the one-stop shop will not apply anymore and that referrals from and to the Commission will no longer be available?[185] Will it be feasible to continue to rely on a voluntary notification system?

More fundamentally, the UK would be free to abolish or fundamentally reshape its conceptions of competition law. Despite the theoretical possibility, there seems little danger that the UK would go back to the times when cartels were seen as a mere modality of business—although these days are not that long gone, as the House of Lord recalled in the *Norris* decision.[186] Today, the UK competition law and policy debate is too firmly rooted in the modern competition law discourse to revert to the state of (or before) the 1980s. If anything, competition lawyers in the UK today are more influenced by the US American and in particular Chicago school discourse and the more economic approach than their continental counterparts, generally preferring an effects-based approach over form-based approaches. Also, the UK is too involved in international cooperation efforts such as the OECD

[183]Clause 6 of the Bill applies to section 60 of the Competition Act 1998 because this section falls under the definition of "retained EU law" in clause 6(7) of the Bill; section 60 of the Competition Act 1998 is "EU-derived domestic legislation" as defined in clause 2(2)(d) of the Bill, because it is an "enactment [. . .] relating otherwise to the EU or EEA".

[184]For the binding effect of infringement decisions see sections 47A and 58A of the Competition Act 1998; for the prima facie effect of foreign NCA decisions see paragraph 35 of Schedule 8A to the Competition Act 1998, inserted by The Claims in respect of Loss or Damage arising from Competition Infringements (Competition Act 1998 and Other Enactments (Amendment)) Regulations 2017, Statutory Instrument 2017 No. 385, made on 8 March 2017. For the implementation of the Damages Directive in various Member States, see e.g., Bien et al. (2017).

[185]See already Whish (2016).

[186]See the overview in *Ian Norris v Government of the United States of America* [2008] UKHL 16, [2008] 1 A.C. 920, and in particular 934–935, para. 18 referring to *British Airways Board v Laker Airways Ltd.* [1985] AC 58.

and ICN, and too proud of its "special relationship" with (or dependence on) the United States, to discard the modern competition law regime they have built over the past two decades. While it is difficult to predict whether a UK "freed from the shackles of Brussels" would become more statist and protectionist, or on the contrary more libertarian, the paradigm of effective competition law seems here to stay. If and to the extent the UK changes its competition laws, instead of choosing to mirror EU competition law in the future on a voluntary basis, I would expect that it would shift in the direction of US federal antitrust law, that is, taking a more lenient stance on vertical restrictions than the EU does and more generally erring on the side of false negatives instead of false positives.

Any such developments in UK competition law, however, depend on the choices that would be made post-Brexit by Parliament (or, if the European Union (Withdrawal) Bill is enacted, by a Minister of the Crown under the Henry VIII powers envisaged in clause 7). Even the immediate consequences of Brexit seem nebulous, and such potential future changes to competition law are so completely unpredictable that speculation is useless. What is predicable, however, is that EU competition law would no longer be the "law of the land", and the next section discusses some of the consequences of this effect.

EU Competition Law in the UK post Brexit

An immediate consequence of Brexit would be that competition law infringements committed in the UK would become extraterritorial from the EU's perspective. Of course, we have been there before, *ICI Dyestuffs* being the EU's paradigm case for extraterritorial jurisdiction.[187] Since then the EU's position to extraterritorial enforcement has evolved. The implementation test in its broad interpretation by the CJEU in *Wood Pulp I* would facilitate finding prescriptive jurisdiction of the EU institutions in most cases, especially given that the UK economy and the EU economy are much more intertwined than used to be the case before UK accession to the (then) European Communities. Should the CJEU follow Advocate General *Wahl's* Opinion in the *Intel* case that the qualified effects test applies, it seems likely that in most cases in which UK undertakings are involved and the restriction may affect trade between Member States, EU law would still apply (extraterritorially) to infringements committed in the UK after Brexit.

Of course, there will be some cases in which the restriction merely affects trade between the UK and *one* Member State of the EU, in which today EU competition law is applicable, while it would not be applicable after Brexit. Nevertheless, for most economically important cases this is unlikely to be a serious problem, given the close relationship between the economies within the EU. Even in these cases,

[187]Commission Decision 69/243/EEC, *Dyestuffs*, OJ 1969 L 195/11; AG Mayras's opinion in CJEU, case 48/69, *ICI v Commission*, ECLI:EU:C:1972:32; CJEU, case 48/69, *Imperial Chemical Industries Ltd. v Commission,* ECLI:EU:C:1972:70.

the affected Member States' competition law, whose content will be largely shaped by EU competition law, may well be applicable extraterritorially.

Prescriptive jurisdiction is therefore unlikely to be a serious limitation to the applicability of substantive EU competition law to competition law infringements committed in the UK post Brexit. This is just a specific application of the recognition above that the modern law and practice on extraterritorial enforcement has largely moved to a qualified effects test, making prescriptive jurisdiction in many cases unproblematic. As was pointed out above, the same cannot be said about enforcement jurisdiction, to which we now turn.

5.2.2 Enforcement Cooperation Post Brexit

One of the most pressing issues for the practical workings of competition authorities following a hard Brexit would be ensuring the continued cooperation between the UK competition authorities on the one hand and the EU Commission and EFTA Surveillance Authority as well as the National Competition Authorities (NCAs) of the other Member States on the other, as well as between the UK and EU courts, and between the respective courts and authorities. Currently, the information flow is governed in antitrust cases by Regulation 1/2003—in particular Articles 11–16—,[188] the Network Notice,[189] and the Notice on cooperation between the Commission and the courts of the Member States,[190] and in merger cases by Regulation 139/2004, in particular its Article 19.

Brexit would deprive the UK authorities and the EU Commission (and National Competition Authorities) of practically all of the benefits of these rules on cooperation. The UK competition authorities would of course cease to be part of the European Competition Network (ECN).[191] Notifications, the ability of the UK competition authorities to consult the Commission, the close information exchange between the Commission and the NCAs on the one hand and the UK competition authorities, including confidential information,[192] and the UK participation in the Advisory Committee would all come to an end. UK courts will no longer have the right to ask the Commission to transmit information to them under Regulation 1/2003. From the EU's perspective, and the perspective of the remaining Member States, the ability to conduct inspections in the UK or to request the UK authorities

[188]Council Regulation (EC) No 1/2003 of 16 December 2002 on the implementation of the rules on competition laid down in Articles 81 and 82 of the Treaty, OJ 2003 L 1/1.

[189]Commission Notice on cooperation within the Network of Competition Authorities, OJ 2004 C 101/43.

[190]Commission Notice on the co-operation between the Commission and the courts of the EU Member States in the application of Articles 81 and 82 EC, OJ 2004 C 101/54.

[191]Whish (2016).

[192]Article 12(1) Regulation No 1/2003.

to conduct such inspections under Articles 20–22 of Regulation 1/2003, will be a major disadvantage.

With regard to private enforcement, a number of changes would result, which may have an impact on the UK as a preferred forum of choice for damages actions.[193] In particular, as described above, clause 6 of the European Union (Withdrawal) Bill would make it impossible to rely on the binding effect of Commission decisions as a basis for follow-on actions. If one wanted to find a silver lining, the UK would no longer be bound by the provisions in the Damages Directive.[194] While the Damages Directive may facilitate private damages actions in many continental jurisdictions, its provisions for the most part either reflect or fall behind the standards already used in English private and civil procedure law.[195] It is true that the Damages Directive seeks, for the most part, only minimum harmonisation, so that it is for the most part merely *not facilitating* damages actions. In some respects, however, the Damages Directive makes private enforcement *more difficult*, for example with regard to the prohibition of over-compensatory damages (Article 3(3) of the Directive) and the absolute limits of disclosure with regard to leniency statements and settlement submissions (Articles 6(6), 7(1) of the Directive). English law may, after Brexit, use over-compensatory damages, in particular exemplary damages, in exceptional cases again, a practice that is prohibited by Article 3(3) of the Damages Directive.[196] With regard to disclosure rules, the provisions in Article 5 of the Damages Directive did not extend the scope of available disclosure in English law, but those in Article 6 and 7 of the Damages Directive restricted the available disclosure[197]; after Brexit, disclosure can be extended to leniency statements and settlement submissions, if this were to be considered desirable. Nor would the English legislator be constrained by the

[193]Until now, the UK was one of the most frequently chosen venues for damages actions—alongside Germany and the Netherlands, see the references in Wagner-von Papp (2015a), p. 29 in fn. 62. The Consumer Rights Act 2015 with its section 81 and schedule 8 strengthening the Competition Appeal Tribunal and allowing various forms of collective redress was expected to consolidate this position.

[194]Directive 2014/104/EU of the European Parliament and of the Council of 26 November 2014 on certain rules governing actions for damages under national law for infringements of the competition law provisions of the Member States and of the European Union, OJ 2014 L 349/1. For the implementation in various Member States, see, e.g., Bien et al (2017).

[195]Cf. Wagner-von Papp (2015a).

[196]See Wagner-von Papp (2015a), p. 30 et seq. For the question in which exceptional cases exemplary damages may be awarded under the cases *Devenish Nutrition* (*Devenish Nutrition Ltd. v Sanofi-Aventis SA* [2007] EWHC 2394 para. 48, an issue that was not appealed), *Cardiff Bus* (*2 Travel Group plc (in liquidation) v Cardiff City Transport Services Ltd.* [2012] CAT 19 paras. 448–598) and *Albion Water* (*Albion Water Ltd. v Dŵr Cymru Cyfyngedig* [2010] CAT 30). See now paragraph 36 of Schedule 8A to the Competition Act 1998, implementing the Damages Directive ("A court or the Tribunal may not award exemplary damages in competition proceedings").

[197]For details see Wagner-von Papp F, Access to Evidence and Leniency Materials, 18 February 2016, https://ssrn.com/abstract=2733973 (last accessed 16 July 2017); for an overview Wagner-von Papp (2015a), p. 31 et seq.

Directive's framework regarding leniency applicants: it could choose a completely different approach, such as following the suggestion in the literature to give full immunity from damages obligations to the immunity recipient and oblige the immunity recipient to disclose all its information to the claimants.[198] All these changes, however, fall into the category of speculative, merely possible changes post-Brexit.

More immediately, a number of Regulations in the field of private international law would cease to be applicable: in our context in particular Brussels I (Recast), the Taking of Evidence Regulation, and the Rome I and Rome II Regulations.[199] The subject matter covered by these Regulations was in some cases dealt with by Conventions before the Regulations started to apply, such as the Brussels Convention, the Lugano Conventions, and the Rome Convention. In these cases the question arises whether the Conventions are revived once the Regulations cease to apply.[200] With regard to jurisdiction, recognition and enforcement, the Brussels I (Recast) Regulation[201] would cease to apply and the UK would have to rely on the 1968 Brussels Convention[202] instead. It has been pointed out that the Brussels Convention has a more limited geographical scope and does not contain the improvements that the Brussels I and Brussels I (Recast) Regulations made, such as addressing (at least partially) the *Italian Torpedo* issue and doing away with the *exequatur* requirement.[203] It has also been pointed out[204] that with regard to jurisdiction, recognition and enforcement in relation to Denmark, Iceland, Norway and Switzerland, the situation is even more difficult: while the UK was a Contracting Party to the original 1988 Lugano Convention, this Convention was replaced by the 2007 Lugano Convention—and the 2007 Lugano Convention was negotiated, concluded and ratified by the European Community (EC) and only mentions the EC and its Member States, Denmark, Iceland, Norway and Switzerland.[205] The 2007 Lugano Convention has thus arguably terminated the applicability of the 1988 Lugano Convention to the UK by virtue of its Article 69(6), but will

---

[198] Buccirossi P, Marvão C, Spagnolo G, Leniency and Damages, CEPR Discussion Paper No DP10682, June 2015, http://ssrn.com/abstract=2624637 (last accessed 16 July 2017).

[199] For an excellent discussion see in particular Dickinson (2016); see also Lehmann and Zetzsche (2016).

[200] Dickinson (2016), pp. 203–207.

[201] Regulation (EU) No 1215/2012 of the European Parliament and of the Council of 12 December 2012 on jurisdiction and the recognition and enforcement of judgments in civil and commercial matters (recast), OJ 2012 L 351/1.

[202] 1968 Brussels Convention on jurisdiction and the enforcement of judgments in civil and commercial matters, OJ 1972 L 299/32.

[203] Lehmann and Zetzsche (2016), pp. 29–31, *inter alia*, with a discussion why the Brussels Convention "survived" the Brussels I and II (Recast) Regulations, and the advantages of the Regulations over the Convention; Dickinson (2016), p. 201 et seq.

[204] By Dickinson (2016), p. 206 et seq.; Lehmann and Zetzsche (2016), p. 31.

[205] Convention on jurisdiction and the recognition and enforcement of judgments in civil and commercial matters (2007 Lugano Convention), OJ 2007 L 339/3.

itself no longer apply to the UK once it ceases to be an EU Member State.[206] In our context, the Hague Convention on Choice of Court Agreements[207] could *not* act as a complement to the Brussels and Lugano Conventions in any event because it excludes competition matters from its scope.[208]

In contrast to the Lugano Convention, it is clearer that the Rome Convention[209] on the applicable law will revive,[210] but in our context it is notable that the Rome Convention only covers contractual obligations and therefore can at best be a replacement for the *Rome I* Regulation,[211] and not for the Rome II Regulation,[212] which covers non-contractual obligations.

The Taking of Evidence Regulation[213] would also cease to apply, although the experience with this Regulation in the competition law case *National Grid* was not necessarily an unmitigated success anyway.[214] Vis-à-vis several jurisdictions, the UK courts could at least continue to rely on the Hague Convention on Taking Evidence.[215]

It should be noted that the "European Union (Withdrawal) Bill" (informally called the "Great Repeal Bill") introduced in Parliament on 13 July 2017 would be of very limited use with regard to most of these aspects. The Great Repeal Bill could not ensure the continued access to information and cooperation that is available under Regulation 1/2003 in the ECN, in the Advisory Committee and through judicial cooperation. Nor would it allow the continuation of the benefits of the Brussels I (Recast) Regulation (although, as noted above, the Brussels Convention would revive and provide limited relief). Nor would the Great Repeal Bill allow courts in the UK to make use of the Taking of Evidence Regulation (although again there is a partial substitute in the Hague Convention on Taking Evidence). The only aspect the Great Repeal Bill addresses in clause 2 is the unilateral replication of the provisions in the various Regulations (in the version in force on the day before exit day) in domestic law; this would mean, for example, that UK courts and tribunals continue to be bound (until further legislative action) by the

[206]Dickinson (2016), p. 207; Lehmann and Zetzsche (2016), p. 31.

[207]Hague Convention on choice of court agreements of 30 June 2005.

[208]Article 2(2)(h) of the Hague Convention on choice of court agreements.

[209]Convention 80/934/EEC on the law applicable to contractual obligations, OJ 1980 L 266/1.

[210]Dickinson (2016), p. 203.

[211]Regulation (EC) No 593/2008 of the European Parliament and of the Council of 17 June 2008 on the law applicable to contractual obligations (Rome I), OJ 2008 L 177/6.

[212]Regulation (EC) No 864/2007 of the European Parliament and of the Council of 11 July 2007 on the law applicable to non-contractual obligations (Rome II), OJ 2007 L 199/40.

[213]Council Regulation (EC) No 1206/2001 of 28 May 2001 on cooperation between the courts of the Member States in the taking of evidence in civil or commercial matters, OJ 2001 L 174/1.

[214]Cf. Wagner-von Papp F, Access to Evidence and Leniency Materials, 18 February 2016, https://ssrn.com/abstract=2733973 (last accessed 16 July 2017), p. 71.

[215]Hague Convention on the Taking of Evidence Abroad in Civil or Commercial Matters, concluded on 18 March 1970.

jurisdictional provisions etc in the Brussels I (Recast) Regulation, and by the provisions on the applicable law in the Rome I and Rome II Regulations.[216]

5.2.3 Enforcement Cooperation Models for the Post-Brexit UK

Time has to show how acrimonious or amicable the divorce of the UK from the EU will be more generally. With regard to competition law enforcement, however, there is little doubt that a very close, and if possible uninterrupted, cooperation especially between the UK authorities and the ECN should be in the mutual interest of both sides. The EU has no interest in going back to the times of *Dyestuffs*, and the CMA is likely keen to cooperate as closely as possible with the EU Commission and the ECN as well, given that its enforcement resources are limited.

In some respects, the circumstances are particularly conducive to agreeing on enforcement cooperation between the UK and the EU. Capobianco and Nagy have recently summarised factors that may impede enforcement cooperation: differences in the enforcement scheme (civil/criminal); differences in the substantive law; differences in procedural rules; and differences in size and economic development.[217] The CMA itself, while young in its current emanation, is the successor of the OFT and so a well-developed competition authority, and the UK economy is as advanced as the economies of the remaining EU Member States. On exit day, the substantive and procedural provisions in UK law will be in full compliance with EU law (or so one would hope), so that substantive or procedural divergences should not prevent cooperation at that time. No further "approximation" of the laws would be required. Whether this state of affairs will continue into the future depends largely on the question to what extent UK competition law will be allowed by the legislator to use EU competition law as a guiding star. A sensible approach would be to aim at the greatest possible harmonisation with EU developments, but such an approach may be questioned by those whose main aim is to "take back control", and the European Union (Withdrawal) Bill does not give great hope in this regard.

There is a certain danger that this emphasis on taking back control and sovereignty in the Brexit campaign may even lead to a revival of the UK's resistance against extraterritorial enforcement of EU (and other foreign) competition law that led to conflicts in the 1970s and 1980s,[218] with a potential application of the

---

[216]See already Dickinson (2016), p. 210.

[217]Capobianco and Nagy (2016), pp. 3–6.

[218]In *Dyestuffs*, the United Kingdom submitted an *aide-mémoire* of 20 October 1969, which is reprinted in Lowe (1983), pp. 144–147. In *Wood Pulp I*, the UK again objected to the effects test: CJEU, joined cases 89/85, 104/85, 114/85, 116/85, 117/85 and 125/85 to 129/85, *Ahlström v Commission*, ECLI:EU:C:1988:447. Also, see Note No 196 of the British Embassy at Washington, DC, which was presented to the US Department of State on July 27, reprinted in Marston (1978), p. 390 et seq. It states that "in the present state of international law there is no basis for the extension of one country's antitrust jurisdiction to activities outside that country by foreign nationals". See also Sweeney (2010), p. 245 et seq.; Lowe (1988), p. 179; but see Whish and

Protection of Trading Interests Act 1980. While it is unlikely that *the CMA* would support such actions impeding the European Commission's antitrust enforcement, it is not unthinkable that the *UK Government* will choose to protect UK undertakings against EU competition law enforcement to advance their industrial policy or protect national champions.[219]

With these caveats, it would seem that both the EU and the UK have a substantial mutual interest to cooperate as closely as possible in competition matters. Even if both parties are willing, however, and despite the current substantive and procedural harmony between the UK and EU competition regimes, the UK will not get the same access to information and cooperation that it currently has by virtue of Regulation 1/2003. The best that could be hoped for after Brexit even by incorrigible optimists would be a cooperation agreement along the lines of Protocol 23 to the EEA Agreement concerning the cooperation between the Surveillance Authorities (Article 58) and Protocol 24 on cooperation in the field of control of concentrations; a close second would be a second-generation intergovernmental agreement along the lines of the Agreement between Switzerland and the EU of 17 May 2013. It would be desirable to start immediate negotiations for an intergovernmental cooperation agreement along these lines. Given the enormity of the task of negotiating Brexit, the limited available time, and the very limited resources for negotiations that the UK Government has at its disposal, it appears unlikely that competition law cooperation will be high on the list of priorities. Under these conditions it does not seem feasible to get to a full-blown intergovernmental agreement between the EU and the UK on competition enforcement cooperation in time to ensure a smooth transition—at least assuming that the 2-year period is not extended. It would be desirable, therefore, that the UK competition authority and the EU Commission immediately start negotiations aiming at an interim interagency cooperation agreement.

Re-establishing cooperation with the EU itself is only part of the task. Section 4 above outlined the network of cooperation agreements on which the EU can rely. Many of these agreements, such as most SAAs, EMAs and PCAs are essentially institution-building tools that are meant to induce the partners in these agreements to introduce and maintain competition rules at least broadly similar to the EU competition rules. To this extent, there is no need to replicate these agreements

---

Bailey (2015), p. 533, indicating a move towards a more favourable attitude to extraterritorial application in the Enterprise and Regulatory Reform Act 2013.

[219]One of the more prominent business leaders donating to the Leave Campaign and speaking out in favour of Brexit before the Referendum was Lord Bamford, the chairman of JCB. It has been speculated that the fine of some €40 million for antitrust infringements imposed by the Commission in 2000 and eventually largely upheld by the CJEU in 2006 (although with a reduced fine of approximately €31 million), "which he [scil: Lord Bamford] called 'disappointing and wrong'" is "likely to have exacerbated" his pre-existing eurosceptic views, see Mance H, Brexit donors guided by bitter experience with EU, Financial Times, 15 June 2016. See Commission Decision of 21 December 2000 relating to a proceeding under Article 81 of the EC Treaty Case COMP.F.1/35.918, *JCB*, OJ 2002 L 69/1; GC, case T-67/01, *JCB Service v Commission*, ECLI:EU:T:2004:3; CJEU, case C-167/04 P, *JCB Services v Commission,* ECLI:EU:C:2006:594.

on the UK side. However, other intergovernmental cooperation agreements with increasingly active antitrust jurisdictions, such as the ones with the US, Switzerland, Turkey, Japan, and Korea, as well as the Memoranda of Understanding with the competition authorities of Brazil, Russia, China, India, and South Africa, are of increasing strategic importance for a competition authority. In establishing links to other third countries, the UK will have to begin largely, save existing general mutual legal assistance treaties and extradition treaties, from scratch.

Even greater difficulties may be expected in the negotiations with the EU with regard to cooperation when it comes to private enforcement. The difficulties will be greater for two reasons. First, jurisdictions within the EU have been competing with each other to attract private enforcement cases, and the disadvantages that the UK will face from not being able to rely on, for example, the Brussel I (Recast) Regulation's provisions on jurisdiction, recognition and enforcement may be considered as a boon by continental jurisdictions. The second reason is that these issues transcend competition law. While it seems likely that in the competition law sector there will be a mutual interest in cooperation to the greatest possible extent, the private international law instruments mentioned above are cross-sectoral, and this means that negotiations will be multipolar. Continental jurisdictions have sought for some time to cannibalise London's dominance in the provision of commercial legal services.[220] It cannot be excluded that the continental jurisdictions will see the difficulties which English law faces in the area of private international law post Brexit with a certain degree of glee.

6 Conclusion

Free trade and competition law, for the most part, mutually reinforce each other by breaking up entrenched positions of market power and creating competitive pressures. Competition law enforcement (as does most public international law) still adheres mostly to the nineteenth century paradigm of sovereign nation states. National competition law enforcers face an increasingly transnational economy, and, for the reasons outlined in Sect. 2, globalisation makes unilateral competition law enforcement based on territorial enforcement jurisdiction difficult. The increase in free trade, the increasing sophistication of the economies of many developing nations, and competition advocacy have resulted in a proliferation of national competition law regimes and national competition enforcement agencies. The patchwork

[220]See Bundesnotarkammer (BNotK), Bundesrechtsanwaltskammer (BRAK), Deutscher Anwaltverein (DAV), Deutscher Industrie- und Handelskammertag e.V. (DIHK), Deutscher Notarverein (DNotV), Deutscher Richterbund (DRB), Law made in Germany, 3rd edn. 2014, http://www.lawmadeingermany.de/Law-Made_in_Germany_EN.pdf (last accessed 16 July 2017). This is a brochure published by an initiative that was founded in reaction to the Law Society's promotion of English law as the best in the world. I have spent several years each in Germany, the UK and the US. Interestingly, all three have the best legal system in the world, at least according to their own assessment.

of multiple national unilateral enforcement leads to enforcement gaps and enforcement overlaps. Some commentators are of the view that such global problems have to be addressed by global solutions, and advocate a global competition agency, or at least acceptance of the decision of a lead agency. Apart from the question whether such centralised enforcement would be desirable, such proposals face an insurmountable (political) feasibility constraint. If neither a global solution nor independent unilateral enforcement is the answer, then there must be an intermediate path.

This path consists in increasing cooperation and coordination of enforcement activities. Arguably the closest integration of sovereign nation states for more than 50 years has been what is today the EU and the extended EEA. Regional cooperation along similar lines, albeit not (yet) in the same depth, is developing all over the world. Ideally, joining forces at a regional level leads to internally (relatively) homogeneous clusters, and reduces complexity—instead of considering all 130 individual competition regimes, regionalisation allows us to treat the (today) 28 Member States of the EU as one cluster, and Australia-New Zealand as another one. To be sure, as always in comparative law the *praesumptio similitudinis* only holds at a high degree of abstraction: of course the competition regimes of the 28 Member States are far from identical.

Around the extremely close cooperation in such regional cooperation agreements, there can be a penumbra of gradually decreasing cooperation, such as the area covering the EU and the states affiliated by the various bilateral agreements described in Sect. 4 of this paper, in particular the second-generation intergovernmental cooperation agreement with Switzerland, the Comity agreements between the EU and the US, and the various SAAs, PCAs and EMAs, as well as the Customs Union with Turkey.

This regional cooperation with an extended penumbra is complemented by cooperation with antitrust regimes that are geographically further apart but are larger economies. Together, we find a network of nodes consisting of regional cooperation with strengthening bonds to neighbouring areas, which are interconnected amongst each other by bilateral or biregional agreements.

Extrapolating this development into the future, the result would eventually be a network of clusters around the nodes. Within each cluster, issues of gaps and overlaps can be reduced to the greatest possible extent—externalities between Member States can be dealt with on the EU level so that gaps are avoided, and one-stop shops, as in Article 21(3) of the European Merger Control Regulation 139/2004, or at least case allocation rules, such as the ones in the Network Notice, help to avoid overlaps. Between clusters, cooperation and coordination may not resolve all gaps and overlaps, but as global heterogeneity in views on competition policy decreases, gradual progress is made here as well.

Until June 2016, this description of the development of cooperation seemed an accurate representation of reality. Then the UK chose to break with the pattern. The attempt to "take back control" and insist on unfettered sovereignty in the tradition of the nineteenth century by going it alone will face steep hurdles in the transnational economy of the twenty-first century. For all the insistence that Brexit will make the UK more and not less open to the world, this fails to understand the complexity of the global economy in the twenty-first century (quite apart from failing to understand the perception the vote for Brexit has created, rightly or wrongly, that it is a signal of isolationism). The presidential election in the US in November 2016 has raised further questions going to the very existence of the transnational economy in its current form.[221] Time will tell whether the events of June 2016 and November 2016 will remain isolated bumps in the road towards greater global cooperation that allows us to face the challenges and reap the fruits of an international economy based on free trade and competitive markets, or whether the world will regress into a collection of protectionist nation states of the nineteenth century. Of course, the retrenchment of the United States, and even the leaving of the United Kingdom, could give the European Union a chance to fill the void by pushing forward with its trade agenda.

References

Baker DI, Rushkoff B (1990) The 1988 Justice Department international guidelines: searching for legal standards and reassurance. Cornell Int Law J 23:405–440

Baudenbacher C (2012) Swiss economic law facing the challenges of international and European law. Zeitschrift für Schweizerisches Recht 146:419–673

Becker F (2007) The case of export cartel exemptions: between competition and protectionism. J Compet Law Econ 3(1):97–126

Bien F et al (2017) Conference proceedings: implementation of the EU Damages Directive into Member State law (Würzburg, May 5, 2017). Concurrences No. 3-2017 (forthcoming)

Bradford A, Büthe T (2015) Competition policy and free trade: antitrust provisions in PTAs. In: Dür A, Elsig M (eds) Trade cooperation—the purpose, design and effects of Preferential Trade Agreements. Cambridge University Press, Cambridge, pp 246–273

Bradford A, Chilton A (2017) Are antitrust laws and trade liberalization substitutes or complements? Draft, 16 March 2017 (on file with the author)

Budzinski O (2008) The governance of global competition. Edward Elgar, Cheltenham

Capobianco A, Nagy A (2016) Developments in international enforcement co-operation in the competition field. J Eur Compet Law Pract 7(8):566–583

Dabbah M (2010) Future directions in bilateral cooperation: a policy perspective. In: Guzman A (ed) Cooperation, comity, and competition policy. Oxford University Press, Oxford, pp 287–299

Dickinson A (2016) Back to the future: the UK's EU exit and the conflict of laws. J Priv Int Law 12 (2):195–210

Evenett S, Fritz J (2015) The tide turns? Trade, protectionism, and slowing global growth: the 18th Global Trade Alert Report. CEPR Press, London

Geradin D, Reysen M, Henry D (2010) Extraterritoriality, comity, and cooperation in EU competition law. In: Guzman A (ed) Cooperation, comity, and competition policy. Oxford University Press, Oxford, pp 21–44

[221]McCain J, Donald Trump retreats from trade deals at his peril, Financial Times, 6 December 2016. For the EU reaction, see European Commission, Reflection paper on harnessing globalisation, COM(2017) 240 of 10 May 2017, https://ec.europa.eu/commission/sites/beta-political/files/reflection-paper-globalisation_en.pdf (last accessed 16 July 2017).

Gerber D (2010) Global competition: Law, markets, and globalization. Oxford University Press, Oxford

Guzman A (2004) The case for international antitrust. Berk J Int Law 22(3):355–374

Guzman A (2010) Competition law and cooperation: possible strategies. In: Guzman A (ed) Cooperation, comity, and competition policy. Oxford University Press, Oxford, pp 345–362

Hoekman B, Mavroidis P (1996) Dumping, antidumping, and antitrust. J World Trade 30(1):27–52

Hoekman B, Mavroidis P (2003) Economic development, competition policy and the World Trade Organisation. J World Trade 37(1):1–27

Immenga U (1995) Export cartels and voluntary export restraints between trade and competition policy. Pac Rim Law Policy J 4(1):93–151

Jenny F (2012) Export cartels in primary products: the Potash case in perspective. In: Evenett S, Jenny F (eds) Trade, competition, and the pricing of commodities. CEPR, London, pp 124–130

Kagitani K, Harimaya K (2015) Safeguards and voluntary export restraints under the World Trade Organization: the case of Japan's vegetable trade. Jpn World 36:29–41

Lehmann M, Zetzsche D (2016) Brexit and the consequences for commercial and financial relations between the EU and the UK. Eur Bus Law Rev 27(7):999–1027

Levenstein M, Suslow V (2005) The changing international status of export cartel exemptions. Am Univ Int Law Rev 20:785–828

Lowe A (1983) Extraterritorial jurisdiction: an annotated collection of legal materials. Grotius Publications, Cambridge

Lowe A (1988) Extraterritorial jurisdiction: the British practice. Rabels Zeitschrift für ausländisches und internationales Privatrecht 52:157–204

Marsden P (2010) The curious incident of positive comity – the dog that didn't bark (and the trade dogs that just might bite). In: Guzman A (ed) Cooperation, comity, and competition policy. Oxford University Press, Oxford, pp 301–318

Marston G (1978) United Kingdom materials on international law 1978. Br Yearb Int Law 49:329–437

Martyniszyn M (2012a) A comparative look on foreign state compulsion as a defence in antitrust litigation. Compet Law Rev 8(2):143–167

Martyniszyn M (2012b) Export cartels: is it legal to target your neighbour? Analysis in light of recent case law. J Int Econ Law 15(1):181–222

Martyniszyn M (2016) How high (and far) can you go? On setting fines in cartel cases involving vertically-integrated undertakings and foreign sales. Eur Compet Law Rev 37(3):99–107

Melamed A (1998) International antitrust in an age of international deregulation. George Mason Law Rev 6:437–446

Morita M (1991) Structural impediment initiative: is it an effective correction of Japan's antimonopoly policy? Univ Pa J Int Bus Law 12(4):777–809

Noland M, Hufbauer GC, Robinson S, Moran T (2016) Assessing trade agendas in the US presidential campaign. Peterson Institute for International Economics Briefing 16-6

Papadopoulos A (2010) The international dimension of EU competition law and policy. Cambridge University Press, Cambridge

Papadopoulos A (2013) External competition law of the EU. In: Hermann C, Krajewski M, Terhechte J (eds) European yearbook of international economic law, vol 4. Springer, Heidelberg, pp 87–108

Pereira V (2016) The seven deadly sins: shortfalls of a "true European solution" for a "one-stop leniency shop". Eur Compet Law Rev 37(5):186–192

Scherer F (1994) Competition policies for an integrated world economy. Brookings Institution, Washington

Sokol D (2008) What do we really know about export cartels and what is the appropriate solution? J Compet Law Econo 4(4):967–982

Solano O, Sennekamp A (2006) Competition provisions in regional trade agreements. OECD Trade Policy Paper Series No. 31. OECD Publishing, Paris

Sweeney B (2007) Export cartels: is there a need for global rules? J Int Econ Law 10(1):87–115
Sweeney B (2010) The internationalisation of competition rules. Routledge, Abingdon
Taladay J (2012) Time for a global "one-stop" shop for leniency markers. Antitrust 27(Fall):43–49
Trebilcock M (1996) Competition policy and trade policy: mediating the interface. J World Trade 30(4):71–106
Trebilcock M, Iacobucci E (2004) National treatment and extraterritoriality: defining the domains of trade and antitrust policy. In: Epstein R, Greve M (eds) Competition laws in conflict: antitrust jurisdiction in the global economy. AEI Press, Washington, pp 152–176
Tschaeni H, Engammare V (2013) The relationship between trade and competition in free trade agreements: developments since the 1990s and challenges. In: Hermann C, Krajewski M, Terhechte J (eds) European yearbook of international economic law, vol 4. Springer, Heidelberg, pp 39–69
Wagner-von Papp F (2012) Competition law and extraterritoriality. In: Ezrachi A (ed) Research handbook on international competition law. Edward Elgar, Cheltenham, pp 21–59
Wagner-von Papp F (2015a) Implementation of the damages directive in England & Wales. Concurrences No. 2-2015:e29–34
Wagner-von Papp F (2015b) Should Google's secret sauce be organic? Melb J Int Law 16:609–646
Wagner-von Papp F (2016) Compliance and individual sanctions for competition law infringements. In: Paha J (ed) Competition law compliance programs – an interdisciplinary approach. Springer, Heidelberg, pp 135–188
Whish R (2016) Brexit and EU competition policy. J Eur Compet Law Pract 7(5):297–298
Whish R, Bailey D (2015) Competition law, 8th edn. Oxford University Press, Oxford
Wils W (2013) Ten years of regulation 1/2003 – a retrospective. J Compet Law Pract 4(4):293–301

The European Union's Policy on Public Procurement in Preferential Trade Agreements

Stephen Woolcock

Abstract The European Union's policy on public procurement in the preferential trade agreements (PTAs) has to be seen against the broader EU aims of shaping international trade rules and ensuring market access to key markets. The EU policy on procurement has both shaped and has been shaped by international norms. Initially pressure from the United States (US) led to international discussions in the OECD. These shaped the initial EU Directives aimed at creating a Europe wide procurement market in the early 1970s. But it was not until the late 1980s, as part of the EU Single Market programme, that EU moved to create a competition based, comprehensive regional procurement market. From this point on the EU became a proponent of stronger international rules on procurement. This shift by the EU paved the way for a significant extension of the international rules in the 1996 revision of the World Trade Organisation's Government Procurement Agreement (GPA). EU policy now has two main components. First, to achieve an equally comprehensive international regime that can ensure access to other major economies, including the emerging markets. Second, to promote the adoption of international best practice in the government procurement, which accounts for a important share of GDP in all economies but it too often subject to a lack of transparency and due process and thus a potential source of abuse and corruption. In these efforts the EU has had partial success in the face of significant opposition. The EU pressed for multilateral negotiations on procurement rules in the WTO's Doha Development Agenda (DDA), but without success. It had some more success in the plurilateral negotiations to extend the coverage of the (non-MFN) GPA, but this was very largely in the form of greater commitments by existing developed signatories to that agreement. Preferential trade agreements (PTAs) have offered an alternative means of fulfilling the EU's objectives and in these the EU has had some success, but there remains considerable opposition. Public procurement arguably marks the high tide

S. Woolcock (✉)
London School of Economics, Houghton Street, London WC2A 2AE, UK
e-mail: S.B.Woolcock@lse.ac.uk

M. Bungenberg et al. (eds.), *European Yearbook of International Economic Law 2017*, European Yearbook of International Economic Law 8,
DOI 10.1007/978-3-319-58832-2_11

mark for the extension of the liberal paradigm of an open, rules-based order into national policy autonomy. It remains to be seen whether recent developments in leading OECD economies, such as the call for more Buy America policies by the incoming *Trump* Administration will threaten the scope of the existing rules.

Contents

1 Introduction

This chapter looks at the European Union's (EU) approach to government procurement in the preferential trade and investment agreements (PTAs). In order to understand the EU policy it is necessary to first discuss the nature of public procurement markets, and thus the challenges involved in establishing rules governing the operation of and access to such market. It is also necessary to see how the EU policy in PTAs fits with the debate on international procurement rules and policy in general.

After covering these points the chapter summarizes the nature of international agreements in public procurement. This is necessary in order to gauge how effective the EU has been in pursuing its aims. The scope of the existing EU bilateral PTAs is then summarized, after which there is a discussion of the issues in procurement in the on-going PTAs. The conclusions return to assess the success of EU policy and the limitations it faces.

2 The Nature of the Procurement Markets

Public procurement constitutes an important share of national GDP in all countries, but is often characterised by limited competition as national and sub-national government or public enterprises provide *de facto* or formal *de jure* preferences for local suppliers. There is generally a lack of data on procurement markets, but the most reliable and extensive data provided by the OECD shows that public contracts account for on average 13% of GDP across the OECD economies.[1] The importance of public procurement in developing economies can be even greater and account for a large share of government expenditure.[2] While a lot of public procurement may not be subject to potential competition, as the figures include expenditure on national health schemes, small efficiencies from increased competition can represent significant welfare gains compared to some other issues in PTA negotiations. Enhanced transparency in public contracts can also promote integrity in the use of public expenditure and reduce the scope for corrupt practices.

In many countries procurement represents the most important part of national economies that is not subject to a great deal of international competition. This is due to continued resistance to extending a rules-based order that facilitates competition. Such resistance has a number of sources. Existing national suppliers may have become reliant on secure access to national public contracts and will resist any increase in competition, whether from other national suppliers, local affiliates of international companies or direct imports from other countries. Purchasing entities, such as government departments or agencies and especially state owned enterprises, may resist the adoption of international rules covering procurement, because these can result in increased compliance costs. This is the case when comprehensive rules are introduced in order to close off the numerous ways in which national governments find to favour national suppliers. Generally speaking the EU has sought comprehensive rules on procurement in line with its internal rules. Resistance to international rules may also result from a desire to use procurement to promote other policy objectives. First and foremost would be the promotion of national champions or support for the development of national supply capacity, a motive that is present in all countries, but is especially prevalent in developing economies. Procurement is also increasingly used to promote other policy objectives such as environmental policies,[3] small and medium sized companies or redistribution such as in the form of regional policy.

It also has to be recognized that there is not just an economic utility function at work in public procurement, but also a political utility function. As a major source of discretionary funding, public contracts can be used as a means of winning votes, or retaining political support by providing local jobs or contracts. In some regimes contracts for public works provide the means by which those in power retain patronage and support for the prevailing regime. Politicians are therefore not always enthusiastic about liberalization, but political leadership is required to drive through reform. In this respect reform of public procurement policy can be

---

[1]See http://www.oecd-ilibrary.org/sites/gov_glance-2015-en/09/01/index.html (last accessed 1 March 2017).

[2]World Bank, Benchmarking Public Procurement, 2017, Assessing Public Procurement Regulatory Systems in 180 Economies, 2016, https://worldbank/Benchmarking-Public-Procurement-2017.pdf (last accessed 1 March 2017).

[3]UNEP, Sustainable Public Procurement: A Global View, December 2013, https://www.globalecolabelling.net/assets/Documents/unep-spp-report.pdf (last accessed 1 March 2017).

seen as a classic example of the political economy of protection in which decision makers in government must balance the welfare gains from the more defuse benefits of more efficient, competition based public procurement and how this might eventually feed through to political support, against the more immediate political costs of local taxes being used to fund contracts for foreign companies and thus provide jobs abroad.

The forces that resist reform in public procurement are important because they illustrate the challenge of extending rules-based, competitive procurement policies via international agreements including EU PTAs. The opposition comes from developing countries, which see market opening vi-a-vis the EU as unbalanced given the limited domestic supply capacity in their economies. It is seen as a threat by emerging markets, such as India or China, that have large public sectors or state owned enterprises and therefore also see the inclusion of rules on procurement as favouring the EU. Even in developed economies, using tax dollars to award contracts to EU suppliers can be seen as a vote loser, hence the pressure for Buy American policies in the US Congress, US state governments or now in the US Administration. These impediments to procurement markets mean that many companies seeking access will do so via the establishment of an affiliate in the target market or via a local contractor. This is called indirect access as opposed to direct access by means of exports of goods or services. It is generally easier to access markets in this way because public contracts are still seen as contributing to the economy of and providing jobs in the host market.

3 The Elements of Procurement Provisions

Before discussing the EU's policy on procurement in PTAs it is necessary to sketch out the substance of typical procurement chapters. This reflects the prevailing international norms that have been developed over a number of years and is reflected in the WTO Government Procurement Agreement, most recently revised in 2012 with entry into force in 2014,[4] and the UNCITRAL model law on procurement dating from 1994 and revised in 2011.[5] The inclusion of procurement chapters in EU PTAs can be seen as a means of extending the coverage of these internationally agreed rules.

In assessing the degree to which EU PTAs are successful in incorporating such norms one can distinguish between four key elements. *Transparency* is an essential

[4]See WTO Government Procurement Agreement, 2014 https://www.wto.org/english/news_e/news14_e/gpro_07apr14_e.htm (last accessed 1 March 2017).

[5]UNCITRAL Model Law on Public Procurement 2011 http://www.uncitral.org/uncitral/uncitral_texts/procurement_infrastructure/2011Model.html (last accessed 1 March 2017).

condition for access to procurement markets and provisions on transparency feature in the GPA, the Model Law and the chapters on procurement in PTAs. Transparency covers to provision of information on national procurement laws and implementing regulations. Transparency provisions can also include requirements to use standard bidding documents and set out the procedures to be followed in awarding contracts. There are usually three types of contract award procedure; open tendering based on price for uniform or low value supplies; selective or restricted tendering when it is important to ensure that the suppliers are technically qualified to fulfill the contract; and negotiated contracts in special cases for which greater diligence is needed to ensure due process is followed.

Potential suppliers also need to know when there are calls for tender. So agreements require covered purchasing entities to publicise calls for tender and to specify the contract award criteria. Increasingly there are efforts to provide this information in electronic form via a central procurement portal and there may be requirements to provide the information in an international language. Potential suppliers will also benefit from the provision of procurement plans that indicate what type of contracts will come from a purchasing entity (i.e. government department or nationalized industry) over the coming year. Post contract award transparency is also considered important and features, in particular, in the UNCITRAL Model Law, as a means of helping to ensure compliance. Post contract award transparency typically requires the provision of information on who has won the contract and provision for unsuccessful bidders to request an explanation of why a bid failed. Data on the distribution of contracts also shows when contracts are awarded to the same suppliers. Generally speaking greater transparency should help to ensure more open markets, but at a cost in terms of compliance.

Technical specifications can be used to favour national suppliers. The rules on procurement, developed in the GPA and included in the EU approach, therefore require the use of performance standards and prohibit design standards or the use of trade marks in drawing up specifications. In other words the specifications should be based on what the good or service should perform not how it is designed. In line with EU policy on standards the norm is to use international standards when these are available. When they are not national standards should be used. More extensive coverage of transparency in line with the EU norm would therefore be seen as a success for the EU.

Coverage determines which purchasing entities will be covered by transparency and/or the liberalization provisions in any agreement. So greater coverage can be seen as a success for EU policies. A distinction is made between three types of purchasing entities: central government entities (type I), sub-central entities, such as state, provincial government or municipal government (type II), and other entities, such as state owned enterprises (type III). Generally speaking sub-central government accounts for more than central government, especially in federal states, such as the USA, Canada and India. Type III procurement can be very important in countries that still have major state owned enterprises, such as China and India. But all countries have some state-owned or public enterprises. Taking the average for the 34 OECD economies nearly a third of all public procurement is accounted for by state-owned utilities, or nearly 5% of GDP.[6] The EU's internal regime for public procurement covers all levels from the EU institutions, through central governments in the Member States, to regional, provincial and municipal levels as well as public utilities. In the negotiation of procurement chapters in PTAs the EU has therefore long sought to include sub-central government level coverage.

Coverage is also determined by thresholds. In order to limit the compliance costs, thresholds are set so as to cover the most important contracts, but exclude the many thousands of smaller contracts where compliance with detailed procedural and transparency rules would constitute a major cost. Thresholds are also used to limit the scope of liberalization. The norm for thresholds has been established by the GPA at 130,000 SDR (Special Drawing Rights) for goods and services contracts, and 5 million SDR for construction/works contracts. There are higher thresholds for sub-central government for goods and services (200,000 SDR) and for state owned enterprises (400,000 SDR). Thresholds can and do vary as will be shown below in the discussion of some EU PTA partners but these constitute the norm. Finally, there are generally exclusions for reasons of security such as defence. The EU internal regime has sought to restrict this to weapons and not have it used to exclude general-purpose equipment purchased by the military or police.

The concept of *liberalisation* commitments in public procurement chapters of PTAs is generally seen to be commitments to provide national treatment for covered entities. In other words there should be no discrimination between national and foreign suppliers. In practice this covers only explicit, *de jure* preferences such as price preferences, in which local suppliers are preferred unless the price is more than a set percentage above the competing international bid. Liberalisation also prohibits set-asides such as making the award of a contract conditional upon a set percentage of the work going to national suppliers. But national treatment seldom guarantees that there will be no *de facto* preference for local suppliers. This is because of the scope for discretion that remains in the application of all national contract award procedures.

Experience has shown that without *effective compliance* rules on public procurement will have little effect. Given the thousands of contracts awarded every day, central compliance monitoring is impracticable. Rules therefore provide bidders who believe they have not been fairly treated with an opportunity to seek an independent review of a contract award decision. Penalties in the case of non-compliance may involve project cancellation or financial penalties (limited to the costs of bids or exemplary damages). These provisions are called bid-challenge or compliance provisions and the EU has sought their inclusion in PTAs since the introduction of a compliance Directive for EU procurement as part of the Single Market Programme.

---

[6] OECD National Accounts Database and Eurostat. Data for Australia are based on a combination of Government Finance Statistics and National Accounts data provided by the Australian Bureau of Statistics.

4 The Existing Preferential Trade Agreements

The content of procurement chapters in EU PTAs has varied between negotiating partners. Table 1 provides a summary of the procurement content in the existing PTAs negotiated by the EU.

The first PTA to include comprehensive provisions on procurement was with Mexico in the agreement implementing the 2000 EU-Mexico agreement. In this Mexico committed to provisions that were in line with its commitments on procurement in NAFTA. Indeed the Mexican text followed the NAFTA text, which had been adopted in 1994 before the 1996 revision of the WTO's GPA.[7] So in procurement, as in other aspects of the EU-Mexico agreement, the EU was matching NAFTA commitments. Importantly, Mexico was not and is still not a signatory to the GPA. Coverage was limited to central government entities because NAFTA coverage was limited to central government due to the position of the US rather than Mexico. The agreement with Chile, which can be seen as of equivalent to a "generation of PTAs" was also striking in that Chile had been one of the most outspoken opponents of the GPA, arguing that the provisions were unnecessarily onerous given the generally liberal approach of Chile.

In PTAs with developing country partners such as in the EPAs with the African and Pacific States or in the earlier agreements with South Africa or the North African partners, the EU has included only a general rendezvous clause or a simple short article urging the opening of procurement markets.

In 2006 the EU shifted to a more active policy of negotiating PTAs as expressed in the Global Europe policy statement.[8] This policy included an effort to extend the coverage of PTAs to include comprehensive provisions on procurement. It should of course be recalled that the EU had favoured the inclusion of public procurement in the Doha Development Agenda as one of the so-called Singapore issues. When the EU was obliged to accept the omission of procurement for the DDA following the Cancun WTO Ministerial meeting,[9] the emphasis shifted to the use of PTAs to further this aim.

The EU-CARIFORUM was the first agreement with developing/middle income states that included a comprehensive chapter on procurement. This is however, limited to transparency provisions with only a rendezvous clause for liberalization. In other words the commitment to national treatment for specified entities will only happen when the Joint CARFORUM-European Union Council agrees to this. On transparency the CARIFORUM states have legislation in place and are working

[7]The GPA is reviewed at regular intervals. These reviews have generally increased coverage by the existing signatories rather than increasing membership. In the 2012 revision, which came into force in 2014 coverage was increased and a new provision added on special and differential treatment as an encouragement for more developing countries to sign up.

[8]European Commission, Global Europe: competing in the world, 2006, http://trade.ec.europa.eu/doclib/docs/2006/october/tradoc_130376.pdf (last accessed 1 March 2017).

[9]Clarke and Evenett (2003).

Table 1 Summary of procurement provisions in PTAs concluded by the EU

PTA	GPA signatory	Transparency	Coverage	Liberalisation	Bid challenge/ compliance
EU-Mexico	No	Broadly equivalent to GPA	Central government	Yes	Yes
EU-Chile	No	Broadly equivalent to GPA	Central government	Yes	Yes
EU-CARIFORUM	No	Yes; UNCITRAL compatible, but no post award transparency	Central government; but this covers most given the size of the economies	Rendezvous clause; Extension of national treatment to be agreed by the parties	Requirement for bid challenge
EU-Central America (and the EU Colombia-Peru provisions are very similar)	No	Extensive transparency provisions, broadly GPA/UNCITRAL level	Central government and some sub-central government such as for Colombia	Yes	Yes
EU-Vietnam	No	Broadly in line with UNCITRAL norm	Central government plus Ho Chi Minh City, hospitals and rail. But phased in from high threshold down to the 130,000 and 5 million SDR over 16 years	Yes, but see phasing of thresholds	Yes
EU-Korea	Yes	GPA rules apply	GPA coverage plus build and operate contracts	GPA coverage	GPA rules
EU-Singapore	Yes	GPA rules apply	GPA	GPA	GPA
CETA	Yes	GPA rules	GPA plus in the form of provincial and municipal procurement	GPA plus	GPA rules

towards the full application of UNCITRAL type rules. Coverage is of central government only, but given the small size of most of the economies this means that most procurement is covered. Here as for other middle-income partners, the EU effectively offers asymmetric access to its procurement market by offering near to full GPA coverage. The CARIFORUM agreement also envisages that there be regional opening in the Caribbean first, thus effectively suggesting the EU would accept a regional preference.[10]

In the later agreements negotiated with Colombia and Peru and Central America the EU was able to get both transparency and liberalization commitments. Again the transparency provisions are in line with the prevailing international norms of the GPA and UNCITRAL texts. But the EU was also successful in getting commitments on national treatment and thus "liberalization" in the case of these agreements. These agreements therefore set the standard for procurement chapters in PTAs with countries that are not signatories to the GPA.

In the case of Vietnam[11] the EU negotiated a high standard in terms of transparency and liberalization, but with a long transition period of 16 years starting from a very high threshold and arriving at the international norm only after this period.[12]

5 EU Preferential Trade Agreements with Existing Signatories to the Government Procurement Agreement

The EU agreements with countries that are signatories to the GPA effectively incorporate the existing GPA provisions on rules, in other words the transparency and procedural elements, into these PTAs, so the question is whether it is possible for the EU to negotiate any GPA-plus provisions on coverage. In the case of the EU-Korea agreement, which was concluded before the revision of the GPA, the EU was able to add build-to-operate contracts to the coverage and thus an extent the then coverage of the GPA. The PTA concluded with Singapore is awaiting a ruling of the European Court of Justice on the issue of the scope of EU exclusive competence on investment. As a GPA member however, Singapore simply incorporated the GPA in the agreement with the EU.

EU-Singapore does include a central web portal for the publication of contract notices for all types of entities, and addresses discrimination based on the obligation show prior experience of procurement in the territory. Coverage of Singapore entities is estimated to have increased from about one half to three quarters. The

[10]Woolcock (2008).

[11]For text of the EU-Vietnam Agreement, see http://trade.ec.europa.eu/doclib/press/index.cfm?id=1437 (last accessed 1 March 2017).

[12]See the annex to the EU-Vietnam FTA specifying coverage, http://trade.ec.europa.eu/doclib/docs/2016/february/tradoc_154219.1.2016%20-%20for%20publication.pdf (last accessed 1 March 2017).

added entities in central government and certain utilities adding 10–12 billion euro in annual opportunities.[13]

5.1 The CETA

In the case of the CETA with Canada the inclusion of the Provinces and Territories in the scope of the agreement was one of the EU's major aims. Indeed it had been the apparent inability of the Canadians to deliver the Provinces that resulted in the breakdown of negotiations in 2006. Only when the Federal government was able to persuade the provinces to be included in the negotiations was it possible to reopen negotiations.[14] CETA goes beyond the GPA by including coverage of procurement by the Canadian sub-federal entities. There remain some general exceptions or exclusions in CETA but these are in line with those in the GPA. On rules, the procurement chapter of CETA (chapter 21)[15] is very closely modelled on the GPA. For the most part the GPA text is simply carried over into CETA. This means that CETA would be consistent with eventual TTIP chapter on procurement.

The thresholds applicable in CETA for the EU are those used in the GPA in other words 130,000 SDR for goods and services and 5 million SDR for works/construction at the federal level. At the sub-federal level there are the slightly higher thresholds at 200,000 and 5 million respectively. For other (type III) procurement there are thresholds of 355,000 or 400,000 for goods and services and 5 million for works.[16]

Almost all types of procurement above the thresholds listed above are covered. At the federal level, the CETA schedules add a further 28 central entities to the GPA schedule, but these are mostly small with the exception of the inclusion of the Space Agency, and even here coverage is limited to satellites.[17] The most significant extension comes at the sub-federal level and in particular to the coverage of the so-called MASH sector (municipal, academic institutions, school boards and hospitals) in terms of goods. But health and other public services are excluded for Canada and there are some restrictions on mass transit in which Ontario and Quebec may require 25% local (Canadian) content. This is linked to developments in NAFTA and whether the US will lower its local content requirement which is

---

[13]European Commission, The economic impact of the EU-Singapore Free Trade Agreement, 2013, http://trade.ec.europa.eu/doclib/docs/2013/september/tradoc_151724.pdf (last accessed 1 March 2017).

[14]Woolcock (2011).

[15]See http://trade.ec.europa.eu/doclib/docs/2014/september/tradoc_152806.pdf (last accessed 1 March 2017).

[16]Appendices to CETA, http://www.international.gc.ca/trade-agreements-accords-commerciaux/agr-acc/ceta-aecg/text-texte/21_01.aspx?lang=eng (last accessed 1 March 2017).

[17]See Heilman Grier J, Update: EU-Canadian Trade Pact Now Public, Perspectives on Trade, 6 October 2014, http://trade.djaghe.com/?p=890 (last accessed 1 March 2017).

also 25% for these products. Canada also agreed to include the 'Crown corporations' in other words state owned or controlled bodies.

The rules elements of chapter 21 are summarised as follows:

- Article IV(1) on general principles contains the national treatment provision and thus the liberalisation element. EU suppliers in Canada or Canadian suppliers in the EU have to be treated no less favourably than local suppliers.
- Normal rules of origin are to be used to determine which suppliers can benefit from of preferential access to EU or Canadian procurement markets.
- Article IV(6) prohibits offsets.
- CETA adopts the transparency requirements in the GPA (Article VI) word for word in Articles V and VI and elsewhere and requires post contract award transparency.
- An important addition is that Canada follows the EU practice by providing a single central point of information, but the provinces and municipalities have 5 years to apply this.
- There is flexibility with regard to the criteria for awarding a contract (Article XI.9) This allows for example, to include environmental criteria provided this is specified in advance.
- Article XVIII of CETA provides for bid challenge/compliance equivalent to Article XVIII of the GPA. These may be administrative or judicial reviews and must provide for remedies including the setting aside of a contract award decision (something that is very rare) and costs, which can be limited to the costs of the bid or of challenging the decision.
- CETA also takes on some of the GPA's weak provisions: Article IX, which seeks to preclude the use of technical specifications to favour a specific supplier, but uses best endeavours wording only. Performance or functional specifications rather than design standards should be used "where appropriate". Moreover, CETA follows the GPA in providing a good deal of flexibility in the scope for limited tendering, in other words "a procurement method whereby the procuring entity contacts a supplier or suppliers of its choice".

The EU was successful in its main aim of extending coverage to the sub-federal level. Coverage of Canadian procurement is therefore comprehensive, with relatively few explicit exceptions. The thresholds remain at the level of the GPA, which makes sense in terms of consistency, but it means that a significant share of Canadian procurement will not be subject to the rules. The thresholds for internal trade within Canada remain significantly lower thus providing an effective preference for Canadian suppliers. Having said this, "indirect" access via affiliates of EU companies in Canada (and vice-versa) will be eased by the general extension of transparency provisions. The introduction of a centralised electronic source for all information on procurement and tenders will, when implemented, provide improved information. This will be especially important for EU small and medium sized companies that do not have the resources to invest in local production in Canada to supply that market and must supply directly by means of exports.

One important factor in the case of Canada is that there had already been reform at a national level that facilitated the inclusion of sub-federal level procurement. This took the form of an Agreement on Internal Trade that opened the procurement markets of the provinces and territories to supplies from other Canadian Provinces. There was also broad support for the coverage of procurement in CETA from Canadian businesses as potential suppliers. Opposition to the procurement provisions in Canada has focused on the extension of procurement to the MASH entities but for goods and construction rather than services. Health and other public services remain excluded from coverage. There was also some criticism of the loss of the ability to provide preferences to local suppliers by sub-central government. On balance then the climate in Canada favoured reform. This is unlikely to be the case in other PTA partners such as the United States, where extension of coverage to the sub-federal level is likely to be much more difficult.

5.2 EU-Japan

The EU is seeking GPA plus commitments from Japan in the PTA negotiations that were underway at the time of writing. The negotiations with Japan are an example of how the EU is seeking to achieve effective reciprocal access. The EU public procurement market is larger than that of Japan. OECD data shows public procurement to be equivalent to 13% of GDP in Japan and the EU at a higher share in line with the overall OECD average.[18] The Commission figures based on WTO data show an EU market of 370 billion euro compared to 96 billion euro for Japan. As the EU has a unified regime covering all levels and types of procurement it is argued that this makes it more transparent and thus more open to both direct and indirect supply of public contracts, i.e. through local affiliates. Japanese companies have for example, gained access to the EU market for rail equipment through its local affiliates in the UK. Going the other way EU suppliers have been much less successful in accessing the important Japanese rail sector. In terms of access to the Japanese market therefore confidence in the effective application of transparency and non-discrimination is vital if EU suppliers are to invest.

Japanese data suggests that foreign suppliers account for 3.1% of the Japanese government procurement markets.[19] This is a little below the level for the EU and appears to apply to direct supply of Japan's procurement markets from imports. The figure for foreign goods and services in central government procurement is given as 7.9% by value or 14.5% by contracts. The share for foreign goods is given as 14%

[18]Concrete data on the size of procurement markets and their degree of openness are difficult to get. These OECD figures are in the recent OECD work on procurement but they largely relate to 2008. This is an unsatisfactory basis for negotiating.

[19]See Prime Minister's Office, Japan's Government Procurement: Policy and Achievements Annual Report (FY 2012 version), http://japan.kantei.go.jp/96_abe/documents/2013/procurement2012_e.html (last accessed 1 March 2017).

and that for foreign services 1.8%. Note these figures are for central government purchasing only and do not include sub-central procurement, procurement by government related entities (type III) and do not include the important construction sector. In terms of the origin of these foreign supplies of goods and services the US accounts for 46% and the EU 36%.[20]

Japan is a signatory of the GPA and has applied GPA compatible rules in its PTAs. But there remain gaps in coverage and questions concerning the effective transparency of Japanese procurement markets. Under the GPA Japan covers central and sub-central government including procurement in all 47 Prefectures, but only 19 designated cities (up from 12 at the time the 1996 GPA was agreed) and there is no coverage of many cities or lower levels of government. Japan has also maintained significantly higher thresholds for works/construction contracts at the sub-central level of procurement. This threshold is out of line with the international norm at 15 million SDR (Special Drawing Rights) compared to the 5 million SDR that is used in the EU and in most other GPA signatories. See Table 2 for a comparison of the GPA thresholds for a range of parties.

Compared to the EU, transparency of Japanese procurement markets is arguably less effective even though Japan complies with the transparency rules of the GPA and Japan has made additional efforts to improve information on Japanese public procurement procedures and calls for tender. Information about Japanese procurement is not uniform at the sub-central level and is not always fully available in English. Japan, perhaps more than most public procurement markets, is characterised by de facto barriers to competition in public contracts, so transparency is important. The importance of the de facto barriers is illustrated by the railway case. Coverage of Japan Railways was negotiated under the 1994 GPA as part of a reciprocal negotiation on "liberalization". But it provides an illustration of how effective market access can be affected by technical specifications. It has been argued by EU suppliers that whilst Japan Railways were covered the attachment of an Operational Safety Clause, which stated that procurement would not be open or liberalised if it could affect the operational safety of the railways. The GPA requires technical specifications to be based on performance standards, but when there are no agreed international standards national standards can apply hence the scope for de facto preference for local suppliers in Japan.

In the negotiations with Japan therefore the issues have included an aim to reduce in the 15 million SDR threshold for construction contracts as well as a reduction in the relatively high threshold for architectural services for central government. As the table shows the EU has somewhat higher thresholds for type III procurement. This provides scope for reciprocal commitments on coverage that will be GPA plus. Efforts on the part of the EU to gain what its suppliers would see as effective access to Japan Railways has also been a focus.

In the case of Japan the EU could also improve coverage of Japanese sub-central entities and utilities. Decisions to cover more sub-central entities and local

[20]Prime Minister's Office, Japan's Government Procurement: Policy and Achievements Annual Report (FY 2012 version).

Table 2 Comparison of thresholds under the GPA in SDR (Special Drawing Rights)

		Japan	EU	US	Canada	Korea
Goods/suppliers	Type I	130,000	130,000	130,000	130,000	130,000
	Type II	200,000	200,000	355,000	355,000	200,000
	Type III	130,000	400,000	180,000 or 400,000	355,000	450,000
Services	Type I	100,000	130,000	130,000	130,000	130,000
	Type II	200,000	200,000	355,000	355,000	200,000
	Type III	130,000	400,000	180,000–400,000	355,000	450,000
Construction/works	Type I	4.5 million	5 million	5 million	5 million	5 million
	Type II	15 million	5 million	5 million	5 million	15 million
	Type III	15 million	5 million	5 million	5 million	15 million
Architectural and engineering services	Type I	450,000	130,000	130,000	130,000	130,000
	Type II	1.5 million	200,000	355,000	355,000	200,000
	Type III	450,000	400,000	180,000–400,000	355,000	450,000

Source: SIA 2016
Type I = central government; Type II = sub-central government; Type III = government related/regulated entities

authorities is a politically difficult decision in Japan as elsewhere. The structure of utilities markets in the EU and Japan are substantially different with significant parts of some utility markets still controlled by state-owned companies. The Japanese utilities market is more diverse, including a larger part of private companies placed in de facto/de jure monopoly situation that are, in contrast to EU utilities, not subject to any legal obligation to organise public tenders.[21]

Negotiating greater coverage will not however, mean guaranteed access to the Japanese procurement market where *de facto* impediments have probably always been more important. Continued efforts to improve transparency and information on procedures and calls for tender will be needed. This could be achieved through the sort of voluntary cooperation that exists already, but the establishment of a sub-committee on public procurement could be a means of ensuring that such cooperation leads to results. A commitment to a single centralised digital portal for all Japanese procurement in English, following the precedent set by CETA, would seem to be a reasonable expectation. Although there are various websites and cooperative initiatives to help enhance transparency, a single portal would still be useful and a realisable objective.

[21]European Commission, Trade Sustainable Impact Assessment of a Free Trade Agreement Between Japan and the European Union, Final Report, 2016, http://trade.ec.europa.eu/doclib/docs/2016/may/tradoc_154522.pdf (last accessed 1 March 2017).

5.3 The Trans-Atlantic Trade and Investment Agreement (TTIP) Negotiations

The prospects for the conclusion of the TTIP are uncertain at best at the time of writing with the incoming *Trump* Administration likely to oppose PTAs except narrow bilateral agreements. This comes on top of some severe criticism of the TTIP from within the EU.

In terms of the rules aspects of procurement, namely transparency provisions and the structure of agreements, the US and EU have long cooperated. This dates back to the 1960s in the OECD, so the approach of the EU and US in their respective PTAs are the same. Where the EU and US have had difficulties is in negotiating reciprocal coverage and liberalization commitments. The TTIP negotiations on procurement were marked by a dispute over whose market is the more open with both the US and EU claiming to be the more open. In global terms they would appear to be about the same. For example, the share of total government consumption accounted for by imports is about 4.5% in both cases.[22] But these figures are too general as they include all government consumption including for example public sector wages rather and not just those elements of public procurement that are potentially open to international competition. Nor do these figures capture the indirect access via local affiliates. In the EU this accounts for 11% of public contracts, with US owned companies featuring significantly. There are no equivalent figures for the US. This is another example of the general lack of comparable data on public procurement data.

In bilateral negotiations with the US the EU aim has been to increase coverage to include the sub-federal or state and city level. In this respect the federal government has been constrained by the fact that it has not had competence to negotiate the inclusion of the states or municipal entities. In the previous GPA negotiations it was possible to persuade the state governors to agree to be included. But the trend in recent years has been towards state legislatures removing the discretion of state governors to do this. The coverage of 37 states under the GPA is therefore unlikely to be extended very easily. Nor it is going to be easy to remove a range of exclusions for those states that have agreed to be covered by the rules (see Table 3). These relate to construction services and steel in particular.

With the change in the federal government and a Trump Administration stressing Buy America it also seems much less likely that the remaining Buy America provisions will be removed, but more likely that new restrictions will be added.

In order to maintain reciprocal coverage the EU has withheld coverage of large parts of the utilities sector (except electricity) and services at the sub-national level.

[22] Messerlin P and Miroudot S, EU public procurement market: How open are they? Groupe d'Economie Mondiale, Policy Brief, 10 August 2012, http://gem.sciences-po.fr/content/publications/pdf/Messerlin-Miroudot_EU_public_procurement072012.pdf (last accessed 1 March 2017).

6 The Impact of Brexit

The UK procurement market accounts for about a quarter of the total EU procurement market, so the exit of the UK from the EU will potentially upset the existing reciprocity calculations that have been made in existing EU agreements in public procurement. At the level of the GPA EU negotiating partners have agreed to reciprocal coverage based on EU commitments that include the UK. If the UK is now removes itself, these partners may seek an adjustment of their commitments under their agreement with the EU and an adjustment to reduce coverage. The UK is also likely to have to negotiate its own reciprocal coverage within the GPA. Indeed, it appears that the UK will first have to become a signatory to the revised 2014 GPA. In this respect as in the UK's general approach to its WTO schedules, the UK may well seek to simply continue to apply the coverage it has offered as part of the EU. In the GPA and the EU PTAs the schedules for entity coverage are listed by EU Member State.

For the coverage of procurement in the EU's PTAs there is a similar position. In agreements negotiated with GPA signatories this will be important if the coverage is significantly GPA plus. This is not the case for most agreements, but in the case of CETA with the inclusion of the sub-federal level it is important. For those PTA partners that are not signatories to the GPA, such as Central America, Mexico, Colombia etc. it will presumably be necessary to renegotiate coverage. As the EU has offered asymmetric coverage there would be a less compelling case for these EU's PTA partners to reduce their coverage. Here as with most other aspects of Brexit there is an element of uncertainty, so whether there will be a general reopening of the reciprocal coverage question in EU PTAs will depend on the EU's partners. However, given the narrow application of reciprocity applied to the entity coverage in procurement it would be surprising if this was not a serious possibility.

7 Other Possible Preferential Trade Agreements

With the state of the TTIP negotiations uncertain, attention may turn to other possible PTAs. The EU is about to start negotiations with Australia and New Zealand, two OECD countries that did not sign the GPA when it was first negotiated on the grounds that they had liberal regimes and the compliance costs of the GPA were too high. In 2015 New Zealand became a signatory of the GPA and Australia is negotiating accession to the GPA. The conclusion of a PTA with Australia with a procurement chapter would therefore offer the promise of binding commitments on the part of Australia on procurement. But this is likely to run parallel to the negotiations on the accession of Australia to the GPA.

The main procurement markets of interest to the EU however, are in the emerging powers, just as these constitute the main area of potential future growth

Table 3 US States covered under GPA and 1995 exchange of letters

State	GPA	State-specific exclusions in GPA	1995 exchange of letters
Arizona	X	None	
Arkansas	X	Construction services	
California	X	None	
Colorado	X	None	
Connecticut	X	None	
Delaware	X	Construction-grade steel (including requirements on subcontracts), motor vehicles, coal	
Florida	X	Construction-grade steel (including requirements on subcontracts), motor vehicles, coal	
Hawaii	X	Construction services; software developed in state	
Idaho	X	None	
Illinois	X	Construction-grade steel (including requirements on subcontracts), motor vehicles, coal	X
Iowa	X	Construction-grade steel (including requirements on subcontracts), motor vehicles, coal	
Kansas	X	Construction services, automobiles, aircraft	
Kentucky	X	Construction services	
Louisiana	X	None	
Maine	X	Construction-grade steel (including requirements on subcontracts), motor vehicles, coal	
Maryland	X	Construction-grade steel (including requirements on subcontracts), motor vehicles, coal	
Massachusetts	X	None	
Michigan	X	Construction-grade steel (including requirements on subcontracts), motor vehicles, coal	
Minnesota	X	None	
Mississippi	X	Services	
Missouri	X	None	
Montana	X	Goods	
Nebraska	X	None	
New Hampshire	X	Construction-grade steel (including requirements on subcontracts), motor vehicles, coal	
New York	X	Construction-grade steel (including requirements on subcontracts), motor vehicles, coal; procurement by public authorities and public benefit corporations with multi-state mandates; transit cars, buses and related equipment	
North Dakota		None	X
Oklahoma	X	Construction services, construction-grade steel (including requirements on subcontracts), motor vehicles, coal	
Oregon	X	None	

(continued)

Table 3 (continued)

State	GPA	State-specific exclusions in GPA	1995 exchange of letters
Pennsylvania	X	Construction-grade steel (including requirements on subcontracts), motor vehicles, coal	
Rhode Island	X	Boats, automobiles, buses, related equipment	
South Dakota	X	Beef	
Tennessee	X	Services, including construction services	
Texas	X	None	
Utah	X	None	
Vermont	X	None	
Washington	X	Fuel, paper products, boats, ships, vessels	
West Virginia		None	X
Wisconsin	X	None	
Wyoming	X	Construction-grade steel (including requirements on subcontracts, motor vehicles, coal	

Sources: Heiman Grier J, State Procurement Restrictions in Agreements, Perspectives on Trade, 14 October 2014, http://trade.djaghe.com/?p=906 (last accessed 1 March 2017)

in trade in goods and services. The EU will therefore have an interest in including procurement chapters in an agreement with Mercosur, negotiations on which have recently been restarted.

India has been one of the major opponents of including public procurement in multilateral negotiations such as the DDA. Indeed, in the discussions in the WTO Working Group on Transparency in Government Procurement in the late 1990s India was one of the members that argued most strongly against any binding provisions. Whilst it accepted the case for transparency in procurement, it did not accept that there was a need for binding provisions on transparency. The EU is looking for a "meaningful chapter" on procurement in the PTA negotiation with India. There could be scope for mutual benefits in the sense that India has supply capacity in a range of sectors, including services in particular. But what the scope of any agreement would be remains to be seen. It may cover transparency provisions, but will it get beyond the federal government in terms of coverage?

When China joined the WTO it made a commitment to negotiate accession to the GPA, but efforts to bring China into the agreement failed in 2012. It remains unclear how much progress can be made in the near future. Progress in extending the GPA would require the support of all major WTO members. Whilst the EU is likely to support a further extension to include China, there is uncertainty about the US. The Buy America rhetoric of the *Trump* Administration will not help to generate a positive climate.

8 A Need for More Negotiating Leverage?

Difficulties negotiating international agreements on procurement and a perception that the EU procurement market is more open than other major economies, has given rise to some pressure to adopt a more unilateral approach to procurement. There has been a debate for some time on whether the EU should strengthen its leverage by threaten to close or restrict access to its market if others do not open theirs. This is an unusual and controversial proposal, because the EU seldom makes such threats. In 2012 the Commission proposed the introduction of a Regulation that would strengthen the EU's negotiating leverage in negotiations on public procurement (Woolcock 2012).[23] To date there has been no agreement on this Regulation due to differences between the Member States on the desirability of such a unilateral instrument.[24] The rationale for the Regulation was to strengthen the EU's negotiating leverage and to ensure more uniformity in how the various EU purchasing entities apply the existing provisions in Article 58 of Directive 17/2004/EC.[25] This includes provision for purchasing entities to exclude bids from countries that do not offer reciprocity in the utilities sector. Under the proposed Regulation purchasing entities would be able to request approval from the Commission to exclude bids for large contracts (5 million euro) from countries that do not offer "substantial reciprocity", defined as "serious and recurring discrimination of Union economic operators" (Article 6(4)).

The draft Regulation proposes coverage of all procurement, unlike Directive 17/2004/EC. The Regulation would only apply to procurement that falls outside of the coverage of agreements such as the GPA or any procurement chapters in PTAs. Goods or services provided by countries that have signed agreements with the EU will be treated "equally" to goods and services originating within the EU, which presumably means national treatment. Developing countries, defined as those that qualify under the EU GSP scheme, would also not be covered by the Regulation. So it is clearly targeted at the major emerging markets or large developing countries. It may also be seen as strengthening the EU's negotiating leverage vis-à-vis countries such as Japan where some interests in the EU believe EU suppliers do not get de facto equivalent access.[26]

[23]European Commission, Proposal for a Regulation on the European Parliament and Council on the access of third-country goods and services to the Union's internal market in public procurement and procedures supporting negotiations on access of Union goods and services to the public procurement markets of third countries, COM (2012) 124 final, 21 March 2012.

[24]For a discussion of the issues and options with regard to this proposed Regulation see European Parliament, Public Procurement in International Trade, PE 457.123, 2012.

[25]Directive 2004/17/EC of 31 March 2004 coordinating the procurement procedures of entities operating in the water, energy, transport and postal services sectors, OJ 2004 L 134/1.

[26]See COM (2012) 124 final.

9 Conclusions

As for other major traders, such as the USA, the EU has moved to use PTAs as a means of furthering its objective of strengthening international rules on public procurement. It has done so only after seeking to include procurement in multilateral negotiations and finding limited success to date in extending the signatories to the plurilateral GPA. The EU rationale for promoting stronger rules are ambiguous. On the one hand it is argued that such rules promote international best practice, competition and fairness in public procurement, which makes up a significant share of GDP in all countries and especially in developing economies. Due process and transparency resulting from the adoption of rules on procurement are therefore seen as beneficial for development and a means of reducing the scope for abuse and corruption.

On the other hand, the EU has clearly seen stronger rules as a means of gaining better access to the procurement markets of other OECD economies or to those of the major emerging market economies.

The EU's success in this endeavour has been mixed. There is evidence of some progress in extending coverage to sub-federal entities, such as in the case of the CETA agreement. But it is much less likely that this will provide a precedent for similar extension of coverage to the sub-federal level in other federal states, such as the USA. In PTAs with middle income countries the EU has also been successful in extending international norms in procurement as reflected in the GPA approach and in some important first steps in liberalization.

However, extending a rules based liberal order to public procurement remains a very challenging task. This is true for developing countries that see it as benefitting the developed economies that have more supply capacity. It is true for the emerging markets, such as India and China that either have extensive state-owned enterprises or federal systems, or both. It is also true for the most advanced economies, such as the USA, which appears to be moving away from opening up it procurement market and towards a return to more "But America" policies.

References

Clarke JL, Evenett SJ (2003) The Singapore issues and the world trading system: the road to Cancun and beyond. Secrétariat d'Etat à l'économie (SECO), Bern

Woolcock S (2008) Government procurement provisions in CARIFORUM EPA and lessons for other ACP states. LSE, London

Woolcock S (2011) European Union trade policy: the Canada – EU comprehensive economic and trade agreement (CETA) towards a new generation of FTA's? In: Huebner K (ed) Europe, Canada and the comprehensive economic partnership. Routledge, London, pp 21–40

Woolcock S (2012) Public procurement in international trade, European Parliament, Directorate-General for external policies of the Union, Brussels

Good Raw Materials Governance: Towards a European Approach Contributing to a Constitutionalised International Economic Law

Karsten Nowrot

Abstract The European Union is currently in the process of adopting a regulation on so-called "conflict minerals". Against this background, the contribution provides some thoughts on this evolving European approach towards the promotion of good raw materials governance. For that purpose, it first assesses the concept of good global governance stipulated as one of the foreign policy objectives in Article 21 TEU with particular emphasis on its regulatory content and the respective scope of application. Subsequently, the contribution specifically addresses the normative steering relevance of this principle for the regulatory design of international trade in raw materials. In the third part an attempt will be made to outline and evaluate the respective EU governance processes aimed at translating the abstract concept of good governance into specific legal instruments and practices, thereby primarily taking recourse to the ongoing deliberations among EU institutions on the said conflict minerals regulation. Finally, the concluding section of the contribution provides a kind of bird's-eye view on some of the expected implications of the European good raw materials governance for the future development of what is here referred to as a constitutionalised international economic law.

Contents

K. Nowrot (✉)
University of Hamburg, Von-Melle-Park 9, 20146 Hamburg, Germany
e-mail: Karsten.Nowrot@wiso.uni-hamburg.de

M. Bungenberg et al. (eds.), *European Yearbook of International Economic Law 2017*, European Yearbook of International Economic Law 8,
DOI 10.1007/978-3-319-58832-2_12

1 Introduction

Stipulating a common set of overarching principles and objectives governing all European Union (EU) external action, and thus first and foremost also including the in practical and doctrinal terms still most important area of EU external relations, the common commercial policy,[1] on the basis of Article 21(3) TEU as well as Articles 205 and 207(1) 2nd sentence TFEU, has been and continues to be frequently and rightly regarded—at least from the perspective of foreign trade and investment policy—as one of the principal innovations brought by the Treaty of Lisbon.[2] Thereby, it hardly needs to be recalled that in practice the incorporation of non-economic concerns like the promotion of democracy, the protection of human rights, issues of supra- and international security as well as the protection of the environment into the law-making processes of the Union's contractual as well as autonomous foreign commercial policy[3] has been already prior to the entry into force of the Reform Treaty in December 2009 certainly not without precedents.[4] Nevertheless, it is equally well-known that among legal scholars the now—for the first time in the process of European integration—explicitly made and EU primary law based self-commitment[5] of this supranational organisation to pursue the principles and objectives enshrined in Article 21(1) and (2) TEU also within the context of implementing the common commercial policy was and still is not only met with approval. Aside from the occasionally voiced perceptions of this stipulated list of external policy goals as for example "lengthy and wide-ranging",[6] as a mere "wish list for a better world" or even as "redolent of motherhood and apple pie",[7] it is in particular the alleged dangers of, first, an increasing "politication" of the EU trade and investment policy as well as, second and closely related, of a notable (and thus undesirable) "downgrading" of the specific trade policy objectives aimed at a gradual trade and investment liberalisation as enshrined in Article 206 TFEU that have at times given cause to serious concern and criticism.[8]

Since this is not the appropriate place for a detailed engagement with that debate and the individual arguments brought forward in this connection, I will confine

[1] See also already, e.g., Krajewski (2005), p. 92: "the common commercial policy was and still is the most important constitutional battleground for European external relations".

[2] On this perception see for example also Cottier and Trinberg (2015), para. 7.

[3] Generally on the distinction between the contractual and the autonomous trade policy in the area of the EU common commercial policy see, e.g., Khan (2015), para. 17 et seq.; Oppermann et al. (2016), p. 653 et seq.; Lenaerts and Van Nuffel (2011), p. 963 et seq.

[4] See thereto, e.g., Vedder (2013), p. 127 et seq.; Weiß (2014), p. 527.

[5] Vedder (2013), p. 137, with further references.

[6] Cremona (2004), p. 568: "the lengthy and wide-ranging list of external policy objectives [. . .] is unlikely to bring about a greater policy focus".

[7] See the references provided by Larik (2016), p. 168.

[8] See thereto for example also Tietje (2009), p. 19 et seq.; Hahn (2016), para. 5 et seq.; Bungenberg (2010), p. 128; Terhechte (2012), para. 7.

myself to two more general remarks intended to at least relativize the respective reservations and objections voiced in the legal literature. On the one hand we should not forget that just as transboundary economic relations never develop—and as a consequence should never be considered—in isolation from, and thus uninfluenced by, the respective political relationship between the states concerned,[9] foreign trade policy measures and regulations have not infrequently been, and continue to be, used also as governmental means to promote and protect non-economic interests and objectives.[10] On the other hand it seems worth recalling the quite broad consensus in the scholarly literature—confirmed by the case law of EU courts[11]—on the for a number of reasons rightly assumed existence of a wide margin of appreciation enjoyed by EU institutions with regard to the practical means and feasibility of implementation as well as the prioritisation of the principles and objectives stipulated in Article 21(1) and (2) TEU.[12] Despite this last-mentioned observation, however, the legally binding character of this provision—as well as of Article 205 and Article 207(1) 2nd sentence TFEU—as normative guidelines for the EU common commercial policy is in principle clearly beyond reasonable doubt.[13] The same applies to their judiciability and thus to the possibility of judicial review by EU courts, since Article 275 TFEU limiting the jurisdiction of the Court of Justice of the EU does only cover the provisions relating to the common foreign and security policy and its scope of application consequently cannot be extended to the supranational policies dealing with the Union's external actions as regulated in Part Five of the TFEU, prominently among them the common commercial policy.[14]

In accordance with Article 205 and Article 207(1) 2nd sentence TFEU in connection with Article 21(2)(h) second alternative TEU, these findings first and foremost also apply to the allegedly "most ambitious of the objectives" listed in Article 21 TEU[15] in the form of the orientation of the EU common commercial policy towards the promotion of an international system based on good global governance.[16] Taking into account that the realisation of good (global) governance

[9]Meng (1997), p. 271 et seq.; Boor and Nowrot (2014), p. 241.

[10]See also, e.g., Krajewski (2012), p. 297; Boysen (2014), p. 468 et seq.; Nettesheim and Duvigneau (2012), paras. 37 et seq.

[11]See for example GG, case T-512/12, *Front Polisario/Council*, ECLI:EU:T:2015:953, para. 164 et seq.

[12]See also, e.g., Dimopoulos (2010), p. 165; Herrmann and Müller-Ibold (2016), p. 647; Hahn (2016), para. 4; Tietje (2015a), p. 802; Krajewski (2016), p. 243.

[13]See also for example Larik (2016), p. 154 et seq.; Dimopoulos (2010), p. 165; Krajewski (2016), p. 242; Nettesheim and Duvigneau (2012), para. 24; Cremer (2016), para. 2.

[14]Thereto among others also for example Terhechte (2012), para. 8; Lachmayer (2015), para. 11; Nettesheim and Duvigneau (2012), para. 24; Krajewski (2016), p. 242.

[15]Vedder (2013), p. 127.

[16]Generally on the importance of this normative steering principle in the context of the Union's common commercial policy see, e.g., Dimopoulos (2010), p. 165: "Last but not least, Article 21 TEU identifies multilateralism and good governance as basic objectives of EU external action. The recognition of these objectives plays a very significant role for the orientation of the CCP."

as a legally binding steering principle for the EU common commercial policy applies in light of this provision also, among others, to the normative frameworks dealing with the transboundary aspects of the extractive industries sector including the international trade in raw materials, the following assessment is intended to provide some thoughts on the currently evolving European approach towards the promotion of good raw materials governance, thereby also reflecting on the questions whether and how the EU's common commercial policy influences in this regard the progressive development of the international economic legal order as a whole. For these purposes, the present contribution is divided into four main parts. The first section is intended to provide some thoughts on the concept of good governance with particular emphasis on its regulatory content and the respective personal scope of application. Building up on the findings made in the first part, the following second section addresses the normative steering relevance of the principle of good governance as enshrined in Article 21(2) TEU for the regulatory design of the international trade in raw materials. Subsequently, in the third part an attempt will be made to outline and evaluate the respective EU governance processes aimed at translating the abstract concept of good governance into specific legal instruments and practices, thereby primarily taking recourse to the ongoing deliberations among EU institutions on the adoption of a regulation on so-called "conflict minerals". Finally, the concluding section of the contribution will provide a kind of bird's-eye view on some of the expected implications of the European good raw materials governance for the future development of what is here referred to as a constitutionalised international economic law.

2 The Normative Guiding Principle of Good Governance: Some Thoughts on Its Regulatory Content and Personal Scope of Application

Successfully identifying and assessing the steering relevance of good global governance in the sense of Article 21(2) TEU for the transnational regulatory design of the extractive industries sector requires first of all an understanding of the normative content rightly to be associated with this ordering principle. Ever since its emergence in the activities of international financial and development institutions such as the World Bank in the end of the 1980s,[17] good governance occupies an occasionally even quite prominent position in the practices of numerous global and regional international organisations like the United Nations (UN) and its specialized agencies, the Organisation for Economic Co-operation and Development

[17]See in particular World Bank, Sub-Saharan Africa, From Crisis to Sustainable Growth—A Long-Term Perspective Study, Washington D.C., November 1989; IMF, Good Governance—The IMF's Role, approved by the IMF Executive Board on 25 July 1997, Washington D.C., August 1997. See thereto also, e.g., Wouters and Ryngaert (2005), p. 71 et seq.

(OECD), the African Union, the Association of Southeast Asian Nations (ASEAN), the Organization for Security and Co-operation in Europe (OSCE), the Council of Europe as well as the Organization of American States.[18] In addition, the Council of the European Communities adopted as early as in November 1991 a resolution that emphasised the importance of good governance in the context of the European development policy.[19] Irrespectable of whether this steering principle can by now already be regarded as a norm of customary international law,[20] good governance has at least insofar found recognition in the international legal order as it is also incorporated in international agreements.

Respective normative manifestations are also particularly noticeable in the treaty-making practice of the EU. This applies not only to agreements concluded under the European development cooperation policy as for example evidenced by Article 2(c) of the Interim Agreement with a view to an Economic Partnership Agreement between the European Community and its Member States, of the one part, and the Central Africa Party, of the other part, signed in January 2009.[21] Rather, good governance as a legal term and concept is also for quite some time quite present in the instruments of the EU common commercial policy itself. For example in Article 2 of the Agreement on Trade, Development and Cooperation between the European Community (EC) and South Africa of October 1999, the parties "reaffirm their attachment to the principles of good governance".[22] Furthermore, this normative ordering idea is enshrined, *inter alia*, in Article 1(3) of the free trade agreement between Chile and the EC of November 2002[23] as well as, more

[18]For a more detailed assessment of these activities see for example Maldonado Pyschny (2013), p. 127 et seq.; Nowrot (2014), p. 571 et seq., each with further references.

[19]Resolution on Human Rights, Democracy and Development, Council and Member States, Meeting within the Council, 28 November 1991, http://archive.idea.int/lome/bgr_docs/resolu tion.html (last accessed 1 March 2017), para. 5: "The Council stresses the importance of good governance. While sovereign States have the right to institute their own administrative structures and establish their own constitutional arrangements, equitable development can only effectively and sustainably be achieved if a number of general principles of government are adhered to: [...]. The Community and Member States will support the efforts of developing countries to advance good governance and these principles will be central in their existing or new development cooperation relationships." For subsequent recourses to this ordering idea see, e.g., Commission of the European Communities, Report on the Implementation of the Resolution of the Council and of the Member States Meeting in the Council on Human Rights, Democracy and Development, adopted on 28 November 1991, SEC(92) 1915 final of 21 October 1992; Commission of the European Communities, Democratization, the Rule of Law, Respect for Human Rights and Good Governance: The Challenges of the Partnership between the European Union and the ACP States, COM (1998) 146 final of 12 March 1998, para. 12 et seq.; Commission of the European Communities, Governance and Development, COM (2003) 615 final of 20 October 2003, para. 2 et seq.

[20]See thereto, e.g., Rudolf (2006), p. 1026 et seq.; Seppänen (2003), p. 123; Maldonado Pyschny (2013), p. 147 et seq.

[21]OJ 2009 L 57/2. Generally on the role of good governance in the EU development policy see for example Kuon (2010), p. 17 et seq.; Hilpold (2002), p. 53 et seq.

[22]OJ 1999 L 311/3.

[23]OJ 2002 L 352/3.

recently, in several provisions of the partnership and cooperation agreement between the EU and Iraq of May 2012,[24] of the EU-Central America association agreement signed in June 2012,[25] of the EU-Moldova association agreement of June 2014[26] as well as of the EU-Georgia association agreement that entered into force on 1 July 2016.[27] With regard to the realm of the autonomous common commercial policy, let it suffice to draw attention to the "special incentive arrangement for sustainable development and good governance" (GSP+) established under the Articles 9–16 of Regulation (EU) 978/2012 of 25 October 2012 applying a scheme of generalised tariff preferences[28] in order to illustrate the presence of good governance in the Union's foreign trade activities.

Despite its relative "fame" in international as well as supranational practices and discourses (or potentially also precisely because of this fact), good governance is often perceived as a rather vague, multi-faceted and indeterminate ordering idea.[29] Nevertheless, and although certain difficulties in defining its normative content cannot be denied, a closer look at this principle reveals that these findings apply primarily to the peripheral meanings of this concept. As for example more recently emphasised by the so-called "Venice Commission" of the Council of Europe, a broad consensus has by now emerged "on a definition concerning some key elements" of good governance.[30] Prominently among them are the expectation that in particular public officials, but potentially also all other citizens, feel responsible for the common good of a political community as well as, and closely related, the prevention and combatting of corrupt practices. Other notable components of this guiding principle are the need for civic participation in public affairs and, as a necessary prerequisite of the aforementioned element, the transparency of the exercise of public powers.[31]

---

[24]OJ 2012 L 204/20.

[25]OJ 2012 L 346/3.

[26]OJ 2014 L 260/4.

[27]OJ 2014 L 261/4.

[28]OJ 2012 L 303/1. Generally on this steering instrument see, e.g., Turksen (2009), p. 927 et seq.

[29]On this perception see, e.g., Verhey (2005), p. 66: "Many issues are discussed under the broad umbrella of 'good governance'." Kuon (2010), p. 252; Weiss and Steiner (2007), p. 1547.

[30]Council of Europe, European Commission for Democracy through Law (Venice Commission), Stocktaking on the Notions of "Good Governance" and "Good Administration", CDL-AD(2011) 009 of 8 April 2011, para. 66. See also for example Rudolf (2006), p. 1020: "In sum, these considerations show that despite some terminological uncertainties, central substantive elements of Good Governance are universally acknowledged irrespectable of the context in which the term is used." Brown Weiss E, Sornarajah A, Good governance (last updated June 2013), The Max Planck Encyclopedia of Public International Law, Online edition, http://opil.ouplaw.com/home/EPIL (last accessed 1 March 2017), para. 15: "However, it is possible to identify common elements of good governance, which are referenced by international institutions, non-governmental organizations, donor countries, and countries that are donees."

[31]On these normative elements of good governance see also, e.g., Brown Weiss E, Sornarajah A, Good governance (last updated June 2013), The Max Planck Encyclopedia of Public International Law, Online edition, para. 15 et seq.; Esty (2006), p. 1530; Nowrot (2014), p. 581 et seq.

Turning finally to the addressees of these normative requirements, it is today almost generally recognized that the principle of good governance, originally developed as a standard primarily taken recourse to by multilateral and regional financial and development institutions in their relations with developing countries, has since then evolved into a global ordering concept whose above-mentioned legal sub-elements are applicable to all developing, transition and industrialised states.[32] In addition, this principle has more recently experienced another broadening of its scope of application by also giving rise to normative expectations with regard to the conduct of international and supranational organisations themselves.[33] This is of course quite vividly demonstrated by Article 21 TEU but also, *inter alia*, exemplified by the World Bank Policy on Access to Information of 1 July 2010, last modified on 1 July 2015, whose introductory section highlights the interrelationship between transparency and good governance as well as the role played by the World Bank therein.[34] Whereas the applicability of this principle to state actors and inter- as well as supranational institutions can thus be regarded as rather firmly established in the international legal order, the—already in light of the considerable structural changes taking place in the international system and its legal order in recent decades[35] not entirely illegitimate—question whether the ordering idea of good governance also stipulates legal obligations and/or normative expectations vis-à-vis some of the increasingly important categories of transnational private steering subjects like multinational enterprises, business associations or non-governmental organisations (NGOs) has so far only rarely been subjected to a closer evaluation in the legal literature.

Interestingly enough, it is precisely also the practice of EU institutions that provides some notable evidence for such a broader understanding of good governance including normative expectations concerning the conduct of business actors and civil society. The comparatively famous White Paper "European Governance" published by the European Commission on 25 July 2001 stresses in the context of demands for an increased civic participation in the decision-making processes of

[32]See for example Herdegen (2011), p. 230; Maldonado Pyschny (2013), p. 182.

[33]See for example United Nations General Assembly, United Nations Millennium Declaration, A/RES/55/2 of 18 September 2000, para. 13: "good governance at the international level"; Commission of the European Communities, European Governance, COM (2001) 428 final of 25 July 2001, p. 10: "Five principles underpin good governance [. . .] they apply to all levels of government – global, European, national, regional and local." Final Report of the International Law Association (ILA) Committee on Accountability of International Organisations, 2004, www.ila-hq.org/en/committees/index.cfm/cid/9 (last accessed 1 March 2017), p. 8 et seq.: "The principle of good governance (or of good administration), which is of an evolving nature, provides the necessary guidance as to the institutional and operational activities of an IO." Brown Weiss E, Sornarajah A, Good governance (last updated June 2013), The Max Planck Encyclopedia of Public International Law, Online edition, para. 63 et seq.

[34]World Bank Policy on Access to Information of 1 July 2010, Introduction, http://documents.worldbank.org/curated/en/391361468161959342/pdf/548730Access0I1y0Statement01Final1.pdf (last accessed 1 March 2017), para. 1.

[35]Generally thereto for example Delbrück (2001), p. 1 et seq., with further references.

the Union the belief that "[w]ith better involvement comes greater responsibility. Civil society must itself follow the principles of good governance, which include accountability and openness."[36] In order to further support a respective additional normative dimension of good governance from an overarching terminological and conceptual perspective, attention might be drawn to the observation that the well-known approach of "global governance" describes and covers in particular also the interactions and networks of state actors, supra- and international governmental institutions, intermediate ordering regimes as well as first and foremost also non-governmental steering subjects.[37] Against this background, a valid argument could be made that also the term and concept of good global governance in accordance with Article 21(2)(h) TEU—contrary to the idea of a "good (global) government"—is with regard to its scope of application not exclusively confined to actors that exercise public authority at the domestic, supranational or international level.

Irrespectable of whether the ordering principle of good governance can already be regarded as a source of direct legal obligations for influential transnational private actors under public international law and/or the supranational legal order of the EU, it seems by now undeniable that this concept at least gives rise to certain indirect obligations of conduct for non-governmental entities in the sense that state actors and supranational organisations are normatively expected and required to consider and adopt measures aimed at regulating as well as guiding the behaviour of relevant private actors in order to promote their "civic" responsibility for public interest concerns.[38] This regulatory technique of indirect obligations and other normative expectations of conduct thereby also finds its manifestation in the Union's common commercial policy, albeit not always with explicit reference to

---

[36]Commission of the European Communities, European Governance, COM (2001) 428 final of 25 July 2001, p. 10. See in this context also, e.g., Commission of the European Communities, Towards a reinforced culture of consultation and dialogue—General principles and minimum standards for consultation of interested parties by the Commission, COM (2002) 704 final of 11 December 2002; as well as Obradovic and Vizcaino (2006), p. 1049 et seq.

[37]See in particular the influential characterization of global governance given by the Commission on Global Governance, Our Global Neighbourhood, 1995, p. 2 et seq.: "[. . .] the sum of the many ways individuals and institutions, public and private, manage their common affairs. It is a continuing process through which conflicting or diverse interests may be accommodated and co-operative action may be taken. It includes formal institutions and regimes empowered to enforce compliance, as well as informal arrangements that people and institutions either have agreed to or perceive to be in their interest. [. . .] At the global level, governance has been viewed primarily as intergovernmental relationships, but it must now be understood as also involving non-governmental organizations (NGOs), citizens' movements, multinational corporations and the global capital market. [. . .] There is no single model or form of global governance, nor is there a single structure or set of structures. It is a broad, dynamic, complex process of interactive decision-making that is constantly evolving and responding to changing circumstances." Moreover, e.g., Nowrot (2004), p. 5 et seq., with further references.

[38]Generally on the regulatory technique of indirect obligations of conduct see already Nowrot (2015), p. 1165 et seq.; specifically on the importance of this approach in the present context Nowrot (2016a), p. 228 et seq.

the principle of good governance. Article 13.6(2) 2nd sentence of the EU-Korea free trade agreement that took effect in July 2011 stipulates in this regard that the parties "shall strive to facilitate and promote trade in goods that contribute to sustainable development, including goods that are the subject of schemes such as fair and ethical trade and those involving corporate social responsibility and accountability".[39] The Joint Declaration concerning Guidelines to Investors attached to the free trade agreement between Chile and the EC of November 2002 states that the parties "remind their multinational enterprises of their recommendation to observe the OECD Guidelines for Multinational Enterprises, wherever they operate".[40] Furthermore, Article 271(3) of the trade agreement concluded by the EU with Colombia and Peru on 26 June 2012 proscribes that the parties "agree to promote best business practices related to corporate social responsibility"[41] and, to mention but one additional example, Article 295 of the EU-Ukraine association agreement of March/June 2014 contains the following notable stipulation:

> Taking into account the importance of ensuring responsible management of fish stocks in a sustainable manner as well as *promoting good governance in trade*, the Parties undertake to work together by: [. . .].[42]

3 Of "Natural Resource Curses" and "Conflict Minerals": Steering Relevance of Good Governance in International Trade in Raw Materials

The specific relevance of good governance and its normative elements for the transnational regulatory framework on the extractive industries sector in general and the international trade in raw materials in particular hardly needs to be emphasised and illustrated in further details. It is sadly well-known that the "natural resources wealth" of many countries, among them often developing states, has from the perspective of economic and societal development as a whole frequently rather turned out to be a kind of "natural resource curse" for the respective political communities, taking into account that the often noticeable focussing on the production, extraction and exportation of certain raw materials results in practice not infrequently in neglecting to establish an own raw materials processing industry, and visibly contributes to the creation and perpetuation of authoritarian regimes, widespread corruption, serious and systematic violations of international human

[39]OJ 2011 L 127/6.

[40]OJ 2002 L 352/1444. Generally on the OECD Guidelines see OECD Guidelines for Multinational Enterprises, 2011 edition, https://www.oecd.org/corporate/mne/48004323.pdf (last accessed 1 March 2017).

[41]OJ 2012 L 354/3.

[42]OJ 2014 L 161/3 (emphasis added).

rights and labour standards as well as severe damages to the natural environment, to mention only a few negative consequences.[43]

Against this background and in order to remedy—or at least mitigate—these undesirable effects, the transnational regulatory structure with regard to commodity markets has undergone in recent decades considerably modifications with many of the new international steering mechanisms, established on the basis of hard law as well as—more frequently—soft law, now aiming more broadly at promoting changes in the general political, economic and societal conditions of the resource producing and exporting countries. An illustrative example is the Extractive Industries Transparency Initiative (EITI), a coalition of governments, companies, NGOs, investors and international governmental organisations launched in 2002 at the initiative of the former UK Prime Minister *Tony Blair*. The central purpose of this transnational good governance regime is promoting improved governance structures and activities in resource-rich countries through the full disclosure and verification of company and investor payments as well as government revenues from the extractive industries sectors of oil, gas and mining.[44] In a broader sense, EITI thereby supports the achievement of an objective that is commonly referred to—in particular also in the field of the EU common commercial policy—as the realization of "good governance in the tax area"[45] and thus serves as a clear indication that the international community as a whole, most certainly including the EU, more recently approaches the economic and societal challenges connected with the international trade in raw materials in a more holistic manner.

The same underlying considerations also strongly influence the regulatory approaches towards societal and political implications arising from the phenomenon of so-called "conflict raw materials" in general and "conflict minerals" in particular. Disputes over natural resources are comparatively rarely the primary reason for the outbreak of civil wars and the accompanying formation of armed rebel groups. Nevertheless, it is generally recognised that resource-rich countries, in particular those that rely heavily on the export of primary commodities, face an overall higher risk of prolonged and even increasingly intensified non-international armed conflicts precisely due to the fact that the production of and international trade in raw materials such as diamonds and other gemstones, gold, timber, rare

---

[43]Generally on the phenomenon of the so-called "natural resource curse" see for example WTO, World Trade Report 2010: Trade in Natural Resources, 2010, p. 91 et seq.; DeKoninck (2015), p. 134 et seq., each with numerous further references.

[44]For a more in-depth assessment of this transnational steering regime see, e.g., Brouder (2009a), p. 849 et seq., with further references. For an overview and evaluation of other related normative instruments see for example Al Faruque (2006), p. 72 et seq.

[45]See for example Article 280 of the EU-Georgia association agreement: "The Parties shall cooperate to enhance good governance in the tax area, with a view to the further improvement of economic relations, trade, investment and fair competition." See also, e.g., the Resolution of the European Parliament of 10 February 2010 on promoting good governance in tax matters, OJ 2010 C 341E/94; European Commission, Tax and Development Cooperating with Developing Countries on Promoting Good Governance in Tax Matters, COM (2010) 163 final.

minerals, oil or (illegal) narcotics often presents itself as one of the primary sources of funding for insurgents and other organised armed groups. In order to illustrate and substantiate the proposition that natural recourses have thus a clear potential to "fuel" ongoing civil wars, one only needs to refer to the respective conditions prevailing in the armed conflicts in Angola, Colombia, Myanmar, Sierra Leone, Peru, Cambodia, Iraq, Libya and—last but unfortunately surely not least—in the Democratic Republic of Congo.[46] In particular in the last two decades a number of transnational steering mechanisms have been created with the aim to suppress or at least limit this funding of parties to internal armed conflicts by means of international trade in natural resources and to prevent for example the accompanying human rights violations in the interest of good global governance. The probably most famous example is the Kimberley Process Certification Scheme, a joint initiative of governments, NGOs as well as representatives from the diamond industry formally launched in 2003 as what has already been appropriate characterised in the legal literature "a means of promoting good governance".[47] This regime portraits itself as an attempt to curb the transboundary trade in so-called "rough" or "blood" diamonds that are used by armed insurgent groups to finance the continuation of civil wars, in particular in Africa.[48]

The fact that the respective steering instruments, in the interest of effectiveness most certainly rightly, first and foremost also include and directly or at least indirectly address the activities of non-state business enterprises as the primary actor in the international trade in (conflict) raw materials is specifically in the context of the ongoing conflict in the Eastern Democratic Republic of Congo for example also illustrated by the respective UN Security Council resolutions. In resolution 1952 (2010), for example, the members of this primary organ of the UN call upon "all States to take appropriate steps to raise awareness of the due diligence guidelines referred to above, and to urge importers, processing industries and consumers of Congolese mineral products to exercise due diligence by applying the aforementioned guidelines, or equivalent guidelines, containing the following steps [...]: strengthening company management systems, identifying and assessing supply chain risks, designing and implementing strategies to respond to identified risks, conducting independent audits, and publicly disclosing supply

[46]See thereto as well as generally on the correlation between natural resources and civil wars Ross (2004), p. 35 et seq.; Smillie (2013), p. 1003 et seq.; as well as specifically with regard to the violent conflict in the Democratic Republic of Congo more recently Final Report of the Group of Experts on the Democratic Republic of the Congo of 26 November 2014, UN Doc. S/2015/19 of 12 January 2015, paras. 73 et seq. and 156 et seq.

[47]Meessen (2015), p. 173.

[48]Generally on the Kimberley Process Certification Scheme see, e.g., Brouder (2009b), p. 969 et seq.; Meessen (2015), p. 173 et seq.; Vidal (2012), p. 505 et seq. On the role of the EU in this regime see, e.g., Council Regulation (EC) No 2368/2002 of 20 December 2002 implementing the Kimberley Process certification scheme for the international trade in rough diamonds, OJ 2002 L 358/28; and Fernandez Arribas G, The European Union and the Kimberley process, CLEER Working Papers 2014/3, http://www.asser.nl/media/1645/cleer14-3_web.pdf (last accessed 1 March 2017), p. 7 et seq.

chain due diligence and findings".[49] In addition, and already with a view to the proposed EU regulation on conflict minerals discussed in the next section of this contribution, reference can be made in the present context to the OECD Due Diligence Guidance for Responsible Supply Chains of Minerals from Conflict-Affected and High-Risk Areas, adopted by OECD Council at Ministerial level on 25 May 2011 and subsequently amended on 17 July 2012, whose central purpose is "to help companies respect human rights and avoid contributing to conflict through their mineral sourcing practices"[50] and which can thus also appropriately be characterised as a more recent approach in the field of good raw materials governance aimed at promoting responsible business practices in the context of so-called "conflict minerals".

4 The Process of Translating Normative Principles into Practice: Finalising an EU Regulation on Conflict Minerals

Firmly located within the last-mentioned field of good raw materials governance are also the current efforts among EU institutions to reach a consensus on and adopt a conflict minerals regulation. The main external regulatory impulse from the other side of the Atlantic Ocean and general role model for this controversially perceived initiative has been the—at least equally contentious—provision of section 1502 of the Dodd-Frank Wall Street Reform and Consumer Protection Act (Dodd-Frank Act) that became effective on 21 July 2010 following its approval by the United States Congress.[51] Section 1502(b) Dodd-Frank Act, a provision that is, however, currently the subject of legal proceedings in US federal courts in particular with regard to its conformity with the freedom of speech guaranteed under the First

[49]UN Security Council Resolution S/RES/1952 of 29 November 2010, para. 8, with reference to the Final Report of the Group of Experts on the Democratic Republic of the Congo of 26 October 2010, S/2010/596 of 29 November 2010, para. 356 et seq. See also subsequently for example UN Security Council Resolution S/RES/2198 of 29 January 2015, para. 20 et seq.

[50]OECD Due Dilligence Guidance for Responsible Supply Chains of Minerals from Conflict-Affected and High-Risk Areas, Second edition, November 2012, https://www.oecd.org/corporate/mne/GuidanceEdition2.pdf (last accessed 1 March 2017), p. 3.

[51]Dodd-Frank Wall Street Reform and Consumer Protection Act, Public Law 111–203—July 21, 2010, 124 Stat. 1375 (2010), https://www.congress.gov/111/plaws/publ203/PLAW-111publ203.pdf (last accessed 1 March 2017). The steering influence exercised by this legislation on the current EU initiative is for example illustrated by European Commission, SWD(2014) 53 final, pp. 8, 13 and *passim*; European Commission, Assessment of Due Dilligence Compliance Cost, Benefit and Related Effects on Selected Operators in Relation to the Responsible Sourcing of Selected Minerals, Final Report by Böhme K, Bugajski-Hochriegl P, Dos Santos M, September 2013, p. 9.

Amendment of the US Constitution,[52] stipulates that all companies required to file periodic reports with the United States Securities and Exchange Commission (SEC), among them in particular publicly traded companies including foreign issuers with securities registered in the United States,[53] have to make annual disclosures to the SEC regarding the origins of covered conflict minerals as well as the respective measures and precautions taken by the corporation to exercise due diligence on the source and chain of custody of such minerals. In addition, respective enterprises are also obliged to make this reported information available to the public on their internet website (section 1502(b)(1)(E) Dodd-Frank Act).

The provision's material scope of application is for the time being confined to the minerals columbite-tantalite (coltan), cassiterite, gold, wolframite and their derivatives, among them in particular also tin, tantalum and tungsten (section 1502(e)(4)(A) Dodd-Frank Act).[54] With regard to its territorial focus, it is important to note that this provision exclusively applies to conflict minerals that originate in the Democratic Republic of Congo or an adjoining country in the sense of section 1502(e)(1) Dodd-Frank Act. Among these nine states that share an internationally recognized border with the Democratic Republic of Congo are Angola, Burundi, the Republic of the Congo, South Sudan, Rwanda, Tanzania, the Central African Republic, Uganda and Zambia. The personal scope of application of the reporting requirements covers all corporations—to which the other stipulations of section 1502 Dodd-Frank Act apply, among them in particular the classification as a publicly traded company in the United States—involved in the entire supply chain for conflict minerals in all industrial sectors (e.g. automotive, electronics, packaging, aerospace, construction, lighting, industrial machinery and tooling as well as jewellery),[55] thus potentially including the so-called "upstream" activities of miners, traders and smelters/refiners as well as the "downstream" activities of traders, component producers, manufacturers and end-users.[56] Finally, with regard to the regulatory content of section 1502 Dodd-Frank Act, it seems appropriate to

[52]See thereto for example Conflict Minerals and Resource Extraction: Dodd-Frank, SEC Regulations, and Legal Challenges, Congressional Research Service Report, April 2015, http://www.fas.org/sgp/crs/misc/R43639.pdf (last accessed 1 March 2017), p. 3 et seq.; Cullen (2016), p. 767 et seq.; Van Marter (2015), p. 297 et seq.; Schuele (2015), p. 769 et seq.; Schwartz (2016), p. 140 et seq., with further references to the respective proceedings and judgments.

[53]For a more detailed description of the personal scope of application of this provision see, e.g., Nelson (2014), p. 227 et seq.

[54]On the possibility to expand the list of covered conflict minerals and its derivatives based on a respective determination by the US Secretary of State see section 1502(e)(4)(B) Dodd-Frank Act.

[55]For a more detailed analysis of section 1502 Dodd-Frank Act and its regulatory content see already Nanda (2014), p. 288 et seq.; Nelson (2014), p. 219 et seq.; Harline (2015), p. 441 et seq.; Factor (2014), p. 93 et seq., each with further references.

[56]For a vivid description of the supply chain for conflict minerals see for example European Commission/High Representative of the European Union for Foreign Affairs and Security Policy, Joint Communication to the European Parliament and the Council: Responsible Sourcing of Minerals Originating in Conflict-Affected and High-Risk Areas—Towards an Integrated EU Approach, JOIN(2014) 8 final of 5 March 2014, p. 6.

re-emphasise that this provision "only" stipulates legally binding obligations of respective companies to make annual disclosures regarding the their use of certain conflict minerals and the due diligence exercised in this respect. The regulation thus neither prohibit or restrict imports of these raw materials nor does it create any specific due diligence requirements that the covered enterprises are legally obliged to observe in connection with their respective business activities.[57] Viewed from an overarching perspective, the regulatory approach manifested in section 1502 Dodd-Frank Act therefore serves as a further indication that legal regulations are with regard to their implementation approaches increasingly shaped by the broader concept of law-realization.[58] In contrast to the traditional "command and control style of legislation",[59] the approach of law-realization is characterised by more indirect steering mechanisms such as cooperative implementation structures, a recourse to economic steering models that rely on incentives and positive as well as adverse reputational effects and, last but not least, the provision of disclosure requirements[60]; a regulatory approach that finds its manifestation in the EU legal order for example in the so-called "Corporate Social Responsibility (CSR)" or "Non-Financial Reporting" Directive 2014/95/EU of October 2014.[61]

Almost immediately after the adoption of the Dodd-Frank Act in the summer of 2010, the European Parliament in a resolution of 7 October 2010 not only welcomed this legislative act but also asked the Commission and the Council "to examine a legislative initiative along these lines".[62] This request for a suitable legislative proposal by the Commission, supported by numerous representatives of civil society, was subsequently reiterated on a number of occasions.[63] On 5 March 2014 the Commission finally presented its proposal for an EU regulation setting up a Union system for supply chain due diligence self-certification of responsible

[57]See also already Brackett et al. (2015), p. 75; Ochoa and Keenan (2011), p. 137; Prenkert and Shackelford (2014), p. 475.

[58]Generally on the notion of "law-realization" as being distinct from the considerably narrower concept of "law enforcement" see Tietje (1998), p. 132 et seq.

[59]Zerk (2006), p. 36.

[60]Specifically with regard to section 1502 Dodd-Frank Act see thereto also, e.g., Ochoa and Keenan (2011), p. 138 et seq.

[61]Directive 2014/95/EU of the European Parliament and of the Council of 22 October 2014 amending Directive 2013/34/EU as regards disclosure of non-financial and diversity information by certain large undertakings and groups, OJ 2014 L 330/1.

[62]Resolution of the European Parliament of 7 October 2010 on failures in protection of human rights and justice in the Democratic Republic of Congo, P7_TA(2010)0350, para. 14.

[63]See for example European Parliament resolution of 5 July 2011 on increasing the impact of EU development policy, P7_TA(2011)0320, para. 60: "Calls on the Commission to make a legislative proposal with a similar objective to the new US 'Conflict Minerals Law', namely to combat the illegal exploitation of minerals in developing countries, in particular in Africa, which fuels civil war and conflicts, and to ensure traceability of imported minerals in the EU market". European Parliament resolution of 26 February 2014 on promoting development through responsible business practices, including the role of extractive industries in developing countries, P7_TA (2014)0163, para. 45 et seq.

importers of tin, tantalum and tungsten, their ores, and gold originating in conflict-affected and high-risk areas, an instrument in the realm of the autonomous common commercial policy based on Article 207 TFEU.[64] This legislative proposal's material scope of application was virtually identical to section 1502 Dodd-Frank Act, covering with tin, tantalum, tungsten and the respective ores as well as gold in accordance with its Article 1 and Article 2 lit. a and b basically the same conflict minerals. For the rest, however, many of the regulatory approaches foreseen in the 2014 Commission's draft regulation differed considerably from its previously adopted US pendant. Three aspects seem to be particularly worth at least briefly drawing attention to in this regard.[65]

First, the territorial scope of application of the proposed regulation was not confined to the Democratic Republic of Congo and nine adjoining countries but intended to extend to respective minerals from all "conflict affected and high-risk areas" in the world. In accordance with the definition provided in Article 2(e) of the 2014 Commission's draft regulation, this term covers all "areas in a state of armed conflict, fragile post-conflict as well as areas witnessing weak or non-existent governance and security, such as failed states, and widespread and systematic violations of international law, including human rights abuses".[66] This regulatory approach aiming not at any specific region of the world but establishing potentially a global geographical applicability should first and foremost also be seen as an attempt to avoid one of the major regulatory challenges arising in connection with section 1502 Dodd-Frank Act, namely the—indeed at least partially materialized—possibility that companies might altogether avoid conflict minerals from the targeted region thereby creating a kind of de facto embargo with often disastrous socio-economic consequences in particular for artisanal miners and their families.[67]

Second, and in contrast to the broad territorial coverage stipulated in the proposal, the personal scope of application was envisioned to be quite narrow in comparison to section 1502 Dodd-Frank Act. The draft regulation was not intended

[64]COM (2014) 111 final.

[65]For a more in-depth evaluation of the 2014 Commission's draft regulation see also already for example Brackett et al. (2015), p. 80 et seq.; Vyboldina (2015), p. 341 et seq.; Nowrot (2016a), p. 240 et seq.

[66]On this definition see in principle also already OECD Due Diligence Guidance for Responsible Supply Chains of Minerals from Conflict-Affected and High-Risk Areas, Second edition, November 2012, https://www.oecd.org/corporate/mne/GuidanceEdition2.pdf (last accessed 1 March 2017), p. 13.

[67]See thereto, e.g., Commission/High Representative of the European Union for Foreign Affairs and Security Policy, Joint Communication to the European Parliament and the Council: Responsible Sourcing of Minerals Originating in Conflict-Affected and High-Risk Areas—Towards an Integrated EU Approach, JOIN(2014) 8 final of 5 March 2014, p. 7; European Commission, SWD (2014) 52 final, p. 3; Conflict Minerals—An Evaluation of the Dodd-Frank Act and other Resource-Related Measures, Öko-Institut e.V., August 2013, p. 27; Centre for Research on Multinational Corporations (SOMO), Conflict Due Dilligence by European Companies, SOMO Paper, October 2013, p. 3; Veale (2013), p. 533 et seq.; Brackett et al. (2015), p. 74 et seq.; for a more optimistic perception see, however, also Schwartz (2016), p. 171 et seq.

to apply to all companies in the whole supply chain but only to "importers" of respective conflict minerals, defined—pursuant to Article 2 lit. g of the proposal—as "any natural or legal person declaring minerals or metals within the scope of this Regulation for release for free circulation within the meaning of Article 79 of Council Regulation (EEC) No 2913/1992". The Commission estimated in 2014 that, while there were some 880,000 companies in the EU trading or processing tin, tantalum, tungsten or gold, only "about 300 EU traders and around 20 smelters/refiners importing ores and metals derived from the four minerals and more than 100 EU component manufacturers importing derived metals" existed at that time.[68] Third, and at least equally noteworthy, the 2014 Commission's proposal differed from its US pendant in particular also insofar as it did not stipulate mandatory disclosure obligations for respective EU companies. Rather, its Article 3 only foresaw for the quite limited number of covered enterprises—and exclusively for them[69]—the option of a voluntary self-certification as "responsible importer". As proscribed by Article 3 of the 2014 proposal, interested companies were for that purpose envisioned to declare to a member state competent authority that they adhere to the supply chain due diligence obligations as set out in the Articles 4–6 that were closely modelled after and in part even explicitly referring to the above mentioned OECD Due Diligence Guidance for Responsible Supply Chains of Minerals from Conflict-Affected and High-Risk Areas. Finally, it were only these "responsible investors" that were subjected to respective disclosure obligations in accordance with Article 7 of the draft regulation.[70]

Since an EU regulation on conflict minerals as part of the Union's autonomous common commercial policy is subject to the ordinary legislative procedure with the European Parliament and the Council acting as co-legislators, the 2014 Commission's proposal was submitted to these two EU institutions in accordance with Articles 207(2) and 294(2) TFEU.[71] Bearing in mind that many members of the European Parliament originally envisioned and also explicitly asked for a regulation creating legally binding due diligence obligations for a large number of

[68]European Commission/High Representative of the European Union for Foreign Affairs and Security Policy, Joint Communication to the European Parliament and the Council: Responsible Sourcing of Minerals Originating in Conflict-Affected and High-Risk Areas—Towards an Integrated EU Approach, JOIN(2014) 8 final of 5 March 2014, p. 6.

[69]See thereto already my critical evaluation in Nowrot (2016a), p. 243.

[70]For a more detailed evaluation, also on the envisioned incentives for as well as control mechanisms in case of participation in this self-certification process, see for example Brackett et al. (2015), p. 80 et seq.; Nowrot (2016a), p. 243 et seq.; Schuele (2015), p. 772 et seq.

[71]Generally on the Union's ordinary legislative procedure see, e.g., Schütze (2015), p. 243 et seq.; Streinz (2016), p. 196 et seq.

companies involved in the trading or processing of respective raw materials,[72] it is hardly surprising that not only numerous civil society groups but also the representatives of this EU institution were in their majority considerably less than entirely pleased with the draft presented by the Commission. On 20 May 2015, the European Parliament during the first reading of the proposal under Article 294(3) TFEU favourably considered and approved a significant number of in part quite fundamental amendments. Among them is the regulatory approach of imposing on all EU importers of covered conflict minerals legally binding supply chain due diligence obligations (amendment 154: new version of Article 1(2) of the EU regulation). Furthermore, and inspired by section 1502 Dodd-Frank Act, all "downstream" companies are asked to take "all reasonable steps to identify and address any risks arising in their supply chains for [covered] minerals and metals" and, in this connection, will be legally required to "provide information on the due diligence practices they employ for responsible sourcing" (amendment 155: new Article 1(2)(d) of the regulation).[73] In light of these substantial "modifications", which in fact amounted to fundamentally changing the proposed regulation's underlying regulatory approach from "voluntary" to "mandatory", the European Parliament ultimately decided on the same day by a vote of 343–331, with nine abstentions, to postpone the final vote on the draft legislative resolution in accordance with Article 61(2) of the Rules of Procedure of the European Parliament (RoP EP) and thus not to close the first reading position under Article 294(3) TFEU.[74] Officially, the matter is thus under Article 61(2) RoP EP deemed to be referred back to the committee responsible, in the present case the EP Committee for International Trade (INTA Committee).

Less officially, but surely no less important, this course of action was intended to open the way for informal tripartite meetings between representatives of the Parliament, the Council and the Commission ("trialogue") aimed at seeking a political understanding on the regulatory approach and content of an EU regulation

[72]See for example European Parliament resolution of 26 February 2014 on promoting development through responsible business practices, including the role of extractive industries in developing countries, P7_TA(2014)0163, para. 46(a): "create a legally binding obligation for all upstream companies operating in the EU that use and trade natural resources sourced from conflict-affected and high-risk areas and all downstream companies that act as the first placer on the European market to undertake supply chain due diligence to identify and mitigate the risk of conflict financing and human rights abuse".

[73]Thereto as well as with regard to all other amendments see Amendments adopted by the European Parliament on 20 May 2015 on the proposal for a regulation of the European Parliament and of the Council setting up a Union system for supply chain due diligence self-certification of responsible importers of tin, tantalum and tungsten, their ores, and gold originating in conflict-affected and high-risk areas, P8_TA(2015)0204.

[74]On the respective voting at the initiative of the Chair of the INTA Committee, Bernd Lange, see PV 20/05/2015—10.7.

on conflict minerals.[75] Following the Council clarifying its own position on the draft legislation, the trialogue process commenced in early 2016. On 16 June 2016 the three institutions announced that they had reached an agreement with regard to the broad framework and regulatory design of a future conflict minerals regulation.[76] At the time of writing (September 2016), the technical details are apparently still in the process of being worked out and agreed upon by the relevant actors. In particular, an updated—or more likely in many parts almost entirely new—textual proposal on an EU conflict minerals regulation by the Commission still awaits publication. Nevertheless, based on the information provided in the official press releases as issued by the three EU institutions in June 2016, we have already a pretty good—albeit most certainly still slightly blurred—picture of what this political understanding means for the general structure and content of the planned legislative act to be adopted "in the coming months".[77] Again, three main issues deserve to be highlighted in this connection.

First, despite early intentions by the Parliament to extend the material scope of application of the envisioned steering instruments to literally "all natural recourses, without exception",[78] the EU regulation is likely to cover only tin, tantalum, tungsten, their ores and gold as already stipulated in the 2014 Commission's proposal and in line with section 1502 Dodd-Frank Act. Second, the political understanding reached in June 2016 foresees with regard to the territorial application that the future EU regulation retains the broad geographical coverage as also already suggested in the 2014 draft. The Parliament's press release specifies in this regard that "the Commission will select experts via a tender procedure to draw up an indicative and non-exhaustive list of areas" to be at a given time qualified as "conflict affected and high-risk areas" in the sense of the EU regulation.[79] Already

[75]On the approach of institutional trilogues in the EU legislative procedures see European Parliament/Council/Commission, Joint Declaration on Practical Arrangements for the Codecision Procedure, OJ 2007 C 145/5; as well as, e.g., Schütze (2015), p. 249 et seq.; Chalmers (2015), p. 322 et seq., with further references.

[76]See European Parliament, Conflict Minerals: MEPs Secure Mandatory Due Diligence for Importers, Press release of 16 June 2016, http://www.europarl.europa.eu/pdfs/news/expert/infopress/20160615IPR32320/20160615IPR32320_en.pdf (last accessed 1 March 2017); European Council/Council of the EU, EU Political Deal to Curb Trade in Conflict Minerals, Press release 342/16 of 16 June 2016, http://www.consilium.europa.eu/de/press/press-releases/2016/06/16-conflict-minerals/ (last accessed 1 March 2017); European Commission, Press release IP/16/2231.

[77]See European Commission, Press release IP/16/2231.

[78]European Parliament resolution of 26 February 2014 on promoting development through responsible business practices, including the role of extractive industries in developing countries, P7_TA(2014)0163, para. 46(c).

[79]European Parliament, Conflict Minerals: MEPs Secure Mandatory Due Diligence for Importers, Press release of 16 June 2016; see also for example already Directorate-General for External Policies, Briefing—EU Initiative on Responsibly Importing Minerals from Conflict-Affected Regions, December 2014, DG EXPO/B/PolDep/Note/2014_195, p. 6: "To help 'responsible importers' determine whether their sources are in conflict-affected or high-risk areas, the European Commission will establish an expert group."

in the interest of legal certainty and practicability, it surely deserves applause that a respective—albeit not necessarily exhaustive[80]—list of respective areas will be compiled by the Commission or a respective expert group. Nevertheless, it should not be left unmentioned that this approach again potentially entails the danger—already partially realised in connection with section 1502 Dodd-Frank Act—that such a list will be interpreted and "misapplied" by covered companies as identifying something like current de fact "no-trade areas" for the minerals in question,[81] most certainly with severe consequences for artisanal miners and their families.

And this danger of ultimately turning the intended socio-economic effects of an EU conflict minerals regulation quasi "on their head"[82] is in fact quite real, even more so because—and this is the third notable aspect—the political understanding of June 2016 between the three EU institutions profoundly modifies the legislative act's personal scope of application as well as the respective legal obligations and other normative expectations arising for covered companies. Contrary to the 2014 Commission's proposal, the EU regulation will apply in principle to all corporate actors in the whole supply chain of conflict minerals. Thereby, the distinction between direct EU importers of these raw materials on the one hand and the "downstream" activities of other traders, component producers, manufacturers and sellers on the other hand will nevertheless be retained as far as the respective obligations and normative expectations are concerned. Direct EU importers at the "upstream" part of the conflict minerals supply chain, the roughly 420 EU companies referred to above, are no longer merely encouraged to undertake a voluntary self-certification but will be legally required to comply with a due diligence scheme conducted according to the OECD Due Diligence Guidance for Responsible Supply Chains of Minerals from Conflict-Affected and High-Risk Areas with the EU member states' competent authorities being "responsible for ensuring compliance by companies, and also for determining penalties for non-compliance, to be monitored by the EU Commission".[83] Only small volume importers, for example for dentistry, will be exempted from these obligations. Some additional limitations or modifications with regard to the scope of application of these obligations are provided for by the understanding that, first, recycled materials are excluded from the EU regulation and, second, the possibility of recognising existing and future

[80]The fact that the respective list will likely be non-exhaustive gives rise to a number of legal issues that cannot be addressed in the course of this comparatively short contribution (and can, in any case, only be dealt with in a meaningful way once a new draft proposal for an EU regulation on conflict minerals has been published).

[81]See also already Brackett et al. (2015), p. 83 et seq.; Nowrot (2016a), p. 241 et seq.

[82]For a vivid description with regard to the potentially adverse effects of section 1502 Dodd-Frank Act see Brackett et al. (2015), p. 76: "The result could in fact exacerbate the harm the Conflict Minerals Rule is seeking to address by increasing smuggling, weakening governance, and depressing prices for ore. Together, these factors make the violation of human rights even more likely."

[83]European Parliament, Conflict Minerals: MEPs Secure Mandatory Due Diligence for Importers, Press release of 16 June 2016.

industry due diligence schemes like the Conflict-Free Smelter Program developed by the Conflict-Free Sourcing Initiative (CFSI)[84] or the International Tin Supply Chain Initiative (iTSCi) Programme[85] as equivalent to the respective OECD Due Diligence Guidance will be given subject to certain conditions to be laid down in the regulation.

To the contrary, "downstream" EU companies, in particular those larger firms with more than 500 employees that are subject to the already mentioned "Non-Financial Reporting" Directive 2014/95/EU of October 2014, will be subject to normative expectations quite similar to the once originally envisioned by the 2014 Commission's proposal for "responsible importers". According to the 2016 political understanding, these corporations will be "encouraged to report on their sourcing practices based on a new set of performance indicators to be developed by the EU Commission". Furthermore, they will be "able to join a registry to be set up by the Commission and report voluntarily on their due diligence practices".[86] This underlying regulatory approach of distinguishing between mandatory obligations for "upstream" businesses and a normative encouragement of "downstream" companies to voluntarily engage in due diligence practices also seems in principle not to be implausible, especially bearing in mind the well-known fact that the "upstream" part of the conflict minerals supply chain is of critical importance since in particular smelters and refiners are normally the last stage where it is still technically feasible to identify the origin of minerals and thus to effectively assure due diligence.[87]

Many of the details of the future EU regulation on conflict minerals are probably still under discussion or at least until now unknown to the public (most certainly including the author). In addition, a more in-depth evaluation of the regulatory design should preferably be based on—and thus wait for—a new draft regulation the publication of which was in June 2016 indicated to occur "in the coming months".[88] Nevertheless, already based on the information included in the official press releases of the three EU institutions and adopting a comparative perspective, it seems quite safe to predict that the EU conflict minerals regulation will ultimately in a number of ways turn out to be a kind of "Dodd-Frank Act plus" or even "super Dodd-Frank Act" piece of legislation. In order to support this proposition, one only

[84]For additional information see http://www.conflictfreesourcing.org/conflict-free-smelter-program/ (last accessed 1 March 2017).

[85]For respective information on this initiative see https://www.itri.co.uk/itsci/frontpage (last accessed 1 March 2017).

[86]European Parliament, Conflict Minerals: MEPs Secure Mandatory Due Diligence for Importers, Press release of 16 June 2016.

[87]See also draft recital 13 in European Commission, COM (2014) 111 final, p. 4; European Commission/High Representative of the European Union for Foreign Affairs and Security Policy, Joint Communication to the European Parliament and the Council: Responsible Sourcing of Minerals Originating in Conflict-Affected and High-Risk Areas—Towards an Integrated EU Approach, JOIN(2014) 8 final of 5 March 2014, p. 6.

[88]European Commission, Press release IP/16/2231.

needs to refer for example to the considerably broader territorial scope of application, the fact that the planned EU regulation is not confined to publicly traded companies as well as to the already above made observation that section 1502 Dodd-Frank Act only foresees mandatory annual disclosures but does not stipulate any specific due diligence obligations that covered businesses are legally bound to fulfil. Time will tell whether the quite far-reaching and ambitious approach recently agreed upon for the EU conflict minerals regulation is able to establish an effective legal framework to successfully address the complex and multi-faceted challenges arising in connection with the conflict minerals "dilemma".

5 A Brief Bird's-Eye (Out-)Look: European Good Raw Materials Governance and the Emergence of a Constitutionalised International Economic Law

Leaving aside the technical peculiarities as well as the future fate and uncertain effects of the coming EU conflict minerals regulation, it seems appropriate to conclude this contribution with a kind of brief bird's eye view on some of the implications arising from this legislative endeavour in the realm of the EU common commercial policy for the progressive development of the international economic legal order as a whole. In this regard it is submitted that the currently emerging European approach to good raw materials governance serves as an indication for the evolution of what is here referred to as a more constitutionalised international economic law. Already—but most certainly not only—in light of the recently noticed "global constitutional cacophony"[89] there is undoubtedly an expectation arising on the side of the readers that I at least briefly explain and substantiate this finding. In order to do so, it appears once more, and thus one last time, useful to highlight three main aspects or characteristics.

First, the term and concept of constitutionalised international economic law entails the perception that the most influential actors in the law-making processes of the international economic system, namely states and supranational organisations, should preferably no longer enjoy a basically almost unlimited discretion in the legal design of their foreign (economic) relations but rather be normatively obliged to contribute to the realisation of common interest concerns in their respective activities on the basis of economic and in particular also non-economic foreign policy objectives as codified in their individual domestic constitutional frameworks. And indeed, contrary to the traditional understanding of foreign policy as an almost exclusive prerogative of the executive branch largely unconstraint by substantive constitutional requirements,[90] the stipulation of legally binding foreign

[89]Mac Amhlaigh (2016), p. 173 et seq.

[90]See thereto, e.g., Krajewski (2013), p. 68 et seq.; Tietje and Nowrot (2016), p. 1469 et seq.; Larik (2016), p. 55 et seq., each with further references.

policy objectives is today no longer an unusual phenomenon in national constitutional law. Quite to the contrary, an increasing number of states, among them EU member states as well as several third countries, provide at the top level of their domestic hierarchy of norms a range of objective pertaining to their external action.[91] In particular also with regard to the realm of international economic relations, this trend is obviously supported and further strengthened by the substantive constitutionalisation of the EU external action, most certainly including the common commercial policy and thus also encompassing what has already been qualified as the "external economic constitution of the Union",[92] on the basis of the foreign policy objectives stipulated in Article 21 TEU.[93] This constitution-based value-orientation of important law-making entities like the EU[94] is of course primarily intended to—and as evidenced by the deliberations on an EU conflict minerals regulation in practice also does—contribute to an increasing value- and thus common interest-orientation of the international economic legal order as a whole. Against this background, this first central characteristic of a constitutionalised international economic law furthermore illustrates a notable correlation between this approach focussing initially and primarily on the internal constitutional design of states and supranational organisations on the one hand and other by now already almost traditional perceptions of the international economic legal order being in a process of constitutionalisation on the other hand, since it is well-known that these last mentioned conceptions or findings are also precisely first and foremost relying on an ever-growing value-orientation of the normative framework governing international economic relations.[95]

Second, albeit closely related to the first aspect, the present concept is based on the understanding that a constitutionalised international economic law presupposes an increasing parliamentarisation of the law-making processes in the international economic system. This proposition, again a deviation from the classical perception of the separation of powers in foreign (trade and investment) relations,[96] is initially inspired by the view that a constitutionally strengthened influence of parliaments is likely to foster the implementation of the (non-economic) constitutional foreign policy objectives in the practice of international trade and investment agreements and the adoption of other foreign economic policy instruments. And again, it is

[91]Larik (2016), p. 88 et seq.: "This chapter shows that foreign policy objectives abound in contemporary constitutional law. They are not the exception, but rather the rule, both within and outside the EU."

[92]Vedder (2013), p. 143 et seq.

[93]Generally on the idea of a constitutionalisation of the EU foreign (trade) policy on the basis of constitutional-like foreign policy objectives see also for example von Arnauld (2014), p. 54; Krajewski (2016), p. 248; Larik (2016), p. 125 et seq.

[94]See in this connection specifically with regard to the EU also for example Vedder (2013), p. 144: "constitutional commitment to a value-based global governance".

[95]See thereto, e.g., Nowrot (2006), p. 457 et seq.; Nowrot (2016b), p. 187 et seq., each with numerous further references.

[96]See for example Tietje and Nowrot (2016), p. 1469 et seq.; Krajewski (2013), p. 68 et seq.

indeed first and foremost also the more recently reformed EU common commercial policy including the enhanced powers enjoyed by the European Parliament therein in general as well as the outlined process leading to a political understanding on a conflict minerals regulation in particular that clearly seem to support this line of reasoning.[97]

Nevertheless, it is not only the—in the recent practice of the EU common commercial policy already partially realised—prospect of more effectively promoting the implementation of constitutional foreign policy goals that makes a parliamentarisation of foreign trade and investment relations an important element of the concept of constitutionalised international economic law. Rather, this feature also has to be regarded as a reflexion of as well as reaction to—and this constitutes the third notable aspect—the more recently changing character of international economic law as an increasingly political law. While from a global perspective many areas of the international economic legal order admittedly always have—and continue to be—contested among states, in particular those adhering to different ideologies,[98] the normative design of foreign economic relations has—viewed from the domestic perspective of most countries—for a long time primarily been the concern of a comparative small circle of experts. As evidenced not only by the public discussions accompanying the drafting of a EU conflict minerals regulation, maybe not even primarily, taken into account the considerably more intensive public debates on the Comprehensive Economic and Trade Agreement (CETA) between the EU and Canada or the negotiations of a Transatlantic Trade and Investment Partnership (TTIP) with the United States, this situation has changed in an unprecedented way.[99] Foreign trade and investment policy today often enjoys

---

[97]Generally on the correlation between the considerably increased parliamentarisation of the EU common commercial policy on the basis of the Lisbon Treaty on the one hand and the effective realization of the EU (non-economic) foreign policy goals see, e.g., Krajewski (2013), p. 83 et seq.; Bungenberg (2010), p. 129 et seq.; Tietje (2009), p. 21.

[98]See for example US Supreme Court, *Banco Nacional de Cuba v. Sabbatino*, Judgment of 23 March 1964, 376 U.S. 398, 428 et seq. (1964): "There are few if any issues in international law today on which opinion seems to be so divided as the limitations on a state's power to expropriate the property of aliens. [. . .] It is difficult to imagine the courts of this country embarking on adjudication in an area which touches more sensitively the practical and ideological goals of the various members of the community of nations." International Court of Justice, *Barcelona Traction Case*, ICJ Reports 1970, 3, 47 et seq.: "Considering the important developments of the last half-century, the growth of foreign investments and the expansion of international activities of corporations, in particular of holding corporations, which are often multinational, and considering the way in which the economic interests of states have proliferated, it may at first sight appear surprising that the evolution of the law has not gone further and that no generally accepted rules in the matter have crystallized on the international plane. Nevertheless, a more thorough examination of the facts shows that the law on the subject has been formed in a period characterized by an intense conflict of systems and interests."

[99]On this observation see also for example European Commission, Trade for All–Towards a More Responsible Trade and Investment Policy, October 2015, p. 18: "Trade policy is more debated today than at any time in recent years, with many asking whether it is designed to support broad European interests and principles or the narrow objectives of large firms."

a high degree of public attention including controversial deliberations among and within political parties and has thus obviously turned into a politicised area of law in the true sense of the meaning.[100] This finding has been for example more recently quite vividly expressed by *Michael J. Trebilcock* stating that "popular and scholarly debates over the virtues and vices of economic globalization ensure that international trade policy has forever forsaken the quiet and obscure corners of trade diplomacy that it once occupied, and become a matter of 'high politics'".[101] The transformation into a more politicised field of law, although occasionally viewed with suspicion, is in principle to be welcomed because it brings with it the possibility of realising the central overarching objective of a constitutionalised international economic law, namely supporting the continued conversion of the normative framework dealing with international economic relations into a more human-oriented legal order. The current emergence of a European approach towards good raw materials governance is another notable step on an admittedly long way still to go.

References

Al Faruque A (2006) Transparency in extractive revenues in developing countries and economies in transition: a review of emerging best practices. J Energy Nat Resour Law 24:66–103

von Arnauld A (2014) Das System der Europäischen Außenbeziehungen. In: von Arnauld A (ed) Europäische Außenbeziehungen. Nomos, Baden-Baden, pp 41–101

Boor F, Nowrot K (2014) Von Wirtschaftssanktionen und Energieversorgungssicherheit: Völkerrechtliche Betrachtungen zu staatlichen Handlungsoptionen in der Ukraine-Krise. Die Friedens-Warte 89:211–248

Boysen S (2014) Das System des Europäischen Außenwirtschaftsrechts. In: von Arnauld A (ed) Europäische Außenbeziehungen. Nomos, Baden-Baden, pp 447–514

Brackett A, Levin E, Melin Y (2015) Revisiting the conflict minerals rule. Glob Trade Cust J 10 (2):73–86

Brouder A (2009a) Extractive industries transparency initiative. In: Tietje C, Brouder A (eds) Handbook of transnational economic governance regimes. Martinus Nijhoff, Leiden/Boston, pp 849–863

Brouder A (2009b) Kimberley process certification scheme. In: Tietje C, Brouder A (eds) Handbook of transnational economic governance regimes. Martinus Nijhoff, Leiden/Boston, pp 969–987

Bungenberg M (2010) Going global? The EU common commercial policy after Lisbon. In: Herrmann C, Terhechte JP (eds) European yearbook of international economic law 2010. Springer, Heidelberg, pp 123–151

Chalmers D (2015) The democratic ambiguity of EU law making and its enemies. In: Arnull A, Chalmers D (eds) The Oxford handbook of European Union law. Oxford University Press, Oxford, pp 303–326

[100]Generally on the notion of "political law" see, e.g., Isensee (2014), p. 483 et seq.

[101]Trebilcock (2015), p. 9. On the perception of international economic law as political law see also, e.g., Tietje (2015b), p. 3; Nowrot (2016c), p. 1 et seq.

Cottier T, Trinberg L (2015) Artikel 207 AEUV. In: von der Groeben H, Schwarze J, Hatje A (eds) Europäisches Unionsrecht, 7th edn. Nomos, Baden-Baden, pp 310–351
Cremer HJ (2016) Artikel 205 AEUV. In: Calliess C, Ruffert M (eds) EUV/AEUV, 5th edn. Beck, Munich, pp 1995–1996
Cremona M (2004) The Union as a global actor: roles, models and identity. Common Mark Law Rev 41(2):553–573
Cullen H (2016) The irresistible rise of human rights due diligence: conflict minerals and beyond. George Wash Int Law Rev 48(4):743–780
DeKoninck H (2015) Breaking the curse: a multilayered regulatory approach. Indiana J Glob Legal Stud 22(1):121–148
Delbrück J (2001) Structural changes in the international system and its legal order: international law in the era of globalization. Swiss Rev Int Eur Law 11:1–36
Dimopoulos A (2010) The effects of the Lisbon Treaty on the principles and objectives of the common commercial policy. Eur Foreign Aff Rev 15(2):153–170
Esty DC (2006) Good governance at the supranational scale: globalizing administrative law. Yale Law J 115:1490–1562
Factor A (2014) Dodd-Frank's specialized disclosure provisions 1502 and 1504: small business, big impact. Ohio State Entrepreneurial Bus Law Journal 9:89–117
Hahn M (2016) Artikel 207 AEUV. In: Calliess C, Ruffert M (eds) EUV/AEUV, 5th edn. Beck, Munich, pp 2004–2070
Harline MS (2015) Can we make them obey? U.S. reporting companies, their foreign suppliers, and the conflict minerals disclosure requirements of Dodd-Frank. Northwest J Int Law Bus 35 (2):439–467
Herdegen M (2011) Der Beitrag des Internationalen Wirtschaftsrechts zu *Good Governance* und Rationalität des Staatshandelns. In: Giegerich T (ed) Internationales Wirtschafts- und Finanzrecht in der Krise. Duncker & Humblot, Berlin, pp 229–239
Herrmann C, Müller-Ibold T (2016) Die Entwicklung des europäischen Außenwirtschaftsrechts. Europäische Zeitschrift für Wirtschaftsrecht 27:646–653
Hilpold P (2002) EU development cooperation at a crossroads: the Cotonou agreement of 23 June 2000 and the principle of good governance. Eur Foreign Aff Rev 7(1):53–72
Isensee J (2014) Verfassungsrecht als "politisches Recht". In: Isensee J, Kirchhof P (eds) Handbuch des Staatsrechts der Bundesrepublik Deutschland, 3rd edn, vol XII. C.F. Müller, Heidelberg, pp 483–555
Khan DE (2015) Article 207 TFEU. In: Geiger R, Khan DE, Kotzur M (eds) European Union treaties – a commentary. Beck/Hart, Munich, pp 756–765
Krajewski M (2005) External trade law and the Constitution Treaty: towards a federal and more democratic common commercial policy? Common Mark Law Rev 42(1):91–127
Krajewski M (2012) The reform of the common commercial policy. In: Biondi A, Eeckhout P, Ripley S (eds) EU law after Lisbon. Oxford University Press, Oxford, pp 292–311
Krajewski M (2013) New functions and new powers for the European Parliament: assessing the changes of the common commercial policy from the perspective of democratic legitimacy. In: Bungenberg M, Herrmann C (eds) Common commercial policy after Lisbon. Springer, Heidelberg, pp 67–85
Krajewski M (2016) Normative Grundlagen der EU-Außenwirtschaftsbeziehungen: Verbindlich, umsetzbar und angewandt? Eur Secur 51:235–255
Kuon D (2010) Good Governance im europäischen Entwicklungsrecht. Nomos, Baden-Baden
Lachmayer K (2015) Artikel 205 AEUV. In: von der Groeben H, Schwarze J, Hatje A (eds) Europäisches Unionsrecht, 7th edn. Nomos, Baden-Baden, pp 267–269
Larik J (2016) Foreign policy objectives in European constitutional law. Oxford University Press, Oxford
Lenaerts K, Van Nuffel P (2011) European Union law, 3rd edn. Sweet & Maxwell, London
Mac Amhlaigh C (2016) Harmonising global constitutionalism. Glob Constitutionalism 5 (2):173–206

Maldonado Pyschny N (2013) Good Governance: Begriff, Inhalt und Stellung zwischen allgemeinem Völkerrecht und Souveränität. Heymanns, Cologne

Meessen KM (2015) Kimberley as a means of promoting good governance: the role of business. In: Bungenberg M, Hobe S (eds) Permanent sovereignty over natural resources. Springer, Heidelberg, pp 173–186

Meng W (1997) Wirtschaftssanktionen und staatliche Jurisdiktion – Grauzonen im Völkerrecht. Zeitschrift für ausländisches öffentliches Recht und Völkerrecht 57:269–327

Nanda VP (2014) Conflict minerals and international business: United States and international responses. ILSA J Int Compar Law 20:285–304

Nelson AL (2014) The materiality of morality: conflict minerals. Utah Law Rev 219–241

Nettesheim M, Duvigneau JL (2012) Artikel 207 AEUV. In: Streinz R (ed) EUV/AEUV, 2nd edn. Beck, Munich, pp 1933–1983

Nowrot K (2004) Global governance and international law. Beiträge zum Transnationalen Wirtschaftsrecht Heft 33. Institut für Wirtschaftsrecht, Halle/Saale

Nowrot K (2006) Normative Ordnungsstruktur und private Wirkungsmacht. Berliner Wissenschaftsverlag, Berlin

Nowrot K (2014) Das Republikprinzip in der Rechtsordnungengemeinschaft. Mohr Siebeck, Tübingen

Nowrot K (2015) Obligations of investors. In: Bungenberg M, Griebel J, Hobe S, Reinisch A (eds) International investment law. Beck/Hart/Nomos, Munich, pp 1154–1185

Nowrot K (2016a) Rohstoffhandel und Good Governance. In: Bungenberg M, Herrmann C (eds) Die gemeinsame Handelspolitik der Europäischen Union. Nomos, Baden-Baden, pp 214–250

Nowrot K (2016b) Global public authority in today's international economic legal order: towards substantive and institutional convergence à la Pacem in Terris? In: Justenhoven HG, O'Connell ME (eds) Peace through law – reflections on Pacem in Terris from philosophy, law, theology, and political science. Nomos, Baden-Baden, pp 187–214

Nowrot K (2016c) Regulatorische Zusammenarbeit als normatives Steuerungskonzept moderner Freihandelsabkommen: Betrachtungen zu einer umstrittenen Ordnungsidee der internationalen Gesetzgebungslehre. Zeitschrift für Gesetzgebung 31:1–23

Obradovic D, Vizcaino J (2006) Good governance requirements concerning the participation of interest groups in EU consultations. Common Mark Law Rev 43(4):1049–1085

Ochoa C, Keenan PJ (2011) Regulating information flows, regulating conflict: an analysis of United States conflict minerals legislation. Goettingen J Int Law 3:129–154

Oppermann T, Classen CD, Nettesheim M (2016) Europarecht, 7th edn. Beck, Munich

Prenkert JD, Shackelford SJ (2014) Business, human rights, and the promise of polycentricity. Vanderbilt J Transnational Law 47:451–500

Ross ML (2004) How do natural resources influence civil war? Evidence from thirteen cases. Int Organ 58:35–67

Rudolf B (2006) Is 'good governance' a norm of international law?. In: Dupuy PM et al. (eds) Völkerrecht als Wertordnung – Festschrift für Christian Tomuschat. Engel, Kehl, pp 1007–1028

Schuele CK (2015) Healing the Congo's colonial scars: advocating for a hybrid approach to conflict minerals reporting regulations in the European Union. Wisconsin Int Law J 33:755–786

Schütze R (2015) European Union law. Cambridge University Press, Cambridge

Schwartz J (2016) The conflict minerals experiment. Harv Bus Law Rev 6:129–183

Seppänen S (2003) Good governance in international law. University of Helsinki, Helsinki

Smillie I (2013) Blood diamonds and non-state actors. Vanderbilt J Transnational Law 46:1003–1023

Streinz R (2016) Europarecht, 10th edn. C.F. Müller, Heidelberg

Terhechte JP (2012) Artikel 205 AEUV. In: Schwarze J (ed) EU-Kommentar, 3rd edn. Nomos, Baden-Baden, pp 1894–1896

Tietje C (1998) Normative Grundstrukturen der Behandlung nichttarifärer Handelshemmnisse in der WTO/GATT-Rechtsordnung. Duncker & Humblot, Berlin
Tietje C (2009) Die Außenwirtschaftsverfassung der EU nach dem Vertrag von Lissabon. Beiträge zum Transnationalen Wirtschaftsrecht Heft 83. Institut für Wirtschaftsrecht, Halle/Saale
Tietje C (2015a) Außenwirtschaftsrecht. In: Tietje C (ed) Internationales Wirtschaftsrecht, 2nd edn. de Gruyter, Berlin/Boston, pp 792–862
Tietje C (2015b) Begriff, Geschichte und Grundlagen des Internationalen Wirtschaftssystems und Wirtschaftsrechts. In: Tietje C (ed) Internationales Wirtschaftsrecht, 2nd edn. de Gruyter, Berlin/Boston, pp 1–66
Tietje C, Nowrot K (2016) Parlamentarische Steuerung und Kontrolle des internationalen Regierungshandelns und der Außenpolitik. In: Morlok M, Schliesky U, Wiefelspütz D (eds) Parlamentsrecht – Handbuch. Nomos, Baden-Baden, pp 1469–1505
Trebilcock MJ (2015) Advanced introduction to international trade law. Edward Elgar, Cheltenham/Northampton
Turksen U (2009) The WTO law and the EC's GSP+ arrangement. J World Trade 43(5):927–968
Van Marter KD (2015) Between a rock and a hard place: the unintended consequences of the conflict minerals rule. Tulane J Int Compar Law 24:291–313
Veale E (2013) Is there blood on your hands-free device? Examining legislative approaches to the conflict minerals problem in the Democratic Republic of Congo. Cardozo J Int Compar Law 21:503–544
Vedder C (2013) Linkage of the common commercial policy to the general objectives for the Union's external action. In: Bungenberg M, Herrmann C (eds) Common commercial policy after Lisbon. Springer, Heidelberg, pp 115–144
Verhey L (2005) Good governance: lessons from constitutional law. In: Curtin DM, Wessel RA (eds) Good governance and the European Union. Intersentia, Antwerp, pp 49–67
Vidal V (2012) Informal international lawmaking: the Kimberley process' mechanism of accountability. In: Berman A, Duquet S, Pauwelyn J, Wessel RA, Wouters J (eds) Informal international lawmaking: case studies. Torkel Opsahl Academic EPublisher, The Hague, pp 505–525
Vyboldina E (2015) Solving the conflict minerals puzzle. Glob Trade Cust J 10(10):338–345
Weiß W (2014) Vertragliche Handelspolitik der EU. In: von Arnauld A (ed) Europäische Außenbeziehungen. Nomos, Baden-Baden, pp 515–586
Weiss F, Steiner S (2007) Transparency as an element of good governance in the practice of the EU and the WTO: overview and comparison. Fordham Int Law J 30:1545–1586
Wouters J, Ryngaert C (2005) Good governance: Lessons from international organizations. In: Curtin DM, Wessel RA (eds) Good governance and the European Union. Intersentia, Antwerp, pp 69–104
Zerk JA (2006) Multinationals and corporate social responsibility. Cambridge University Press, Cambridge

Part II
Regions: Ongoing Bi- and Multilateral Negotiations of the European Union

Bilateral Developments in EU Trade Policy Seven Years After Lisbon: A Look into the Spaghetti-Bowl à la Bruxelloise (2010–2016)

Frank Hoffmeister

Abstract The author reviews the EU's bilateral free trade agenda since the entry into force of the Lisbon Treaty. He shows that the number of partner countries has grown significantly, nowadays covering all major regions of the world. The review covers neighbourhood countries, emerging economies, G-7 partners, ASEAN and ACP countries, as well as Latin American countries plus Australia and New Zealand. Afterwards, he describes the major trends in a typical EU FTA on trade in goods, services, investment protection, public procurement, IPRs, competition and sustainable development. In his conclusion, the author argues that EU trade policy has become increasingly politicised over the past 7 years and is regularly dealt with nowadays at the level of Heads of States and Governments.

Contents

The views expressed are personal.

F. Hoffmeister (✉)
European Commission, DG Trade, Brussels, Belgium
e-mail: Frank.Hoffmeister@ec.europa.eu

M. Bungenberg et al. (eds.), *European Yearbook of International Economic Law 2017*, European Yearbook of International Economic Law 8,
DOI 10.1007/978-3-319-58832-2_13

1 Introduction

Already 20 years ago, the famous Indian economist *Bhagwati* pointed to the disadvantages of concluding bilateral trade agreements. If more and more WTO members conclude among themselves preferential treaties, which derogate *per definitionem* from most-favoured treatment in Article I GATT international trade relations would come to a stage, where they can be compared to a spaghetti bowl. Between all these preferences, exceptions and transitional periods, nobody could find the thread, especially not the companies who should normally benefit from the concessions. Rather to the opposite: more and more complicated rules of origin would prevent that companies would actually use the negotiated preferences.[1]

The analysis of *Bhagwati* cannot be denied. Also the European Union has engaged in bilateral free trade negotiations. While it traditionally put its emphasis multilateral liberalisation under the auspices of the WTO, it got more cautious after the failed Ministerial Conference in Cancun (2003). This trend got even stronger after the entry into force of the Lisbon Treaty. For the European Commission had confirmed the strategic priority for the Doha Development Agenda in its strategy for the EU's commercial policy in 2010.[2] But in spring 2011, after another unsuccessful attempt to bring the NAMA negotiations in the WTO forward, it had to accept that new market access could only be negotiated in a bilateral or regional setting. The question was thus whether one was ready to remain hungry or whether one is satisfied with a spaghetti-bowl since the globally accessible meat of the Doha Development Agenda was still a couple of rounds away. Brussels gave a clear reply. Especially in times of the financial crisis, it would have been irresponsible for Europe not to liaise stronger with other countries which create more growth than the old continent. The Commission often referred in this context to the fact that roughly 10 million export jobs had existed in 1995, while the figure increased three times for 2012, reaching 30 million export-related jobs.[3] Against that background, further efforts to deepen free trade with other nations could not be made dependent on the success of the Doha Round.

[1]Bhagwati (1995).

[2]European Commission, Trade, Growth and World Affairs – Trade Policy as a core component of the EU's 2020 strategy, COM (2010) 612 final, 9 November 2010, p. 9.

[3]European Commission, Trade, Growth and Jobs, Commission contribution to the European Council, 7–8 February 2013, p. 2.

Drawing on and expanding an earlier contribution published in German,[4] the present article will review how the Brussels trade agenda evolved in the time between 2010–2016. It will thus cover the entire *Barroso II* Commission with Trade Commissioner *De Gucht* (2010–2014) and the first 2 years of the *Juncker* Commission with Trade Commissioner *Malmström* (2015–2016). How does the spaghetti bowl *à la bruxelloise* look like at *Comme chez soi*?[5] What are the recipes and in which way sauces on the plate are different?

In order to respond to these queries, we first look at the partner countries with which negotiations were started, continued or concluded. Afterwards, we will review the topics, which are typically dealt with in an EU Free Trade Agreement. Some remarks about the institutional balance in the EU's common commercial policy and its politicisation will follow before concluding.

2 Partner Countries

2.1 Neighbourhood

2.1.1 Mediterranean Countries

Since the entry into force of the Lisbon Treaty, the specific situation of the neighbouring countries to the EU is secured in Article 8 TEU. The European Union aims at creating special relations and concluding neighbourhood agreements. Mostly, such agreements take the form of Association Agreements. Usually, they contain next to other policy areas a chapter about deepening trade. These chapters comply with the requirements of Article XXIV GATT to cover substantially all trade between the EU and its neighbours.

As a result of the Barcelona process, the European Union concluded such Association Agreements with the Mediterranean countries already a couple of years ago (Tunisia 1998, Morocco 2000, Israel 2000, Jordan 2000, Lebanon 2003, Egypt 2004, Algeria 2005, Interim-agreement with the Palestine Authority 1997). There were no agreements with Syria or Libya. After the Arab spring in 2011 the question arose whether the EU should build a new dynamic with some of them. This idea met immediately resistance, as many products of these neighbours are in direct competition with the agricultural products of the EU-Mediterranean countries. The political appetite for such a "green revolution dividend" was thus relatively small, as the bitter dispute about the ratification of the agricultural protocol with Morocco[6] in the years 2011–2012 showed.

[4]Hoffmeister (2016a).

[5]Literal translation: "Like at home". At the same time, "Comme Chez Soi" is supposedly the most distinguished Gourmet restaurant in the city of Brussels.

[6]OJ 2012 L 241/4.

Nevertheless, in December 2011, the Council authorised the Commission to negotiate deep and comprehensive' free trade agreements with Morocco, Egypt, Jordan and Tunisia. The purpose was to include new areas such as trade in services, public procurement, the protection of intellectual property rights and investment protection into the existing framework. The negotiations started with Morocco in mid-2013, whereas the respective Sustainability Impact Assessments for Tunisia (2013), Jordan and Egypt (2014) were available later on the side of the EU. Until mid-2016, no significant progress could be recorded with any of the countries. The only commercial highlight was the entry into force on the Regional Convention on pan-Euro-Mediterranean preferential rules of origin (covering countries of the Western Balkans, the EU, the EFTA States, and the Barcelona process countries) in 2012. The EU had signed the document in April 2011 and ratified it in March 2012.[7] From the southern Mediterranean neighbours Morocco and Algeria signed the next in 2012, whereas Jordan (2013), Egypt (2014) and Tunisia (2015) ratified it as well. It has thus become operational for some of the EU's southern neighbours.

2.1.2 Turkey

A special case is Turkey. The country is linked to the EU since 1995 with a customs union and has started accession negotiations in 2015. These are stagnating, however. All the more important is thus a close commercial relationship. However, it is currently jeopardised by the fact that the dispute-settlement arrangements date back to a system established under the Association Agreement of 1963, according to which unanimity is needed in the Association Council. That leads *de facto* to a blockade when the EU and Turkey disagree about the compliance with the customs union rules. Moreover, important areas are wholly excluded from the customs union, for example agriculture, services or public procurement. In return, Turkey sees an inconvenience of the customs union in the fact that the Union concludes more and more free trade agreements with third states. As it is bound to harmonise its external tariffs to the EU tariffs, market openings granted by the EU to third countries become relevant for Turkey as well. Ankara, though, is not a party to the EU FTA with that third country and thus does not benefit from the concessions given by that country to the EU. Such asymmetry can only be rectified, when Turkey concludes a similar FTA with the third country in question, or when the EU FTA is open to a Turkish accession. All this increases the need for closer cooperation between Ankara and Brussels on the current FTA negotiations between the EU and other countries.

Whereas these topics were discussed, but not solved in 2010–2014, the two sides achieved a breakthrough in March 2015. EU Trade Commissioner *Malmström* and

[7]Council Decision 2013/94/EU of 26 March 2012, OJ 2013 L 54/4.

the Turkish Minister of Economy *Zeybekci* announced that both sides wish to deepen the customs union.[8] The Council is currently discussing draft negotiation directives but has not yet authorised the Commission to formally launch this process. Moreover, in view of the political controversies around the Turkish domestic political development after the failed coup d'état of 15 July 2016 and around the EU-Turkey migration pact, it is currently uncertain how realistic a further deepening of the customs union with Turkey has become.

2.1.3 Countries of the Western Balkans

As of the year 2000, the Union granted the autonomous trade preferences to the countries of the Western Balkans.[9] The Stabilization and Association Agreements also contain comprehensive trade chapters, which facilitate the market access of European companies to markets of that region. That is true for the Former Yugoslav Republic of Macedonia (2004), Bosnia-Herzegovina (2008), Albania (2009), Montenegro (2010) and Serbia (2013). After the normalisation of relations between Belgrade and Pristina, it was also possible to conclude a similar agreement with Kosovo[10] in 2016. A further need for the EU to become active under its common commercial policy did thus not arise.

2.1.4 Countries of the Eastern Partnership

In return, the relations with the Eastern neighbours Ukraine, Belarus, Moldova, Georgia, Armenia and Azerbaijan called for very high political attention.

The three countries from the Caucasus expressed their wish to deepen their relations with the EU early on and started negotiations about an Association Agreement. While Baku stopped the process in 2013 (and was eliminated from the EU's General System of Preferences in 2014[11]), Yerevan and Tbilisi negotiated with full energy. The respective agreements were initialled in summer 2013. However, in September that year, the Armenian President announced upon Russian pressure not to sign the agreement. Rather, his country, which needs Russian support in the Nagorno-Karabakh conflict, would accede to the Eurasian Customs Union between Russia, Kazakhstan and Belarus. On the other hand, Georgia kept its pro-Western course. The trade part of the Association Agreement

[8]European Commission, EU and Turkey announce modernisation of Customs Union, Press release, 12 May 2015.

[9]The Regulation was prolonged in 2005 and 2011. See the last Regulation (EU) No 1336/2011, OJ 2011 L 347/1.

[10]Council Decision (EU) 2016/342 of 12 February 2016 on the conclusion of the SAA with Kosovo, OJ 2016 L 71/1.

[11]Regulation (EU) No 978/2012, OJ 2012 L 303/1.

signed in June 2014 started being provisionally applied as of September that year.[12]

The biggest challenge occurred in the relations with Ukraine. After the decision of the former President *Yanoukovich* not to sign the Association Agreement (and the trade chapter therein) with the EU at the Vilnius Summit of November 2013, protests against his government grew at the Euro-Maidan in Kiev. Leaving aside details of the subsequent crisis,[13] we can observe that the new President *Porochenko* then kept his election promises to bring the Agreement into force. First, the interim-government signed the political part of the agreement in March 2014 (on the same day on which Russia annexed the Crimea), followed by a signature of the remaining parts of the agreement in June 2014. This, in turn, mobilised resistance in Moscow, which maintained that the deepened EU-Ukraine trade relations would have a negative impact on the Russian economy.

This allegation was then verified at the highest level. EU Trade Commissioner *De Gucht* travelled to the Minsk Summit in August 2014, in which also the outline of the first cease-fire agreement ("Minsk I") was negotiated. In the subsequent trilateral negotiations in Brussels between *De Gucht*, the Ukrainian Foreign Minister *Klimkin* and the Russian Minister of Economy *Ulyukayev* of 12 September 2014 a compromise was found. The EU-Ukraine Association Agreement[14] would be ratified by the Parliaments on both sides, but the trade chapter would only be provisionally applied as of 2016. Exactly this was then laid down in a Council Decision,[15] which had been politically covered by the ratification through the European Parliament of 16 September 2014. At the same time, technical discussions about specific Russian concerns[16] and the autonomous EU trade preferences for the Ukraine continued. As of 1 January 2016, after notification on both sides, also the trade chapter of the EU-Ukraine agreement is now provisionally applied.

However, an unexpected set-back occurred shortly thereafter, when the Dutch people held a consultative referendum in April 2016 on the ratification of the treaty by the Netherlands. With a low participation rate of 32%, 64% of the voters voted against the text. As the political parties in the Parliament had previously announced that they would regard the result as authoritative for them, the ratification process is halted in the Dutch Parliament. This led to the awkward situation that all EU countries, but the Netherlands have deposited their instrument of ratification by October 2016. However, the Dutch government has not stopped provisional application after the referendum. Rather, it prepared a Decision of the Heads of State or Government of the 28 EU Member States, meeting within the European Council to give certain interpretations to the Association Agreements which would meet certain concerns voiced during the campaign. This Decision was adopted at the

[12]OJ 2014 L 261/4.

[13]For more details see Wiegand and Schulz (2015), pp. 321–326.

[14]OJ 2014 L 161/3.

[15]Council Decision 2014/691/EU of 29 September 2014, OJ 2014 L 289/1.

[16]See European Commission, EU-Ukraine-Russia Trilateral Talks – State of play, Press release, 5 August 2015.

European Council meeting on 15 December 2016, thus paving the way for Dutch ratification.

2.2 *Emerging Economies*

Whereas the strong links with its neighbours form part of the Union's quasi-constitutional program, the EU institutions enjoy a large margin of discretion how to handle the relations with other parts of the world. In its trade strategy of 2010, the Commission stated the principle that the EU should primarily aim at negotiating with partners with high growth rates.[17] This brings the focus automatically to the emerging economies. At the same time, it became clear in practice that the "BRICs" are not a homogenous group. Even though Brazil, India, China and South Africa try to co-ordinate their positions in G-20 meetings, their interests differ considerably in many aspects. This is exactly also the reason why they have always approached the EU for bilateral free trade negotiations rather than together.

The EU managed to have a good start with South Korea. The text, which had still been negotiated by the former Trade Commissioner *Ashton*, was the first one presented to the European Parliament after the Lisbon Treaty had entered into force. The representatives gave their consent to the treaty with a large majority, after an accompanying safeguard regulation[18] had catered for the fear about too many Korean car exports. Being in provisional application since July 2011,[19] the agreement exceeded expectations. Three years later, the Commission could announce that the volume of European exports to Korea had risen by 30%. In the other direction, imports of Korean cars had grown by 53%,[20] but that had not created any disturbance.

With respect to India, Brussels had to digest a stand-still. After initial euphoria in 2010–2011, there was a growing disappointment that the Indian negotiators did not touch a number of important sectors. Moreover, one could not avoid the impression that the political control of Trade Minister *Sharma* over his administration was not strong enough to overcome a number of reservations. The erratic positions of India was also manifest at the WTO, when India's insistence to shield its agricultural subsidies first dominated the Bali summit in 2013 and then lead to a half-year delay in the signature of the relevant legal texts on trade facilitation.[21] The only prospect of giving new dynamic to the negotiations thus seems to be connected with a significant levelling down of ambition.

---

[17]COM (2010) 612 final, p. 4.

[18]Regulation (EU) No 511/2011, OJ 2011 L 145/19.

[19]OJ 2011 L 127/6.

[20]European Commission, Annual Report on the Implementation of the EU-Korea Free Trade Agreement, COM (2015) 139 final, 26 March 2015, p. 5.

[21]See Hoffmeister (2015a), p. 59.

There were also political problems with *Mercosur*. When Brazil, Argentina, Uruguay and Paraguay sent positive signals in spring 2010 to replace the cooperation agreement of 1995 with a comprehensive free trade agreement, the negotiations re-started after a decision at the Madrid Summit in May 2010. The negotiators met for nine rounds, but when President *Kirchner* took over power in Buenos Aires, Mercosur was unable to present a market access offer. Instead, political tensions grew, culminating when the Argentinian government expropriated the Spanish company Repsol without any compensation in April 2012. Moreover, the EU suffered from new trade restrictions in the form of non-automatic import licences. The Commission, together with the USA, Mexico and Japan, brought a case before the WTO against these Argentinian measures—and won.[22] In return, Argentina attacked the EU because of anti-dumping measures against the export of Argentinian bio-diesel. A panel report largely sided with the plaintiff, confirmed by the Appellate Body in October 2016.[23]

With China, the situation is different. Albeit there are frictions in several sectors—every second trade defence case deals with Chinese imports—, there are also earnest attempts to deepen the trade relations. Next to regular consultations in the framework of High Level Economic Dialogue between the EU Commission and the Chinese government, which also address trade irritants,[24] the two sides also exchange views in the Joint Trade Committee. This body was established by the cooperation agreement of 1985. For some time, Beijing asks now for a replacement of this old text with a modern free trade agreement, pointing also to its free trade agreement with Switzerland. However, the official position of the EU at summit level is to first conclude negotiations on an investment agreement, before engaging into a full FTA. The European perspective is that China already reduced classical tariffs for its WTO accession in 2001, while European companies complain about restrictions on establishment, regulatory barriers or non-respect for intellectual property rights. Such issues can be tackled and tested in an investment agreement. Since November 2013, these important negotiations are on their way. However, as of the end of 2016, China has not yet made a comprehensive market access offer. Moreover, when the Commission announced in its Trade Communication of October 2015 to "explore launching negotiations on investment with Hong Kong and Taiwan",[25] Beijing's reaction was forcefully sceptical.

---

[22]Panel Report, *Argentina – Measures Affecting the Import of Goods*, WT/DS438/R, adopted 22 August 2015; Appellate Body Report, WT/DS438/AB/R, adopted 15 January 2015.

[23]Panel Report, *EU – Anti-Dumping Measures Affecting the Imports of Bio-Diesel from Argentina*, WT/DS473/R, adopted 29 March 2016; Appellate Body Report, WT/DS473/AB/R, adopted 6 October 2016.

[24]The 6th HED took place 18 October 2016 in Brussels, see European Commission, Press release IP-16-3441, 18 October 2016.

[25]European Commission, Trade for All – Towards a more responsible trade and investment policy, COM (2015) 497 final, chapter 5.2.2.

2.3 *G7 Partner Countries*

In order not to undermine the attractiveness of the multilateral WTO rounds there was an unwritten understanding between the G7 countries not to engage in bilateral free trade deals. However, also this approach eroded because of the experience with the stalled Doha round.

2.3.1 Canada

The first test case in this respect was Canada. After 5 years of negotiations, Brussels and Ottawa agreed on a text in October 2014, which was then published by the Commission.[26] During legal scrubbing, the text got further refined, in particular in the investment chapter. That was an important step to appease intra-EU opposition against the classical approach on investor-state dispute settlement. With the agreement of Canada, the Commission was able to introduce into the final CETA text its new approach, favouring a fully-fledged Investment Court System, rather than ad hoc tribunals. In July 2016, the Commission proposed signature and provisional application of CETA[27] as well as its conclusion[28] as a mixed agreement.

This was a remarkable U-turn. Just a week before, in the end of June 2016, Commission President *Juncker* had still declared at the European Council that he regarded the agreement as an EU-only agreement. However, after severe criticism in some capitals, he adjusted his position. The reason advanced in the Commission proposal was as follows:

> CETA has identical objectives and essentially the same contents as the Free Trade Agreement with Singapore (EUSFTA). Therefore, the Union's competence is the same in both cases. In view of the doubts raised with regard to the extent and the nature of the Union's competence to conclude EUSFTA, in July 2015 the Commission requested from the Court of Justice an opinion under Article 218(11) TFEU (case A-2/15). In case A-2/15 the Commission has expressed the view that the Union has exclusive competence to conclude EUSFTA alone and, in the alternative, that it has at least shared competence in those areas where the Union's competence is not exclusive. Many Member States, however, have expressed a different opinion. *In view of this, and in order not to delay the signature of the Agreement*, the Commission has decided to propose the signature of the Agreement as a mixed agreement. Nevertheless, this is without prejudice to the views expressed by the Commission in Case A-2/15. Once the Court issues its opinion in case A-2/15, it will be necessary to draw the appropriate conclusions.[29]

This political decision is not without consequences. While a vote under Article 207(4) first subparagraph TFEU could be done by qualified majority, a

[26]Consolidated CETA text of 26 September 2014, http://trade.ec.europa.eu/doclib/docs/2014/september/tradoc_152806.pdf (last accessed 1 March 2017).

[27]COM (2016) 444, 5 July 2016.

[28]COM (2016) 443, 5 July 2016.

[29]COM (2016) 444, p. 4.

mixed agreement needs the positive vote of every single EU government on the allegedly remaining "national part". The stakes were thus high when the German Constitutional Court was seized by the matter on an individual complaint brought by a number of citizens. They claimed that the German government was prevented from signing the agreement, in particular because there was no sufficient democratic German participation in the joint CETA Committee between the EU and Canada. The Karlsruhe Court decided on 13 October 2016 not to issue an injunction which would have prohibited the German government from going ahead, arguing that such move would jeopardize the Union's ability to act on the international trade scene. On the other hand, it also reserved the rights to look in more detail at the merits. It thus interpreted Article 30.7(3) of the CETA Agreement as allowing the unilateral termination of CETA's provisional application by Germany if the agreement would turn out to be breaching Germany's fundamental constitutional principles.[30]

After this "up" for CETA on 1 day, the next day produced a "down", though, at the Parliament of Wallonia. On 14 October 2016, the predominantly socialist regional assembly of the Belgian region of roughly three million inhabitants voted against the Agreement,[31] although it had not even been asked to ratify it! Rather, the Socialist Prime Minister of Wallonia *Magnette* had made its own support to the federal government dependent on a positive vote in his assembly. Lacking such support from Wallonia, also the Belgian Foreign Minister *Reynders* was unable to vote in favour of the Council's decision in the extra-ordinary Trade Council meeting on 18 October 2016.[32] Moreover, direct negotiations between *Magnette* and the Canadian Trade Minister *Freeman* in Brussels on 22 October 2016 failed, leading to the cancellation of the EU-Canada summit a few days later.

Only on 27 October 2016, Belgium came to terms with CETA. Federal and regional representatives worked out a Belgian declaration to be annexed to the Council decision on signature. This document, which would later become Declaration No. 37,[33] contains a number of important points. First, the regions engaged themselves to monitor the social-economic and environmental effects of CETA during provisional application—and keep a reserve on their respective ratification. If only one region decides against ratification, Belgium as a whole will be forced to notify non-ratification to the Council.[34] Second, Belgium took note that the investment chapter is not covered by provisional application and—echoing the Karlsruhe judgment—that each party could end provisional application under Article 30.7 CETA Agreement; moreover, Belgium will demand an opinion of the Court of

[30]German Constitutional Court, cases 2 BvR 1368/16, 2 BvR 1444/16, 2 BvR 1823/16, 2 BvR 1482/16 and 2 BvE 3/16, Judgment 13 October 2016.

[31]Parlement wallon, Session 2016–2017, Document 606 (2016–2017) – Project to motion déposé en conclusion du débat sur les projets de Traité CETA et de Déclaration interprétatitve du traité.

[32]See http://www.consilium.europa.eu/en/meetings/fac/2016/10/18/ (last accessed 1 March 2017).

[33]Declaration No. 37 to the Council decision of 28 October 2016 on signature of CETA, http://data.consilium.europa.eu/doc/document/ST-13463-2016-REV-1/fr/pdf (last accessed 1 March 2017).

[34]Declaration No. 37, point A.

Justice of the European Union on the compatibility of investor-to-state dispute settlement clauses with the EU treaty.[35] Amazingly, the non-Flemish regions also declare in advance that they will not ratify the current chapter 8 of CETA on investment, unless their Parliaments decide otherwise.[36] Third, all the regions reiterate that decisions in the CETA Joint Committee, which would fall within national competence and—under Belgian constitutional law—within the competences of the regions would be submitted to their Parliaments first before taking a position.[37] Fourth, Belgium reserves its right to trigger a safeguard mechanism on agriculture if there is a disturbance of the EU market. It reiterates also that no GMO's will be authorised and that the precautionary principle will be safeguarded.[38]

With this Belgian declaration in the bag, the Council finally adopted its decision on signature on the following day in written procedure. Interestingly, the decision quotes as legal basis Article 43(2)—agriculture, Articles 91/100(2)—transport, Article 153(2)—social policy, Article 192—environmental policy and Article 207(4), first subparagraph TFEU as legal bases. As all of them allow for internal decision-making under ordinary legislative procedure, this means that the decision in the Council was actually done under qualified majority voting rules. It was thus indeed only the characterisation as a "mixed agreement" which led to the need to seek unanimous support from the representatives of the Member States, meeting in the Council.

CETA was then actually signed at the postponed summit on 30 October 2016 in the presence of the Canadian Prime Minister *Trudeau*. Pending its ratification by the European Parliament and all 28 national Parliaments, most parts of CETA can now be provisionally applied. The Council decision on provisional application exempts in particular those parts which are said to fall under national competence. These concern parts of the investment protection chapter (including the special provisions on financial services and taxation measures[39]), a criminal provision on camcording,[40] and administrative proceedings, review and appeal at Member State level.[41] In order to uphold its legal position before the Court in the *Singapore* opinion, the Council also declared that chapters 22 (sustainable development), 23 (trade and labour) and 24 (trade and environment) of CETA should be applied in "respect of the allocation of competences between the Union and the Member

[35]Declaration No. 37, point B, first and second subparagraph.

[36]Declaration No. 37, point B, third subparagraph.

[37]Declaration No. 37, point C.

[38]Declaration No. 37, point D.

[39]Article 1(a), (b) and (c), third indent of the Council decision on provisional application.

[40]Article 1(c), first indent of the Council decision on provisional application.

[41]Article 1(c), second indent of the Council decision on provisional application.

States".[42] For the interpretation of CETA, a "joint interpretative instrument between Canada and the European Union and its Member States"[43] is relevant. It shortly summarises the main innovations of CETA and clarifies some legal concepts used in the investment chapter. Curiously, as its legal value had been put in doubt by the Wallonian Parliament as well,[44] the Legal Service of the Council even made another declaration on the value of declarations! Not surprisingly, it stated that by virtue of Article 31(2)(b) of the Vienna Convention on the Law of Treaties, this Joint Interpretation forms context of CETA and thus can be used in the interpretation of its terms. To this effect, it has legal force and binding character.[45]

The next step at European level followed on 15 February 2017. After a positive vote of all relevant committees, the European Parliament approved the text with the large majority of 408 votes to 254, with 33 abstentions. This means that at least the parts covered by EU competence can be provisionally applied as of October 2017, pending the full ratification of the mixed agreement in all Member States.

2.3.2 United States of America

Clearly, the hesitation about concluding CETA as an EU-only agreement and the Belgian declaration had also something to do with the parallel negotiations with the United States on the Transatlantic Trade and Investment Partnership (TTIP). These negotiations had been launched in June 2012, but quickly ran into remarkable opposition in parts of the German, French and Austrian public, fuelled by a number of NGO's and political factions. A glimpse of the many points and prejudices made against TTIP can be found in the above-mentioned resolution of Wallonia's Parliament of 14 October 2014. Echoing the words of many protesters, it deplored the negative impacts "on the protection of public services, the right to regulate of States, the protection of privacy, the rights of workers, small and medium sized enterprises, the respect for social and environmental norms and the organisation of public health services" allegedly brought about by both CETA and TTIP.[46]

However, a closer look reveals that also TTIP follows the usual patterns of the EU's bilateral trade policy. Accordingly, fears about lowering environmental or social standards or setbacks for the cultural or public health sector seem to be

---

[42]Article 1(d) of the Council decision on provisional application.

[43]Council Document 13,541/16, 27 October 2016.

[44]Resolution of the Wallonian Parliament of 14 October 2016, Document 606 (2016–2017), preamble point J.

[45]Declaration No. 38 to the Council decision of 28 October 2016 on signature of CETA, http://data.consilium.europa.eu/doc/document/ST-13463-2016-REV-1/fr/pdf (last accessed 1 March 2017).

[46]Resolution of the Wallonian Parliament of 14 October 2016, Document 606 (2016–2017), preamble point F.

exaggerated. As in previous FTAs, TTIP is likely to also contain specific clauses protecting public services.[47] Moreover, regulatory cooperation is no attack on democracy, as it is mainly about laying down horizontal principles of good regulatory practices.[48] In contrast, legally binding decisions on mutual recognition will only be taken on a sector-specific basis and in line with the regulatory process of either side. It follows that concerns about an alleged automatic recognition of genetically modified organisms (GMOs), hormone-treated beef, or asbestos, are unfounded.[49] Nevertheless, the future of TTIP has become more uncertain at the time of writing, as negotiations were not concluded with the Obama administration in 2016. That means that any progress will lie in the hands of the newly elected *Trump* administration, whose stance on the matter is unknown.

2.3.3 Japan

In contrast, the Japanese government is strongly pushing for a free trade agreement with the EU. Since the start of the negotiations in March 2013, the EU-Japanese agreement makes progress in the shadow of TTIP dominating the public media. Interestingly, there is no public opposition against these negotiations, although the topics are largely similar. It seems that some political motives in the TTIP, such as anti-Americanism and the fear to be dwarfed by a stronger power, are missing in the Japanese context. Therefore, the first *rendez-vous* in March 2014 finding sufficient progress by Tokyo in tackling non-tariff barriers was not further noticed in the public debate. Moreover, even after the decision of the United Kingdom to leave the European Union in June 2016, the EU-Japanese negotiations were kept on track. It can thus be expected that the next big EU Trade agreement in 2017 will be the one with Japan.

2.4 ASEAN Countries

With respect to the Asian tiger states, the focus is now directed towards the ASEAN region. Whereas efforts to negotiate a region-to-region agreement between 2007 and 2009 failed due to the disparities in the ASEAN, individual countries signalled their interest to the Union to negotiate on a bilateral basis. The leader was Singapore. The island-state concluded its negotiations with the EU in October 2014 when the last details on the investment chapter ware agreed. However, as the Commission

[47] Treier and Wernicke (2015), p. 338.

[48] In detail Pitschas (2015), p. 141.

[49] For more detail see Hoffmeister (2015b), p. 34.

asked the Court of Justice for an opinion about the scope of the EU's external competence,[50] the signature of the agreement will be delayed for some time.

As the second ASEAN country, Viet Nam closed negotiations with the EU in June 2015. There are many hopes that this text will foster further economic reforms in the country. In contrast, the negotiations with Malaysia (launched in 2010) and Thailand (launched in 2013) are blocked. More positive is that the Commission could start negotiations with the Philippines in December 2015 and with Indonesia in July 2016. Finally, negotiations with Myanmar about an investment agreement (only) are underway as well.

2.5 *African-Pacific-Caribbean Countries*

While the relations between the EU and the ACP-countries have been built over 40 years, the partners intensified their trade regime only more recently. The starting point was the expiry of the WTO waiver[51] for the preferential regime for these countries in year 2000. In order to still grant commercial advantages deviating from most-favoured nation treatment (Article I GATT), another justification was needed. The Union found this justification in Article XXIV GATT and envisaged regional free trade agreements with seven sub-groups of the ACP group.[52] Thus, in 2001 the EU launched an initiative to negotiate the so-called Economic Partnership Agreements (EPAs), which would replace the previous asymmetric trade regimes and cover new areas such as services. In order to get negotiating space, the EU asked for another prolongation of the WTO waiver, which was granted in November 2001 till the end of 2007.

In practice, this endeavour proved very difficult. Only the Caribbean countries went ahead with the CARIFORUM EPA from 2008,[53] and a study of 2013 found that the implementation thereof showed a mixed picture.[54] In the Pacific region, an

[50]The Barroso II Commission took the decision of principle during its penultimate meeting in October 2014 under the pressure of the then Trade Commissioner De Gucht. The Juncker Commission confirmed that decision in May 2015 and the request was presented to the Court at the end of September 2015. The Court handed down its opinion 2/15 in May 2017.

[51]The Fourth ACP-EEC Convention of Lomé, Decision of the Contracting Parties of 9 December 1994, L/7604, 19 December 1994 (the "Lomé Waiver"); and The Fourth ACP-EC Convention of Lomé, Extension of Waiver, Decision of the WTO General Council of 14 October 1996, WT/L/186, 18 October 1996.

[52]For more detail see Zimmermann (2009), p. 1 et seq.

[53]OJ 2008 L 289/3.

[54]Singh RH et al., Monitoring the Implementation & Results of the CARIFORUM – EU EPA Agreement, September 2013, http://trade.ec.europa.eu/doclib/docs/2014/october/tradoc_152825.pdf (last accessed 1 March 2017).

interim-agreement with Papua New Guinean and Fiji[55] is provisionally applied from all three sides since 2014.

On the other hand, the African countries entered the negotiations with defined, but little ambition. This also had to with the fact that the EU had granted them unilateral market access with a specific regulation[56] hoping that they would sign and ratify the EPAs early on. When it became clear that the African side did not share this objective, the then Trade Commissioner *De Gucht* convinced the EU legislator to abolish this wrong incentive. Hence, the market access regulation came to an end in October 2014.[57] That created a new dynamic in the region, when falling-back into MFN treatment became a real prospect. Hence, the countries of south-east Africa have been applying an EPA since 2012. Another EPA with countries of the Southern African Development Community (SADC) was brought to a close in July 2014 and formally signed in June 2016. After a positive vote in the European Parliament, the EU and Botswana, Lesotho, Namibia, South Africa and Swaziland, and Mozambique are applying the EPA now provisionally as of October 2016. The Western African States endorsed the signature of their EPA in July 2014 (but the actual signature is still outstanding). Even the reluctant countries of the Eastern-African Community (EAC) agreed to a text in the last minute in October 2014, and in September 2016 Kenya and Rwanda actually signed it. Only central Africa (with the exception of Cameroon, which signed an interim EPA back in 2009, which got ratified by both sides in 2013/2014) is still left without a trade agreement with the EU.

On substance, the EPAs are reciprocal trade agreements. However, they remain strongly asymmetrical. While the EU promises complete market access with provisional application, the partner countries usually have less coverage or benefit from long transition periods. For example, under the recent SADC EPA, the EU will guarantee Botswana, Lesotho, Mozambique, Namibia, and Swaziland 100% free access to its market. The EU has also fully or partially removed customs duties on 98.7% of imports coming from South Africa. The SADC EPA states do not have to respond with the same level of market openness. Instead, they can keep tariffs on products sensitive to international competition. For that reason the Southern African Customs Union (SACU) removes customs duties on only around 86% of imports from the EU and Mozambique only 74%.

2.6 Latin American Countries

The first deep and comprehensive free trade agreement in Latin America was concluded with Peru and Colombia in 2011. However, in the European Parliament,

[55]OJ 2009 L 272/2.

[56]Regulation (EC) No 1528/2007, OJ 2007 L 348/1.

[57]Amending Regulation (EU) No 527/2013, OJ 2013 L 165/59.

the text became controversial for political reasons. In particular, the protection of trade unionists in Columbia against alleged attacks and killings from para-military groups was a specific concern to the parliamentarians. The EP thus asked for an action plan from the Colombian government before voting in favour of the agreement in December 2012.[58] It then went into provisional application in 2013.

In contrast, the Council exercised some sort of economic conditionality with respect to the agreement with Central-America, initialled in 2011. When it decided in principle in June 2012 to accept provisional application, the Council took the unprecedented step to reserve the precise date for the start thereof.[59] Only in 2013, when it was satisfied that the partner countries had taken necessary steps for the protection of European geographical indications, was it finally ready to put the text into application.[60]

Under Trade Commissioner *Malmström* the EU also accepted Mexico's wish to upgrade the old trade agreement negotiated before 2001. Accordingly, formal negotiations with the US's neighbour were launched in 2016.

2.7 Australia and New Zealand

Finally, in its communication "Trade for All" of October 2015, the *Juncker* Commission also announced its willingness to strengthen economic ties with Australia and New Zealand.[61] Accordingly, scoping exercises have been launched with both countries, although some Member States with agricultural interests are not looking forward to an early conclusion of this exercise.

3 Free Trade Agreement Topics

After this *tour d'horizon* about the partner countries with which the European Union has started or concluded bilateral free trade agreements, it has become clear that the picture changed dramatically in the last 7 years. Whereas a FTA was an exception in 2005, nowadays it is the rule. At the same time, DG TRADE has reached the limits of its capacity. This is because negotiations nowadays do not only require some specialists about trade in goods. Rather, many more experts need

[58]For more details see Hoffmeister (2013), p. 396 et seq.

[59]Article 3(2) of the Council Decision 2012/734/EU of 25 June 2012, OJ 2012 L 346/1.

[60]See http://ec.europa.eu/trade/policy/countries-and-regions/regions/central-america/ (last accessed 1 March 2017).

[61]European Commission, Trade for All – Towards a more responsible trade and investment policy, COM (2015) 497 final, chapter 5.2.2.

to cover a lot of additional topics in line with the strategy announced in 2006[62] to conclude „deep and comprehensive free trade agreements—DCFTAs. "Modern trade agreements are "deep" insofar as they included additional disciplines in traditional areas, so-called "WTO-pluses". But they are also "comprehensive" by regulating new areas such as public procurement, intellectual property rights, competition law, sustainable development and investment protection (since 2009). Without giving details for any individual agreement, the following observations should sketch some general ideas and trends on the recurrent topics in EU FTAs post Lisbon.

3.1 Trade in Goods

In the chapter about goods, the reduction or abolition of tariffs is the natural focus. In order to satisfy the requirements under Article XXIV GATT to catch "substantially all trade", the EU usually does not wish to have exceptions for entire sectors. That means that roughly 90% of all trade should be liberalised between the partners. This traditional approach is sometimes not successful. For example, in the above-mentioned EPAs the goods covered were sometimes not exceeding 75% on the side of the African counterparts, which can be explained by their developing country status.

When dealing with non-tariff barriers, the crucial points relate to technical standards and food safety. As the WTO TBT and SPS agreements already contain horizontal standards, the partners usually try to elaborate sector-specific rules. But that is not tantamount to a large-scale harmonisation. Rather, while respecting the sovereignty of both sides to determine their own level of protection (the "Whether"), the partners try to find simplifications about the way in which such protection is achieved (the "How"). Accordingly, the relevant chapters often contain more procedural rules than substantive decisions recognizing the applicable standard of the trading partner.

3.2 Trade in Services

Many countries still are reluctant to negotiate about the liberalisation of services. A good indicator in this respect can be drawn from plurilateral negotiations in Geneva on an "International Service Agreement" (TISA). Out of the over 160 WTO members, only 23 are participating in the discussions on further disciplines on services. Once the EU meets an interested partner, there are regularly important

[62]European Commission, Global Europe: competing in the world, COM (2006) 567 final, 4 October 2006, p. 11 et seq.

technical questions with some political significance. One option is to liberalise all services, but to exempt those which are explicitly listed ("negative list approach"). In the alternative, one can only list those sectors which should be liberalised ("positive list approach"). Although the result should be the same, a "negative list approach" nurtures the suspicion of sceptics[63] that it would cover consciously or unconsciously services which should not be included. In practice, a pragmatic approach prevailed. When dealing with market access, the EU favours a positive list (as under the GATS). But it also accepts a negative list to outlaw discrimination of foreign services. Accordingly, specific privileges for domestic service providers must explicitly listed, which in turn creates in an internal need to verify whether such privileges are still needed. Apart from this, the EU services chapters are silent about property questions. In none of the EU DCFTAs did the EU ever require to privatise certain utilities or other service providers or to prohibit a previously privatised service to come back to public control, contrary to certain rumours spread with respect to TTIP or CETA. For the avoidance of doubt, this point has now been even put in the interpretative declaration on CETA.[64]

3.3 Investment Protection

With the entry into force of the Lisbon Treaty, the European Union became exclusively competent on investment protection. While Commission and Council are still not in agreement about the precise scope of this transfer of competence[65]—a matter which the CJEU will decide in the pending opinion on the Singapore agreement –, the EU negotiated in practice a couple of new investment chapters already. While the FTA with Korea (as a pre-Lisbon text which may be updated) is silent about the matter, the relevant negotiations with Canada, Singapore and Viet Nam were successful. In relation to TTIP, the Commission under *De Gucht* also conducted a public consultation in 2014 and received almost 150,000 replies. The

[63]See for example Resolution of the Wallonian Parliament of 14 October 2016, Document 606 (2016–2017), preamble point O.

[64]Joint Interpretative Instrument on CETA between Canada and the European Union and its Member States, point 4: "(a) The European Union and its Member States and Canada affirm and recognise the right of governments, at all levels, to provide and support the provision of services that they consider public services including in areas such as public health and education, social services and housing and the collection, purification and distribution of water. (b) CETA does not prevent governments from defining and regulating the provision of these services in the public interest. CETA will not require governments to privatise any services nor prevent governments from expanding the range of services they supply to the public. (c) CETA will not prevent governments from providing public services previously supplied by private service suppliers or from bringing back under public control services that governments had chosen to privatise. CETA does not mean that contracting a public service to private providers makes it irreversibly part of the commercial sector."

[65]See for example Reinisch (2010), pp. 99–112.

new Trade Commissioner *Malmström* then published a concept paper in May and made the first concrete proposals during the TTIP negotiations in September 2015.[66]

Comparing the EU chapters[67] and the traditional bilateral investment treaties of EU Member States[68] one can recognize continuity and change. On the one hand, the EU took the BIT standard clauses from Member States as a starting point. On the other hand, it also refined those standards and added new language. Depending on the political point of view of a spectator, this was then either seen as a deplorable lowering of protection for the investor or as a laudable clarification on the right to regulate of States. Moreover, the EU made a strong push for reforming the enforcement mechanism. While confirming the right of an investor to bring cases directly against the host State ("Investor-to-State Dispute Settlement"—ISDS), it anchored this right much more into public law concepts than before. For example, it makes the UNCITRAL rules on transparency mandatory, takes a stronger influence on the selection of judges, and clarifies that awards are limited to declaring compensation rather than restitution. Most importantly, the EU also proposed a fully-fledged Investment Court System (ICS) in the TTIP negotiations.[69] This should link the appeals instance from each bilateral agreement to a multilateral investment court to be founded among a coalition of willing states—the idea was already accepted in CETA[70] and the EU Viet Nam FTA, both from 2016. Moreover, EU chapters on investment are usually part of a wider agreement which also contains chapters about sustainable development or references to the social responsibility of companies. These objectives can also be taken into account in the interpretation of the investment chapter. Accordingly, all the reform efforts of the EU contribute to a further development of international investment law at large.[71]

3.4 Public Procurement

Somehow comparably with trade in services, the number of countries interested in opening up their procurement market is limited. The plurilateral Government Procurement Agreement (GPA) in the WTO was updated after some tedious negotiations between Canada, Hong-Kong, Israel, Iceland, Japan, Lichtenstein,

[66]See European Commission, Commission proposes new Investment Court System for TTIP and other EU trade and investment negotiations, Press release IP-15-5651.

[67]For the EU standard clauses see Hoffmeister and Alexandru (2014).

[68]See an overview at Gaffney and Akcay (2015).

[69]Commission draft text on investment in TTIP, September 2015, http://trade.ec.europa.eu/doclib/docs/2015/september/tradoc_153807.pdf (last accessed 1 March 2017). For a first discussion of the proposal see Schill (2016).

[70]Article 8.29 of the CETA Agreement.

[71]See Hoffmeister (2016b).

Aruba (the Netherlands), Singapore, Taiwan, USA and Norway in 2010.[72] The revised GPA entered into force in spring 2014. It modernised the rules and contained additional market openings, as more public bodies were covered by the new commitments. Moreover, the revised GPA lowered the thresholds and included all construction services.[73]

Nevertheless, there is still room left in bilateral relations for the EU and its partners. For the EU, the starting point is defined by its directives on public procurement. Its principles on non-discrimination inside the single market also protect foreign bidders. Only the directive about public utilities contains exceptions[74]—but they are not applied in practice and a proposal which would give the Commission the right to close the EU market when EU companies face serious access problems in a third country is pending.[75] Against that background, the European Union can be regarded as a rather open market for third-country bidders. In contrast, some of the EU's partners maintain access barriers for EU companies that are also not removed in the GPA. Thus, the negotiation of a bilateral chapter on public procurement is usually in the interest of the Union. For example, in CETA, this issue played an important role. Here, it is particularly positive that Canada opened up the procurement market also at provisional and local level, in a manner which had not been granted to any other G20 country.[76] Whether or not a similar step can be expected by the United States in TTIP remains to be seen. Some US States are very protectionist and the federal government has little influence over them. Hence, a more indirect opening of the US market is more probable: once the US federal government finances State or local procurement it can also make instructions, which should exclude the discrimination of European companies in the future.

3.5 *Protection of Intellectual Property Rights*

In the context of the WTO TRIPS agreement, a great number of intellectual property rights are protected. A relatively low level of protection is granted for geographical indications ("GIs") under Articles 22 and 23 TRIPS, as only wines and spirits are protected through a specific registry. For all other GIs every State has the right under its domestic law to organise protection by law or to empower private parties to stop others from (ab)-using a GI.

---

[72]WTO, GPA/W/313 of 16 December 2010 – Decision on the Outcome of Negotiations under Article XXIV.7 of the Agreement on Government Procurement. The protocol entered into force in spring 2014.

[73]Prieß (2015), p. 110.

[74]Article 58 et seq. Directive 2004/17/EC, OJ 2004 L 134/1.

[75]See Hoffmeister (2016c), p. 82 et seq.

[76]See Prieß (2015), p. 144.

This explains why the EU is traditionally keen on upgrading the protection of GIs in its bilateral FTA chapters. A good example is the Association Agreement with Central America.[77] Under Articles 244 and 245, the partner countries committed to introduce legislation to protect GIs in the future. This includes a registry which has the advantage to protect a registered GI *erga omnes* in the entire country. Moreover, the EU negotiates with partner countries to provide for the protection of a number of specific European GIs. That can even go so far as to make the provisional application of the entire agreement dependent on this point. Some of the EU Member States used for example the relevant link made by Article 353(5) of the EU-Central American Association Agreement. Although the process was legally questionable (the Council determined the date of the provisional application without a proposal from the Commission),[78] it showed at the same time how important this chapter is in particular for the southern EU member States.

Moreover, the EU negotiates a number of "TRIPS plus" provisions, for example on the protection of clinical data or on patent protection.[79] As laid down in Article 10.2 of the IP chapter in the EU-Korea FTA, these provisions are meant to complement and specify the TRIPS.

3.6 Competition

Another important area is competition policy. Trade and competition have failed as a Singapore-issue in the WTO,[80] but can be a valid topic in a bilateral FTA. In this respect, it is important whether a partner country is closely linked to the EU or not. For example, the EU can go much further in this chapter with a neighbouring country which wishes to approximate itself to European standards than with other countries. Moreover, it plays a role whether a country is used to have an effective competition policy already itself. Against that background one can distinguish roughly between three different models.

The neighbouring countries are usually ready to apply EU competition norms concerning certain practices that could undermine bilateral trade. That is valid for both anti-trust law as well as merger control. In both cases, the country wishes to take over the *EU-acquis*. The authorities of both sides should share also relevant information. As an example, we can cite Articles 253–261 of the EU-Ukraine Association Agreement.[81] Moreover, there is an obligation to introduce a system of national state aid control to be enforced by an independent body (Article 267

[77]The Text of 2012 is available at http://trade.ec.europa.eu/doclib/press/index.cfm?id=689 (last accessed 1 March 2017).

[78]Hoffmeister (2013), p. 399.

[79]See also Drexl et al. (2014).

[80]See Drexl (2004).

[81]OJ 2014 L 161/3.

(1) EU-Ukraine Association Agreement). That provision is remarkable, as the EU acquis itself does not go so far with respect to the EU Member States themselves. State aid control is exercised at the level of the European Commission, but European law does not require Member States to operate an own independent body to scrutinise national subsidies. All this shows that the effect of the competition chapter on the domestic reform agenda of a country such as the Ukraine may be considerable.[82]

A second model exists with respect to industrialised countries. For example, the FTA with Korea contains an elaborate competition chapter.[83] In Articles 11.3 und 11.4 of the EU-Korea FTA, the parties agreed on formulations that resemble the EU *acquis*, but which do not oblige Korea to apply the rules for purely national situations. Rather, the provisions aim at curbing anti-competitive behaviour which has an effect on EU-Korean trade. For subsidies, the agreement takes the WTO SCM agreement as a point of reference.

Third, the substantial standards for conducting a competition policy are further reduced with respect to the EPAs. True, there is a common reference point in Article 45 of the Cotonou agreement.[84] However, the EPAs themselves are not going much further. For example, Article 126 of the EU-CARIFORUM EPA outlaws cartels and the abuse of dominant positions, but does not contain any discipline on state aid.[85] This echoes the general principle already contained in Article 45(2) of the Cotonou Agreement, which also speaks in favour of cooperation between competition authorities (Article 45(3) of the Cotonou-Agreement).

3.7 Sustainable Development

Finally, the EU regularly negotiates a chapter about sustainable development. Starting with the CARIFORUM EPA and building on the text of the EU-Korea FTA, Title IX of the agreement with Peru and Colombia further advanced on the matter.[86] The Contracting Parties underline their efforts for achieving high labour and environmental standards (Article 268 of the FTA). In addition, investments shall not be attracted by lowering such standards, according to Article 277 of the FTA. There is also a list of international Conventions which are already binding on

[82]Croce and Stakheyeva (2014), p. 28.

[83]OJ 2011 L 127/6.

[84]Cotonou Agreement, OJ 2000 L 317/3.

[85]Economic Partnership Agreement between the CARIFORUM States, of the one part, and the European Community and its Member States, of the other part, OJ 2008 L 289/3.

[86]The text is available at http://trade.ec.europa.eu/doclib/press/index.cfm?id=691 (last accessed 1 March 2017).

both sides and whose implementation in good faith is re-affirmed. In the 2015 FTA with Vietnam,[87] the parties go a step further. Next to the commitment to properly comply certain core labour standards, there is even a best endeavour clause to ratify a couple of specifically mentioned international Conventions, which had *not* been binding on the country so far. Article 3(3) and (4) of the relevant chapter 15 reads:

> 3. Each Party will make continued and sustained efforts towards ratifying, to the extent it has not yet done so, the fundamental ILO conventions, and the Parties will regularly exchange information in this regard.
>
> 4. Each Party, will also consider the ratification of other conventions that are classified as up to date by the ILO, taking into account its domestic circumstances. The Parties will exchange information in this regard.

When it comes to enforcement, the EU is counting on domestic mechanisms and a structured civil society dialogue (Articles 281–282 of the EU-Columbia/Peru FTA). This also means that the chapter cannot be used to justify the suspension of the agreement.[88] However, this issue is subject to debate. In TTIP, there are many voices in the EU which wish to see stronger enforcement mechanisms in the sustainable development chapter.

4 Politicisation of the EU's Trade Policy

This overview about the bilateral developments since Lisbon would be incomplete without a short word about the internal constitutional changes. First, Article 207 (1) second sentence TFEU introduced the new point that also the commercial policy should foster the general objectives of the EU in its external diplomacy. This means that a couple of non-trade topics, such as the protection of human rights, the promotion of democracy or the strengthening of international environmental protection should be taken into account in trade policy-making. Clearly, trade sanctions for foreign policy goals have been long in the Union's tool box—the most recent case are the sanctions against Russia because of the annexation of the Crimea and the destabilisation of Eastern Ukraine.[89] But it has also used trade to help countries for humanitarian reasons. For example, when Pakistan was hit a natural disaster in summer 2010, the Commission proposed in October that year to grant specific trade concessions to the country.[90] However, the necessary WTO waiver

[87] The text is available at http://trade.ec.europa.eu/doclib/press/index.cfm?id=1437 (last accessed 1 March 2017).

[88] Hoffmeister (2012), p. 257.

[89] For details on the EU reaction in the Russia-Ukraine conflict see Hoffmeister (2016d), pp. 281–284.

[90] COM 2010 (522) final, 7 October 2010.

for this exercise was only granted in February 2012,[91] i.e. one and a half years later! This example shows rather powerfully that the political space for supportive trade measures is relatively small under the WTO framework. Nevertheless, in the Commission's 2015 trade policy communication, the "trade and" topics play a much bigger role than before.

Second, the European Parliament rose to become an important actor of the EU's trade policy. It is not only co-legislator in ordinary law-making under Article 218 (2) TFEU. As it also has to give consent to EU Trade agreements under Article 218 (6)(a)(v) TFEU, it plays a central role for those agreements. For them to pass, it is thus necessary that not only the Council, but also the Parliament supports their content. In turn, this means that the Commission must take into account the views of the EP with respect to controversial issues, such as trade in services, investment or sustainable development. If, however, the EP is split itself, the conducting of negotiations is more difficult for the Commission. Accordingly, resolutions taken by the EP plenary prior to the launch or during the course of negotiations, such as the one on TTIP[92] in 2015, have become an important reference point.

5 Conclusion

The trade relations between Europe and the rest of the world are changing dramatically. Ten years ago, it would have been unthinkable that the EU is conducting parallel FTA negotiations with the United States, Japan, Mercosur and India. At the same time, the bilateral net with Asian and Latin American countries extends. Only the Economic Partnership Agreements with the ACP countries lagged behind as long as the Union had been granting them unilateral preferences. Under the Belgian Trade Commissioner *De Gucht* (2010–2014) the spaghetti bowl *à la bruxelloise* lost its former regional focus on the neighbouring countries and received additional recipes from all around the world. The Swedish Trade Commissioner *Malmström* (2015–2016) continued with this trend, while putting more emphasis on some horizontal topics such as transparency and integration of non-trade policy objectives into the EU's trade policy.

At the same time, the noodles have become thicker and longer—as the EU FTAs reach many matters of domestic self-regulation and impose rules which should foster a positive trade and investment climate much beyond the mere question of market access. Hence, it is not surprising that the political debate about the scope and reach of such trade liberalisation has intensified over the last years, both in the European Parliament and in EU Member States. In order to describe the EU trade policy 7 years after Lisbon, one may therefore wish to use a more contemporary

[91] See https://www.wto.org/english/news_e/news12_e/good_02feb12_e.htm (last accessed 1 March 2017).

[92] Resolution of the European Parliament of 8 July 2015 concerning TTIP, A8-0175/2015.

image: it does not constitute the spaghetti for the Ministers of Economy any more, but has become the main dish of the Heads of States and Governments in almost every diplomatic summit of the European Union with third countries. Probably, the most obvious example of this trend is CETA. When the Council did not agree to sign this agreement, the EU summit with Canada was postponed until the very moment that the EU had overcome its internal division. The price to pay, though, was a considerable exposure of the EU's increasingly narrow domestic policy space to negotiate modern trade agreements.

References

Bhagwati J (1995) U.S. trade policy: the infatuation with FTAs. Columbia University Department of economics discussion paper series no. 726

Croce R, Stakheyeva H (2014) Competition law and state aid reform in light of the EU-Ukraine association agreement and its impact on business in Ukraine. Eur Compet Law Rev 35:23–28

Drexl J, Ruse-Khan HG, Nadde-Phlix S (2014) EU bilateral agreements and intellectual property: for better or worse?. MPI Studies on Intellectual Property and Competition Law, Springer, Berlin

Drexl J (2004) International competition policy after Cancún: pacing a Singapore issue on the WTO development Agenda. World Compet 27:419–457

Gaffney JP, Akcay Z (2015) European bilateral approaches. In: Bungenberg M, Griebel J, Hindelang S, Reinisch A (eds) International investment law and EU law. C.H. Beck, München, pp 186–201

Hoffmeister F (2016a) Bilaterale Entwicklungen in der EU-Handelspolitik in den ersten fünf Jahren nach Lissabon – ein Blick in die Spaghettischüssel à la bruxelloise (2010–2014). In: Bungenberg M, Herrmann C (eds) Die Gemeinsame Handelspolitik der Europäischen Union – Fünf Jahre nach Lissabon – quo vadis? Nomos, Baden-Baden, pp 190–213

Hoffmeister F (2016b) The contribution of EU bilateral investment agreements to the development of international investment law. In: Hindelang S, Krajewski M (eds) Shifting paradigms in investment law. Oxford University Press, Oxford, pp 357–376

Hoffmeister F (2016c) The EU procurement regime for third-country bidders – setting the cursor between openness and reciprocity. In: Kalimo H, Jansson M (eds) European economic law in times of crisis. Edward Elgar, Northampton, pp 76–88

Hoffmeister F (2016d) The practice of the European Union with respect to the territorial integrity of and border disputes between states. In: d'Argent P (ed) Droit des frontières internationales – the law of international borders, Paris, pp 277–290

Hoffmeister F (2015a) Die Verhandlungsagenda und -führung zwischen Stillstand und Modernisierung. In: Ehlers D, Pitschas C, Wolffgang HM (eds) Die WTO nach Bali – Chancen und Risiken. Fachmedien Recht und Wirtschaft, Frankfurt, pp 51–60

Hoffmeister F (2015b) Wider die German Angst – Ein Plädoyer für die Transatlantische Handels- und Investitionspartnerschaft. Archiv des Völkerrechts 53(1):47–50

Hoffmeister F, Alexandru G (2014) A first glimpse of light on the emerging invisible EU model BIT. J World Invest Trade 15:379–401

Hoffmeister F (2013) Aktuelle Rechtsfragen in der Praxis der europäischen Außenhandelspolitik. Zeitschrift für Europarechtliche Studien 16(4):385–401

Hoffmeister F (2012) Der Beitrag der EU zur Entwicklung des besonderen Völkerrechts. Europarecht-Beiheft 2:247–262

Pitschas C (2015) Transatlantic trade and investment Partnership und regulatorische Konvergenz. In: Ehlers D, Pitschas C, Wolffgang HM (eds) Die WTO nach Bali – Chancen und Risiken. Fachmedien Recht und Wirtschaft, Frankfurt, pp 152–154

Prieß HJ (2015) Neuerungen des Agreement on Government Procurement. In: Ehlers D, Pitschas C, Wolffgang HM (eds) Die WTO nach Bali – Chancen und Risiken. Fachmedien Recht und Wirtschaft, Frankfurt, pp 105–116

Reinisch A (2010) The division of powers between the EU and its member states "after Lisbon". In: Bungenberg M, Griebel J, Hindelang S (eds) Internationaler Investitionsschutz und Europarecht. Nomos, Baden-Baden, pp 99–111

Schill S (2016) The European Commission's Proposal of an "Investment Court System" for TTIP: Stepping Stone or Stumbling Block for Multilateralizing International Investment Law?. ASIL 20(9)

Treier V, Wernicke S (2015) Die transatlantische Handels- und Investitionspartnerschaft, Trojanisches Pferd oder steiniger Weg zum Olymp? Europäische Zeitschrift für Wirtschaftsrecht 26(9):334–340

Wiegand G, Schulz E (2015) The EU and its Eastern Partnership: political association and economic integration in a rough neighbourhood. In: Herrmann C, Simma B, Streinz R (eds) Trade policy between law, diplomacy and scholarship. Liber amicorum in memoriam Horst G. Krenzler. Springer, Heidelberg, pp 321–359

Zimmermann A (2009) Die neuen Wirtschaftspartnerschaftsabkommen der EU – WTO-Konformität versus Entwicklungsorientierung? Europäische Zeitschrift für Wirtschaftsrecht 20(1):1–6

Negotiating CETA with the European Union and Some Thoughts on the Impact of Mega-Regional Trade Agreements on Agreements Inter Partes and Agreements with Third Parties

Armand de Mestral

Abstract The negotiation of the CETA between the EU and Canada took a surprisingly long time given the many common interests of the two parties. The final stages of the negotiation involved last minute changes, the decision to agree on provisional application and the threat of a veto from Belgium. This was in part due to public concerns concerning investor-state arbitration, to the political decision to treat CETA as a mixed agreement under EU law and due to the rather surprising understanding that even the decision to adopt CETA on a provisional basis was subject to a rule of unanimity. The second part of this paper considers the legal consequences of CETA and other mega-regional trade agreements on relations between parties *inter se*, relations with third party states and the complex implications of a decision to withdraw.

Contents

The author thanks Lukas Vanhonnaeker, PhD candidate McGill University for his assistance.

A. de Mestral (✉)
McGill University, New Chancellor Day Hall, 3644 Peel Street, Room 517, Montreal, QC, Canada, H3A 1W9
e-mail: armand.de.mestral@mcgill.ca

M. Bungenberg et al. (eds.), *European Yearbook of International Economic Law 2017*, European Yearbook of International Economic Law 8,
DOI 10.1007/978-3-319-58832-2_14

1 Introduction

Canada finally completed negotiations and signed the Comprehensive Economic and Trade Agreement (CETA)[1] with the European Union on 30 October 2016. The negotiations began formally 7 years earlier[2] although the initial overtures by Canada were first made some years before that time.[3] This has probably been a learning experience for both sides. Canada has long experience of the difficulties of negotiating treaties with the United States but very little in dealing with the European Union (EU), especially under the new rules of the Treaty on the Functioning of the European Union (TFEU) which entered into force only in 1 December 2009. The EU, for its part, was breaking new ground on a number of trade issues, particularly those relating to its new competence over the protection of foreign direct investment and the related issues posed by the design of systems of investor-state arbitration (ISA). There were moments when it appeared that a successful outcome would require a miracle, but in the end both sides are relatively happy with the outcome of CETA. However, the agreement is only provisionally approved, and both sides are nervously struggling to understand the full legal implications of provisional application of a mixed treaty, and neither is absolutely certain that provisional application is certain to lead to permanent application.

The Canada-EU negotiation is a significant phenomenon in itself, but it reflects a broader reality, the emergence of mega-regional agreements. CETA is in many respects part of the phenomenon of mega-regional agreements reflected in the negotiation of the Trans-Pacific Partnership (TPP),[4] the Transatlantic Trade and Investment Partnership (TTIP)[5] and the Regional Comprehensive Economic Partnership (RCEP).[6] The scope of the CETA and the fact that it involves Canada on one side and the 28 member states of the EU, as well as the fact that many saw it as a precursor to the TTIP, makes it in every way comparable to these other even larger and more controversial trade agreements. The CETA negotiation therefore reflects much of the dynamics of these agreements and helps to understand the problems to which they give rise.

This paper therefore first covers the Canada-EU negotiation of CETA and then considers the broader questions posed by mega-regional agreements. The paper

[1]Comprehensive Economic and Trade Agreement between Canada and the European Union (CETA), signed 30 October 2016, to enter into force provisionaly on September 21, 2017.

[2]The negotiations were officially launched on 6 May 2009 at the Canada-EU summit in Prague.

[3]In particular, the CETA was negotiated as a result of a joint study by the European Commission and the Government of Canada titled "Assessing the costs and benefits of a closer EU-Canada economic partnership" that was released in October 2008. See http://trade.ec.europa.eu/doclib/docs/2008/october/tradoc_141032.pdf (last accessed 1 March 2017).

[4]Trans-Pacific Partnership (TPP), https://ustr.gov/trade-agreements/free-trade-agreements/trans-pacific-partnership/tpp-full-text (last accessed 1 March 2017).

[5]Regional Comprehensive Economic Partnership (RCEP), under negotiation.

[6]Transatlantic Trade Investment Partnership (TTIP), under negotiation.

then moves to the second prominent issue of the legal dimensions that emerge from the phenomenon of multilateral trading agreements. In this section among the debatable legal issues raised are those turning on the CETA treaty text itself in addition to questions on EU law relevant to mixed treaties and EU and public international law relevant to provisional application of treaties. In the next section, we shed light on the fact that the CETA negotiation also raises a broader range of issues involved in negotiating similar mega-regional agreements concerning the impact of mega-regional agreements on the parties inter se as well as their impact on third party states. Lastly, we evaluate if it is recognised that withdrawal from mega-regional agreements raises almost as many thorny problems as does their entry into force.

2 History of the CETA Negotiations

Canada was the original demander of a trade agreement with the EU. The 1968 Framework Agreement between Canada and the European Economic Community[7] had long outlived its usefulness, and apart from two agreements dealing with the sale of EU alcoholic drinks in Canada,[8] trade relations between the two parties were governed by WTO law and six outmoded investment protection agreements with Eastern European states dating back to the communist era.[9] Canada thus found itself with no special trade agreement governing access of its goods, services and investments into its second major trading partner at a time when other states were seeking agreements with the EU and when WTO commitments on goods, services and investments were not considered sufficiently extensive. Canada had been pressing its case with the EU Commission for some time without much success until the EU began to envisage the need for an agreement with the United States. At that point a negotiation with Canada became a more inviting prospect as a means of setting a precedent for broader access to the North American market. The two parties agreed to conduct an economic analysis of their relations with a view to determining the advantages and the feasibility of a trade agreement. The Scoping Exercise[10] conducted jointly by the parties, concluded in 2009, proved to be

[7]Framework Agreement for Commercial and Economic Cooperation Between Canada and the European Community, signed 6 July 1976, entered into force 1 October 1976, http://www.canadainternational.gc.ca/eu-ue/commerce_international/agreements-accords.aspx?lang=eng (last accessed 1 March 2017).

[8]Agreement between the European Economic Community and Canada concerning trade and commerce in alcoholic beverages, signed 28 February 1989, entered into force 28 February 2009, OJ 1989 L 71/42; Agreement Between Canada and the European Community on Trade in Wine and Spirit Drinks, concluded 16 April 2003, entered into force 1 June 2004, OJ 2004 L35/3.

[9]It is noteworthy, however, that most of these agreements were renegotiated after 2000.

[10]Joint Report on the EU-Canada Scoping Exercise, 5 March 2009, http://trade.ec.europa.eu/doclib/docs/2009/march/tradoc_142470.pdf (last accessed 1 March 2017).

positive and it was then agreed to commence negotiations in 2010 with a view to concluding a "comprehensive economic and trade agreement" on an ambitious scale.

Negotiations involved the usual twists and turns of trade agreements. It was clear from the start that both parties wished to cover virtually all aspects of their trading relationship. To make that point the EU insisted that the Canadian Provinces actually be at the negotiating table to ensure that provincial procurement and services markets be fully covered. Canada agreed to this unusual stipulation, something it does not normally do in WTO or bilateral trade and investment negotiations[11] and which the EU itself does not allow either in the composition of negotiating teams. The negotiations went through many negotiating rounds and produced a final text in 2014[12] which was and still is the most far-reaching free trade agreement (FTA) ever concluded between two parties. CETA may well become the standard against which other FTAs will be measured, very much as NAFTA became the most widely copied FTA after its adoption in 1994.

CETA covers trade in goods and services in greater depth than other contemporary FTAs. It opens services and procurement markets of both parties in ways that go well beyond other FTAs to which they are parties. Virtually all tariffs are eliminated and many service markets are opened for the first time. Investments are also protected in new and original ways, defining foreign investment broadly and covering pre and post-investment phases, but which importantly innovate with respect to the protection of the sovereign right of to regulate to protect public health, the environment, human rights, safety standards, labour standards etc. Canada agreed to protect a number of appellations d'origine and other trade mark protections sought by the EU. Entire chapters are included to ensure that trade does not endanger environmental or labour standards. CETA heralds the search for more harmonisation of regulatory standards and a common philosophy of regulation. There are extensive provisions for the establishment of joint committees to monitor and advance the achievement of the agreement. The whole agreement is subject to binding compulsory dispute settlement.

The negotiation of the CETA was not an easy process but it succeeded in the space of 4 years.[13] Paradoxically it was the process of formal adoption which caused the most difficulty. The first surprise was the length of time required for formal signature. Both parties announced that they had an agreement in 2014, but, with Canada very much the bemused onlooker, the EU then began a period of confused but intensive debate over the wisdom of concluding trade agreements. This period saw the successful adoption of the EU-Singapore[14] and the

[11]See de Mestral (2013a, b).

[12]After the negotiations were concluded on 1 August 2014 and the agreement presented on 25 September 2014 during the EU-Canada Summit in Toronto, the text became public on 26 September 2014.

[13]See http://europa.eu/rapid/press-release_STATEMENT-14-288_en.htm (last accessed 1 March 2017).

[14]EU-Singapore Free Trade Agreement, http://trade.ec.europa.eu/doclib/press/index.cfm?id=961 (last accessed 1 March 2017).

EU-Vietnam[15] FTAs, but also the potential derailing of the important EU—Ukraine Partnership Agreement[16] as well as an intense and very public debate over the wisdom and the apprehended dangers of concluding the TTIP with the United States. CETA was caught up in this debate and early adoption was its first victim.

The debate was both political and legal. An increasing number of EU citizens appeared to be uncertain as to the benefits of new FTAs in particular and of economic globalisation generally. The epicentre of the debate appeared to be the negotiations with the United States designed to lead to a major bilateral trade agreement—the TTIP. Some proponents of CETA suggested that it was being used by opponents of the TTIP as a stalking horse, on the assumption that if CETA were killed the TTIP would automatically be killed. Some suggested that opponents of CETA, motivated by increasing scepticism over the benefits of globalisation, were fundamentally opposed to international trade liberalisation as a basic trade policy. Other critics focussed on more specific issues such as agriculture, as traditional stumbling block in trade negotiations, or on the increasing public concern about the apprehended dangers of investor-state arbitration—a feature of CETA and the other agreements under negotiation. The Commission initially defended its position in favour of the FTAs as negotiated and sought to defend the integrity of its exclusive competence over the common commercial policy (CCP), including foreign direct investment, which had been added in 2009. However, it was faced with fierce public debate and diminishing political support, even from France and Germany, where the Ministers of Trade of both member states adopted a critical stance with respect to investor-state arbitration being kept in the investment chapters of the FTAs.

The first sign of serious danger to the FTAs was the agreement to refer the EU-Singapore FTA to the CJEU for an opinion as to its compatibility with EU competence.[17] The second and more serious problem for Canada took the form of increasing challenge to the idea that CETA fell entirely within exclusive EU competence over the CCP. This debate focussed particularly on the investor-state arbitration and the standards of protection afforded foreign investors, but it was not clear that the debate ended there. A number of member states were involved in a

[15]Framework Agreement on Comprehensive Partnership and Cooperation between the European Union and its Member States, of the one part, and the Socialist Republic of Vietnam, of the other part, signed 27 June 2012, http://investmentpolicyhub.unctad.org/Download/TreatyFile/3244 (last accessed 1 March 2017).

[16]Partnership and Cooperation Agreement between the European Communities and Their Member States and Ukraine, signed 14 June 1994, entered into force 1 March 1998, http://investmentpolicyhub.unctad.org/Download/TreatyFile/2430 (last accessed 1 March 2017).

[17]See CJEU, opinion 2/15, *Request for an opinion submitted by the European Commission pursuant to Article 218(11) TFEU*, OJ 2015 C 363/18. While the Court did not render its opinion, AG Sharpston rendered her opinion on this question on 21 December 2016. AG Sharpston considers that the Singapore Free Trade Agreement can only be concluded by the European Union and the Member States acting jointly. See AG Sharpston to CJEU, opinion 2/15, *Singapore Agreement*, ECLI:EU:C:2016:992. The CJEU rendered its decision on May 16, 2017. The decision is broadly in support of a wide reading of the EU's authority over foreign direct investment, but holds that authority over investor-state dispute settlement is largely reserved to Member States.

complex legal debate over the continued legal validity of some 190 bilateral investment agreements concluded with new member states before their entry into the EU, when they had been members of the communist bloc of states. The Commission argued that these BITs now fell under the CCP and should be abrogated. Several member states argued that these BITs constituted a separate legal regime which they had the right to maintain. Among these states was Germany, which took the position that the provisions of CETA on foreign investment protection and arbitration fell partially within national jurisdiction and thus maintained that CETA must be treated as a mixed agreement. The consequence of this position is that the adoption of CETA could not simply follow the procedures set out in the Article 218 TFEU but would require joint ratification by both the EU and by each member state.

CETA was thus caught up in a larger political and legal debate occurring within the EU and over which it had very little influence. Almost 2 years had passed since the conclusion of negotiations when in 2016 the Commission and Canada took a political and legal step designed to assuage some of the public criticism of the agreement and hopefully encourage its adoption. In October 2016 Canada and the Commission announced that the legal review of the text had finally been concluded after some 2 years. Apart from the usual drafting modifications and harmonisation of the language between the many chapters of a complex agreement, chapter 8 contained some surprising and rather extensive changes. The original chapter 8 provided for investor-state arbitration between dissatisfied foreign investors and the EU the new "scrubbed" version provided that disappointed foreign investors would have to take their disputes to an "Investment Tribunal" formed of Members named by the two parties and no longer could investors invoke arbitration. The Investment Tribunal would proceed according to arbitral rules but would clearly be a very different entity from the traditional panel of investment arbitrators. This was made all the more clear by the fact that the revised chapter 8 also provides for the constitution of a court of appeal from decisions of the Investment Tribunal. The fact that the adoption of an Investment Tribunal was a major policy initiative for the EU was brought home by the fact that the EU-Vietnam FTA was similarly modified—although this could not happen to the Singapore FTA which was already in process of formal adoption. Canada appeared to be a willing party to this change although the amendment came as a complete surprise to all commentators and appeared in the final text without any prior notification. Canada was left to hope in 2016 that the adoption of the Investment Tribunal would satisfy critics of the CETA and hasten its adoption by the EU.

The adoption of the Investment Tribunal was only the beginning of the surprises afforded by the saga of the adoption of the CETA. Chapter 32 of the CETA makes specific provision for "provisional application" of the agreement. This mirrors Article 218 of the TFEU which also provides for the possibility of provisional application. But arguably, provisional application under the TFEU is designed to speed the process of adoption of agreements where unanimous consent of all member states is clearly required, such as the accession of new members. It is not designed to deal with a political dispute where the Commission claims that the treaty falls under exclusive EU competence under Article 207 TFEU, nor is it designed to provide cover for a purely political decision to deem a treaty to be mixed in order to avoid offending the political susceptibilities of certain member states. But this is what happened. In the face of mounting opposition in some states, the decision was taken to deem CETA to be a mixed treaty, with the consequence that all 28 member states would be called upon to ratify. CETA chapter 32 about provisional application was invoked and it was proposed that the treaty be provisionally applied pending completion of the process of ratification.

But the saga did not end there. Instead it became clear that not only final ratification of the CETA required the approval of the 28 member states but also that the decision to authorise signature and provisional application would require unanimous consent in the Council. Arguably, this flies in the face of Article 218 TFEU, but much to Canada's surprise towards the end of 2016 it became clear that the Council would not authorise formal signature and provisional entry into force without unanimous consent. This unfortunate and legally questionable decision opened the door to opponents of the CETA in Belgium to seek to impede signature. Opponents of the CETA in the Region of Wallonia, some allege for partisan reasons or out of fears of new trade agreements, especially the much feared TTIP, sought to deny the consent of that Region and hence make impossible Belgian approval of CETA. The debate in Wallonia became so embroiled and confused that Canada was encouraged by Belgium and the EU to dispatch a former trade minister, then a Parliamentary Assistant to the Minister of International Trade and finally the Minister of International trade herself. The Minister was drawn into an unseemly and totally unprecedented negotiation with a subdivision of the Belgian federation of a declaratory document designed to allay the fears of local dairy farmers and opponents of investor-state dispute settlement. But all to no avail. The Minister had to return to Canada discouraged and empty handed.[18] Only the collective efforts of Belgian politicians and the heads of State of the EU succeeded in producing a tortured Belgian consent to signature and provisional application of CETA.

But the saga did also not end there. The final statement on provisional application[19] required the exclusion of provisions concerning investor-state dispute settlement in chapter 8 and related provisions on the financial services chapter and were communicated to Canada early in 2017. On top of this, to add to the general uncertainty, the Wallon authorities issued a statement that they could decide against continued provisional application of the whole of CETA and when and if they did so the process of Belgian approval and hence of EU approval of CETA should be

[18]See McGregor J, Canada-EU trade talks with Wallonia collapse as Freeland heads home, CBC New, 21 October 2016, http://www.cbc.ca/news/politics/canada-eu-ceta-brussels-friday-1.3815332 (last accessed 1 March 2017).

[19]Council Decision on the provisional application of the Comprehensive Economic and Trade Agreement (CETA) between Canada, of the one part, and the European Union and its Member States, of the other part, 2016/0220 (NLE). The Canadian bill to implement CETA was granted royal assent in May 2017 and the EU Parliament approved CETA in February 2017.

ended.[20] This final assertion is legally questionable but it serves to leave Canada entirely at the mercy of confused Belgian and EU politics. This is hardly a solid basis for entry into force of CETA and leaves Canada and presumably many in the EU even more uncertain than they were before as to the legal implications of a mixed treaty either in EU law or in international law, let alone for the text of CETA itself.

Canada thus only learned at the beginning of 2017 what provisions of the CETA text would be excluded from provisional application, or whether the promise of provisional application is conditional on the whim of any member state and even more uncertain as to whether and when CETA will enter definitively into force. For the EU some questions have been answered by the CJEU. The CETA and other trade agreements like it are mixed treaties. But is the decision to declare a treaty "mixed" a political or a legal decision? Is unanimity required for both the signature and the formal ratification of a mixed treaty? Clearly Canada still has much to learn about making treaties with the EU, and it appears that the EU has much to learn about its own law.

3 Challenges Posed by Mega Regional Trade Agreements

The fact of becoming party to a free trade agreement[21] or a customs union has always had multiple consequences both between the parties and for third parties. With the recent emergence of so called "mega-regional" trade agreements such as the Trans-Pacific Partnership (TPP)[22] or the negotiation of the EU-USA (TTIP)[23] or the East Asian Regional Commercial and Economic Partnership[24] (RCEP), these consequences have become even more evident than in previous years. The consequences are both economic and legal. The recent Brexit vote in the UK to leave the EU has served to highlight the fact that as many consequences may well attend the leaving as the joining of a mega-regional trade agreement. As mentioned before, we seek to discuss both the consequences of leaving and joining mega-regionals as a central question in this paper.

The expression mega-regional has only recently been applied to regional trade agreements (RTAs)[25] with the emergence of the TPP, TTIP, RCEP and CETA. It is

[20]See Déclaration du Royaume de Belgique relative aux conditions de pleins pouvoirs par l'Etat fédéral et les Entités fédérées pour la signature du CETA, http://ds.static.rtbf.be/article/pdf/ceta-belgique-ok-1477479201.pdf (last accessed 1 March 2017).

[21]Generally designated as regional trade agreements (RTAs) by the World Trade Agreement (WTO).

[22]The TPP negotiations were concluded and the text has been signed in Auckland, New Zealand on 4 February 2016. Subsequently, President Trump withdrew the signature of the United States.

[23]Transatlantic Trade and Investment Partnership, currently under negotiations.

[24]The TPP negotiations were concluded and the text has been signed in Auckland, New Zealand on 4 February 2016.

[25]The expression regional trade agreement is used by the WTO database to cover all bilateral and plurilateral trade agreements whether customs unions or free trade agreements; the expression

designed to capture the situation which occurs when a regional trade agreement is made between a significant number of parties, as in the case of the TPP, or between two extremely important trading partners, as with the TTIP. There is no universally accepted definition of the term. One may well assert that CETA, which is potentially the model for other agreements, must rightly be included in the category. Despite the recent emergence of the term, there have in fact been mega-regionals for many years. The European Union, a customs union rather than a free trade agreement, can certainly be described as mega-regional, as can the *Mercado Común Sudamericano* (MERCOSUR),[26] the Association of South-East Asian Nations (ASEAN),[27] the Andean Pact[28] and the various African regional trade agreements.[29] There is really very little to differentiate the modern mega-regionals from those major RTAs that have come before. The recently coined designation of mega is used largely to differentiate these agreements from the host of bilateral regional trade agreements which have been concluded in recent years. In the contemporary context, the designation mega-regional is meant to capture the increasing scope, importance and number of parties in comparison to less broad or significant agreements.

The focus of this part of the paper is on the consequences of conclusion of a mega regional agreement on the parties to the agreement but we also seek to evaluate a relatively unfamiliar question of the consequences that flow with respect to the relation of the parties to the agreement with third party states. More familiar is the question of the impact of adhesion to an RTA on existing multilateral commitments, particularly the WTO, which is governed by Article XXIV GATT and has been the object of considerable discussion over the years among trade law scholars, although many questions remain unresolved.[30] Similar questions are raised by the withdrawal of a state from a mega-regional FTA.

"preferential trade agreements" (PTAs) is used by the WTO to cover the relatively small number of non-reciprocal aid agreements.

[26]Additional Protocol to the Treaty of Asuncion on the Institutional Structure of Mercosur, entered into force 29 November 1991.

[27]ASEAN Free Trade Agreements, signed 28 January 1992, http://www.worldtradelaw.net/fta/agreements/afta.pdf (last accessed 1 March 2017).

[28]Codification of the Andean Subregional Integration Agreement (Cartagena Agreement), 25 June 2003, http://www.worldtradelaw.net/fta/agreements/cartagenafta.pdf (last accessed 1 March 2017).

[29]See e.g. Southern African Development Community (SADC) Free Trade Agreement, signed 17 August 1992, entered into force 5 October 1992, http://www.worldtradelaw.net/fta/agreements/sadcfta.pdf; Common Market for Eastern and Southern Africa (COMESA), signed 5 November 1993, http://www.worldtradelaw.net/fta/agreements/comesafta.pdf; East African Community Free Trade Agreement, http://www.worldtradelaw.net/fta/agreements/eacfta.pdf; Economic Community of West African States (ECOWAS) Revised Treaty, http://www.worldtradelaw.net/fta/agreements/ecowasfta.pdf; Economic and Monetary Community of Central Africa (CEMAC), http://www.worldtradelaw.net/fta/agreements/cemacfta.pdf (all last accessed 1 March 2017).

[30]See de Mestral (2013a, b).

The increasing number of parties to these agreements, their increased complexity, plus the inclusion of several forms of dispute settlement pose questions which may be answered by the terms of the treaties themselves or by the general law of treaties, but in the circumstances many potential problems must be the object of speculation and will only be fully recognized as they arise subsequent to the entry into force of the treaty.

These issues are highlighted by the provisions of the TPP and the CETA, which seek to anticipate and provide answers to these questions.

The CETA contains the following provisions:

> Article 1.5 Relation to the WTO Agreement and other agreements
> The Parties affirm their rights and obligations with respect to each other under the WTO Agreement and other agreements to which they are party.
> Article 1.6 Reference to other agreements
> When this Agreement refers to or incorporates by reference other agreements or legal instruments in whole or in part, those references include:
> (a) related annexes, protocols, footnotes, interpretative notes and explanatory notes; and
> (b) successor agreements to which the Parties are party or amendments that are binding on the Parties, except where the reference affirms existing rights.

The TPP approaches the issue in the following terms:

> Article 1.2: Relation to Other Agreements
> 1. Recognising the Parties' intention for this Agreement to coexist with their existing international agreements, each Party affirms:
> (a) in relation to existing international agreements to which all Parties are party, including the WTO Agreement, its existing rights and obligations with respect to the other Parties; and
> (b) in relation to existing international agreements to which that Party and at least one other Party are party, its existing rights and obligations with respect to that other Party or Parties, as the case may be.
> 2. If a Party considers that a provision of this Agreement is inconsistent with a provision of another agreement to which it and at least one other Party are party, on request, the relevant Parties to the other agreement shall consult with a view to reaching a mutually satisfactory solution. This paragraph is without prejudice to a Party's rights and obligations under Chapter 28 (Dispute Settlement).

The affirmation of their rights under the WTO and other agreements in CETA and the assertion of the intention to ensure the coexistence of the TPP with the Parties' other international agreements, suggests strongly that the Parties were fully aware of the existence of the issues, but that they were unable to resolve them in more explicit terms. The formulations adopted leave as many questions as they resolve and imply that many questions will only be resolved in the process of dispute resolution in subsequent years. It was open to the Parties to both agreements to make a detailed review of all potentially related commitments and to cover them by way of explicit exceptions or more explicit interpretative provisions. This they did only in a partial and incomplete fashion, either because of time or political constraints.

Interestingly, in two cases common to both treaties, taxation and air transport agreements, explicit provisions governing the relationship of these more specific agreements to the more general are provided giving precedence to the other treaties. The CETA also contains provisions in its final chapter 30 stating that it replaces the six investment protection treaties listed in Annex 30-A,[31] the Agreement on Mutual Recognition 1998[32] and the Veterinary Agreement 1998.[33] Since the CETA provides for a period of interim application it is stated that these agreements will cease to be in force during that period, but it is also stated that they would revive should the interim application not lead to permanent entry into force.[34] A further caveat is placed on the application of the investment agreements during the period of provisional application. Any dispute arising in that period may be continued or a claim for arbitration launched within a 3 year period after for facts occurring in the period of interim application.[35] Finally, Annex 30-A incorporates two pre-existing agreements between the EU and Canada on trade in alcoholic beverages into CETA and states that they "prevail" in the case of any inconsistency between them and the text of CETA.[36] Another example is the principle states in Article 351 TFEU that on joining the EU a new member State may maintain its existing treaties with third states but it must "eliminate incompatibilities" that may exist between these agreements and its commitments under EU law. These provisions serve to show that it is perfectly possible to deal with the relationship of pre-existing agreements between parties with great precision.

4 Relationships inter se

When a large number of states enter into a mega-regional trading relationship it is almost inevitable that these parties will already have pre-existing agreements between themselves. As a minimum they will be parties to the WTO which provides a minimum standard of treatment below which they are not entitled to go. Measures have to be taken to ensure that preferential rights of parties to the mega-regional agreement over and above WTO rights and duties are duly granted.

The larger the number of parties the more likely it is that they will already have concluded various trade commitments on a bilateral or even regional basis. For example, among the future TPP partners, the United States, Canada and Mexico are already partners in the 1994 North American Free Trade Agreement (NAFTA)[37] and, were NAFTA to be abrogated, the United States and Canada would revert to

[31] Article 30.8(1) CETA.
[32] Article 30.8(7) CETA.
[33] Article 30.8(8) CETA.
[34] Article 30.8(7) and (8) CETA.
[35] Article 30.8(3) and (4) CETA.
[36] Article 30.8(6) CETA.
[37] North American Free Trade Agreement (NAFTA), signed 17 December 1992, entered into force 1 January 1994.

the 1988 Canada US FTA.[38] Beyond this, the three states have a variety of bilateral border agreements designed to facilitate trans-border movement of goods while dealing with threats to security. The United States and Australia concluded a trade agreement in 2004[39] governing many aspects of their economic relationship but specifically excluding, at the Australian request, investor-state arbitration, yet investor-state arbitration is included in the TPP.[40] Japan has a number of trade and investment agreements with various South-East Asian countries which are signatories of the TPP.[41] Many of these agreements provide a lower standard of trade advantages than those guaranteed by the TPP but some provide for a higher standard on a bilateral or regional basis, and the countries involved may not wish to see these advantages abandoned after the entry into force of the TPP. In the case of the ASEAN countries, a number of special agreements have been concluded inter se dealing with a range of trade and investment issues including a general investment protection agreement.[42] Determining whether these agreements provide for advantages superior to those of the TPP may be a complex process which apparently has not yet been carried out.

Canada and the EU have concluded the CETA which is to enter into force provisionally on September 21, 2017.[43] CETA will require Canada to protect appellations d'origine on a range of European products when exported to Canada. NAFTA does not protect any appellations d'origine but it guarantees access of American products to Canadian markets. How will American producers react when their products have trouble entering the Canadian market because they violate the EU names or trade-marks to be protected under the CETA? CETA will open Canadian provincial service and government procurement markets to trade from the EU. How will American trading interests, accustomed to working very closely with Canadian clients, react when they find that Europeans have better access to provincial markets than they do?

None of the questions raised above appear to have received definite answers. The Canadian Chamber of Commerce has suggested a simple and straightforward approach: in every case the importer should be free to choose the least onerous terms of entry to the Canadian market. This approach may work for tariff rates, but

[38]Free Trade Agreement between Canada and the United States of America, signed 2 January 1988.

[39]Free Trade Agreement between Australia and the United States of America, signed 18 May 2004, entered into force 1 January 2005, http://investmentpolicyhub.unctad.org/Download/TreatyFile/2682 (last accessed 1 March 2017).

[40]Chapter 9, Section B TPP.

[41]See http://investmentpolicyhub.unctad.org/IIA/CountryBits/105#iiaInnerMenu (last accessed 1 March 2017).

[42]ASEAN Comprehensive Investment Agreement, signed 26 February 2009, entered into force 29 March 2012, http://investmentpolicyhub.unctad.org/Download/TreatyFile/3095 (last accessed 1 March 2017).

[43]European Parliament, CETA: MEPs back EU-Canada trade agreement, Press release, 15 February 2017.

does this imply that importers of products comparable to Emmental de Savoie[44] cheese from the United States into Canada need not respect the new protections which will be enjoyed by this French designated cheese in the Canadian market under CETA? Nor does it work so obviously for services. The TPP guarantees that no investor-state arbitral claim can be made against a party arising out of the regulation of tobacco.[45] But the TPP also guarantees MFN and national treatment in respect of investments.[46] Does this mean that tobacco companies wishing to launch a claim against a NAFTA party would not be bound by the TPP rule and thus could do so under Chapter 11 of NAFTA, which contains no such limitation and which is therefore to be considered the more favourable standard for North American tobacco companies?

One of the most far-reaching of the tariff commitments made under the TPP relates to automobiles and autoparts. The future TPP rules, which were negotiated by the United States and Japan on a bilateral basis before being discussed with Canada and Mexico, came as a very unpleasant surprise to the two countries which have benefitted from the relatively high North American content rules under Chapter 3 Annex B of NAFTA.[47] These content rules have ensured that it would be lucrative for companies to expand parts production in Canada and automobile production in Mexico. The new TPP rules considerably lower the content requirement on parts and autos from other TPP countries, thus ensuring that Japanese parts and autos produced in Japan using parts derived from supply chains in countries such as Thailand, will now qualify for access into the American market, thereby threatening existing automotive investments in Canada and Mexico previously made under NAFTA.

5 Relationships with Third Parties

While CETA refers to commitments to "each other" the TPP text refers more broadly to "their existing international agreements" thus encompassing trade agreements inter se and with third parties. The most significant are no doubt the commitments made under the WTO, to be discussed below, but a cursory examination of the WTO data base on RTAs makes it plain that many TPP Parties have other commitments with a wide range of parties whose interests can be affected either by the emergence of the TPP or other mega-regional agreement as a new phenomenon affecting international trade patterns or commitments made on a bilateral basis. Most TPP Parties have trade and investment agreements with a

[44]Annex 20-A CETA.

[45]Article 29.5 TPP.

[46]Articles 9.4 and 9.5 TPP.

[47]Chapter B, Annex 300-B (Textile and Apparel Goods) NAFTA.

number of non-TPP states. Canada has an investment agreement with China[48]—a state which apparently was not invited to join the TPP circle. Should China feel that its interests in Canada have been diminished by the advantages that the TPP Parties will enjoy? Equally, should China be concerned that European investors will enjoy more extensive protection and market access in Canada under CETA than those set out in the Canada-China FIPA? Should the United States and the EU ultimately conclude the TTIP, will this be deemed to create a new and over-mighty trading block able to set regulatory standards for the rest of the world? At the very least, there are issues of competitive relationships and broad political calculus caused to third parties by the emergence of a new mega-regional agreement. Developing countries may also suffer negative impacts as a consequence of the negotiation and conclusion of mega-regionals. If mega-regionals lead to regulatory convergence, their impact will likely not be limited to the member states but will have systematic impacts and could lead poorer nations that are not parties to the mega-regional being forced to adopt rich-nation standards in order to remain competitive.

The impact of the emergence of a mega-regional trade agreement may also be felt on the strictly bilateral level. Mexico, by virtue of NAFTA, or Chile and Peru and Colombia by virtue of their bilateral trade agreements with Canada,[49] have become major suppliers of fruit and vegetables in the Canadian market. It is not impossible that some agricultural and fisheries products from TPP Parties in South East Asia might compete with South American products in Canada. The same may be true for certain fisheries and agricultural products from Europe as a result of CETA. The United States has concluded bilateral agreements on trade and investment with a considerable number of countries.[50] These states are too numerous and varied to be able to highlight the potential impact of the entry into force of the TPP upon them all. Suffice it to say that the impact would be considerable given the importance of the US market as a destination for their imports. The broad implication is that the value of a bilateral trade agreement with a mega-regional member state may be seriously diluted for the third party state. An excellent example of this is Korea, which has RTAs and investment protection agreements with a number of

---

[48]Agreement Between the Government of Canada and the Government of the People's Republic of China for the Promotion and Reciprocal Protection of Investments, signed 9 September 2012, entered into force 1 October 2014, http://investmentpolicyhub.unctad.org/Download/TreatyFile/3476 (last accessed 1 March 2017).

[49]Free Trade Agreement between the Government of Canada and the Government of the Republic of Chile, signed 5 December 1996, entered into force 5 July 1997, http://investmentpolicyhub.unctad.org/Download/TreatyFile/2456; Free Trade Agreement between Canada and Peru, signed 29 May 2008, entered into force 1 August 2009, http://investmentpolicyhub.unctad.org/Download/TreatyFile/2568; Free Trade Agreement between Canada and Colombia, signed 21 November 2008, entered into force 15 August 2011, http://investmentpolicyhub.unctad.org/Download/TreatyFile/2569 (all last accessed 1 March 2017).

[50]See http://investmentpolicyhub.unctad.org/IIA/CountryBits/223#iiaInnerMenu (last accessed 1 March 2017).

TPP parties, and which has expressed concern that these agreements will diminish in value. This concern may well lead Korea to seek to be admitted to the TPP should the TPP go forward despite the United States.[51]

Non-member states to mega-regionals can pursue several strategies, some being better than others, either by pursuing one specific agenda or by combining different strategies. First, non-member states can do nothing. The "wait and see" option is certainly not the best but one that countries often converge to. In particular, small countries that do not have the power to influence negotiations of mega-regionals are often left with no other option. A second option for non-member states could consist in starting to withdraw from existing trade agreements as a sign of protest for not being included in mega-regionals. Third, they can engage in autonomous reforms. While not likely and not necessarily efficient, engaging in such unilateral regulatory reforms can help responding to and mitigating the effects of mega-regionals to which a given country is not a party to by reducing distortions in order to prepare the domestic firms to bigger markets created by mega-regionals. A fourth strategy could consist in joining the mega-regionals. This option is not without its pitfalls, however. While being most appealing for smaller countries, the danger is that these countries have less if no bargaining power compared to the larger countries parties to a given mega-regional and it might lead the former to be subjected to high standards established between the members of the mega-regionals. Accordingly, a better strategy might be to enter into bilateral negotiations with the members of the mega-regionals instead of becoming a party to the RTA as such. Because it means being subject to previously negotiated terms, larger countries are less likely to opt for this option. A fifth strategy would consist in competing with mega-regionals. Thus the TTIP can be seen as a way for the United States to compete with Canada and the CETA, other countries might engage in parallel negotiations to enter in a mega-regional agreement of their own. China appears to have chosen this strategy in leading negotiations for a Regional Comprehensive Economic Partnership (RCEP) which competes with the TPP. A final strategy could consist in re-engaging in WTO negotiations. While the progress on this front has been less than satisfactory during the last few years, the growing number of mega-regionals being negotiated and a certain harmonization of standards taking place, may provide the impulsion needed to make progress for negotiations at the multilateral level.

The situation of countries having bilateral relations with a free trade area (FTA) and a customs union (CU) may differ considerably; a member of a FTA remains free to entertain bilateral relations with third states with no legal duty of consideration to other FTA parties, while members of a CU are bound to third states as a single unit and are not free to make bilateral agreements. Thus states with agreements with individual TPP Parties must consider their agreements with all Parties, while states with agreements with the EU have only one agreement to consider.

[51]See Solis M, South Korea's Fateful Decision on the Trans-Pacific Partnership, Brookings, 18 September 2013, https://www.brookings.edu/research/south-koreas-fateful-decision-on-the-trans-pacific-partnership/ (last accessed 1 March 2017).

This simplifies matters with a CU at the time of conclusion of the agreement but, as will be discussed below, may greatly complicate matters if a state leaves a CU.

6 Departure from a Mega-Regional

The recent referendum vote in the United Kingdom to leave the EU has brought the consequences of departure from a mega-regional trade agreement into sharper focus. The complexity of the issues posed has doubtless been heightened by the fact that the EU is a customs union which has authority to negotiate relations with third states and, in the process of these negotiations, has supplanted the UK as the responsible negotiator and in many cases has set aside previously existing trade agreements of the UK. The UK is thus in a position that it will have to make new agreements on a range of issues such as the future terms of its WTO membership and bilateral trade relations, and in many cases air transport and investment. Where agreements have not been set-aside over the years as a consequence of EU membership there may be older and possibly unsuitable agreements which subsist but which will have to be reviewed and updated.

The UK is a founding member of the GATT and the WTO but since its relationship to other WTO Members is currently governed by the EU's bound tariff it will be necessary for the UK to renegotiate its relationship with other WTO parties. It is conceivable that the UK would be willing to accept all the existing EU tariffs as they are and it is possible that all other WTO Members will accept this arrangement, but it is by no means certain that this arrangement would be satisfactory to the UK or that others would find it acceptable. Since older Friendship, Commerce and Navigation (FCN) treaties or bilateral trade agreements or arrangements for Imperial or Commonwealth preferences have all disappeared with the UK's membership in the EU, the UK will have to negotiate new trade agreements with those states with which it plans to seek preferential agreements under Article XXIV GATT. It is conceivable that the UK may wish to remain subject to the bilateral arrangements made or being negotiated by the EU with Canada,[52] Mexico,[53] Singapore,[54] Vietnam,[55] the Ukraine[56] and others in recent years, but again this will depend on the UK's calculus of its trade interests and the

[52]CETA.

[53]Economic Partnership, Political Coordination and Cooperation Agreement between the European Community and its Member States, on the one part, and the United Mexican States, on the other part, signed 27 February 2001, entered into force 1 March 2001, http://investmentpolicyhub.unctad.org/Download/TreatyFile/2409 (last accessed 1 March 2017).

[54]EU-Singapore FTA.

[55]EU-Vietnam FTA.

[56]Association Agreement between the European Union and its Member States, of the one part, and Ukraine, of the other part, signed 27 June 2014, entered into force 1 January 2016, http://investmentpolicyhub.unctad.org/Download/TreatyFile/3123 (last accessed 1 March 2017).

reaction of the other parties. It is quite possible that these relationships will have to be renegotiated. A long and arduous negotiating process may well be before the UK if it wishes to establish such relationships.

Further examples of the difficulties that lie ahead for the UK are provided by air transport services agreements and investment protection agreements. As a result of a series of decisions of the European Court of Justice[57] followed by a succession of Regulations and Directives[58] the EU has assumed very broad competence over air transport services in and out of its territory. As part of this process the EU has replaced air transport bilateral agreements of its Member States with a number of countries such as the United States and Canada. Should the UK leave the EU it will no longer have air transport bilateral agreements with many of its most important partners and will have to renegotiate these agreements. It is by no means certain that the new UK bilaterals can be based on exactly the same terms as those negotiated by the EU, as the interests of states whose aircraft fly to and from the UK may not be the same as those prevailing while the UK was part of the EU. Something similar has occurred with the transfer from EU Member States to the EU of competence over "foreign direct investment" with the adoption of the Treaty on the Functioning of the European Union in 2009.[59] The EU has negotiated new trade agreements with Singapore,[60] Vietnam[61] and Canada[62] which all contain investment chapters. These agreements replace all pre-existing investment agreements made by Member States with third states. Fortunately for the UK perhaps, this process is not as far advanced as is the case with respect to air transport bilateral agreements and most investment protection agreements made by the UK in previous years are still in force.

7 Regionalism v Multilateralism

Mega-regional agreements are subject to Article XXIV GATT like all other RTAs and all WTO Members must meet the requirements of that article. Equally, measures taken pursuant to a mega-regional which are deemed to violate the rights of third states under the WTO are subject to WTO dispute settlement.[63] The

[57]See e.g. CJEU, case 167/73, *Commission v French Republic*, ECLI:EU:C:1974:35; CJEU, case 13/83, *Parliament v Council*, ECLI:EU:C:1985:220; CJEU, joined cases 209/84 to 213/84, *Ministère public v Asjes*, ECLI:EU:C:1986:188.

[58]See e.g. the first package of Regulations and Directives, OJ 1987 L 374/1; the second package of Regulations and Directives, OJ 1990 L 217/1; and the third package of Regulations and Directives, OJ 1992 L 240/1.

[59]Articles 206 and 207 TFEU.

[60]EU-Singapore FTA.

[61]EU-Vietnam FTA.

[62]CETA.

[63]See WTO, Understanding on the Interpretation of Article XXIV of the General Agreement on Tariffs and Trade, https://www.wto.org/english/docs_e/legal_e/10-24.pdf (last accessed 1 March

phenomenon of mega-regional trade agreements presents both broader policy questions as well as a number of interesting legal questions.

Given the difficulty that has been encountered over the last 15 years in bringing the Doha Round of Multilateral Trade Negotiations to a successful conclusion, one may well ask what may be the impact of the conclusion of several major mega-regionals? Should the CETA and the TPP be followed by successful conclusion of the RCEP and TTIP negotiations significant elements of the international trading community will have committed themselves to trade disciplines on a range of similar issues. The commitments in these mega-regionals go beyond those required of all WTO Members. It is not unreasonable to think that, despite the differences between these agreements, their conclusion might facilitate the search for new common standards at the WTO. Even if the process does not evolve on a voluntary basis with many states making similar commitments, should the EU and the United States agree on common approaches to regulation and standard setting in a future TTIP, the standards that they adopt is bound to have a significant impact on the whole international trading community, whether they become the formal WTO standard or not. The impact of these mega-regionals could well be similar to the adoption of a plurilateral trade agreement by a number of leading trading countries: the whole WTO membership would not be bound but the influence could be very significant.

A further complication can be posed by the incorporation into mega-regional trade agreements of different dispute settlement procedures. The more extensive the agreement and the greater the number of members the more potential there is for conflict between these provisions and those of the WTO DSU.[64] Agreements such as the TPP attempt to resolve potential conflicts by incorporating a binding choice of forum clause requiring respect for the forum chosen by the complainant. Article 28.4(2) TPP states that: "the forum selected (by the complainant) shall be used to the exclusion of other fora." The difficulty of such provisions is that while it is a clear rule of the TPP it is not necessarily going to be recognized as binding on a dispute settlement panel under the WTO DSU. Efforts to plead *forum non conveniens* before the WTO have always failed[65] and despite criticism of this position the most recent WTO decision[66] suggests that WTO panels and the Appellate Body are not ready to change this approach. The result is that it appears to be possible to take a dispute arising under the TPP or other such agreement to the WTO whenever the WTO agreement and covered agreement contain similar rules. Until the WTO AB indicates a willingness to take the existence of RTA dispute

2017); Appellate Body Report, *Turkey – Restrictions on Imports of Textile and Clothing Products*, WT/DS34/AB/R, 22 October 1999.

[64]See de Mestral (2013a, b).

[65]See e.g. Appellate Body Report, *Mexico – Tax Measures on Soft Drinks and Other Beverages*, WT/DS308/AB/R, 6 March 2006; Panel Report, *Argentina – Definitive Anti-Dumping Duties on Poultry from Brazil*, WT/DS241/R, 22 April 2003.

[66]Appellate Body Report, *Peru – Additional Duty on Imports of Certain Agricultural Products*, WT/DS457/AB/R, 20 July 2015.

settlement procedures and decisions into account, as it suggested might be possible in the *Brazil Retreaded Tires* case.[67] But subsequently this suggestion has yet to be followed.

For the reasons discussed above the relationship of RTAs and the WTO remain complicated, with the WTO quite reasonably claiming primacy, but rather unreasonably not proposing a viable modus vivendi. The emergence of mega-regionals may possibly force the issue of coexistence between RTAs and the WTO legal order, but it is by no means clear what might be the outlines of a more harmonious relationship.

References

de Mestral A (2013a) Dispute settlement under the WTO and RTAs: an uneasy relationship. J Int Econ Law 16(4):777–825

de Mestral A (2013b) The role of the Canadian provinces in the negotiation of the CETA: Canadian and European perspectives. In: Bungenberg M, Reinisch A, Tietje C (eds) EU and international investment agreements – open questions and remaining challenges. Nomos, Baden-Baden, pp 145–164

[67] Appellate Body Report, *Brazil – Measures Affecting Imports of Retreaded Tyres*, WT/DS332/AB/R, 3 December 2007.

Characteristics of EU Free Trade Agreements in a Legal Context: A Japanese Perspective

Yumiko Nakanishi

Abstract The European Union (EU) has concluded; it is currently negotiating Free Trade Agreements (FTAs) with third countries and has been negotiating an FTA with Japan since 2013. These FTAs have certain specific characteristics (related to competences, values and objectives) emerging from the EU's legal order. Bilateral and multilateral FTA negotiations are occurring all over the world and these negotiations and transactions are all influencing one another. Global multilateral negotiations form a soft coherence of the agreement texts, which in turn leads to a kind of approximation of the text of FTAs worldwide. The EU is an important trade partner that accounts for 10% of Japanese total import and export values (the third largest value after China and USA). In the negotiations regarding the EPA between the EU and Japan the specific characteristics of the EU can be permeated. The content of negotiations are influenced by other FTAs of the EU.

Contents

Y. Nakanishi (✉)
Graduate School of Law, Hitotsubashi University, Tokyo, Japan
e-mail: yumiko.nakanishi@r.hit-u.ac.jp

M. Bungenberg et al. (eds.), *European Yearbook of International Economic Law 2017*, European Yearbook of International Economic Law 8,
DOI 10.1007/978-3-319-58832-2_15

1 Introduction

The European Union (EU) has concluded and is negotiating Free Trade Agreements (FTAs) with third countries. For example, the EU concluded an FTA with Canada, i.e. the Comprehensive Economic and Trade Agreement (CETA) and FTAs with South Korea, Singapore and Vietnam. The Union is negotiating an FTA with the US, i.e. the Transatlantic Trade and Investment Partnership Agreement (TTIP) and an FTA with Japan, i.e. the Economic Partnership Agreement (EPA). Those agreements have similar elements because they have influenced and continue to influence each other. At the same time, those FTAs have some specific characteristics that come from the Union's Treaties and the Union's legal system.

This chapter aims to analyse the FTAs of the Union and show specific characteristics from a third country perspective, especially a Japanese perspective. The EU and Japan agreed to start a scoping process to conclude an FTA on 28 May 2011. After that, both sides began to negotiate in April 2013. The Eighteenth Round of FTA/EPA negotiations between the EU and Japan took place from April 3 to 5 2017 in Tokyo. About four years later, on 6 July 2017 the EU and Japan reached an agreement in principle on the main elements of the EPA. Issues regarding Investor-to State Dispute Settlement (ISDS) and invstment court should continue to be negotiated. In the website of the Ministry of Foreign Affairs of Japan (MOFA), you can find a factsheet regarding the EPA between the EU and Japan in Japanese, although there are still no draft texts of the EPA.[1] Soon, it will be easier to find detailed information regarding the negotiations on the MOFA website and that of the Ministry of Economy, Trade and Industry in Japan (METI). Japan respected the framework of the World Trade Organisation (WTO) and hesitated to conclude bilateral and/or multilateral agreements with the third countries and regions. Therefore, in comparison with the other countries, Japan got off to a late start. Now, however, Japan is eager to negotiate and conclude trade and investment agreements with other countries and regions.

First, this study will discuss how EU-specific ideals strongly permeate both the negotiations and the text of the agreements, which the EU has concluded and is negotiating. Second, this study will examine the mutual influences between the FTAs of the EU and the TPP as well as the role that the EP and public opinion play in negotiations. Finally, based on those discussions, negotiations between the EU and Japan will be explored.

[1]Ministry of Foreign Affairs of Japan, http://www.mofa.go.jp/mofaj/files/000270758.pdf (last accessed 13 July 2017).

2 Specific Characteristics of the Free Trade Agreements and the EU Treaties

2.1 *Competences*

2.1.1 Competences and Mixed Agreements

From a third-country perspective, it is hard to understand the division of competences between the EU and its Member States. Japanese ministries have difficulties recognizing with whom they should negotiate and which parties are responsible and have competences. Recently, the chief negotiator for the EU, *Mauro Petriccione*, Deputy Director-General for Trade and the chief negotiator for the Japanese, Ambassador *Yoichi Suzuki*, were in their eightteenth round of negotiations. *Petriccione* has been the chief negotiator since the first round of negotiations in 2013. The Commission asked the Council for a mandate for Japan-EU negotiations in July 2012 and since then the Commission has been responsible for the negotiations.

The Union can be active so far as competences are conferred to it by the EU Treaties (the principle of conferral, Article 5 TEU). If the Union wishes to conclude an FTA, it needs competence to do so. If the Union does not have comprehensive competence to conclude the FTA and the necessary competences for concluding it are shared between the EU and its Member States or some competence remains in the Member States, the Union cannot then conclude it alone but is obliged to do so with the EU Member States together. The form of the FTA will be a mixed agreement. For example, the FTA between the EU and South Korea is a mixed agreement.[2] The FTA was signed on 6 October 2010 in Brussels, ratified by the EU and its Member States and entered into force on 13 December 2015. The legal bases for concluding it are Articles 91, 100(2), 167(3) and 207 TFEU. Articles 91 and 100 TFEU are related to transport, Article 167(3) TFEU is related to culture and Article 207 TFEU concerns common commercial policy. The name of the FTA is "trade" agreement, but in fact the FTA is a comprehensive agreement. The Commission is eager to let the Union conclude agreements alone, but in fact agreements are often concluded in the form of mixed agreements. Opinion 2/15 addresses competence issues regarding the FTA between the EU and Singapore. The Court delivered the Opinion on 16 May 2017. According to it, the EU has exclusive competence except ISDS issues and non-direct investment.[3]

2.1.2 Mixed Agreements and Brexit

If subject matters of a FTA do not only cover trade, but also investment, intellectual property rights, transport, sustainable development, environment and others and as

[2] OJ 2011 L 127/1.

[3] CJEU, case Opinion 2/15, ECLI:EU:C:2017:376.

a result the EU does not have exclusive competence to conclude it then the FTA might be a mixed agreement with the EU Member States. Understanding the division of competences between the EU and its Member States can be problematic.[4] Even in the case of shared competences, pre-emption may occur if the EU takes measures in certain fields.

A real problem might now happen because of the Brexit. The UK will be the first country to withdraw from the Union according to Article 50 TEU. It is uncertain how the Brexit will affect existing FTAs and their ongoing negotiations. The third countries that concluded FTAs with the EU and its Member States and want to continue the relationship with the UK now must negotiate regarding application of the FTAs and their effect on tariffs, conditions and other concerns with the UK and the Union again. Keidanren, the Japan Business Federation, is afraid that the Brexit would delay the ongoing negotiations. Japanese companies are concerned about the influence of the Brexit because more than 1000 companies including Toyota, Nissan, Honda and Hitachi invest money in the UK. They have enjoyed and expected merits from the UK's membership in the Union, i.e. a single market. Japan is obliged to continue to negotiate an EPA with the EU and at the same time consider an agreement with the UK.

2.1.3 Enlargement of Competences and Subject Matters of the Free Trade Agreements

The EU (formerly the Commission) has been conferred competences through the Treaties. At the beginning of the European Economic Community in 1958, the Community (now the Union) had competences in certain limited fields such as agriculture and the common market. The custom union launched on 1 July 1968 and the common customs tariff was introduced. It was unclear whether the Community could conclude agreements other than trade agreements (Article 113 TEEC) and association agreements (Article 238 TEEC) until a series of case law in 1970.[5] After this series of case law, the existence of implied external powers was accepted and the Community was able to conclude agreements so far as the Community had internal competences.

The Single European Act (SEA) conferred some new competences to the Community in 1987. According to the SEA, the Community procured explicit competences in the fields of public health, environment, research and development and economic and social cohesion. The Treaty of Maastricht transformed the EEC into the European Community (EC) in 1993. The Community was no longer just an economic community but was conferred further new competences in the fields of the economic monetary union, social policy, consumer protection, trans-European

---

[4]Cf. Rosa (2014).

[5]CJEU, case 22/70, *AETR*, ECLI:EU:C:1971:32; CJEU, joined cases 3/76, 4/76 and 6/76, *Kramer*, ECLI:EU:C:1976:114; CJEU, opinion 1/76, ECLI:EU:C:1977:63.

networks, industry, development cooperation, culture and education. The Treaty of Amsterdam introduced new areas of freedom, security and justice in 1999 and the Treaty of Nice made institutional changes resulting in the enlargement of the EU in 2002. Further, the Treaty of Lisbon, which commenced on 1 December 2009, conferred the Union some new competences in the fields of intellectual property, sports, civil protection, humanitarian aid, tourism, administrative cooperation, energy, space and common commercial policy.

Those Treaties have enlarged the scope of the Union's (formerly the Community's) competences. As a result, subject matters of agreements that the Union concludes are becoming more comprehensive. The Treaty of Lisbon added new competences to the EU in the field of common commercial policy and now the EU has exclusive competences regarding trade in service, the commercial aspects of intellectual property as well as foreign direct investment (Articles 207 and 3 TFEU).[6]

The TTIP between the EU and the US, the CETA between the EU and Canada and the EPA between the EU and Japan cover not only trade but also intellectual property rights (including geographical indication), investment, environment and sustainable development and others. Those changes happened with the enlargement of the Union's competences.

2.2 *Values, Objectives and Standards*

Specific characteristics of the FTAs derive from the EU's own values, objectives and standards.

2.2.1 Political Principles and the Free Trade Agreements

Particularly since the Treaty of Maastricht, the EU has used political conditionality when it gives economic assistance to the African, Caribbean and Pacific countries (ACP countries). Amended Article 5 of the Lomé IV agreement of 1995 introduced so-called human rights clauses (i.e. essential element clauses) stating that they must respect human rights, democratic principles and the rule of law. If a contracting country fails to fulfil its obligations, the country cannot receive assistance from the Union. This is the so-called "carrot and stick" approach. The EU has concluded such an agreement with not only the ACP countries but also other countries in the context of the enlargement policy, the neighbourhood policy, the development policy, the economic and technical cooperation and so forth.[7]

[6]See Bungenberg and Herrmann (2013).

[7]European Commission, COM (95) 216, p. 7 et seq.: "On the inclusion of respect for democratic principles and human rights in agreement between the Community and third countries". Nakanishi (2014), p. 13.

After the Treaty of Lisbon, the TEU laid down the Union's own values in Article 2 TEU—respect for human dignity, freedom, democracy, equality, the rule of law and respect for human rights. Article 21 TEU establishes political principles that are applied in the EU's external action. The Union's values and political principles are almost the same, meaning that the EU applies its own values in its external activities. As a result, the Union is eager to negotiate and conclude binding political agreements in parallel with FTAs. For example, the EU concluded a Framework Agreement with South Korea, which is a comprehensive agreement that includes political elements.[8] The EU concluded a Partnership and Cooperation Agreement (PCA) with Singapore and a new PCA with Vietnam. These documents and how they came to be—including their increased focus on human rights issues—are coming to bear on negotiations between the EU and Japan.

As for Japan, it was only interested in concluding an FTA with the EU. However, the EU requested that Japan negotiate a binding political agreement and a strategic partnership agreement (SPA) in a parallel manner. Therefore, recently, the EU and Japan agreed in principle on the SPA as well as the EPA.[9]

2.2.2 Sustainable Development

The concept of sustainable development and the protection of nature and the future generation came from the 1987 book "Our Common Future," i.e. the Brundtland report. In the EU the Treaty of Maastricht introduced the idea of sustainable development. The fifth environmental action programme in 1993 was titled "toward sustainability" and the Treaty of Amsterdam used the word "sustainable development." Now, after the Treaty of Lisbon, the concept of sustainable development is a key concept for the EU. The preamble of the TEU states

> [the Member States] determined to promote economic and social progress for their peoples, taking into account the principle of sustainable development.

Article 3 TEU establishes that

> [the Union] shall work for the sustainable development of Europe [...] aiming at full employment and a high level of protection and improvement of the quality of the environment.

Current FTAs that the EU concluded or is negotiating have a specific chapter for sustainable development.[10] The concept of sustainable development is used not

[8]European External Action Service, http://eeas.europa.eu/korea_south/docs/framework_agreement_final_en.pdf (last assessed 1 March 2017).

[9]Ministry of Foreign Affairs of Japan, http://www.mofa.go.jp/erp/ep/page25e_000107.html (last accessed 1 March 2017); as for SPA, e.g., Prado CD, Prospects for the EU-Japan Strategic Partnership, 2014, http://cdnsite.eu-japan.eu/sites/default/files/publications/docs/eujpstrategicpartnership.pdf (last accessed 1 March 2017).

[10]Bartels (2015), p. 82.

only in the context of environmental protection but also in the context of economic and social development. For example, Article 22.1(1) in chapter 22 (trade and sustainable development) of the CETA states

> [t]he Parties recognise that economic development, social development and environmental protection are interdependent and mutually reinforcing components of sustainable development.

Paragraph 2 of the same Article states that

> [t]he Parties underline the benefit of considering trade-related labour and environmental issues as part of a global approach to trade and sustainable development.

The CETA establishes the rights and obligations related to labour and environmental protection in chapter 23 (trade and labour) and 24 (trade and environment). All of this demonstrates that the concept of sustainable development has become wider and more comprehensive than in the past.

2.2.3 Environment

The EEC aimed for economic integration at the beginning, but environmental protection became increasingly important.[11] After SEA, the Community has an explicit individual legal basis for environmental protection. In addition, the principle of environmental integration was introduced in Article 130r TEEC and stated that environmental protection requirements shall be a component of the Community's other policies. Now, after the Treaty of Lisbon, Article 11 TFEU regulates,

> environmental protection requirements must be integrated into the definition and implementation of the Union's policies and activities with a view to promoting sustainable development.

The principle of environmental integration must now apply to common commercial policy. As a result, the EU is obliged to take environmental protection into consideration in negotiating FTAs with third countries. In fact, all current FTAs include environmental elements.

2.2.4 Animal Welfare

The concept of animal welfare does not belong to the Union's values which are published in Article 2 TEU. However, the concept of animal welfare has a special position in the EU's legal order.

Measures on animal welfare already existed in the 1970s.[12] The Treaty of Maastricht annexed declaration stated that the government conference required EU institutions and Member States to fully consider the welfare requirements of

[11] As for development of EU environmental law, see Krämer (2015), p. 4 et seq.

[12] Nakanishi (2016b), pp. 88–91.

animals when drafting and implementing Community measures on common agricultural policy, transport and the internal market. This declaration was known as the "soft" integration clause.[13] The Treaty of Amsterdam includes a special protocol on the protection and welfare of animals. Article 13 TFEU regarding animal welfare is unique. According to the Treaty of Lisbon, the provision establishes that the Union and the Member States shall pay full regard to the welfare requirements of animals because animals are sentient beings. The Treaties were based on economic integration and the idea of anthropocentrism, but the Union now pays attention to animal pains.

Some FTAs that the EU concluded or is negotiating refer to animal protection and welfare, obliging the third countries to consider the concept of animal welfare.[14]

2.2.5 Standards

It is said that the EU has normative power, which means that the Union's standards would be global standards. Regulations such as the EU measures have general application and are directly applicable in the Member States (Article 288 TFEU). Regulation (EC) No 1907/2006 concerning the Registration, Evaluation, Authorisation and Restriction of Chemicals (REACH)[15] is an EU internal measure. However, companies in third countries' are obliged to comply with the standards of the REACH regulation if they export goods to the EU Member States. A recommendation by Keidanren states that given the fact that regulations similar to the EU REACH rules prevail as a global standard, Japan needs to make its Act on the Evaluation of Chemical Substances and Regulation of Their manufacture, etc. (the Chemical Substances Control Law) commensurate with international trends in chemicals management.[16] METI, the Ministry of the Environment, Japan External Trade Organization (JETRO) and other chemical-related organisations provide information to help Japanese companies understand the REACH regulation.[17] Regulation (EC) No 1223/2009[18] on cosmetic products (and former Directives 76/768/EEC,[19] 93/35/EEC,[20] 2003/15/EC[21]) has influenced Japanese cosmetic

[13]Edward and Lane (2013), p. 419.

[14]Nakanishi (2016c), pp. 138–141.

[15]OJ 2006 L 396/1.

[16]Keidanren, Recommendations for Japan-EU Regulatory Cooperation, 17 March 2015, http://www.keidanren.or.jp/en/policy/2015/024_recommendations.html (last accessed 1 March 2017), p. 10; cf. Nakanishi (2017), p. 303 et seq.

[17]Ministry of Economy, Trade and Industry of Japan, http://www.meti.go.jp/policy/chemical_management/int/files/reach/080526reach_kaisetusyo.pdf (last accessed 1 March 2017); see also http://www.chemicalmate.jp/cm/reach4/ (last accessed 1 March 2017).

[18]OJ 2009 L 342/59.

[19]OJ 1976 L 262/169.

[20]OJ 1993 L 151/32.

[21]OJ 2003 L 66/26.

companies.[22] Most of them stopped animal testing for cosmetic products in order to comply with the EU measures. As for data protection, the European Parliament and Council adopted Regulation (EU) 2016/679 on the protection of natural persons with regard to the processing of personal data and on the free movement of such data (General Data Protection Regulation) on 27 April 2016.[23] According to Article 45 of the Regulation

> a transfer of personal data to a third country or an international organisation may take place where the Commission has decided that third country [. . .] ensures an adequate level of protection.

This provision is related to Japanese companies who handle consumers' data on their websites. The level of the EU's data protection is now the highest in the world. It is not easy for third countries to ensure the required level of protection.[24]

In the report of impact assessment regarding the FTA between the EU and Japan the following phrases can be found, "there are two issues dealt with in the FTAs that fall within the broad ambit of human rights but without explicitly invoking that term: data privacy (that links to the right to privacy) and the related questions of cultural diversity and freedom of expression" and "EU FTAs have also regulated exchange of personal data in e.g. EU Korea, CETA under e-commerce and financial services annexes."[25] Those standards can directly or indirectly affect negotiations with third countries.

3 EU Free Trade Agreements with Third Countries

3.1 *Mutual Influences*

3.1.1 Overview: EU Free Trade Agreements and the TPP

The EU began to negotiate an FTA with South Korea on 23 April 2007 and the parties initialled the FTA on 15 October 2009. Entering into force on 1 July 2011, it was the first FTA between the EU and Asian countries. South Korea was eager to conclude FTAs with third countries and succeeded in concluding an FTA with the US as well. At the beginning, in 2007, the Union tried to negotiate for a region-to-region FTA with the Association of South East Asian Nations (ASEAN), but it did not succeed in this. Thereafter, the EU started negotiating with each ASEAN

---

[22] Nakanishi (2016b), p. 109.

[23] OJ 2016 L 119/1.

[24] Cf. as for the US, CJEU, case C-362/14, *Schrems v Data Protection Commissioner*, ECLI:EU:C:2015:650.

[25] European Commission, Trade Sustainability Impact Assessment of the Free Trade Agreement between the European Union and Japan, 2015, http://trade.ec.europa.eu/doclib/docs/2015/june/tradoc_153541.pdf (last accessed 1 March 2017), pp. 67 and 85.

country individually. The negotiations with Singapore launched in 2007 and the FTA was concluded on 17 October 2014, but it is still not formally signed as the competences issue regarding the FTA is pending before the Court of Justice of the EU. The negotiations between the EU and Vietnam began in June 2012 and finished in December 2015. The EU and Canada launched CETA negotiations in May 2009. The CETA was singed on 30 October 2016 and approved by the European Parliament on 15 February 2017. The EU and the US began to negotiate TTIP in June 2013.

Japan began to negotiate the EPA with the EU in April 2013 and the negotiations are ongoing. On the other hand, Japan was accepted to participate in negotiations of the Trans-Pacific Partnership (TPP) on 20 April 2013. The TPP was signed on 4 February 2016.[26] There are 12 signatory countries of the TPP: Australia, Brunei, Canada, Chile, Japan, Malaysia, Mexico, New Zealand, Peru, Singapore, the US[27] and Vietnam. Some of them have concluded or are negotiating FTAs with the EU.

3.1.2 Mutual Influence Between the EU Free Trade Agreements: Investment Court as an Example

The EU and Canada finished CETA negotiations in August 2014. The draft text of the CETA did not cover investment-related and appellate tribunals at that time. After that, in 2015, there were discussions in the EP regarding the investor-state dispute settlement (ISDS), which was related to TTIP. The following is decided as a recommendation toward the Commission,

> to ensure that foreign investors are treated in a non-discriminately fashion, while benefiting from no greater rights than domestic investors, and to replace the ISDS system with a new system for resolving dispute between investors and states which is subject to democratic principles and scrutiny, where potential cases are treated in a transparent manner by publicly appointed, independent professional judges in public hearings and which includes an appropriate mechanism, where consistency of judicial decision is ensured, the jurisdiction of courts of the EU and of the Member States is respected, and where private interests cannot undermine public policy objectives.[28]

ISDS is considered a threat to democracy. Facing such a recommendation by the European Parliament, the EU's proposal for Investment Protection and Resolution of Investment Disputes for the TTIP was published on 12 November 2015 by the Commission. It contains the investment court system (Articles 9–30, sub-section 4, section 3 Resolution of Investment Disputes and Investment Court System). The

---

[26]As for the text of the TPP, see Ministry of Foreign Affairs and Trade of New Zealand, https://www.mfat.govt.nz/en/about-us/who-we-are/treaty-making-process/trans-pacific-partnership-tpp/text-of-the-trans-pacific-partnership (last accessed 1 March 2017).

[27]The US withdrew from the TPP on 23 January 2017.

[28]European Parliament resolution of 8 July 2015 containing the European Parliament's recommendations to the European Commission on the negotiations for the Transatlantic Trade and Investment Partnership (TTIP), 2014/2228(INI).

text of the CETA as of September 2016[29] establishes tribunals for investment issues (Article 8.27) and appellate tribunals (Article 8.28) in chapter eight, "investment". Further, Article 8.29 governs the establishment of a multilateral investment tribunal and appellate mechanism, which is not contained in the proposal of the TTIP. According to Article 8.29, the Parties shall pursue with other trading partners the establishment of a multilateral investment tribunal and appellate mechanism for the resolution of investment disputes. It is a new idea.

The EU and Singapore concluded their FTA in October 2014, which was before the proposal for the investment tribunal of the TTIP. On the other hand, the FTA between the EU and Vietnam contains the investment tribunal provisions. Although the negotiations between the EU and Vietnam began in June 2012, they finished in December 2015. As a result, the investment tribunal was taken into consideration. Sub-section 4 "Investment Tribunal System" of section 3 "Resolution of Investment Disputes" establishes a permanent investment tribunal (Article 12) and a permanent Appeal Tribunal (Article 13). This investment tribunal system is similar to that of the TTIP proposal (Article 9 and 10 of the investment chapter of the TTIP).

Mutual influences among the FTAs of the EU can be detected. In fact, the negotiations of the EPA between the EU and Japan are also influenced by this series of investment tribunal issues. It will be referred to later.

3.1.3 Mutual Influences Between the Free Trade Agreements and the TPP

The WTO does not function well except in dispute settlement. The number of FTAs, both bilateral and multilateral, is increasing to fill this shortfall. FTAs are becoming more comprehensive and mega-FTAs are appearing, all of them seemingly influenced by each other. Sustainable development including labour and environment protection is an important subject matter of the FTAs of the EU. For example, CETA has chapters for sustainable development, labour and environment. The TPP has chapter 19 "labour" and chapter 20 "environment". In chapter 20 the concept of sustainable development is discussed, while in chapter 19 the concept does not appear, implying that the concept is used only in the context of environmental protection. It differs from the FTAs of the EU. The TPP includes a chapter for investment and one for intellectual property. Chapter 18 also contains geographical indication, the protection of which has been a request from the EU that the parties of the TPP subsequently recognized. The TPP was already signed and published and therefore, the content, composition and style of the text might affect future negotiations between the EU and third countries, especially when using the US and Japan as a model.

[29]Council of the European Union, http://data.consilium.europa.eu/doc/document/ST-10973-2016-INIT/en/pdf (last accessed 1 March 2017).

The report of the Commission states

> various recent agreements, such as CETA, have introduced specific procedural measures to strengthen cooperation. The TPP and TTIP negotiations are considering similar measures.[30]

Multilateral negotiations might form a soft coherence between the texts of agreements. It can be understood as a kind of approximation of law through them.

3.2 The European Parliament and Public Opinion

It is customary that negotiations and related draft texts are disclosed. The decision to make public only a few documents during the negotiations of the TPP was criticised, although the parties did so in order that they could hold their cards close to their chest during the negotiations.

However, as for the TTIP, there was (and still is) strong criticism of the lack of transparency by the NGO and the parliamentarians of the European Parliament and national governments. Facing such criticism, more and more documents are published through the website of the Commission, thereby increasing the transparency of the negotiation process.

The EP and the NGO have participated in debates of the EU's FTAs. One example is the investment court/tribunal as mentioned above. Another example is the so-called "right to regulate". The importance of this right is emphasized by many non-governmental organisations (NGO) and consumer-protection advocates. These organisations are concerned about the deterioration of the EU regulation standards regarding environmental, consumer or social protection during negotiations with the US. Article 2(1) of section 2 of chapter II "Investment" in "Trade in services, investment and e-commerce" of the TTIP lays down that "the provisions of this section shall not affect the right of the Parties to regulate". As mentioned later, the right to regulate is a discussion topic in the negotiations between the EU and Japan.

4 Negotiations Between the EU and Japan

4.1 Free Trade Agreements of Japan

Japan concluded and ratified FTAs with nine Asian countries[31] and ASEAN, Pacific (Australia), Central and South America (Mexico, Chile and Peru) and a European

[30]European Commission, Trade Sustainability Impact Assessment of the Free Trade Agreement between the European Union and Japan, 2015, p. 21.

[31]Singapore, Malaysia, Thailand, Indonesia, Brunei, Philippines, Vietnam, India and Mongolia; see Ministry of Economy, Trade and Industry of Japan, http://www.meti.go.jp/policy/trade_policy/epa/english.html (last accessed 1 March 2017).

country (Switzerland). Japan also signed the TPP. Currently, Japan is engaged in negotiation with South Korea (suspended), China, Regional Comprehensive Economic Partnership (RCEP),[32] Gulf Cooperation Council (GCC) (negotiation postponed), Turkey, Canada, Columbia and the EU.

Japan concluded TPP and is now negotiating EPA with the EU. Its participation in and the negotiations of the TPP influenced the negotiations with the EU. A report titled "Trade Sustainability Impact Assessment of the Free Trade Agreement between the European Union and Japan" states

> [i]t must be recognised however that the EU Japan negotiations are taking place against a background of other preferential trade (PTA) negotiations, such as in particular the Transpacific Partnership (TPP) [...] The outcome of the TPP could well affect Japan's PTA norm on regulatory provisions. This could in turn impinge on the EU-Japan negotiations, especially as TPP is expected to be concluded first.[33]

Japan did not try to conclude FTAs with the third countries at the beginning because it respected the WTO system. The number of FTAs that Japan concluded or is negotiating is increasing. It will draw on the experience of negotiations with the EU and the Parties of the TPP in future negotiations and renegotiations with third countries, which may lead to a kind of approximation of law in a wider sense.

4.2 *Transparency of the Negotiations*

The lack of transparency of the negotiations regarding the TTIP was strongly criticised by the public and others as mentioned above, and as a result more documents are becoming publicly available. In contrast, there was and is little criticism of the transparency of the EPA negotiations between the EU and Japan while there was a strong backlash against the TPP especially from the agricultural and medical industries and consumer-protection organisations. Neither Japan nor the EU published negotiation-related documents. However, there have been some changes on the EU side since March 2016, when it published a report about the 15th EU-Japan negotiating round, and short reports of the 15th, 16th, 17th and 18th EU-Japan FTA/EPA negotiating round can also be found on the website of the Commission.[34] Until recently, there remains no change on the website of MOFA and METI in Japan, and no documents regarding the negotiations except basic

[32]The members of RECEP are ten ASEAN countries, Japan, China, South Korea, India, Australia and New Zealand.

[33]European Commission, Trade Sustainability Impact Assessment of the Free Trade Agreement between the European Union and Japan Interim Technical Report, http://trade.ec.europa.eu/doclib/docs/2015/june/tradoc_153541.pdf (last accessed 1 March 2017), p. 20.

[34]European Commission, http://trade.ec.europa.eu/doclib/cfm/doclib_section.cfm?sec=127 (last accessed 13 July 2017).

minimum information (when, who, where and what) were available to the public, however it will be more open in the future.[35]

4.3 Individual Sectors

4.3.1 General

According to the METI, the EU is an important trade partner that accounts for 10% of the Japanese total import and export value. Japan's investment in the EU is the second largest investment destination behind the US, and investment from the EU is the largest in Japan. Japan's main areas of interest are 1. tariff elimination of EU industrial goods, 2. movement of persons and other barriers and 3. transparency and improvement of the operation of regulations.[36] On the other hand, the EU's interests are 1. Japan's non-tariff measures (NTMs) on cars, drugs, medical devices, food safety, and processed food, etc., 2. public procurement and 3. geographical indications.

According to the Reports of the 15th, 16th and 17th EU-Japan ETA/EPA negotiating round,[37] the negotiations were divided between various working groups covering the following areas: 1. trade in goods, 2. non-tariff measures and technical barriers to trade, 3. rules of origin, 4. customs and trade facilitations, 5. sanitary and phytosanitary measures, 6. trade in services, 7. investment, 8. procurement, 9. intellectual property (including geographical indications), 10. competition policy, 11. other issues (general and regulatory cooperation, business environment, animal welfare, 12. trade and sustainable development, 13. dispute settlement, 14. general, institutional and final provisions and transparency.

4.3.2 Human Rights

The report of impact assessment regarding Japan refers to privacy rights and cross-border data flow.[38] According to the report, Japan was not a third country to which

[35]Ministry of Foreign Affairs of Japan, http://www.mofa.go.jp/policy/economy/page6e_000013.html; http://www.meti.go.jp/policy/trade_policy/epa/epa_en/eu/ (last accessed 1 March 2017).

[36]Nakanishi (2016a), p. 19; Ministry of Economy, Trade and Industry of Japan, http://www.meti.go.jp/policy/trade_policy/epa/epa_en/eu/index.html (last accessed 1 March 2017).

[37]European Commission, Report of the 15th EU-Japan FTA/EPA negotiating round, http://trade.ec.europa.eu/doclib/docs/2016/march/tradoc_154368.pdf; European Commission, Report of the 16th EU-Japan FTA/EPA negotiating round, http://trade.ec.europa.eu/doclib/docs/2016/may/tradoc_154554.pdf; European Commission, Report of the 17th EU-Japan FTA/EPA negotiating round, http://trade.ec.europa.eu/doclib/docs/2016/october/tradoc_155060.pdf (all last accessed 1 March 2017).

[38]European Commission, Trade Sustainability Impact Assessment of the Free Trade Agreement between the European Union and Japan, 2015, p. 85.

personal data can be transferred, but Japan may undertake reforms in this area in the near future. The Japanese government is afraid that the existence of capital punishment might hinder the negotiations, but the report does not mention this specifically. More comprehensive human rights issues are being discussed at the negotiations for SPA between the EU and Japan.

4.3.3 Intellectual Property

According to the report of the 16th round of EU-Japan negotiations, Japan and the EU were able to consolidate the text in some areas (notably general provisions and trademarks) and reach a preliminary agreement on other provisions regarding copyright, design and civil enforcement. Further, the report of 17th round of EU-Japan negotiations stated that the Parties advanced in the consolidation of the text concerning general provisions and civil enforcement.

The EU has requested the protection of geographical indications. As a result of this, the Act of Protection of Names of Designated Agricultural, Forestry and Fishery Products and Foodstuffs (Geographical Indication Act) was enforced in Japan in June 2015, illustrating how negotiations themselves can influence domestic law.[39] The reports of the 15th and 16th rounds of negotiation stated that there was a draft text regarding geographical indications, but no discussions or progress on alcoholic beverages took place. In the report of the 17th rounds of negotiation there is though no reference to the alcoholic beverages.

4.3.4 Investment

After the Treaty of Lisbon, the EU was conferred exclusive competence in the field of direct foreign investment. This was a huge change in the common commercial policy. Investment became one of the most important subject matters of the EU's FTAs. In the negotiation text of the TTIP, CETA and others, phrases such as "the right to regulate" and "the investment court/tribunal" can be found, as mentioned above.

Investment is also an important topic in the negotiations between the EU and Japan. According to the report of the 15th EU-Japan round, the EU has explained its new approach on the right to regulate and made reference to the TTIP and CETA texts. As for investment dispute resolution in the report, Japan asked for clarifications on several aspects of the EU proposal for an Investment Court System (ICS). According to the report of the 16th EU-Japan round, there was a discussion aimed at

[39]Ministry of Foreign Affairs of Japan, http://www.maff.go.jp/e/japan_food/gi_act; http://www.maff.go.jp/e/japan_food/gi_act/pdf/gi_pamph.pdf; see also http://www.japaneselawtranslation.go.jp/law/detail/?ft=1&co=01&ia=03&x=70&y=12&ky=geographical+indication&page=4&re=02 (all last accessed 1 March 2017).

bringing further clarification of the interplay between the EU's proposal for ICS and the ICSID convention. The report states that good progress was made on the investment definitions, and the right to regulate was explained and discussed. Facing those discussions, Japan might prioritise the right to regulate when negotiating FTAs or investment agreements with third countries in the future. Further, according to the report of the 17th EU-Japan round, both sides discussed also methods for appointing tribunal members and questions relating to the review and enforcement of awards.

4.3.5 Animal Welfare

The EU ban of cosmetic products based on animal testing has definitely affected Japanese companies. In fact, major Japanese companies announced a stop to animal testing. In Japan, the Act on Animal Protection and Management of Animals was enacted in 1975 and was thereafter amended several times, the final one in 2012.[40] The name of the act was changed as well and is now referred to as the Act on Welfare and Management of Animals. Article 13 TFEU states that "animals are sentient beings", while Article 2 of the Act on Welfare and Management of Animals includes phrases such as "animals are living beings" and "symbiosis between humans and animals". Although there are differences in the viewpoints about animals and the development of animal law Japanese animal protection law is developing rapidly. In addition, the negotiations between the EU and Japan may incentivise further development in this field.

Animal welfare is one area of negotiation. According to the report of the 15th round of negotiations, animal welfare is a sensitive issue in Japan, but the EU recalled the content of the scoping paper, foreseeing the inclusion of cooperation activities regarding animal welfare. According to the report of the 16th round of negotiations, internal consultations are still required for the scope and possibility of creating an ad hoc working group. Further, according to the report of the 17th round of negotiations, both sides discussed on a possible compromise text on "Cooperation on animal welfare".

4.3.6 Others

The report of impact assessment regarding Japan states that in contrast to the EU, the Japanese government has preferred to pursue voluntary rather than regulatory measures in the context of legal and sustainable timber.[41] This tendency can be generally seen in Japan.[42]

[40]Aoki (2016), Nakanishi (2016b), pp. 105–109.

[41]European Commission, Trade Sustainability Impact Assessment of the Free Trade Agreement between the European Union and Japan, 2015, p. 88.

[42]See for cutting emission, Morita (2016), p. 70.

5 Conclusion

The ongoing EPA between the EU and Japan is one of the FTAs that the EU is negotiating. Third countries including Japan have difficulties negotiating with the EU because of certain specific characteristics arising from the EU legal order. One is the division of competences between the EU and its Member States. The EU and its Member States often conclude FTAs with third countries in the form of a mixed agreement because the EU's competences do not cover the subject matters of those FTAs. The Brexit might affect existing FTAs as well as current negotiations.

The EU has its own values and objectives and establishes its own standards. After the Treaty of Lisbon, Article 2 TEU set forth certain values and Article 21 TEU certain political principles in the Union's external action. The EU then eagerly concluded political agreements with third countries in addition to FTAs. Japan is negotiating an EPA and an SPA in parallel. In the 1990s, after the Treaty of Amsterdam, the concept of sustainable development became a key concept in the EU. The concept concerned not only sustainable development in the context of the environment but also in the context of social development. The EU's FTAs began including chapters on "trade and sustainable development". The EU has normative power, and its standards tend to be global standards. The REACH regulation, cosmetic products measures and data protection regulation have all affected Japan and Japanese companies.

EU FTAs—such as TTIP, CETA and the FTA between the EU and Singapore, the FTA between the EU and Vietnam, and the EPA between the EU and Japan—all influence each other. The introduction and the text of an investment court/tribunal is a good example of such mutual influence. Mutual influence can also be seen in the FTAs of the EU and the TPP. Further, the EP and public opinion have definitely influenced FTA negotiations. Multilateral negotiations form a soft coherence of the agreement texts, which in turn leads to a kind of approximation of the text of FTAs worldwide.

Almost all negotiation documents regarding the EPA between the EU and Japan were not available to the public. The EU has published some documents related to the 15th negotiating round however these published documents are limited, and the Japanese government has not yet published any documents. Even through these limited documents, the influence of the EU legal order is discernible, as is the influence that other EU negotiations have on its EPA negotiations with Japan, especially in the field of investment, geographical indications and animal welfare.

References

Aoki H (2016) Japanese animal law, 2nd edn. Tokyo University Press, Tokyo

Bartels L (2015) Human rights and sustainable development obligations in the EU free trade agreements. In: Wouters J, Marx A, Geraets D, Natens B (eds) Global governance through trade. Edward Elgar, Cheltenham

Bungenberg M, Herrmann C (2013) Common commercial policy after Lisbon. Springer, Heidelberg
Edward D, Lane R (2013) Edward and Lane on European Union law. Edward Elgar, Cheltenham
Krämer L (2015) EU environmental law, 8th edn. Sweet & Maxwell, London
Morita K (2016) Polices towards tackling climate change and their compatibility with the WTO. In: Nakanishi Y (ed) Contemporary issues in environmental law. The EU and Japan. Springer, Heidelberg, pp 63–86
Nakanishi Y (2014) Political principles in Article 21 TEU and constitutionalism. Hitotsubashi J Law Polit 42:11–23
Nakanishi Y (2016a) Economic partnership agreement between Japan and the European Union and legal issues – a focus on investment. Hitotsubashi J Law Polit 44:19–30
Nakanishi Y (2016b) The principle of animal welfare in the EU and its influence in Japan and the world. In: Nakanishi Y (ed) Contemporary issues in environmental law. The EU and Japan. Springer, Heidelberg, pp 87–113
Nakanishi Y (2016c) Animal welfare in the European Union's external relations law. In: Weaver J (ed) Animal welfare, assessment. Challenges and improvement strategies. Nova Science, Hauppauge, pp 125–145
Nakanishi Y (2017) Japanese environmental law in the context of globalisation – a focus on chemical law. In: Hebeler T, Hofmann E, Proelß A, Reiff P (eds) Protecting the environment for future generations-principles and actors in international environmental law. Erich Schmidt Verlag, Berlin, pp 283–304
Rosa A (2014) Exclusive, shared and National Competence in the context of EU external relations. In: Govaere I, Lannon E, Elsuwege PV, Adam S (eds) The European Union in the world: essays in honour of Marc Maresceau. Martinus Nijhoff, Leiden, pp 17–43

The China-EU BIT as a Stepping Stone Towards a China-EU FTA: A Policy Analysis

Manjiao Chi

Abstract China and EU are negotiating a BIT while envisaging an FTA as a long term goal for deepening bilateral economic relations. The two parties are determined to negotiate a comprehensive BIT that will provide a high level of investment protection and feature broad market access and deep investment liberalisation commitments. Although China has not developed a clear FTA-making strategy, a brief empirical study of the relationship between China's BITs and its existing FTA investment chapters suggests that China has adopted the "from BIT to FTA" approach. In recent years, China has also sped up its FTA-making and tried to engage in making high level and multilateral FTAs. The negotiation and conclusion of the China-EU BIT may, when considered from various different perspectives, serve as a "stepping stone" for a China-EU FTA. It is helpful in terms of providing a methodological reference, in furnishing an important source of substantive content as well as in building a favourable political and legal environment for the negotiation of the FTA. Further, the making of a China-EU FTA can be a sensible strategic option in order for China to enhance its engagement in global trade governance.

Contents

The author sincerely thanks Prof. Andrea K. Bjorklund, Faculty of Law, McGill University, for her insightful comments on the previous draft, and Prof. Marc Bungenberg, Europa-Institut, Saarland University, for his kind invitation and unfailing support. The author is solely responsible for the opinions and errors of the article.

M. Chi (✉)
Law School, Xiamen University, Xiamen, China
e-mail: chimanjiao@xmu.edu.cn

M. Bungenberg et al. (eds.), *European Yearbook of International Economic Law 2017*, European Yearbook of International Economic Law 8,
DOI 10.1007/978-3-319-58832-2_16

1 Introduction

The People's Republic of China (China) and the European Union (EU) are among the most important economies in the world. A close and healthy economic relationship between the two parties is of profound bilateral and global significance. Since the establishment of formal diplomatic relations in 1975, China and the European Economic Community (EEC) have made progressive efforts in developing bilateral economic relations.[1] For instance, a trade agreement was signed by China and the EEC in 1978. Some years later, in 1985, China and the EU concluded the Agreement on Trade and Cooperation.[2] A notable recent step in deepening economic relations between China and the EU is the launch of the negotiation of a bilateral investment treaty (BIT), known as the Comprehensive Agreement on Investment (CAI) in 2013, with the first round of negotiation held in January 2014.[3] Up to August 2016, China and the EU had completed eleven rounds of negotiations.

While the China-EU BIT is under negotiation, the parties have shown an interest in negotiating a free trade agreement (FTA) as a long term goal. Such interest has been stated in the EU-China 2020 Strategic Agenda for Cooperation ("2020 Agenda"), adopted during the Summit of the two parties in 2013.[4] It is of some interest to study how the negotiation and conclusion of a China-EU BIT would impact the future making of a China-EU FTA, despite the fact that such a study is highly speculative.

2 The Making of a China-EU FTA as an Engagement Strategy

China has a short history of FTA-making and has not until now developed a clear strategy. As *Q. Kong* has observed, China's decisions with respect to FTAs are mainly based on economic and political calculations on a partner-specific basis.[5] Yet, this does not mean China's FTA-making is without a clear intention.

Recently, especially amid the "FTA proliferation", China deemed the making of a China-EU FTA as an effective strategy for engaging and enhancing its role in global investment and trade rule-making. Due largely to the inherent insufficiency of WTO negotiations and decision-making mechanisms as well as the stagnancy of

[1]Pelkmans et al. (2016), p. 35.

[2]European External Action Service, EU-China Relations: Chronology, http://www.eeas.europa.eu/china/docs/chronology_2012_en.pdf (last accessed 1 March 2017).

[3]European Commission, EU and China Begin Investment Talks, Press release IP-14-33, 20 January 2014.

[4]European Commission, EU-China 2020 Strategic Agenda for Cooperation, 2013, http://eeas.europa.eu/china/docs/eu-china_2020_strategic_agenda_en.pdf (last accessed 1 March 2017).

[5]Kong (2012), p. 1205.

the Doha round, some WTO members conclude FTAs in order to seek further trade and investment liberalization.[6] WTO law allows WTO members to negotiate Regional Trade Agreements (RTAs), the provisions of which may to some extent deviate from WTO law.[7] FTA-making has become an important discourse in global trade and investment governance. The world is now witnessing a rapid increase of FTAs. It is particularly the case as some mega-FTAs involve the world's major economies and are broad in terms of their geographical scope, comprehensive in terms of sectoral coverage and deep in terms of investment and trade liberalisation and market access.

The Trans-Pacific Partnership (TPP) and Transatlantic Trade and Investment Partnership (TTIP) are widely deemed as typical examples of so-called mega-FTAs.[8] For instance, the newly signed TPP covers a dozen economies, including the US, Canada, Japan and Australia, is home to around 40% of the world's population and nearly 60% of global GDP.[9] TPP consists of 30 chapters, touching upon a wide range of trade-related issues. Compared with the WTO Agreement and many existing FTAs, the TPP appears "unique" in that it also deals with certain "non-traditional" trade and investment issues, such as state-owned enterprises,[10] labour rights,[11] environment protection,[12] regulatory coherence,[13] and anti-corruption.[14] For similar reasons, TTIP, once concluded, is also likely to profoundly impact global trade and investment governance, especially when combined with the TPP.[15]

While the EU is involved in TTIP negotiations and the US is a member of the TPP, China as the world's second largest economy is not a party of any mega-FTA. Although the China-ASEAN FTA, the first FTA of China, may be deemed as a multilateral FTA, it is concluded primarily for geopolitical reasons and its global impacts are limited.[16] Practically speaking, China's absence in mega-FTAs would mean that the WTO will remain the major way for China to engage in global trade and investment governance, which seems to be not sufficiently attractive for China for two major reasons.

---

[6]Henckels (2008), p. 571.

[7]Article XXIV GATT 1994.

[8]The full text of TPP is available at https://www.tpp.mfat.govt.nz/text (last accessed 1 March 2017).

[9]See Williams B, Trans-Pacific Partnership (TPP) Countries: Comparative Trade and Economic Analysis, Congressional Research Service R42344, 2013.

[10]Chapter 17 of the TPP.

[11]Chapter 19 of the TPP.

[12]Chapter 20 of the TPP.

[13]Chapter 25 of the TPP.

[14]Chapter 26 of the TPP.

[15]Freytag et al. (2014), p. 19.

[16]See Gao H, China's Strategy for Free Trade Agreements: Political Battle in the Name of Trade, Asian Regional Workshop on Free Trade Agreements: Towards Inclusive Trade Policies in Post-crisis Asia, 8–9 December 2009, pp. 3–6; Wang (2005).

Firstly, it would be difficult for the WTO to serve as the primary means of discourse in global investment rule-making in the current situation. In fact, during the WTO Singapore Ministerial Conference of 1996, some developed members proposed that the WTO should admit some new issues, including investment, competition, transparency in government procurement and trade facilitation. Because of the objection of developing members in Seattle, Doha and Cancun Ministerial Meetings, these issues, with the exception of trade facilitation, were ultimately dropped from the Doha Round Agenda.[17] At this point in time, there is no clear consensus as to whether investment issues will be negotiated in the next WTO round, although such a possibility shall not be hastily excluded.

Second, China's overall attitudes towards the WTO as a rule-making entity seem complicated. After 15 years of hard negotiation, China was finally accepted as a WTO member in 2001. China views this process as a "bittersweet" experience: while China hails its WTO membership as a major "victory" in its economic development, the "victory" is mixed with a sense of frustration. Because China, a non-founding WTO member, is required to accept WTO agreements "in a package", China senses that it has been deprived of the opportunity to be involved in the making of WTO agreements, the cornerstone of the current multilateral trade regime.[18] While drawing lessons from the past, China feels it is important to make sure that it will not be excluded or marginalised in the "new round" of global trade and investment rule-making in the twenty-first century.

Today, the world still lacks a set of multilateral rules on investment. The failed efforts of negotiating the Multilateral Agreement on Investment (MAI) under the auspices of the Organization of Economic Cooperation and Development (OECD) illustrate that there are "both normative and political impediments" to a broad multilateral international investment treaty.[19] At this point in time, it is unclear whether, when and how the international community will negotiate a multilateral investment treaty. As the regionalisation of trade rule-making becomes increasingly important, making FTAs seems to be a practical and sensible way of engaging in global investment rule-making. In this respect, China has already taken serious steps, which is shown not only by the ongoing negotiations of the historical BITs with the US and the EU, but also through China's recent change of its FTA-making practice.

On the one hand, China now adopts a proactive approach to FTA-making. Specifically, China has not only accelerated its pace of FTA-making, but is also actively engaged in negotiating high-level FTAs in the last few years. To a large extent, this represents a change of China's FTA-making practice. In its early years of FTA-making, China only signed FTAs with neighbouring developing countries. These FTAs mainly codify the parties' commitments to tariff cutting and trade

[17]Khor (2008).

[18]See Kong (2012), p. 1199 et seq.

[19]See Malli (2015), p. 509; UNCTAD, Lessons from the MAI, UNCTAD Series on Issues of International Investment Agreements, UNCTAD/ITE/IIT/MISC.22, 1999.

facilitation, while investment liberalisation is less explored. Since 2010, China has somehow shifted its focus towards negotiating high level FTAs with developed countries and upgrading existing FTAs. China's most recent FTAs are all concluded with developed countries, especially European ones. Because developed countries often have a strong demand for trade and investment liberalisation, especially market access, FTAs with developed countries are deemed to be high level as they feature deeper investment liberalisation and broader market access. For instance, after the China-Switzerland FTA was signed in 2013, the Ministry of Commerce of the People's Republic of China (MOFCOM) stated that "this is the first comprehensive FTA China has ever concluded with a European continent country, which covers a wide range of aspects including traditional trade, service, finance and intellectual property".[20] Similarly, after the conclusion of the China-Australia FTA in 2015, MOFCOM also stated that this FTA "represents the highest level of trade and investment liberalisation among all Chinese FTAs" because it features broad market access, lowered threshold for investment limits and unprecedented tariff cuts.[21] More recently, the Prime Ministers of China and Canada have agreed to launch the feasibility study on the China-Canada FTA as early as possible.[22]

On the other hand, China has also shown increasing interest in negotiating multilateral FTAs and even tries to play a leading role in the negotiations. It has been suggested that "as China is presently excluded from the TPP and [...] the TPP does not necessarily represent the best approach to economic integration in Asia, China has been active in promoting its own FTA strategy in the Asia-Pacific region".[23] China is a strong proponent of the Regional Cooperation and Economic Partnership (RCEP) and the Free Trade Area of the Asia Pacific (FTAAP).[24] It has even been opined that the RCEP and the TPP may converge to make a pathway to the FTAAP.[25] China also hopes to play a leading role in the negotiations of these Asia-based FTAs and hopes they will "offset" the potential impacts of the TPP.[26]

Besides this, China has also proposed its own version of a "mega-regional economic partnership", the "One Belt One Road" (OBOR) initiative,[27] which

---

[20]See http://www.mofcom.gov.cn/article/i/ck/201307/20130700205811.shtml (last accessed 1 March 2017).

[21]International Business Daily, China-Australia FTA Coming into Effect, 31 December 2015, http://fta.mofcom.gov.cn/article/chinaaustralia/chinaaustraliagfguandian/201512/30077_1.html (last accessed 1 March 2017).

[22]MOFCOM, China and Canada Plan to Start Feasibility Study of an FTA as Early as Possible, 1 September 2016, http://fta.mofcom.gov.cn/article/fzdongtai/201609/33178_1.html (last accessed 1 March 2017).

[23]Du (2015), p. 424.

[24]See Lewis (2013), p. 375.

[25]Petri et al. (2014), p. 78 et seq.

[26]See Hamanaka (2014), p. 163; Aggarwa (2016), p. 5 et seq.

[27]National Development and Reform Commission, Vision and Actions on Jointly Building Silk Road Economic Belt and twenty-first-Century Maritime Silk Road, March 2015, http://www.sdpc.gov.cn/gzdt/201503/t20150330_669392.html (last accessed 1 March 2017).

could transform the political and economic landscapes of Eurasia and Africa.[28] As trade and investment issues are a core issue of this initiative, it is possible, at least in theory, that China and countries involved would negotiate a mega-FTA as the legal framework for regional economic development in the long term perspective. More recently, China has shown an interest in making global investment rules. During the G20 Ministerial Meeting under China's presidency in July 2016, trade ministers of the world's largest economies agreed on a set of non-binding Guiding Principles for Investment and Policymaking, aiming to "promote coherence in national and international investment policymaking in the absence of a global governance regime".[29]

The unprecedented FTA proliferation necessitates China's enhanced engagement in the "new round" of global trade and investment rule-making. In particular, the making of mega-FTAs brings about pressure on non-member countries to negotiate their own deals to partially compensate for being excluded from deals among the FTA members.[30] As China is not a party to any mega-FTAs, the TPP and TTIP in particular, pressure on China will grow fast in the future. In this sense, negotiating a China-EU FTA could provide a precious opportunity for China to alleviate such pressure and to make its own version of a mega-FTA.

3 The Relationship Between Chinese BITs and FTA Investment Chapters

While investment chapters were seldom included in the early FTAs, they are frequently seen in modern FTAs,[31] either as an integrated part or a standalone agreement under the FTA framework agreement. The relationship between BITs and FTA investment chapters can be quite complicated. On the one hand, they can be similar or even identical. Essentially, investment issues are not only the subject of BITs; they are often regulated by FTA investment chapters. This is especially the case considering the growing recognition of the change of the nature of investment due to the fact that more and more investment matters are considered as trade-related or as trade themselves.[32] On the other hand, BITs and FTA investment chapters may also be different in many ways. Generally speaking, BITs focus primarily on investment protection and promotion by granting foreign investments

[28]Winter T, One Belt, One Road, One Heritage: Cultural Diplomacy and the Silk Road, The Diplomate, 29 March 2016.

[29]UNCTAD, UNCTAD facilitates G20 consensus on Guiding Principles for Global Investment Policymaking, 11 July 2016; MOFCOM, Trade Minister Gao Hucheng Attends the G20 Ministerial Meeting Outcome Delivery Meeting, 10 July 2016, http://www.mofcom.gov.cn/article/ae/ai/201607/20160701355815.shtml (last accessed 1 March 2017).

[30]Li et al. (2014), p. 15.

[31]Lo (2008), p. 153 et seq.

[32]Lo (2008), p. 165.

Table 1 FTA-BIT relationship in a Chinese context

	Trade partner	FTA signed	BIT signed	FTA-BIT relationship
1	ASEAN	2002	N/A	N/A
2	Chile	2005	1994	FTA Terminates and replaces BIT
3	Pakistan	2006	1989	FTA does not mention BIT
4	Costa Rica	2007	2007	FTA reaffirms the commitments of BIT
5	New Zealand	2008	1988	FTA does not mention BIT
6	Singapore	2008	1985	FTA Incorporates China-ASEAN Investment Agreement
7	Peru	2009	1994	FTA does not mention BIT
8	Iceland	2013	1994	FTA recognizes BIT
9	Switzerland	2013	2009	FTA does not mention BIT
10	Korea	2015	2007	FTA does not mention BIT
11	Australia	2015	1988	FTA review includes BIT

Here, it should be noted that for the purpose of this paper, only concluded FTAs between China and foreign states are studied, while Mainland and Hong Kong Closer Economic Partnership Arrangement as well as Mainland and Macau Closer Economic Partnership Arrangement, collectively referred to as CEPA, are excluded. This is because CEPA is concluded between China and its two special administrative regions and its conclusion is obviously politically driven, and has limited value of reference in discussing China's FTA-making with foreign states. Besides, when discussing Chinese BITs, only BITs that are currently in force will be studied

and investors certain treatment and allowing investors direct recourse to international arbitration in order to settle disputes with the host states. In comparison, while FTA investment chapters also deal with investment protection and promotion like BITs, they focus more on investment facilitation and liberalisation.

According to the China FTA Network, the official website of Chinese FTAs maintained by MOFCOM, up to the present day, China has concluded thirteen FTAs and one Preferential Trade Agreement (PTA), and is engaged in negotiations and upgrading of eight FTAs as well as conducting feasibility of negotiating five FTAs.[33] Such statistics convincingly show that China now holds a proactive attitude towards FTA-making in general, although it did not conclude its first FTA with ASEAN until the new millennium.

As can be seen in Table 1, China has adopted an implied "from BIT to FTA" approach in its FTA-making, essentially meaning that China would conclude a BIT prior to the conclusion of an FTA with its trade partners. The only exception is Costa Rica. China concluded an FTA and a BIT with Costa Rica in the same year (2007), while the FTA came into force in 2011, earlier than the BIT's coming into effect in 2016.

In international investment law-making, the "from BIT to FTA" approach is often adopted, especially in negotiations of FTAs between developed and developing countries. Although the conclusion of a BIT will not necessarily lead to the

[33]See China FTA Network, http://fta.mofcom.gov.cn/english/ (last accessed 1 March 2017).

conclusion of an FTA, the pragmatic merits of this strategy are obvious. Since modern FTAs often include investment chapters, having already signed a BIT would make any subsequent FTA negotiations simpler.[34] This could particularly be the case given that in many countries, the responsible authorities and even the negotiators of BITs and FTAs are often the same.[35] Besides, a BIT negotiation could also indicate whether the developing country partner is sufficiently and truly prepared to enter into the much more complex and time-consuming FTA negotiations.[36]

In general, this article identifies three major modes of the FTA-BIT relationship in the Chinese context. Firstly, the FTA "replaces" the BIT. This is the case with the China-Chile FTA.[37] This means that China-Chile BIT shall cease to be in force, subject to its "survival clause", while the FTA investment chapter shall "play the role of the BIT" instead. Thus practically speaking, Chilean and Chinese investors can only rely on the FTA investment chapter to raise their claims, unless otherwise allowed.[38]

Secondly, the FTA stays on its relationship with the existing BIT. This applies to five Chinese FTAs in general, i.e. the China-Pakistan FTA, the China-New Zealand FTA, the China-Peru FTA, the China-Switzerland FTA and the China-Korea FTA. These FTAs are silent on the relationship between their investment chapters and the corresponding BITs. Such silence would mean that these FTAs and BITs shall stay in force and function separately, and that investments and investors will be subject to two parallel sets of rules (BITs and FTA investment chapters). This will give rise to some important questions. Are these two sets of rules identical, similar or different? How can the discrepancy between them, if it exists, be reconciled? None of the five FTAs provides clear answers to these questions. Thus, whether and to what extent discrepancy exists between the FTA investment chapters and BITs shall be determined after careful analysis and comparison of the two sets of rules and in accordance with the relevant rules regarding successive treaties in the Vienna Convention on the Law of Treaties (VCLT).[39]

The third alternative or option is that the FTA "absorbs" the BIT. Here, the term "absorb" shall be understood in flexible terms. There are three different situations of FTAs absorbing BITs.

In the first situation, the parties expressly incorporate an existing BIT (or a similar investment agreement) as their FTA investment chapter, thus avoiding the need to negotiate the latter. For instance, the China-Singapore FTA does not have

---

[34]Poulsen L, Bilateral Investment Treaties and Preferential Trade Agreements: Is a BIT really better than a lot?, Investment Treaty News, 23 September 2010.

[35]For instance, in China, MOFCOM is in charge of the negotiations of BITs and FTAs, and European Commission Directorate-General is the authorised organ for BIT and FTA negotiations.

[36]Poulsen L, Bilateral Investment Treaties and Preferential Trade Agreements: Is a BIT really better than a lot?, Investment Treaty News, 23 September 2010.

[37]Article 1 Annex 4 of the Supplementary Agreement on Investments of the China-Chile FTA.

[38]Article 3 Annex 4 of the Supplementary Agreement on Investments of the China-Chile FTA.

[39]See Article 30 VCLT; see also Orakhelashvili (2016).

an investment chapter, but incorporates the investment agreement of the China-ASEAN FTA.[40]

In the second situation, the parties "confirm" their commitments in an existing BIT in their FTA investment chapter, also avoiding negotiation of the latter. This is the case of the China-Iceland FTA and the China-Costa Rica FTA. For instance, the investment chapter (section) of the China-Costa Rica FTA does not contain any substantive provision, but merely states that "[t]he parties reaffirm their commitments under the China-Costa Rica BIT of 2007".[41] Similarly, the very succinct investment chapter of the China-Iceland FTA does not contain any substantive provisions, but includes a clause titled "bilateral investment agreement", stating that "the parties recognize the importance of China-Iceland BIT in creating favorable conditions for investments between the parties, and thus its contribution to creation of the free trade area established by this Agreement".[42] Although the relevant terms used in the two FTAs appear vague ("reaffirm" and "recognize"), the parties show a clear joint intention of integrating their existing BITs into the substance of the FTA.

In the third situation, the FTA contains an investment chapter independent of a BIT, but the parties take steps to harmonise the BIT and the FTA investment chapter. The China-Australia FTA is an illustrative example. This FTA contains a comprehensive investment chapter that appears quite different from the China-Australia BIT. To reconcile the potential normative conflict between these two agreements, the FTA investment chapter requires that "the parties shall conduct a review of the investment legal framework between them no later than three years after the date of entry into force of the FTA" and such review shall include consideration of this Chapter and the China-Australia BIT.[43] Although in the strict sense the investment chapter of the China-Australia FTA and the China-Australia BIT are independent, one can reasonably expect that the BIT shall be brought into conformity with the substance of the FTA investment chapter as a result of the review in the near future.

By absorbing a BIT (or investment agreement) into an FTA either formally (meaning that the BIT shall be deemed as the FTA investment chapter) or substantively (meaning that the contents of the BIT and the FTA investment chapter shall be synchronised), the FTA investment chapter and the BIT will be made, despite their separate legal status, similar or identical in terms of substantive content. In practice, although foreign investors may select either an FTA or a BIT as the applicable law for their claims, such treaty shopping is not likely to make a substantive difference to the final outcome of the claims given the similarity of the substantive contents of the two agreements.

[40] Article 84 China-Singapore FTA.

[41] Article 89 China-Costa Rica FTA.

[42] Article 92 China-Iceland FTA.

[43] Article 9.9 China-Australia FTA.

4 The Making of a Comprehensive China-EU BIT

While on the presumption that the "from BIT to FTA" approach will be followed in the future China-EU FTA negotiations, what China and the EU agree to in their BIT, especially with regard to the investment chapter, is likely to profoundly influence their FTA-making.

The China-EU BIT will be the first standalone BIT at the EU level after the Treaty of Lisbon came into to force, which is intended to replace existing BITs between China and EU member states.[44] In addition, given the fact that EU has many member states and that China maintains BITs with all but one EU member state (Ireland),[45] the China-EU BIT as the first BIT at the EU level will need to accommodate the different needs of the EU member states and streamline the existing BITs into a single and coherent text.[46] Both China and the EU attach great importance to the negotiation of this BIT. According to the Communication "Trade for All – Towards a More Responsible Trade and Investment Policy", the negotiation of the China-EU BIT is among EU's top priorities in developing China-EU economic relations.[47] The Chinese government has also stated that the negotiation of this BIT and the China-US BIT are currently its most important engagements.[48]

As China and the EU have different economic conditions, it is natural that they have different priorities and expectations of their BIT.[49] Although it is not sufficiently clear what issues are on the negotiation agenda due to the inadequacy of information released officially, both parties have agreed in the 2020 Agenda that this BIT should be "comprehensive".[50] Indeed, the alternative title of this BIT, CAI, clearly indicates its comprehensiveness. Such a characteristic also helps distinguish the China-EU BIT from existing BITs between China and EU member states.

Strictly speaking, "comprehensive" is not a legal term in international investment law. It should be understood in the specific context of the BIT-making practices of China and the EU. The majority of Chinese and EU BITs are in the "European style", which are simple in content and narrow in coverage, focusing mainly on the protection of foreign investments in the post-establishment stage,

---

[44]Article 9.9 China-Australia FTA.

[45]Despite the occurrence of Brexit, this article deems UK as an EU member state, since legally speaking UK's membership will not cease until the legal procedures are duly completed.

[46]European Commission, Commission Proposes to Open Negotiations for an Investment Agreement with China, Press release IP-13-458, 23 May 2013.

[47]European Commission, Trade for all – Towards a More Responsible Trade and Investment Policy, 2015, p. 31.

[48]MOFCOM, The Negotiations of China-US BIT and China-EU BIT, 2015, http://history.mofcom.gov.cn/?newchina=%E4%B8%AD%E7%BE%8E%E3%80%81%E4%B8%AD%E6%AC%A7bit%E8%B0%88%E5%88%A4-2 (last accessed 1 March 2017).

[49]See Ewert (2016).

[50]European Commission, EU-China 2020 Strategic Agenda for Cooperation, 2013, http://eeas.europa.eu/china/docs/eu-china_2020_strategic_agenda_en.pdf (last accessed 1 March 2017).

while clauses relating to investment liberalisation (such as market access based on national treatment of pre-establishment investment) as well as public interest protection (such as environment measures, labour protection, national security and general exceptions) are often excluded. Yet, the recent conclusion of the China-Canada BIT and the Canada-EU Comprehensive Economic and Trade Agreement (CETA) seem to suggest that China and the EU have changed their treaty-making paradigm from "European style" to "American style".[51] Compared with the "European style" IIAs, "American style" IIAs are much more comprehensive and complicated. In addition to the provisions commonly seen in "European style" IIAs, a typical "American style" IIA also incorporates provisions relating to market access and general exceptions (for public interest protection purpose) plus a standalone investor-state dispute settlement (ISDS) section (or chapter) dealing with a wide range of procedural issues. In the context of international trade agreement-making, it is often opined that the incorporation and harmonisation of these provisions in a trade agreement represents a "deeper" integration than the mere achievement of trade liberalisation.[52]

As the China-EU BIT will be a comprehensive one, it is supposed to cover a much wider range of issues than existing BITs between China and EU member states. Both EU and China have confirmed that this BIT shall boast broad coverage and various "novel" provisions relating to some outstanding issues, such as market access (especially in the field of trade in service), labour rights, state-owned enterprises (SOEs), general exceptions and dispute settlement.[53] For the purpose of this study, it would neither be possible nor necessary to explore in detail each and all of the legal issues pertaining to the BIT negotiation. A brief discussion of a few outstanding issues will be provided.

First and foremost, the China-EU BIT is likely to feature unprecedentedly broad market access provisions. China and the EU have confirmed on various occasions that this BIT will codify the parties' commitments to market access and national treatment of foreign investments at the pre-establishment stage, which will be achieved through a "negative list" formula. For instance, China and the EU have both voiced their concerns over investment liberalisation, particularly market access. The European Commission has stated that "[t]he EU and China agreed in particular that the future deal should improve market access opportunities for their investors by establishing a genuine right to invest and by guaranteeing that they will not discriminate against their respective companies".[54] While Chinese investors

[51]Chi (2015a), pp. 378–381.

[52]Krishna (2009), p. 26.

[53]MOFCOM, The Negotiations of China-US BIT and China-EU BIT, 2015, http://history.mofcom.gov.cn/?newchina=%E4%B8%AD%E7%BE%8E%E3%80%81%E4%B8%AD%E6%AC%A7bit%E8%B0%88%E5%88%A4-2 (last accessed 1 March 2017); European Commission, EU and China Begin Investment Talks, Press release IP-14-33, 20 January 2014; Shan and Wang (2015), pp. 261–263.

[54]European Commission, EU and China Agree on Scope of the Future Investment Deal, 15 January 2016.

also complain that strict legal requirements, especially labour and environmental standards, cultural barriers and high costs in some EU countries may constitute an obstacle for Chinese investment when entering the EU market, although it is generally agreed that EU countries are already quite open and friendly to foreign investment.[55] To address this issue, China and the EU have agreed to make broad market access commitments in the BIT by granting national treatment to EU investments covering both pre- and post-establishment stages subject a negative list.

Secondly, the China-EU BIT is also likely to include a reformed ISDS clause or section. In recent years, the existing ISDS system has been subjected to strong criticism for various reasons, such as a lack of transparency, unduly limiting the host states' regulatory power and the inconsistency of arbitral awards.[56] While some countries tend to exclude ISDS provisions from their future IIAs, the EU has proposed to reform this system. During the TTIP negotiation, the EU put forward a proposal that would substantively deviate from the current ISDS system and would lead to the establishment of an investment court system.[57] Though China has not put forward any specific request or clear roadmap for reforming the existing ISDS system, it did express concerns over the limiting effects of this system on host states' regulatory power. For instance, *Yongjie Li*, one of China's key IIA negotiators, has insightfully observed that the current ISDS system has some "inherent disadvantages" due chiefly to its hybrid nature and thus should be reformed to reduce inconsistency of arbitral awards and to provide non-disputing states with the opportunity to express their views on treaty interpretation during the dispute settlement proceedings.[58] At this point in time, although it is not certain what kind of ISDS system China and EU will design in their future BIT, the parties' consensus in terms of reforming the current system has become quite obvious. Consequently, one may have reason to expect that the ISDS provisions of a China-EU BIT will be different from those embodied in the existing BITs of China and the EU member states.

Last but not the least, it is also likely that more sustainable development provisions will be included in the China-EU BIT. The EU consistently stresses and promotes sustainable development in its internal and external trade policy-making as the EU "wants its trade policy to support economic growth, social development, and environmental protection".[59] China has also started in recent years to realise the

[55]See, e.g., European Union Chamber of Commerce in China, Chinese Outbound Investment in the European Union, January 2013, https://www.kpmg.de/docs/Chinese_Outbound_Investment_European_Union.pdf (last accessed 1 March 2017).

[56]See, e.g., UNCTAD, Reform of Investor-State Dispute Settlement: In Search of a Roadmap, No. 2, June 2013.

[57]European Commission, Why the new EU proposal for an Investment Court System in TTIP is beneficial to both States and investors, MEMO-15-6060, 12 November 2015.

[58]Li (2014), pp. 177–179.

[59]See European Commission, Sustainable Development, http://ec.europa.eu/trade/policy/policy-making/sustainable-development/ (last accessed 1 March 2017).

importance of sustainable development, especially as a response to the worsening environmental situation. There is a clear trend in Chinese BITs, which are becoming increasingly environmentally friendly in that more types and higher quality environmental provisions are incorporated into Chinese BITs, especially those concluded recently, such as the China-Canada BIT.[60] In light of the growing global consensus for promoting sustainable development in IIA-making ("balanced IIAs"), it can be expected that the China-EU BIT will be open to more types of sustainable development provisions.

Admittedly, the above three issues do not amount to an exhaustive list of outstanding issues with the China-EU BIT negotiation. Although China and the EU agree on these issues at policy level, it remains a difficult legal task for the parties to negotiate the relevant provisions. Notwithstanding the potential difficulties of the negotiation of the China-EU BIT, it is almost certain that this BIT will hold fundamental differences from the existing BITs between China and EU member states and will have profound implications for both parties in their future trade and investment treaty-making.

5 The Prospect of China-EU FTA Negotiation

Given that a China-EU BIT is likely to be concluded in the near future, it is of interest to discuss why they would want an FTA in addition to the BIT. This question essentially explores the justifications for a favourable decision to negotiate a China-EU FTA. It is true that when making the decision, both parties need to take into consideration a wide range of factors, including but not limited to potential economic benefits and losses, social and labour impacts, the international situation, negotiating capacity, domestic law compatibility, international trade regime, domestic interest groups and national security.[61] It is difficult to assess which factors have prompted China and the EU to negotiate an FTA and what weight the parties attach to such factors when making a decision. As mentioned, China and the EU share a common political aspiration to negotiate an FTA as a long-term goal to strengthen their economic cooperation, "once the conditions are right".[62] Although, strictly speaking, the parties have not made clear whether the conclusion of the BIT is a precondition of the FTA negotiation, they have nonetheless implied that the conclusion of the BIT is important in assessing whether and how they should negotiate an FTA.

[60]See Chi (2015b), p. 514.

[61]See Salidjanova N, China's Trade Ambitions: Strategy and Objectives behind China's Pursuit of Free Trade Agreements, US-China Economic Security Review Commission Staff Research Report, 28 May 2015, pp. 23–35.

[62]European Commission, EU-China 2020 Strategic Agenda for Cooperation, 2013, http://eeas.europa.eu/china/docs/eu-china_2020_strategic_agenda_en.pdf (last accessed 1 March 2017), p. 5.

Firstly, a China-EU BIT may provide a helpful methodological reference for the negotiation of a China-EU FTA. This is based on the temporal perspective of the "from BIT to FTA" approach, meaning that an FTA should be made after the conclusion of BIT. As mentioned, a well negotiated BIT may serve as a good basis or starting point for the negotiation of an FTA investment chapter. Practically, the process of BIT negotiation is also a rare opportunity for effective information sharing, clarifying positions and interest exchanging. The parties' enhanced knowledge of the details of each other's investment governance regimes will be very helpful to the negotiation of the China-EU FTA.

Secondly, the "from BIT to FTA" approach also has a substantive perspective, meaning that the FTA uses BIT provisions as a source of content. As shown by the above empirical study of the BIT-FTA relationship, almost all of China's existing FTA investment chapters are heavily reliant on its BITs as an important source of content, regardless of whether this is intended by the negotiators. Especially, as a China-EU BIT will be comprehensive and of a high level, it will not only feature a high level of investment liberalisation and broad market access, but also various "novel" provisions relating to SOEs and public interest protection. As these issues are also likely to be addressed in the negotiation of a China-EU FTA in the broader context of trade, it is almost certain that what has been agreed in the BIT may serve as the source of content for the FTA. Even if the parties wish to pursue further investment commitments in the FTA, the BIT may still serve as a good starting point for the negotiations.

This article further opines that China and the EU are likely to opt for the third mode in negotiating the China-EU FTA investment chapter, meaning that the FTA will absorb the main contents of the China-EU BIT. This viewpoint is shared by experts of economic and international relations in both China and the EU. For instance, a prominent Chinese think tank has recently called for China and the EU to conclude an FTA by 2020 through the "merging" of China-EU BIT negotiation with the negotiation of the China-EU FTA, stating that "negotiating only for BIT cannot meet the need of development of the economic and trade relations between China and the EU" and that without an FTA, even if a BIT is signed, its benefits will be limited.[63] Some EU experts have also suggested that the China-EU FTA should "integrate" the BIT as a policy option.[64]

Last but not the least, the successful conclusion of a China-EU BIT may also help build a favourable political and social environment for the negotiation of a China-EU FTA. It is almost self-evident that the conclusion of this historical BIT will demonstrate the two parties' strong commitments to deepening bilateral economic relations and cooperation; it will also mean that the parties have reached consensus with regard to certain thorny legal issues that are plaguing their bilateral economic relations, especially the issues of SOE and market access. In addition, the

[63]China Institute for Reform and Development, China-EU FTA – Decisive Option for Deepening China-EU Cooperation by 2020, 2016, p. 22 et seq.

[64]Pelkmans et al. (2016), p. 224 et seq.

implementation of the China-EU BIT would necessitate China's internal reform of its investment governance regime towards a deeper level of investment and trade liberalisation. The achievement of these factors, to some extent, would imply that "the right conditions" have been met for China and the EU to launch the FTA negotiation. In such a situation, as suggested by a recent report, it will be "logical and worthwhile" for the two parties to negotiate an FTA once their BIT is concluded.[65]

6 Concluding Remarks

China and the EU are now engaged in unprecedented BIT negotiations. The parties share the ambition to make this BIT a comprehensive and high level one. Different from the existing BITs between China and EU member states, a China-EU BIT will not only feature a higher degree of investment protection, but will also boast broad market access and a deep level of investment liberalisation.

The ambitions of China and the EU do not end with the conclusion of a BIT. Rather, the two parties have shown an interest in negotiating an FTA as a long-term goal. This makes sense for China and the EU as both have political aspirations and will benefit economically from closer trade relations. Further, negotiating an FTA with the EU is also consistent with China's current need to engage in the new round of global trade and investment governance as a policy response to the recent global FTA proliferation. Considering China's consistent adoption of the "from BIT to FTA" approach, the comprehensiveness of the China-EU BIT and recent focus on negotiating high level and multilateral FTAs, one may have reason to expect that the successful negotiation and conclusion of a China-EU BIT could provide helpful methodological references, furnish important sources of substantive content and build a favourable political and legal environment for the future negotiation of a China-EU FTA.

References

Aggarwa V (2016) Mega-FTAs and the trade-security nexus: the Trans-Pacific Partnership (TPP) and Regional Comprehensive Economic Partnership (RCEP). Asia Pacific issues analysis of the East-West Center No. 123

Chi M (2015a) A long march towards compatibility, coherence and consistency: the future of China's investment treaties. Zeitschrift für Europarechtliche Studien 18(4):373–389

Chi M (2015b) The "Greenization" of Chinese BITs. J Int Econ Law 18(3):511–542

Du M (2015) Explaining China's tripartite strategy towards trans-pacific partnership agreement. J Int Econ Law 18(3):407–432

[65] Pelkmans et al. (2016), pp. 209–224.

Ewert I (2016) The EU-China bilateral investment treaty: between high hopes and real challenges. Egmont Security Policy Brief No. 68

Freytag A, Draper P, Fricke S (2014) The impact of TTIP. Volume 2: Political consequences for EU economic policymaking, transatlantic integration, China and the world trade order. Konrad-Adenauer-Stiftung, Berlin

Hamanaka S (2014) TPP versus RCEP: control of membership and agenda setting. J East Asian Econ Integration 18(2):163–186

Henckels C (2008) Overcoming jurisdictional isolationism at the WTO – FTA nexus: a potential approach for the WTO. Eur J Int Law 19(3):571–599

Khor M (2008) The "Singapore Issues" in the WTO: evolution and implications for developing countries. TWN Trade & Development Series No. 33

Kong Q (2012) China's unchartered FTA strategy. J World Trade 46(5):1191–1206

Krishna P (2009) The economics of PTAs. In: Lestor S, Mercurio B (eds) Bilateral and regional trade agreements. Cambridge University Press, Cambridge, pp 11–27

Lewis MK (2013) The TPP and the RCEP (ASEAN+6) as potential paths towards deeper Asian economic integration. Asian J WTO Law Public Health Law 8(2):359–378

Li Y (2014) Factors to be considered for China's future investment treaties. In: Wenhua S (ed) China and international investment law: twenty years of ICSID membership. Brill, Leiden, pp 171–179

Li C, Wang J, Whalley J (2014) China and global mega trade deals, CIGI Papers No. 34

Lo CF (2008) A comparison of BIT and the investment chapter of free trade agreement from policy perspective. Asian J WTO Int Health Law Policy 3(1):147–170

Malli M (2015) Minilateral treaty-making in international investment law. In: Bjorklund A (ed) Yearbook on international investment law & policy (2013–2014). Oxford University Press, Oxford, pp 507–528

Orakhelashvili A (2016) Article 30 of the 1969 Vienna Convention on the law of treaties: application of the successive treaties relating to the same subject-matter. ICSID Rev 31 (2):344–365

Pelkmans J, Hu W, Mustilli F, Di Salvo M, Francois J, Bekkers E, Manchin M, Tomberger P (2016) Tomorrow's silk road: assessing an EU-China Free Trade Agreement CEPS 04/2016

Petri P, Plummer M, Zhai F (2014) The TPP, China and the FTAAP: the case for convergence. In: Tang G, Petri P (eds) New directions in Asia-Pacific economic integration. East-West Center, Honolulu, pp 78–89

Shan W, Wang L (2015) The China-EU BIT and the Emerging Global BIT 2.0. ICSID Rev 30 (1):260–267

Wang VW (2005) The logic of China-ASEAN FTA: economic statecraft of "Peaceful Ascendancy". In: Ho K, Ku S (eds) Southeast Asia and China: global changes and regional challenges. Institute of Southeast Asia Studies, Singapore, pp 17–41

The Proposed European and Australian Free Trade Agreement: And the Importance for Small and Medium-Sized Enterprises

Leon Trakman, Robert Walters, and Bruno Zeller

Abstract This chapter investigates how Free Trade Agreements (FTAs) can assist the small and medium-sized enterprise sector (SME) to benefit from reduced tariffs and opening overseas markets. It identifies the importance of SMEs when negotiating the proposed European Union Australian Free Trade Agreement (EU-Australian FTA) which commenced in 1995 when the EU and Australia agreed on a political framework to establish an FTA. This chapter argues how promoting SME trade emanating from Australia into the EU can strengthen economic ties with the EU and benefit Australian SMEs and that, just as the single EU market has benefitted SME's across member states, Australian SMEs can benefit significantly through an EU-Australian free trade agreement that encourages and stimulates bilateral SME trade.

Contents

L. Trakman (✉)
University of New South Wales, Union Road, Kensington Campus, Sydney, NSW, Australia
e-mail: l.trakman@unsw.edu.au

R. Walters
European Faculty of Law, Nova Gorica, Slovenia
e-mail: Robert.Walters2@live.vu.edu.au

B. Zeller
University of Western Australia, 35 Stirling Highway, Crawley, Perth, WA, Australia
e-mail: Bruno.zeller@uwa.edu.au

M. Bungenberg et al. (eds.), *European Yearbook of International Economic Law 2017*, European Yearbook of International Economic Law 8,
DOI 10.1007/978-3-319-58832-2_17

1 Introduction

Free Trade Agreements (FTAs) can produce material economic and social benefits for signatory countries and their citizens. FTAs can help to facilitate economic growth, benefitting consumers and generating employment opportunities. FTAs can also strengthen links between countries by allowing their citizens to interact with each other through exporting and importing of goods and services by small and medium-size enterprises (SMEs).

However, economic and legal roadblocks currently impede the trade prospects of Australian SMEs. This includes trade regulations governing international trade that are imposed by a number of government agencies, both commonwealth and state. "One of the major blocks is regulation in the respective jurisdictions at the point of departure to the final destination that also includes the import and release process and recipient of the goods."[1]

This chapter examines small and medium-sized enterprises (SMEs) and argues that the benefits of SMEs are insufficiently—or arguably not at all—exploited in Australia. The work currently underway to develop a FTA between Australia and the European Union provides a valuable opportunity to promote SMEs by placing greater emphasis on harmonizing rules and laws directed at increasing trade between these two Parties. The EU and Australia can accomplish these goals by drafting and negotiating an FTA that draws on the experiences of other countries in regulating SMEs, notably the FTAs between China and Switzerland,[2] as well as between China and New Zealand.[3] These FTAs can maximize the potential for SMEs in these countries to trade effectively in each other's markets including harmonizing the principles, standards and rules used to regulate enable such trade.

This chapter will demonstrate how the European Union, European Economic Area and the European Free Trade Association can provide robust opportunities for Australian SMEs to prosper in European markets. Australia can also draw from comparatively from its trade and investment negotiations with other countries, such as New Zealand and the United States.[4]

Importantly, the Australian government can develop regulatory policies that promote awareness among SMEs of the economic benefits derived from exporting their goods and services into the EU. It can provide them with much needed access to information on how to overcome internal and external barriers to such trade. It

[1]See http://www.gadens.com/publications/Pages/Reduction-in-Iran-sanctions-not-the-end-of-the-issue.aspx (last accessed 1 March 2017), originally published by Lloyds List, 31 March 2016.

[2]China and Switzerland Free Trade Agreement, https://www.ige.ch/fileadmin/user_upload/Juristische_Infos/e/Switzerland_China_FTA_Main_Agreement.pdf (last accessed 1 March 2017).

[3]New Zealand and China Free Trade Agreement, https://www.mfat.govt.nz/en/trade/free-trade-agreements/free-trade-agreements-in-force/china-fta/ (last accessed 1 March 2017).

[4]Australia-New Zealand Closer Economic Relations Trade Agreement, http://dfat.gov.au/trade/agreements/anzcerta/Pages/australia-new-zealand-closer-economic-relations-trade-agreement.aspx (last accessed 1 March 2017).

can assist them to balance the costs of regulatory compliance with savings in customs duties under an EU-Australia FTA. Importantly, the Australian government can critically examine current barriers to SME trade and where appropriate, reduce or abolish those barriers in negotiating strategically with the EU.

In seeking to address how the Australian Government can provide for SMEs in its FTA with the EU, the chapter will consider internal and external barriers faced by SME's in engaging in export markets, including "all those attitudinal, structural, operational and other constraints that hinder a firm's ability to initiate, develop or sustain international operations".[5] It will illustrate internal barriers to trade faced by SMEs, including safety and other standards which inhibit SMEs from exporting due to the cost of the initial investment. It will address external barriers to trade outside the control of SMEs, such as complex documentation, regulation, exchange rates and tariffs.[6] It will stress that "barriers specific to individual SMEs, [in] the sector in which they operate, and other barriers outside SMEs' control can prevent them from reaching international markets."[7]

The chapter will propose how the Australian government can frame its regulatory principles, standards and duties in a manner that is compatible with EU requirements that enable SMEs to limit current barriers to their trade into the EU. Beyond the fact that the EU has developed policies to protect SMEs including in its FTAs, it would provide Australian SMEs with access to EU markets that include 500 million people compared to Australia's 24 million.

In accomplishing these goals, the Australian government will need to skillfully construct market entry points for SMEs into the EU, while reducing their exposure to volatility in market supply and demand, such as was suffered by the Australian automobile industry. It will also be required to develop a managed regulatory and advisory framework that limits the exposure of SMEs to the harsh market impact of foreign governments. It will need, as well, to address EU regulatory requirements, such as relating to biosecurity and quarantine measures.

Most importantly, the Australian government will need to assist SMEs to overcome both internal barriers to trade arising from their limited understanding of export markets in general, and in responding to external and regulatory barriers that impede SME access to particular EU markets.[8] The Australian Government will also need to consult key domestic stakeholders, including SMEs, Business Councils, Chambers of Commerce and academics. The chapter will suggest that the approach adopted by the Australian Government towards SMEs to date has been largely deficient. Its ultimate goal is to redress that deficiency.

---

[5]Leonidou (1995).

[6]European Parliament, European SMEs and International Trade, February 2012, p. 15.

[7]Cernat L, Norman-López A and Duch T-Figueras A, SMEs are more important than you think! Challenges and Opportunities for EU exporting SMEs, Chief Economist Note, Issue 3, September 2014, p. 2.

[8]Cernat L, Norman-López A and Duch T-Figueras A, SMEs are more important than you think! Challenges and Opportunities for EU exporting SMEs, Chief Economist Note, Issue 3, September 2014, p. 2.

Section 2 of the chapter will identify the growth of SMEs globally and in Australia and the barriers they face in gaining access to international markets. Sections 3–5 will explore how SMEs can gain access to European markets through an EU-Australian Free Trade Agreement. Sections 6–8 will evaluate issues to be addressed in negotiating, drafting and implementing an FTA that protects and promotes SME trade, including in exporting from and importing into Australia. Sections 9 and 10 will examine market and research strategies, including the development of FTAs elsewhere, that the Australian government might consider in ensuring greater protection of its SMEs in European markets, and indeed, internationally.

2 How Free Trade Agreements Can Benefit Small and Medium-Sized Enterprises

Recent examinations by economists[9] indicate that the actual gains for the Australian economy has been far less than was anticipated at the time that FTAs, such as between the United States and Australia (US-Australia FTA), were negotiated. As an example, following the US-Australia FTA, "the data shows that [. . .] Australia and the United States [. . .] are worse off than they would have been without the agreement."[10] The main argument is that there is a gap between trade diplomacy and economic reality, and that future FTAs should be subject to cost benefit analyses before negotiating and ratifying such FTAs.[11]

Concluding an EU-Australia FTA will therefore require recognition by the negotiating parties of the value of globalisation both politically and economically. That will entail, at the macro level, an appreciation of the value of opening borders to trade and transcending restrictive national barriers to trade. Concluding such an FTA, at the micro-level, will also require recognition of the direct economic benefits arising from it, such as for SMEs in the agricultural trade.

In negotiating a EU-Australia FTA, therefore, Australia will need to be aware of the political and economic background predating the FTA, including how to harness its economic benefits in general, but also how to do so for particular sectors that are likely to be impacted by it. As an example, Switzerland is aware that, should the Transatlantic Trade and Investment Partnership (TTIP) between the EU and the US be resurrected in a comparable or different form, Switzerland would expect to join it. However, joining would pose a challenge for Switzerland's agricultural sector which is currently the beneficiary of significant state protections. *Wasescha*, a past Swiss diplomat and trade negotiator, has argued that only two possibilities exist. Switzerland could do nothing and decline to join, or it could start

[9]For a full analysis see The Australian, 24 August 2016, p. 11.

[10]The Australian, 24 August 2016, p. 11.

[11]The Australian, 24 August 2016, p. 11.

to prepare its agricultural industry to facilitate changes needed to sign onto such an FTA.[12] Whether or not Switzerland acceded to a TTIP, the short-term consequences would be a loss, in particular for SMEs in the agricultural sector, of 600 million Swiss Francs particularly in markets in which produce is not differentiated. However, insofar as farmers produce value added products that can be differentiated in a TTIP market, those farmers would benefit from it.[13]

Arguably this lesson for Switzerland and the EU could be a lesson for Australia in negotiating the EU-Australian FTA. What is essential, therefore, is being able to determine *a priori* how such an FTA can only "secure the gains in national wealth from engaging in trade on the basis of what we do best",[14] but also benefit SMEs.

In addition, Australia would also need to take advantage of the political and economic relationship between regionalism, represented by the EU and globalisation, represented by an expansion beyond that region to include global partners such as Australia. The EU has long adopted the principle of regionalism, as a cornerstone principle in forging a borderless Federal State (*Bundesstaat*).[15] That concept entails overcoming national boundaries through the development of effective regional governance, reflected in the history of the EU and manifest in closer political and economic integration among its member states.[16] However, a number of political and economic factors have led to a jaded view of regionalism as a means towards globalism. This is reflected today in hesitation among elite members of the EU to argue for further opening borders to trade going forward.[17] This is evident in the shockwaves created by Brexit and a threat it has posed to the conception of a viable and united Europe.[18] Coupled with this development has been cynicism about economic and political globalism in the EU. This cynicism was epitomized in an interview with the daughter of EU luminary, *Altiero Spinelli*, in the Italian newspaper La Repubblica:

> Honestly, today I do not see any politicians with class but only statesmen who wander aimlessly through Europe fearful that they could lose the next election.[19]

[12]Neue Züricher Zeitung, 24 August 2016, p. 13.

[13]Neue Züricher Zeitung, 24 August 2016, p. 13.

[14]The Australian, 24 August 2016, p. 11.

[15]Neue Züricher Zeitung, 24 August, 2016, p. 13.

[16]Zimmer O, Geschichtsphilosophisch taub, Meinung und Debatte, Neue Züricher Zeitung, 25 July 2016, p. 8.

[17]Neue Züricher Zeitung, 24 August 2016, p. 13.

[18]Toggenburger Tagblatt, 23 August 2016, p. 6.

[19]Toggenburger Tagblatt, 23 August 2016, p. 6.

3 The Importance of Small and Medium-Sized Enterprises

The importance of SMEs to the Australian economy is significant. The Australian Treasury has noted that "small business contributed around 33% of private industry value added in 2012-13."[20] In addition, small business employed "around 4.5 million people in 2014–2015, approximately 43% of private sector employment."[21] Yet, even though the small business sector contributes materially to the Australian economy, SMEs can play an even more significant economic role as Australia transitions from a mining to a more diverse economy.[22] For example, Australian agricultural exports continue to be an important part of that transition. However, Australia's growing primary industry sector is likely to contribute disproportionately to its economic growth, including in exports.[23] This industrial growth is already evident in the role of the processed and unprocessed sectors (value adding parts of the Australian economy) which includes current annual exports of approximately $37 billion of such products.[24] SMEs, too, have an expanding role to play in the value added supply chain that is associated with these sectors of the Australian economy.

Despite their expanding contributions to the Australian economy, SMEs struggle to maintain their economic base not only in international trade, but also domestically. The SME Association of Australia refers to SME's as "the back bone" of the Australian economy, but that SMEs "battle every day for growth and sustainability".[25] Coupled with this is recognition that, to sustain market capacity, SMEs need to "look abroad, particularly in the services sector, with low-interest rates supporting economic activity."[26]

The primary obstacles faced by SMEs gaining market entry are the intrusive and costly internal and external barriers in gaining entry to foreign markets, along with complex regulations which constrain such entry. As *Dean Pearson* notes, based on research into Australian SMEs:

> It has been determined in many cases that the level and complexity of regulation is a real deterrent to trade, especially for SMEs which, for example, can reduce the use of FTAs and other trade initiatives.[27]

---

[20]See http://www.treasury.gov.au/PublicationsAndMedia/Publications/2012/sml-bus-data (last accessed 1 March 2017).

[21]See http://www.treasury.gov.au/PublicationsAndMedia/Publications/2012/sml-bus-data (last accessed 1 March 2017).

[22]Australian Trade Commission, Investment opportunities in Australian agribusiness and food, October 2015.

[23]Australian Trade Commission, Investment opportunities in Australian agribusiness and food, October 2015.

[24]Australian Trade Commission, Investment opportunities in Australian agribusiness and food, October 2015, p. 7.

[25]See https://www.smea.org.au/ (last accessed 1 March 2017).

[26]See Pearson D, Where are the opportunities for Australian SMEs in 2016?, NAB, Business Research and Insights, Economic Commentary, 23 December 2015, http://business.nab.com.au/where-are-the-opportunities-for-australian-smes-in-2016-14529/ (last accessed 1 March 2017).

[27]See Pearson D, Where are the opportunities for Australian SMEs in 2016?, NAB, Business Research and Insights, Economic Commentary, 23 December 2015.

Redressing impediments to SMEs participating profitably in foreign markets is unlikely to be easily achieved. In particular, SMEs need to develop strategies by which to overcome internal barriers to securing access to foreign markets. Governments, including the government of Australia, need to provide guidance to SMEs on how to secure such access, as well as to assist them in gaining a foothold in foreign markets including through carefully negotiated and drafted FTAs.

Making provision for SMEs in treaties, such as the EU-Australia FTA, can help SMEs to reduce external barriers to trade. However, the Australian government will need to understand those barriers to trade that are specific to industries in which SMEs participate, the EU market to which export or from which they import goods and services, and the EU regulatory policies that apply to them.[28] In effect, SMEs will need guidance from the Australian Government on how to avoid and limit legal and economic barriers to entry into foreign markets which are unfamiliar to them, or in which their rates of participation to date has been low. Moreover, for Australian SMEs to enter new EU markets for products not sold extensively in Australia, they need to acquire the know-how and skill sets to gain EU and through it, global market access. As an example of such an achievement, the Swiss firm of Heiniger exports quality shearing equipment all over the world despite the fact that the sheep industry in Switzerland is insignificant.[29]

Trade barriers that impede Australian SMEs gaining access to EU markets are also faced by SMEs in the EU gaining access to Australian markets. As *Cernat et al.* suggest:

> SME exporters suffer from relatively higher costs and challenges than larger exporters due to less human resources and capital. These barriers include tariffs, quotas and stringent rules of origin [...][as well as] differences in standard-related measures [which] remain one of the main obstacles to deepening the participation of SMEs in international trade not only in the EU but also in the United States.[30]

However, EU policy makers already address such barriers to trade. EU regulators recognize their need to disseminate detailed information, including statistical data, by which to identify not only external, but also internal barriers to SMEs importing and exporting goods and services. As *Mayer* and *Ottaviano* observe:

> This simple truth makes it clear that understanding the firm-level facts is essential to good policy making in Europe.[31]

As a result, the EU is proactive in promoting FTAs to facilitate SME trade, notably in sectors in which key trade irritants, such as tariff barriers, are sometimes imbedded within regulatory systems. In contrast, Australian regulators are far less pro-active in

---

[28]Cernat L, Norman-López A and Duch T-Figueras A, SMEs are more important than you think! Challenges and Opportunities for EU exporting SMEs, Chief Economist Note, Issue 3, September 2014, p. 9.

[29]Heiniger AG, Industrieweg 8, 3360 Herzogenbuchsee, Switzerland.

[30]Cernat L, Norman-López A and Duch T-Figueras A, SMEs are more important than you think! Challenges and Opportunities for EU exporting SMEs, Chief Economist Note, Issue 3, September 2014, p. 10.

[31]Mayer and Ottaviano (2007).

redressing the barriers to Australian SMEs engaging in trade abroad. It follows that Australia and its SMEs can gain benefit from an EU-Australian FTA which articulates rules and standards by which to facilitate export trade by SMEs that is not yet prevalent in Australia's FTA. In appreciating the ambit of these rules and standards, the Australian government can help, not only to open up new markets for SME goods and services in the EU, but also to expand into other foreign markets as well.

4 A Single European Market

The EU is by far the largest exporter in the world and exported 1.6 trillion euro of goods and services in 2009, which is about 13% of GDP.[32] In order to sustain its export markets, it has developed sustainable policies in order to retain, but also expand into, foreign markets.[33] Since its establishment the single EU market has grown geometrically. It currently provides 500 million Europeans with access to goods and services.[34] The EU has sustained a 15% increase in annual trade growth for more than 10 years. Working through a single EU regulatory system, it has effectively harmonized rules and standards governing imports and exports and harmonized the applicable law both internally among its member states and externally with its trading partners.[35] In doing so, it has created approximately 2.5 million jobs in the EU.[36]

The EU has also developed global markets for its SMEs in a strategic manner.[37] For example, the EU has established a common legal framework by which to regulate trade in industrial products that includes SMEs.[38] It has enacted the Small Business

[32]European Commission, COM (2010) 612 final, p. 4.

[33]European Commission, COM (2010) 612 final, p. 2.

[34]For trade purposes the European Union includes all member states and those other countries the make up the European Economic Area (EEA) and the European Free Trade Association (EFTA) (Iceland, Liechtenstein and Norway). Switzerland is not a member of the EEA but is a member of the EFTA and has established bilateral agreements with the European Union to ensure there is effective and efficient trade.

[35]European Parliament, Fact Sheets on the European Union, The internal market: general principles, http://www.europarl.europa.eu/atyourservice/en/displayFtu.html?ftuId=FTU_3.1.1.html (last accessed 1 March 2017).

[36]European Parliament, Fact Sheets on the European Union, The internal market: general principles.

[37]The European Commission defines SMEs as: "The category of micro, small and medium-sized enterprises (SMEs) is made up of enterprises which employ fewer than 250 persons and which have an annual turnover not exceeding 50 million euro, and/or an annual balance sheet total not exceeding 43 million euro." See Commission Recommendation of 6 May 2003 concerning the definition of micro, small and medium-sized enterprises, OJ 2003 L 124/36.

[38]Regulation (EC) No 765/2008 setting out the requirements for accreditation and the market surveillance of products, OJ 2008 L 218/30; Regulation (EC) No 264/2008 laying down the procedures relating to the application of certain technical rules to products lawfully marketed in another Member State, Decision 768/2008/EC on a common framework for the marketing of

Act for Europe (SBA) which focuses specifically on SMEs and which it has integrated into the EU's Europe 2020 strategy.[39] The SBA, in turn, has sought to promote entrepreneurship among SMEs across the EU. It has also developed consultative and regulatory frameworks to ensure that SMEs are not disproportionately disadvantaged in engaging in such trade. Typifying such a framework, the SBA initiated a program in 2008 directed at promoting access by SMEs to a wider range of EU products. That program sought to attain reasonable SME access through rules governing market surveillance, accreditation and conformity assessment.

Nevertheless, the EU faces new challenges, impeded by recent dislocation in EU economies.[40] As a result it has the economic incentive to facilitate the expansion of SME markets abroad beyond its current markets. To accomplish this expansion, it needs to harmonize standards, rules, accreditation systems, mutual recognition arrangements, protocols and treaties with new treaty partners. It also needs to address economic, legal, political and geographic barriers to entering markets, such as Australia, that are geographic distant from the EU and that have common law legal systems that diverge from the dominant civil law system of the EU.

The EU has already embarked on such market expansion for its SMEs. It has stressed the importance of building global markets in the Europe 2020 Communication on Industrial Policy and the EU 2010 Trade, Growth and World Affairs strategy.[41] Working through the European Commission, it has identified the fundamental objective of promoting SMEs in the Communication of its "Small Business Act" for Europe[42] and "Small Business, Big World",[43] Importantly, it has stressed that, by removing direct and indirect barriers to trade facing SMEs, it can meet its inclusive targets for market growth.[44]

In its Report on the public consultation on its "New SME Policy", the EU has stressed the need to reduce the administrative burden borne by SMEs, to provide SMEs across the EU with access to finance, to promote market access for SMEs, and to encourage entrepreneurial innovation directed at market growth.[45] The EU has also released policy papers on the expanding role of SMEs in global exports of goods and services, including by defining a SME in its directives.[46] Importantly, the

---

products, which includes reference provisions to be incorporated whenever product legislation is revised, and repealing Council Decision 93/465/EEC, OJ 2008 L 218/21.

[39]European Commission, "Think Small First"—A "Small Business Act" for Europe, COM (2008) 394 final.

[40]European Commission, Growth, Internal Market, Industry, Entrepreneurship and SMEs, http://ec.europa.eu/growth/smes_en (last accessed 1 March 2017).

[41]European Commission, COM (2010) 612 final.

[42]European Commission, COM (2008) 394 final, responding to the needs of small and medium-sized enterprises.

[43]European Commission, COM (2011) 702 final.

[44]European Commission, COM (2011) 702 final.

[45]European Commission, Report on the public consultation on the "New SME Policy", Ref. Ares (2015)812234–25/02/2015.

[46]See European Commission, Smart regulation—Responding to the needs of small and medium-sized enterprises, COM (2013) 122 final.

EU has championed the principle of inclusive growth that aims to promote high-employment and the delivery of economic and social benefits.[47]

In addressing market growth, the European Commission released the EU 2010 Trade, Growth and World Affairs strategy[48] as a core component in the EU's plan to expand trade abroad into the 2020s. In the foreword the EU Commissioner for Trade noted that:

> with the right policies in place we can fuel growth in Europe. By completing the trade deals on the table and engaging more closely with our strategic partners, trade policy can increase the size of our economy by around €150 billion. This would make a major contribution to the Union's wider agenda for smart, sustainable and inclusive growth.[49]

The European Commission has also recognized that "[t]rade and investment flows are key to the diffusion of innovation and new technologies across the EU and in the rest of the world." Conversely, it has stressed that "[r]egulatory barriers to trade in goods, services and investment are especially harmful, particularly to our major trading partners."[50]

5 Australian Small and Medium-Sized Enterprises in the EU

An important question arises as to how Australian SMEs can fit within the EU's focus on international markets for goods and services? How can the EU and Australia create a single market in which they harmonize their legal principles, standards and rules consistently with the harmonization of principles, standards and rules within the EU? And how can they do so, given Australia's geographic distance from the EU, and its legal and cultural differences with the EU, notably post Brexit? How too, can Australian negotiators—given the appropriate time frame—engage in parallel negotiations with the UK given that it is the fifth largest global economy?

At the macro-economic level, Australia is already a significant trading partner with the EU. Even though Australia is located closer to South East Asia than the EU, the benefits of trading with the EU and its member states cannot be underestimated. Take the example of one of the smallest EU states, Slovenia. Australia has a long standing relationship with Slovenia which began in 1855, when the first recorded Slovene arrived on Australian soil. Even, though trade between the two countries is small, there has been a steady flow of Slovenians and trade from Slovenia into Australia since World War II which includes SMEs. While 70% of Slovenia's exports are to EU member states, an EU-Australia FTA will

[47]European Commission, Europe 2020: A strategy for smart, sustainable and inclusive growth, COM (2010) 2020.

[48]European Commission, COM (2010) 612 final.

[49]European Commission, COM (2010) 612 final.

[50]European Commission, COM (2010) 612 final, para. 7.

provide more harmonized access to SMEs in Slovenia, as to SMEs in other EU member states. Were Australia to frame its SME policy in light of EU regulations and standards governing SMEs, Australia could extend those trade links into the EU and countries like Slovenia in particular. Australia would thereby be able to harmonize its regulation of SME trade with the EU, without having to develop a wholly new regulatory framework.

Australian trade into the EU member states would also likely extend beyond the EU to trade between EU member states and third party states. For example, despite being an EU member state, Slovenia has a long history of trade partnerships with South Eastern Europe which represent a market of 20 million people. By leveraging off an EU-Australia FTA, Australia could extend trade relations, directly or indirectly through Slovenia, into such third party states in South Eastern Europe. The result could be enhanced regulatory cooperation with these states arising through Australia's partnership with EU members, not limited to smaller states like Slovenia. As the European Commission stressed, such regulatory cooperation "is an important aspect of our trade relationships particularly with our key partners, or as part of FTA or similar negotiations."[51]

6 An EU-Australian Free Trade Agreement?

In negotiating an FTA with Australia, the EU is likely to insist that SMEs are specifically included in the resulting FTA. In adopting this course of action, EU negotiators will be guided by the fact that, in 2011, SMEs accounted for more than a third of total EU exports and represented 81% of the firms exporting outside the EU.[52] They will be motivated by the fact that the EU provides both direct and indirect support to SMEs, through infrastructure assistance, a market access strategy, a customs information portal, and centres providing financial advice to SMEs on securing access to foreign markets.[53] EU negotiators will also be guided by established EU policies directed at promoting the effective harmonization of EU and Australian legal principles, standards and rules regulating SMEs in bilateral trade.

More specifically, the EU has recognized its strong market-specific reasons to accommodate SMEs in negotiating an EU-Australia FTA.[54] This is particularly so in promoting innovation in the technology and service sectors. An example of such

[51]European Commission, COM (2010) 612 final, para. 7.

[52]Cernat L, Norman-López A and Duch T-Figueras A, SMEs are more important than you think! Challenges and Opportunities for EU exporting SMEs, Chief Economist Note, Issue 3, September 2014, p. 4.

[53]European Parliament, European SMEs and International Trade, February 2012, p. 19.

[54]See http://ec.europa.eu/trade/policy/countries-and-regions/countries/australia/ (last accessed 1 March 2017).

innovation is the benefit of promoting startups that evolve into SMEs in the renewable energy sector. In particular, an FTA could assist both the EU and Australia to collaborate with SMEs in decoupling energy from traditional energy resources in favor of low carbon and renewable energy that encompass multiple industries that involve SMEs.[55]

Most importantly, the EU appreciates the economic benefits that arise from extending SME trade beyond EU member states, not limited to Australia. For example, the Directorate-General for External Policies of the EU at a workshop entitled "European SMEs and International Trade",[56] observed from a survey that only 13% of EU SMEs were active outside the EU through trade, investment or other forms of cooperation with non-EU partners. This observation suggests that there is significant unfulfilled potential for EU SMEs to extend their involvement in non EU markets.[57] It also provides an incentive for the EU to expand SMEs exports to Australia, aided by advances in technology that offset geographic barriers.

However, to accommodate the interests of SMEs in both the EU and Australia, FTA negotiators will need to redress economic barriers to achieving these results. The EU will need to be assured that Australia is willing to harmonize its legal principles, standards and rules relating to SMEs with those of the EU. It will also be required to be cognizant of differences between regulatory regimes and EU and the Australian legal systems.

7 Is Australia Ready for a Free Trade Agreement with the EU?

An important question is whether Australian negotiators can rely on current Australian governmental policies to represent the interests of the Australian SME sectors in EU-Australia negotiations. Importantly, will the Australian regulatory regime be ready for an EU-Australia FTA that provides for SMEs?

In answering this question, it will be necessary for the Australian Government to enable its negotiators to take a proactive stance in support of SMEs, consistent with the approach adopted by the EU. An evident difference is that, while EU regulators have highlighted the importance of SMEs in determining EU export policies, Australian regulators have not done so to date. A crude but glaring illustration of this difference is the fact that the Australian Department of Foreign Affairs and Trade (DFAT) dedicates only one somewhat cursory page in its website to SMEs.[58] In contrast, the EU office of the Chief Economist and Trade Analysis Unit

[55]See http://ec.europa.eu/trade/policy/countries-and-regions/countries/australia/ (last accessed 1 March 2017).

[56]European Parliament, European SMEs and International Trade, February 2012.

[57]European Parliament, European SMEs and International Trade, February 2012, p. 13.

[58]See http://dfat.gov.au/pages/default.aspx (last accessed 1 March 2017).

elaborates in detail on the significance of SMEs to such trade. In particular, it notes that "SMEs have an untapped export potential, given the intrinsic and trade-specific hurdles that SMEs still face."[59]

Nevertheless, there are several arguments to indicate that Australia is ready for an EU-Australia FTA. First, the EU has a regulatory platform which Australian negotiators can adopt selectively in negotiating an FTA. Second, the EU has an established policy framework to govern SMEs that Australian negotiators can adapt in concluding an EU-Australia FTA. Third, an EU-Australia FTA entails bilateral negotiations even though there are multiple countries involved in the EU, thereby avoiding the complexity of a multilateral trade agreement with multiple parties. Fourth, the EU and Australia share somewhat comparable democratic values.[60] These four reasons provide a strong basis for productive negotiations and sustainable FTA outcomes.

Notwithstanding these advantages in negotiating an FTA, it is necessary to recognize that the EU has faced barriers in concluding trade agreements with other countries, notably in negotiating the TTIP. For example, the European Parliamentary Research Service (at the request of the European Parliament) noted that

> [t]he empirical economic analysis underlying the European Commission's Impact Assessment (IA) of the Transatlantic Trade and Investment Partnership (TTIP) is particularly difficult because the TTIP is an unusual bilateral trade agreement.[61]

In particular, the Parliamentary Research Service highlighted that regulatory heterogeneity between the US and the EU gave rise to "trade costs" in securing market access for both Parties. It added that it is exceedingly difficult to assess authoritatively the nature and consequences of those trade costs on the export of goods or services under the TTIP.[62]

FTA negotiators will also need to address the costs of protectionism, or conversely, the refusal to protect domestic markets, notably in the agriculture sector. The current Victorian milk crisis is an excellent example of a crisis triggered by global over-supply of agricultural goods, falling commodity prices, the nature of governmental regulation of cross-border agricultural trade generally, and control of domestic dairy markets by foreign corporations in particular. However, domestic "public interest" concerns about maintaining food security and regional viability of

---

[59] Cernat L, Norman-López A and Duch T-Figueras A, SMEs are more important than you think! Challenges and Opportunities for EU exporting SMEs, Chief Economist Note, Issue 3, September 2014.

[60] McMillan (2015), p. 98.

[61] European Parliamentary Research Service, EU-US Transatlantic Trade and Investment Partnership, Detailed Appraisal of the European Commission's Impact Assessment, 2014, http://www.europarl.europa.eu/RegData/etudes/etudes/join/2014/528798/IPOL-JOIN_ET%282014%29528798_EN.pdf (last accessed 1 March 2017), p. 9.

[62] European Parliamentary Research Service, EU-US Transatlantic Trade and Investment Partnership, Detailed Appraisal of the European Commission's Impact Assessment, 2014, p. 9.

farming communities, among others, is an issue that extends beyond Victoria and its SMEs engaged in the dairy sector. A more pervasive and potentially divisive issue is that overseas corporations, acting under the guise of trade liberalization, have become increasingly active in buying farmland, controlling supply chains and determining prices of agricultural produce. Typifying these issues was how Fonterra, an essentially non-New Zealand corporation, defended falling milk prices on the grounds that it was repatriating profits for the benefit of its New Zealand shareholders.[63] In adopting a hands-off approach, the New Zealand government declined to intervene, affirming a "free market" approach to resolve the issue, an approach which is somewhat replicated in Australia. In contrast, the EU and the United States have both provided assistance through subsidies or incentives to SMEs in the dairy sector, despite deregulating it.

In contrast to such protectionism, the Australian and New Zealand governments have recognized the importance of harmonizing their legal frameworks in their mutual relations so as to accommodate mutual trade, particularly in such services sector as accountancy, business law and therapeutics. Among other actions, they have entered into memoranda of understanding, joint statutory authorities, mutual accreditation systems, mutual recognition arrangements, single economic market initiatives, as well as though treaties and protocols.[64] What is absent from their trade agreements, however, is explicit provision for SMEs, despite the free movement of goods and services between the two countries.

In contrast, the EU has used such tools as protocols to its trade agreements to encourage SME trade in sectors such as agriculture, while still protecting itself from pests and disease arising from imported agricultural goods.[65] The question arises as to how FTAs in general can redress barriers faced by SMEs in seeking to access to foreign markets. In particular, to what extent can bilateral and regional trade agreements reduce barriers to SME trade across national boundaries, while still protecting local markets from foreign trade that threatens public health, the environment and for that matter, national security?

---

[63]Lockhart J, Donaghy D, Gow H, Murray Goulburn and Fonterra are playing chicken with dairy farmers, The Conversation, 23 May 2016, http://www.smartcompany.com.au/industries/agribusiness/69284-murray-goulburn-and-fonterra-are-playing-chicken-with-dairy-farmers/ (last accessed 1 March 2017).

[64]The Parliament of the Commonwealth of Australia, Standing Committee on Legal and Constitutional Affairs, Harmonisation of Legal Systems, within Australia and between Australia and New Zealand, 2006, chapters 1–3.

[65]The Parliament of the Commonwealth of Australia, Standing Committee on Legal and Constitutional Affairs, Harmonisation of Legal Systems, within Australia and between Australia and New Zealand, 2006, chapters 1–3.

8 Small and Medium-Sized Enterprises in Free Trade Agreements Generally

There is very little evidence of SMEs being provided for in FTAs generally, with the exception of FTAs involving China. For example, chapter 4 of the Swiss-China FTA on Customs Procedures and Trade Facilitation, provides that:

> Each Party shall consult its respective business community on its needs with regard to the development and implementation of trade facilitation measures, noting that particular attention should be given to the interests of small and medium-sized enterprises.[66]

Even more explicitly, Article 173 of the New Zealand-China FTA states: that

> the objectives of this Chapter are to facilitate the establishment of close cooperation aimed, inter alia, at: (c) creating new opportunities to encourage small and medium-sized enterprise ('SME') business growth and management development.

Furthermore, Article 176, states that the aims of Small and Medium-Sized Enterprises are:

> (a) to build on existing agreements or arrangements already in place for trade and economic cooperation;
>
> (b) to promote a favourable trading environment for the development of SMEs; and
>
> (c) to build the capacity of SMEs to trade effectively under this Agreement.
>
> 2. In pursuit of the objectives in paragraph 1, the Parties will encourage and facilitate, as appropriate, inter alia, the following activities:
>
> (a) promoting cooperation and information exchange between government institutions, business groups and industrial associations;
>
> (b) exploring jointly effective strategies and support policies for the development of SMEs, including financial support and intermediary services;
>
> (c) holding trade fairs and investment marts and promoting other mechanisms for exchanging goods and services involving SMEs of both Parties; and
>
> (d) promoting training and personnel exchange between SMEs of both Parties and relevant business advisors and industrial associations.
>
> 3. Cooperation activities will be oriented to improve knowledge and good practices among SMEs and to facilitate bilateral trade by SMEs, including through exchanges of information about regulatory regimes, local markets and regional and national economies of both Parties.[67]

Apart from this formal recognition of SMEs, the New Zealand-China FTA highlights the need for the exchange of information regarding different regulatory environments that include SMEs.[68]

---

[66] See https://www.eda.admin.ch/countries/china/de/home/vertretungen/botschaft/aufgaben/wirtschaft-finanzen/china-switzerland-free-trade-agreement.html (last accessed 1 March 2017).

[67] See https://www.mfat.govt.nz/assets/_securedfiles/FTAs-agreements-in-force/China-FTA/NZ-ChinaFTA-Agreement-text.pdf (last accessed 1 March 2017).

[68] See https://www.mfat.govt.nz/assets/_securedfiles/FTAs-agreements-in-force/China-FTA/NZ-ChinaFTA-Agreement-text.pdf (last accessed 1 March 2017).

In contrast, the China-Australian Free Trade agreement does not mention SMEs. The Instructions and Guidelines published by the Australian Government in relation to that FTA also do not indicate how SMEs can engage in exporting or importing under that FTA. Nor does the ASEAN-Australia-New Zealand Free Trade Agreement[69] provide expressly for trade involving SMEs.

The question therefore arises as to what criteria need to be satisfied in order to provide for SMEs in an EU-Australia FTA. For example, to what extent can Australia draw from its trade relationship with New Zealand in concluding an FTA with the EU that provides for SMEs? Even more significantly, to what extent can Australia rely on the EU to support Australian SMEs seeking access to EU markets under an EU-Australia FTA?

Such questions can be answered, in part, by reflecting on the opportunities of SMEs provided for in the G20 Agenda for growth.

9 The G20 Agenda for Growth: Opportunities for Small and Medium-Sized Enterprises

There is no doubt that promoting SME trade involves a higher overall regulatory cost than promoting trade involving large corporations. This is the unavoidable product of the multiplicity of SMEs and the multiple barriers to trade they face when compared to large enterprises. In 2014, the G20 Agenda for Growth: Opportunities for SMEs Conference[70] concluded that the compliance costs associated with international trade for SMEs can be 10–30 times greater than for larger firms.[71] While these costs of regulating SMEs are formidable, they are arguably outweighed by the economic benefits derived from expanding SME trade regionally and internationally. The benefit of enhancing SME trade, notwithstanding the costs of compliance, is potentially geometric. For example, Germany's recent trade surplus of 200 billion euros arose in large part from profitable trade generated by its 10,000 "*Mittelstand*" SME companies. Italy's medium-sized companies have also contributed significantly to its otherwise struggling economy.[72]

Nevertheless, it is important to identify the nature of compliance costs for governments in order to reduce them by managing compliance requirements directly, and by enlisting the cooperation of SMEs in order to reduce the burden of such management.

[69]See http://dfat.gov.au/trade/agreements/aanzfta/pages/asean-australia-new-zealand-free-trade-agreement.aspx (last accessed 1 March 2017).

[70]The G20 Agenda for Growth: Opportunities for SMEs, Conference, 20 June 2014, http://www.globalaccesspartners.org/G20-SME-Conference.pdf (last accessed 1 March 2017).

[71]The G20 Agenda for Growth: Opportunities for SMEs, Conference, 20 June 2014, p. 6.

[72]The G20 Agenda for Growth: Opportunities for SMEs, Conference, 20 June 2014, p. 21.

In accomplishing these compliance goals in relation to SMEs, it is important to so stipulate in an EU-Australia FTA and to provide mechanisms for doing so. Ideally and as a matter of both policy and process, the FTA should provide for SMEs in a separate chapter which outlines policies relating to SMEs and processes through which to implement them. These aspirations already have governmental support among G20 countries. Indeed, a key recommendation on the G20 Agenda for Growth is to encourage SMEs and industry organisations to submit specific examples of existing red tape requiring reform, for review by the executives of G20 members.[73]

How much time and energy to devote to redressing such impediments to SME trade, however, is potentially contentious. On the one hand, reducing the red tape that impedes SMEs from having effective access to foreign markets is the key to securing their cooperation and limiting the costs of managing their compliance. However, the pledge that "two parliamentary days each year will be dedicated to removing superfluous Acts and regulations"[74] is hardly enough time to debate issues of cutting red tape associated with promoting SME trade.

10 Australian Research and Organizations

It is debatable whether Australia has engaged sufficiently actively in the research and development of SME trade across national borders. Illustrating this concern about the limited involvement of universities in such research, in 2013, *Sir Whitty*[75] "called for universities to accept a third mission, in addition to teaching and research, to engage with SMEs through local enterprise partnerships."[76] Similarly, at the governmental level, organized collaboration between the Australian government and SMEs has only occurred on an *ad hoc* basis. Indeed "Australia ranks last out of 33 OECD countries in relations between business and academia."[77] Clearly, more needs to be done in the research and academic sphere to ensure there are tangible benefits to Australian SMEs when negotiations commence for an EU-Australia FTA.

What is also needed are regulatory policies in Australia that encourage SME trade in a manner that increases domestic output and employment.[78] What is

---

[73]The G20 Agenda for Growth: Opportunities for SMEs, Conference, 20 June 2014, p. 10.

[74]The G20 Agenda for Growth: Opportunities for SMEs, Conference, 20 June 2014, p. 10.

[75]Encouraging a British Invention Revolution: Sir Andrew Witty's Review of Universities and Growth, Final Report and Recommendations, October 2013, https://www.gov.uk/government/uploads/system/uploads/attachment_data/file/249720/bis-13-1241-encouraging-a-british-invention-revolution-andrew-witty-review-R1.pdf (last accessed 1 March 2017).

[76]Encouraging a British Invention Revolution: Sir Andrew Witty's Review of Universities and Growth, Final Report and Recommendations, October 2013, p. 24.

[77]Encouraging a British Invention Revolution: Sir Andrew Witty's Review of Universities and Growth, Final Report and Recommendations, October 2013, p. 29.

[78]Encouraging a British Invention Revolution: Sir Andrew Witty's Review of Universities and Growth, Final Report and Recommendations, October 2013, p. 20.

required is, not only the removal of regulatory red tape faced by SMEs,[79] but also provision for green tape that enables SMEs to gain access to foreign markets, including by addressing artificial trade barriers and unfair competition.

These positive developments are already partly underway. One of the more significant SME developments in Australia consists of a partnership between the Export Council and the Manufacturing Excellence Taskforce Australia. In particular, the Export Council of Australia (ECA), in conjunction with the "Manufacturing Excellence Taskforce Australia (META), has established the META Deregulation Hub to investigate reducing the regulation that adversely affects the ability of Australian manufacturers to compete internationally."[80]

The META Deregulation Hub has been established by META and ECA to connect manufacturing businesses with industry experts in order to identify and quantify the regulatory burdens and costs imposed on exports and their impact on Australian manufacturing companies.[81]

The META has published a Report and the ECA has published survey results relating to that Report. Of particular relevance, in 2014 META consulted 57 organizations in focus groups. The single most frequent issue raised by those surveyed concerned the application of standards and the need for certification.[82] Survey participants also commented on the excessive volume of documentation which was required of SMEs and the time it took to complete them in the presence of multiple and constantly changing export licensing requirements.[83]

Comparable issues emerged in evaluating the usefulness of information on addressing trade barriers and costs that are provided to SMEs under FTAs. Importantly, survey respondents indicated that FTAs are often not equitably implemented as Australian SOEs are held to a higher standard than overseas companies with branches in Australia.[84] Sadly, the META Hub which was funded by the Australian Government was disbanded once its funding period had expired.

It is arguable that a successor organization should be established and funded, including to develop research on an EU-Australia FTA. Alternatively, funding could be provided to the European Australian Business Council to undertake such research on behalf of the Australian Government. The purpose should be to enable both regulators and the business community to better understand whether such inequities exist in relation to SMEs and how they should be redressed. Doing so

---

[79]Encouraging a British Invention Revolution: Sir Andrew Witty's Review of Universities and Growth, Final Report and Recommendations, October 2013, p. 20.

[80]Export Council of Australia, META Deregulation Hub, see http://mtest.dynamicexport.com.au/article/meta/New-Deregulation-Hub-to-slash-regulatory-costs-for-exporters (last accessed 1 March 2017). Unfortunately the government decided to stop funding META. The author represented his university on META as an observer and has the report on file.

[81]Export Council of Australia, META Deregulation Hub.

[82]Export Council of Australia, META Deregulation Hub.

[83]Export Council of Australia, META Deregulation Hub.

[84]See https://www.mfat.govt.nz/assets/_securedfiles/FTAs-agreements-in-force/China-FTA/NZ-ChinaFTA-Agreement-text.pdf (last accessed 1 March 2017).

would enhance EU-Australian FTA negotiations by providing important data and information on the cost of SME's engaging in mutual trade and in SMEs developing the capacity to satisfy the regulatory requirements of both FTA parties.

A final consideration for Australia is not to be in a rush to sign up to the EU-Australia FTA. For instance, the recent FTA concluded between Australia and Japan has provided a significant political bonanza for both Governments. However, many of the provisions in that FTA will not take effect for at least 15 years.[85] In addition, industry councils in Australia, such as the Australian Dairy Industry Council, have voiced their disapproval of the small gains in tariff reductions provided for under the FTA, eschewing them as little more than symbolic. For example, the tariff reduction for beef exports from Australia to Japan, would be marginal, leaving beef in the light 19.5–23.5% tariff range.[86] An FTA with such limited scope is unlikely to stimulate further trade activity in general, and will definitely not assist smaller farmers and related SMEs.

Drawing an inference for Australia's FTA with Japan, what is required is an EU-Australia FTA that provides real opportunities for Australian and EU SMEs. This includes an FTA that significantly reduces tariff barriers to SME trade, and that come into effect long before 15 years from entering into such an FTA.

11 Conclusion

Using a proposed EU-Australia FTA as its framework, this chapter has argued that the Australian government has attempted, to a limited degree, to reduce red tape in order to promote export trade by Australian SMEs. However, it has done so in a generic manner, not through specific provisions in FTAs directed at promoting SME trade. Nor has it made serious attempts to determine the best way in which to assist SMEs engage in importing and exporting, and in reducing red tape obstacles to SME trade. Arguably, too many regulators are involved in such trade initiatives, there is an absence of coordination among them, and efforts to promote and benefit SMEs in particular have disintegrated, insofar as they were ever started.

A concentrated effort is needed to harness the potential of Australian SMEs to fully exploit their contribution to the Australian economy, and to increase trade and employment through them. It is worth noting that, at the G20 conference in Melbourne, it was noted that:

> The SME sector must be supported by better research, improved access to information and a renewed emphasis on the commercialisation of Australian innovation.[87]

---

[85]See http://www.abc.net.au/news/2015-01-15/japan-free-trade-agreement-takes-effect/6018760 (last accessed 1 March 2017).

[86]See http://www.abc.net.au/news/2015-10-06/agriculture-tariffs-to-fall-under-tpp/6830138 (last accessed 1 March 2017).

[87]The G20 Agenda for Growth: Opportunities for SMEs, Conference, 20 June 2014.

To this was added:

> The Australian Government is scrutinising the financial, legislative and tax requirements faced by SMEs and removing or reforming those which act against the public interest.[88]

However, Australian SMEs have not gained much benefit from these assertions. Primary barriers to Australian SME participating in foreign markets arise are not only from their limited funding, or even from the lack of skilled personnel in the sector that can address complex regulatory and other barriers to trade. Limited access to foreign markets stems materially from the lack of government support in address the deficient understanding and confidence of SMEs in gaining access to such markets.

There are now viable opportunities for Australian SMEs to redress these deficiencies. Indeed, it is arguable that physical barriers they have faced in seeking access to foreign markets have receded with the development of important new opportunities enabling them to participate more effectively in global markets in new technologies, not least of all through the use of the Internet. However, Australian SMEs need more Government support to utilize these technologies in order to engage effectively in those foreign markets.

An important means of Australian SMEs acquiring the confidence and resources to enter foreign markets, such as the EU, is through a comparative investigation of the treatment accorded to SMEs by other countries, including through their FTAs. For example, it would be instructive to compare the manner in which the China-New Zealand and China-Switzerland FTAs address SMEs, as Australia prepares itself for FTA negotiations with the EU.

Importantly too, the Australian government and its SMEs have some strategic advantages in seeking access to EU markets at this time. The Australian dollar is low, making exports by SMEs into the EU cheaper. It is generally known that Federal and State governments in Australia have imposed safety regulations on SMEs in manufacturing and supplying goods and services. Such knowledge would be reassuring to the EU. In addition, the EU is currently seeking new trade markets, not least of all with the exit of the UK from that Union.

A challenge ahead is for the Australian Government to demonstrate its willingness to assist SMEs to redress both internal and external obstacles to trade, and to provide them with viable opportunities to export goods and services to the EU on a sustained basis. To meet these challenges, Australian SMEs have to demonstrate that they are both innovative and competitive in EU markets, and that they can outperform competitors in their sectors. However, if they are to establish beachheads in EU markets, they require material assistance from the Australian government to promote their exports of manufactured goods, agricultural products and new technologies. The Australian government, in turn, needs to recognise the value of repositioning its export sector to include SMEs in relation to the EU, notably in recognition of the economic fallout arising from the continuing global retreat from

[88]The G20 Agenda for Growth: Opportunities for SMEs, Conference, 20 June 2014.

the pre-existing mining boom that had fuelled the Australian economy. Further supporting an EU-Australia FTA is the value of Australia diversifying into important markets beyond China and the United States. The EU, along with the exiting UK, provides such export opportunities. They are well worth exploring as Australia strives to enhance access to such international markets.

Finally, it is necessary that an EU-Australia FTA include real and effective tariff reductions that are more than symbolic. A timeframe of between 5 and 10 years in which to action such an FTA would better ensure that trade benefits including to Australia's SMEs flow more timeously and profitably than they have with other agreements that Australia has signed, including the US-Australia FTA and Australia's recent FTA with Japan.

References

Leonidou L (1995) Empirical research on export barriers: review, assessment, and synthesis. J Ind Mark 3(1):29–43

Mayer T, Ottaviano G (2007) The happy few: the internationalisation of European firms. New facts based on firm-level evidence. Bruegel Blueprint Series, vol III, Brussels

McMillan K (2015) Moving freely, but taking a different route: comparing Trans-Tasman and European Union norms of human mobility. In: Biörkdahl A, Chaban N, Leslie J, Masselot A (eds) Importing EU norms: conceptual framework and empirical findings. United Nations University Series on Regionalism, vol 8. Springer International Publishing, pp 97–113

EU-Taiwan: New Partners in International Trade Negotiations

Roy Chun Lee

Abstract This paper examines the possible trade negotiation agendas between the EU and Taiwan in lieu of a comprehensive Free Trade Agreement (FTA). The EU and Taiwan are both important trade and investment partners to each other; trade in goods, for example, shows a strong production network relationship. A number of notable impediments also exist, arising mainly in the areas of TBT, SPS and domestic regulatory practices. Ideally, an FTA following the EU standards would underpin further enhancement of the already robust relationship, yet such an undertaking is barred by the EU's political constrains in light of China's likely opposition. A Bilateral Investment Agreement (BIA) has been considered as a substitution, but there are questions regarding the value of a BIA in terms of substance and timing. This paper argues that if the EU and Taiwan intend to capture the benefits of deep integration, it would require "out-of-the-box" thinking. Taking into account the nature of the bilateral barriers, this paper puts forward proposals in pursuing bilateral TBT and SPS Agreement as the priority, with collaboration in the Trade in Services Agreement (TiSA) as well as in the sectoral initiatives in the WTO.

Contents

R.C. Lee (✉)
Taiwan WTO & RTA Center, Chung-Hua Institution for Economic Research (CIER), Taipei City 106, Taiwan
e-mail: roy.lee@cier.edu.tw

M. Bungenberg et al. (eds.), *European Yearbook of International Economic Law 2017*, European Yearbook of International Economic Law 8,
DOI 10.1007/978-3-319-58832-2_18

1 Introduction

The economic relationship between the EU and Taiwan is uniquely distorted. Bilateral trade and investment is intense and growing. At a macroeconomic level, Taiwan is the EU's 18th largest trading partner worldwide and was 7th in Asia in 2015; at the product level, Taiwan is the primary supplier of semiconductors and other capital goods in the EU. At the same time, the EU is Taiwan's number one source of foreign investment and their 5th largest trading partner. Intuitively, this close relationship would normally prompt the EU and Taiwan to seriously consider the removal of unnecessary impediments through binding and institutionalised mechanisms such as the negotiation of a Free Trade Agreement (FTA). Yet still constrained by political realities, Taiwan is the only top trading partner that is excluded from the EU's trade negotiation agenda in Asia.[1] This is unique especially given the fact that the EU is actively pursuing strategic engagements in Asia and the Pacific region.[2]

Recent FTAs are no longer agreements merely focusing on the market opening of tariff and investment liberalisation. Rather they involve many behind-the-border "deep integration" elements that are aimed at creating harmonised rules and coherence in decision-making process.[3] Specifically, this reflects the desire by participating countries to enhance the competitiveness and efficiency of the production networks through the removal of behind-the-border obstacles in technical regulations, conformity assessment procedures, services regulations, competition policy, regulatory practices,[4] and more recently, in cross-border data movement. With the units of integration increasingly determined by production networks rather than national boundaries, it will be efficient-maximising if FTA networks integrated fully with production networks. To the contrary, if a key player in the Asia

[1]As of 2016, the EU has concluded or initiated FTA negotiations with most of its main Asian trading partners, namely Japan, South Korea, Malaysia Singapore, Thailand, Vietnam and India, and the discussions of a Bilateral Investment Agreement (BIA) with China and Myanmar is ongoing. This would include all except one (Hong Kong) of the EU's top 10 trading partners in Asia. The EU's FTA negotiation status update is available at http://trade.ec.europa.eu/doclib/docs/2006/december/tradoc_118238.pdf (last accessed 1 March 2017).

[2]European Commission, Trade for all: Towards a more responsible trade and investment policy, 2015, p. 31.

[3]WTO, World Trade Report 2011, The WTO and preferential trade agreements: From co-existence to coherence, p. 145.

[4]WTO, World Trade Report 2011, The WTO and preferential trade agreements: From co-existence to coherence, pp. 146–148.

Pacific production networks such as Taiwan is omitted from the FTA network,[5] the trade and investment diversion effects are likely to bring distortion and extra cost to both the EU and Taiwan.[6]

It is however increasingly clear that the traditional framework for economic integration does not work fully in the EU-Taiwan context. A comprehensive FTA appears to be unlikely in the near future, and a Bilateral Investment Agreement (BIA) is likely to be seriously delayed under the EU's "China-first" stance. These limitations suggest that if the EU and Taiwan intend to capture the benefits of deep integration underpinned by binding commitments and institutionalised cooperation mechanisms, it would require "out-of-the-box" thinking and tailor-made approaches with pragmatic perspectives and flexibility in ways and means. This is the topic that this paper intends to explore.

This paper starts with a review of the bilateral trade and investment relationship between the EU and Taiwan. Part 3 of the paper examines the barriers and impediments that are hindering the economic relationship. Part 4 discusses the benefits and limitations of traditional negotiation agendas, namely the FTA and BIA approach, and several new negotiation ideas are offered in part 5.

2 The EU-Taiwan Trade and Investment Relationship

2.1 Overview

Bilateral trade and investment ties between the EU and Taiwan are intimate and robust. In 2015, total trade with Taiwan accounts for 1.3% of the EU's total world trade, making Taiwan the EU's 18th trading partner globally and the 5th in Asia.[7] While the EU runs a deficit in trade in goods, services trade between the EU and Taiwan has been expanding and the EU has continued to enjoy a trade surplus. From Taiwan's perspective, the trade and investment relationship with the EU is more prominent. In 2015 the EU was Taiwan's fifth largest trading partner next to

[5]WTO and IDE-JETRO, Trade patterns and global value chains in East Asia: From trade in goods to trade in tasks, 2011, p. 6. For a case study on Taiwan's role in the global production networks, see Chen SH and Wen PC, A Longitudinal View on Global Production Network, Trade and Economic Integration. Paper presented at the Conference on Trade and Development Symposium, the Ninth WTO Ministerial Conference, Bali, Indonesia 3–5 December 2013, http://www.cier.edu.tw/public/Data/2014-2.pdf (last accessed 1 March 2017).

[6]Copenhagen Economics, EU-Taiwan Trade Enhancement Measures: Update of the 2008 report "Taiwan: Enhancing Opportunities for European Business", 20 September 2012, http://www.ecct.com.tw/file/userfiles/files/2012%20TEM%20Update%20Study(1).pdf (last accessed 1 March 2017).

[7]European External Action Services, EU-Taiwan Factfile 2016, https://eeas.europa.eu/sites/eeas/files/eufactfile2016.pdf (last accessed 1 March 2017).

China, ASEAN, the US and Japan.[8] More importantly, the EU is Taiwan's largest source of Foreign Direct Investment (FDI). In 2015, for instance, FDI from the EU reached US$1.02 billion, accounting for 20% of Taiwan's total FDI, only next to the British Caribbean Islands (29%).[9] Accumulatively, however, EU's FDI stock accounted for 25% of total FDI stock in Taiwan, making the EU the largest investor in Taiwan.

2.2 *Trade in Goods with a Strong Production Network Characteristic*

Despite the fact that the total bilateral trade value between the EU and Taiwan only represents a small portion of EU's external trade vis-à-vis other main trading partners in the Asia region, it has been on the rise in recent years (Table 1), and the trade surplus Taiwan has enjoyed is declining. However, not withstanding the EU's trade surplus in some product categories (e.g. pharmaceuticals, organic chemicals and automotive products), the overall trade deficit for the EU remains high, reaching US$9.7 billion in 2015. Significant trade deficit has always been a policy concern for most governments, yet such concern derived mainly from a traditional approach in understanding bilateral trade relationships, in which the gain of one country is considered the loss of the other with the assumption that the pair is competing horizontally in the downstream final product market. From a production network perspective, however, trade balance gradually becomes just a simple indication of the direction and degree of vertical collaboration and complementarity in a production network relationship.[10] This is evidently the case for the EU-Taiwan trade relationship, and it is an indication that there will be more common interest than competition in considering trade policy.

Indeed the composition of products traded bilaterally denotes a strong production network relationship. As demonstrated in Table 2 below, Taiwan's export to the EU is dominated by a small group of products. These include electrical machinery and its parts, telecom equipment, mechanical appliances, computers, and non-railway vehicles. Together these categories of products account for over 60% of Taiwan's export to the EU in recent years. The trade pattern between the EU and Taiwan is directly associated with Taiwan's economic re-structuring efforts. Particularly, Taiwan has restructured its industrial position during the last two decades from a major producer of final products to the supply of intermediary goods.[11] Consumer Information and Communications (ICT) products that

[8]Taiwan Bureau of Foreign Trade, Ministry of Economic Affairs, International trade database, http://www.trade.gov.tw/Pages/List.aspx?nodeID=1376 (last accessed 1 March 2017).

[9]Taiwan Bureau of Foreign Trade, Ministry of Economic Affairs, International trade database, http://www.trade.gov.tw/Pages/List.aspx?nodeID=1376 (last accessed 1 March 2017).

[10]Athukorala (2010), p. 17 et seq.

[11]Dreyer et al. (2010), p. 9.

Table 1 Trade in goods between Taiwan and the EU

	Total trade		Taiwan's export		Taiwan's import		Balance	
Year	Value	Growth rate (%)	Value	Growth rate (%)	Value	Growth rate (%)	Value	Growth rate (%)
2010	48.7	31.3	27.3	27.9	21.3	36.0	6.0	5.7
2011	52.6	8.0	28.6	4.5	24.0	12.5	4.6	−23.7
2012	48.7	−7.4	26.2	−8.3	22.5	−6.3	3.7	−18.6
2013	49.1	0.8	25.3	−3.7	23.9	6.1	1.4	−62.8
2014	50.9	3.7	26.5	4.9	24.4	2.4	2.1	48.4
2015	46.5	−8.8	23.7	−10.5	22.8	−6.9	0.97	−52.9

Source: Republic of China (Taiwan), Ministry of Economic Affairs, Trade Statistics: http://cus93.trade.gov.tw
Unit: US$ billion

Table 2 Taiwan's main export and import product with the EU

	August 2016		August 2015	
Product category	Value	% of total trade	Value	% of total trade
Total export to EU	*21.7*		*20.9*	
Electrical Machinery and equipment/parts, telecom equip., sound and TV recorders	6.7	31.1	6.7	32.1
Machinery and mechanical appliances, computers	3.7	17.2	3.9	18.7
Vehicles other than railway or tramway rolling stock	2.6	12.0	2.5	12.0
Iron and steel articles	1.5	6.9	1.5	7.2
Plastics & plastic articles	0.9	4.3	1.0	5.0
Metal tools and parts	0.7	3.1	0.7	3.2
Optical and precision equipment, medical or surgical instruments & accessories	0.7	3.1	0.6	2.9
Others	3.2	14.6	3.0	14.4
Total import from EU	*20.4*		*22.7*	
Machinery & mechanical appliances, computers	4.9	23.9	4.5	19.6
Electrical Machinery and equip. & parts	2.9	14.4	2.3	10.3
Vehicles other than railway or tramway rolling stock	2.0	9.6	3.3	14.5
Pharmaceutical products	1.4	6.8	1.4	6.2
Optical and precision equipment, medical or surgical instruments & accessories	1.1	5.6	1.2	5.2
Organic chemicals	0.9	4.4	1.1	5.1
Beverages, spirits & vinegar	0.9	4.3	1.1	4.7
Others	4.8	23.5	5.7	25.0

Source: Republic of China (Taiwan), Ministry of Economic Affairs, Trade Statistics: http://cus93.trade.gov.tw
Unit: US$ 100 million; %

historically accounted for more than half of Taiwan's total export have declined rapidly since 1998 to just around 15% in 2006. Instead, ICT parts and components became the primary export products.[12] This is also evident in the trade pattern between the EU and Taiwan.

Taking integrated circuit (semiconductors) as the example, Taiwan has been the EU's top supplier of semiconductors in the last decade and in 2015, Taiwan was EU's number one source of supply of semiconductors outside EU, occupying over 17% of the market share in the imported semiconductors market. Computer and accessories is another group of ICT products for which Taiwan is the EU's main supplier. Interestingly, Taiwan's most competitive intermediate products in the EU market are not hi-tech: screws, bolts, nuts and washers and related products from Taiwan account for over a quarter of the market share in the EU (followed by the US with 16% market share).[13] Other main product trades between the EU and Taiwan, including machinery, mechanical appliances, transport equipment, plastics and chemicals are also indications of the existence of strong production networking between the EU and Taiwan (Table 2).

2.3 *Trade in Services and Investment with Room to Improve*

Compared with trade in goods, the value of bilateral trade in services between the EU and Taiwan is relatively small.[14] Total trade value in services between the EU and Taiwan was 7.3 billion Euros in 2014, with the EU's services export values at 4.3 billion Euros and imports from Taiwan valued at 3.1 billion Euros (Table 3).

Table 3 Taiwan's services trade value with the EU

	Total trade		Taiwan's export		Taiwan's import		Balance	
Year	Value	Growth rate (%)	Value	Growth rate (%)	Value	Growth rate (%)	Value	Growth rate (%)
2010	6.99	–	2.47	–	4.53	–	2.07	–
2011	6.25	−10.7	2.36	−4.4	3.89	−14.1	1.53	−26.1
2012	6.94	11	2.67	13.1	4.26	9.5	1.59	3.9
2013	7.34	5.8	3.08	15.3	4.26	−0.1	1.18	−25.8
2014	7.34	0.1	3.05	−1.0	4.30	0.9	1.25	5.9
Average	6.972	1.55	2.76	5.8	4.2	−0.95	1.524	−0.11

Source: EUROSTAT—Data available only for 2010–2014
Unit: Billion Euros

[12]World Trade Organization and IDE-JETRO, Trade patterns and global value chains in East Asia: From trade in goods to trade in tasks, 2011, https://www.wto.org/english/res_e/booksp_e/stat_tradepat_globvalchains_e.pdf (last accessed 1 March 2017), p. 11.

[13]Taiwan Bureau of Foreign Trade, Ministry of Economic Affairs, International trade status and development 2015, http://www.trade.gov.tw/App_Ashx/File.ashx?FilePath=../Files/Doc/46fc1c3a-44ff-4f45-bd82-24e05970c6a3.pdf (last accessed 1 March 2017).

[14]As Taiwan does not collect bilateral services trade data, this paper relies on the EU's statistics from EUROSTAT for the analysis in this section.

Table 4 EU direct investment in selected Asian economies

	2010	2011	2012	2013	2014
Singapore (GDP: US$292.7 billion)	109,532	104,184	92,550	91,875	102,914
Japan (GDP: US$4123 billion)	98,053	100,933	96,130	81,259	72,958
South Korea (GDP: US$1377 billion)	37,480	36,306	35,206	32,308	43,720
Malaysia (GDP: US$296.2 billion)	22,063	23,067	17,208	20,046	21,654
Taiwan (GDP: US$523.6 billion)	10,618	10,521	11,011	9389	10,725

Sources: EUROSTAT and CIA World Fact book
Note: EURO STAT adopted new data collection methodology in 2013 with the fourth edition of the OECD Benchmark Definition of Foreign Direct Investment (BD4), thus data from 2013 onwards is not comparable with previous years
Unit: Euros Million

Contrary to trade in goods, the EU has maintained a surplus with Taiwan in services trade; in 2015, the positive balance was 1.3 billion Euros. It is of note that while total services trade value continued to increase during the last 5 years, the trade surplus enjoyed by the EU is volatile and diminishing. A decrease of more than 25% was recorded in the EU's services exports for both 2011 and 2013, and until 2014, the export value was still 40% less than the figure in 2010. Further, the growth rate for Taiwan's services export to the EU, on average over 5% growth between 2010 and 2014, has out-performed EU's export growth (−1% over the 5-year period).

The investment relationship between the EU and Taiwan is more intense yet asymmetric. Over the past decade, the EU has been the most important source of inbound FDI for Taiwan. In 2014, FDI stock from the EU stood at 10.7 billion Euros, which accounts for nearly 25% of total foreign investment in Taiwan and is considerably higher than the rest of foreign investors[15] (Table 4). The investment from Taiwan to the EU, on the other hand, is far less significant. In 2014, the EU received just 2% of Taiwan's total FDI stock globally. According to Taiwan's Ministry of Economic Affairs (MOEA) statistics, on average over 61% of Taiwan's outward FDI went to China for the last 20 years, followed by British Caribbean (11.9%) the US (5.1%) and Singapore (4.3%). The U.K. is the EU Member State that has hosted most of Taiwan's investment in the EU, receiving half of the FDI stock from Taiwan.[16]

Although the EU has already been the most active investor in Taiwan, there is still significant room for improvement if compared with the EU's participation in other Asian countries. As shown in Table 4, the level of EU's investment in Taiwan is significantly lower than that of Singapore, Japan, South Korea and Malaysia, after taking into account the relative GDP size. South Korea, for example, with a GDP around 2.6 times larger than Taiwan, attracts four times more FDI from the EU as at

[15]British Caribbean, which is the second largest investor in Taiwan, accounted for 19% of FDI stock in 2014, followed by the US (17%) and Japan (13%).

[16]Taiwan Investment Commission, 2015 Annual Inflow and outflow investment Statistics, http://www.moeaic.gov.tw/download-file.jsp?id=CSJffQHprx8%3d (last accessed 1 March 2017).

2014. The case for Malaysia is even clearer. With a GDP size only 57% of that of Taiwan, the EU's investment in Malaysia is 200% higher vis-à-vis that of Taiwan. This implies that it remains a key policy agenda for Taiwan to continue refining its attractiveness to EU investment. Vice versa, more effort is required for the EU to elevate the level of Taiwanese investment interest in the EU region.

3 Major Bilateral Trade Concerns Between the EU and Taiwan

3.1 Non-Tariff Measures (NTMs) Are the Key Potential Barriers

Admittedly both the EU and Taiwan are already among the most open economies in the world,[17] but there are still issues and impediments that prevent further deepening of the relationship. Some of the issues are more systematic and persistent than others. Identifying these obstacles would be the first step to underpinning a focused orientation for any future EU-Taiwan trade negotiations. Tariffs are unlikely to be the primary barriers hindering the bilateral trade in goods, as even duties levied on a most-favoured-nation (MFN) basis are already low for both the EU and Taiwan.[18]

As for the openness in the services sectors, one quantitative study found that the overall level of services restrictions in Taiwan is equivalent to a tariff rate of 37.3%, which is significantly higher than that of EU (17.3%) but lower than that of Korea (46.4%).[19] Another research measuring the level of services liberalization among the 21 APEC Economies found that Taiwan's openness is higher than, for instance, that of the US, Japan and South Korea.[20] This suggests that the most likely areas of trade and investment impediments are in the form of Non-Tariff Measures (NTMs).

The European Commission periodically publishes reports on potentially trade restrictive measures adopted by trading partners. In the latest version of the

[17]In the 2016 Economic Freedom Index published by the Heritage Foundation, Taiwan is identified as a "Mostly Free" Economy and ranked 14th out of 178 countries reviewed, before the Netherlands (16) and Germany (17). The full ranking is available at http://www.heritage.org/index/ranking (last accessed 1 March 2017).

[18]Based on World Trade Organization (WTO) tariff profiles, the trade weighted average applied tariffs for Taiwan and the EU are 1.9% and 3.6% respectively. See WTO Tariff and Trade Indicator https://www.wto.org/english/res_e/statis_e/statis_maps_e.htm (last accessed 1 March 2017).

[19]Copenhagen Economics, Taiwan: Enhancing Opportunities for European Business, August 2008, http://www.ecct.com.tw/file/userfiles/files/Copenhagen%20EU-Taiwan%20Study%20Aug2008%20Final.pdf (last accessed 1 March 2017), p. 27.

[20]Foster et al., Trade in Services in the APEC Region: Challenges and Opportunities for Improvement, USC-ABAC Joint Research, University of Southern California, September 2012, p. 51.

report,[21] Taiwanese measures identified as such by the European Commission can be categorised into three main policy areas, namely those relating to sanitary and phytosanitary (SPS) regulations,[22] market access restrictions for government procurement participation, and restriction on foreign participation in the cable radio and TV services sector.[23]

A further and more comprehensive set of information on potential trade and investment impediments in Taiwan is available in the annual European Chamber of Commerce Taiwan (ECCT) Position Paper.[24] Trade and investment policy-related issues reflected in the 2017 Position Paper, for instance, are mostly NTMs in nature. Further categorisation and simple counting of the frequency of issues reported under each category reveal that Technical Barriers to Trade (TBT), i.e. measures relating to mandatory standards or technical regulations and conformity assessment procedures, is the most challenging policy area encountered by EU firms in Taiwan (Table 5). There is a broad range of TBT-related issues included in the 2017 Position Paper, ranging from inconsistency in mandatory standards and testing procedurals with international standards, non-recognition of test report and certifications, burdensome testing and authorization/registration requirements, to unnecessary labeling regulations. The second group of issues is those concerning domestic regulations in services sectors. EU banking operators in Taiwan, for example, complained about the regulator's conservativeness in approving internet-based new services.[25] Problems in other areas, such as SPS, government procurement and intellectual property protection, are significantly less in quantity if not the level of seriousness.

On the other hand, trade and investment concerns revealed by Taiwan exporters are mainly associated with the tariff discrimination for products that are competing with Korean exports after the EU-Korea FTA came into force in 2012. For instance, exporters of petroleum resin and polyester filament yarn have repeatedly expressed

---

[21]European Commission, Overview of Potentially Trade Restrictive Measures Identified between 2008 and the End of 2015, May 2016, http://trade.ec.europa.eu/doclib/docs/2016/may/tradoc_154568.pdf (last accessed 1 March 2017).

[22]For instance, the Commission identified Taiwan's removal of Poland from the list of non-infected countries for African Swine Fever is inconsistent with WTO and the Organisation for Animal Health (OIE). See European Commission, Overview of Potentially Trade Restrictive Measures Identified between 2008 and the End of 2015, May 2016, p. 39.

[23]European Commission, Overview of Potentially Trade Restrictive Measures Identified between 2008 and the End of 2015, May 2016, pp. 70 and 95.

[24]European Chamber of Commerce Taiwan, 2017 Position Paper: Gearing up Taiwan's Revivals, November 2016, http://www.ecct.com.tw/file/Publications/201611171256325377.pdf (last accessed 1 March 2017). The position paper is formulated by members of the ECCT's 29 industry committees and its board of directors, representing the interests of some 400 companies and organizations and over 800 individual members.

[25]European Chamber of Commerce Taiwan, 2017 Position Paper: Gearing up Taiwan's Revivals, 2016, pp. 16 and 32.

Table 5 Frequency and content of restriction faced by EU Firms in Taiwan

Policy areas involved	No. of issues raised	Description of the issues
TBT related (including labelling)	24	Automotive: Safety, emission and noise testing standards and procedures not compatible with international standards, restriction on forging laboratory participation. Agro-chemical: product registration procedural, testing requirement. Beverage alcohol: Labelling regulations. Cosmetics: Pre-market registration requirement, labelling requirement. Electronic equipment: Repetition of testing and certification, harmonisation of international standards. Pharmaceutical and medical device: unnecessary testing, market authorisation and registration requirements.
Sectoral domestic regulation for services sectors	21 (2/3 of which relates to financial sector)	Banking regulation: Relaxation of regulations on new banking (especially internet-based) and asset management services and setting up new outlets by foreign banks. Insurance regulation: Relaxation of regulations on the approval and registration of new insurance products, expedite approval procedural. Telecom: Spectrum allocation, base-station deployment. Movement of natural persons: Rigidity in visa and work permit.
SPS related	6	The SPS approval process is excessive. Taiwan's food standards, procedures and testing methods are inconsistent with international standards. Review process for import of organic food is cumbersome and redundant. Discriminatory rules on food supplements. Slowness in updating the list of approved food additives. Standards and processes to measure Maximum Residue Limits (MRLs) of pesticide not consistent with international standards and best practices.
Government procurement	5	Unbalanced risk allocation, unlimited liability and not using arbitration as a dispute resolution mechanism in GPA contracts. Lack of procurement supervision and collaboration between central and local authorities. Limited use of "most advantageous tender selection process" (as contrary to lowest tender system). Transparency in dispute procedures.

(continued)

Table 5 (continued)

Policy areas involved	No. of issues raised	Description of the issues
IPR	4	The government's intervention in royalty rates and interfered with the normal rights of parties to negotiate rates. Ineffective handling of online copyright infringements: Inadequate trademark/trade dress protection. Confusion of the definition of "process patent protection" and "Patent linkage").
Customs procedurals	3	Simplifying export procedures. No buffer period for the implementation of new regulations. Over-stringent criteria for International Logistics Centre requirements.
General admin. procedural	2	Transparency and consistency of government policies. Administrative measures which may exceed the authorisation of the law or even be in conflict with other laws.
Tariffs	1	Tariff rate on Champagne higher than those for regular grape wine
Others	1	The reimbursement pricing mechanism for pharmaceutical and medical devices is efficient and discourages innovation.

Note: The frequency of issues raised is based on author's own calculation Source: European Chamber of Commerce Taiwan, 2016

their disadvantageous positions (with tariff rates of 6.5% and 4.5% respectively) to their Korean competitors, who pay no tariffs when entering the EU market.[26]

3.2 *The Implications*

Superficially, insofar as the quantity of potentially trade and investment impeding measures is concerned, the asymmetry between the EU and Taiwan is clearly recognisable. Intuitively, the most direct implication from this result is that Taiwan would qualify, by the EU's own standard, as an ideal candidate for FTA negotiation. It is of note, however, that there are disagreements by competent authorities in Taiwan in terms of classifying some of the aforementioned issues as trade barriers.[27] For issues involving regulatory treatment in the financial sector, the

[26]Chinese (Taiwan) National Confederation of Industries, 2015 Export Barriers Industry Survey Report, 2016, http://wto.cnfi.org.tw/admin/upload/12/2015report.pdf (last accessed 1 March 2017).

[27]The Taiwan government officially responds to most of the issues raised in each year's Position Paper. The latest responses to the 2016 Position Paper see http://www.ndc.gov.tw/Content_List.aspx?n=D7D3AA1846E85A23 (last accessed 1 March 2017).

Taiwanese regulator has rejected many of the reform proposals put forward by the ECCT Position Paper on prudential grounds.[28] Likewise, quarantine and food safety authorities also argued that their zoning, registration and other practices are in line with relevant international standards and disciplines.[29]

This paper does not intend nor has it the ability to make judgment on the justification and consistency of all the measures at issue. Rather the categorisation serves as a benchmark for prioritising policy areas for future EU-Taiwan trade negotiations. As such, some interesting observations can be drawn from the analysis. First, while a comprehensive FTA remains the ideal mechanism to address all the barriers discussed, the distinctive characteristics of the restrictions existing between the EU and Taiwan suggest that the priority of future negotiation, FTA or not, should be given to mechanisms in tackling and removing unnecessary and unjustified behind-border NTMs, especially in the area of TBT, services domestic regulations and SPS issues.

Second, for many NTMs, the problems are not only concerned with rules and regulations *per se*. Instead the challenges reside more in the regulatory decision-making process, i.e. the case-by-case interpretation of the regulations, the deliberation of data/information and the consultation (or lack of) with stakeholders to reach a positive conclusion on individual circumstances. In other words, the solution to many of the aforementioned issues is to improve the regulatory quality through introducing regulatory best practices. As such, it highlights the need to include regulatory cooperation, experience-sharing and capacity-building as essential negotiation agenda items.

4 The EU-Taiwan Negotiation Agenda: The Conventional Approach

4.1 The EU-Taiwan Free Trade Agreement

Many ideas have been put in place to explore possible avenues for further enhancing the EU-Taiwan economic relationship, with the negotiation of an FTA the favourable option. In 2008, the ECCT commissioned a study to examine the economic benefits of a potential FTA between the EU and Taiwan. Referred to as "trade enhancement measures" to avoid the political sensitivity of a former FTA, the research estimated that an EU-Taiwan FTA would bring an extra GDP

[28]Taiwan Financial Supervisory Commission, Response of the 2016 ECCT Recommendations, 2016, http://www.ndc.gov.tw/Content_List.aspx?n=D7D3AA1846E85A23 (last accessed 1 March 2017).

[29]Bureau of Animal and Plant Health Inspection and Quarantine and the Taiwan Food and Drug Administration, Response of the 2016 ECCT Recommendations, 2016, http://www.ndc.gov.tw/Content_List.aspx?n=D7D3AA1846E85A23 (last accessed 1 March 2017).

increase of 2 billion Euros for the EU and 4 billion Euros for Taiwan. Combined goods and services exports from the EU will increase to the extent of 12 billion Euros per year and 10 billion for Taiwan.[30] There will be longer-term economic gains for EU firms through enhanced access to the broader Asian and Chinese markets.[31] Others argued that the gains for the EU would be the greatest in the services sectors.[32]

By all means an EU-Taiwan FTA would be the preferred approach in removing both trade and investment barriers. By projecting the EU-Korea FTA as the benchmark for a possible EU-Taiwan FTA, both the EU and Korea are committed to remove the tariff duties for 98% of all product lines within 7 years of implementation of the FTA.[33] Equally as important, there are also comprehensive investment/services liberalisation commitments and chapters regulating the TBT, SPS, competition policy, IPR and government procurement that dealt with behind-border NTMs. Taking the TBT chapter in the EU-Korea FTA as an example, there are a number of new rules that go beyond the WTO Agreement on Technical Barriers to Trade (TBT Agreement), many of which appear to be equally applicable in addressing the EU's concerns with Taiwan.

The unique feature of the EU-Korea FTA is that there are two chapters that address TBT-related issues, namely chapter 4 (TBT) and chapter 2 (National Treatment and Market Access for Goods).[34] Building upon the general principles of the TBT Agreement, provisions in the TBT Chapter of the EU-Korea FTA include several WTO-plus elements that could serve as best practices for future EU-Taiwan negotiation as well. The first example is the enhancement to improve stakeholders' participation in the process of formulating technical regulations. Article 4.4.2 of the EU-Korea FTA requires TBT authorities to offer national treatment for interested persons from other parties to participate in formal public consultative processes concerning the development of technical regulations. This obligation has to be read in tandem with the general obligations on administrative proceedings as stipulated in Article 12.3.2(c) and (d), which further require both the EU and Korea to provide reasonable opportunities and sufficient time for interested

[30]Copenhagen Economics, Taiwan: Enhancing Opportunities for European Business, August 2008, p. 5 et seq.

[31]Copenhagen Economics, Taiwan: Enhancing Opportunities for European Business, August 2008, p. 7.

[32]Krol and Lee-Makiyama (2012); Kerneis P, Lamprecht P, Messerlin P, Taiwan and European Union Trade and Economic Relations: The case for a Comprehensive Bilateral Investment Agreement, Report by the European Services Forum, November 2016, http://www.esf.be/new/wp-content/uploads/2016/11/ESF-Report-Taiwan-EU-Economic-Relations-Components-of-a-trade-investment-agreement-Final.pdf (last accessed 1 March 2017).

[33]Decreux Y, Milner C, Péridy N, The Economic Impact of the Free Trade Agreement (FTA) between the European Union and Korea, May 2010, htttp://trade.ec.europa.eu/doclib/docs/2010/may/tradoc_146174.pdf (last accessed 1 March 2017), p. 22.

[34]The Free Trade Agreement between the EU and Republic of Korea (EU-Korea FTA), OJ 2011 L 127/6.

persons to comment on proposed measures of general application, and should endeavour to take into account the comments received from interested persons with respect to such proposed measures.[35]

While the TBT Agreement also has rules regarding transparency and information provisions, the "right to participate" is in principle reserved only for governments from other WTO members[36]; there is lack a of allowance for direct participation of stakeholders/interest persons in the rule making process. The only provision that barely takes into account the interest of stakeholders is Article 2.9.1 of TBT Agreement, in which WTO members are obliged to publish a proposed technical regulation that is not based on international standards so that interested parties can "become acquainted" with it.

Another example would be the WTO-plus disciplines concerning marking and labelling regulations. Article 4.9(a) of the EU-Korea FTA provided that if labelling is required for purposes other than informing consumers or users (e.g. for fiscal purposes), a necessity test is applied to ensure that such requirements are not more trade restrictive than necessary to fulfill a legitimate objective. In addition, Article 4.9(b) forbids the EU and Korea to require prior approval, registration or certification of marking or labelling marking. Finally Article 4.9(d) provides that the simultaneous use of other languages shall not be prohibited, as long as the information provided is identical to the official language, and will not constitute a deceptive statement. To the contrary, the TBT Agreement does not have any specific disciplines on labelling and marking.

Finally, and perhaps the most unique design of the EU-Korea FTA, is the inclusion of product-specific NTMs rules applied to consumer electronic products, motor vehicles, pharmaceutical products and medical devices, and chemicals.[37] For the TBT disciplines on consumer electronic products (Annex 2-B), Korea agrees to both apply simplified conformity assessment procedural (i.e. the acceptance of Supplier's Declaration of Conformity or SDoC) for the testing of electromagnetic compatibility (EMC) and safety requirements under specified conditions.[38] In addition, during the transitional period (3 years after the implementation of the FTA), a test report issued by conformity assessment bodies designated by both the EU and Korea will be accepted by both sides, and at the end of the transitional period, both parties shall eliminate the EMC testing requirement altogether (with some positively listed carved out products). For automotive and components products (Annex 2-C), the EU and Korea agree to harmonise nation standards so they are compatible with standards set by the World Forum for Harmonization of Vehicles Regulations. In terms of safety standards, both parties agree that vehicles

---

[35]EU-Korea FTA, OJ 2011 L 127/6.

[36]For example, Article 2.9.4 of the TBT Agreement requires WTO members to "allow reasonable time for other *members* to make comments in writing, discuss these comments upon request, and take these written comments and the results of these discussions into account" (emphasis added).

[37]EU-Korea FTA, OJ 2011 L 127/6, p. 1134 et seq.

[38]EU-Korea FTA, OJ 2011 L 127/6, p. 1134 et seq.

manufactured under the UNECE Code will be recognised as in compliance with their respective national codes. Lastly, there are disciplines on transparency in reimbursement and pricing decision for pharmaceutical products and medical devices deals.

Moreover, the WTO-plus clauses in the SPS chapter on the regionalisation or zoning determination process in the EU-Korea FTA is an equally valuable reference point for a possible EU-Taiwan FTA.[39] Article 5.8.3 of the EU-Korea FTA establishes a cooperation mechanism to acquire confidence in the process on the determination of pest-or disease-free areas and areas of low pest or disease prevalence within about 2 years from the entry into force of the agreement. Article 5.8.4 further requires the importing party to take into consideration the determination made by the exporting party regarding regionalisation. In circumstances where the importing party does not accept the determination made by the exporting party, the former is obliged to offer an explanation and the latter can request consultation to discuss the non-acceptance.

Important lessons can also be drawn from the EU-Korea FTA's WTO-plus disciplines on domestic regulations for services.[40] Specifically, in addition to the general principles of domestic regulations applied horizontally to the services sectors, the EU-Korea FTA establishes sectoral disciplines for computer services, postal and courier services, telecom, financial and maritime transport services.[41] Taking financial services as the example, Article 7.42 of the EU-Korea FTA stipulates that each party shall provide national treatment in approving new financial services, under the condition that such approval does not require a new law or modification of an existing law. Rules on telecom also include regulatory principles concerning, inter alia, competitive safeguards and allocation of scare resources.

One will be surprised to observe the similarity between the scope of NTM and domestic regulatory barriers these WTO-plus disciplines intend to mitigate and the restrictions EU businesses face in Taiwan summarised in the preceding section. Most of the items covered under the product-specific NTM rules under the

---

[39]As defined in Article 6 of the WTO Agreement on the Application of Sanitary and Phytosanitary Measures (SPS Agreement), zoning or regionalization is the recognition of an area (all of a country, part of a country, or all or parts of several countries) as pest-or disease-free areas and areas of low pest or disease prevalence.

[40]Article VI of the WTO General Agreement on Trade in Services (GATS) already provides some horizontal principles relating to domestic regulations to ensure all measures of general application affecting trade in services are administered in a reasonable, objective and impartial manner. Article VI.4 also mandates WTO members to develop disciplines to ensure measures relating to qualification requirements and procedures, technical standards and licensing requirements do not constitute unnecessary barriers to trade in services. There are no sectoral regulatory principles under the GATS except the Reference Paper on Basic Telecom, the Annex on Financial Services and the Disciplines on Domestic Regulation in the Accountancy Sector. As of 2016, WTO members have not reached consensus on the Article VI.4 horizontal disciplines. For the progress and development of the negotiation, see https://www.wto.org/english/tratop_e/serv_e/dom_reg_negs_e.htm (last accessed 1 March 2017).

[41]Section E (regulatory framework), chapter 7 of the EU-Korea FTA, OJ 2011 L 127/6.

EU-Korea FTA are almost identical to the product list reported in the ECCT Position Paper. Similarly, sectoral regulatory disciplines on new financial services and telecom appeared to be able to tackle the same set of issues in Taiwan. These non-quantifiable benefits of the EU-Korea FTA further highlight the value of an EU-Taiwan FTA. By the same token, rules on intellectual property protection, competition policy, government procurement and administrative procedure as provided for in most EU FTAs are equally important policy tools in underpinning more long-term and dynamic economic gains for both the EU and Taiwan.

4.2 The EU-Taiwan Bilateral Investment Agreement

It is unfortunate that despite all the merits of an FTA, an EU-Taiwan agreement appears to be unlikely in the foreseeable future. The European Commission put forward its criteria for the selection of FTA partners in 2006, which include market potential (economic size and growth), the level of protection against EU export interests (tariffs and non-tariff barriers) and FTAs with EU competitors.[42] Based on these criteria, the Commission explicated nominated FTAs with ASEAN, Korea and Mercosur as priorities, as well as with India, Russia and the Gulf Co-operation Council. China was also on the list yet the Commission argued that special attention is required because of the risks.[43] The EU Commission has added further conditions such as the completing of ongoing trade negotiations and focusing on the EU's strategic partners in 2010.[44]

In both documents, Taiwan was not on the list. Reasons for the omission varied. Some pointed to the fact that it will be considered a political provocation to launch an FTA negotiation with Taiwan before China.[45] Other argued that it is because of Taiwan's economic size, growth potential and relatively low level of barriers.[46] Moreover, there appears to be a tendency if not a former policy by the EU to require a political agreement, i.e. a Partnership and Cooperation Agreement (PCA) or Strategic Partnership Agreement (SPA), often signed prior to or in tandem with FTA negotiations, as a precondition of an FTA negotiation.[47] If this continues to be

[42]European Commission, Global Europe: Competing in the world—A contribution to the EU's Growth and Jobs Strategy, COM (2006) 567 final, 4 October 2006, p. 11.

[43]COM (2006) 567 final, p. 11.

[44]European Commission, Trade, Growth and World Affairs—Trade Policy as a core component of the EU's 2020 strategy, COM (2010) 612 final, 9 November 2010, p. 10 et seq.

[45]Kerneis P, Lamprecht P, Messerlin P, Taiwan and European Union Trade and Economic Relations: The case for a Comprehensive Bilateral Investment Agreement, Report by the European Services Forum, November 2016, p. 44.

[46]Dreyer et al. (2010), p. 9.

[47]Okano-Heijmans et al. (2015), p. 12. The EU has indeed either concluded or initiated the negotiation of a PCA or SPA with all FTA partners in the Asia Pacific region, including China. Information regarding the status of PCA/SPA negotiation is available at https://eeas.europa.eu/headquarters/headquarters-homepage/area/geo_en (last accessed 1 March 2017).

the case, then the political economy complexity behind the EU-Taiwan-China triangle relationship could plausibly prevent the EU from considering the initiation of a PCA with Taiwan as a prerequisite or stepping-stone for a trade agreement.

Consequently, the possibility of negotiating a Bilateral Investment Agreement (BIA) as a substitution has surfaced and has been lobbied by Taiwan since 2014.[48] The idea of utilising a BIA as a building block for a future FTA is somehow encouraged by the launch of the EU-China BIA negotiation in 2013.[49] To this end, the Commission has also stated in its latest trade and investment strategy that it will conclude the ongoing investment negotiations with China and explore launching negotiations on investment with Taiwan.[50] From a "better-than-nothing" or building block viewpoint, a BIA is indeed a good starting point. There are however a number of uncertainties overshadowing the value and gains for both the EU and Taiwan in this BIA-first strategy.

The first uncertainty is the value of a Taiwan BIA in terms of timing. Implicitly, there is a "China-first" sequential arrangement in which the Commission will have to wait until the BIA with China is completed, a stance that has been confirmed by a top EU trade official.[51] Thus the progress of the BIA with China will have a direct bearing on the future of the EU-Taiwan BIA. Unfortunately, in spite of twelve rounds of negotiation of the EU-China BIA that have taken place since 2013, the scope of the BIA was only agreed in January 2016. The differences in objective and priorities are likely to further delay the process. For the EU, meaningful improvement in market access conditions is the top priority.[52] On the other hand, the already liberal EU investment rules suggest that China is more interested in consolidating its existing 26 individual BIAs with the EU Member States,[53] and in demonstrating its readiness as a credible negotiating partner to underpin a future FTA deal with the EU.[54] The EU's refusal to accord China's Market Economy Status (MES) in relation to anti-dumping investigations at the end of 2016 is envisaged to bring

[48]Taiwan National Development Council, The 2014 National Development Masterplan, 2013, http://www.ey.gov.tw/Upload/RelFile/26/706546/43d04638-5ca6-4e33-9e68-408986b28764.pdf (last accessed 1 March 2017), p. 81.

[49]European Commission, EU and China begin investment talks, Press release IP/14/33, 20 January 2014.

[50]European Commission, Trade for all: Towards a more responsible trade and investment policy, 2015, p. 32.

[51]Statement made by Trade Commissioner Malmström indicating that the negotiations with Taiwan would be launched "only once the talks of the BIA with China would be done". See http://www.europarl.europa.eu/ep-live/en/committees/video?event=20151015-0900-COMMITTEE-INTA (last accessed 1 March 2017).

[52]Ewert (2016).

[53]For the status of China's BIA's, see http://tfs.mofcom.gov.cn/article/Nocategory/201111/20111107819474.shtml (last accessed 1 March 2017).

[54]Ewert (2016), p. 4.

even more political challenges to the BIA negotiation.[55] All these complications suggest that a swift negotiation with China is highly questionable, which consequently puts the BIA with Taiwan in doubt as far as time is concerned.

The second uncertainty is over the substantive value of a potential BIA with Taiwan. The Lisbon Treaty grants the European Union exclusive competence to negotiate a BIA on behalf of the Member States.[56] To this end, the Commission has pointed out the following direction and principles in which it will exercise this new negotiation authority in the 2010 Communication titled "Towards a comprehensive European international investment policy".[57] The first agenda is to harmonise and elevate the level of investment protection standards of existing Bilateral Investment Treaties (BITs) previously concluded by individual EU Member States. The second agenda is to include the liberalisation of "pre-entry" treatment,[58] i.e. market access and investment liberalisation commitments, as part of future BIA negotiations. The third is to set the standards for investment protection that go beyond non-discriminatory treatment. This will include, *inter alia*, fair and equitable treatment post-entry, protection of contractual rights, rules ensuring the proportionality principle is observed in expropriation measures with timely and adequate compensation, and to ensure the effective enforcement of commitments through investment dispute settlement mechanisms. Of note is that the Commission also indicates that as the one-size-fits-all model might not be feasible or desirable in all circumstances, it will take into consideration the special conditions applied to each specific negotiating context.

In practice, the development of the EU-China BIA provides a useful reference for the possible table of contents for a BIA with Taiwan. As disclosed on the public consultation website, the EU's objectives of the negotiation for the BIA, in addition to the aforementioned items, are to address key challenges of the regulatory environment, including those related to transparency, licensing and authorisation procedures, as well as disciplines encouraging responsible investment and promoting core environmental and labour standards.[59] There is also a clear indication that the objective and key provisions of the EU-China BIA will be guided by the EU-Canada Comprehensive Economic and Trade Agreement (CETA) and the EU-Singapore Free Trade Agreement (FTA), as well as by the EU text proposal for the Investment Chapter of the Transatlantic Trade and Investment Partnership (TTIP) with the US.

---

[55]China insisted that, in accordance with section 15(a)(ii) of its accession agreement, the 15-years "transitional" clause that allows other WTO members to use a surrogate price in light of an anti-dumping investigation expired after 11 December 2016.

[56]Article 206 and 207 TFEU.

[57]European Commission, Towards a comprehensive European international investment policy, COM (2010) 343 final, 7 July 2010.

[58]COM (2010) 343 final, pp. 5–9.

[59]See European Commission, Public Consultation on the Trade in Services Agreement (TiSA), http://trade.ec.europa.eu/consultations/index.cfm?consul_id=177 (last accessed 1 March 2017).

Table 6 Comparison of key elements of the investment chapters

Key elements	EU-Canada CETA	EU-Singapore FTA
Definition	§ 8.1	§ 9.1
Scope of application	§ 8.2	§ 9.2
Market access	§ 8.4	§ 8.10
Performance requirements	§ 8.5	–
National treatment	§ 8.6	§§ 9.3 & 8.11
Most-favoured national treatment	§ 8.7	–
Senior management and boards of directors	§ 8.8	–
Investment and regulatory measures	§ 8.9	Preamble
Treatment of investors and covered investments (i.e. fair and equitable treatment)	§ 8.10	§ 9.4
Compensation for losses	§ 8.11	§ 9.5
Expropriation	§ 8.12	§ 9.6
Transfers	§ 8.13	§ 9.7
Subrogation	§ 8.14	§ 9.8
Reservations and exceptions	§ 8.15	§ 8.12
Denial of benefits	§ 8.16	–
Formal requirements	§ 8.17	–
Investors and states investment disputes settlement (through mediation and the investment court system with appeal mechanism)	Section F	Section B
Schedule of commitments	Yes	Yes

Source: Summarised by author

It will not be difficult therefore to conceive the possible structure, scope and key provisions of a EU model BIA, as there is a high degree of intersection between the content of the investment chapters in the EU-Canada CETA and the EU-Singapore FTA (see Table 6 for comparison). Based on this, we can safely envisage the salient features of an EU BIA will include investment liberalisation clauses (with a schedule of commitments), treatment of investments/investors, investment protection rules as well as the establishment of an investment court system with appeal mechanism. This is in fact consistent with what was denoted in the Commission's 2010 Communications.

There are undoubtedly benefits if Taiwan is able to advance a BIA with the EU. The uncertainty of the substantive value of a future BIA, however, derives not so much from the BIA *per se*, but from the fact both the EU and Taiwan are currently participating in the Trade in Services Agreement (TiSA) negotiation.[60]

[60]The TiSA is currently being negotiated by 23 WTO members (50 countries, with the EU representing all 28 Member states), including Australia, Canada, Chile, Colombia, Costa Rica, the European Union, Hong Kong China, Iceland, Israel, Japan, Korea, Liechtenstein, Mauritius,

Started in 2013, the TiSA completed the 21st round of negotiating in November 2016. In addition to market access negotiation and general principles, there are also 17 Annexes on regulatory disciplines that have been proposed and discussed by TiSA members. Some TiSA Annexes are horizontal disciplines that would be applied to all measures affecting trade in services, such as transparency, domestic regulation localisation, e-commerce, state owned enterprises, and government procurement. Sectoral Annexes include regulatory rules for telecom, financial, transport, energy, professional services and a mode-specific Annex on the temporary entry and stay of professionals.[61]

Compared with TiSA, a stand-alone BIA has the following deficiencies that would compromise its importance. With regard to market access, a BIA covers only liberalisation in establishments (i.e. commercial presence or mode 3 under GATS and TiSA), whereas TiSA includes additional market access commitments for other modes of supply, i.e. cross border supply of services and the movement of professionals. As the internet-based cross-border services provisions rapidly become a dominating mode of supply for the international services trade,[62] this shortcoming could render the BIA relatively obsolete over time. Even for the liberalisation of investment, considering the likelihood that the TiSA concludes right before/after the initiation of the EU-Taiwan BIA negotiation, the proximity in terms of timing could undermine both parties' ability to offer new and meaningful concessions under the BIA. Another area of shortcoming is the lack of disciplines on domestic regulations under a BIA. As discussed, EU firms in Taiwan have suggested that substantial impediments in the services sector are associated domestic regulations. This disadvantage implies that even if the BIA is implemented, its ability to offer additional assistance in alleviating restrictions will be limited. Moreover, this drawback also extends to a common restriction that both BIA and TiSA share, i.e. the inability to tackle trade issues relating to trade in goods, especially in TBT, SPS and other MTNs. Overall, the value of a EU-Taiwan BIA could be confined predominately to investment protection and the investor-to-state dispute settlement elements, and this requires further thinking on the objective and rationales of pursuing a BIA, and the BIA's relationship with other possible trade agendas.

Mexico, New Zealand, Norway, Pakistan, Panama, Peru, Switzerland, Taiwan, Turkey and the United States. TiSA members account for around 70% of the world trade in services. For the latest update on the progress, see http://ec.europa.eu/trade/policy/in-focus/tisa/ (last accessed 1 March 2017).

[61]European Commission, Report of the 21st TiSA negotiation round, 2–10 November 2016, http://trade.ec.europa.eu/doclib/docs/2016/november/tradoc_155095.pdf (last accessed 1 March 2017).

[62]This is one of the primary rationales underpinning the EU's Digital Single Market (DSM) policy. For further elaborations on the background and implications of the DSM, see https://ec.europa.eu/priorities/digital-single-market_en (last accessed 1 March 2017).

5 The New EU-Taiwan Trade Negotiation Agendas: Thinking Out-of-the-Box

Considering the economic and political constrains for a comprehensive FTA between the EU and Taiwan, and the decreasing value of a BIA in light of the TiSA progress, there is a need to revisit the trade negotiation agenda at this juncture. The new agenda should be designed to serve at least two objectives. First it must be able to accommodate and alleviate current bilateral trade and investment concerns that are hindering the EU and Taiwan. Second it must underpin a future FTA negotiation should the window of opportunity become available. In this final section, we put forward the following new approaches as the possible avenues for achieving these objectives.

5.1 Pursuing TBT and SPS Cooperation Agreements

TBT is the top policy area where most of the potentially trade and investment restrictive measures are reflected by EU firms. Disagreements between the competent authorities across a number of past and new SPS issues also remain a persistently outstanding agenda. This clearly signifies that systematic instead of *ad hoc* cooperation frameworks in the TBT and SPS areas are both pragmatic and desirable. Cooperation in these two areas would also be able to deliver targeted resolutions in response to the practical problems that EU business and regulators are encountering. Bilateral cooperation in the TBT area is not new to both the EU and Taiwan; to date each has included a TBT chapter in most of their respective FTAs, and concluded a number of bilateral Mutual Recognition Agreement (MRA) with trading partners. For the EU, MRAs were with Australia, Canada, Japan, New Zealand, the USA, Israel and Switzerland,[63] and Taiwan's MRA partners include Australia, Canada, Japan, New Zealand, Singapore and the US.[64]

As early as 1997, the Council instructed the Commission to place greater emphasis on using mutual recognition as a vehicle for greater harmonization,[65] and all of the existing EU MRAs were concluded between 1998 and 2002. Interestingly, there is no new stand-alone MRA concluded by the EU after 2002. Some of the possible explanations for the EU's slowness in pursuing stand-alone MRAs include the fact that mutual recognition issues are now mainly being dealt with in

[63]Information regarding EU's MRA coverage and status is available at https://ec.europa.eu/growth/single-market/goods/international-aspects/mutual-recognition-agreements_en (last accessed 1 March 2017).

[64]See www.bsmi.gov.tw/bsmiGIP/wSite/public/Data/f1369367729015.doc (last accessed 1 March 2017).

[65]Council conclusions of 26 June 1997—Communication from the Commission on Community external trade policy in the field of standards and conformity assessment, OJ 2001 C 8/1.

comprehensive FTAs, and the trade-encouraging, cost-saving effects of stand-alone MRAs are not significant.[66] In reality, however, TBT-related issues remain the top obstacles for international trade, and they remain an important part of a comprehensive FTA. As discussed in the preceding section, TBT cooperation in the EU-Korea FTA is not limited to procedural simplification and mutual recognition; there are also WTO-plus provisions on stakeholder participation and regulatory coherence rules for specific products. As an FTA appears to be a mission impossible for the time being, flexibility and innovation is required in this particular context. A quick and effective option to achieve the objective of enhancing TBT cooperation will be to consider a stand-alone TBT Cooperation Agreement with its structure and content benchmarking the EU-Korea FTA model. Specifically, taking into account the nature and frequency of TBT issues raised by EU businesses in Taiwan, the scope of the bilateral TBT Cooperation Agreement should transcend the traditional MRA to include enhanced transparency requirements, deeper participation of stakeholders in rule-making processes, rules on labelling practices, product-specific harmonisation disciplines (with the introduction or broader application of Suppliers' Declaration of Conformity scheme) and the creation of a framework for further dialogue and regulatory coherence.

The last part on regulatory cooperation, in tandem with the establishment of a TBT committee, can serve not only as a mechanism to exchange views and experiences in regulatory best practices and capacity-building process but also as a platform for the EU and Taiwan to seek an alliance in pursuing TBT cooperation beyond the bilateral level. One such instance will be the negotiation of disciplines in reducing Non-Tariff Barriers (NTBs) under the WTO Information Technology Agreement (ITA). The ITA expansion concluded in 2015 only includes tariff elimination commitments. Regarding NTBs, the participating parties only agree to intensify consultations concerning non-tariff barriers in the information technology sector. To this effect, the parties support the possible development of an upgraded work programme on non-tariff barriers.[67] In an ex post economic assessment of the ITA Expansion, the EU's DG Trade indicates that it would benefit the EU to focus future negotiation on broadening country coverage and the reduction of NTBs.[68] An equally major beneficiary of the ITA Expansion,[69] Taiwan also has

[66]This is the general conclusion made in a report commissioned by the DG Trade and Enterprises. See Hogan and Hartson LLP, The Economic Impact of Mutual Recognition Agreements on Conformity Assessment—A Review of the Costs, Benefits, and Trade Effects Resulting from the European Community MRAs Negotiated with Australia and New Zealand, 9 May 2003, http://trade.ec.europa.eu/doclib/docs/2006/december/tradoc_131416.pdf (last accessed 1 March 2017).

[67]WTO, The Ministerial Declaration on the Expansion of Trade in Information Technology Products (WT/MIN(15)/25), 16 December 2015, para. 10.

[68]European Commission, The Expansion of the Information Technology Agreement: An Economic Assessment, 2016, http://trade.ec.europa.eu/doclib/docs/2016/april/tradoc_154430.pdf (last accessed 1 March 2017).

[69]The global shares of export of the products covered by the ITA Expansion for EU and Taiwan are 14.7% and 7.1% respectively. See WTO, Information Technology Agreement—an explanation, https://www.wto.org/english/tratop_e/inftec_e/itaintro_e.htm (last accessed 1 March 2017).

Table 7 Comparison of key elements in SPS agreements/chapters concluded by EU

Agreement partners	New Zealand	Canada	Chile	Korea (FTA)	Canada (FTA)
Year came into force	1996	1999	2003	2012	2016
Scope	Live animal and animal products		Sanitary and phytosanitary		
Relationship with WTO SPS Agreement	V	V	V	V	V
Adaptation of regional conditions	V	V	V	V	V
Recognition of equivalence and the right to request for consultation	V	V	V	X	V
Trade conditions (Made available of the SPS-related import requirements)	X	X	X	X	V
Authorization or certification	X	X	V	X	V
Audit by importing partners	X	V	X	X	V
Verification	X	X	V	X	V
Import checks and fees	V	V	V	X	V
Notification and consultation	V	V	V	V	V
Exchange of information	V	V	V	V	V
Provision of scientific data	V	X	X	X	X
Safeguard (emergency) measures	V	V	V	X	V
Outstanding issues	V	V	V	X	X
SPS committee	V	V	V	V	V

Source: Summarised by author based on European Commission information: https://ec.europa.eu/food/safety/international_affairs/agreements_en (last accessed 1 March 2017)

strong incentives to further lowering NTBs associated with ITA products, and this creates a nature negotiation partnership on this particular subject matter.

By the same token, bilateral SPS Cooperation Agreement would be a similar building-block possibility. As a matter of fact, the EU has previously concluded a number of bilateral agreements on sanitary measures with Canada, Chile, New Zealand and the US.[70] Cross agreement comparison demonstrates that there is a common set of disciplines applied to all agreements, with additional rules attached to individual agreements. Some of the stand-alone SPS Agreements have broader scope and issue-coverage than that of the EU-Korea FTA, but the SPS chapter in the EU-Canada CECA appears to be the most up-to-date and comprehensive yardstick to follow (Table 7). It is true that most of the EU's SPS agreements were concluded with agricultural exporting countries, but chapters with similar effects are also found in the FTAs with Korea and Singapore. Therefore, by drawing from these experiences, the EU and Taiwan can work out a tailor-made bilateral SPS agreement by selecting from this menu of topics (especially the EU-Canada CETA), with additional emphasis on specific issues that are of particular interest in the EU-Taiwan context. This would for example include provisions

[70]See https://ec.europa.eu/food/safety/international_affairs/agreements_en (last accessed 1 March 2017).

on the recognition of regional conditions and equivalence, harmonisation of certification procedures and a list of outstanding issues identified bilaterally as priority areas to be addressed by the SPS committee.

5.2 Partnership in TiSA Negotiation Focusing on the Disciplines of Domestic Regulations and E-Commerce

As discussed above, there are merits and constraints in pushing for further liberalisation through an EU-Taiwan BIA. To compensate the deficiencies, it would be preferable, especially for Taiwan, to fully utilise the TiSA opportunity in making ambitious commitments in the following areas. The first of these is market access liberalisation with special attention paid to the opening of cross border supply across most services sectors. The second area would be to facilitate the inclusion of a set of high standard disciplines on domestic regulations, both horizontal and sector-specific. Bearing in mind the services trade concerns expressed by EU businesses in Taiwan, harmonisation and coherence in financial services regulatory principles, as well as facilitation rules in the movement and temporary stay of professionals will be top negotiation priorities. Further, taking into account the development of e-commerce and digital trade, the TiSA disciplines on e-commerce will also be a critical area of the EU-Taiwan partnership.

In fact, there is also a multilateral dimension in the collaboration on the e-commerce agenda. As summarised in a recent submission by the EU and other members to the WTO General Council on the Work Programme on E-commerce,[71] possible e-commerce related elements to be considered in the WTO include sound regulatory frameworks for transparency, consumer protection, privacy cyber security and the cross-border flow of data. With regard to ensuring market openness, the submission recommends that WTO members advance discussions on liberalising the cross-border supply of services, the elimination of tariffs on ITA-related products and on electronic transmissions, and the disciplines in localisation requirements. There are also trade facilitation measures in addressing access to and use of the internet, electronic payment, IPR protection and the recognition of e-authentication. The benefits of partnership in promoting these e-commerce/digital trade elements—most of which are in line with the obligations in the Trans Pacific Partnership Agreement (TPP) that Taiwan is preparing to join[72]—at the multilateral

[71]WTO, Work Programme on Electronic Commerce, Trade Policy, the WTI and the Digital Economy, Communication from Canada, Chile, Colombia, Côte d'Ivoire, the European Union, the Republic of Korea, Mexico, Montenegro, Paraguay, Singapore and Turkey (JOB/GC/97/Rev.3), August 2016.

[72]For a summary of the rules and obligations covering digital trade related issues, see United States Trade Representative, The Digital Two Dozen, https://ustr.gov/sites/default/files/Digital-2-Dozen-Final.pdf (last accessed 1 March 2017).

level extend beyond economic gains. The lessons and experiences in the EU in addressing civil society's concerns on how to ensure the effective protection of data and privacy can also contribute positively to Taiwan's readiness for negotiating next generation FTAs with the EU and others.

5.3 Partnership in Multilateral Sectoral Initiatives in Tariff Elimination

None of the above potential undertakings touch upon tariff elimination, which remains a key issue especially for Taiwanese manufacturers facing stiff competition in the EU market from Korea and other EU FTA partners. As a rule of thumb, preferential tariff liberalisation requires a FTA in accordance with Article XXVI of GATT, an undertaking that is currently politically impractical to realise. That said, this should not prevent Taiwan from pursuing non-discriminatory tariff liberalisation initiatives in the WTO that would create similar benefits. One pragmatic approach would be to explore possible partnership under the WTO "sectoral initiatives", in which tariff reduction is negotiated voluntarily and plurilaterally for a cluster of products. This can be done through informal "zero-for-zero" negotiations or by a formal plurilateral agreement such as the ITA.[73] Under both modalities the zero-tariff treatment offered by participating members will be extended to all WTO members on a MFN basis with or without reciprocal commitments.[74]

There are 14 proposed sectors under consideration in the WTO's Doha Development Round (DDA) agenda, and the EU and Taiwan have co-sponsored for the chemicals, gems and jewellery products, healthcare related products, industrial machinery and textiles/clothing/footwear initiatives.[75] With reference to the trade structure between the EU and Taiwan, many of the co-sponsored sectors under consideration would cover many of the top traded items between the EU and Taiwan. This indicates that, in spite of the potential cost of free-riding by non-participating members, there should be sufficient economic incentives, at least from the Taiwanese perspective, to revisit the benefits of the sectoral initiatives currently stalled by the deadlocked DDA.

---

[73]WTO, Handbook on Accession to the WTO: chapter 5, Substance of Accession Negotiations, https://www.wto.org/english/thewto_e/acc_e/cbt_course_e/c5s3p1_e.htm (last accessed 1 March 2017).

[74]WTO, Handbook on Accession to the WTO: chapter 5, Substance of Accession Negotiations, https://www.wto.org/english/thewto_e/acc_e/cbt_course_e/c5s3p1_e.htm (last accessed 1 March 2017).

[75]The 14 sectors are: automotive and related parts; bicycles and related parts; chemicals; electronics/electrical products; fish and fish products; forestry products; gems and jewellery products; raw materials; sports equipment; healthcare related products, pharmaceutical and medical devices; hand tools; toys; textiles, clothing and footwear; and industrial machinery. See WTO, Annex 6 on Sectoral Proposals, the Fourth Revision on the Draft Modalities for Non-Agricultural Access (TN/MA/W/103/Rev.3), 6 December 2008.

A formal plurilateral agreement on the covered goods similar to the ITA would be the preferable choice, as such an agreement will be enacted only after trade represented by participating members reaches a "critical mass" threshold,[76] and thus help to minimise the free-riding problem. Nevertheless, the critical mass criterion is also a challenge; it implies the need to attract a sufficiently large number of members, or at least all major exporting members, to join the membership. The diversity in trade interest and priorities across WTO members often renders the critical mass condition a fundamental obstacle to success. Alternatively, Taiwan can also opt for the zero-for-zero modality with the EU. A zero-for-zero undertaking could be time-efficient, as it does not require the critical mass condition to be met, yet it still faces the dilemma of finding the right balance in reciprocity and the impact of free-riding. However, with other options limited, both approaches are worth considering for the EU and Taiwan.

References

Athukorala P (2010) Production networks and trade patterns in East Asia: regionalization or globalization? ADB Working Paper Series on Regional Economic Integration No. 56

Dreyer I, Erixon F, Lee-Makiyama H, Sally R (2010) Beyond geopolitics: the case for a free-trade accord between Europe and Taiwan. ECIPE Occasional Paper No. 3, Brussels

Ewert I (2016) The EU-China bilateral investment agreement: between high hopes and real challenges. Egmont Security Policy Brief No. 68

Kerneis P, Lamprecht P, Messerlin P (2016) Taiwan and European Union trade and economic relations: The case for a comprehensive bilateral investment agreement. A survey sponsored by the European Services Forum and BOFT (Taiwan)

Krol M, Lee-Makiyama H (2012) A EU-Taiwan trade accord from EU member states perspective: rebalancing regional trade. ECIPE Policy Brief No. 12

Okano-Heijmans M, Wit S, van der Putten FP (2015) Cross-strait relations and trade diplomacy in East Asia: towards greater EU-Taiwan economic cooperation? Clingendael Report, The Hague

[76]In the case of the ITA, the critical mass threshold is set at 90% of world trade in IT products. See Para. 4, Annex of the WTO Ministerial Declaration on Trade in Information Technology Products (WT/MIN(96)/16), 13 December 1996.

Part III
The European Union in International Organizations/Institutions

The European Union in United Nations Economic Governance Fora

Anna-Luise Chané and Jan Wouters

Abstract Despite being one of the "heavyweights" in international trade, finance and development, the European Union's (EU) presence in the economic governance fora of the United Nations (UN) continues to be fraught with difficulties. Faced with the legal and political hurdles of multilateral diplomacy in a state-centric environment, the EU has had to deal with a lack of status and participation rights, the complexities of an internal coordination process involving 28 Member States, and the challenges of ensuring a cohesive external representation. This contribution provides a brief overview of the legal basis for EU engagement in the UN, the Union's internal coordination process, as well as the framework governing its external representation. To highlight the patchwork of legal statuses and modes of engagement, we subsequently take a closer look at the EU's relations with a select number of UN bodies in the area of economic governance. This allows us to illustrate the respective challenges in three scenarios: UN fora where the EU and the EU Member States hold membership rights, where we look at FAO; UN fora where the EU holds an observer or full participant status while its Member States have membership rights, where we look at ECOSOC, its subsidiary bodies, and UNCTAD; and UN fora where the EU Member States are members but where the EU has no formal status: here we look at the World Bank.

Contents

A.-L. Chané (✉) • J. Wouters
Leuven Centre for Global Governance Studies, KU Leuven, Deberiotstraat 34, 3000 Leuven, Belgium
e-mail: annaluise.chane@kuleuven.be; jan.wouters@ggs.kuleuven.be

M. Bungenberg et al. (eds.), *European Yearbook of International Economic Law 2017*, European Yearbook of International Economic Law 8,
DOI 10.1007/978-3-319-58832-2_19

1 Introduction

The European Union (EU) ranks among the major economic powers in the world. It is one of the world's largest economies in terms of nominal Gross Domestic Product (GDP),[1] the largest exporter of manufactured goods and services, the biggest export market for around 80 countries, and one of the principal sources of foreign direct investments (FDI).[2] The Euro has been considered as the most important currency after the US Dollar,[3] and the EU and its Member States continue to be among the major donors of development aid.[4] While the EU ranks among the heavyweights in international trade, finance and development, it experiences difficulties when it comes to translating this economic clout into political influence in global multilateral organizations. The EU has often been perceived to "punch below its weight" at the multilateral level, and has even been termed a "political dwarf".[5]

This section of the Yearbook discusses the EU's engagement with a number of international economic governance organizations and institutions. It addresses the persistent difficulties associated with the engagement of a regional organization—the EU—in a state-centric environment, including the questions of legal status, internal coordination and external representation. While other contributions in the Yearbook focus specifically on the International Monetary Fund (IMF) and the World Trade Organization (WTO), this contribution only addresses the EU's engagement with (other) bodies of the United Nations (UN) and the UN family of organizations. Its findings therefore do not necessarily apply to the EU's position in the IMF and WTO[6] and in more informal bodies of global economic governance, such as the G7 and the G20.[7]

The UN's own role in global economic governance is not exactly a success story. Although pursuant to its Charter the organization was also set up "to promote social progress and better standards of life in larger freedom" and "to employ international machinery for the promotion of the economic and social advancement of all peoples",[8] and though one of its purposes is to "achieve international cooperation

[1]World Bank, data of 2015, http://data.worldbank.org/indicator/NY.GDP.MKTP.CD (last accessed 1 March 2017).

[2]European Commission, EU position in world trade, http://ec.europa.eu/trade/policy/eu-position-in-world-trade/ (last accessed 1 March 2017).

[3]Hervé (2012), p. 143.

[4]OECD, Development aid in 2015 continues to grow despite costs for in-donor refugees, 13 April 2016, www.oecd.org/dac/stats/ODA-2015-detailed-summary.pdf (last accessed 1 March 2017).

[5]Hervé (2012), p. 143. This assessment is not unique to the EU's engagement with economic governance institutions, see e.g. Thomas (2012) on the EU and the International Criminal Court; and Smith (2010) on the EU at the UN Human Rights Council.

[6]For earlier writings on the EU-IMF relationship, see Wouters and Ramopoulos (2016), pp. 21–37; Wouters et al. (2013a), pp. 306–327; Wouters and Van Kerckhoven (2012), pp. 221–233. On the EU-WTO relationship, see Wouters (2013), pp. 373–383.

[7]On the EU-G20 relationship, see *inter alia* Wouters et al. (2013b), pp. 259–271.

[8]Charter of the United Nations (UN Charter), fourth and eighth recital of the preamble.

in solving international problems of an economic [...] character",[9] these aims have in practice been overshadowed by the UN's goal to maintain international peace and security.[10] Two of the UN's principal organs were mandated to work on economic governance: the General Assembly (which was *inter alia* tasked to "initiate studies and make recommendations for the purpose of [...] promoting international cooperation in the economic [...] field [...]")[11] and, under the authority of the latter,[12] the Economic and Social Council (ECOSOC). Neither of them fully lived up to the Charter's aspirations. There are many reasons for the UN's marginalization as an actor in global economic governance, including its primary focus on peace and security and its institutional design, which has often obstructed communication and coordination between the various organs, agencies and other bodies in the UN system.[13] Historically, the UN was quickly side-lined by the IMF and the World Bank, and now stands in the shadow of the G20.

There have been numerous proposals to strengthen the UN's role in global economic governance.[14] The EU itself has traditionally been a strong advocate of the UN and the UN system.[15] As the European Security Strategy of 2003 underlined, "[s]trengthening the United Nations, equipping it to fulfil its responsibilities and to act effectively, is a European priority".[16] The Lisbon Treaty additionally strengthened the Union's commitment to multilateralism in general and to the UN in particular. Article 21 of the Treaty on European Union (TEU)[17] provides that the EU "shall promote multilateral solutions to common problems, particularly in the framework of the United Nations", and it enshrines the promotion of an "international system based on stronger multilateral cooperation and good global governance" as an objective of the Union's foreign policy. The EU institutions are

---

[9]Article 1(3) UN Charter. Article 55 UN Charter develops this objective further: "With a view to the creation of conditions of stability and well-being which are necessary for peaceful and friendly relations among nations based on respect for the principle of equal rights and self-determination of peoples, the United Nations shall promote: (a) higher standards of living, full employment, and conditions of economic and social progress and development; (b) solutions of international economic [...] problems [...]."

[10]Kirton J, The United Nations, Global Economic Governance and the G20. Lecture given at the University of Leuven, 10 December 2015, www.g20.utoronto.ca/biblio/kirton-un-g20-151210.html (last accessed 1 March 2017).

[11]Article 13(1)(b) UN Charter.

[12]Article 60 UN Charter.

[13]Article 60 UN Charter.

[14]See *inter alia* UN General Assembly, The United Nations in global economic governance, Resolution 67/289, 9 July 2013; UN General Assembly, The United Nations in global governance, Resolution 66/256, 16 March 2012; UN General Assembly, The United Nations in global governance, Resolution 65/94, 8 December 2010; UN Secretary General Report, The United Nations in global economic governance, A/71/378, 16 September 2016.

[15]See for more details Wouters and Chané (2016), pp. 299–323.

[16]European Council, European Security Strategy: A Secure Europe in a Better World, Brussels, 12 December 2003, p. 9.

[17]Consolidated Version of the Treaty on European Union, OJ 2016 C 202/13.

tasked to comply with the commitments entered into within the UN framework, and to cooperate with UN bodies where appropriate.[18] Also the EU's 2016 Global Strategy underlines the EU's determination to "promote a rules-based global order with multilateralism as its key principle and the United Nations at its core."[19]

However, despite the EU's economic clout, on the one hand, and its commitment to the UN system, on the other, the EU's role in UN economic governance fora continues to be fraught with obstacles. This contribution seeks to provide a brief overview of the legal basis for EU engagement in the UN, the Union's internal coordination process, as well as the framework governing its external representation. To highlight the patchwork of legal statuses and modes of engagement, we subsequently take a closer look at the EU's relations with a select number of UN bodies in the area of economic governance. This allows us to illustrate the respective challenges in three scenarios: UN fora where the EU and the EU Member States hold membership rights, where we look at FAO (Sect. 4.1); UN fora where the EU holds an observer or full participant status while its Member States have membership rights, where we look at ECOSOC, its subsidiary bodies, and UNCTAD (Sect. 4.2); and UN fora where the EU Member States are members but where the EU has no formal status: here we look at the World Bank (Sect. 4.3).

2 Legal Framework for EU Engagement with the UN and the UN System

The EU's engagement with the UN and the UN system is governed both by EU law and by the treaties, resolutions, rules of procedure and other instruments that together constitute the legal framework of the UN. EU engagement with the UN, therefore, not only depends on the Union's external relations competences as provided for in the EU Treaties, but also on whether and to what extent UN bodies permit the participation of the EU.

Within the EU's legal framework, Article 220(1) of the Treaty on the Functioning of the European Union (TFEU)[20] provides that the "Union shall establish all appropriate forms of cooperation with the organs of the United Nations and its specialised agencies", thus recognizing the importance of EU-UN cooperation. Indeed, EU engagement with multilateral fora is vital in order to ensure effective EU external action, in particular in areas of exclusive EU competence. Similar provisions exist for a variety of policy areas, e.g. on environmental policy

[18]See e.g. Articles 208(2), 214(7), 220(1) TFEU.

[19]Shared Vision, Common Action: A Stronger Europe. A Global Strategy for the European Union's Foreign and Security Policy, June 2016, http://eeas.europa.eu/archives/docs/top_stories/pdf/eugs_review_web.pdf (last accessed 1 March 2017).

[20]Consolidated Version of the Treaty on the Functioning of the European Union, OJ 2016 C 202/47.

(Article 191(4) TFEU), development cooperation (Article 211 TFEU), and economic, financial and technical cooperation (Article 212(3) TFEU). While these provisions empower and oblige the Union to cooperate with the UN and other international organizations, they only cover organizational relations,[21] whereas substantive agreements negotiated within the framework of the UN must be concluded in line with the requirements and procedure outlined in Articles 216 and 218 TFEU. As Article 216 TFEU provides, the Union may enter into a binding legal agreement with an international organization if either one of four requirements are met: where (1) the Treaties so provide; (2) where the conclusion of an agreement is necessary in order to achieve one of the objectives referred to in the Treaties; (3) where this is provided for in a legally binding Union act; or (4) where this is likely to affect common rules or alter their scope. The first category merely declaratorily provides that the Union may enter into agreements if this is already provided for elsewhere in the Treaties. For example, Article 207(3) TFEU grants the Union this competence in the area of the common commercial policy, as does Article 212(3) TFEU in the area of economic, financial and technical cooperation. The third category mirrors this provision at the level of secondary EU law. Categories 2 and 4 grant the Union implicit treaty making powers, in line with established case law of the Court of Justice of the European Union (CJEU).[22]

However, the EU's competence to cooperate with the UN and the UN system does not necessarily correspond to actual cooperation between both organisations. The UN remains a predominantly state-centric institution, thus limiting the possibilities for formal participation of the EU. As Article 4(1) UN Charter provides, "[m]embership in the United Nations is open to all other peace-loving *states*" (emphasis added), which is widely understood as limiting membership of the main organization to states, thus excluding non-state entities such as the EU.[23] However, UN agencies and other fora are free to include different provisions in their constituent treaties, rules of procedure etc. The Constitution of the Food and Agriculture Organization (FAO), for example, was amended in 1991 to include a regional economic integration organization (REIO) clause, permitting the EU (in those days the European Economic Community) to join the FAO as a "member organization".[24] Today, the EU holds a variety of different statuses in the various bodies of the UN system, ranging from membership status, to full participant, enhanced observer, observer or no status. Only membership grants the EU the full range of participatory rights, including the right to vote. As an observer, the EU may usually attend (formal) meetings and make interventions—though its speaking time slots will often be later and shorter than those of members. Observers

[21]Geiger (2015), para. 4.

[22]CJEU, opinion 1/03, *Lugano Convention*, ECLI:EU:C:2006:81; CJEU, opinion 1/76, *European laying-up fund for inland waterway vessels*, ECLI:EU:C:1977:63; CJEU, opinion 1/94, *WTO*, ECLI:EU:C:1994:384. See Kuijper et al. (2015), pp. 1–11.

[23]Hoffmeister (2007), p. 41.

[24]Article II(3) FAO Constitution.

are usually seated apart from the Member States, may not raise points of order or propose candidates. In a number of UN bodies, the EU has no formal status at all, forcing it to rely entirely on representation through the EU Member States. This patchwork of statuses and participation rights has long been considered as unsatisfactory among EU policy makers. In 2003, the Commission demanded that the Community "should be given the possibility to participate fully in the work of UN bodies where matters of Community competence are concerned, and Member States should contribute effectively towards this".[25] With full participation out of reach, in 2012 the then European Commission President *Barroso* and Vice-President *Ashton* proposed a more sober "Strategy for the progressive improvement of the EU status in international organisations and other fora in line with the objectives of the Treaty of Lisbon".[26] Though still calling for an "improvement of the EU status and its alignment with the objectives of the EU Treaties", it avoided any reference to concrete negotiation goals.[27] In practice, EU efforts for status upgrades have faced serious political resistance, both internally and externally. The saga around the EU's enhanced participation rights in the UN General Assembly[28] appears to have had a dampening effect on similar efforts in other fora.

3 Internal Coordination and External Representation

As a Union of (still) 28 Member States, internal coordination is an essential aspect of EU external action. Its primary function is to ensure the coherent presence of the EU at the international level, meaning that all EU actors—EU and EU Member States representatives—speak with one voice and vote cohesively. In those fora where the EU itself does not have a formal status, internal coordination serves to ensure that the EU Member States represent existing Union positions, and in fora where both the EU and the EU Member States have membership status, internal coordination is vital to clarify the internal division of competences and, thus, who will exercise the participation rights with regard to each individual agenda item.[29]

In line with the principle of sincere cooperation (Article 4(3) TEU), the EU Member States must refrain from any act that may run counter to obtaining the EU's

[25]European Commission, The European Union and the United Nations: The choice of multilateralism, COM (2003) 526 final, 10 September 2003, p. 23.

[26]President and Vice-President of the European Commission, Strategy for the progressive improvement of the EU status in international organisations and other fora in line with the objectives of the Treaty of Lisbon, C(2012) 9420 final, 20 December 2012, on file with the authors.

[27]See for a detailed analysis of the Barroso-Ashton Strategy, Wouters et al. (2015), pp. 45–74.

[28]In 2011 the EU's was granted additional participation rights in the UN General Assembly, UN Doc A/RES/65/276, 3 May 2011. For a detailed analysis see *inter alia* Brewer (2012), pp. 181–225; Wouters et al. (2011), pp. 166–170; Wouters et al. (2013c), pp. 211–223.

[29]In case of "mixity", membership rights can only be exercised on an alternative basis by either the EU or its Member States, see e.g. Article II(8) FAO Constitution.

objectives and instead assist the Union in fulfilling its tasks. On the basis of this principle, Member States are required to coordinate their actions in international organisations, especially for those competences that refer to "integrated policies"—previously called Community competences. It is interesting to point to the original Article 116 of the Treaty establishing the European Economic Community (EEC Treaty),[30] which required that, "[f]rom the end of the transitional period onwards, Member States shall, in respect of all matters of particular interest to the common market, proceed within the framework of international organisations of an economic character only by common action." This provision was deleted by the Maastricht Treaty, albeit in somewhat ambivalent circumstances and against the will of the European Commission.[31] It is important to note that, from a strictly legal point of view, for the EU's actions on economic, financial and trade matters within global governance fora, including of the UN, the legal principles and doctrines applicable are fundamentally those of the TFEU, combined with the principle of sincere cooperation, and not those laid down in Articles 24(3) and 34 TEU, which only apply to the EU's Common Foreign and Security Policy (CFSP).[32] In practice, the distinction does not always appear to be made consistently in the context of EU coordination efforts at the UN.[33]

Coordination between the EU and the EU Member States is a complex process, from strategy development in Brussels, to the fine-tuning on the ground in New York, Geneva, Rome and other UN venues. In Brussels, the Commission and several working parties of the Council prepare the Union's positions at the UN, depending on the subject matter and the forum. At a general level, the United Nations Working Party (CONUN) develops the Union's UN policy, with a focus on strengthening and reforming the UN system, and maintaining international peace and security. Other Council working parties have regional and thematic portfolios.

[30]Treaty establishing the European Economic Community, 25 March 1957, 298 U.N.T.S. 11.

[31]Cloos et al. (1993), p. 345 et seq.

[32]Article 24(3) TEU provides: "The Member States shall support the Union's external and security policy actively and unreservedly in a spirit of loyalty and mutual solidarity and shall comply with the Union's action in this area. The Member States shall work together to enhance and develop their mutual political solidarity. They shall refrain from any action which is contrary to the interests of the Union or likely to impair its effectiveness as a cohesive force in international relations." This provision aims at ensuring the effectiveness of the EU at the international stage by obliging the EU Member States to ensure a cohesive external façade through cooperation and coordination. It consequently limits, in the area of CFSP, the Member States' freedom to take unilateral action in UN fora. This duty to cooperate and coordinate in the framework of international organisations, as far as CFSP is concerned, is enshrined in Article 34(1) TEU. It provides that "Member States shall coordinate their action in international organisations and at international conferences" and that they "shall uphold the Union's positions in such forums". Article 34(1), second paragraph and 34(2), first paragraph, TEU also makes special provisions for those international fora where not all EU Member States are represented. The rules on the UN Security Council in Article 34(2), second paragraph, constitute a remarkable derogation from these principles.

[33]This could be regarded as a form of "intergovernmentalisation" of the external dimension of EU integrated policy areas.

The Coordination Working Party of the Agriculture and Fisheries Council, for example, coordinates EU and EU Member States positions at meetings of the FAO, whereas the Working Party on Forestry prepares issues discussed in the FAO Committee on Forestry (COFO), and the Codex Alimentarius Working Party coordinates positions in the Codex Alimentarius Commission, where the EU and EU Member States have membership status. The Union Delegations in New York, Geneva, Washington DC, Rome etc. chair the local coordination process, having taken over this role from the rotating Council Presidency since the entry into force of the Lisbon Treaty.[34]

With regard to the external representation of the Union, much has changed with the entry into force of the Lisbon Treaty. The reform of the Union's external relations architecture, including among others the creation of the High Representative for Foreign Affairs and Security Policy and the establishment of the European External Action Service, is aimed at increasing the effectiveness of EU foreign policy. Ideally the EU should now be represented by its own officials, leaving only a limited role for the rotating Council Presidency. In practice, however, the EU's limited participation rights in most UN bodies still force it to rely on representation through the Member States, usually the one holding the Council Presidency. The EU's external representation at the UN is, therefore, still spread on many shoulders. Depending on the subject-matter and on the level of the meeting, the EU will be represented by the Commission (in matters that do not fall under the CFSP), the President of the European Council and the High Representative (in CFSP matters) and/or the EU Delegation. The Member States continue to speak on their own behalf and will speak "on behalf of the EU" whenever the Union's lack of participation rights so requires. If a matter falls within an area of both EU and national competence, the EU's representative will be determined on the basis of whether the "thrust" of the issue falls under EU or national competence.[35]

4 EU Engagement with UN Economic Governance Fora

Over time, the EU has acquired a patchwork of legal statuses and participation rights in the various UN bodies. Membership, such as in the FAO (Sect. 4.1) is still the exception. In most bodies, the EU holds observer status, for example in ECOSOC and its subsidiary bodies, as well as in the UN Conference on Trade and Development (UNCTAD), which is a subsidiary body of the UN General Assembly (Sect. 4.2). Finally, there remain a number of bodies within the UN

[34]Council of the European Union, Presidency report to the European Council on the European External Action Service, 14,930/09, 23 October 2009, para. 31.

[35]Cf. Arrangement concerning preparation for the meetings of the FAO as well as interventions and voting, 18 December 1991, unpublished, reproduced in Frid (1995), Annex VI, Article 2.3. The 1991 Arrangement was updated in 1992 and 1995.

framework, where the EU has no formal status, such as the World Bank, although its Member States may be members (Sect. 4.3).

4.1 Member Status: The EU in the FAO

The FAO is one of the very few UN organizations where the EU has obtained membership status. Founded in 1945 as a specialized agency of the UN, the FAO pursues the threefold aim to eradicate hunger and poverty, to promote economic and social progress, and to contribute to the sustainable management of natural resources.[36] First contacts between the FAO and the European Economic Community (EEC) were already established in the 1950s, reflecting the Union's competences in the area of agriculture and fisheries.[37] Though a formal agreement between the EEC and the FAO was initially considered, it was at that time rejected as not feasible.[38] Instead, the EEC was granted observer status through an exchange of letters between the Director-General of the FAO and the President of the European Commission in 1962.[39] As the letters provided, cooperation between the EEC and the FAO was supposed to take the form of information exchange, consultation, participation of observers in meetings of common interest (upon invitation), and the potential creation of mixed committees to examine topics of common interest. These participation rights were soon considered as insufficient by the European Commission. The Commission deplored in particular that it "could not table any proposals, did not take part in the policy making of the organization, and was not able to fully participate in technical bodies established in the framework of the FAO".[40] After exploratory talks, the Council of the European Community decided on 22 October 1990 to send a letter requesting the formal opening of accession negotiations.[41] The negotiations were formally initiated on 1 February 1991. In June 1991, the FAO Council debated the necessary amendments to the FAO Constitution, which would allow for the accession of a REIO as a member organisation. Among others, a clause was inserted that provided:

---

[36]FAO, About FAO, www.fao.org/about/en/ (last accessed 1 March 2017).

[37]Agriculture has been one of the core competences of the EU since the Treaty establishing the European Economic Community tasked the EEC with the creation of a common agricultural policy ("CAP"), Articles 3(d), 38–47 EEC Treaty.

[38]Schild (2013), p. 225.

[39]Exchange of letters between the Director-General of the FAO, Sen, and the President of the European Commission, Hallstein, 25 October 1962 and 11 December 1962, reprinted in Commission of the European Communities, The European Community, international organizations and multilateral agreements, 3rd edn. January 1983, pp. 97–99.

[40]Frid (1993), p. 241.

[41]See Commission of the European Communities, Proposal for a Council decision on the access of the European Community to the FAO at the 26th session of the FAO Conference, COM (91) 387 final, 18 October 1991; Frid (1993), p. 246.

> The Conference may by a two-thirds majority of the votes cast, provided that a majority of the Member Nations of the Organization is present, decide to admit as a Member of the Organization any regional economic integration organization meeting the criteria set out in paragraph 4 of this Article, which has submitted an application for membership and a declaration made in a formal instrument that it will accept the obligations of the Constitution as in force at the time of admission.[42]

Eligibility was limited to REIOs which are

> constituted by sovereign States, a majority of which are Member Nations of the Organization, and to which its Member States have transferred competence over a range of matters within the purview of the Organization, including the authority to make decisions binding on its Member States in respect of those matters.[43]

This provision, though referring to REIOs generally, was clearly tailored towards the EEC, and it is doubtful whether there is currently any other international organization which would meet the required level of integration. On 25 November 1991 the Council of the European Community requested admission, which was accepted the next day by the FAO Conference with 98 states voting in favour, 6 against, and 3 abstentions.[44]

As a "Member Organization", the EU enjoys generally the same participation rights as Member States, including the right to vote. However, owing to its particular nature, several exceptions were made. In particular, as a Member Organization, the EU may not participate in certain restricted committees[45] and the committees responsible for the internal working of the Conference. Since the EU does not contribute to the budget of the FAO but only pays a sum that covers the administrative expenses of its membership, it does not have voting rights on budget matters.[46] The EU may not hold office in the Conference, the Council and their subsidiary bodies, nor does it have the right to vote for elective places in both organs.[47]

In addition, several arrangements were made to deal with the parallel membership of both the EU and the EU Member States ("mixity"). As Article II(8) of the FAO Constitution provides, a Member Organization "shall exercise membership rights on an alternative basis with its Member States that are Member Nations of the Organization in the areas of their respective competences". It therefore needs to be established on a case by case basis whether the EU or the Member States will exercise their participatory rights, which requires a high degree of internal coordination. In order to increase the effectiveness of this process, the Commission and the Council adopted an internal "Arrangement Regarding Preparation for FAO

[42]Article II(3) FAO Constitution.

[43]Article II(4) FAO Constitution.

[44]Frid (1993), p. 246.

[45]Programme Committee, Finance Committee, Committee on Constitutional and Legal Matters, see Article II(9) FAO Constitution and Rule XLVI FAO General Rules.

[46]Article XVIII(6) FAO Constitution.

[47]Article II(9) FAO Constitution; Rules XLIII(3) and XLIV FAO General Rules.

Meetings and Statements and Voting".[48] It provides that the EU will exercise membership rights if an issue falls in the area of exclusive EU competence, and that the EU Member State holding the rotating Council Presidency will represent the Union in case of Member State competence. In cases of mixed competence, a common position should be sought, based on whether the "thrust" of the issue falls in exclusive EU or Member States competence,[49] with the Permanent Representatives Committee of the Council (COREPER) deciding in case of a disagreement.[50] Nevertheless, internal coordination remained cumbersome and has prompted the Commission to propose a set of revised amendments in 2013.[51] Among others, the draft arrangements proposed that full statements should only be prepared in exceptional cases, while the new default modus operandi for EU positions in the FAO should be the one of "lines to take".[52] These draft arrangements have since been under discussion in the Council, and as of early 2017 adoption did not yet appear to be in sight.

In addition, the FAO Constitution and General Rules oblige the EU and the EU Member States to be transparent about their internal division of competences. At a general level, the EC had to submit a declaration of competence when it applied for membership, specifying its internal division of competences.[53] Any subsequent changes in the division of competences must be communicated to the FAO.[54] In addition, the EU and the EU Member States must indicate before any meeting of the FAO who is competent with regard to which agenda item and who will exercise the right to vote.[55] Other Member States of the FAO may at any time request the EU and the EU Member States to disclose their internal division of competences with regard to any specific matter.[56] These transparency requirements place an additional burden on the EU—one with which it does not always comply. For example, the EU's current declaration of competences still dates back to 1994, despite the

[48]Arrangement concerning preparation for the meetings of the FAO as well as interventions and voting, 18 December 1991, unpublished, reproduced in Frid (1995), Annex VI, Article 2.1–2.2.

[49]Frid (1995), Annex VI, Article 2.3; Schild (2013), p. 228.

[50]Frid (1995), Annex VI, Article 1.12.

[51]European Commission, The role of the European Union in the Food and Agriculture Organisation (FAO) after the Treaty of Lisbon: Updated Declaration of Competences and new arrangements between the Council and the Commission for the exercise of membership rights of the EU and its Member States, COM (2013) 333 final, 29 May 2013.

[52]COM (2013) 333 final, Annex 2, chapter 2.3.

[53]Article II(5) FAO Constitution.

[54]Article II(7) FAO Constitution. See Council Decision of 25 November 1991, Declaration of Competence by the European Union in respect of matters covered by the constitution of the Food and Agriculture Organization of the United Nations (Pursuant to the General Rules of the Organization); updated by a letter sent on 4 October 1994 from the President of the Council to the Director-General of the FAO, cf. European Commission, Notification of a change in the distribution of competence between the EC and its Member States pursuant to Article II(7) of the FAO Constitution, SEC 94 (437) final; Schild (2013), p. 226, note 35.

[55]Rule XLII(2) General Rules of the FAO.

[56]Rule XLII(1) General Rules of the FAO.

subsequent developments in EU primary and secondary law. An updated draft declaration was only proposed by the Commission in 2013 and is still under consideration in the Council.[57]

4.2 *Observer Status: The EU in ECOSOC, Its Subsidiary Bodies, and UNCTAD*

In most (but not all) UN organs, bodies, programmes, funds and specialized agencies the EU has been granted an observer status in the course of time: ECOSOC is one of them. Unlike the FAO, ECOSOC is a body with limited membership. Its 54 members are elected by the UN General Assembly for a term of three years, taking into account geographical representation. To coordinate the membership bids of EU Member States, the EU has developed a complex system which determines the election intervals for each EU Member State.[58]

Relations between ECOSOC and the EEC began on an informal basis and were progressively strengthened in the 1960s and 1970s. On 3 August 1967 ECOSOC adopted Resolution 1267 (XLIII), which recognized the increasing number of intergovernmental organisations active in the areas of economic and social governance and the fact that many of these organisations had already established informal and formal collaboration with various UN bodies.[59] Considering that the development of "further contacts on a more systematic basis" would be "useful", ECOSOC requested the UN Secretary General to propose intergovernmental organisations outside the UN framework which should be granted observer status in the ECOSOC. It was considered that these organisations should be entitled to participate in the debates of the Council, without having the right to vote. Following the UN Secretary General's report, ECOSOC extended a standing invitation to the EEC, granting it the right to "participate, with the approval of the Council and without the right to vote, in the Council's debates on questions of [its] concern".[60] The EEC's *ad hoc* participation subject to invitation was consequently turned into a permanent observer status. Rule 79 of the ECOSOC Rules of Procedure today provides:

---

[57]Draft Declaration of competences by the European Union in respect of matters covered by the Constitution of the Food and Agriculture Organisation of the United Nations (FAO), see European Commission, The role of the European Union in the Food and Agriculture Organisation (FAO) after the Treaty of Lisbon: Updated Declaration of Competences and new arrangements between the Council and the Commission for the exercise of membership rights of the EU and its Member States, COM (2013) 333 final, 29 May 2013, Annex 1.

[58]Winkelmann (2000), p. 425 et seq.

[59]ECOSOC Resolution 1267 (XLIII), Relations with non-United Nations intergovernmental organisations in the economic and social field, 3 August 1967.

[60]Decision reprinted in Commission of the European Communities, The European Community, international organisations and multilateral agreements, 3rd edn. January 1983, p. 35.

> Representatives of intergovernmental organisations accorded permanent observer status by the General Assembly and of other intergovernmental organisations designated on an ad hoc or a continuing basis by the Council on the recommendation of the Bureau, may participate, without the right to vote, in the deliberations of the Council on questions within the scope of the activities of the organisations.

A similar provision can be found in the joint Rules of Procedure of the currently eight functional commissions[61] of ECOSOC.[62] Here, the EU is equally entitled to participate as an observer without voting rights.

An exceptional case, however, was the former Commission on Sustainable Development (CSD), which was established in 1993 as a functional commission of ECOSOC, tasked with ensuring the follow-up to the 1992 United Nations Conference on Environment and Development (Rio Conference) and monitoring the implementation of the Agenda 21.[63] The EC had participated as a "full participant" in the Rio Conference, a status which was then perpetuated in the CSD.[64] As a "full participant", the EC enjoyed more rights than in the other functional commissions of ECOSOC, including the right to speak, the right of reply, the right to introduce proposals and amendments, as well as the right to take part in informal (and not merely formal) meetings.[65] While the EC did not receive the right to vote, it was granted the right to submit proposals that had to be voted on, if CSD Members so requested.[66] In return, the EC committed to ensuring transparency about its internal division of competences between the Community and the Member States, by submitting a general declaration of competence.[67] In line with UN General Assembly Resolution 66/288, the CSD was replaced by a High-level Political Forum on Sustainable Development (HLPF) in 2013.[68] The EU retained its "full participant" status in those meetings convened under the auspices of the ECOSOC, while its "enhanced observer" rights apply in meetings convened under the auspices of the UN General Assembly. UN General Assembly Resolution

---

[61] Statistical Commission, Commission on Population and Development, Commission for Social Development, Commission on the Status of Women, Commission on Narcotic Drugs, Commission on Crime Prevention and Criminal Justice, Commission on Science and Technology for Development, United Nations Forum on Forests, see ECOSOC, Subsidiary bodies of ECOSOC, www.un.org/en/ecosoc/about/subsidiary.shtml (last accessed 1 March 2017).

[62] Rules of Procedure of the Functional Commissions of the Economic and Social Council, Rule 74: "Representatives of intergovernmental organisations accorded permanent observer status by the General Assembly and of other intergovernmental organisations designated on a continuing basis by the Council or invited by the commission may participate, without the right to vote, in the deliberations of the commission on questions within the scope of the activities of the organisations".

[63] ECOSOC Decision, UN Doc E/1993/207, 12 February 1993.

[64] Sack (1995), p. 1249.

[65] ECOSOC Decision, UN Doc E/1995/201, 8 February 1995.

[66] ECOSOC Decision, UN Doc E/1995/201, 8 February 1995.

[67] Sack (1995), p. 1250.

[68] UN General Assembly Ressolution, UN Doc A/RES/66/288, 27 July 2012, para. 84.

67/290 explicitly provides that the arrangements of UN General Assembly Resolution 65/276 and ECOSOC decision 1995/201 apply.[69]

The EU also has observer status in the regional commissions of ECOSOC.[70] Cooperation between the EEC and the UN Economic Commission for Europe (UNECE) began in an informal manner, based on an exchange of letters between the Executive Secretariat of UNECE and the EEC Commission in 1958.[71] Both organisations agreed to exchange information and to consult on issues of common interest. In addition, it was agreed that the EEC could participate as an observer in meetings of UNECE subject to invitation. Subsequently, the EEC's participation rights were progressively expanded[72] and in 1975 the EEC was granted regular observer status.[73] Beyond that, and thanks to REIO clauses, the EU has become a party to several international conventions that were negotiated under the auspices of UNECE. For example, the EU and the EU Member States are parties to the Convention on Long-Range Transboundary Air Pollution.[74] Here again, the abovementioned issues associated with "mixity" arise. As provided for in Rule 29(7) and (8) of the Rules of procedure for sessions of the Executive Body for the Convention on Long-range Transboundary Air Pollution, the EU and the EU Member States must exercise their voting rights on an alternative basis, to avoid that a vote counts twice.[75] This, again, requires the EU and the EU Member States to determine on a case by case basis who will exercise voting rights in the Executive Body.

[69]UN General Assembly Resolution, UN Doc A/RES/67/290, 9 July 2013, para. 10.

[70]For a more detailed analysis of the Union's role in UNECE see Schmidt (2015), pp. 40–43.

[71]Exchange of letters between the Executive Secretary of the UNECE, Tuomioj, and the European Commissioner for External Relations, Rey, 30 September and 7 October 1958, reprinted in Commission of the European Communities, The European Community, international organisations and multilateral agreements, 3rd edn. January 1983, pp. 44–46.

[72]Scheffler (2011), p. 360, note 210.

[73]UNECE Decision L (XXX), 15 April 1975, reprinted in Commission of the European Communities, The European Community, international organisations and multilateral agreements, 3rd edn. January 1983, p. 43.

[74]Convention on Long-Range Transboundary Air Pollution, 13 November 1979, entry into force 16 March 1983, 18 ILM 1442 (1979). See the REIO clause in Article 14 of the Convention which provides: "The present Convention shall be open for signature [...] by regional economic integration organisations, constituted by sovereign States members of the Economic Commission for Europe, which have competence in respect of the negotiation, conclusion and application of international agreements in matters covered by the present Convention". See also Council Decision on the conclusion of the Convention on long-range transboundary air pollution, 81/462/EEC, 11 June 1981.

[75]Rules of procedure for sessions of the Executive Body for the Convention on Long-range Transboundary Air Pollution as adopted by decision 2010/9 and amended by decision 2013/1, https://www.unece.org/fileadmin/DAM/env/documents/2016/AIR/Decision2010_9and2013_1.pdf (last accessed 1 March 2017).

UNCTAD is another body where critics observed that the EU's observer status did not reflect the major competences it had been granted internally.[76] UNCTAD was established in 1964 as a subsidiary body of the UN General Assembly, tasked with promoting international trade and economic development, policy formulation and initiating the negotiation of international legal instruments in the field of trade.[77] UNCTAD's mandate also foresaw that it establish links and cooperate with "intergovernmental bodies whose activities are relevant to [UNCTAD's] functions",[78] the representatives of which should then be allowed to "participate, without vote, in its deliberations and in those of the subsidiary bodies and working groups established by it".[79] In line with this, the EU participates as an observer in the sessions of the Conference, the Trade and Development Board, as well as the subsidiary organs and working groups.[80] In the latter, the EU is de facto able to participate as a full participant.[81] In addition, the EU consults and exchanges documentation with the UNCTAD Secretariat. Post-Lisbon, the EU's external representation and internal coordination mechanisms have been amended to reflect the Union's new external relations architecture. The EU Delegation in Geneva now represents the EU and its Member States in UNCTAD, with the exception of the Working Party on the Strategic Framework and the Programme Budget.[82] The EU Delegation also chairs the internal coordination process among EU Member

[76]Emerson et al. (2011), p. 78.

[77]UN General Assembly Resolution, UN Doc A/RES/1995(XIX), 30 December 1964, Article II(3).

[78]UN General Assembly Resolution, UN Doc A/RES/1995(XIX), 30 December 1964, Article II (18) and (19).

[79]UN General Assembly Resolution, UN Doc A/RES/1995(XIX), 30 December 1964, Article II(11). See also UNCTAD, Rules of Procedure, rule 80: "Representatives of [...] the intergovernmental bodies referred to in paragraphs 18 and 19 of General Assembly resolution 1995 (XIX) which are designated for this purpose by the Conference or the Board may participate, without the right to vote, in the deliberations of the Conference, its main committees and other sessional bodies upon the invitation of the President or Chairman, as the case may be, on questions within the scope of their activities." See also the similar wording in UNCTAD, Rules of Procedure of the Trade and Development Board, rule 76 and UNCTAD, Rules of Procedure of the Main Committees of the Trade and Development Board, rule 74.

[80]See UNCTAD, List of intergovernmental organisations participating in the activities of UNCTAD, TD/B/IGO/LIST/11, 27 October 2014, p. 4.

[81]Emerson et al. (2011), p. 78; Scheffler (2011), pp. 446 and 619.

[82]Barone B, The United Nations and the EU Trade Policy: the case of UNCTAD, DGEXPO/B/PolDep/Note/2016_34, January 2016, p. 6. See also Permanent Delegation of the European Union to the UN office and other international organisations in Geneva, Working with UNCTAD, http://collections.internetmemory.org/haeu/content/20160313172652/http://eeas.europa.eu/delegations/un_geneva/eu_un_geneva/economic_social/unctad/index_unctad_en.htm (last accessed 1 March 2017).

States.[83] Beyond that, the EU has become a party to a number of commodities agreements that were negotiated under the auspices of UNCTAD. Initially, these negotiations were only open to States, while the EEC was merely granted a consultative status,[84] despite its far-reaching competences in these areas. Since the 1960s this has gradually changed,[85] and today the EU is a member of several commodities organisations, sometimes to the exclusion of EU Member States.[86]

In their 2012 "Strategy for the progressive improvement of the EU status in international organisations and other fora in line with the objectives of the Treaty of Lisbon", then European Commission President *Barroso* and Vice-President *Ashton* argued that this patchwork of limited participation rights "restrict[ed the] EU's ability to effectively represent and participate".[87] They proposed that an "enhanced observer status", similar to the one obtained in the UN General Assembly, should be the goal for EU participation also in other UN bodies, in particular ECOSOC and its subsidiary bodies.

> There should also be an effort to examine the political (and legal) feasibility to achieve enhanced rights along the lines of those in UNGA resolution 65/276 in certain UN programmes and funds and specialized agencies, where the EU usually enjoys observer status. In the case of UN principal organs, the focus should be on the Economic and Social Council (ECOSOC) and at a later stage possibly also its subsidiary bodies (e.g. UNECE).[88]

Interestingly, UNCTAD was not explicitly mentioned. In any case, so far, these plans appear to have remained theoretical—the 2012 Strategy was even taken off-line by the Commission—and no efforts like the ones made in the UN General Assembly seem to be underway.

---

[83]See for the internal division of competences in the EU Delegation to the UN and other international organisations in Geneva, About the EU Delegation in Geneva, 12 May 2016, https://eeas.europa.eu/delegations/un-geneva/659/about-eu-delegation-geneva_en (last accessed 1 March 2017).

[84]Scheffler (2011), p. 341 et seq.

[85]See e.g. Schermers and Blokker (2011), para. 1773; Scheffler (2011), pp. 340–350.

[86]For example in the International Coffee Organization, the International Cocoa Organization and the International Olive Council. In the International Organisation of Vine and Wine (OIV), on the other hand, only (some) EU Member States are represented. However, as the Court of Justice of the EU held, the fact that the EU is not itself a member of the OIV does not preclude it from establishing a position to be adopted on its behalf by the EU Member States with regard to OIV recommendations, if these recommendations are "capable of decisively influencing the content of the legislation adopted by the EU legislature in the area of the common organisation of the wine markets", see CJEU. Case C-399/12, *Germany v Council*, ECLI:EU:C:2014:2258, para. 63.

[87]European Commission, Strategy for the progressive improvement of the EU status in international organisations and other fora in line with the objectives of the Treaty of Lisbon, 20 December 2012, C(2012) 9420 final, on file with the authors, p. 1.

[88]President and Vice-President of the European Commission, Strategy for the progressive improvement of the EU status in international organisations and other fora in line with the objectives of the Treaty of Lisbon, 20 December 2012, C(2012) 9420 final, on file with the authors, p. 4.

4.3 No Formal Status: The EU and the World Bank

Finally, there are a number of UN bodies active in global economic governance where the EU has no formal status. For example, despite being a major donor of Official Development Assistance in general and ranking third among the contributors to World Bank trust funds,[89] the EU has no formal status in the World Bank and only observer status in the "Joint Ministerial Committee of the Boards of Governors of the World Bank and the International Monetary Fund on the Transfer of Real Resources to Developing Countries" (better known as Development Committee).[90] The World Bank only recognizes States as members. The Member States' ministers of finance or development sit on the World Bank's Board of Governors, and they appoint the World Bank's 25 Executive Directors, who, together with the President of the World Bank Group, make up the Boards of Directors.[91] Three of the EU Member States are among the World Bank's largest members and may consequently appoint their own Executive Director (France, Germany and the United Kingdom).[92] The other EU Member States are spread across seven constituencies, five of which are currently led by an Executive Director from an EU Member State (Belgium, Denmark, Italy, the Netherlands and Spain).[93]

Development policy is a "parallel" shared competence of the EU and its Member States (Article 4(4) TFEU). While the exercise of the competence by the Union does not prevent the Member States from exercising their competences, the principle of sincere cooperation requires them to refrain from any action that may run counter to obtaining the EU's objectives.[94] Consequently, if a matter at the World Bank falls into an area that has become increasingly "communitarised" or governed by agreements between the EU and third states, EU Member States should represent the position of the Union.[95]

---

[89] Viilup E, The role of the World Bank in international trade policy, DGEXPO/B/PolDep/Note/2016_29, January 2016, p. 3.

[90] Wouters et al. (2006), p. 403. Here, the EU is represented by its Development Commissioner, see Baroncelli (2011), p. 641.

[91] See for more details World Bank, Organization, www.worldbank.org/en/about/leadership (last accessed 1 March 2017).

[92] See International Bank for Reconstruction and Development, International Finance Corporation, International Development Association, Executive Directors and Alternatives, 26 January 2017, http://siteresources.worldbank.org/BODINT/Resources/278027-1215526322295/BankExecutiveDirectors.pdf, and Multilateral Investment Guarantee Agency, Directors and Alternates, 26 January 2017, http://siteresources.worldbank.org/BODINT/Resources/278027-1215526322295/MIGADirectors.pdf (both last accessed 1 March 2017).

[93] See International Bank for Reconstruction and Development, International Finance Corporation, International Development Association, Executive Directors and Alternatives, 26 January 2017, http://siteresources.worldbank.org/BODINT/Resources/278027-1215526322295/BankExecutiveDirectors.pdf, and Multilateral Investment Guarantee Agency, Directors and Alternates, 26 January 2017, http://siteresources.worldbank.org/BODINT/Resources/278027-1215526322295/MIGADirectors.pdf (both last accessed 1 March 2017).

[94] See Sect. 3.

[95] Baroncelli (2013), p. 209.

Compared to other international organisations, however, EU coordination at the World Bank is less developed and more recent. In particular, there is no permanent structure of coordination in Brussels, such as exists for example with regard to EU participation in the FAO (see above) or the UN human rights fora (Human Rights Working Group of the Council of the European Union, COHOM).[96] However, coordination takes place in Washington between the EU Executive Directors and EU Member State representatives. In 2003, under the Italian Presidency, the Italian Executive Director established an informal consultation process of the EU Executive Directors in Washington, to coordinate European positions on the Board of Directors, exchange information and agree on joint positions.[97] The EU Delegation in Washington participates in these meetings as an observer.[98] Coordination is hampered in particular by the lack of a permanent forum in Brussels, the disparate representation of EU Member States in the World Bank (with ministers covering a diverse range of portfolios), the quick reaction times necessitated by World Bank projects, and the governance structure of the World Bank, which disperses EU Member States across different constituencies.[99]

Nevertheless, the EU has developed a strong partnership with the World Bank, as indicated by the EU's financial contributions to the World Bank's funds. In 2001, both organisations concluded a "Trust Funds and Co-Financing Framework Agreement", subsequently renewed and revised in 2009,[100] 2014[101] and 2016,[102] which governs the use of EU budget money for World Bank development projects. The European Commission and the World Bank exchange information and coordinate

[96]Eurodad, European Coordination at the World Bank and International Monetary Fund: A Question of Harmony?, 2016, p. 13.

[97]Baroncelli (2013), p. 205; Baroncelli (2011), note 6.

[98]Eurodad, European Coordination at the World Bank and International Monetary Fund: A Question of Harmony?, 2016, p. 13.

[99]Eurodad, European Coordination at the World Bank and International Monetary Fund: A Question of Harmony?, 2016, p. 14.

[100]Trust Funds and Cofinancing Framework Agreement between the European Community, represented by the Commission of the European Communities, and the International Bank for Reconstruction and Development, the International Development Association and the International Finance Corporation, Brussels, 20 March 2009, http://ec.europa.eu/europeaid/sites/devco/files/agreement-cofinancing-ec-wb-2009bis_en.pdf (last accessed 1 March 2017).

[101]Framework Agreement between the European Commission on behalf of the European Union and the International Bank for Reconstruction and Development, the International Development Association, the International Finance Corporation and the Multilateral Investment Guarantee Agency, signed in Brussels on 30 July and in Washington on 15 August 2014.

[102]World Bank, European Commission and World Bank sign agreement to boost development cooperation, Press release, 15 April 2016, www.worldbank.org/en/news/press-release/2016/04/15/european-commission-and-world-bank-sign-agreement-to-boost-development-cooperation (last accessed 1 March 2017).

on development cooperation, conduct policy dialogues on trade and agriculture and cooperate in the area of global public goods.[103]

However, the gap between the EU's financial contribution and its representation in the World Bank persists and proposals to combine the various EU Member State Executive Directorates into a single EU seat on the Board of Directors have so far received little support from EU Member States.

5 Conclusions

Despite the Union's major role in international trade, finance and development, its political influence in many UN economic governance fora remains limited. While recent reforms have contributed to making EU internal coordination and external representation more effective, external obstacles, in particular the Union's limited participation rights in most UN bodies, remain. As the 2010–2011 negotiations on the upgrade of the EU's observer status in the UN General Assembly have shown, political willingness to strengthen the Union's rights is often lacking—both in the EU Member States who may fear a silent "competence creep" and in third countries which may be concerned about setting a precedent. Even in those rare fora where the EU has obtained membership status, cumbersome coordination and transparency requirements may place a strain on effective EU participation. In a changing political environment—both within the EU and abroad—divisions and political resistance are only likely to grow. If the EU wants to be a "player", and not just a "payer", at the UN level,[104] it needs to continue pushing for a stronger EU presence and to build on the positive dynamics created with the Lisbon Treaty.

References

Baroncelli E (2011) The EU at the World Bank: institutional and policy performance. J Eur Integr 33(6):637–650

Baroncelli E (2013) The World Bank. In: Jørgensen KE, Laatikainen KV (eds) Routledge handbook on the European Union and international institutions: performance, policy, power. Routledge, Abindgon, pp 205–220

Brewer E (2012) The participation of the European Union in the work of the United Nations: evolving to reflect the new realities of regional organisations. Int Org Law Rev 9(1):181–225

Cloos J, Reinesch G, Vignes D, Weyland J (1993) Le Traité de Maastricht. Genèse, analyse, commentaires. Bruylant, Brussels

[103]Viilup E, The role of the World Bank in international trade policy, DGEXPO/B/PolDep/Note/2016_29, January 2016, p. 4.

[104]Wouters and Chané (2016), p. 322.

Emerson M, Balfour R, Corthaut T, Wouters J, Kaczynski PM, Renard T (2011) Upgrading the EU's role as global actor: institutions, law and the restructuring of european diplomacy. Centre for European Policy Studies, Brussels

Frid R (1993) The European economic community: a member of a specialized agency of the United Nations. Eur J Int Law 4(2):239–255

Frid R (1995) The relations between the EC and international organisations – legal theory and practice. Kluwer, The Hague

Geiger R (2015) Article 220 TFEU. In: Geiger R, Khan DE, Kotzur M (eds) European Union treaties: treaty on European Union treaty on the functioning of the European Union. Hart, Oxford

Hervé A (2012) The participation of the European Union in global economic governance fora. Eur Law J 18(1):143–161

Hoffmeister F (2007) Outsider or frontrunner? Recent developments under international and European law on the status of the European Union in international organisations and treaty bodies. Common Mark Law Rev 44(1):41–68

Kuijper PJ, Wouters J, Hoffmeister F, De Baere G, Ramopoulos T (2015) The law of EU external relations: cases, materials and commentary on the EU as an international legal actor. Oxford University Press, Oxford

Sack J (1995) The European community's membership of international organisations. Common Mark Law Rev 32(5):1227–1256

Scheffler J (2011) Die Europäische Union als rechtlich-institutioneller Akteur im System der Vereinten Nationen. Springer, Heidelberg

Schermers HG, Blokker NM (2011) International institutional law: unity within diversity. Nijhoff, Leiden

Schild FD (2013) The influence of the Food and Agriculture Organization (FAO) on the EU legal order. In: Wessel RA, Blockmans S (eds) Between autonomy and dependence: the EU legal order under the influence of international organisations. Springer, Dordrecht, pp 217–241

Schmidt M (2015) The position of the European Union in the United Nations: a United Nations perspective. In: Kaddous C (ed) The European Union in international organisations and global governance. Hart, Oxford, pp 33–43

Smith KE (2010) The European Union at the Human Rights Council: speaking with one voice but having little influence. J Eur Publ Policy 17(2):224–241

Thomas DC (2012) Still punching below its weight? Coherence and effectiveness in European Union Foreign Policy. J Common Mark Stud 50(3):457–474

Winkelmann I (2000) Europäische und mitgliedstaatliche Interessenvertretung in den Vereinten Nationen. Zeitschrift für ausländisches öffentliches Recht und Völkerrecht 60:413–445

Wouters J (2013) The European Union and the World Trade Organization: partners or competitors? In: Govaere I, Hanf D (eds) Scrutinizing internal and external dimensions of European law: liber Amicorum Paul Demaret. Lang, Brussels, pp 373–383

Wouters J, Chané AL (2016) Brussels meets Westphalia: The European Union and the United Nations. In: Eeckhout P, Lopez-Escudero M (eds) The European Union's external action in times of crisis. Hart, Oxford, pp 299–323

Wouters J, Ramopoulos T (2016) Time to reconsider status: the IMF, the EU, the Euro Area and its sovereign Debt Crisis. In: Guderzo M, Bosco A (eds) A Monetary Hope for Europe. The Euro and the struggly for the creation of a new global currency. Firenze University Press, Florence, pp 21–37

Wouters J, Van Kerckhoven S (2012) The International Monetary Fund. In: Joergensen KE, Laatikainen KV (eds) Routledge handbook on the European Union and international institutions: performance, policy, Power. Routledge, Abindgon, pp 221–233

Wouters J, Hoffmeister F, Ruys T (2006) The United Nations and the European Union: an ever stronger partnership. Asser, The Hague

Wouters J, Ramopoulos T, Odermatt J (2011) The Lisbon Treaty and the Status of the European Union in the International Arena: The May 2011 Upgrade at the UN General Assembly. IEMed. Mediterranean Yearbook, pp 166–170

Wouters J, Van Kerckhoven S, Ramopoulos T (2013a) The EU and the Euro Area in international economic governance: the case of the IMF. In: Amtenbrink F, Kochenov D (eds) The European Union's shaping of the international legal order. Cambridge University Press, Cambridge, pp 306–327

Wouters J, Van Kerckhoven S, Odermatt J (2013b) The EU at the G20 and the G20's impact on the EU. In: Van Vooren B, Blockmans S, Wouters J (eds) The EU's role in global governance: the legal dimension. Oxford University Press, Oxford, pp 259–271

Wouters J, Odermatt J, Ramopoulos T (2013c) The status of the European Union at the United Nations General Assembly. In: Govaere I, Lannon E, Van Elsuweghe P, Adam S (eds) The European Union in the world: essays in Honour of Marc Maresceau. Nijhoff, Leiden/Boston, pp 211–223

Wouters J, Chané AL, Odermatt J, Ramopoulos T (2015) Improving the EU's status in the UN and the UN system: an objective without a strategy? In: Kaddous C (ed) The European Union in international organisations and global governance. Hart, Oxford, pp 45–74

On the Duty of Cooperation, Consistency and Influence in the External Relations of the Euro-Zone: Representation of EU and EU Member States in the International Monetary Fund

Päivi Leino

Abstract The question of unified representation by the euro area in international financial institutions has been discussed more or less since the introduction of the common currency. In 2015 the Commission adopted a new proposal for a Council decision laying down measures in view of progressively establishing unified representation of the euro area in the IMF. This paper introduces the IMF and its key functions in light of the EU Member State competence division. Second, it discusses the IMF decision-making structures and EU participation in them following the 2010 IMF governance reforms. It explores the current arrangements for ensuring EU coherence and the current proposals for their improvement in light of the broader legal framework relating to external competence, with a focus on EU influence and its meaning in the IMF context. The Commission proposal focuses largely on the political justifications relating to unified representation while disregarding the legal arguments that would support the objective. While focusing on unified representation of the euro area, the proposal disregards the question of Member States outside the euro. Finally, the paper argues that the mechanisms of unified representation should build on the realistic understanding that often there will not be a common position, and there might not even be justified reasons to aim for one.

Contents

I thank Daniel Wyatt for research assistance, and Marise Cremona, Joni Heliskoski and Tuomas Saarenheimo for discussions and comments on an earlier draft. I also thank the experts at the Finnish permanent mission in Geneva and at the EU for answering my queries concerning some of the practical arrangements.

P. Leino (✉)
UEF Law School, Helsinki, Finland
e-mail: paivi.leino-sandberg@uef.fi

M. Bungenberg et al. (eds.), *European Yearbook of International Economic Law 2017*, European Yearbook of International Economic Law 8,
DOI 10.1007/978-3-319-58832-2_20

1 Why Should Euro-Zone Representation in the IMF be Discussed?

The question of unified representation by the euro area in international financial institutions (IFIs) in general, and in the International Monetary Fund (IMF), in particular, has been discussed more or less since the introduction of the common currency. In 1999 *Jacqueline Dutheil de la Rochère* predicted that "this question of the external representation of economic and monetary union will be one of the most difficult to face during the years to come [. . .]."[1] The December 1997 and 1998 European Council conclusions specifically addressed the issue. The European Council placed responsibility for the external representation of the euro on the Council and the European Central Bank (ECB),[2] and encouraged the EU institutions and the Member States to "ensure a timely and effective preparation of common positions and common understandings that can be presented to third parties in international fora."[3] In 1998 the Commission presented a proposal for a Council decision relating to the matter, but it was never adopted by the latter.[4]

Institutional and academic concern in the EU has been directed specifically at a perceived lack of EU influence in IFIs. While EU policy decisions and economic developments are increasingly relevant for the world economy, in the IFIs, the EU and the euro area are still not represented as one:

> The situation of the EU and the Euro area at the IMF is characterised by an overrepresentation of European/EU Member States, a poor ex ante coordination of positions and, as a result, a weak identification and a limited influence of the euro area in the organs of the IMF.[5]

Discussion concerning the role of EU States in IFIs also takes place at global level, but for the opposite reason: relating to the perceived disproportionate weight

[1]De la Rochère (1999), p. 445.
[2]Luxembourg European Council, Presidency Conclusions, 12 and 13 December 1997, para. 46.
[3]Vienna European Council, Presidency Conclusions, 11 and 12 December 1998, para. 15.
[4]See European Commission, COM (1998) 637 final.
[5]Louis (2013), p. 193.

of certain advanced countries,[6] as a result of which "[t]he institution's major shareholders" are seen to be "gambling, perhaps unwittingly, with the IMF's legitimacy and credibility".[7] While the recent 2010 IMF governance reforms have aimed at diminishing the power of advanced economies including the EU states in the IMF, on the EU side they have been seen to provide increased momentum to create a unified EU voice at the IMF.[8] Therefore, a key question arises as to whether the purpose of unifying EU representation in IFIs is in fact more about limiting EU power e.g. through the limitation of the number of EU seats around the negotiating table (the global discussion) or about strengthening EU power (the argument with which the EU Commission justifies its proposals). In other words, what counts as "influence", and how do you gain it?

In 2015 the Commission adopted a new proposal for a Council decision laying down measures in view of progressively establishing unified representation of the euro area in the IMF.[9] In the draft Council decision, the Commission points out how a more coherent representation is not only about maximizing EU influence; instead, it is a win-win scenario that also benefits third countries, "in particular by a stronger and more consistent euro area contribution to global economic and financial stability".[10] The Commission puts forward several concrete suggestions for improving the current situation in the short and longer term (by 2025). In the short term, attempts should be made to secure observer status for the euro area in the Executive Board, and representation of the euro area through the appointment of a euro area Member State Executive Director. Attempts should also to be made to secure a right to address the International Monetary and Financial Committee by the President of the Eurogroup, the Commission and the ECB "as appropriate". All questions relating to constituency arrangements are to be "fully coordinated and agreed in advance", and "consistent with the objective of increasing coherence". Finally, euro area Member States are to "closely coordinate and agree on common positions on all matters of euro area relevance for the IMF Executive Board and Board of Governors meetings and shall use common statements on those issues". In the long term, the scope of coordination expands beyond matters that are of euro area relevance to "all positions to be taken, orally or through written statements, within IMF organs", which "shall be fully coordinated in advance" in the relevant EU bodies (Article 4). The euro area Member States, supported by the Commission

[6]International Monetary and Financial Committee of the IMF, Statement by Guido Mantega, Minister of Finance, Ministerio de Fazenda, Brazil, 16 April 2011, https://www.imf.org/External/spring/2011/imfc/statement/eng/bra.pdf (last accessed 1 March 2017), paras. 14–16.

[7]International Monetary and Financial Committee of the IMF, Statement by Guido Mantega, Minister of Finance, Ministerio de Fazenda, Brazil, 20 April 2013, https://www.imf.org/External/spring/2013/imfc/statement/eng/bra.pdf (last accessed 1 March 2017), para. 14.

[8]Wouters and Van Kerckhoven (2013), p. 227.

[9]European Commission, Proposal for a Council Decision laying down measures in view of progressively establishing unified representation of the euro area in the International Monetary Fund, COM (2015) 603 final.

[10]European Commission, COM (2015) 603 final.

itself and the ECB should "take all necessary actions for the establishment, by 2025 at the latest, of a unified representation of the euro area within the IMF" (Article 3). This includes in particular the presentation of a unified view by the President of the Eurogroup in the Board of Governors. In the Executive Board the euro area should be represented by its own Executive Director representing one or several constituencies consisting of euro states.

In December 2015 the European Council adopted conclusions, where it established that work towards the completion of the EMU was to advance rapidly, in particular as regards the euro area's external representation, "to better reflect its weight in the world economy".[11] While discussions concerning the proposal have not advanced in the Council—reflecting the general reluctance of governments to engage in the matter—the ECB issued an opinion concerning the proposal in April 2016, giving its broad support to strengthening euro area policy coordination but making a number of proposals for amendments, primarily relating to its own position in the envisaged mechanisms.[12]

The proposal raises a number of questions that are more political than legal in nature, such as the willingness of the Member States to create euro area constituencies, and whether forming one constituency is in fact beneficial in terms of power even though this would mean that Member States would no longer have the ability to influence discussions in several constituencies. The matter has been dressed as one relating to external representation, which is not identical to the question of who has competence in matters falling under the IMF agenda. However, the key aspect in the proposals relates less to the more symbolic question of who delivers a speech in a particular IMF session or which name plate is to be used, and more to the question of how the substance of that speech is to be decided. Therefore, the attempt to move into position-building that would be more or less binding on the euro states, and the justifications provided in support of this agenda, raise a number of key considerations relating to the scope and influence of EU competence in matters falling under the IMF. To a certain degree, these are matters of interpretation. There are no general rules in the Treaties that would address the question of adoption of positions under agreements that fall partly under EU (exclusive or shared) and partly under national competence. Many of the relevant questions have however been addressed in Court jurisprudence. These questions are touched upon only lightly by the Commission proposal.

In the following, after a brief description of the legal and factual background, I will first introduce the IMF and its key functions in light of the EU-Member State competence division, followed by a discussion of the IMF decision-making structures and EU participation in them following the 2010 governance reforms. I will

[11]European Council, European Council meeting (17 and 18 December 2015) Conclusions, EUCO 28/15, 18 December 2015, para. 14.

[12]See Opinion of the European Central Bank of 6 April 2016 on a proposal for a Council Decision laying down measures in view of progressively establishing unified representation of the euro area in the International Monetary Fund (CON /2016/22).

then explore the current arrangements for ensuring EU coherence and the current proposals for their improvement in light of the broader legal framework relating to external competence. My focus is on EU influence in the IMF. In addition to the roles of Member State and the EU, this discussion points to a third dimension of power that is relevant for the study: the question of institutional power.

2 Legal and Factual Background: The Coherence Agenda

Euro area representation in the IFIs returned to the discussion agenda with new force following the decisions taken to develop the Economic and Monetary Union (EMU) during and after the financial crisis. The Commission blueprint for a deep and genuine EMU, adopted in 2012, argued that a "strengthened voice of the Economic and Monetary Union is an integral part of the current efforts to improve the economic governance of the euro area". Therefore, further internal integration would need to be reflected externally, notably through progress towards united external economic representation of the EU and of the euro area, in particular in the IMF: The logic is that

> it is the size of the euro area that matters in influencing the type of policy responses that will be taken in international financial institutions and fora [...]. However, because of the current fragmentation of its representation in international financial institutions and fora, the euro area does not have an influence and leadership commensurate to its economic weight.[13]

The Five Presidents' Report published in June 2015 also advocates for a gradual process towards increasingly unified external representation for the euro area, beginning in the short term. For the Five Presidents,

> [t]his fragmented voice means the EU is punching below its political and economic weight as each euro area Member State speaks individually. This is particularly true in the case of the IMF despite the efforts made to coordinate European positions.[14]

The Five Presidents' Report was followed by a Commission Communication adopted in October 2015 laying down a roadmap for moving towards a more consistent external representation of the euro area in international fora[15] as well as a proposal for a Council decision laying down measures in view of progressively

[13]European Commission, A blueprint for a deep and genuine economic and monetary union Launching a European Debate, COM (2012) 777 final.

[14]European Commission, The Five Presidents' Report: Completing Europe's Economic and Monetary Union, https://ec.europa.eu/commission/publications/five-presidents-report-completing-europes-economic-and-monetary-union_en (last accessed 1 March 2017).

[15]European Commission, A roadmap for moving towards a more consistent external representation of the euro area in international fora, COM (2015) 602 final.

establishing unified representation of the euro area in the International Monetary Fund.[16] The proposal is based on Article 138 TFEU, which establishes that

> 1. In order to secure the euro's place in the international monetary system, the Council, on a proposal from the Commission, shall adopt a decision establishing common positions on matters of particular interest for economic and monetary union within the competent international financial institutions and conferences. The Council shall act after consulting the European Central Bank.
>
> 2. The Council, on a proposal from the Commission, may adopt appropriate measures to ensure unified representation within the international financial institutions and conferences. The Council shall act after consulting the European Central Bank.
>
> 3. For the measures referred to in paragraphs 1 and 2, only members of the Council representing Member States whose currency is the euro shall take part in the vote.
>
> A qualified majority of the said members shall be defined in accordance with Article 238(3)(a).

Article 138 TFEU is one of the specific Treaty provisions that only apply to euro area Member States. The first paragraph creates a special legal basis for taking positions in IFIs. It does not stipulate as to its relationship with Article 218(9) TFEU, which refers more generally to Union positions in international bodies on matters that have legal effects. It can be seen as a *lex specialis*, which in particular adds the duty to consult the European Central Bank to that procedure, which reflects its particular role in questions falling under monetary policy. Another difference with Article 218(9) TFEU is that while that Article refers to the adoption of Union positions concerning acts that have legal effects, Article 138(1) only refers to the adoption of common positions relating to "matters of particular interest" for the EMU. This might be seen as a reflection of the type of decisions adopted in the IFIs, which might be significant and yet without formal legal effect. However, the first paragraph establishes that common positions "shall" be adopted, thus imposing an obligation of coordination on the euro area Member States. Relevance is defined with reference to the EMU as a whole and not only to the euro area. The second paragraph refers to more general arrangements of representation in IFIs, which is more loosely formulated as "appropriate measures that "may" be adopted. This is what the new Commission proposal aims to do as far as the IMF is concerned. However, the formulation of the Article suggests that the Council need not be compelled to agree to such arrangements; it may instead opt for using common positions when "matters of a particular interest" for EMU appear on the IFI agendas.

On an even broader scale, ensuring the consistency of multifaceted EU action has been a "recurring concern in the EU external relations narrative".[17] The Laeken declaration on the Future of Europe adopted in 2001 specifically raised questions on how the coherence of European foreign policy could be enhanced and whether the external representation of the Union in international fora should be extended

[16]European Commission, Proposal for a Council Decision laying down measures in view of progressively establishing unified representation of the euro area in the International Monetary Fund, COM (2015) 603 final.

[17]See Hillion (2008).

further.[18] The Lisbon Treaty provisions on developing EU external representation were one of the most prominent rationales for the Treaty.[19] The Commission argued,

> the EU's impact falls short when there are unresolved tensions or a lack of coherence between different policies. There is a need for strong and permanent efforts to enhance the complementary interaction of various policy actions and to reconcile different objectives [. . .]. For the EU, there is the additional challenge in ensuring coherence between EU and national actions. Unsatisfactory co-ordination between different actors and policies means that the EU loses potential leverage internationally, both politically and economically.[20]

Several post-Lisbon Treaty Articles stress the need to ensure consistency between the different areas of Union external action and between these policy areas and other Union policies with a more internal orientation (Article 21(3) TEU). The obligation for ensuring this consistency is placed on the Council and the Commission, assisted by the High Representative of the Union for Foreign Affairs and Security Policy (Article 18 TEU), who acts as one of the Vice-Presidents of the Commission with a special responsibility for consistency in Union external action. The establishment of the European External Action Service (EEAS) under Article 27(3) TEU is also intended to contribute to this objective through assisting the High Representative to fulfil her mandate.[21] These provisions however focus on consistency between different EU policies, not consistency between EU policies and Member State policies.[22] Questions of policy consistency between the latter two dimensions have been treated more as falling under the principle of loyal cooperation in Article 4(3) TEU.[23]

But instead of solving the issue, recent reports argue that the new strengthened coherence framework has done little to enhance EU performance. In fact, it has led to

[18]The Convention drafting the provisions also discussed specifically the issue of European representation in IFIs. See The European Convention Praesidium, EU External Action, CONV 161/02, 3 July 2002. The Treaty included Article 111(4) TEC, which enabled the Council to decide on a joint position "at international level as regards issues of particular relevance to economic and monetary union and on its representation, in compliance with the allocation of powers laid down in Articles 99 and 105". No measures were adopted on that legal basis.

[19]The European Convention Praesidium, EU External Action, CONV 161/02, 3 July 2002, discusses how "[t]here is widespread acknowledgement amongst Europe's citizens of the potential benefits to be gained when the European Union acts collectively on the global stage. At the same time, there is criticism that the Union's international impact currently falls short of what might reasonably be expected given its economic weight, its high degree of internal integration and the resources collectively at its disposal."

[20]European Commission, Europe in the World – Some Practical Proposals for Greater Coherence, Effectiveness and Visibility, COM (2006) 278 final.

[21]Article 2 Council Decision establishing the organisation and functioning of the European External Action Service, OJ 2010 L 201/30.

[22]See however Articles 208 and 212 TFEU relating to development cooperation and technical assistance, which specifically refer to how the "Union's development cooperation policy and that of the Member States complement and reinforce each other" and how the "Union's operations and those of the Member States shall complement and reinforce each other".

[23]On this, see Heliskoski (2010) and Larik (2018).

serious inter-institutional conflicts between the Member States and the Commission in international institutions covering areas of shared/mixed competence.[24] While the Lisbon Treaty has "probably improved the Union's institutional structures, these structures alone will not ensure coherence of foreign policy or the unity of the Union as an international actor".[25] The legal provisions cannot answer why choices are made for the benefit of a certain competence or why member states are reluctant to hand over powers, or explain their possible unwillingness to be represented by the EU.[26] Considering the way in which the discussion concerning euro area representation in IFIs has not really advanced during the past 20 years, the issue might be one relating more to such considerations rather than to the lack of formal procedures for position-building or questions of principle relating to coherence. Joint external representation is unlikely to settle problems in position-building or lack of interest in allowing the EU to take over matters that have so far been dealt with by the Member States. These problems are often blamed on the complex division of competences between the EU and its Member States, which are seen to block the EU from fully taking over and thus diminish its relevance as an international actor.[27] The European External Action Service has also recently noted how the "situation has in general been more challenging in multilateral delegations given the greater complexity of legal and competence issues".[28] While the Treaties already allow for the EU to engage in international institutions and to become a full member of them, the possibilities for doing so are often hampered either by the rules of the institution—such as in the case of the IMF—or by the reluctance of EU Member States to allow the EU to act on their behalf.[29] While in principle Member States should aim at enabling EU participation in international organizations and agreements in its own name, in practice they are often reluctant to do so.

In 2011 the Council adopted a number of General Arrangements relating to EU Statements to be presented in multilateral organizations, which reflect on the difficulties experienced:

> The Treaty of Lisbon enables the EU to achieve coherent, comprehensive and unified external representation. The EU Treaties provide for close and sincere cooperation between the Member States and the Union. Given the sensitivity of representation and potential expectations of third parties, it is essential that, in conformity with current practice, the preparation of statements relating to the sensitive area of competences of the EU and its Member States should remain internal and consensual.[30]

[24]Jørgensen et al. (2011), p. 612.

[25]Cremona (2011), p. 58.

[26]Wessel (2011), p. 17 et seq.

[27]Wessel (2011), p. 17 et seq.

[28]European External Action Service, Report by the High Representative to the European Parliament, the Council and the Commission, 22 December 2011, http://eeas.europa.eu/images/top_stories/2011_eeas_report_cor_+_formatting.pdf (last accessed 1 March 2017), para. 17.

[29]Wessel (2011) p. 18.

[30]Council of the European Union, EU Statements in multilateral organisations – General Arrangements, 15901/11, 22 October 2011, para. 2.

The General Arrangements further stress the importance of competence considerations.[31] First, the "EU can only make a statement in those cases where it is competent and there is a position which has been agreed in accordance with the relevant Treaty provisions". Second, "[e]xternal representation and internal coordination does not affect the distribution of competences under the Treaties nor can it be invoked to claim new forms of competences". Furthermore, while action in international organizations is to be coordinated "to the fullest extent possible", "ensuring that there is adequate and timely prior consultation", the responsibility is to a large extent with the Member States who "agree on a case by case basis whether and how to co-ordinate and be represented externally". Further, when the General Arrangements were adopted, several key Member States stressed how the Member States were still fully entitled to "continue to exercise their rights in International Organisations, including by making national statements, participating in statements with other states, or representing EU positions".[32] Unified representation is used in particular in strategically important matters, irrespective of whether they fall under EU or national competence but especially in the latter case and decision-making with respect to the substance of the statements takes place with consensus. While national statements repeating an identical message are avoided, such statements can be added after the delivery of the EU statement, and in a manner that does not challenge the substance of the common position. The question of who then presents the common statement depends on the rules of the international organization in question: it can be the Head of EU Delegation, but it can also be the EU Presidency, or, especially in their absence from that organization, the representative of another EU Member State.

The recent Commission Communication and proposal for Council decision aim at attacking these problems in the specific context of the IMF. However, consistency is just as much a political as it is a legal concept. The political dimension, in particular the willingness of Member States to be represented by the EU institutions, is something that the 2012 and 2015EMU Reports, with their focus on new procedures, fail to discuss. Questions relating to unified representation are often more political than legal in character and reach beyond the surface of a unified voice to the absence of a common position and to a fear of external representation having repercussions on the division of competences. The Commission is not entirely innocent in this regard. The recent EMU Reports are also weak on questions relating to competence. Representation is not the same as competence; therefore, unified representation through the EU institutions or through a Member State acting in the name of the Union can be relied upon even in the absence of EU competence. In various international organizations this is also common practice.

[31] Council of the European Union, EU Statements in multilateral organisations – General Arrangements, 15901/11, 22 October 2011, para. 3.

[32] See Council of the European Union, EU Statements in multilateral organisations – General Arrangements – United Kingdom Statement, 15855/11 ADD2, 21 October 2011. See also Council of the European Union, EU Statements in multilateral organisations – General Arrangements – German Statement, 15855/11 ADD3, 22 October 2011.

However, the weaker the EU competence, the stronger that Member State objections to unified EU representation tend to become. Competence also affects the degree to which Member States are bound to establish, and then be bound by, a common position. In brief, legal competences matter[33]; therefore, attempting to run a discussion of representation in isolation from the broader framework of EU competence would be difficult. The focus of this contribution is in particular on the competence issue, which has so far received limited attention.

There are various reasons for why EMU and EMU-related matters discussed in IFIs have been a particularly difficult case for consistency and external representation. First, EU competence in these areas varies from exclusive competence in monetary policy, shared competence in internal market matters (such as financial market legislation or free movement of capital) to soft coordination competence in economic and fiscal policy, which primarily remains a national competence.[34] Moreover, IMF actions are funded from national budgets. As far as external competence is concerned, Article 3(2) TFEU establishes that

> [t]he Union shall also have exclusive competence for the conclusion of an international agreement when its conclusion is provided for in a legislative act of the Union or is necessary to enable the Union to exercise its internal competence, or in so far as its conclusion may affect common rules or alter their scope.

Therefore, the relevant question for IMF representation relates in particular to the last parts of the paragraph: the existence of EU implied external powers in matters covered by the IMF.

Second, EMU is a prime example of differentiated integration. This is also reflected in the arrangements envisaged under Article 138 TFEU, which foresees a separate arrangement for euro area states. The obligations of states belonging to the euro area and those of states outside of it have fundamental differences, not only as regards monetary policy, but also as regards economic policy, where obligations of euro states reach deeper.[35] Differences between euro area and non-euro area Member States are also relevant for banking union and EU-related, but non-EU law based, commitments, such as the European Stability Mechanism (ESM). However, it is not entirely clear why the attempts to coordinate EU positions should be only limited to euro area states, even if this is the arrangement for which the Treaty specifies powers. Even in the absence of common currency, various questions relating to EU legislation and its external effects are also relevant for other EU Member States. These concern, for example, financial market legislation or the influence of EU economic policy competence on an individual Member State's room to maneuver, discussed below.

Third, EMU external relations encompass a number of IFIs where membership is limited to states, and where membership varies between those involving all Member States and those where only a few are represented. The EU role and institutional

---

[33]See Wessel (2011).

[34]Leino and Salminen (2017).

[35]Leino and Salminen (2017).

presence also differ. In many IFIs, such as the OECD, G7, G20 or Financial Stability Board (FSB), only a limited number of EU Member States are represented. This contribution focuses on the IMF, which has been identified as a priority issue in the EU Reports, but many of the questions raised in the current paper are also relevant for other IFIs. Finally, the institutional setting for external relations in the EMU is also more complex than in other EU external relations: the role of the ECB in the external relations of monetary policy is central,[36] while the roles of the EU High Representative and the European External Action Service—which generally operate as the fundamental tool of external policy coherence—are limited. Therefore, when discussing external representation of the euro area, it is obvious that something other than the mainstream solution is called for.

3 IMF and EU Representation

3.1 IMF Membership and Functions

The IMF exists to ensure the stability of the international monetary system. Its purposes are enumerated in Article 1 of the IMF Articles of Agreement (AoA) and include promoting international monetary cooperation, facilitating the expansion and growth of international trade, promoting exchange stability and making resources available to members under adequate safeguards.[37] The IMF pursues its goal of stability through four primary mechanisms: surveillance, financial assistance, technical assistance and Special Drawing Rights (SDRs). Membership in the IMF is based on the concept of a quota subscription, which is meant to reflect an individual country's position within the world economy and also settles the power and financial liability of those countries within the IMF. The IMF apportions votes to a member country based on their quota as a percentage of the total of all member countries' quotas of the IMF.[38] The quota also has an impact on a member country's ability to borrow from the IMF. Decisions regarding quota allocation and membership are taken by the Board of Governors. All Member States are members of the IMF. The EU is not a member of the IMF, since its membership is limited to states.[39] There has been limited discussion about the need to amend the Articles of

[36]The ECB Statute also includes a specific provision on International cooperation in Article 6, which empowers the ECB to decide how the ESCB is to be represented in the field of international cooperation involving the tasks entrusted to the ESCB, and to participate in international monetary institutions, without prejudice to Article 138 TFEU. In fact, some authors have promoted the membership of the ECB in the IMF—a somewhat odd suggestion considering that it is not an organization for central banks but for states. See Horng (2005).

[37]The expansive wording of these purposes has enabled the IMF to weather challenges posed by "diverse economic circumstances", see Lasta (2000), p. 512.

[38]See Smaghi (2004).

[39]Article II, section 2 of the IMF AoA.

Agreement to enable its membership. The ECB opinion concerning the Commission proposal indicates its support for a "fully unified representation of the euro area in the IMF", but points out that this would ultimately require full EU membership, which is not currently on the Commission agenda.

Substantial governance reforms were instigated in the IMF in 2010. In the background was the acknowledgement that the economically powerful countries of 1944 when the IMF was created, notably the USA and various European countries, had a distinct overrepresentation in the IMF as compared to modern economic powers, for example China and Russia, or developing economies. The reforms introduced in 2010 were primarily aimed at curing these disproportionate representation issues: to diminish the power of those member countries seen as overrepresented[40] and to increase the power of the underrepresented developing countries. The key element of the 2010 reform was the doubling of all members' quotas, thus making substantially more resources available to the IMF. The reform package also included a 6% quota shift from overrepresented member countries to underrepresented dynamic emerging market and developing member countries.[41] Following a lengthy period of inactivity by important major economic powers,[42] the rollout of the 2010 reforms officially began in January 2016.[43]

Article IV IMF AoA, section 1, establishes the general obligations of Members,

> [...] each member undertakes to collaborate with the Fund and other members to assure orderly exchange arrangements and to promote a stable system of exchange rates. In particular, each member shall:
>
> (i) endeavor to direct its economic and financial policies toward the objective of fostering orderly economic growth with reasonable price stability, with due regard to its circumstances;
>
> (ii) seek to promote stability by fostering orderly underlying economic and financial conditions and a monetary system that does not tend to produce erratic disruptions;
>
> (iii) avoid manipulating exchange rates or the international monetary system in order to prevent effective balance of payments adjustment or to gain an unfair competitive advantage over other members; and
>
> (iv) follow exchange policies compatible with the undertakings under this Section.

Considering the substance, these provisions fall partly under Member State competence, partly under shared competence and partly under Union exclusive competence in respect of monetary policy for euro area states. But even in areas falling under shared competence, Article 3(2) TFEU quoted above indicates that the EU might have implied exclusive external competence in questions that affect "common rules or alter their scope". This finding is also relevant for Article VIII

---

[40] Smaghi (2004), p. 203 regarding comments about Europe being overrepresented.

[41] For a full list of voting shares post-2010 reform see IMF, Quota and voting shares before and after implementation of reforms agreed in 2008 and 2010 (in percentage shares of total IMF quota), http://www.imf.org/external/np/sec/pr/2011/pdfs/quota_tbl.pdf (last accessed 1 March 2017).

[42] For example the US Congress did not approve the reforms until December 2015. See IMF, Press release No. 15/573, 18 December 2015.

[43] See IMF, Press release No. 16/25, 27 January 2016.

IMF AoA, which includes further general obligations on Members, including obligations relating to restrictions on capital movements, which fall under shared or exclusive EU competence. Such provisions include obligations relating to the avoidance of restrictions on the making of payments and transfers for international transactions without IMF authorization, certain kinds of exchange contracts or discriminatory currency practices. The remaining parts of the Article include provisions on the convertibility of foreign-held balances, duties to provide information, consult and collaborate.

An important function of the IMF is to engage in surveillance of financial systems. This surveillance takes two different forms: overseeing the international monetary system, known as multilateral surveillance, and monitoring the economic and financial policies of its member countries, known as bilateral surveillance.[44] Multilateral surveillance takes the form of the IMF monitoring international and regional economies as well as analyzing the impact of individual member country financial policy on the greater global economy. Bilateral surveillance involves IMF economists visiting member countries, usually annually, to discuss financial issues with that country's government and central bank in what is known as an Article IV consultation. IMF economists also meet with various other stakeholders (such as labour unions or business representatives) during this process to assess the functioning of the country's economy. IMF staff then prepare a report, which forms the basis for discussion by the Executive Board. The member country prepares a position referred to as the "Buff statement" on the report, presented in the Executive Board by the relevant Executive Director. After approval in the Executive Board the report is sent to the member state in question. Article IV is formulated as a "best endeavors" clause, which primarily commits the contracting parties to listen and make their best efforts to follow the advice of the IMF, which are in effect recommendations addressed to the member countries. There is no formal follow-up on the reports.

As far as the EU states are concerned, the IMF also holds consultations annually for the euro area as a whole, whereby it exchanges views with the ECB and the Commission relating to monetary and exchange rate policies and regional fiscal policies, financial sector supervision and stability, trade and cross-border capital flows, as well as structural policies. A separate report concerning the entire euro area is ultimately produced.[45] The Financial Sector Assessment Program (FSAP) is used to provide input to the Article IV consultation through a comprehensive and in-depth assessment of a country's financial sector. Since 2013, this analysis has been also done on an EU wide basis.[46]

[44]The IMF is tasked with surveillance responsibilities and member countries with compliance responsibilities pursuant to Article IV, section 3 of the IMF AoA.

[45]For the most recent one concerning the euro area, see IMF Country Report No. 16/219, July 2016.

[46]IMF, Press release No. 13/79, 15 March 2013.

Currently EU positions to the euro area reports are coordinated (see below) while positions to EU member state Article IV consultations are not. This builds on the presumption that the IMF, when preparing the reports, takes into account the relevant competence division. However, for example, the recent IMF Staff Concluding Statement of the 2016 Article IV Mission concerning Finland takes up several issues that are of a relevance for EU legislation. These include a need to strengthen banking supervision and expand the macroprudential toolkit as well as the compatibility of the current state of affairs with the EU Stability and Growth Pact, including progress on structural reforms and the need to make structural fiscal adjustments and consolidate in the context of EU rules.[47] Initiating an amendment of EU legislation is naturally an EU Commission prerogative, as is monitoring the implementation of the Stability and Growth Pact and taking measures to ensure Member State compliance with them. From a competence point-of-view, the extent to which a provision actually creates directly binding outcomes—a matter that is always relative in international law—might not be decisive. In the recent *OIV* case, for example, the CJEU found that recommendations, while not directly binding, were still "capable of influencing the content of the legislation adopted by the EU legislature".[48] Such an effect would be difficult to exclude in the case of the IMF—why would such recommendations be given other than to affect Member State rules and behaviour?

Financial assistance is arguably the most prominent, and perhaps also the most politically charged, of the IMF's functions. The IMF can provide loans to member countries suffering real or potential balance of payment problems. IMF loans are conditional upon the effective implementation of economic policies and measures agreed with the country involving a series of measures designed to correct the relevant member country's balance-of-payments imbalances. The IMF also provides technical assistance and training to member countries with respect to the development of their institutions, laws and policies to enable greater economic stability and growth.

Several euro area states have received financial support from other euro area Member States, the IMF, the European Financial Stability Facility and the ESM during and after the crisis. As far as non-euro area states are concerned, obligations relating to monetary policy tend to be a part of the program, including provisions on currency regime, foreign exchange reserves and possible limitations of capital movements. In the case of euro states however, such requirements have not in practice been set, on the understanding that such provisions would fall under EU competence.[49] The programs generally also include provisions on measures in the

---

[47]IMF, Finland: Staff Concluding Statement of the 2016 Article IV Mission, 4 October 2016, https://www.imf.org/en/News/Articles/2016/10/03/MS100416-Finland-Staff-Concluding-Statement-of-the-2016-Article-IV-Mission (last accessed 1 March 2017).

[48]CJEU, case C-399/12, *Germany v Council*, ECLI:EU:C:2014:2258, para. 63.

[49]This conclusion is founded on data that can be found in the IMF Monitoring of Fund Arrangements (MONA) Database, https://www.imf.org/external/np/pdr/mona/Country.aspx (last accessed 1 March 2017). Since 2000 there have been altogether 170 programs funded by the IMF.

financial sector, the relevant legislation and supervision, all of which are increasingly touched upon by EU legislation and joint supervision at EU level as far as the euro area states are concerned. The relevant question from a competence perspective is the extent to which the new EU legislation can give recourse to implied exclusive external competence under Article 3(2) TFEU.

It would seem obvious that if the IMF Articles of Agreement was concluded now, and if it enabled participation of the EU as a contracting party, the agreement would be concluded as a mixed agreement. The fact that it has not been concluded as a mixed agreement is however not decisive for today's competence division in the EU. The fact that the EU is not

> a member of an international organisation in no way authorises a Member State, acting individually in the context of its participation in an international organisation, to assume obligations likely to affect Community rules promulgated for the attainment of the objectives of the Treaty. Moreover, the fact that the Community is not a member of an international organisation does not prevent its external competence from being in fact exercised, in particular through the Member States acting jointly in the Community's interest.[50]

It would seem that even though the IMF Articles of Agreement is concluded by the Member States alone, it contains significant provisions that fall under EU competence either through express powers or through implied powers because they are "capable of decisively influencing the content of the legislation adopted by the EU legislature".[51] But since the IMF Articles of Agreement predates the existence of the EU, the exact competence division has never been subject to a thorough discussion. However, even if the Articles of Agreement were to be formally concluded as a mixed agreement, it is unlikely that it would have drawn any systematic distinction between the exclusive or non-exclusive competence of the EU and its effects at the stage of implementing the agreement.[52] International agreements seldom engage in such discussion, especially since the exact division of competence changes with developments in EU legislation. As far as the implementation of the IMF Articles of Agreement is concerned, it would seem that the competence dimension is currently mostly observed based on a gentleman's agreement within the IMF and that matters falling under EU competence are to be discussed separately in the reports prepared for the euro area, for which coordination mechanisms exist (see below). However, as the Finnish example shows, the division between the two is, in practice, difficult to draw. Still, considering the legal effect of IMF reports, there might be some room for a debate on whether these reports in fact have the capacity to "decisively influence the content of the legislation adopted by the EU legislature", and thus whether they require binding position-building in EU bodies as far as Member State reports are concerned. If

[50]CJEU, case C-45/07, *Commission v Greece*, ECLI:EU:C:2009:84, para. 30 et seq.

[51]CJEU, case C-399/12, *Germany v Council*, ECLI:EU:C:2014:2258, para. 63.

[52]On this, see Heliskoski (2010), p. 150.

this question is answered in the negative, then this finding has direct implications for any duties of coordination that Member States might have.

3.2 IMF Governance Bodies

The power structure of the IMF is split into two main governance bodies: the Board of Governors and the Executive Board. The Board of Governors is the pinnacle body of the IMF and is responsible for taking decisions on the fundamental institutional aspects of the IMF, e.g. quota increases, allocating SDRs, admitting new members as well as amending the IMF's Articles of Agreement.[53] The membership of the Board of Governors consists of a governor, usually the member country's Finance Minister or central bank Governor, and one alternate governor, from each member country. The Board of Governors is also formally responsible for appointing or electing Executive Directors for the Executive Board. The Board of Governors has delegated most of its powers to the Executive Board to enable the day-to-day management of the IMF.[54] The International Monetary and Financial Committee (IMFC) advises the Board of Governors generally on matters affecting, or potentially affecting, the international monetary system. The Committee has no formal decision-making power, but nevertheless exerts influence, particularly with respect to the policy direction of the IMF. The IMFC meets twice per year and its composition essentially mirrors that of the Executive Board.[55] The Commission has observer status at the IMFC and the IMF Development Committee.[56]

The voting structure at the IMF is weighted according to an individual member country's quota. As the main rule, the Board of Governors decides by a majority of votes cast.[57] However, the Executive Board engages predominately in consensus-based decision-making.[58] Therefore, the "sense of the meeting" is usually seen to reflect the position that would have achieved a majority of votes if a formal vote were taken—something that in fact "equals a de facto potential veto for smaller countries".[59] This system also enables the removal of those parts of decisions that may be considered uncomfortable.

---

[53]On this, see Brandner and Grech (2009), p. 11.

[54]Article XII, section 2(b) of the IMF AoA; Brandner and Grech (2009), p. 11.

[55]See IMF, Factsheet: A guide to committees, groups and clubs, 26 September 2016, http://www.imf.org/external/np/exr/facts/groups.htm (last accessed 1 March 2017).

[56]Wouters and Van Kerckhoven (2013), p. 224.

[57]Section 11 of the IMF By-Laws. For the Executive Board, sections C10 and C11 of the Rules and Regulations of the International Monetary Fund.

[58]For a full exploration of consensus-based decision-making at the IMF see, Van Houtven (2002), pp. 20–31.

[59]Van Houtven (2002), pp. 20–31.

The Executive Board operates in continuous session, is the body responsible for the daily business of the IMF and exercises all powers delegated to it by the Board of Governors.[60] The Executive Board is divided into constituencies made up of one singular member country or, often seemingly random, blocs of member countries, which group together for the purpose of electing an Executive Director.[61] Under Article XII of the Articles of Agreement, the Executive Board consists of "twenty Executive Directors elected by the members, with the Managing Director as chairman"; however, the "Board of Governors, by an eighty-five percent majority of the total voting power, may increase or decrease the number of Executive Directors", and has every 2 years opted to increase the amount of seats to 24 for the following 2-year period.

Each constituency is headed by an Executive Director who—even though an official of the IMF—acts as the voice of their constituency, wielding the combined voting power of all of their constituency's member countries.[62] The IMF Articles of Agreement include no provisions on replacing an Executive Director during his 2 years in office, and they continue in office until their successors are elected. This means that while the Executive Director is elected by a constituency, the latter has limited means to punish the Executive Director if she fails to follow instructions given. Re-election of Executive Directors is possible and common, but can also be excluded already at the time of election. The Executive Board is also responsible for nominating a Managing Director who acts as the head of IMF staff as well as the chair of meetings of the Executive Board.

EU representation is currently fragmented in eight different constituencies. Currently two of the euro area Member States—France and Germany—elect their own Executive Directors, while the other euro area Member States are spread over six multi-country constituencies, with some being represented through constituencies with non-EU Executive Directors. In addition, the ECB has observer status at the Executive Board,[63] where it is permitted to speak on matters pertaining to the ECB's mandate. The 2010 governance reforms entailed that advanced European nations committed to giving up two of their IMF Executive Director seats to transitioning, developing and emerging market member countries. The political agreement on the issue was reached outside the IMF governing bodies in a G20 meeting. The question of which EU Member States will give up their Executive Director chairs was not addressed.[64] In 2012 Belgium agreed to move into the

[60]Article XII, section 3(a) of the IMF AoA.

[61]Prior to the 2010 reforms, the five countries with the largest IMF quotas could appoint their Executive Director. The remaining Executive Directors were elected by the countries unable to appoint their own Executive Director.

[62]IMF Finance Department, Financial Organization and Operations of the IMF, IMF Pamphlet Series No. 45, Fifth Edition 1988, p. 4.

[63]See Decision No. 11875 (99/1), 21 December 1998; substituted by Decision No. 12925 (03/1), 27 December 2002; as amended by Decision No. 13414 (05/01), 23 December 2004, Decision No. 13612 (05/108), 22 December 2005, and Decision No. 14517 (10/1), 5 January 2010; Wouters and Van Kerckhoven (2013), p. 224.

[64]See Wouters and Van Kerckhoven (2013), p. 227.

Netherlands' constituency group and share one Executive Director seat.[65] The seat formerly controlled by Belgium is currently controlled by Turkey. Switzerland agreed to share its seat with Poland, and the Nordic countries agreed to include the Baltic countries in their seat rotation. Altogether, these changes add to some 1.64 seats relinquished by advanced European countries. There does not appear to be any movement with respect to the freeing up of the remaining fraction of a seat. The fact that much of the change has been achieved by shifting representation to EU countries that do not (or did not, at the time of the agreement) fall into the category of "advanced" has been derided by some: "The modest reshuffling announced so far indicates that this reduction will be effected mostly by cosmetic changes, namely by upgrading "emerging markets" of the European Union. This of course fails to correct the overrepresentation of Europe in the board, sending yet another negative signal to the outside world".[66] It is evident that if the actual size of the Executive Board was indeed diminished to 20 seats, this would necessitate a serious round of musical chairs.

In Europe, the problems relating to mixed constituencies have been seen as one of the key factors for Europe "punching below its weight" in the IMF[67]; a single EU constituency is believed to enable EU Member States to have a strong impact on IMF policies.[68] Through the reforms, the previous ceiling for constituency size was abolished,[69] which in principle would make it possible for all euro area states to form one constituency. In this regard, the Commission 2015 proposal would be legally possible to realize; the question is now more about its political attractiveness.

While a significant part of IMF work falls under or is affected by EU competence, the presence of Union institutions has remained limited to functions enabled by the IMF rules. Therefore the key issue has become how EU coherence can be guaranteed in the absence of an effective institutional presence.

---

[65]See, DNB, IMF governance reform: open economies have a place at the table, DNBulletin, 17 October 2012, http://www.dnb.nl/en/news/news-and-archive/dnbulletin-2012/dnb279658.jsp (last accessed 1 March 2017).

[66]International Monetary and Financial Committee of the IMF, Statement by Guido Mantega, Minister of Finance, Ministerio de Fazenda, Brazil, 13 October 2012, https://www.imf.org/External/AM/2012/imfc/statement/eng/bra.pdf (last accessed 1 March 2017), p. 3.

[67]See Wouters et al. (2014).

[68]See Smaghi (2004), p. 247.

[69]The IMF AoA previously included a provision prohibiting the election of Executive Directors representing more than 9%, see Brandner and Grech (2009), p. 9.

4 Euro Area (and EU) Coherence in the IMF

There are two primary bodies for EU coordination: the Brussels-based Subcommittee on IMF-Related Issues, which falls under the Economic and Financial Committee (SCIMF), and the Washington-based EU Representatives to the IMF (EURIMF). All EU Member States currently participate in these bodies, irrespective of whether they belong to the euro area or not.

SCIMF is made up of two representatives each from EU Member States—a representative from the Ministry of Finance and central bank—two representatives from the Commission Directorate-General for Economic and Financial Affairs (DG ECFIN) and two representatives from the ECB. The Commission is in charge of running the Secretariat. SCIMF meets eight to ten times per year and operates on a general consensus basis.[70] Euro area states agreed in 2007 to prepare common euro area statements on issues that relate directly and exclusively to euro area common policy.[71] SCIMF prepares the EU statements delivered by the EU Presidency at certain meetings of the IMFC, prepares the common response (the Buff) in the context of the Article IV review of the Eurozone, issues formal joint positions and may draft common policy papers called "common understandings" reflecting long term and broad strategies for the EU at the IMF.[72] Documents agreed to at SCIMF are sent to the EFC for endorsement and then sent to the European Executive Directors at the IMF for use at EURIMF meetings, or at IMF Executive Board meetings generally. Executive Directors are not, however, formally obliged to comply with the contents of these documents.[73] This links with the broader question of the extent to which Executive Directors in fact effectively represent their constituencies and can be controlled by them.

EURIMF is the EU's primary day-to-day IMF-based coordination vehicle and meets approximately three times per week. It consists of EU Executive Directors and various other EU IMF representatives, as well as an observer from the ECB and the Commission delegation to Washington. The Commission has no formal coordination role, which is seen to reflect its competence limitations with respect to issues dealt with at the IMF.[74] The same limitations, logically, apply to the ECB, which can only speak on issues within the realm of its competence. The purpose of

---

[70]See e.g., Hervé 2012 p. 11 et seq.; Eurodad, European Coordination at the World Bank and International Monetary Fund: A Question of Harmony?, January 2006, http://www.eurodad.org/uploadedfiles/whats_new/reports/eurodad%20euifigovernance.pdf (last accessed 1 March 2017), p. 11 et seq.

[71]For a reference to the earlier practices, see European Commission, COM (2015) 602 final, para. 4.1(a).

[72]Eurodad, European Coordination at the World Bank and International Monetary Fund: A Question of Harmony?, January 2006, p. 12.

[73]Eurodad, European Coordination at the World Bank and International Monetary Fund: A Question of Harmony?, January 2006, p. 11 et seq.

[74]Eurodad, European Coordination at the World Bank and International Monetary Fund: A Question of Harmony?, January 2006, p. 10.

EURIMF is to act as an informal information exchange between concerned EU parties about the current IMF agenda, with the hope that these discussions lead to EU position coordination.[75] EURIMF is chaired by one of the EU Executive Directors for periods of 2 years at a time.[76] Due to the large size of EURIMF, a "mini-EURIMF" has been set-up, which consists only of EU Executive Directors and their alternates and meets on an ad-hoc basis.[77] EURIMF also coordinates EU Executive Director opinions regarding Article IV Consultations. Prior to an IMF Executive Board meeting, the primary Member States of their constituency prepare what is known as a "grey" paper, which reflects the positions of their constituency regarding the Executive Board agenda and serve as the basis of discussion at EURIMF.[78] There is no formal voting at EURIMF meetings,[79] which in practice indicates the use of consensus as the decision-making rule. The EU Presidency will also prepare European grey papers to be discussed at EURIMF on matters of relevance to the EU.[80]

The success of these bodies in coordinating common EU positions has however in practice been seen as modest. The capacity of SCIMF to form strong common positions on matters relevant to the EU at the IMF has proved limited, and it does not take binding decisions.[81] In practice, the EU Presidency statement prepared in SCIMF is complemented by Member States offering statements reflecting their national agendas.[82] This also points to some difficulties in establishing what exactly should be coordinated. The IMF obviously discusses some issues that clearly fall under the "relevant for euro area" definition for the purposes of Article 138 TFEU. However, many highly contentious issues—such as the future lending framework involving questions relating to debt restructuring for states—are matters that divide EU Member States in a fundamental manner, beyond the euro—non-euro divide. While there is currently no EU legislation on the matter, it would be difficult to treat them as matters that are in no way "relevant for the euro area". These divergences are undoubtedly among those that have provoked the Commission to act on the issue of unified representation. And yet, divergences in Member State positions are

[75]Hervé (2012), p. 8 et seq.

[76]Wouters and Van Kerckhoven (2013), p. 225.

[77]Eurodad, European Coordination at the World Bank and International Monetary Fund: A Question of Harmony?, January 2006, p. 9.

[78]Wouters and Van Kerckhoven (2013), p. 225; Eurodad, European Coordination at the World Bank and International Monetary Fund: A Question of Harmony?, January 2006, p. 9.

[79]Eurodad, European Coordination at the World Bank and International Monetary Fund: A Question of Harmony?, January 2006, p. 9.

[80]Eurodad, European Coordination at the World Bank and International Monetary Fund: A Question of Harmony?, January 2006, p. 9.

[81]European Parliament, External Representation of the Euro Area, IP/A/ECON/FWC/2010_19, May 2012, p. 36.

[82]Eurodad, European Coordination at the World Bank and International Monetary Fund: A Question of Harmony?, January 2006, p. 12.

unlikely to be overcome in the short term no matter how the EU coordination regime is designed and enforced.

The 2012 Commission blueprint included a separate annex 2 on "External representation of the euro area". According to the blueprint, the external representation of the euro area should be strengthened to allow it to play a more active role, which "should result in delivering a single message on issues such as economic and fiscal policy, macroeconomic surveillance, exchange rate policies, and financial stability". Therefore, euro area coordination infrastructure in Brussels and in Washington was in need of further development: "The euro area coordination process should be improved, and Member States should follow common messages on a compulsory basis". Constituencies needed to be rearranged and an observer status in the IMF Executive Board sought for the euro area.

In the Five Presidents Report, and the 2015 Commission Communication and proposal for a Council decision,[83] this argumentation is developed further. So far, formal Council decisions based on Article 138 TFEU (or Article 218(9) TFEU) have not been used. Somewhat curiously, the Commission's 2015 proposal does also not directly refer to the adoption of Council decisions, even if these are the instruments mentioned in Article 138(1) TFEU, and that would provide the formally legally binding effect the Commission is aiming for. Article 138 TFEU itself seems to require such decisions to be adopted by using "shall". Instead, the draft refers more generally to taking common positions and coordinating them fully. The draft decision is limited to euro area representation, it limits to "all positions taken, orally or through written statements, within IMF organs", and that these are to be "fully coordinated in advance within the Council, the Eurogroup, the EFC and/or the Euro Working Group (EWG) as appropriate", but without defining the instrument or the decision-making procedure to be applied. In many international organizations consensus is used in practice. Article 138 TFEU however establishes qualified majority voting of euro area Member States as the voting pattern in the Council. Moreover, the proposal includes no suggestions concerning the EU states outside the euro area. How about their obligations of coordination?

5 How Far do the Requirements of Consistency and Duty of Cooperation in External Action Stretch in the Question of IMF?

The broader framework that is relevant for an analysis of the recent Commission proposals relates partly to the Treaty provisions on the need to ensure consistency in Union external representation and partly to the Court's jurisprudence interpreting these provisions and the duty of cooperation, particularly in the context of mixed agreements. While the questions relating to coherence and consistency are

[83]European Commission, COM (2015) 602 final; European Commission, COM (2015) 603 final.

ultimately more political or institutional in character,[84] the latter questions are more legal in nature. As noted above, representation ultimately has a strong linkage with questions of competence. These considerations form the substance of this section.

In the Commission proposal for a Council decision, the competence dimension is explained only in broad terms, with reference to the increased political relevance of the euro area and the combined effect of the European Semester, six-pack and two-pack legislation as well as the Fiscal Compact,[85] which "have integrated, strengthened and broadened EU-level surveillance of Member State policies in essential areas of macroeconomic and budgetary relevance". The draft Council decision points out how the IMF has

> played a key role, together with the Commission and the ECB, in shaping the programmes aimed at rescuing Member States hit by the sovereign debt crises. In addition, the strengthened governance framework for economic policy coordination and strong convergence of financial sector regulation and supervision in the context of the Banking Union mean that, in the future, the IMF will need to go well beyond a national perspective in its assessment of supervision and crisis management in the euro area.[86]

The Commission also refers to the establishment of the ESM, and the decision to put in place a Banking Union with centralized supervision and resolution for banks in the euro area. In the Commission's view, external representation has not kept up with those developments, which limits the effectiveness of the euro area voice in IFIs.[87] In the argumentation of the ECB, which concurs with the Commission analysis, these developments have also been seen as "transfer of competences", which must have implications for representation in international fora.[88] The Court's case law in *opinion 1/78* and *opinion 2/91* on external competence has been invoked as a further justification. In these Opinions the Court has established that

> when it appears that the subject-matter of an agreement or contract falls in part within the competence of the Community and in part within that of the Member States, it is important to ensure that there is a close association between the institutions of the Community and the Member States both in the process of negotiation and conclusion and in the fulfilment of the obligations entered into. This duty of cooperation [. . .] results from the requirement of unity in the international representation of the Community.[89]

This jurisprudence—which largely relates to mixed agreements—indicates that there is a duty for the Member States and EU institutions to orchestrate their performance on the international scene.[90]

---

[84]See also Cremona (2011), p. 59.

[85]Treaty on the Stability, Coordination and Governance in the Economic and Monetary Union.

[86]European Commission, COM (2015) 603 final.

[87]European Commission, COM (2015) 603 final.

[88]See e.g. ECB, The external representation of the EU and EMU, ECB Monthly Bulletin 05/2011.

[89]See CJEU, opinion 2/91, *Convention N° 170 of the International Labour Organization*, ECLI: EU:C:1993:106, para. 36.

[90]See Hillion (2009).

Competence considerations are highly relevant for the objectives that the draft Council decisions aim to achieve.

The explanation of Union competence illustrated in the Commission and ECB argumentation however appears slightly superficial and partly misleading. First, it is evident that a transfer of competence can only take place through a Treaty amendment; apart from the limited amendment to Article 136(3) TFEU confirming Member State competence to conclude the ESM Agreement, no Treaty amendments have taken place widening EU competence in the policy areas where the IMF is active. Instead, since the crisis the EU has used some of the shared competence, in particular in the area of the internal market, which can give recourse to exclusive competence in external relations under Article 3(2) TFEU. In the areas where the recent developments quoted as a main justification for a re-think may have had an impact on Union competence are the new instruments relating to financial supervision and Banking Union. In these policy areas the Union's implied internal market competence has now been exercised—thus confirming an understanding that such internal competence in fact exists. As such, it may give recourse to implied external competence and thus also affect the division of responsibilities in IFIs such as the IMF.

Second, the jurisprudence invoked as a justification for the new arrangements largely relates to the existence of exclusive EU external competence and mixed agreements where competence to conclude the agreement is shared by the EU and the Member States. Based on jurisprudence, the starting point would be in matters falling under EU competence—exclusive or shared. Common positions can and should be formed following EU decision-making structures based on Article 218(9) TFEU, or in the case of IFIs, Article 138(2) TFEU. This conclusion is supported by the Court's recent jurisprudence concerning the application of Article 218(9) TFEU in the *OIV* case, which concerned the 2001 Agreement Establishing the International Organisation of Vine and Wine of which 21 Member States are members, but of which the EU is not. Until June 2010, the Member States, on their own initiative, had coordinated their positions within the OIV's working group on wines and alcohol. After several failed Commission attempts to propose a Council decision formulating a Union position, such a decision was finally adopted, with Germany voting against, and later challenging the decision before the CJEU with reference to how the EU was not a member of the said organization; therefore Article 218(9) TFEU was in its view not applicable. The Court confirmed that as far as an area of law falls within a competence of the European Union, Article 218(9) TFEU was indeed the correct legal basis for adopting an EU position.[91] Even though the *OIV* case concerns the implementation of 218(9) TFEU—and not Article 138 TFEU specifically—one could assume that just as Member States were required to act via Article 218(9) TFEU procedures, they are also required to act via Article 138 TFEU when its conditions are fulfilled. Case law establishes even more generally that to the extent that "the matter falls either wholly or in part within the Union's *exclusive* competence, the position

[91]CJEU, case C-399/12, *Germany v Council*, ECLI:EU:C:2014:2258.

adopted must be one of the Union".[92] The existence of Union exclusive competence "does not preclude the Member States from actively participating" in the international organization, "provided that the positions adopted by those States within that international organization are coordinated at [Union] level beforehand".[93] This case law is of relevance for questions relating to monetary policy or the possible implied external powers relating to the internal market legislation, including the Banking Union.

In the areas of shared competence, case law points to obligations of consultation, coordination or even abstention to act that fall primarily on the Member States in the name of a duty of sincere cooperation.[94] Based on jurisprudence, a duty of genuine cooperation is of general application and is, as such, not dependent on the exclusivity of EU competence, or the right of the Member States to enter into obligations towards non-member countries.[95] Once a position has been coordinated at EU level, a Member State should not depart from it: "That obligation to cooperate flows from the requirement of unity in the international representation". Therefore, Member States can be subject to "special duties of action and abstention in a situation in which the Commission has submitted to the Council proposals which, although they have not been adopted by the Council, represent the point of departure for concerted Community action." Unilateral Member State action "is likely to compromise the principle of unity in the international representation of the Union and its Member States and weaken their negotiating power with regard to the other parties to the Convention concerned".[96] However, the Court left open the degree to which there is an obligation to establish a common position or an obligation to attempt to do so. The key principle seems to be that in matters where EU competence is not exclusive and it has not decided to exercise its non-exclusive (shared) competence, the Member States have the freedom to exercise their competence either collectively or individually.[97]

As far as national competence is concerned, there is no case law establishing binding obligations for Member States in areas falling purely under national competence, and such obligations would be difficult to justify with duties relating to loyal cooperation or consistency. Therefore, Member States ultimately decide on

[92]See Heliskoski (2010), p. 159 (emphasis in original).

[93]CJEU, case C-45/07, *Commission v Greece*, ECLI:EU:C:2009:84, para. 28.

[94]Den Hertog and Stroß (2013), p. 388. Even the powers falling under CFSP must be exercised in a "manner consistent with Community law": "Consequently, while it is for Member States to adopt measures of foreign and security policy in the exercise of their national competence, those measures must nevertheless respect the provisions adopted by the Community in the field of the common commercial policy provided for by Article 113 of the Treaty". CJEU, case C-124/95, *The Queen, ex parte Centro-Com v HM Treasury and Bank of England*, ECLI:EU:C:1997:8, paras. 24–26.

[95]See CJEU, case C-266/03, *Commission v Luxembourg*, ECLI:EU:C:2005:341, para. 58; CJEU, case C-433/03, *Commission v Germany*, ECLI:EU:C:2005:462, para. 64.

[96]CJEU, case C-246/07, *Commission v Sweden*, ECLI:EU:C:2010:203, paras. 103–105. For a discussion, see Casteleiro and Larik (2011).

[97]Heliskoski (2010), p. 154.

matters falling under national competence,[98] but subject to duties of good and loyal cooperation, which prevent them from jeopardizing Union objectives. Moreover, both the ESM and the Fiscal Compact referred to by the Commission are international agreements specifically concluded under national competence. And while the Commission and the ECB have—together with the IMF—played a core role in crisis management in the euro area, they have done so under the special mandate of the ESM, thus involving no exercise of EU competence.[99]

IMF obligations are also highly relevant for budgetary powers, not only because IMF monitoring is directed at their exercise, but also because its actions are funded by the Member States. In addition to a discussion concerning the obligations flowing from the requirement of unity in international representation, *opinion 1/78* quoted above also addresses the exclusivity of Union competence in concluding the agreement in a situation where its execution involves the finances of the Member States as undertakings that cannot be entered into without their participation. In this case the Commission argued that the "question of competence precedes that of financing and that the question of Community powers cannot therefore be made dependent on the choice of financial arrangements". The Court specifically rejected this with reference to the way in which financing constituted an essential element of the arrangement; therefore,

> If the financing of the agreement is a matter for the Community the necessary decisions will be taken according to the appropriate Community procedures. If on the other hand the financing is to be by the Member States that will imply the participation of those States in the decision-making machinery or, at least, their agreement with regard to the arrangements for financing envisaged and consequently their participation in the agreement together with the Community. The exclusive competence of the Community could not be envisaged in such a case.[100]

The relevance of this finding in the IMF context would be difficult to explain away. As far as the IMF is funded by the Member States, the relevant decision-making procedures are those found in the Member States.[101]

---

[98]Further on this, see Heliskoski (2010).

[99]See CJEU, case C-370/12, *Pringle v Ireland*, ECLI:EU:C:2012:756; and more recently, CJEU, joined cases C-8/15 P to C-10/15 P, *Ledra Advertising v Commission and ECB*, ECLI:EU:C:2016:701, para. 52: "It should be recalled that, as is apparent from the statement by the Eurogroup of 27 June 2012, the Commission and the ECB were entrusted with the task of negotiating with the Cypriot authorities a macro-economic adjustment programme to be set out in the form of a memorandum of understanding. When the Commission and the ECB participated in the negotiations with the Cypriot authorities, provided their technical expertise, gave advice and provided guidance, they acted within the limits of the powers granted to them by Article 13(3) of the ESM Treaty. Participation of the Commission and the ECB, as envisaged by that provision, in the procedure resulting in the signature of the Memorandum of Understanding of 26 April 2013 does not enable the latter to be classified as an act that can be imputed to them."

[100]CJEU, opinion 1/78, *International Agreement on Natural Rubber*, ECLI:EU:C:1979:224, para. 60.

[101]A study on the "External representation of the Euro Area" commissioned in 2012 by the European Parliament proposes that the ESM could be used in the longer run as the institution channelling the fiscal aspects of euro states' relations with the IMF, for example by merging their quotas in the ESM and through representation at the IMF by its Managing Director. European Parliament, External Representation of the Euro Area, IP/A/ECON/FWC/2010_19, May 2012, p. 30.

Falling between these categories—exclusive competence where the position must be an EU one; shared competence where the Member States have a choice but act subject to duties of good cooperation, and national competence where no clear obligations exist based on jurisprudence—is the area of economic policy. It is not on the Treaty list of exclusive or shared competences, and by definition is *sui generis* in nature. Economic policy competence continues to rest with the Member States, even if its exercise is affected by the requirements of the EU coordination framework.[102] There is no case law on whether economic policy competence is capable of creating EU exclusive external competence. This would seem unlikely and, in any case, could not reach beyond those elements that are "capable of decisively influencing the content of the legislation adopted by the EU legislature".[103]

Therefore, what can be said about the Commission proposal based on jurisprudence?

The IMF Articles of Agreement is formally not a mixed agreement, but one where the Member States continue as contracting parties. In matters falling under EU competence (exclusive or shared) they are bound by an obligation to act in accordance with their EU law obligations, which in practice entails a duty to follow jointly agreed EU positions. This duty exists irrespective of how EU external representation is organized. Case law does not indicate what happens if no attempt to coordinate positions is made, or if coordination fails, and no decision to disagree and go different ways is taken. Advocate General *Tesauro* has suggested that obligations might extend beyond the process of negotiation and conclusion of the agreements, to the fulfilment of the commitments: Member States and the Community institutions "must endeavour to adopt a common position".[104] For Advocate General *Tesauro*,

> the absence of close cooperation between Community institutions and Member States – in view of the ineffectiveness that would inevitably result from a failure to speak with one voice and, above all, from a lack of common rules of conduct and common procedures – would certainly be a considerable drawback in any future negotiations [. . .].[105]

However, the Court's jurisprudence has not placed the Member States and the EU institutions in the mixed agreements context under obligations concerning the result: not all measures are needed to ensure "unity". Instead, the principle operates as a "best endeavours" obligation of conduct.[106] While in areas of exclusive competence "no EU position" means "no position", in areas falling under shared

[102]On this, see e.g. Leino and Saarenheimo (2017).

[103]CJEU, case C-399/12, *Germany v Council*, ECLI:EU:C:2014:2258, para. 63.

[104]Opinion by AG Tesauro to CJEU, case C-53/96, *Hermès International v FHT Marketing Choice BV*, ECLI:EU:C:1991:539, para. 21.

[105]See Opinion by AG Tesauro to CJEU, case C-53/96, *Hermès International v FHT Marketing Choice*, ECLI:EU:C:1991:539, fn. 33, referring to the WTO context and matters governed by the TRIPs Agreement.

[106]Hillion (2009), p. 20.

competence case law does not require Member States in the Council to actually agree on a common position; instead, the Council also has the possibility of not forming one[107] and leaving the Member States the possibility to adopt their own positions. The competence division also affects the voting pattern—the Council could certainly not decide on matters falling under Member State competence with qualified majority voting.

The current Commission proposal, however, seems to reach beyond current jurisprudence by setting obligations of result even in matters falling under national competence. Moreover, in questions where EU competence is limited to coordination measures at EU level, the question becomes what the effect of its competence might be in international fora, and how much duties of cooperation and the objective of unified EU representation can be seen to limit Member State behaviour, and whether the obligation is positive or negative in character. In matters involving Member State budgetary or fiscal powers, it is unlikely that EU positions could be used to replace Member State action. These matters would also be beyond the reach of duties of sincere cooperation. As far as these parts of the Commission proposal are concerned, the proposal appears legally unsustainable. The same conclusion should apply to questions falling under national competence (such as questions involving the ESM, or questions relating to the details of Member State economic and fiscal policies covered by Article IV consultations): duties of cooperation can hardly reach to these questions in the sense of creating obligations to commit to a certain outcome.

However, even Member State competence needs to be exercised in accordance with EU law. They need to

> collaborate and consult with the institutions (that is, in practice the Commission) before they establish a national position or otherwise take action under a mixed agreement. So even in the exercise of national competence the Member States are acting firmly within the confines of Union law.[108]

Several of these elements have clearly been lacking in the context of EU coordination at the IMF. A somewhat similar conclusion is likely to apply to many other IFIs including the G20, the Basel Committee on Banking Supervision[109] and the Financial Stability Board,[110] which deal with issues where EU competence is even stronger than in the matters covered by the IMF and have a direct impact on the development of EU legislation. What in the IMF context seems particularly problematic is that in practice the limits of competence are settled by the IMF economists when preparing their reports. There seems to be no internal mechanism for sorting out these questions. Such mechanisms do exist in the context

[107]See Heliskoski (2010).

[108]Heliskoski (2010), p. 159.

[109]Membership in the Basel Committee is limited to the central banks of nine EU states, the ECB and the Single Supervisory Mechanism.

[110]Participation in the FSB is limited to national authorities from France, Germany, the Netherlands, Spain, the UK and the ECB.

of other international organisations, and case law suggests that such internal coordination arrangements are binding on the institutions. The *FAO* case concerned the Council and the Commission arrangement "regarding preparation for FAO meetings, statements and voting". The arrangement set up a coordination procedure between the Commission and the Member States for the purpose of deciding on the exercise of responsibilities or on statements on particular agenda points on the FAO agenda based on the competence division. In its ruling, the Court reiterated the obligation to cooperate: the "institutions and the Member States must take all necessary steps to ensure the best possible cooperation in that regard". The Court noted that section 2.3 of the Arrangement represented the fulfilment of that duty of cooperation, and that the two institutions had intended to enter into a binding commitment towards each other.[111]

The exact way in which the EU is represented—through a single Executive Director, through individual Member States, through the President of the Eurogroup or occasionally by the Commission or the ECB—is of less relevance from a competence point-of-view, and is also affected by the rules of the international organization in question. In its opinion, the ECB points out how in a majority of euro area states the Governor of the national central bank operates as the Governor or Alternate Governor in the IMF Board of Governors, and therefore proposes to add the President of the ECB to those representing the euro area in the IMF Governance bodies. Moreover, the ECB is concerned about the proposed coordination mechanisms affecting the independence of the Eurosystem as operated by the ECB. As the ECB opinion points out, unified representation must be achieved by taking into account the EU allocation of competences and the mandates of each institution.[112] Whether this in fact contributes to a further extension of the role of the ECB itself is another thing.

Article 138 TFEU empowers the Council to "adopt appropriate measures to ensure unified representation within the international financial institutions and conferences". It is left to the Council to settle what counts as "appropriate". In the Commission proposal, the key role would be allocated to the President of the Eurogroup, simultaneously allocating a key role in position-building to the Eurogroup. In addition to getting rid of mixed constituencies, Commission

---

[111]CJEU, case C-25/94, *Commission v Council*, ECLI:EU:C:1996:114, para. 7, section 2.3: "Where an agenda item deals with matters containing elements both of national and of Community competence, the aim will be to achieve a common position by consensus. If a common position can be achieved:—the Presidency shall express the common position when the thrust of the issue lies in an area outside the exclusive competence of the Community. Member States and the Commission may speak to support and/or to add to the Presidency statement. Member States will vote in accordance with the common position;—the Commission shall express the common position when the thrust of the issue lies in an area within the exclusive competence of the Community. Member States may speak to support and/or add to the Commission's statement. The Commission will vote in accordance with the common position." For further discussion concerning the FAO case, see Heliskoski (2000).

[112]On this, see also the court's recent ruling in CJEU, case C-660/13, *Council v Commission*, ECLI:EU:C:2016:616.

emphasis is on the presentation of a unified view by the President of the Eurogroup in the Board of Governors. This probably refers to the Eurogroup chair—presuming that he acts as the designated IMF Governor for his own country—issuing an annual meeting speech on behalf of all euro area countries, since in the Board of Governors each contracting party is represented by its own Governor, who also exercises its right to vote. As long as the EU is not a full member, Member State Governors will remain the channel of true influence.

The CJEU has recently reminded us of the fact that the Eurogroup consists of the ministers of those Member States whose currency is the euro who are to meet informally to discuss questions related to the specific responsibilities they share with regard to the single currency. It is therefore not a decision-making body, and cannot be equated with a configuration of the Council or classified as an EU body, office or agency.[113] Therefore, while the Eurogroup could certainly be used for informal and even factual position-building, it could not be used to adopt EU positions under Article 138(2) TFEU, which empowers the Council to adopt the decisions.

The role of the Eurogroup links with a broader question of whether it in fact should be the euro area states or EU states as a whole that should be subject to tighter coordination in the IMF. True, the existence of Article 138 TFEU does give the indication that the tighter coordination of euro area state positions might be justified. However, based on the jurisprudence discussed above, there is little indication as to why non-euro area states would escape such coordination, and they do participate in the currently existing coordination mechanisms. If the recent Article IV Staff Report on Finland discussed above is taken as an example, it is difficult to see why the EU-relevant matters such as the need to tighten the macroprudential toolkit or ensure compliance with the SGP raised in the Report would not be equally relevant for, say, Sweden, and their coordination therefore equally justified with reference to Court jurisprudence. Thus, in case full coordination of EU positions is in fact aimed at, three separate decisions might be needed: one coordinating euro area positions based on Article 138 TFEU; another one coordinating non-euro area positions based on Article 218(9) TFEU and the relevant substantive legal bases in matters where the EU has exclusive competence—presuming that the decision to be adopted in the IMF can in fact be seen to have legal effects—and a third decision by Representatives of the Governments of the Member States meeting within the Council, which can be used to coordinate matters falling under national competence, adopted unanimously.[114]

[113]CJEU, joined cases C-105/15 P to C-109/15 P, *Mallis and Malli v Commission and ECB*, ECLI:EU:C:2016:702, paras. 46–48 and 61.

[114]See CJEU, case C-28/12, *Commission v Council*, ECLI:EU:C:2015:282.

6 Conclusions

Several of the choices made by the Commission in presenting its 2015 proposal are interesting both with a view to the applicable framework and political realities. It would seem that the Commission proposal reaches partly too far in proposing binding coordination of all matters. At the same time, the proposal is in some respects too narrow in scope, since it leaves the non-euro area states without consideration. Finally, to the extent the proposal is justified, it fails to rely on the grounds that could be used to justify the objective.

First, why does the Commission focus on the (political) question of representation, and disregard the legal arguments that would support its objective?

It seems that from a purely legal point of view it can be argued that the "EU presence" in the IMF could be strengthened, but not to the extent that the Commission proposes. Even if there is no jurisprudence concerning Article 138 TFEU as such, the existing jurisprudence does demonstrate that there is a duty to at least try to achieve an EU position in matters falling under exclusive EU competence, and that coordination duty in these cases is a consequence of the fact that the EU is not a member of the IMF and therefore cannot express the position itself but needs to be represented through the Member States. Moreover, even shared and Member State competence would need to be exercised in a manner that is compatible with their EU law obligations, keeping in mind that the threshold under Article 138 TFEU is lower, and refers to an obligation to coordinate matters that are "relevant for the EMU". Current coordination mechanisms do not seem to reach quite this far. In particular, they include no internal mechanism for settling the competence division internally.

Instead, in the IMF context the matter seems to have primarily been settled through having Article IV consultations separately for the euro area and involving the EU institutions in these discussions, and as far as programs are concerned, by excluding such elements from the IMF conditionality that would fall under EU competence. Legally this is an unorthodox solution—also because the EU and national spheres are often rather fundamentally intertwined, for example through the implementation of EU legislation in national systems—but one that has been enabled by the IMF decision-making structures. Therefore, while a legal justification would exist to some elements that the Commission has defined as objectives, these justifications do not reach to the whole spectrum of proposals on the table, in particular as regards the binding coordination of positions falling under Member State competence, to be decided by qualified majority.

However, this finding is to some extent however dependent on whether the IMF measures adopted are capable of affecting EU legislation in the manner that jurisprudence specifies. If that criterion is fulfilled, it would seem that based on jurisprudence, in manners falling under EU exclusive competence there is a need to formulate a common position. Article 138 TFEU indicates that common positions should be used even in other cases that fulfil the criteria in the first paragraph: that the matters are relevant for the EMU. In the absence of one, no one is in principle entitled to speak, and the Commission is in principle at liberty to raise infringement proceedings against disobedient Member States that act without EU authorization in matters falling under EU exclusive competence. That this has so far not taken place indicates both that the Commission has some understanding of political realities, but also that this might not be the best avenue to strengthen EU influence in the IMF. Moreover, lack of action can also reflect uncertainties relating how responsibility for Member State positions can be concretized, in particular whether the Executive Directors—who in fact take all the relevant decisions in the IMF—can be seen to effectively represent the Member States so that their action or non-action can be traced back to the states forming their constituency and as such be subjected to infringement proceedings.

Second, what is influence and how can it be gained?

The question of EU influence has been discussed in all IFIs. While participation in G20 is more limited than in the IMF, there have been many complaints about European overrepresentation diminishing the weight of everything that European nations say,[115] as this quote from *Pascal Lamy*, former Director-General of the WTO, demonstrates. His concerns feel familiar to the IMF context:

> If one European takes the floor on one topic, and then another European takes the floor on the same topic, nobody listens. Nobody listens because either it's the same thing and it gets boring, or it's not the same thing and it will not influence the result at the end of the day [. . .]. So the right solution, if I may, is at least to make sure that they speak with one mouth. Not one voice – one mouth – on each topic on the agenda. That would be a great improvement.[116]

In the EU debates the key issue relates to power and influence. As demonstrated above, the legal framework would enable—and to some extent even require—solutions that are different from those used today.

However, prior to that there should be some agreement on what counts as "influence" and how it can be maximized. More particularly, does the current way in which euro area states are divided in different constituencies in fact diminish EU power? Would joint EU representation in fact strengthen it? Do Executive Directors effectively represent their constituencies in a manner that would secure the presentation of EU positions in all circumstances?

There is, in fact, little empirical evidence that would support the "one-mouth conclusion" promoted by *Pascal Lamy* above. Instead, the question might be more about the lack of one common position. Blaming the difficulties in finding agreement on too many mouths or the complex division of competences is an attempt to find a legal explanation to a problem that is fundamentally political in nature, and one that can only be solved through political means. The real problems as far as influence is concerned emerge in the situations where Member State views are

[115]See, e.g., Wouters et al. (2012), p. 6.

[116]The Economist, World to Europe: If you must hog G20 seats, could you at least talk less? 28 March 2010, http://www.economist.com/blogs/charlemagne/2010/03/too_many_europeans_g20 (last accessed 1 March 2017).

divided and they are effectively arguing for opposite positions. In these cases deciding that the "EU should take over" is unlikely to solve the actual problem. The formal creation of procedures does not solve the political question. While a decision-making procedure based on qualified majority voting concerning matters falling under EU competence could formally be created, the EU tradition is still to settle sensitive matters by consensus. Consensus is also an absolute requirement for matters falling under national competence. This would minimize the EU common position to the smallest common denominator, which is unlikely to influence the negotiations much. It is specifically this sort of situations where euro area Executive Directors will feel tempted to distance themselves from the "common position" by formally supporting it, but simultaneously providing a few additional remarks containing the substantive comments. In particular in questions that fall under national competence—and in particular considering those that are close to Member State sovereignty such as those relating to economic, fiscal and structural policies—the question becomes whether it is realistic to think there could be a common position. Finding common positions becomes even more difficult in broad questions relating to the global system as a whole.

In matters where the EU States have a common position, the way in which competence is divided—in a complex or simple manner—is unlikely to constitute a problem, and consequently, has not hindered efficient influencing of discussions in the IMF. And if the same position is repeated in discussions several times, and also influences discussions in mixed constituencies, it is unlikely that this in fact reduces EU influence. Instead, this might just count as efficient repeat playing.

Third, whose representation should be unified in the IMF?

It is not evident that, to the extent coordination mechanisms are created, their scope should be limited to euro area states only. Many of the IMF matters are equally relevant for those EU states that are outside the euro area. Coordination in relation to them cannot be undertaken based on Article 138 TFEU, but instead Article 218(9) TFEU could be invoked as a legal basis. If there is a wish to coordinate matters falling under national competence, a third decision by Member State representatives is needed, to be adopted by consensus.

The question is even more complex if the broader spectrum of IFIs is considered. After all, as the example concerning IMF governance reforms demonstrates, the IMF is also often faced with a fait accompli settled in G20, where only large Member States (UK, Germany, Italy, France and the EU) are represented.[117] This setting provokes complaints from other EU Member States regarding the perceived power of the Big Four.[118]

---

[117] At the heads of state level the EU is represented in G20 by the President of the Commission and the President of the Council, whereas at the finance ministers level the EU is represented by the Commissioner for Economic and Monetary Affairs, the rotating Council presidency and the Head of the ECB.

See also Wouters et al. (2012), p. 5.

[118] Debaere and Orbie (2013), p. 316. Wouters et al. (2012), p. 5.

Finally, what would be a realistic objective?

After all, as the Commission already noted 10 years ago, the success of EU external action depends first and foremost on political agreement among Member States, "a strong partnership between the EU institutions and a clear focus on a limited number of strategic priorities where Europe can make the difference, rather than dispersing efforts across the board. This is the condition sine qua non".[119] This realism is also reflected in the 2011 General Arrangements, which make reference to common statements being used in matters in which the EU is competent and in fact has a common position.

The draft Council decision includes no provisions relating to the (realistic) situation of when no EU common position is reached, which might—as already demonstrated by case law—ultimately prevent the Member States from acting. In such cases EU coordination is not likely to improve effective influencing of international discussions. Alternatively, binding EU coordination might result in a finding that there is indeed no common position, and let the Member States wander their own ways. Further, the deeper into national competence that "binding" EU coordination reaches, the less likely it is that Member States are willing to comply with common positions they substantively disagree with. While there is no harm in EU discussions and even coordination, the mechanism should be built on realistic premises, which the current proposal building on a "binding in all matters" principle is not representative of. Instead, the mechanisms should build on the understanding that often there will not be a common position, and there might not even be justified reasons to try to attempt to achieve one.

References

Brandner P, Grech H (2009) Unifying EU representation at the IMF – a voting power analysis. Austrian Federal Ministry of Finance Working Paper 2/2009

Casteleiro A, Larik J (2011) The duty to remain silent: limitless loyalty in EU external relations? Eur Law Rev 36(4):524–541

Cremona M (2011) Coherence in EU foreign relations law. In: Koutrakos P (ed) European foreign policy: legal and political perspectives. Edward Elgar, Cheltenham, pp 55–92

De la Rochère J (1999) EMU: constitutional aspects and external representation. Yearb Eur Law 19(1):427–446

Debaere P, Orbie J (2013) The European Union in the Gx system. In: Jørgensen K, Laatikainen K (eds) Routledge handbook on the European Union and international institutions: performance, policy, power. Routledge, Oxford, pp 221–233

Den Hertog L, Stroß S (2013) Coherence in EU external relations: concepts and legal rooting of an ambiguous term. Eur Foreign Aff Rev 18(3):373–388

Heliskoski J (2000) Internal struggle for international presence: the exercise of voting rights within the FAO. In: Dashwood A, Hillion C (eds) The general law of E.C. external relations. Sweet and Maxwell, London, pp 79–99

[119]European Commission, COM (2006) 278 final.

Heliskoski J (2010) Adoption of positions under mixed agreements (implementation). In: Hillion C, Koutrakos P (eds) Mixed agreements revisited. The EU and its Member States in the World. Hart, Oxford, pp 138–159
Hervé A (2012) The participation of the European Union in global economic governance fora. Eur Law J 18(1):143–161
Hillion C (2008) Tous pour un, un pour tous! Coherence in the external relations of the European union. In: Cremona M (ed) Developments in EU external relations law. Oxford University Press, Oxford, pp 10–36
Hillion C (2009) Mixity and coherence in EU external relations: the significance of the duty of cooperation. CLEER Working Paper 2009/1
Horng DC (2005) The ECB's membership in the IMF: legal approaches to constitutional challenges. Eur Law J 11(6):802–822
Jørgensen K, Oberthür S, Shahin J (2011) Introduction: assessing the EU's performance in international institutions – conceptual framework and core findings. J Eur Integr 33 (6):599–620
Larik J (2018) Pars pro toto: The Member States' obligations of sincere cooperation, solidarity, and unity. In: Cremona M (ed) Structural principles in EU external relations law. Hart, forthcoming
Lasta R (2000) The International Monetary Fund in historical perspective. J Int Econ Law 3 (3):507–523
Leino P, Saarenheimo T (2017) Sovereignty and subordination. On the limits of EU economic policy competence. Eur Law Rev 42(2):166–189
Leino P, Salminen J (2017) A multi-level playing field for economic policy-making: does EU economic governance have impact? In: Beukers T, de Witte B, Kilpatrick C (eds) Constitutional change through euro-crisis law. Cambridge University Press, Cambridge
Louis JV (2013) The euro area and multilateral financial institutions and bodies. In: Govaere I, Lannon L, van Elsuwege P, Adam S (eds) The European Union in the world, essays in honor of Marc Maresceau. Brill, Leiden, pp 193–207
Smaghi L (2004) A single EU seat in the IMF. J Common Mark Stud 42(2):229–248
Van Houtven L (2002) Governance of the IMF: decision making, institutional oversight, transparency, and accountability. IMF Pamphlet Series No 53
Wessel R (2011) The legal framework for the participation of the European Union in international institutions. J Eur Integr 33(6):621–635
Wouters J, Van Kerckhoven S (2013) The International Monetary Fund. In: Jørgensen K, Laatikainen K (eds) Routledge handbook on the European Union and international institutions: performance, policy, Power. Routledge, Oxford, pp 221–233
Wouters J, Van Kerckhoven S, Odermatt J (2012) The EU at the G20 and the G20's impact on the EU. Leuven Centre for Global Governance Studies Working Paper No. 93
Wouters J, Van Kerckhoven S, Ramopoulos T (2014) The EU and the euro area in international economic governance: the case of the IMF. In: Kochenov D, Amtenbrink F (eds) The European Union's shaping of the international legal order. Cambridge University Press, Cambridge, pp 306–327

Overview of WTO Jurisprudence in 2015 Involving the EU as a Main Party and Selected Cases with Third-Party Participation by the EU

Jan Bohanes and Kholofelo Kugler

Abstract This article presents an overview of the World Trade Organization (WTO) disputes resolved in 2015 in which the EU participated as the complaining party or the defending party. These disputes were *China – Measures Imposing Anti-Dumping Duties on High-Performance Stainless Steel Seamless Tubes* (*"HP-SSST"*), *Argentina – Measures Affecting the Importation of Goods* (in both cases the EU as complainant) and *EC – Definitive Anti-Dumping Measures on Certain Iron or Steel Fasteners from China* (EU as defendant). On each of these cases, this article provides an overview of the key Panel and Appellate Body findings, and a few observations. The article also addresses two cases in which the EU participated as third party, namely, *Peru – Additional Duty on Imports of Certain Agricultural Products* and *US – Country of Origin Labelling (COOL) Requirements (Article 21.5)*. For the latter two cases, the article highlights the facts of those disputes, the key rulings by the WTO Panel (and the Appellate Body, where relevant), as well as the most salient positions expressed by the EU as third party.

Contents

J. Bohanes • K. Kugler (✉)
Advisory Centre on WTO Law, Avenue Giuseppe Motta 31-33, 1211, Geneva 30, Switzerland
e-mail: Jan.Bohanes@acwl.ch; Kholofelo.Kugler@acwl.ch

M. Bungenberg et al. (eds.), *European Yearbook of International Economic Law 2017*, European Yearbook of International Economic Law 8,
DOI 10.1007/978-3-319-58832-2_21

1 Introduction

In previous years, this contribution to the European Yearbook of International Economic Law provided a summary of all WTO Panel and Appellate Body reports issued during the previous year. This year's article, however, focusses on the European Union (EU) as a participant in WTO dispute settlement, in keeping with the orientation of this year's EYIEL issue. The article therefore summarizes, first, all the disputes in which the EU was a main party. Surprisingly, this concerns a fairly limited number of disputes in 2015—only three, namely *China – Measures Imposing Anti-Dumping Duties on High-Performance Stainless Steel Seamless Tubes ("HP-SSST")*,[1] *Argentina – Measures Affecting the Importation of Goods*[2] (in both cases the EU as complainant) and *EC – Definitive Anti-Dumping Measures on Certain Iron or Steel Fasteners from China*[3] (EU as defendant). Moreover, in *Argentina – Import Measures*, only the issuance of the Appellate Body Report fell into 2015 (in January), which means that the dispute essentially took place before 2015. The Panel ruling in that dispute was summarized in last year's issue of the Yearbook.[4]

Of course, the EU's participation in the dispute settlement system is not limited to being a complainant or defendant. As one of the key players in the system, the EU systematically participates as a third party, to make its voice heard on issues that it considers of sufficient interest, both to itself as well as from a systemic perspective. To date, the EU has participated in 159 disputes as a third party. This means that the EU has been a third party in almost half of the disputes in which it was not either a complainant or defendant.

The article has therefore selected two disputes from 2015 in which the EU participated as third party. The article summarizes the panel and Appellate Body rulings in those disputes, and then summarizes and analyzes the EU's arguments as third party. These two disputes are *Peru – Additional Duty on Imports of Certain Agricultural Products*[5] and *US – Country of Origin Labelling (COOL) Requirements (Article 21.5)*.[6]

---

[1] DS454 and DS460.

[2] DS438, 444, 445.

[3] DS397.

[4] Bohanes et al. (2016), p. 672 et seqq.

[5] DS457.

[6] DS384, 386.

2 Disputes in Which the EU was a Main Party

The following is an overview of the disputes in 2015 in which the EU was a main party, that is, either the complaining or defending party. We begin with the *Argentina – Import Measures* dispute, in which the EU was a co-complainant with Japan and the United States. Next, we analyse *China – HP-SSST*, in which the EU jointly with the US challenged Chinese anti-dumping measures on certain steel products. Finally, we address the *EC – Fasteners (Article 21.5)* dispute, in which China challenged the EU's compliance measures from the original *Fasteners* dispute; that dispute focused to a large extent on various aspects of the non-market economy (NME) methodology in anti-dumping investigations.

2.1 Argentina: Import Measures (Appellate Body Report)

This case was brought by the EU, Japan, and the United States and was decided by a Panel in 2014. In early 2015, the Appellate Body largely upheld the Panel's rulings. This section describes the key elements of the Appellate Body's findings.

2.1.1 Facts of the Case

The EU, Japan, and the United States challenged Argentine alleged import restrictions covering a broad range of sectors, including foodstuffs, automobiles, motorcycles, mining equipment, electronic and office products, agricultural machinery, medicines, publications, and clothing. The complaint referred to two main measures:

First, an unwritten measure, described by the complainants as a "combination of actions" under the label of "Restrictive Trade-Related Requirements". The complainants argued that the various "actions" taken by the Argentine government created a requirement on importers to agree to certain conditions to import into Argentina. These conditions included five distinct elements, namely, commitments: (1) to export a certain value of goods from Argentina; (2) to limit the volume and value of imports; (3) not to repatriate funds from Argentina to another country; (4) to undertake investments in Argentina; and (5) to use local content in domestic production. The panel referred to each one of these five sets of actions as "trade-related requirements" (TRRs); the panel also referred to the combined single measure, consisting of these five actions taken together, as the "trade-related requirements measure" (TRRs measure).

The second measure was the Advance Sworn Import Declaration (DJAI). The DJAI was in essence an import license that a prospective importer had to fill out and submit, and that a number of Argentine government agencies could review and comment on. A comment by one of these agencies could prevent the completion of the DJAI procedure, and the importer had to submit additional information. Only upon satisfactory completion of the review process would an importer be entitled to import the goods covered by the DJAI.

2.1.2 Summary of the Panel's and the Appellate Body's Findings

The protectionist and trade restrictive nature of the Argentine government's actions was fairly clear. The dispute revolved to a significant extent around evidentiary issues and the definition of a "measure" for purposes of WTO law.

The Trade-Related Requirements (TRR)

Drawing on a broad range of evidence, the panel found that Argentina had imposed the five different unwritten sets of TRRs alleged by the complainants.[7] The Panel also found that these five individual sets of measures together constituted a single overarching measure because they contributed "in different combinations and degrees – as part of a single measure – towards the realization of common policy objectives that guide Argentina's 'managed trade' policy, i.e. substituting imports and reducing or eliminating trade deficits".[8]

The Panel then found that this single TRR measure constituted an "other measure" within the meaning of Article XI of the GATT 1994 that had a limiting effect on imports into Argentina. This was because the various components of the measure either had a direct limiting effect (the balancing, import limiting, and local content requirement) or were linked to the right to import (the investment and non-repatriation requirement). The Panel also highlighted the "uncertainty generated by the unwritten and discretionary nature of the requirements" and the additional costs resulting from activities unrelated to an operator's business activity.[9] The Panel also reflected previous case law that, in order to prove a violation of Article XI, it was not necessary to establish actual trade effects based on data of trade flows.[10] Once the existence of this measure had been determined, the legal analysis was straightforward—the measure was an import restriction that violated Article XI and could not be justified. Certain additional aspects (the local content requirement) also constituted a straightforward violation of the national treatment requirement under Article III:4 of the GATT 1994.

---

[7]Panel Report, *Argentina – Import Measures*, WT/DS438/R, WT/DS444/R, WT/DS445/R, paras. 6.166–6.177 (for the requirement to balance imports with exports); paras. 6.178–6.195 (for the requirement to limit the volume and value of imports); paras. 6.196–6.207 (for the local content requirement); paras. 6.208–6.212 (for the investment requirement); paras. 6.213–6.216 (for the requirement not to repatriate profits from Argentina).

[8]Panel Report, *Argentina – Import Measures*, para. 6.228.

[9]Panel Report, *Argentina – Import Measures*, paras. 6.249–6.263.

[10]Panel Report, *Argentina – Import Measures*, para. 6.264.

On appeal, Argentina challenged the Panel's determination of the existence of the measure. In a nutshell, Argentina argued that the complainants had challenged an unwritten measure "as such", that is, independently of its case-specific application. In the WTO system, this kind of challenge has in the past required complainants to demonstrate the precise content of the measure, its attributability to the government, as well as general and prospective application.[11] According to Argentina, the Panel had failed to apply these criteria.

The Appellate Body rejected Argentina's appeal and held that a complainant is not required to classify every challenge into the "as such" or "as applied" categories and that not every measure need to "fit squarely" into one of these two categories. As to the three criteria above, the Appellate Body found that precise content and attributability to the government were essential for demonstrating the existence of an unwritten measure, but the criterion of general and prospective application was not. That would depend on the way the measure was framed by the complainant. In any event, as the Appellate pointed out, the Panel had analyzed elements that pointed to a systemic, generalized application of the measure and its continued application, such that the third criterion had been fulfilled in any event.[12] The Appellate Body also rejected Argentina's arguments that the panel had not properly analyzed the content of the overarching TRR, as compared to the content of the five individual sets of measures.

In addition to the above ruling, the Panel had also made findings in response to a claim only by Japan, which Japan framed as an "as such" challenge. In analyzing this claim, the Panel had actually applied the three criteria from previous Appellate Body case law. Particularly interestingly, on the criterion of *general* application, the Panel emphasized that the TRR measure affects a wide range of sectors and could affect any sector and was part of a broader policy implemented by the Argentine government, rather than isolated measures taken with respect to individual importers. With respect to *prospective* application, the Panel focused on what it considered the "deliberate policy" character of the measure, its year-long application, and the resulting likelihood that it would continue to be applied in the future.[13]

Argentina acknowledged that the Panel had applied the three criteria from previous case law but argued that the Panel had incorrectly evaluated the evidence, in particular that it had incorrectly determined the precise content of the measure as well as the general and prospective application.

The Appellate Body expressed surprise at the Panel's separate "as such" analysis of Japan's claim. The Appellate Body did not see any value added in these findings, because the Panel had relied on the same evidence and on the same reasoning as in

[11]These criteria had been applied by the Appellate Body in challenges against the United States' unwritten "zeroing" methodology in anti-dumping investigations. See for instance, Appellate Body Report, *US – Zeroing (EC)*, WT/DS294/AB/R, para. 198.

[12]Appellate Body Report, *Argentina – Import Measures*, WT/DS438/AB/R, WT/DS444/AB/R, WT/DS445/AB/R, paras. 5.140–5.145.

[13]Panel Report, *Argentina – Import Measures*, paras. 6.329–6.342.

the general claim presented by all three complainants. Nevertheless, the Appellate Body examined Argentina's objections to the Panel's analysis of the evidence and rejected them in substance. However, it emphasized that rejecting Argentina's argument should be read as an endorsement of the Panel's separate analytical approach to Japan's claim.[14]

The DJAI

With respect to the DJAI—which was a written measure—the complainants relied on Article XI, whereas Argentina argued that the DJAI was an import formality covered exclusively by Article VIII of the GATT 1994. The Panel found that DJAI procedure was not a mere formality, but rather related to the right to import; and that, in any event, even if Article VIII were triggered, this would not exclude the applicability of Article XI, because these two provisions are not mutually exclusive.[15] On substance under Article XI, the Panel found that the DJAI was a necessary condition to import into Argentina and the process of obtaining a DJAI in "exit" status was not automatic. Moreover—as in the case of the TRR measure—the Panel found that uncertainty existed concerning the application of the measure, which uncertainty itself affected import opportunities; and that the operation of the measure also imposed a burden on importers unrelated to their business activity.[16] The Panel also rejected Argentina's argument that, in order to violate Article XI, the measure had to restrict imports by reference to quantity or in a way that was "quantifiable". Rather, the Panel found that Article XI:1 protects Members' expectations as to the competitive relationship between their products and those of other Members in respect of importation itself.[17]

The Panel also found that the local content requirement—one of the five individual sets of TRRs—violated Article III:4 of the GATT 1994, because it resulted in less favourable treatment of imported products when compared to domestic products. In this rather straightforward finding, the Panel confirmed previous case law that origin-based distinctions between products created a presumption that products are "like"; that the requirement affected the level of imports purchased; and that the Argentine measured created an incentive to use domestic products over imported products.[18]

Argentina's appeal centered on challenging the Panel's interpretation of Articles XI and VIII. In a nutshell, as before the Panel, Argentina argued that Articles VIII and XI were mutually exclusive and that Article VIII—rather than Article XI—was the proper provision under which to analyze the DJAI measure at

[14] Appellate Body Report, *Argentina – Import Measures*, paras. 5.151–5.184.

[15] Panel Report, *Argentina – Import Measures*, paras. 6.433–6.445.

[16] Panel Report, *Argentina – Import Measures*, paras. 6.471–6.473.

[17] Panel Report, *Argentina – Import Measures*, paras. 6.476–6.478.

[18] Panel Report, *Argentina – Import Measures*, paras. 6.273–6.294.

issue. The Appellate Body rejected this reading of Article VIII and upheld the Panel's analysis on this point, based on similar reasoning. The Appellate Body also rejected Argentina's appeal against other Panel's findings, e.g. that the DJAI formality was not "automatic", thereby amounting to an import restriction in violation of Article XI of the GATT 1994.

2.1.3 Observations

These Panel and Appellate Body reports are interesting not only because they shed some light on long-standing formal and informal import restrictions imposed by the Argentine government, policies that have for a long time been a source of professed frustration for certain other WTO Members. Once the Panel found that the alleged import restrictions existed and constituted a WTO-law-relevant "measure", the resulting findings were unsurprising. However, getting to a finding that unwritten measures existed represented a challenge for the complainants, because at least with respect to the TRRs, the Argentine government had deliberately not reduced these measures in written form.

Both the Panel and the Appellate Body report are remarkable for their treatment of unwritten measures as well as the flexibility for WTO dispute settlement bodies to accommodate evidentiary challenges faced by complainants against trade-restrictive measures that the defendant government has made a deliberate effort not to enshrine in written measures. Both the Panel and the Appellate Body were visibly sympathetic to the complainants' situation, with the Panel even explicitly acknowledging that the complainants had a "plausible motive" for not submitting certain evidence that was in their possession or in the possession of their economic operators.[19]

The Appellate Body showed further flexibility in holding that a complainant is not always required, when challenging an unwritten measure, to classify its challenge under the "as such" or "as applied" rubric. This also meant that the complainants in this dispute were not required to demonstrate the criterion of general and prospective application. This flexibility may, again, have been driven to a considerable extent by the difficult situation that the complainants found themselves in and by the deliberate attempt by the Argentine government to operate unwritten and opaque trade-restrictive measures. The Appellate Body was clearly concerned that placing procedural and evidentiary hurdles in the complainants' path might encourage other protectionist-minded governments to impose similar measures.

[19]Panel Report, *Argentina – Import Measures*, para. 6.63.

2.2 *China: HP-SSST*

2.2.1 Factual Background

In this dispute, the EU challenged—together with Japan—Chinese anti-dumping duties on certain high performance stainless steel seamless tubes (HP-SSSTs) imposed on EU and Japanese companies. These tubes are used in the construction of high temperature and high pressure industrial boilers. The political economy background for the Chinese anti-dumping measure was a reduction in domestic demand coupled with an increase in the production capacity of the domestic industry. As in the previous dispute, the EU appeared particularly concerned with what it perceived as "procedural defects concerning excessive secrecy, the heavy-handed conduct of verifications, inadequate disclosure and a lack of due explanation".[20]

The Panel made multiple findings of inconsistency, some of which were appealed to the Appellate Body. In the following section, we present what we consider the systemically most interesting findings.

2.2.2 Overview of the Panel and Appellate Body Findings

One part of the Panel findings concerned the dumping determination. Here, the Panel found that the Chinese Ministry of Foreign Commerce (MOFCOM)—which is the Chinese anti-dumping investigating authority—incorrectly constructed the normal value, violating Article 2.2.2 of the Anti-Dumping Agreement (ADA); failed to conduct a fair comparison between normal value and export price, contrary to Article 2.4 of the ADA; and improperly rejected information provided by the investigated companies, on the grounds that it had not been provided prior to the verification visit. Two of these findings were appealed, but the Appellate Body upheld the Panel's findings. The Panel rejected a claim concerning the use of facts available under Article 6.8 of the ADA.

The Panel also addressed claims related to MOFCOM's price undercutting, MOFCOM's analysis of injury factors as well as the causation and non-attribution analysis. The Appellate Body reversed some of these claims, but on completing the analysis also concluded on some of these claims that MOFCOM had acted inconsistently with the relevant ADA provisions.

Finally, the Panel found that MOFCOM had improperly permitted certain information to remain confidential; and had insufficiently disclosed the essential facts to the investigated companies. The Appellate Body reversed some of these findings, but then completed the analysis and found that MOFCOM had violated its ADA obligations.

[20]EU first written submission to the Panel, http://trade.ec.europa.eu/doclib/docs/2014/march/tradoc_152222.doc.pdf (last accessed 1 March 2017).

2.2.3 Selected Panel and Appellate Body Findings in Detail

Fair Comparison Under Article 2.4 of the ADA

The Panel found that MOFCOM failed to respond properly to a request by one of the (EU) investigated companies to exclude certain sales from its normal value calculations because they concerned a product that, unlike the product at issue, was not used in the construction of boilers. The company had initially informed MOFCOM that there were no differences in physical characteristics requiring an adjustment; however, the company subsequently changed its position and made an adjustment request in response to a preliminary determination. The Panel found that an objective investigating authority could not have ignored this request and was required to address it in its determination.[21] The Panel finding demonstrates the rather common-sense proposition that investigating authorities may be required to address matters even if the investigated companies change their position in the course of the proceedings.

Verification Pursuant to Article 6.7 and Annex I of the ADA

The Panel also agreed with the EU's claim that MOFCOM acted inconsistently with Article 6.7 and Annex I of the ADA when it refused to take into account a request by one of the investigated companies. MOFCOM refused to take into account a request for rectification of a document, on the grounds that that information had not been provided prior to the verification visit. The Panel agreed with the EU that MOFCOM acted inconsistently with the very purpose of verification visits, which may include correction of previously-submitted information. In addition, MOFCOM itself had instructed the company to keep that information readily available for verification. The Panel agreed that Article 6.7 and Annex I(7) do not require investigation authorities to simply accept all or large amounts of information during verification, it stated that the case at hand concerned only the rectification of one piece of information and that there appeared to be no "valid reason" why MOFCOM did not accept that information.[22] This finding by the Panel is one of the few findings to date on verification, despite the great practical significance of verification visits and the disclosure of verification results.

Price Undercutting Under Article 3.2 of the ADA

Article 3.2 of the ADA requires investigating authorities to examine whether dumped imports gave rise to undercutting of domestic industry prices. The *China – HP-SSST* dispute added to the case law by the Panel's finding that to ensure a proper

[21]Panel Report, *China – HP-SSST*, WT/DS454/R, WT/DS460/R, paras. 7.83–7.86.

[22]Panel Report, *China – HP-SSST*, para. 7.99 et seq.

comparison of prices, an investigating authority has to take into account differences in volumes of the product sold; thus if on the normal value or export side, the volume of sales is markedly different from that on the other side of the equation, an investigating authority has to consider whether an adjustment is required.[23]

Another aspect of the price undercutting analysis was the Appellate Body's finding that a comparison of prices to determine the existence of price undercutting may not be a "mathematical exercise", based solely on an arithmetic comparison of prices. The Appellate Body read the Panel to have adopted this interpretative approach and therefore reversed the Panel's finding in this regard. It held that a "dynamic assessment of price developments and trends in the relationship between the prices"[24] was required, finding additional textual support in the use of the term "*significant* price undercutting".[25] The Appellate Body then completed the analysis and found that MOFCOM had failed to make a proper "dynamic assessment", thereby acting inconsistently with Article 3.2 of the ADA. The Appellate Body also found fault with the Panel's analysis because the Panel did not require MOFCOM to assess the significance of price undercutting by the dumped imports in relation to the proportion of domestic production for which no price undercutting was found.[26]

Arguably, these findings by the Appellate Body—together with its finding under Article 3.4 (see below)—continue a trend of reading expansively the obligations under Article 3. It would be entirely plausible to read the concept of price undercutting in Article 3.2 as a purely mathematical price comparison. The more qualitative assessment of what this mathematical price difference means, and whether it can be related to any injury suffered by the domestic industry, could fit under Article 3.5. Hence, the Appellate Body has chosen to "frontload", as it were, the analysis under Article 3.2.

This is similar to the Appellate Body's previous findings under Article 3.4, which requires a consideration of various injury factors. In *US – GOES*, the Appellate Body required a form of impact analysis under Article 3.4 that would appear to replicate at least elements of the causation analysis under Article 3.5.[27] Indeed, in this dispute, the Appellate Body confirmed this case law by repeating that, under Article 3.4, an investigating authority must derive understanding of the impact of dumped imports on the state of the domestic industry.[28] The Appellate Body again, however, confirmed that the analysis of the causal link between dumped imports and injury is to be examined under Article 3.5.[29] Once again, the fine distinction between the "impact" analysis under Article 3.4 and the "causal link" analysis under Article 3.5 arguably remains somewhat elusive.

[23]Panel Report, *China – HP-SSST*, para. 7.114.

[24]Appellate Body Report, *China – HP-SSST*, WT/DS454/AB/R, WT/DS460/AB/R, para. 5.164.

[25]Emphasis added.

[26]Appellate Body Report, *China – HP-SSST*, paras. 5.178–5.181.

[27]Appellate Body Report, *US – GOES*, WT/DS414/AB/R, para. 127.

[28]Appellate Body Report, *China – HP-SSST*, paras. 5.202–5.205.

[29]Appellate Body Report, *China – HP-SSST*, paras. 5.202–5.205.

Disclosure of Essential Facts Under Article 6.9 of the ADA

Under Article 6.9 of the ADA, the Panel and the Appellate Body had to grapple with the MOFCOM's decision to refer, by way of disclosure of essential facts, to data that was within the possession of the investigated party. More specifically, the Panel found that the investigating authority's obligation under Article 6.9 could be satisfied if the investigating authority pointed to data that was in the possession of the investigated party. In contrast, the Appellate Body emphasized that Article 6.9 required the disclosure of the essential facts that "form the basis for the decision whether to apply definitive measures." The Appellate Body held that, "[t]o the extent that the Panel suggested that a narrative description of the data used would constitute sufficient disclosure simply because the essential facts that the authority is referring to 'are in the possession of the respondent'," this would not be correct.[30] The reference must be more specific and relate, in particular, to the home market and export sales being used, the adjustments made to these sales prices, as well as the calculation methodology applied by the investigating authority to determine the margin of dumping. The investigated party must be placed in a position to "understand clearly what data the investigating authority has used, and how those data were used to determine the margin of dumping."[31]

This Appellate Body finding reflects a deeper concern for the due process rights of investigated parties than flows from the Panel's approach.

2.3 *EC: Fasteners (Article 21.5 – China)*

2.3.1 Facts of the Case

China initiated the original dispute against the EU in 2009 when it challenged the EU's Council Regulation (EC) No 91/2009 that applied definitive anti-dumping duties on imports of certain iron or steel fasteners originating in China. In 2011, the Appellate Body found the original measure to be inconsistent with WTO law. Subsequent to the initiation of a review investigation in 2012, the EU published Council Implementing Regulation (EU) No 924/2012, which confirmed the "injurious dumping determined in the original investigation".[32] The EU continued to apply definitive anti-dumping duties on fasteners from China.

In the original investigation, the EU Commission had resorted to the "analogue country" methodology in determining the normal values of the products at issue because it considered China a non-market economy (NME). The Commission

[30] Appellate Body Report, *China – HP-SSST*, para. 5.133.

[31] Appellate Body Report, *China – HP-SSST*, paras. 5.129–131.

[32] Council Implementing Regulation (EU) No 924/2012 of 4 October 2012 amending Regulation (EC) No 91/2009 imposing a definitive anti-dumping duty on imports of certain iron or steel fasteners originating in the People's Republic of China, OJ 2012 L 275/1.

chose India as the analogue country and sent questionnaires to Indian fasteners producers. The Commission confirmed that the information provided by the producers would be treated as "strictly confidential" and requested them to provide non-confidential summaries of the information. Two Indian companies cooperated in the investigation, submitting answers to the questionnaires. However, only one of the two companies, Pooja Forge, provided a response that contained sufficiently detailed data to enable the Commission to calculate the normal values of the products at issue. Pooja Forge's initial questionnaire was incomplete and did not contain a detailed domestic sales listing (DMSAL) or the product descriptions. The Commission conducted a verification visit at Pooja Forge's premises to collect the missing information and to confirm its suitability as an analogue country producer.

During visit, the company provided the DMSAL file, which contained information on approximately 80,000 transactions with information on prices, quantities, internal item codes, and product descriptions. Pooja Forge did not provide a non-confidential summary of the DMSAL file, but provided a non-confidential summary of its questionnaire response. The company further provided a brochure containing information on product range, production process and other sensitive details such as production capacity and number of employees.

In the compliance proceedings, China's challenged certain aspects of the review investigation. In particular, China challenged findings based on the list of Pooja Forge's products and the characteristics of such products that was not previously available to its producers.

The Panel and Appellate Body both found that the EU acted inconsistently with various provisions of the ADA.

2.3.2 Selected Panel and Appellate Body Findings in Detail

The current section addresses China's claims under Articles 6.2, 6.4 and 6.5 of the ADA. China had brought other claims under Articles 2.4, 2.4.2, 3.1, and 4.1 of the same agreement; however, these claims will not be discussed.

Treatment of Confidential Information Under Article 6.5 of the ADA

Pursuant to Article 6.5 of the ADA, in relevant parts, any information of a confidential nature or that is provided on a confidential basis during an investigation, upon "good cause" shown, must be treated as confidential by the investigating authorities. Article 6.5.1 provides that the authorities must require interested parties that provide confidential information to provide a non-confidential summary. The summarised information must be sufficient to permit a "reasonable understanding of the substance" of the confidential information. Only in exceptional circumstances may parties indicate that the information cannot be summarised and provide reasons as to why such summarisation is not possible.

The Panel found that the EU acted inconsistently with Article 6.5 because the Commission treated as confidential information submitted by Pooja Forge regarding the list and characteristics of its products. This means that nobody else had access to that information, including the Chinese companies that were affected by the dumping determination and that had no opportunity to defend themselves on the basis of that information The decision to accord Pooja Forge's information confidentiality status was based on an e-mail sent by the company to the Commission. The company simply requested the Commission not to provide the list of products to third parties as it would give an advantage to their competitors.[33]

As it had found a violation of Article 6.5, the Panel did not consider it necessary to make a finding under Article 6.5.1. The Panel insisted that, in finding a violation of Article 6.5, it did not necessarily find that the information was not confidential in nature. The Panel explained that doing so would entail a *de novo* review of the facts at issue, which is beyond the scope of its terms of reference. Nevertheless, the Panel considered that the information on the list and characteristics of Pooja Forge's products did not require confidential treatment, as contemplated by Article 6.5.[34]

On appeal, the Appellate Body explained that "good cause" is a condition precedent for according confidential treatment to information submitted to an authority. If the information is granted confidential status without the presenter of such information showing "good cause", the authority would be acting inconsistently with Article 6.5.[35] The Appellate Body confirmed that the role of the Panel is not to conduct a *de novo* review of the record evidence,[36] and that the Panel did not err in finding that Pooja Forge's e-mail requesting confidential treatment of its information contained no more than a "bald assertion".[37]

Further, the Appellate Body found that the Panel did not err in finding that the Commission never conducted an objective assessment as to whether Pooja Forge had shown "good cause" for the confidential treatment of the information at issue.[38] The Appellate Body also found that the Panel did not err by not assessing whether the information at issue was, indeed, confidential. It was, rather, the duty of the Commission to do so.

Therefore, the Appellate Body upheld the Panel's finding that the EU acted inconsistently with Article 6.5 of the ADA.[39]

[33]Panel Report, *EC – Fasteners (Article 21.5)*, WT/DS397/RW, para. 7.42.

[34]Panel Report, *EC – Fasteners (Article 21.5)*, para. 7.50 et seq.

[35]Appellate Body Report, *EC – Fasteners (Article 21.5)*, WT/DS397/AB/RW, para. 5.38.

[36]Appellate Body Report, *EC – Fasteners (Article 21.5)*, para. 5.54.

[37]Appellate Body Report, *EC – Fasteners (Article 21.5)*, para. 5.55.

[38]Appellate Body Report, *EC – Fasteners (Article 21.5)*, para. 5.62.

[39]Appellate Body Report, *EC – Fasteners (Article 21.5)*, para. 5.72.

Opportunity to Provide Access to Information Under Articles 6.4 and 6.2 of the ADA

The relevant parts of Article 6.4 of the ADA state that, whenever practicable, authorities are obliged to provide timely opportunities for all interested parties to see non-confidential information relevant to the presentation of their cases—such information is used by the authorities in the anti-dumping investigation. Article 6.2 further provides that, throughout the anti-dumping investigation, all interested parties must have a full opportunity to defend their interests. Upon request, the authorities are obliged to provide opportunities for all interested parties to meet those with adverse interests so that opposing views can be presented. The provision of these opportunities must take into account the confidentiality of certain information.

The Panel explained that information falling within the scope of Article 6.4 must be (1) relevant to the presentation of the interested parties' cases; (2) non-confidential, within the meaning of Article 6.5; and (3) must be used by the authorities in the anti-dumping investigation.[40]

The Panel found that the EU acted inconsistently with Article 6.4 because the Commission failed, when requested, to provide Chinese producers with timely opportunities to see information related to the list and characteristics of Pooja Forge's products. The requests were denied even though the information was not confidential within the meaning of Article 6.5. This information could have allowed Chinese producers to request adjustments to their normal values or their export prices. Recalling the legal standard explaining the link between Articles 6.4 and 6.2 established by the Appellate Body in *EC – Tube or Pipe Fittings*,[41] the Panel found that the inability of the Chinese producers to access this information affected their ability to defend their interests within the meaning of Article 6.2.[42]

On appeal, the Appellate Body confirmed the information at issue was relevant,[43] not confidential,[44] and "used" by the Commission in the anti-dumping investigation.[45] The Appellate Body considered that because the Commission did not provide an opportunity to see all information relevant to the presentation of their cases, the question as to whether the opportunities were timely was moot. Nevertheless, whether "timely opportunities" have been granted must be determined on a case-by-case basis.[46] The Appellate Body also did not find that the Panel erred in finding that, by failing to disclose the pertinent information to the Chinese

[40]Panel Report, *EC – Fasteners (Article 21.5)*, para. 7.88 referring to Appellate Body Report, *EC – Tube or Pipe Fittings*, WT/DS219/AB/R, para. 142.

[41]Appellate Body Report, *EC – Tube or Pipe Fittings*, para. 149.

[42]Panel Report, *EC – Fasteners (Article 21.5)*, paras. 7.94 and 7.96.

[43]Appellate Body Report, *EC – Fasteners (Article 21.5)*, paras. 5.108 et seq. and 5.111–5.113.

[44]Appellate Body Report, *EC – Fasteners (Article 21.5)*, paras. 5.101–5.103.

[45]Appellate Body Report, *EC – Fasteners (Article 21.5)*, paras. 5.116–5.118.

[46]Appellate Body Report, *EC – Fasteners (Article 21.5)*, paras. 5.121 et seq.

producers in a manner consistent with Article 6.4, the EU denied the producers full opportunities to defend their interests in a manner inconsistent with Article 6.2.[47]

Therefore, the Appellate Body upheld the Panel's findings with respect to Article 6.4 and 6.2 of the ADA.[48]

Evidence Made Available Promptly to all Interested Parties Under Article 6.1.2 of the ADA

According to Article 6.1.2 of the ADA, subject to the protection of confidential information, the authorities must promptly make available evidence presented in writing by one party to other interested parties participating in the investigation. "Interested party" is defined in Article 6.11 as, *inter alia*, an exporter or foreign producer or the importer of the product under investigation. Members are allowed to include domestic or foreign parties other than those mentioned in the first part of Article 6.11 as interested parties.

China's argument was premised on the fact that (1) the information at issue was not confidential; and (2) Pooja Forge was an "interested party", within the meaning of Article 6.11. As the Panel had already found the information not to be confidential within the meaning of Article 6.5, it relied on its previous finding.[49] However, the Panel rejected China's second argument and found that while it is not disputed that Pooja Forge is an analogue country producer, it is not considered an "interested party" for the purposes of this dispute. A participant in the investigation becomes an "interested party" by virtue of it being accorded this status by the investigating authority.[50]

On appeal, the Appellate Body confirmed that the information at issue was not confidential but reversed the Panel's conclusion, finding that Pooja Forge was an "interested party". The latter finding was based on the following factors: (1) Pooja Forge participated in the investigation at the request of the Commission; (2) the Commission selected Pooja Force as the analogue country producer for the investigation and used its data to determine normal values and calculate dumping margins for the Chinese producers; and (3) the Commission treated Pooja Forge like an "interested party".[51]

The Appellate Body completed the analysis to determine if the EU acted inconsistently with Article 6.1.2. The Appellate Body based its determination on the fact that the Commission failed to make the information concerning the list and characteristics of Pooja Forge's products available to Chinese producers during the

[47]Appellate Body Report, *EC – Fasteners (Article 21.5)*, para. 5.124.

[48]Appellate Body Report, *EC – Fasteners (Article 21.5)*, paras. 5.123–5.125.

[49]Panel Report, *EC – Fasteners (Article 21.5)*, para. 7.116.

[50]Panel Report, *EC – Fasteners (Article 21.5)*, paras. 7.118 et seq. and 7.123.

[51]Appellate Body Report, *EC – Fasteners (Article 21.5)*, paras. 5.150 and 5.152.

review investigation. Consequently, the Appellate Body found the European Union to have acted inconsistently with Article 6.1.2.[52]

2.3.3 Observations

This dispute certainly elucidated interesting points in respect of the responsibility of an investigating authority to properly determine whether information provided to it as confidential is indeed confidential. Failure to do so may curtail the procedural and substantive rights of some parties in the context of an anti-dumping investigation.

However, central to this dispute is the age-old issue of which measures can be brought before a compliance Panel. This perennial issue becomes even more relevant as more and more disputes extend to multiple compliance proceedings. The EU argued that some of China's claims could not be heard in the current proceedings because China should have brought them in the original dispute but failed to do so. In addition, the EU contended that China's claims related to unchanged aspects of the original measure that were adopted to achieve compliance and were thus *res judicata*.

China, however, argued that the EU did not provide proper access to information that was necessary to bring the claims in the original dispute, so the claims could not have been brought then. China also asserted that while the new claims were fundamentally linked to the original ones, the new information changed certain aspects of the original investigation and should be adjudicated in the compliance hearings.

According to established jurisprudence, the scope of claims that may be raised in compliance proceedings is "not unbounded".[53] A complainant may not re-litigate claims raised in the original dispute with respect to which it failed to make a *prima facie* case. A complainant also cannot re-litigate a claim before a compliance Panel "with respect to the unchanged element of the measure".[54] However, in *US – Upland Cotton (Article 21.5 – Brazil)*, the Appellate Body permitted a claim that had not been resolved on its merits in the original proceedings because the Appellate Body had not completed the analysis. The Appellate Body noted that in this situation, allowing such a claim in the compliance phase, would not raise "due process concerns".[55]

In *US – Zeroing (EC) (Article 21.5 – EC)*, the Appellate Body addressed similar jurisdictional issues in the context of anti-dumping proceedings. In the original dispute, the complainant raised claims regarding the "zeroing" methodology and in

[52]Appellate Body Report, *EC – Fasteners (Article 21.5)*, para. 5.153 et seq.

[53]Panel Report, *EC – Fasteners (Article 21.5)*, para. 7.24 referring to Appellate Body Report, *US – Upland Cotton (Article 21.5 – Brazil)*, WT/DS267/AB/RW, para. 210.

[54]Appellate Body Report, *EC – Bed Linen (Article 21.5 – India)*, WT/DS141/AB/RW, para. 93.

[55]Appellate Body Report, *US – Upland Cotton (Article 21.5 – Brazil)*, para. 210.

the compliance proceedings, the complainant raised a claim regarding an alleged arithmetical error in the investigation authority's dumping calculation. This aspect was not related to zeroing and was not raised in the original proceedings. The compliance Panel found this claim outside its terms of reference because it pertained to an unchanged aspect of the original measure. It could have been raised in the original proceedings but it was not.[56] The Appellate Body disagreed and stressed that, in compliance proceedings, the complainant can bring new claims against unchanged aspects of the original measure that are incorporated in the measure taken to comply and are not separable from it.[57]

In the current dispute, the Panel and Appellate Body largely followed established case law but also provide additional clarification. A complainant may bring a measure before a compliance panel if the complainant's ability to litigate that measure in the original dispute was affected by the respondent's failure to correctly assess and provide access to relevant information.

3 Selected Disputes with the EU Acting as a Third Party

This section discusses two selected cases in which the EU was not a main party, but rather a third party. It focusses on the positions taken by the EU concerning the most salient aspects of the case and we provide reflections on the broader context of EU interests into which these positions fit.

3.1 Peru: Agricultural Products

3.1.1 Facts of the Case

In this dispute, Guatemala challenged the Peruvian "price range system" (PRS), a customs charge that applied to four sets of agricultural products. Among these four categories of agricultural products was sugar, which is of significant commercial interest to Guatemala. Under the PRS, the Peruvian government would impose a fluctuating "additional variable duty", the amount of which depended on the precise numerical relationship between a so-called reference price and other PRS parameters. This additional duty applied in addition to any otherwise applicable ordinary duty (however, for most of the covered products the ordinary duty was zero).

Among the key elements of the PRS were a "price range floor" and a "price range ceiling", which together constitute the price range. Both the floor and the

[56] Panel Report, *US – Zeroing (EC) (Article 21.5 – EC)*, WT/DS294/RW, paras. 8.238 et seq. and 8.243.

[57] Appellate Body Report, *US – Zeroing (EC) (Article 21.5 – EC)*, WT/DS294/AB/RW, paras. 427 and 432.

ceiling were based on 5-year world market price data for a given commodity and were updated every 6 months. The third key element of the PRS was the "reference price". This was the average world market price for the previous 2 weeks (fortnight) for a given commodity; it was updated every fortnight. In simplified terms, the reference price was a proxy for the current world market price, whereas the price range floor and ceiling reflected long-term average prices.

The interaction between the price range (floor and ceiling) and the reference price determined the additional duty imposed. If the reference price was below the price range floor, an additional variable duty was imposed, equaling the difference between these two values. Put differently, if the current world market price was below the long-term average price, Peru would impose an additional duty that covered the difference and lifted the price of incoming sugar to the level of that long-term average price. If the reference price was between the price range floor and the price range ceiling, no additional duty was imposed. Finally, if the reference price was above the price range ceiling, the differential was subtracted from the otherwise applicable normal duty, by way of a "duty rebate". However, the rebate could not be higher than the normal duty; in any event, because most of the covered products attracted a zero tariff, the system almost never resulted in a rebate. The below Fig. 1 depicts graphically the functioning of the PRS.

In essence, and by its explicit design, the PRS was a price stabilizing mechanism for imports. When current world market prices were low, in relation to a 5-year average, the value of imports would be artificially elevated to at least the price range floor. When current world market prices were within the pre-defined price band—as desired by the Peruvian government—no additional duty was generated and only the ordinary customs duty (zero for most products) would apply. When the current world market price exceeded the ceiling of the price band, the system would

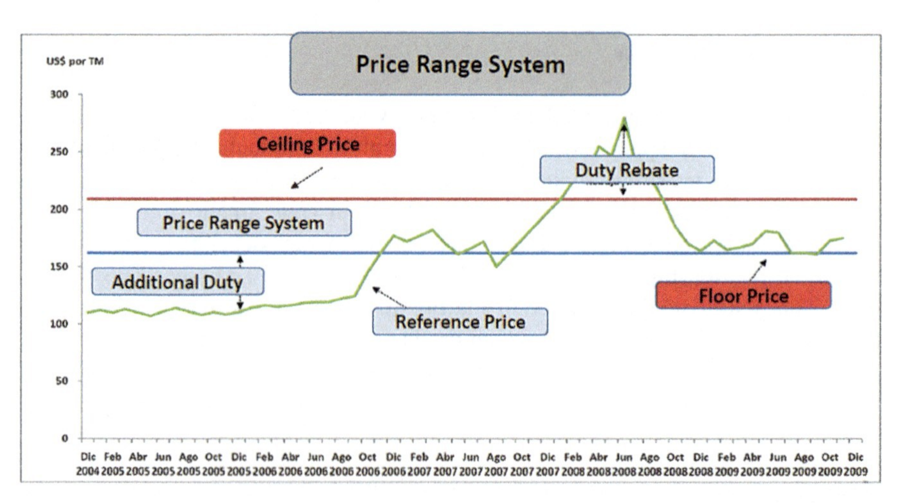

Fig. 1 Functioning of the price range system (PRS). Partially translated version of a chart on the website of the Peruvian Ministry of Economy and Tourism, https://www.mef.gob.pe/es/economia-internacional/politica-arancelaria/franja-de-precios (last accessed 1 March 2017)

generate a rebate from any applicable ordinary customs duty. While the additional variable duty protected producers, the rebate from any applicable customs duty reflected a concern (although much weaker a concern) for consumers.

The PRS bore a conspicuous resemblance to the so-called price band system previously operated by Chile and challenged by Argentina during the 2000s. In two sets of dispute settlement proceedings, WTO Panels and the Appellate Body unambiguously ruled the Chilean system to be a WTO-inconsistent measure similar to a variable import levy or to a minimum import price, as well as an "other duty or charge" that Chile was not entitled to maintain under its Schedule of Concessions.

3.1.2 Panel and Appellate Body Rulings

Both Panel and the Appellate Body agreed with Guatemala that the PRS violated Article 4.2 of the Agreement on Agriculture, on the grounds that it was a variable import levy. The mechanism or formula described above—the interplay between the reference price and the floor and ceiling prices in determining the amount of the additional duty—created a so-called "inherent variability". "Inherent variability" is the defining feature of a variable import levy and distinguishes such a levy from an ordinary customs duty (OCD). An OCD—like any measure—can be varied/modified and there is, in some sense of the word, "variable". However, the variable import levy within the meaning of Article 4.2 is a measure that contains a mechanism or a formula that ensures a periodic fluctuation of the duty, independently of any additional discretionary governmental action. It is precisely this automaticity inherent in this mechanism that sets such a measure apart from any other governmental measure that is variable in the sense that the government can change it whenever it deems it fit.

Both Panel and the Appellate Body also found that, due to being a variable import levy, the measure was an impermissible "other duty and charge" under II of the GATT 1994, because Peru had not registered it in the corresponding column of its good schedule. In any event, recording that measure in the goods schedule would not have shielded the measure from the violation under the Agreement on Agriculture.

From a legal perspective, the findings on the PRS under the Agreement on Agriculture and the GATT 1994 were entirely predictable and fairly anodyne. The Panel and Appellate Body findings that generated much more attention concerned Peru's arguments about a signed, but not fully ratified free trade agreement (FTA) between Peru and Guatemala, as well as the relationship of that FTA to the applicable WTO provisions.

In a nutshell, the FTA—signed well before the WTO dispute began—contained several clauses of relevance for the PRS and the WTO dispute—first, an FTA provision that "Peru may maintain the PRS". Another clause reaffirmed the full scope of both parties' WTO rights and obligations. A "fork in the road" dispute settlement clause stated that, to the extent that a matter could be brought both before the FTA dispute settlement mechanism and the WTO's dispute settlement system, a party had the choice but would permanently forgo the forum not chosen. Finally, a conflicts clause stated that, to the extent a conflict existed, the FTA should prevail to the extent of that conflict. Both parties had signed the FTA, but only Guatemala had ratified it. Peru subsequently refused to ratify the FTA, explicitly citing Guatemala's decision to initiate the WTO dispute as a reason for this refusal.

Peru presented a range of arguments to the Panel and the Appellate Body relating to the FTA. These arguments were based on the allegation that Guatemala had agreed to Peru's maintaining the PRS, thus had lost the right to bring a WTO dispute on this issue and its WTO complaint was thus improper. The more detailed arguments had a procedural and a substantive dimension.

At the procedural level, Peru invoked Articles 3.7 and 3.10 of the DSU, which state that a complainant will exercise judgment whether initiating a dispute would be "fruitful" and that parties will engage in a dispute settlement proceeding in "good faith". Peru argued that Guatemala had acted inconsistently with these provisions and that the Panel thus had no jurisdiction over the dispute. Both Panel and the Appellate Body disagreed, essentially because a complainant is self-regulating in its decision whether to initiate a dispute and there was no evidence that Guatemala had initiated the dispute in anything but good faith.

At the substantive level, Peru argued that the (unratified) FTA had modified WTO obligations between the parties (before the Panel) or that the WTO obligations between the parties had to be *interpreted* in the light of the FTA and of Articles 20 and 45 of the ILC Articles on Responsibility of States for Internationally Wrongful Acts (before the Appellate Body). The Panel took the easy path and relied on the fact that the FTA had not yet entered into force. The Appellate Body in addition ruled that "interpretation" within the meaning of Article 31 of the Vienna Convention on the Law of Treaties (VCLT) cannot go beyond the possible range of meanings of a term. Thus, the phrase "shall not maintain" in Article 4.2 of the Agreement on Agriculture could not, under the rubric of interpretation, be converted into "may maintain". The Appellate Body also did not consider that the provisions invoked by Peru (including ILC Articles 20 and 45) were "relevant" for the interpretation of Articles 4.2 of the Agreement on Agriculture and Article II:1(b) of the GATT 1994.[58] Perhaps most importantly, the Appellate Body also ruled that Article 42 of the VCLT—which allows two or more parties to modify "inter se" a multilateral agreement—has been superseded by the WTO rules on amending the WTO treaty (Articles X of the WTO Agreement). The Appellate Body also found that an FTA could not be a vehicle for WTO members to "roll back" WTO obligations (as opposed to agreeing on further trade liberalization).

Thus, the Appellate Body essentially closed the window on the possibility of WTO Members to "contract out" of the substantive norms of the WTO legal framework. Arguably, the only route not yet explicitly foreclosed by WTO jurisprudence seems to be where an FTA contains a "fork-in-the-road" jurisdictional clause and a WTO complainant initiates a WTO dispute in violation of that FTA clause. For instance, a complainant might have lost an FTA dispute and subsequently, in violation of an FTA jurisdictional clause, initiates a WTO dispute on the

[58] Appellate Body Report, *Peru – Agricultural Products*, WT/DS457/AB/R, para. 5.104.

same issue. If the initiation of the first (FTA) dispute could be interpreted as a waiver of WTO jurisdictional rights—as envisaged by the Appellate Body in *EC – Bananas III (Article 21.5)*—a WTO panel might decline jurisdiction.

3.1.3 The Arguments of the EU as Third Party

On the measure at issue, the EU took a fairly standard view in line with Guatemala's challenge, arguing that inherent variability—the type of variability that violates the Agreement on Agriculture—exists where a measure incorporates a mathematical formula. Indeed, the EU even went a step beyond and questioned whether non-inherent variability—that is, variation in a tariff through autonomous legislative or regulatory decisions, rather than based on a mathematical formula—could, in case of a particular frequency, morph into inherent variability within the meaning of Article 4.2 of the Agreement on Agriculture.[59]

Concerning the significance of the FTA, the EU took a cautious view on Articles 3.7 and 3.10, arguing that WTO Members were largely self-regulating in initiating a WTO dispute. However, it submitted that elements of an FTA, or acts under an FTA, could amount to a "waiver" of procedural rights under the DSU, as previously envisaged by the Appellate Body in *EC – Bananas III (Article 21.5)*.[60] The key question in the instant case, according to the EU, was whether the FTA contained an unambiguous commitment by Guatemala to refrain from challenging the Peruvian PRS.[61] The EU took the view that this was not the case, especially because the FTA had not entered into effect yet.[62] The EU thus appeared to privilege a waiver of procedural rights through non-unilateral acts (e.g. a legally effective FTA), even if it did not exclude that a unilateral declaration could give rise to a valid waiver.[63]

What is interesting in this context is that the EU would apparently accept an *ex ante* waiver of the right to challenge a measure, before an actual dispute has arisen. For instance, the EU would apparently accept a waiver in the shape of an FTA provision that prohibits disputes against a particular measure (or a category of measures). In contrast, the Appellate Body seems more conservative at this point. It suggested, albeit not entirely explicitly, that a waiver of procedural rights could occur only after a dispute has arisen, rather than before.[64]

---

[59]EU's third party submission, http://trade.ec.europa.eu/wtodispute/show.cfm?id=583&code=3#_eu-submissions (last accessed 1 February 2017), para. 17; EU's third party opening statement at the first panel meeting, http://trade.ec.europa.eu/doclib/docs/2014/june/tradoc_152593.doc.pdf (last accessed 1 March 2017), para. 17.

[60]Panel Report, *Peru – Agricultural Products*, WT/DS457/R, para. 7.65.

[61]Panel Report, *Peru – Agricultural Products*, para. 7.65.

[62]EU's third participant submission before the Appellate Body, http://trade.ec.europa.eu/wtodispute/show.cfm?id=583&code=3#_eu-submissions (last accessed 1 March 2017), para. 30.

[63]EU's third participant submission before the Appellate Body, para. 29.

[64]See Appellate Body Report, *Peru – Agricultural Products*, para. 5.26.

Before the Appellate Body, the EU also addressed some of Peru's arguments under Article 31 of the VCLT, concerning the interpretation of WTO provisions in the light of the FTA. To recall, Peru argued that the WTO provisions at issue should be interpreted in the light of the FTA and of ILC Articles 20 and 45. The EU opposed Peru's argument on the FTA, mostly due to the fact that the FTA had not yet entered into effect.[65] Furthermore, the EU appeared to agree with Guatemala that the term "the parties" in Articles 31.3(a) of the VCLT refers to all parties to the treaty, which in this case would mean all WTO Members. Thus, a non-WTO treaty would constitute an agreement about the interpretation of the WTO Agreement only if it were concluded among all WTO Members.[66] Under Article 31.3(c) of the VCLT, the EU took a more nuanced view, referring to the principle of "systemic integration"; under this rubric, the EU suggested that a treaty could be part of the "normative environment" for the interpretation of a treaty even if it has not been ratified by all WTO Members.[67] The EU also invoked examples from prior case law that interpreted the ordinary meaning of a term in the light of non-WTO law to which not all WTO Members were parties.[68]

3.1.4 Reflections on the EU's Position

The EU's arguments reflect an interesting and nuanced view on the relationship between WTO law and non-WTO law. As one of the key WTO Members and one of the most frequent participants in the WTO dispute settlement system, and as an international body rooted in international law, the EU has keen interest in preserving the integrity of the WTO's judicial system, while also ensuring a harmonious relationship between WTO law and other systems of international law. The EU has historically taken a more pro-public international law stance than the United States, which consistently argues for a strict separation between WTO law and other systems of international law.

The EU appears to look favourably, or at least with acceptance, on the emerging WTO case law. That case law rejects the application of non-WTO law in a WTO dispute and also stops short of formally using non-WTO law as a tool for interpreting WTO provisions, for instance as "context" or "together with the context" within the meaning of the Vienna Convention on the Law of Treaties, unless all WTO Members are bound by that non-WTO law. However, non-WTO law that enjoys a sufficiently broad recognition will be considered to determine the ordinary meaning of a WTO term, even if not all WTO Members are party to or bound by that non-WTO legal instrument. A good example in this regard remains the term "exhaustible natural resources" under Article XX(g) of the GATT 1994,

[65] EU's third participant submission before the Appellate Body, para. 53.
[66] EU's third participant submission before the Appellate Body, para. 43.
[67] EU's third participant submission before the Appellate Body, para. 47 et seq.
[68] EU's third participant submission before the Appellate Body, paras. 49–52.

cited by the EU, which the Appellate Body interpreted as encompassing living endangered animal species, relying on a range of international conventions and declarations to which not all WTO Members had subscribed.

This compromise of sorts appears to satisfy both pro-public international law WTO Members like the EU, all the while remaining acceptable to public international law skeptical WTO Members like the United States. For the EU, this entry point for public international law into WTO law remains sufficiently large to ensure a degree of harmonious interpretation and "systemic integration" with non-WTO law. At least in this case, the EU appears to take a more conservative stance than in *EC – Aircraft*, where it argued that a bilateral agreement between the EU and US should be directly relevant for the interpretation and application of the Agreement on Subsidies and Countervailing Measures (SCM Agreement).[69] For the US, in contrast, the "ordinary meaning" approach may be acceptable because the ordinary meaning of a treaty term is determined by a multiplicity of sources—including the famous dictionaries—and is subsequently further cushioned and mitigated by context and other elements under the Vienna Convention.

3.2 US: COOL (Article 21.5)

3.2.1 Facts of the Case

These compliance proceedings are part of the original *US – COOL* dispute initiated by Canada and Mexico in 2009 concerning the US country of origin labelling requirements (the "COOL measure"). In 2012, the Appellate Body declared the COOL measure to be WTO-inconsistent. In 2013, Canada and Mexico subsequently challenged the United States for failing to properly comply with the Appellate Body's findings.

The amended COOL measure is largely similar to the COOL measure. The amended COOL measure establishes country of origin labelling rules for live hogs and cattle, muscle cuts of beef and pork, and ground beef and pork based on five categories (A–E). For meat from animals slaughtered in the United States, labels A, B, and C established point-of-production labelling, which required an indication of the specific production steps that took place in each country.[70] Label D applied to meat from animals that were not slaughtered in the United States, the labels affixed to these products were required to indicate the origin as declared to the United States customs authority at the time the products entered the United States' market.[71] No changes were made to category E.

---

[69] Appellate Body Report, *US – Airbus*, WT/DS316/AB/R, para. 839.

[70] For example, label B would read "Born and raised in Mexico, Raised and Slaughtered in the United States".

[71] Label D would read, for example, "Product of Canada".

The amended COOL measure also contained some flexibilities and exemptions. The three main exemptions were with respect to (i) entities not meeting the definition of "retailer"; (ii) ingredients in "processed food items"; and (c) products served in a "food service establishment".

3.2.2 Panel and Appellate Body Rulings

This discussion focusses on the Panel's and Appellate Body's findings in respect of Articles 2.1 and 2.2 of the Agreement on Technical Barriers to Trade (TBT Agreement) and Articles III:4 and XX of the GATT 1994.

With respect to Article 2.1 of the TBT Agreement, the Panel found that the amended COOL measure was inconsistent with the national treatment obligation of this provision. The Panel adhered to the two-step legal standard established by the Appellate Body in *US – Clove Cigarettes*, i.e. (1) whether a detrimental impact exists, and (2) then whether such impact stems exclusively from a legitimate regulatory distinction.

The Panel explained that a discriminatory technical regulation may still be in conformity with Article 2.1 of the TBT Agreement if it pursues a legitimate objective.[72] The Panel found that the amended COOL measure increased the detrimental impact on imported livestock because it established point-of-production labelling. This increased the administrative burden on upstream producers to keep precise production records, thereby affecting the sourcing decisions of processors to opt for domestic livestock. This, consequently, modified the conditions of competition between domestic and imported livestock.[73]

In analyzing whether the amended COOL measure resulted in "less favourable treatment" under Article 2.1, the Panel examined whether the detrimental impact stemmed exclusively from legitimate regulatory distinctions. The Panel found a "disconnect" between the informational requirements imposed on upstream producers and the information effectively communicated to consumers.[74] The Panel therefore concluded that the detrimental impact caused by the amended COOL measure in respect of categories A–C "does not stem exclusively from legitimate regulatory distinctions".[75]

On appeal, the Appellate Body agreed with the Panel's approach and found that its conclusion that the detrimental impact does not stem exclusively from legitimate regulatory distinctions is based on comparative analysis of the key determinants of the informational "disconnect". The Appellate Body noted that the Panel's findings support the conclusion that the recordkeeping requirement of the amended measure imposes a disproportionate burden on producers and livestock processors that

[72]Panel Report, *US – COOL (Article 21.5)*, WT/DS384/RW, WT/DS386/RW, paras. 7.60–7.62.

[73]Panel Report, *US – COOL (Article 21.5)*, para. 7.167.

[74]Panel Report, *US – COOL (Article 21.5)*, para. 7.266.

[75]Panel Report, *US – COOL (Article 21.5)*, paras. 7.283 and 7.285.

cannot be justified by the need to provide consumers with the point-of-production information.[76] The Appellate Body thus upheld the Panel's findings under Article 2.1 of the TBT Agreement.

With respect to Article 2.2 of the TBT Agreement, like in the original case, the Panel rejected the complainants' claims that the amended COOL measures are more trade restrictive than necessary. The Panel recalled the findings of the Appellate Body in *US – Tuna II (Mexico)* and the original *US – COOL* dispute and addressed the following six factors before reaching a conclusion on the complainants' claims: (1) the amended COOL measure's degree of contribution to a legitimate objective; (2) its trade-restrictiveness; (3) the nature of the risk and the gravity of the consequences that would arise from non-fulfilment of the objective; (4) whether the proposed alternatives are less trade restrictive than the amended COOL measure; (5) whether the proposed alternatives would make an equivalent contribution to the legitimate objective, taking account the risks of non-fulfilment; and (6) whether the proposed alternatives are reasonably available.[77]

The Panel recalled that the amended COOL measure pursued the objective of providing consumer information on origin.[78] While it found that the measure makes some contribution to this objective, and is trade restrictive, the Panel was unable to ascertain the gravity of not fulfilling the amended COOL measure's objective (relational analysis).[79] Therefore, the Panel proceeded to examine the four alternative measures submitted by Canada and Mexico (comparative analysis). The Panel rejected all four alternative measures concluding that the complainants failed to make a *prima facie* case that the amended COOL measure violates Article 2.2 of the TBT Agreement.[80]

The Appellate Body confirmed the Panel's reliance on the weighing and balancing factors set out in *US – Tuna (Mexico)*[81] and its relational and comparative analysis of the amended COOL measure and the alternative measures, respectively.[82] The Appellate Body recalled that the assessment of whether a technical regulation is more trade restrictive than necessary "involves the *holistic* weighing and balancing of all relevant factors".[83] The Appellate Body explained that, recalling its interpretation of "necessity" under Article XX of the GATT 1994, it is not mandatory with respect to Article 2.2 of the TBT Agreement for a Panel to draw a preliminary conclusion on necessity based on factors related to the technical

[76] Appellate Body Report, *US – COOL (Article 21.5)*, WT/DS384/AB/RW, WT/DS386/AB/RW, paras. 5.31–5.44.

[77] Panel Report, *US – COOL (Article 21.5)*, para. 7.303.

[78] Panel Report, *US – COOL (Article 21.5)*, para. 7.331.

[79] Panel Report, *US – COOL (Article 21.5)*, para. 7.424.

[80] Panel Report, *US – COOL (Article 21.5)*, para. 7.614.

[81] Appellate Body Report, *US – COOL (Article 21.5)*, paras. 5.195–5.198.

[82] Appellate Body Report, *US – COOL (Article 21.5)*, paras. 5.231–5.234.

[83] Appellate Body Report, *US – COOL (Article 21.5)*, para. 5.218.

regulation itself before delving further in a comparison with the proposed alternatives.[84] In addition, the Appellate Body found that the Panel erred in not including labels D and E in reaching its conclusion that the amended COOL measure makes a "considerable but necessarily partial" contribution to its objective.[85]

With respect to the interpretation of the phrase "taking account of the risks non-fulfilment would create", the Appellate Body noted that an interpretation that potentially decreases the degree of contribution needed to be made by an alternative measure to be considered equivalent would not comply with Article 2.2 of the TBT Agreement. It could potentially restrain a Member's ability to pursue a legitimate objective "at the levels it considers appropriate".[86] Further, the Appellate Body concluded that, in assessing "the risks non-fulfilment would create" the Panel did not err by failing to take into account the importance of the values or interests[87] or the design, structure, and architecture pursued by the amended COOL measure.[88]

However, the Appellate Body found that the Panel had erred in finding that it was unable to ascertain the gravity of the consequences of non-fulfilment of the amended COOL measure's objective.[89] The Appellate Body therefore reversed the panel's findings that the complainants had not made a *prima facie* case of inconsistency with Article 2.2 of the TBT Agreement. However, the Appellate Body did not complete the legal analysis in respect of the alternative measures.[90]

With respect to the complainant's claims under Article III:4 of the GATT 1994, the Panel followed its findings under Article 2.1 of the TBT Agreement to conclude that the amended COOL measure violates the latter provision.[91]

At the interim review stage, the United States requested the panel to address the availability of Article XX as an exception for Article III:4 with regards to the amended COOL measure.[92] The Panel rejected the United States' request, explaining that, *inter alia*, the United States did not invoke Article XX of the GATT 1994 in the dispute and thus found it inappropriate to address the "hypothetical situation".[93]

On appeal, the United States requested the Appellate Body to reverse the Panel's findings under Article III:4 of the GATT 1994 because it failed to take into account Article IX of the GATT 1994 as the relevant context of the latter provision.[94] The

[84]Appellate Body Report, *US – COOL (Article 21.5)*, paras. 5.232–5.235.

[85]Appellate Body Report, *US – COOL (Article 21.5)*, para. 5.247.

[86]Appellate Body Report, *US – COOL (Article 21.5)*, para. 5.266.

[87]Appellate Body Report, *US – COOL (Article 21.5)*, paras. 5.276–5.281.

[88]Appellate Body Report, *US – COOL (Article 21.5)*, paras. 5.285–5.287.

[89]Appellate Body Report, *US – COOL (Article 21.5)*, para. 5.297.

[90]Appellate Body Report, *US – COOL (Article 21.5)*, paras. 5.302–5.313, 5.322–5.323 and 5.339 et seq.

[91]Panel Report, *US – COOL (Article 21.5)*, para. 7.643.

[92]Panel Report, *US – COOL (Article 21.5)*, para. 6.70.

[93]Panel Report, *US – COOL (Article 21.5)*, paras. 6.71–6.75.

[94]Appellate Body Report, *US – COOL (Article 21.5)*, para. 2.29.

Appellate Body rejected the United States' claim. The Appellate Body considered that the provisions of Article IX of the GATT 1994 set out obligations regarding marking requirements that are separate and additional to the national treatment obligation in Article III:4 of the GATT 1994. The Appellate Body also rejected the United States' claim on the basis that the Appellate Body in *US – Clove Cigarettes* explicitly clarified that the detrimental impact analysis under Article III:4 does not involve an assessment of whether the detrimental impact stems exclusively from a legitimate regulatory distinction.[95]

The Appellate Body also concluded that the Panel did not err in not addressing the United States' interim review request. The Appellate Body thus did not complete the analysis in order to make findings on whether the amended COOL measure would be justified under the general exceptions of Article XX of the GATT 1994.[96]

3.2.3 The EU's Third Party Submission

As both proceedings were opened to the public, certain third parties requested, for confidentiality reasons, not to make their statements public.[97] Perhaps it is due to the same reasons that this dispute is one in respect of which the EU did not post its third party and third participants submissions on the DG Trade's website. The EU made extensive submissions in all aspects of the dispute; however, this section will focus on those that relate to the right that WTO Members have to regulate according to their public interest.

With respect to Article 2.1 of the TBT Agreement, at the Panel stage, the EU was of the view that it would find it difficult to consider the exemptions for, *inter alia*, restaurants and small retailers *de facto* discriminatory. The EU cautioned against an approach that made it impossible for a regulating Member to implement an origin-neutral rule because there may be *de facto* discrimination.[98]

With respect to the Article 2.2 of the TBT Agreement, at the Panel stage, the EU opined that WTO Members have the right to determine their legitimate regulatory objectives. Once the provision of consumer information on origin and points-of-production has been considered a legitimate objective, it is not possible to question the motives of particular consumers in requiring such information. Information about which labels consumers want may be relevant to an assessment under Article 2.2 but is not dispositive.[99]

---

[95]Appellate Body Report, *US – COOL (Article 21.5)*, para. 5.357 et seq.

[96]Appellate Body Report, *US – COOL (Article 21.5)*, paras. 5.376–5.380.

[97]Panel Report, *US – COOL (Article 21.5)*, para. 1.10.

[98]Panel Report, *US – COOL (Article 21.5)*, Annex C-4, Integrated Executive Summary of the Arguments of the European Union, para. 10.

[99]Panel Report, *US – COOL (Article 21.5)*, Annex C-4, Integrated Executive Summary of the Arguments of the European Union, para. 11.

The EU further noted that it is not for WTO adjudicators to rank in general and abstract terms the importance of WTO Members' legitimate regulatory objectives. In WTO law, this is strictly the reserve of the regulating Member because different Members have different values. The WTO has no mandate to apply a pure proportionality test. The EU also questioned Canada and Mexico's value judgement on the non-fulfilment of the origin labelling objective. Based on this, they argued that an alternative measure could make a lesser contribution to the fulfilment of the legitimate objective because, relatively, the consequence of non-fulfilment is not that grave. The EU noted that Article 2.2 of the TBT Agreement does not refer to the *consequences* of non-fulfilment rather the risk thereof. This does not result in diminishing the appropriate level of protection (ALOP) but merely examines if there is a rational relationship between the different parts of the challenged measure or the proposed alternative.[100]

At the appeal phase, the EU submitted that the analysis of whether a measure is more trade restrictive than necessary involves a "relational" and "comparative" analysis, which are closely connected. The assessment of how much a measure contributes to an objective must necessarily involve an assessment of whether the alternatives could contribute more or less.[101] With respect to the phrase "taking account of the risks non-fulfilment would create", the EU agreed with the United States that there is no hierarchy of values in WTO law and it is up to each Member to decide which regulatory objective it wishes to pursue and which extent. While the EU considered that the Panel was correct in that considering consumers' interest and willingness to pay should be taken into account in its "necessity" analysis, these criteria should not have been the only ones to be considered.[102] The EU considered that the proposed alternative measures should, in principle, make a contribution that is equivalent to that of the challenged measure. However, this burden rests on the complainants.[103]

3.2.4 Reflections on the EU's Position

Given the EU's experience with TBT issues in, *inter alia*, *EC – Asbestos* and more recently, *EC – Seal Products*, the EU's stance in this case, and on TBT issues in general, is hardly surprising. There is no question that, with increasing consumer sophistication, WTO members like the EU are faced with mounting pressure to provide more specific information as to the origin and contents of products, particularly food, clothing, and cosmetic products. In this dispute, the EU advocates that WTO adjudicative bodies should be almost completely deferential to Members

[100]Panel Report, *US – COOL (Article 21.5)*, Annex C-4, Integrated Executive Summary of the Arguments of the European Union, para. 16 et seq.

[101]Appellate Body Report, *US – COOL (Article 21.5)*, para. 2.225.

[102]Appellate Body Report, *US – COOL (Article 21.5)*, para. 2.227.

[103]Appellate Body Report, *US – COOL (Article 21.5)*, para. 2.228.

when considering the legitimacy of certain policy objectives and how high the Member can set its ALOP. Members should not be restricted in the design and architecture of the measure, including its exceptions, because they might result in some kind of *de facto* discrimination.

The EU's stance could be read to suggest that panels and the Appellate Body should not even engage in what is already a routine check to see if there is even a semblance of a legitimate objective policy and whether the measure applied remotely contributes to achieving that objective. It appears that the EU would not object if the WTO adjudicators went straight to determining whether the measure at issue results in discrimination or is more trade restrictive than necessary.

The EU's stance also extends the manner and extent of the alternative measures that the complainant can suggest. According to the EU, the complainant cannot make a value judgement on whether the legitimate objective pursued by the regulating Member is relatively important or not. This is not controversial. Of course, it can be argued that providing information on a label on where a pig or a cow was born, raised, and slaughtered is not as important as providing information about the hazardous nature of the contents of products. But to the EU, the complainant should not engage in relative comparisons of the consequences of non-fulfilment of the objective. The duty of the complainant is, instead, to ensure that the proposed equivalent measure makes, in principle, a contribution that is equivalent to the original measure.

The EU's stance requires complainants to really "do their homework" on a proposed measure. It is difficult for any complainant to propose alternatives without somewhat engaging with the objective pursued by the policy. Some Members may believe that the trade inconvenience or barriers far outweigh the need for consumers to know the alkaline content of the water that was used to irrigate their quinoa. Therefore, in suggesting alternatives, those Members may opt for an alternative that is administratively less burdensome, yet providing vital consumer information. The EU would unlikely support the Appellate Body's confirmation that an alternative measure that provides less or less accurate origin information to consumers for a significantly wider product range might achieve an equivalent degree of contribution as the original measure.[104]

The authors believe that the WTO dispute settlement has not seen the last of disputes like *US – COOL* and *EC – Seal Products*. As consumers around the world become more and more sophisticated, Members will increasingly react to demands for consumer protection, which some might consider excessive indulgence to consumer demands. While consumers are not actors for the purposes of WTO law, they determine markets and the more they deem it important to ensure, for example, ethical supply chains, and the more that they are willing to pay for certain information to be reflected on their products, the more clashes like these will arise.

[104]Appellate Body Report, *US – COOL (Article 21.5)*, paras. 5.267–5.270.

Reference

Bohanes J, Sánchez A, Telychko A (2016) Overview of WTO jurisprudence in 2014. In: Bungenberg M, Herrmann C, Krajewski M, Terhechte JP (eds) European yearbook of international economic law 2016. Springer, Heidelberg, pp 651–702

Part IV
Book Reviews

Marise Cremona and Hans-W. Micklitz (eds.), Private Law in the External Relations of the EU

Oxford University Press, 2016, ISBN 9780198744566

Peter Rott

Abstract Hans-W. Micklitz has been one of the most prominent writers on EU private law in all its substantive, procedural and constitutional facets in the past decades, whilst Marise Cremona is among the leading authors on EU external relations; an area that has attracted much attention recently, with the EU Commission's negotiations of highly controversial trade agreements, such as CETA, TTIP and TISA. With their edited volume on "Private Law in the External Relations of the EU", Marise Cremona and Hans-W. Micklitz combine their expertise by making the bold attempt to bring these seemingly unconnected areas of law together. The book presents a number of sub-disciplines and complements them with structural themes such as the competences of the EU in concluding international agreements with effect on internal EU law.

EU private law has been discussed in all its substantive, procedural and constitutional facets in the past decades, and with a broader audience at least since the 1990s; and *Hans-W. Micklitz* was and is one of the most prominent writers in that area.[1] His main theme has been EU private law as regulatory law, as an area of law that goes far beyond the interaction of private parties but that is meant to regulate the market and society. The main dimensions of regulatory private law are the social aspects of private law, in particular in the form of consumer law, and the law related to formerly public services, such as telecommunications services, postal services, electricity, gas and public transport.

EU external relations, on its part, has also been subject to numerous controversies, often turning on the competing relationship between the EU, on the one hand,

[1]See only Micklitz (2009, 2014).

P. Rott (✉)
Faculty of Economics and Management, University of Kassel, Nora-Platiel-Straße 4, 34109 Kassel, Germany
e-mail: rott@uni-kassel.de

M. Bungenberg et al. (eds.), *European Yearbook of International Economic Law 2017*, European Yearbook of International Economic Law 8,
DOI 10.1007/978-3-319-58832-2_22

and its Member States, on the other hand, in the international sphere, and therefore in public international law. It has attracted much attention recently, with the EU Commission's negotiations of highly controversial trade agreements, such as CETA, TTIP and TISA. *Marise Cremona* is among the leading authors in that area.[2]

With this edited volume on "Private Law in the External Relations of the EU", *Marise Cremona* and *Hans-W. Micklitz* combine their expertise by making the bold attempt to bring these seemingly unconnected areas of law together. In fact, individual aspects of EU private law taking effect beyond the borders of the European Union, for example, in the areas of private international law or competition law, are well-known and have been discussed broadly in academic writing within these sub-disciplines. Likewise, the influence of supranational and transnational regimes, such as the international trade law of the World Trade Organization (WTO), on EU law has been subject to academic debate as well as to the case law of the Court of Justice (CJEU), for example in the bananas case of *T. Port*[3] and in relation to the intellectual property regime of the TRIPS Agreement.[4] In recent years, supranational and transnational regulation of the financial market have gained momentum, and the EU is one important actor in that process. Moreover, the EU as such but also individual EU legislation has stood model for other countries or regional organisations worldwide.

The book by *Cremona* and *Micklitz* brings a number of sub-disciplines together and complements them with structural themes such as the competences of the EU in concluding international agreements with effect on internal EU law. It is divided in three parts. Part 1 on "Private Law and EU External Competence" sets the scene, with one chapter each by the two co-editors. Part 2 deals with EU law that takes effect beyond the boundaries of the European Union, whereas part 3 discusses the "Making of International Private Law and the Role of the EU".

As indicated by the editors in the Introduction to the book, the book is meant to initiate research into the relationship between private law and EU external relations law, rather than to present a conclusive analysis of that relationship. The theme and the research agenda are explained in more detail by *Hans Micklitz* in chapter 1. He presents four observations on what he calls the "External European Private Law". First, legal practice does not necessarily reflect the legal rules, one central reason being the various mechanisms to settle disputes out of the ordinary court system, including commercial arbitration, alternative dispute resolution in consumer affairs and the internal conflict management rules of the big online platform operators such as eBay. Second, "experimental governance" is substituting or even replacing formal governance in many areas of law or life. The most prominent emanation of this phenomenon are the technical standards as elaborated nationally, within the framework of the EU's so-called "New Approach" but also at the international

---

[2]See only Cremona (2003, 2008).

[3]CJEU, case C-68/96, *T. Port v. Bundesanstalt für Landwirtschaft und Ernährung*, ECLI:EU:C:1996:452.

[4]See, for example, CJEU, case C-135/10, *SCF*, ECLI:EU:C:2012:140.

level, within organisations such as the International Standardization Organization (ISO), the Basel Committee and the International Organization of Securities Commissions (IOSCO). Third, *Micklitz* sees a shift from substance to procedure. This includes procedures (at EU law level) to protect EU substantive law standards against the outside world but also international agreements on procedure rather than on substantive law. Fourth, the sharp distinction between private law and trade law is vanishing, as international trade agreements impact on the private law relationships of traders.

Marise Cremona then sets out the interactions between international law, EU law and private law, focussing mainly on the competence system of the EU and on its (ever growing) position in the international sphere. She elaborates on the various competence norms of the Treaty on the Functioning of the European Union (TFEU), starting with the basic provision of Article 216(1) TFEU, and then focuses on the effects that international agreements have on internal EU law and on the law of the Member States. The central norm here is Article 216(2) TFEU (ex-Article 300(7) EC), which has triggered rich case law of the Court of Justice relating to the direct effect or otherwise of international agreements in EU law, to the interpretation of EU law in the light of international agreements and to interpretations of EU law that avoid conflicts with international agreements. More complicated is the situation where, due to changes to the allocation of competences between the EU and the Member States, areas of law that used to be in the competence of the Member States migrate into the exclusive or shared competence of the EU; a situation to which EU law and policy have reacted with a number of different solution, such as Article 351 TFEU, provisions of EU secondary law but also rules within the related international agreement.

The second part of the book is mainly concerned with the written and unwritten private international law of the European Union and with substantive law instruments that reach beyond the borders of the EU.

Christiaan Timmermans emphasises and regrets the limitations of the EU competences for an external policy in the field of private law, under the so-called AETR approach,[5] requiring already existing EU legislation in the relevant field, and the necessity test of opinion 1/76, as now codified in Articles 3(2) and 216(1) TFEU. He then, however, discusses three types of "connection clauses" regulating the relationship of EU legislation with existing and possibly also future international agreements entered into by Member States: (1) Incorporation of external EU law by way of reference in an EU instrument, with the consequence of the CJEU acquiring the competence to interpret the referenced external rules; (2) authorization of Member States to conclude or to accede to treaties; and (3) clauses regulating the relationship between EU legislation and treaties concluded by Member States.

Stéphanie Francq focuses on the external dimension of the private international law of the Rome I and Rome II Regulations both of which have universal scope of application; thus, they apply once a court within the EU has jurisdiction. This is, of

[5]See CJEU, case 22/70, *Commission v Council*, ECLI:EU:C:1971:32.

course, not new, but it produces an interesting conflict between the traditional neutrality of private international law and the policy-based EU private law, in particular but not only EU consumer law. Examples are Article 6 Rome I Regulation and Articles 6(3) and 7 Rome II Regulation. *Francq* shows that while EU private international law does not formally distinguish internal and external situations, EU substantive law determines its scope of application in a unilateral fashion and secures the application of EU standards over third states' standards. The Court of Justice also plays a role in this, as illustrated in the famous *Ingmar* case but also more recently in the data protection case of *Google Spain*, where situations that were partly placed outside the EU were subjected to substantive EU law because they somehow affected the EU market. One crucial factor seems to be trust that is (perhaps fictitiously) inherent in the relationship between Member States but surely not omnipresent in the relationship of the EU with third states.

Etienne Pataut looks at an area that is still fairly new in EU private law: family law. The EU's external competence is limited to private international law, which mainly takes place in the Hague Conference, of which the EU became a member on 3 April 2007. Before that date, the competence to sign conventions of the Hague Conference lay with the Member States, although the EU had already gained the competence on private international law with the Amsterdam Treaty that entered into force in 1999. *Pataut* meticulously analyses the complications that arose from that competence shift, internally as well as in the external relations to third states. He also elaborates on the differences between the jurisdiction rules of the Brussels I Regulation (on civil and commercial matters) and the family law regimes of the Brussels II and II*bis* Regulations (on matrimonial matters and matters of parental responsibility) and the Maintenance and Succession Regulations.

CJEU case law on the external reach of EU private law, namely *L'Oréal v. eBay* on trademark law and *Google and Google Spain* on data protection law, is discussed by *Niilo Jääskinen* and *Angela Ward*. In both cases, the CJEU confirmed the applicability of substantive EU law to conduct that originated in third countries. *Jääskinen* and *Ward* begin their discussion with a review of CJEU case law on the circumstances under which EU public law captures legal relations and behaviour that occurred outside the EU, starting with the "effects doctrine" developed in the famous wood pulp case of *Ahlström* and the "entity doctrine" as developed in *Dyestuffs*, both cartel law cases. The authors then analyse CJEU case law concerning the application of the Brussels I Regulation and its predecessor to situations that were partly external. They show how principles developed under both regimes resurface, although in different contexts and related to different legal issues, in *L'Oréal v. eBay* (concerning offers of counterfeit products from locations outside the EU on eBay websites) and *Google and Google Spain* (concerning the protection of data entered in Google search machines, with Google Inc. being a US American company).

Stefan Grundmann poses the question whether EU contract and company law have global reach. He takes up the above-mentioned "effects principle" as developed in competition law and illustrates its relevance in private international law relating to contract law and to company law, where public interest regulation may enjoy global reach. *Grundmann* then looks at substantive law instruments, namely, the European Company Statute and the proposed (and failed) Common European Sales Law (CESL) and states that both are not capable of being used by third country actors. As to incorporation of international regulatory regimes, *Grundmann* refers to the international accounting standards as well as standards on banking supervision and capital market law that are also discussed in other chapters of the book. Finally, he offers reflections on the desired reach of the EU regulatory regime, using the example of the financial crisis triggered by the US sub-prime mortgage crisis.

The third part of the book, dealing with the making of international private law regulation and the role of the EU, begins with a contribution by *Jan Wouters* and *Jed Odermatt* on "International Banking Standards, Private Law, and the European Union". The authors establish that the role of the EU is much weaker in the world of finance than in the world of trade, due to the less formal structures in the global regulation of finance. They point out that the EU participates in two principal agenda-setting bodies, the Group of 20 (G20) and the Financial Stability Board (FSB), but is not a member of some other main drivers of international banking regulations, in particular the International Monetary Fund (IMF) and the World Bank. The European Central Bank (ECB) is a member of the Bank for International Settlements (BIS), based in Basel, where most of the regulatory work is undertaken through committees such as the Basel Committee on Banking Supervision and the Commission on the Global Financial System. The authors describe the work of these and other standard-setting committees and then show how the international standards are transposed into EU law by the EU legislator.

Antonio Maracci discusses one of the financial standard setters, the International Organization of Securities Commissions (IOSCO). He elaborates that although the EU has limited competences in concluding international agreements in the sector of financial services, the same does not apply, according to the case law of the CJEU, to soft law agreements. *Maracci* then describes in detail the origin, mission and membership of IOSCO, which is not an international organisation but can be characterised as a multilateral regulatory network of (usually public) regulators with the formal structure of a private law based non-profit entity (currently under Spanish law), with a self-declared outreach to 95% of the world's securities markets. The European Commission is an associate member of IOSCO, as is the European Securities and Markets Authority (ESMA), since both do not have the regulatory powers required for ordinary membership. Nevertheless, *Maracci* ascribes the EU an increasing, legally informal, role in IOSCO, particularly triggered by the financial crisis. Vice versa, he tracks how subsequent EU law in the area of capital market law share key features with IOSCO documents.

The external dimension of EU consumer law is the topic of *Jules Stuyck* and *Mateja Durovic*. Consumer law, being mainly part of the internal market law of the EU, quite clearly does not belong to the areas in which the EU has external competence, as the authors establish. Nevertheless, they identify ways by which the EU has exported its consumer law, predominantly through bilateral agreements, to third countries, and the reasons they find are that consumer law is an important element of EU law and with its advanced state particularly suitable to serve as a model for other countries, and finally, that divergences in consumer protection standards may constitute an obstacle to trade, within the EU as much as internationally. *Stuyck* and *Durovic* analyse the various types of agreements but also the mechanisms by which the EU supports the material implementation of consumer law in third countries, for example, through financial support and education.

Anna-Alexandra Marhold focuses on EU regulatory private law in the energy sector, where two regulatory bodies are active: the Energy Community Regulatory Board (ECRB) and the Council of European Energy Regulators (CEER). EU energy law serves the primary goal of efficiency through competition, which requires the liberalisation of the markets, but also aims to ensure customer protection. CEER plays a role in rule-making related to small consumers within the EU, which *Marhold* provides evidence of, but also participates in international and regional energy regulators networks, thereby working on the establishment of best practices. Beyond its borders, the EU acts within the Energy Community Treaty framework, which includes the immediate and broader European neighbourhood reaching as far as Moldova and Ukraine. The Energy Community Treaty houses the ECRB, composed of representatives of the national regulatory agencies of the contracting states, observers and participants and concerned, amongst others, with customer protection. *Marhold* shows in much detail how EU-style customer protection is exported, through the co-operation of CEER and ECRB, into the countries of the Energy Community Treaty.

Marco Rizzi's contribution is concerned with the relationship between transnational regulation of pharmaceuticals and private law. For many years, informal transnational regulation of pharmaceuticals between the EU, the US and Japan has taken place within the International Conference on Harmonisation of Technical Requirements for Registration of Pharmaceuticals for Human Use (ICH). Its mission is to make recommendations towards achieving greater harmonization in the interpretation and application of technical guidelines and requirements for pharmaceutical product registration. The EU is represented by the EU Commission and the European Medicines Agency (EMA). At EU level, pharmaceutical regulation has gradually been transferred from the Member States to the European Commission where marketing authorization is now largely centralised for innovative products. *Rizzi* primarily focuses on the organisation and the decision-making processes in the ICH and flags up legitimacy concerns resulting from the exclusion of patients representatives. Finally, he also reminds the reader of the complementary liability system of the Product Liability Directive that may provide for remedies if the pre-market approval procedures fail.

The book is excellent and challenging reading. As stated at the outset, the book intends to provoke thoughts and research, and it fully achieves that goal. The authors provide deep insights in particular sectors of law and regulation and in the variety of mechanisms by which EU law takes influence beyond the borders of the EU and by which EU law is influenced by transnational regulation. This is most valuable information, and one is inclined to suspect that there are informal structures in other economic sectors in which the EU is involved without a clear mandate. The book is concerned with description and analysis, not so much with critique of the phenomena it reveals. A quite obvious concern would be the limited democratic legitimacy of many of the informal bodies that take factual impact on the law and of the way in which the EU Commission or special agencies act in the international sphere; a concern that is raised, in particular, in *Marco Rizzi's* discussion of the role of the ICH. At the same time, it provides important input to the sometimes very optimistic views on emerging transnational law. The stage is set for more research!

References

Cremona M (2003) The enlargement of the European Union. Oxford University Press, Oxford
Cremona M (2008) Developments in EU external relations law. Oxford University Press, Oxford
Micklitz H-W (2009) The visible hand of European private law. Yearb Eur Law 28(1):3–59
Micklitz H-W (2014) Constitutionalisation of European private law. Oxford University Press, Oxford

Hedwig Kavasch, Unterschiedliche Zollpräferenzen für unterschiedliche Entwicklungsländer

Mohr Siebeck, 2016, ISBN 9783161542947

Charlotte Sieber-Gasser

Abstract The legal interdependence between economic development policy, WTO law and the General System of Preferences (GSP) is the topic of the book of Hedwig Kavasch, Unterschiedliche Zollpräferenzen für unterschiedliche Entwicklungsländer. Kavasch focuses on the relatively recent GSP Plus preferences schemes developed and applied by the European Union (EU). The EU uses the GSP as a tool to encourage compliance with obligations in international law in the fields of human and labour rights, environment and good governance. Countries complying with this particular set of policy objectives will be granted more preferential market access to the EU than developing and least-developed countries disregarding said policy objectives. Besides the insights on the GSP Plus scheme of the EU and the legal challenges coming along with economic development policies and "aid for trade", this book provides a powerful example for the crucial role of the WTO system in shaping the economic prospects of developing and least-developed countries in the global market.

In order to encourage and foster economic growth in developing and least-developed countries, UNCTAD introduced the General System of Preferences (GSP) in the 1970s. It allows and encourages countries to grant preferential tariffs to developing and least-developed countries and is based on the concept of fostering economic growth through an increase in exports. Preferential tariffs independent from a Preferential Trade Agreement, however, are not complying with the Most-Favoured Nation Treatment (MFN) obligation of the GATT and the WTO. Thus, the Enabling Clause serves until today the purpose of exempting preferential and discriminatory tariff lines for developing and least-developed countries under the GSP from the MFN obligation in WTO law.

C. Sieber-Gasser (✉)
University of Lucerne, Frohburgstrasse 3, 6002 Lucerne, Switzerland
e-mail: charlotte.sieber@unilu.ch

M. Bungenberg et al. (eds.), *European Yearbook of International Economic Law 2017*, European Yearbook of International Economic Law 8,
DOI 10.1007/978-3-319-58832-2_23

The legal interaction between economic development policy, WTO law and the GSP is the topic of the book of *Hedwig Kavasch, Unterschiedliche Zollpräferenzen für unterschiedliche Entwicklungsländer*, written in German and published in 2016. *Kavasch* focuses on the relatively recent GSP Plus preferences schemes developed and applied by the European Union (EU). The EU uses the GSP as a tool to encourage compliance in developing and in least-developed countries with obligations in international law in the fields of human and labour rights, environment and good governance. Countries complying with this particular set of policy objectives will be granted more preferential market access to the EU than developing and least-developed countries disregarding said policy objectives.

This raises a number of legal questions with regard to WTO compliance of the EU's GSP Plus scheme, which *Kavasch* analyses in great detail in her book. Furthermore, the book feeds into the greater discussion about the role of WTO law and the responsibility of industrialised countries in enabling developing and least-developed countries to escape poverty. Therewith, the book addresses a number of topical legal questions relevant for the role of trade regulation and tariff preferences in reducing global inequality and provides for a thorough basis for subsequent research on the law and policy of "aid for trade".

The book is structured in eight chapters in which the core legal question whether or to what extent the GSP Plus scheme of the EU complies with WTO law is assessed from different angles. In introducing the topic, *Kavasch* rightly points out that conditionality in granting preferential treatment to developing and least-developed countries is as "old and as new as the GSP itself". Such conditionality naturally comes along with the inherent risk of abuse in the interest of the donor country's own foreign policy and trade objectives. Therefore, investigating the legal scope for graduation in the preferential treatment of developing and least-developed countries based on the Enabling Clause promises to clarify the legality of conditionality within the GSP and is of interest to both recipient and donor countries.

In the second chapter, *Kavasch* provides a substantial overview of the history of GSP and of special and differential treatment of developing and least-developed countries in WTO law. She describes the legal, political and economic context in which GSP schemes have to be located and discusses conditionality in the EU's past to current use of the GSP as a sanction and an incentive. Chapter 3 still serves the purpose of clarifying the background of the core question of the legality of the EU's GSP Plus scheme under WTO law and analyses the legal implications of the dispute settlement procedure in *EC — Tariff Preferences*. While the Appellate Body decision clarified to a certain extent the conditions under which developing and least-developed countries may be treated differently under the GSP (differentiation based on objective standards linked with specific development, financial or trade needs of a country), however, it did not investigate to what extent GSP preferences can legally be tied to political objectives as is the case under the EU's GSP Plus scheme. *Kavasch* then demonstrates how the decision in *EC – Tariff Preferences* subsequently led to a reform of the EU's GSP scheme and to the GSP Plus scheme.

However, India reserved the right to return to this matter based on doubts whether the GSP Plus scheme fully complies with the dispute settlement body's decision.

Chapters 4 and 5 then analyse in detail the legal implications of *EC – Tariff Preferences* for the assessment of the legality of the EU GSP Plus scheme under WTO law. In particular, *Kavasch* focuses on the relationship between the MFN principle and the Enabling Clause and on the extent to which the MFN principle applies to the preferential treatment of individual developing and least-developed countries under the GSP. In differentiating between developing and least-developed countries, the GSP infringes upon the MFN principle. In this regard and with reference to the Waiver, *Kavasch* elaborates that differentiation within GSP schemes has to be non-discriminatory in order to be lawful. However, non-discrimination within a GSP scheme does not necessarily require donor countries to use the same tariff for all developing and least-developed countries. While the scope of lawful differentiation was defined as "in line with objective standards of development needs", *Kavasch* critically assesses the larger political and legal context of this decision, as well as its implications for the relationship between WTO and public international law in general. Finally, *Kavasch* looks into the EU's position that donor countries are legally obliged to differentiate between unequal developing and least-developed countries and refutes this argument.

In chapters 6 (the largest chapter) and 7 the findings with regard to the legal scope and conditions for lawful differentiation between recipient countries within the GSP are applied to the EU's GSP Plus scheme. The two chapters elaborate in great detail various aspects of the EU's GSP Plus scheme and its legal relationship with WTO law. Chapter 6 discusses to what extent the GSP Plus incentives constitute a violation of the narrow margin for differentiation in WTO law with regard to the reference to human and labour rights, environment and good governance obligations, and chapter 7 discusses a potential violation with regard to the requirement of certain economic preconditions in potential recipient countries. *Kavasch* highlights the challenges linked with defining objective standards of development needs and critically assesses whether the GSP Plus scheme of the EU complies with objective standards as required in WTO law and jurisprudence. She distinguishes in her analysis between the development objective of the 27 treaties in the GSP Plus scheme and the ratification and implementation of the treaties. Furthermore, the eligibility of the GSP Plus scheme as an incentive to foster and realize economic development as required by WTO law is critically assessed. *Kavasch* identifies in particular the large number of treaties required by the GSP scheme as problematic, along with certain incoherencies in the selection of the relevant treaties and the requirement to demonstrate implementation. She furthermore argues that the requirement to ratify and implement all 27 treaties in the GSP Plus scheme prevents a considerable number of potential recipient countries from benefitting from the GSP Plus scheme due to practical reasons and points out the legal challenge of dealing with incentive systems: they naturally lead to discrimination between developing countries capable but unwilling to implement all of the 27 treaties and developing countries willing to do so. In addition, it is uncertain whether the review process of the implementation of the treaties as required by the GSP Plus scheme of the EU fully complies with the transparency and objectivity requirements in WTO law. Finally, *Kavasch* critically investigates the recourse of the GSP Plus scheme on a number of economic preconditions necessary for qualifying as a potential recipient country and concludes that they do not constitute an objective standard of development needs as required by WTO law.

In her conclusion in chapter 8, *Kavasch* suggests that neither the incentive system nor the economic preconditions of the EU's GSP Plus scheme are per se incompatible with WTO law. However, she makes a strong argument for the reduction of the number of conditions required by the GSP Plus scheme in order to increase WTO compatibility and for the introduction—within the WTO—of neutral and binding criteria for graduation between the different stages of economic development of WTO members.

Besides the insights on the GSP Plus scheme of the EU and the legal challenges coming along with economic development policies and "aid for trade", this book provides a powerful example for the crucial role of the WTO system in shaping the economic prospects of developing and least-developed countries in the global market. Furthermore, *EC — Tariff Preferences* along with the subsequent changes in the GSP scheme of the EU is exemplary for the widespread acceptance of the role of the WTO in defining the minimum standard applicable on the global market and in constraining discriminatory behavior of industrialised countries. While the EU is by far not the only WTO member with a questionable GSP scheme, it remains open to what extent potential discrimination within GSP is considered sufficiently significant to engage in a dispute settlement procedure again in the nearer future, which renders the thorough legal analysis of the legal scope for lawful differentiation within GSP in this book all the more relevant and a valuable contribution to the field.

Billy A. Melo Araujo, The EU Deep Trade Agenda: Law and Policy

Oxford University Press, 2016, ISBN 9780198753384

Wolfgang Weiß

Abstract The Chapter reviews the book The EU Deep Trade Agenda written by Melo Araujo that provides a comprehensive analysis of the legal and political issues of the EU deep trade agenda which started with the pronouncement of the new Global Europe trade strategy of the European Commission in 2006. The overall message of the research presented by the author is the statement of the ambiguous, double-faced character of the EU's trade policy after 2006. For, the then rather new trade policy strategy initiated a turn of the EU towards the interests of EU trade stakeholders in saving the global position of the EU economy amidst the gravitational shifts of World trade since the 1990s, and opening up markets for EU goods and services. The former generally rather altruistic attitude of favouring multilateral approaches in codifying common trade rules over selfish economic orientations has been amended, if not replaced by a much more pragmatic stance which seeks to sustain European shares in world trade by recourse to bilateral or regional FTA.

The book by Melo Araujo is the first comprehensive analysis of the EU DCFTAs and their implementation of the EU Global Europe trade agenda. The author presents a thorough and convincing law and politics examination of the drivers of the formation of the new trade policy and its realisation by way of FTAs. Even though one might not agree with the author's views in every respect, the structure of analysis and the way of argumentation makes the overall conclusions extremely compelling.

The monograph provides a comprehensive analysis of the legal and political issues of the EU deep trade agenda which started with the pronouncement of the new Global Europe trade strategy of the European Commission in 2006. The overall message of the research presented by the author is the statement of the ambiguous, double-faced character of the EU's trade policy after 2006. For, the then rather new

W. Weiß (✉)
German University of Administrative Sciences Speyer, Freiherr-vom-Stein-Straße 2, 67346 Speyer, Germany
e-mail: weiss@uni-speyer.de

M. Bungenberg et al. (eds.), *European Yearbook of International Economic Law 2017*, European Yearbook of International Economic Law 8,
DOI 10.1007/978-3-319-58832-2_24

trade policy strategy initiated a turn of the EU towards the interests of EU trade stakeholders in saving the global position of the EU economy amidst the gravitational shifts of world trade since the 1990s, and opening up markets for EU goods and services. The former generally rather altruistic attitude of favouring multilateral approaches in codifying common trade rules over selfish economic orientations has been amended, if not replaced by a much more pragmatic stance which seeks to sustain European shares in world trade by recourse to bilateral or regional FTA. The ambiguity in EU trade politics results from the contradictions between internal expectations and external demands and between rather generous EU constitutional objectives, in particular those with regard to foreign relations and external commercial policy, on the one hand, and the practical needs and demands of realistic trade politics in the politically multipolar and economically globalized world, on the other hand. There is, in other words, as always the gap between talk (on sustainability, poverty, development, values) and (real trade policy) action to which external policies may be considerably vulnerable due to the lack of a foreign constituency and the gap between external concernment and mainly domestic political accountability, at least until recently.

The book is divided into nine chapters. The first three chapters address—besides the introductory aspects of explaining the research focus and methodological approaches—horizontal issues of the EU trade policy's context and legal framework. The subsequent five chapters then turn to the five substantial regulatory areas which—in view of the author—form the strategically most important policy fields of the EU's endeavour of codifying regulatory disciplines in its deep and comprehensive free trade agreements (DCFTAs) concluded since 2006 that address behind-the-border problems (i.e. services, investment, IP, competition, and public procurement). The final chapter 9 offers the conclusions and the author's overall assessment of the EU deep trade agenda practice since 2006 as being a failure, mainly for two reasons: First, because of the lack of negotiation success as FTAs have not been concluded with the key economic partners identified in the Global Europe strategy (foremost BRICS). Second, because the EU's attempt of entering into regulatory disciplines have met with considerable internal resistance recently.

The first introductory chapter sets the scene as it explains the research question and the approaches adopted and reasons its limitations to the most relevant issues. The core research issue of the book is defined as being the nature and content of the deep regulatory disciplines which the EU uses to implement its trade agenda in its FTAs. From this, the author will derive conclusions about the very essence of the EU as a trading nation. The author promises addressing what type of power the EU is insofar, in view of its sustained promise to further multilateral processes.

In the second chapter, the author explores the driving factors for the development of the deep trade agenda in the EU, starting with the evolution of the international trading system after World War II which with the advent of the WTO definitively went beyond border and mere non-discrimination issues and turned to deeper, more positive economic integration. This turn is analysed with regard to its consequences for domestic regulatory autonomy, for the mandate of the WTO, and for its lax standards for controlling preferential trade agreements. As progress in the Doha Round domestic regulatory disciplines stayed out, trading nations turned to FTAs. The author highlights the gradual temptation this engendered for the EU to opt for the bilateral way as well, finally leading to the Global Europe's "shift to competitive liberalization" (p. 32) similar to the US, but with considerable differences as the EU identified favourite trading partners, strived for deeper regulatory cooperation, and continued with non-trade goals. In the final section, the author gives an account of diverse conceptualisations of the EU's role as an international actor seeking for international trading rules that are more beneficial for its internal market, in which he later will place its assessment of the impact of the EU's change on its (self-)perception.

Chapter 3 sets out the constitutional legal framework for the EU's trade policy, which consists of competence provisions, the related decision making rules and the external policy non-trade objectives whose integration in primary law is assessed by the author as a mere formalization of existing practice. Their limited steering force for shaping the content of FTAs to the benefit of e.g. environmental protection is illustrated with regard to sustainable development; the author shows that the DCFTA provisions are tailored in a way so that they do not compromise trade liberalisation (pp. 71 and 74). The author diligently surveys the current state of exclusive EU external trade competences and the related still unsettled disputes, e.g. as regards portfolio investment or the coverage of investment protection and arbitration. He succinctly highlights the internal constraints for the EU trade policy and the complexities following from there.

Chapter 4 on services addresses the policy area that particularly is in need of deep trade disciplines in order to liberalise trade. The thorough analysis of the author highlights the specific challenges of trade liberalisation in services as even non-discriminatory domestic regulation may hamper cross-border trade and services trade liberalisation necessitates domestic reforms, and presents the relevant regulatory framework of the GATS. Against this legal and political-economic background, the EU's approach to services trade liberalisation aims at fostering the competitive advantages of EU service suppliers, but also at the development of its trading partners. The scrutiny of the services chapters of the EU DCFTAs shows that most DCFTA rules on services merely promote GATS compliance and add some rather general regulatory disciplines which are tailored to the development needs of the developing countries and ensure that services commitments are not undone by domestic regulation. Only the EU-Singapore FTA and the CETA contain rather specific disciplines on domestic regulation (p. 90 et seq.). The EU in some DCFTA also establishes regulatory cooperation mechanism. The authors doubts whether they will successfully draw closer diverse domestic regulatory concepts and approaches.

The subsequent chapter 5 considers the development of the EU's investment policy and provides for a diligent analysis of the respective disciplines in the CETA and the EU Singapore FTA. It situates the EU policy within the evolution of international investment agreements and the more recent attempts to ameliorate their investment protection provisions in order to allow for more respect for the states' right to regulate and their regulatory autonomy and to rectify the pro-investor bias of traditional investment arbitration. Against this backdrop, the author rightly identifies still existing problems in the EU's Singapore and CETA investment provisions and raises doubts about the general meaningfulness of investment protection arbitration. Unfortunately, the author was not able to cover the latest developments in particular with regard to CETA as his analysis still is based on the first version of the CETA investment provisions. The new Investment Court System in the CETA could not be considered, not to mention the latest strive of Canada and the EU for a multilateral investment court.

In chapter 6 on IP rights, the author explores the turn in the EU's Global Europe strategy to enshrine IP rules in its FTAs which aim at a stronger IP standard which comes closer to existing EU rules instead of merely requiring the adoption of IP standards contained in respective international agreements. The author considers the tension between the EU's intention to enhance the respect for IP standards, which it pursues both in bilateral as well as multilateral channels, on the one hand, and the interest of developing countries to set aside IP disciplines for the sake of non-trade objectives. The protection of geographical indications, being an issue of high importance for the EU, receives particular attention. The EU's approach insofar is considerably demanding for its trade partners so that it comes without surprise that its attempts to grant absolute protection to indications protected under EU law have been (partially) successful only in some of its FTAs. In the end, the analysis illustrates that the EU's approach to protection of geographical indications pursues the proliferation of EU domestic regulatory concepts similarly aggressively as the US does; hardly will we see global regulatory approximation insofar. The study highlights further problems of the EU's IP approach with regard to imbalances between the rights of IP holders and that of consumers and competitors, and with regard to human rights in IP enforcement. Taking the EU Korea FTA criminal IP enforcement provisions as an example, the author also warns of including contested regulatory issues in FTAs as they might intensify resistance by parliaments. Having in mind the recent disputes about CETA in some national parliaments, this warning call appears particularly current.

The final substantive chapters 7 and 8 turn to competition policy and public procurement. Again, the author gives a comparatively common analytical structure to these chapters: First, the specific regulatory challenges of dealing with competition rules and public procurement liberalisation are treated from a political economy perspective. Second, the current legal framework of global competition or public procurement rules is explored. Finally, the development of the EU approach is studied against this background, and the relevant rules in the EU FTAs are examined. With regard to competition, the analysis shows that the rules in the EU FTA's are rather weak and symbolic, in contrast to public procurement rules where the EU strives for expansion of the reach of the WTO GPA or revised GPA provisions. Interestingly the EU does not promote its own public procurement rules.

In conclusion, the analysis of the substantive policy areas demonstrates that the EU uses the DCFTAs to enforce its regulatory conceptions and to enter into regulatory disciplines in its self-interest. In this way, it tries to promulgate the EU acquis/its regulatory ideas beyond its territory, hoping for a plurilateralisation and finally multilateralization of the standards reached in its bilateral or plurilateral FTAs. In this view, the failure of multilateral attempts to address regulatory issues more deeply in the WTO is not used by the EU for a critical reflection of its material positions. Instead the EU DCFTAs serve as a circumvention for lack of success in getting its way multilaterally—in the same way as any other trade power behaves (see p. 235; with regard to IP see p. 142, with regard to services see p. 103, with regard to labour and environment standards see p. 71 et seq.).

The book by *Melo Araujo* is the first comprehensive analysis of the EU DCFTAs and their implementation of the EU Global Europe trade agenda. The author presents a thorough and convincing law and politics examination of the drivers of the formation of the new trade policy and its realisation by way of FTAs. Even though one might not agree with the author's views in every respect, the structure of analysis and the way of argumentation makes the overall conclusions extremely compelling. The book is a very valuable and timely contribution to a commencing discussion about the EU's further course in its external trade policy which got new impetus by the occurrences surrounding the signature of the CETA.

Jan Ulrich Heinemann, Die Entwicklung der Außenkompetenzen der Europäischen Union im Vergleich der Rechtslagen vor und nach dem Reformvertrag von Lissabon: Unter besonderer Berücksichtigung der impliziten Außenkompetenzen

Peter Lang, 2016, ISBN 9783631671672

Anja Trautmann

Abstract The reviewed book provides a comprehensive analysis of the external competences of the European Union before and after the Treaty of Lisbon. Thereby, it also deals with the distinction between explicit powers, meaning those clearly defined in the relevant articles of the treaties, and the implicit powers, meaning the competences in external matters that derive from explicit internal competence. Moreover, it takes the intergovernmental competences into consideration.

The monograph provides a comprehensive analysis of the external competences of the European Union before and after the Treaty of Lisbon. While internal competences concern the Union's internal functioning, external competences are those that fall within the framework of the Union's relations and partnerships with non-EU countries and international, regional or global organisations. In addition, the EU may conclude external agreements with non-EU countries or international organisations in accordance with Article 216 TFEU within the framework of its competences. The external relations of the European Union and the distinction of competences between the Union and the Member States in this field have become a controversial and debated topic in European law as well as in the public dialogue especially as a result of the European Commission's negotiations of trade agreements such as CETA, TTIP or TISA. Even the Court of Justice of the European Union had to deal with the question of the division of external competences

A. Trautmann (✉)
Europa-Institut of Saarland University, Campus Geb. B2.1, 66123 Saarbrücken, Germany
e-mail: a.trautmann@europainstitut.de

M. Bungenberg et al. (eds.), *European Yearbook of International Economic Law 2017*, European Yearbook of International Economic Law 8,
DOI 10.1007/978-3-319-58832-2_25

between the Union and the Member States in its opinion on the Singapore Agreement.

Besides introduction and conclusion, the book is divided into two extensive parts which differentiate between the external competences of the European Union before and after the Treaty of Lisbon. Thereby, it also deals with the distinction between explicit powers, meaning those clearly defined in the relevant articles of the treaties, and the implicit powers, meaning the competences in external matters that derive from explicit internal competence. Moreover, it takes the intergovernmental competences into consideration.

The first part of the book addresses the external competences of the European Community and the European Union according to the pre-Lisbon treaties in the Nice consolidated version. After the assessment of the legal capacity of the European Community in an introductory section, the second section concentrates on the external competences and starts with the basic principles in regard to the existence of competences, which means the principles of limited conferral, subsidiarity and proportionality. Subsequently, the author deals with explicit external competences with an exclusive nature and therefore with the common commercial policy (Article 133 TEC), the association agreements (Article 310 TEC) and the monetary policy (Article 111 TEC). Next to these, the implicit external competences are at the centre of the author's examination. Here the book provides a substantial overview of the history of the implicit competences—form the landmark decision in the AETR and Kramer cases, the opinions 1/76, 2/91, 1/94, 2/92, the open skies agreement until the opinion 1/03. After an analysis of these decisions, the author comes to the conclusion that the existence of implicit competences is only recognised in the case of exclusive powers and not, therefore, in the case of parallel powers. Thus, the book further analyses the different explicit competences in parallel powers, e.g. the environment policy (Articles 174 and 175 TEC), development cooperation (Article 181 TEC), international cooperation with third countries (Article 181a TEC), cooperation in research and technological development (Article 170 TEC), agreements in the fields of trade in services and the commercial aspects of intellectual property (Article 133(5) TEC) as well as further external measures in regard to public health (Article 152(3) TEC), culture (Article 151(3) TEC), education and youth policy (Articles 149(3) and 150(3) TECT) and the trans-European networks (Article 155(3) TEC). The last four subsections then handle the special external provision concerning the relations with international organisations (Articles 302–304 TEC), the fields without explicit external competences and, last but not least, the general clause in Article 308 TEC as well as the approximation of laws (Articles 94 and 95 TEC). The question of the legal personality of the European Union and the external competences in the intergovernmental field complete the analysis in the first part of the book and create a comprehensive picture of the external competences before the Treaty of Lisbon.

Adhering to the same structure, the second part of the book addresses the external competences after the Treaty of Lisbon. In the first three sections the author describes the modifications made to Union law by the Treaty of Lisbon, the new legal personality of the European Union as well as the new principles of external relations.

Here the author goes especially into detail about the new categories and areas of Union competence in the Articles 2–6 TFEU, the new consolidated part 5 of the TFEU about the external actions (Articles 205–222 TFEU), the new principles and aims of the European external policy in Articles 21 and 22 TEU as well as the treaty making powers in Article 216 TFEU. The fourth section is then a comprehensive analysis about the external competences of the Union which starts with the exclusive explicit competences in the different areas mentioned in Article 3(1) TFEU. Afterwards, the author deals with the implicit external competences and discusses their exclusive nature based on Article 3(2) TFEU in distinction to the alternatives 2–4 of Article 216(1) TFEU that result in the new established category of implicit shared external competences. Article 216(1) TFEU thereby makes it clear under which circumstances a competence of the Union for concluding international treaties is being granted expressly as well as implicitly and therefore is a provision without having a corresponding provision in former treaties. Subsequently, the author focuses on the explicit shared or parallel external competences. These are especially the following areas of development cooperation (Article 209(2) TFEU), humanitarian aid (Article 214(4) TFEU), international cooperation policy (Art. 212(3) TFEU), environmental protection (Articles 192(1) and 191(4) TFEU), cooperation in research and technological development (Article 186), immigration policy (Article 79(3) TFEU) as well as further external measures in regard to public health (Article 168(3) TFEU), culture (Article 167(3) TFEU), education and youth policy (Articles 165(3) and 166(3) TFEU) and the trans-European networks (Article 171(3) TFEU). The further four subsections, at least, address the special external provision concerning the relations with international organisations (Article 220 TFEU), the fields without explicit external competences and the general clause in Article 352 TFEU as well as the approximation of laws in the internal market in Article 114 TFEU. The final section of the second part focuses on the intergovernmental external competences of the Union.

The book by *Jan Ulrich Heinemann* is a comprehensive list and analysis of the explicit and implicit external competences of the European Union. His analysis of the jurisprudence and the norms of competence shows the preconditions for the conclusion of international agreements and thereby the operational framework of the European Union in its external relations.

The author presents a thorough and convincing legal examination of the important field of external competences with a special focus on the newly codified implicit competences. In addition, the comparison between the legal status before and after Lisbon excellently illustrates the modifications introduced by the Treaty but also the associated problematic points. Even though one might not agree with the author's views in every aspect, the structure of analysis and the method of argumentation make the overall conclusions extremely compelling. The book is a very valuable contribution to the present discussion about the EU's further course in its external relations policy, which is also of particular interest in the context of the recently issued opinion of the Court of Justice of the European Union to the Singapore agreement.

Printed by Printforce, the Netherlands